Anonymous

Kenny's Guide

Containing full information as to railroads, steamboats and their time tables. Vol. 2

Anonymous

Kenny's Guide
Containing full information as to railroads, steamboats and their time tables. Vol. 2

ISBN/EAN: 9783337409227

Printed in Europe, USA, Canada, Australia, Japan

Cover: Foto ©Lupo / pixelio.de

More available books at **www.hansebooks.com**

Kenny's Guide,

CONTAINING FULL INFORMATION AS TO

RAILROADS, STEAMBOATS AND THEIR TIME TABLES; HOTELS AND THEIR CHARGES; ART GALLERIES; THEATRES, WITH DIAGRAMS OF SEATS; PUBLIC INSTITUTIONS, CHURCHES, ASYLUMS, BANKS, ETC., ETC.

FOR THE USE OF

BUSINESS MEN, HOUSEHOLDERS AND OTHERS.

For Index to Contents, see pages 3 and 4.

PUBLISHED BY
F. H. KENNY, 83 Nassau St., New York.
MAY, 1889.

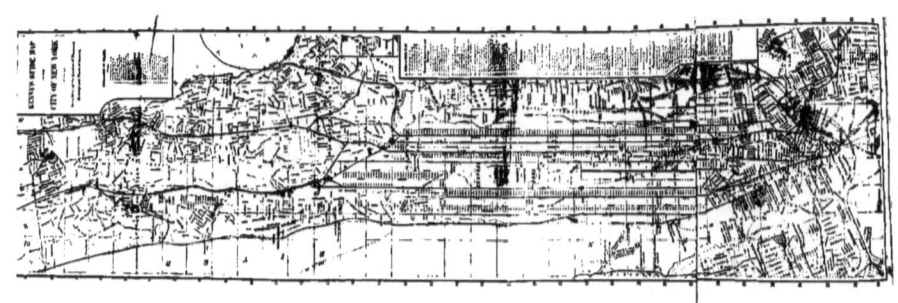

Kenny's Guide,

F. H. KENNY, Publisher, **83 NASSAU STREET.**

TERMS:—Single Number Complete (Each Edition), 50 cents; with Weekly Supplement, issued on Mondays, $4.00 per Annum, in advance.

No. 1. **May 1889.** Vol. I.

INDEX—MISCELLANEOUS INFORMATION.

	Page
Accident Insurance Companies	107
American District Telegraph Offices	128
Amusement, Places of	128, 148
Apartment Houses	31
Armories	94
Arrears and Assessments Bureau	94
Art Galleries and Art Schools	24
Assessors, Board of	94
Associations, Mercantile and Trade	107
Asylums	29
Banks in New York City	95
Banks in Brooklyn	96
Board of Education	28
Brooklyn Annex	125
Building Inspection Bureau	94
Cab and Carriage Fares	128
Canal Lines	109
Car Lines in New York City	18
" " in Brooklyn	124, 125
Cemeteries	27
Charities and Correction Department	94
Churches	25, 27
Clubs	77
Colleges	28
Commissioner of Jurors	94
Conservatories of Music	24
Consuls	51
Coupons—where payable	153, 157
Custom House	94
Dancing Academies	24
Directions for reaching various places	110, 123
Dispensaries	30
Distances in N. Y. City	128
Dividends	153, 157
Dock Masters	102
Elevated Railroads in New York City	38
" " in Brooklyn	64
Exchanges in New York City	107
Excise Department	94
Express Offices	103, 109
Express to various places	112, 123
Fares to all places in United States.	
Via Baltimore & Ohio R. R.	65, 69
" Central R. R. of New Jersey	74, 77
" Delaware, Lackawanna & W. R. R.	65, 69
" Long Island R. R.	73
" N.Y. Central & Hudson River R. R.	65, 69
" New York, Lake Erie&Western R. R.	65, 69
" New York, New Haven&Hartford R. R.	70, 73
" New York, Ontario & Western R. R.	65, 69
" Pennsylvania R. R.	65, 69
" West Shore R. R.	65, 69
Fast Freight Lines	12, 16
Ferries	19
Financial, Coupons, Elections, Meetings	153, 157
Fire Department	94
Fire Insurance Companies	150
Flats	31
Foreign Exchange Quotations	163

	Page.
Foreign Money Equivalents	157
Grand Army Republic—Meeting places, etc.	51
Hack Fares	128
Health Department	94
Homes and Asylums	29
Hospitals	30
Hotels and their Rates	32
Insurance Companies	107, 150
Internal Revenue Officers	16
Investment Companies	95
Libraries	30
Life Insurance Companies	107
Map of New York City	16
Marine Insurance Companies	107
Markets, Location of	46
Money Order, Post Office Rates	17
Money Order, Express Rates	17
Mortgage Companies	95
National Guard	94
Newspaper Offices	64
Office Buildings	19
Piers, Location of	50
Police Stations	29
Port Wardens	103
Post Office Information.	
General Information	21, 24
Domestic and Canada Mails	93
Foreign Mails	154, 156
Money Order Rates	17
Post Office Stations	24
Public Buildings	46
Railroad Depots	12, 16, 110, 111
Safe Deposit Companies	95, 96
Sailing Vessel Lines	104, 106
Savings Banks	95, 96
Schools	28
Seminaries	28
Societies	17
Steamboats—Hudson River Landings	5, 7
do. —Landings not on the Hudson	7, 11
do. —Service from other places	125
Steamships from New York	150, 152
do. from other ports	20
Storage Warehouses	94
Street Cleaning Department	94
Tax Collection Bureau	94
Telegraph Rates, U. S., Canada and Mexico	52, 58
Telegraph Rates, Foreign	78, 80
Theatres and Diagrams	128, 148
Tides at Sandy Hook	90
Transportation Lines	12, 16
Trust Companies	95, 96
Weights and Measures, Inspectors and Sealers of	94
Young Men's Christian Association	17

For Railroad Time Tables, see next page.

RAILROAD TIME TABLE INDEX.

	PAGE		PAGE
Adirondack	35	Meriden, Waterbury & Conn. River	88
"Air Line" to Boston	45	Michigan Central	36, 41
Atlantic Coast Line	98	Newburgh, Duchess & Connecticut	88
Baltimore & Ohio	126, 127	New Haven & Derby	59
Bay Line	99	New Jersey & New York	61
"Bee Line" to the West	38	New Jersey Southern	84
Bennington & Rutland	37	New London Northern	63
Boston & Albany	45, 85	New York & Greenwood Lake	40
Boston & Maine	46	New York & Long Branch	92
Brooklyn Annex	125	New York & Massachusetts	64
Brooklyn, Bath & West End	108	New York & New England	45, 60
Brooklyn & Brighton Beach	108	New York & Northern	64
Brooklyn, Canarsie & Rockaway Beach	111	New York & Rockaway Beach	63
Buffalo, Rochester & Pittsburgh	63	New York & Sea Beach	108
Camden & Atlantic	92	New York Central & Hudson River	33, 38
Cape Charles Route	99	Harlem Division	96
Catskill Mountain & Cairo	108	New York, Lake Erie & Western	39, 41
Central of New Jersey	81, 84	New York, New Haven & Hartford	42, 45
Bound Brook Route (Phila. New Line)	81, 83	Naugatuck Division	44
Lehigh & Susquehanna Division	83	Northampton Division	44
Newark & New York R. R.	82	Valley Division	43
New Jersey Southern Division	84	New York, Ontario & Western	62
Central Vermont	37	New York, Providence & Boston	45, 46
Chateaugay	35	Narragansett Pier R. R.	45
Chicago & Grand Trunk	37	Newport & Wickford R. R.	45
Coney Island & Brooklyn	108	New York, Susquehanna & Western	61
Connecticut River	63	Northern Adirondack	35
Danbury & Norwalk	59	Northern of New Jersey	46
Delaware & Hudson Canal	35	Old Colony	59
Susquehanna Division	35	Passaic & Delaware	87
Delaware, Lackawanna & Western	86, 88	Pennsylvania	97, 102
Bloomsburgh Division	87	Amboy Division	102
Morris & Essex Division	86	Belvidere Division	101
Elevated Railroads in New York	38	Freehold & Jamesburg R. R.	102
" " in Brooklyn	64	Philadelphia & Reading	85
Elmira, Cortland & Northern	108	Philadelphia, Wilmington & Baltimore	127
Erie, see "New York, Lake Erie & W."	39, 41	Piedmont Air Line	98
Fitchburg	37	Port Jervis, Monticello & New York	11
Fonda, Johnstown & Gloversville	60	Prospect Park & Coney Island	89
Freehold & New York	60	Providence & Springfield	89
Grand Trunk	37, 41	Providence & Worcester	46
Hartford & Conn. Western	60	Rome, Watertown & Ogdensburg	36
"Hoosac Tunnel Route"	37	Shepaug, Litchfield & Northern	58
Housatonic	59	"Shore Line" to Boston	45
Danbury & Norwalk R. R.	59	"Springfield Line" to Boston	45
Lake Shore & Michigan Southern	36, 41	Staten Island	91
Lebanon Springs	62	Sussex	87
Lehigh & Hudson River	88	Tuckerton	58
Lehigh Valley	85	Ulster & Delaware	106
Geneva, Ithaca & Sayre Division	60	Kaaterskill R. R.	106
Long Island	47, 50	Stony Clove & Catskill Mountain	106
Atlantic Ave. Branch	50	Wallkill Valley	62
Long Beach Branch. *Not running.*		West Jersey	103
Manhattan Beach Division	49	West Shore R. R.	89, 91

TIME TABLE INDEX TO IMPORTANT PLACES.

Place.	Page.	Place.	Page.	Place.	Page.	Place.	Page.
Albany, N. Y.	33, 90	Duluth, Minn.	149	Mauch Chunk	83, 85	Portland, Oreg.	149
Atchison, Kan.	149	East Saginaw	36, 41	Memphis	98	Providence	45, 60
Atlantic City	81, 99	Fort Wayne	37, 97	Mexico City, Mex.	98	Reading, Pa	85, 101
Asbury Park	92	Galveston	98	Milwaukee	149	Richfield Springs	35, 88
Babylon, L. I.	48	Grand Rapids, Mich.	36, 41	Minneapolis	149	Richmond	99
Baltimore	81, 99	Greenwood Lake	40	Montreal	35, 37	Rochester	33, 41, 90
Bar Harbor	46	Halifax, N. S.	46	Narragansett Pier	45	St. Joseph, Mo	149
Bismarck, Dak	149	Harrisburg	83, 97	Nashville, Tenn.	98	St. Louis	37, 38, 41, 97
Boston	45, 59, 60	Hartford	41, 45, 60	Newark, N. J.	82, 86, 140	St. Paul, Minn.	149
Bridgeport, Conn.	41	Helena, Mont.	149	Newburg, N. J.	40, 89	San Francisco	98
Buffalo	33, 41, 85, 88, 90	Indianapolis	38, 41, 97	New Haven	41	Saranac Lake	35
Burlington, Iowa.	149	Jackson, Mich.	36, 41	New London	44	Saratoga	35
Cape May, N. J.	99	Jacksonville, Fla.	98	New Orleans	98	Savannah	98
Catskill, N. Y.	33, 90	Jamaica, L. I.	47	Newport, R. I.	45	Sharon Springs	35
Charleston, S. C.	98	Kansas City	149	Niagara Falls	35, 41, 85, 90	Springfield, Mass.	41
Chicago	36, 37, 41, 97	Lake George	35	Ocean Grove, N. J.	92	Syracuse	33, 90
Cincinnati	36, 41, 98	Lake Mahopac	64, 96	Old Point Comfort.	99	Terre Haute, Ind	38, 97
Cleveland	36, 38, 41, 98	Lakewood, N. J.	81	Omaha, Neb.	149	Toledo, Ohio	36, 41, 98
Columbus, Ohio.	38, 98	Lenox, Mass.	59	Paterson, N. J.	39, 61, 87	Topeka, Kan.	149
Council Bluffs	149	Logansport, Ind	97	Philadelphia	81, 97	Toronto	37, 41
Denver, Col.	149	Long Branch	92	Pittsburg	97	Trenton	81, 100
Des Moines, Iowa	149	Louisville	98	Pittsfield, Mass	59, 90	Washington	81, 99
Detroit	36, 37, 41	Mansfield, Ohio	97	Portland, Me.	46		

☞ *For Places East of Boston, see page 46; for Places West of Chicago & St. Louis, see page 149.*

STEAMBOATS FOR HUDSON RIVER LANDINGS.

MLS.

145 Albany, N. Y. People's Line leaves Canal St. Steamboat Drew, Monday, Wednesday, Friday, 6 00 p. m. Steamboat Dean Richmond, Tuesday, Thursday, Saturday, 6 00 p. m. Fare $1 50; Exc. Fare $2 50. Freight received to 5 45 p. m. Due at Albany 6 00 a. m. Leave Albany daily except Sunday, 8 00 p. m. Due in New York 7 00 a. m.

145 Albany, N. Y. Citizens' Line leaves Christopher St. Steamboat Saratoga on Sundays only, 6 00 p. m. (For passengers only.) Fare $1 50; Exc. $2.50. Due at Albany, 6 00 a. m. Leave Albany Steamboat City of Troy on Sundays only, 7 00 p. m. Due in New York 7 00 a. m.

120 Athens, N. Y. Catskill and New York Steamboat Co. Steamboat Walter Brett leaves Jay St., Tuesday, Thursday, Saturday, 6 00 p. m. Fare $1 00. Freight received same days to 5 45 p. m. Leave Athens, Monday, Wednesday, Friday, 5 00 p. m. Due in New York, 5 00 a. m.

95 Barrytown, N. Y. New York and Saugerties Transportation Co. Steamboat Ansonia leaves Franklin St. Tuesday, Thursday, Saturday, 6 00 p. m. Freight received same days to 5 15 p. m. Fare $1 00. Leaves Barrytown, Monday, Wednesday, Friday, 8 p. m. Due in New York, 5 a. m.

115 Catskill, N. Y. Catskill and New York Steamboat Co. leave Jay St. Steamboat Catskill, Monday, Wednesday, Friday, 6 00 p. m. Steamboat Walter Brett, Tuesday, Thursday, Saturday, 6 00 p. m. Fare $1 00; Exc. Fare $1 70. Freight received to 5 15 p. m. Leave Catskill daily except Saturday, 6 00 p. m. Due in in New York 5 00 a. m.

115 Catskill, N. Y. Catskill and New York Steamboat Co. Jay St. Propeller W. C. Redfield leaves Catskill for New York, Monday, Wednesday, Friday, 8 00 p. m. Fare $1 00. Due in New York 5 a. m.

54 Cold Spring, N. Y. Catskill and New York Steamboat Co. leave Jay St. Steamboat Catskill, Monday, Wednesday, Friday, 6 00 p. m. Propeller W. C. Redfield, Tuesday, Thursday, Saturday, 6 00 p. m. Fare 50 cts. Freight received to 5 45 p. m. Does not stop at Cold Spring on return trip to New York.

54 Cold Spring, N. Y. Homer Ramsdell Line. Propellers Newburgh and Homer Ramsdell leave Franklin St. daily except Sunday, 5 00 p. m.; on Sundays 9 a. m. Fare 50 cts. Freight received to 5 00 p. m. Leave Cold Spring every day 9 00 p. m. Due in New York 1 30 a. m.

56 Cornwall. Homer Ramsdell, Line. Propellers Newburgh and Homer Ramsdell leave Franklin St. daily except Sunday, 5 00 p. m., on Sundays, 9 00 a. m. Fare 50 cts. Freight received 5 00 p. m. Leave Newburg every day 8 00 p. m. Due in New York 1 30 a. m.

56 Cornwall. Steamboats J. W. Baldwin and City of Kingston leave Harrison St. J. W. Baldwin, Monday, Wednesday, Friday, 4 00 p. m., City of Kingston, Tuesday and Thursday, 4 00 p. m., Saturday, 1 00 p. m. Fare 50 cts. Freight received up to 30 minutes before departure. Leave Cornwall daily except Saturday, 9 20 p. m. Due in New York 2 00 a. m.

125 Coxsackie, N. Y. Propeller Thomas McManus leave Franklin St. Monday, Wednesday, Friday, 6 00 p. m. Fare $1 00. Freight received same days to 5 45 p. m. Leave Coxsackie, Tuesday, Thursday, Sunday, 3 30 p. m. Due in New York 5 00 a. m.

125 Coxsackie, N. Y. Catskill and New York Steamboat Co. Propeller W. C. Redfield leaves Jay St. Tuesday, Thursday, Saturday, 6 p. m. Fare $1 00. Freight received same days to 5 45 p. m. Due in New York 5 00 a. m.

52 Cranstons, (West Point.) Steamboat J. W. Baldwin and City of Kingston, leaves Harrison St. J. W. Baldwin, Monday, Wednesday, Friday, 4 00 p. m.; City of Kingston, Tuesday and Thursday, 4 00 p. m.; Saturday 1 00 p. m. Fare 50 cts. Freight received up to 30 minutes before departure. Leave Cranstons daily except Saturday, 10 00 p. m. Due in New York, 2 00 a. m.

35 Croton, N. Y. Propeller Fanny Woodall leave Harrison St. Tuesday, Thursday, 3 00 p. m.; Saturday, 2 00 p. m. (No passengers carried.) Freight received same days when boat is in. Leave Croton, Monday, Wednesday, Friday, about 4 30 p. m. Time to New York 3 hours.

22 Dobbs' Ferry, N. Y. North River Steamboat Co. Propeller Raleigh leaves Harrison St. daily except Saturday, Sunday, 2 00 p. m.; on Saturday, 1 p. m. (No passengers carried.) Freight received up to time of departure. Leaves Dobbs' Ferry during the night.

8 Edgewater, N. J. Fort Lee Park and Steamboat Co. Boats leave Canal St. daily except Sundays, 10 00 a. m.; 2 00 p. m., 5 15 p. m.; on Sundays, 10 00 a. m., 2 00 p. m., 6 00 p. m. Lands at West 22d St. 10 minutes later. Fare 15 cts.; Exc. Fare 25 cts. Freight received to 2 00 p. m. Leave Edgewater daily except Sundays, 7 40 a. m., 11 40 a. m., 4 10 p. m.; on Sundays, 8 10 a. m., 12 10 p. m., 5 10 p. m. Time to New York, 35 minutes.

84 Esopus, N. Y. Steamboat J. W. Baldwin and City of Kingston leave Harrison St. J. W. Baldwin, Monday, Wednesday, Friday, 4 00 p. m. City of Kingston, Tuesday, Thursday, 4 00 p. m.; on Saturday, 1 00 p. m. Fare $1 00. Freight received up to 30 minutes before departure. Leave Esopus daily except Saturday, 6 30 p. m. Due in New York, 2 00 a. m.

60 Fishkill, N. Y. Homer Ramsdell Line Propellers, Newburgh and Homer Ramsdell. Leave Franklin St. daily, except Sunday, 5 p. m. On Sundays 9 00 a. m. Fare 50 cts. Freight received to 5 00 p. m. Leave Fishkill every day 7 30 p. m. Due in New York 1 30 a. m.

10 Fort Lee, N. J. Fort Lee Park and Steamboat Co. Boats leave Canal St. daily, except Sundays, 10 00 a. m., 2 00 p. m., 5 15 p. m. On Sundays 10 00 a. m., 2 00, 6 00 p. m. Lands at West 22d St. 10 minutes later. Fare, 15c.; Exc. Fare, 25c. Freight received 2 00 p. m. Leave Fort Lee daily, except Sunday, 7 30 a. m., 11 30 a. m., 4. 00 p. m. On Sundays, 8 00 a. m., 12 00 m., 5 00 p. m. Time to New York, 45 minutes.

Fort Lee. Fort Lee Ferry Boats leave West 130th St. (West 125th St.) every day. 16 10 a. m., †6 30 a. m., †7 45 a. m., 8 30 a. m., 9 30 a. m., 10 30 a. m., 11 30 a. m., 12 30 p. m., 1 30 p. m., 2 30 p. m., 3 30 p. m., 4 30 p. m., 5 30 p. m., 6 30 p. m., 7 15 p. m. Trip marked † are not run on Sundays Fare, 10c. Leave Fort Lee every day, *5 45 a. m., †6 30 a. m., †7 15 a. m., 8 00 a. m., 9 00 a. m., 10 00 a. m., 11 00 a. m., 12 noon, 1 00 p. m., 2 00 p. m., 3 00 p. m., 4 00 p. m., 5 00 p. m., 6 00 p. m., are not run on Sundays. Time of trip, 15 minutes.

111 Germantown, N. Y. Catskill and New York Steamboat Co. leave Jay St. Steamboat Catskill, Monday, Wednesday, Friday, 6 00 p. m. Steamboat Walter Brett, Tuesday, Thursday, Saturday, 6 00 p. m. Fare, $1.00; Exc. Fare, $1.70. Freight received to 5 45 p. m. Leave Germantown daily, except Saturday, 7 00 p. m. Due in New York 5 00 a. m.

42 Grassy Point, N. Y. North River Steamboat Co. Steamboat Chrystenah leave Harrison St. daily, except Saturday and Sunday, 3 45 p. m., on Saturday 2 30 p. m. Lands at West 22d St. 15 minutes later. Fare, 40c.; Exc. Fare, 50c. Freight received up to time of departure. Leave Grassy Point, daily, except Sunday, 7 00 a. m. Due in New York 10 00 a. m.

42 Grassy Point, N. Y. Propeller Peekskill leave Harrison St. Monday, Wednesday, Friday, 3 00 p. m. (No passengers carried.) Freight received same days to 2 15 p. m. Leave Grassy Point, Tuesday, Thursday, Saturday and 4 00 p. m. Sunday Time to New York, 3½ hours.

42 Grassy Point, N. Y. Propeller Fanny Woodall leave Harrison St., Tuesday, Thursday, 3 00 p. m. Saturday 2 00 p. m. (No passengers carried.) Freight received when boat is in. Leave Grassy Point Monday, Wednesday, Friday about 4 00 p. m. Time to New York 3½ hours.

21 Hastings, N. Y. North River Steamboat Co. Propeller Raleigh leaves Harrison St. daily, except Saturday and Sunday, 2 00 p. m. On Saturday 1 00 p. m. (No passengers carried.) Freight received up to time of departure. Leave Hastings during the night.

40 Haverstraw, N. Y. North River Steamboat Co. Steamboat Chrystenah leaves Harrison St. daily, except Saturday and Sunday, 3 45 p. m. on Saturday 2 30 p. m. Lands at West 22d St. 15 minutes later. No Freight received for this landing. Leave Haverstraw daily, except Sunday, 7 15 a. m. Due in New York 10 00 a. m.

40 Haverstraw, N. Y. North River Steamboat Co. Propeller Raleigh leave Harrison St. daily, except Saturday, Sunday, 2 00 p. m.; on Saturday 1 00 p. m. (No passengers carried.) Freight received up to time of departure. Leave Haverstraw during the night.

77 Highland, N. Y. Propellers J. L. Hasbrouck and D. S. Miller leave Franklin St. D. S. Miller, Monday, Wednesday, Friday, 6 00 p. m.; J. L. Hasbrouck. Tuesday, Thursday, Saturday, 6 00 p. m. Fare, 75c. Freight received to 5 45 p. m. Leave Highland daily, except Saturday, 7 30 p. m. Due in New York 3 00 a. m.

STEAMBOATS FOR HUDSON RIVER LANDINGS.—Continued.

MLS.

120 **Hudson, N. Y.** Propeller Thomas McManus, leave Franklin St. Monday, Wednesday, Friday, 6 00 p. m. Fare, $1.00. Freight received same days to 5 45 p. m. Leave Hudson, Tuesday, Thursday, Sunday, 7 00 p. m. Due in New York 5 00 a. m.

12 **Hudson, N. Y.** Catskill and New York Steamboat Co. Propeller W. C. Redfield leave Jay St., Tuesday, Thursday, Saturday, 6 00 p. m. Fare, $1.00. Freight received same days to 5 45 p. m. Leave Hudson Monday, Wednesday, Friday, 7 00 p. m. Due in New York 5 00 a. m.

81 **Hyde Park, N. Y.** Catskill and New York Steamboat Co. leave Jay St. Steamboat Catskill, Monday, Wednesday, Friday, 6 00 p. m. Steamboat Walter Brett, Tuesday, Thursday, Saturday, 6 00 p. m. Fare, $1.00; Exc. Fare, $1.70. Freight received to 5 45 p. m. Leave Hyde Park daily, except Saturday, 10 00 p. m. Due in New York 5 00 a. m.

 Linlithgo. N. Y. Catskill and New York Steamboat Co. leave Jay St. Steamboat Catskill, Monday, Wednesday, Friday, 6 00 p. m. Steamboat Walter Brett, Tuesday, Thursday, Saturday, 6 00 p. m. Fare, $1.00; Exc. Fare, $1.70. Freight received to 5 45 p. m. Leave Linlithgo daily, except Saturday, 6 30 p. m. Due in New York 5 00 a. m.

105 **Malden, N. Y.** Catskill and New York Steamboat Co. leave Jay St. Steamboat Catskill, Monday, Wednesday, Friday, 6 00 p. m. Steamboat Walter Brett, Tuesday, Thursday, Saturday, 6 00 p. m. Fare, $1.00; Exc. Fare, $1.70. Freight received to 5 45 p. m. Leave Malden daily, except Saturday, 7 30 p. m. Due in New York 5 00 a. m.

68 **Marlborough, N. Y.** Propellers J. L. Hasbrouck and D. S. Miller leave Franklin St, D. S. Miller, Monday, Wednesday, Friday, 6 00 p. m. J. L. Hasbrouck, Tuesday, Thursday, Saturday, 6 00 p. m. Fare, 75c. Freight received to 5 45 p. m. Leave Marlborough daily, except Saturday, 8 15 p. m. Due in New York 3 00 a. m.

68 **Marlborough, N. Y.** Steamboats J. W. Baldwin and City of Kingston leave Harrison St. J. W. Baldwin, Monday, Wednesday, Friday, 4 00 p. m. City of Kingston, Tuesday, Thursday, 4 00 p. m.; on Saturday 1 00 p. m. Fare, 75c. Freight received up to 30 minutes before departure. Leave Marlborough daily, except Saturday, 8 15 p. m. Due in New York 2 00 a. m.

72 **Milton, N. Y.** Steamboats J. W. Baldwin and City of Kingston leave Harrison St., J. W. Baldwin, Monday. Wednesday, Friday, 4 00 p. m. City of Kingston, Tuesday, Thursday, 4 00 p. m.; on Saturday 1 00 p. m. Fare, 75c. Freight received up to 30 minutes before departure. Leave Milton daily, except Saturday, 7 45 p. m. Due in New York 2 00 a. m.

130 **New Baltimore, N. Y.** Catskill and New York Steamboat Co. Steamboat Walter Brett, leaves Jay St., Tuesday, Thursday, Saturday, 6 00 p. m. Fare $1.00. Freight received same days to 5 45 p. m. Leave New Baltimore, Monday, Wednesday, Friday, 2 00 p. m. Due in New York 3 a. m.

60 **Newburgh, N. Y.** Homer Ramsdell Line. Propellers Newburgh and Homer Ramsdell leave Franklin St, daily, except Sunday, 5 00 p. m. On Sunday 9 00 a. m. Fare 50 cts. Freight received to 4 00 p. m. Leave Newburg every day 8 00 p. m. Due in New York 3 00 a. m.

60 **Newburgh, N. Y.** Steamboats J. W. Baldwin and City of Kingston leave Harrison St. J. W. Baldwin, Monday, Wednesday, Friday, 4 00 p. m. City of Kingston, Tuesday, Thursday, 4 00 p. m. On Saturday 1 00 p. m. Fare 50 cts. No freight received for this landing. Leave Newburg daily, except Saturday, 9 00 p. m. Due in New York, 2 00 a. m.

67 **New Hamburgh, N. Y.** Propellers J. L. Hasbrouck and D. S. Miller leave Franklin St. D. S. Miller, Monday, Wednesday, Friday, 6 00 p. m. J. L. Hasbrouck, Tuesday, Thursday, Saturday, 6 00 p. m. Fare 75 cts. Freight received to 5 45 p. m. Leave New Hamburgh daily, except Saturday, 8 45 p. m. Due in New York 3 00 a. m.

28 **Nyack,** North River Steamboat Co. Steamboat Chrystenah leaves Harrison St., daily, except Saturday and Sunday, 3 45 p. m. On Saturday 2 30 p. m. Lands at West 22d St. 15 minutes later. Fare 30 cts. Exc. fare 50 cts. No freight received for this landing. Leave Nyack daily, except Sunday, 7 55 a. m. Due in New York 10 00 a. m.

28 **Nyack,** North River Steamboat Co. Propeller Raleigh leaves Harrison St. daily, except Saturday and Sunday, 2 00 p. m. On Saturday 1 00 p. m. (No Passengers carried.) Freight received up to time of departure. Leave Nyack during the night.

113 **Oak Hill, N. Y.** Catskill and New York Steamboat Co. Leave Jay St., Steamboat Catskill, Monday, Wednesday, Friday, 6 00 p. m. Steamboat Walter Brett, Tuesday, Thursday, Saturday, 6 00 p. m. Fare $1.00. Exc. Fare $1.70. Freight received to 5 45 p. m. Leave Oak Hill daily, except Saturday, 6 15 p. m. Due in New York 5 00 a. m.

48 **Peekskill, N. Y.** North River Steamboat Co. Steamboat Chrystenah leaves Harrison St. daily, except Saturday and Sunday, 3 45 p. m. On Saturday 2 30 p. m. Lands at West 22d St. 15 minutes later. Fare 40 cts. Exc. Fare 50 cts. Freight received up to time of departure. Leave Peekskill daily, except Sunday, 6 30 a. m. Due in New York 10 00 a. m.

48 **Peekskill, N. Y.** Propeller Peekskill leaves Harrison St., Monday, Wednesday, Friday, 3 00 p. m. (No passengers carried). Freight received same days to 2 15 p. m. Leave Peekskill, Tuesday, Thursday 3 00 p. m. Saturday 5 00 p. m. Time to New York 4 hours 30 minutes.

48 **Peekskill, N. Y.** Propeller Fanny Woodall leaves Harrison St. Tuesday, Thursday, 3 00 p. m. Saturday 2 00 p. m. (No Passengers carried.) Freight received when boat is in. Leave Peekskill Monday, Wednesday, Friday, 3 00 p. m. Time to New York 4 hours 30 minutes.

10 **Pleasant Valley, N. J.** Fort Lee Park & Steamboat Company. Boats leave Canal St. daily, except Sunday, 10 00 a. m., 2 00 p. m., 5 15 p. m. On Sundays 10 00 a. m., 2 00 p. m., 6 00 p. m. Lands at West 22d Street 10 minutes later. Freight received to 2 00 p. m. Leave Pleasant Valley daily, except Sunday, at 7 35 a. m., 11 35 a. m., 4 05 p. m. Sunday 8 05 a. m., 12 05 p. m., 4 05 p. m. Time of trip 40 minutes.

75 **Poughkeepsie, N. Y.** Steamboats J. W. Baldwin and City of Kingston leave Harrison St. J. W. Baldwin, Monday, Wednesday, Friday, 4 00 p. m. City of Kingston, Tuesday, Thursday, 4 00 p. m. Saturday 1 00 p. m. Fare 75 cts. No freight received for this landing. Leave Poughkeepsie daily, except Saturday, 7 30 p. m. Due in New York 2 00 a. m.

76 **Poughkeepsie, N. Y.** Propeller J. L. Hasbrouck and D. S Miller leave Franklin St. D. S. Miller, Monday, Wednesday, Friday, 6 00 p. m. J. L. Hasbrouck, Tuesday, Thursday, Saturday, 6 00 p. m. Fare 75 cts. Freight received to 5 45 p. m. Leave Poughkeepsie daily, except Saturday, 7 00 p. m. Due in New York 3 00 a. m.

90 **Rhinebeck, N. Y.** New York and Saugerties Transportation Co. Steamboat Ansonia leave Franklin St. Tuesday, Thursday, Saturday, 6 00 p. m. Fare $1.00. Freight received same days to 5 45 p. m. Leave Rhinebeck Monday, Wednesday, Friday, 8 30 p. m. Due in New York 5 00 a. m.

31 **Rockland Lake, N. Y.** North River Steamboat Co. Steamboat Chrystenah leaves Harrison St. daily, except Saturday and Sunday, 3 45 p. m. On Saturday 2 30 p. m. Lands at West 22d Street 15 minutes later. Fare 35 cts. Exc. Fare 50 cts. Freight received up to time of departure. Leave Rockland Lake daily, except Sunday, 7 30 a. m. Due in New York 10 00 a. m.

95 **Rondout, N. Y.** Steamboats J. W. Baldwin and City of Kingston leave Harrison St. J. W. Baldwin, Monday, Wednesday, Friday, 4 00 p. m. City of Kingston, Tuesday, Thursday, 4 00 p. m., Saturday 1 00 p. m. Fare $1.00. Freight received up to 30 minutes before departure. Leave Rondout daily except Saturday 6 00 p. m. Due in New York 2 00 a. m.

101 **Saugerties, N. Y.** New York and Saugerties Transportation Co. Steamboat Ansonia leave Franklin St. Tuesday, Thursday, Saturday, 6 00 p. m. Fare $1.00. Freight received same days to 5 45 p. m. Leave Saugerties, Monday, Wednesday, Friday, 7 00 p. m. Due in New York, 5 00 a. m.

7 **Shady Side, N. J.** Fort Lee Park and Steamboat Co. Boats leave Canal St. daily except Sundays, 10 00 a. m., 2 00 p. m., 5 15 p. m.; on Sunday, 10 a. m., 2 00 p. m., 6 00 p. m. Lands at West 22d st. 10 minutes later. Fare 15 cts.; Exc. Fare 25 cts. Freight received to 2 00 p. m. Leave Shady Side daily except Sunday, 7 45 a. m., 11 45 a. m. 4 15 p. m. Sundays 8 15 a. m., 12 15 p. m., 5 15 p. m. Time to New York 30 minutes.

35 **Sing Sing, N. Y.** Propeller S. A. Jenks leaves Franklin St. daily except Sunday, 3 00 p. m. Fare 25 cts. Freight received to 2 15 p. m. Leave Sing Sing daily except Sunday, 7 00 a. m. Due in New York, 10 00 a. m.

100 **Smith's Landing, N. Y.** Catskill and New York Steamboat Co. leave Jay St. Steamboat Catskill, Monday, Wednesday, Friday, 6 00 p. m. Steamboat Walter Brett, Tuesday, Thursday, Saturday, 6 00 p. m. Fare $1 00; Exc. Fare $1 70. Freight received to 5 45 p. m. Leave Smith's Landing daily except Saturday, 7 15 p. m. Due in New York, 5 00 a. m.

STEAMBOATS FOR HUDSON RIVER LANDINGS.—Continued.

MLS.
127 Stuyvesant, N. Y. Catskill and New York Steamboat Co. Steamboat Walter Brett leave Jay St. Tuesday, Thursday, Saturday, 6 00 p. m. Fare $1 00. Freight received same days to 5 45 p. m. Leave Stuyvesant, Monday, Wednesday, Friday, 3 00 p. m. Due in New York, 5 00 a. m.

28 Tarrytown, North River Steamboat Co. Steamboat Chrystenah leave Harrison St. daily except Saturday and Sunday, 3 45 p. m.; on Saturday 2 30 p. m. *Lands at West 22d St. 15 minutes later.* Fare 25 cts.; Exc. Fare 40 cts. *Connects by ferry. No freight received.* Leave Tarrytown *by ferry* daily except Sunday 8 00 a. m. Due in New York 10 00 a. m.

15 Tarrytown, N. Y. Propeller Tarrytown leaves Harrison St. Monday, Wednesday, Friday, 3 00 p. m. (*No passengers carried.*) Freight received some days to 2 45 p. m. Leaves Tarrytown, Tuesday, Thursday, Saturday, 1 00 p. m. Time to New York 3 hours.

100 Tivoli, N. Y. New York and Saugerties Transportation Co. Steamboat Ansonia leave Franklin St. Tuesday, Thursday, Saturday, 6 00 p. m. Fare $1.00. Freight received same days to 5 45 p. m. Leave Tivoli, Monday, Wednesday, Friday, 7 15 p. m. Due in New York 5 00 a. m.

100 Tivoli, N. Y. Catskill and New York Steamboat Co. leaves Jay St. Steamboat Catskill, Monday, Wednesday, Friday, 6 00 p. m. Steamboat Walter Brett, Tuesday, Thursday, Saturday, 6 00 p. m. Fare $1 00; Exc. Fare $1 70. Freight received to 5 45 p. m. Leave Tivoli daily except Saturday 7 45 p. m. Due in New York 5 00 a. m.

41 Tompkins' Cove, N. Y. Propeller Peekskill leave Harrison St. Monday, Wednesday, Friday, 3 00 p. m. (*No passengers carried.*) Freight received same days to 2 45 p. m. Leave Tompkins' Cove, Tuesday, Thursday, about 3 30 p. m.; Saturday about 5 30 p. m. Time to New York 4 hours.

44 Tompkins' Cove, N. Y. Propeller Fanny Woodall leaves Harrison St. Tuesday, Thursday, 3 00 p. m.; Saturday 2 00 p. m. (*No passengers carried.*) Freight received same days when boat is in. Leave Tompkins' Cove, Monday, Wednesday, Friday, 3 30 p. m. Time to New York 4 hours.

151 Troy, N. Y. Citizens' Line leave Christopher St. Steamboat City of Troy, Monday, Wednesday, Friday, 6 00 p. m.; Saratoga, Tuesday, Thursday, Sunday, 6 00 p. m. Fare $1 50; Exc. Fare $2 50. Freight received to 5 45 p. m. Due at Troy 6 00 a. m. Leave Troy daily except Saturday and Sunday, 7 30 p. m.; *on Sundays* 6 00 p. m. Due in New York 7 00 a. m.

95 Ulster Landing, N. Y. New York and Saugerties Transportation Co. Steamboat Ansonia leave Franklin St. Tuesday, Thursday, Saturday, 6 00 p. m. Fare $1 00. Freight received same days 5 45 p. m. Leave Ulster Landing, Monday, Wednesday, Friday, 7 45 p. m. Due in New York 5 00 a. m.

43 Verplanks, N. Y. North River Steamboat Co. Steamboat Chrystenah leave Harrison St. daily except Saturday and Sunday 3 45 p. m.; on Saturday 2 30 p. m. *Lands at West 22d St. 15 minutes later.* Fare 40 cts.; Exc. Fare 50 cts. Freight received up to time of departure. Leave Verplanks daily except Sunday 6 50 a. m. Due in New York 10 00 a. m.

43 Verplanks, N. Y. Propeller Peekskill leave Harrison St. Monday, Wednesday, Friday, 3 00 p. m. (*No passengers carried.*) Freight received 2 45 p. m. Leave Verplanks, Tuesday, Thursday, about 3 45 p. m. Saturday about 5 45 p. m. Time to New York 3 hours, 45 minutes.

43 Verplanks, N. Y. Propeller Fanny Woodall leave Harrison St. Tuesday, Thursday, 3 00 p. m.; Saturday 2 00 p. m. (*No passengers carried.*) Freight received when boat is in. Leave Verplanks, Monday, Wednesday, Friday, 3 45 p. m. Time to New York 3 hours, 45 minutes.

53 West Point, N. Y. Catskill and New York Steamboat Co. Steamboat Catskill, Monday, Wednesday, Friday, 6 00 p. m. Propeller W. C. Redfield, Tuesday, Thursday, Saturday, 6 00 p. m. Fare 50 cts. Freight received to 5 45 p. m. *Does not stop at West Point on return trip to New York.*

53 West Point, N. Y. Homer Ramsdell Line. Propellers Newburgh and Homer Ramsdell leave Franklin St. daily except Sunday, 5 00 p. m.; on Sundays 6 00 a. m. Fare 50 cts. Freight received to 5 00 p. m. Leave West Point every day 9 15 p. m. Due in New York 1 30 a. m.

82 West Park, N. Y. Steamboat J. W. Baldwin leaves Harrison St., Monday, Wednesday, Friday, 4 00 p. m. Fare $1.00. Freight received up to 30 minutes before departure. Leave West Park, Sunday, Tuesday, Thursday, 7 00 p. m. Due in New York 2 00 a. m.

17 Yonkers, N. Y. North River Steamboat Co. Steamboat Chrystenah leave Harrison St. daily except Saturday and Sunday, 3 45 p. m.; on Saturday 2 30 p. m. *Lands at West 22d St. 15 minutes later.* Fare 20 cts.; Exc. Fare 30 cts. Freight received to time of departure. Leave Yonkers daily except Sunday 8 50 a. m. Due in New York 10 00 a. m.

17 Yonkers, N. Y. Propeller C. A. Peene leaves Franklin St. daily except Sunday 3 00 p. m. Fare 15 cts. Freight received up to 2 45 p. m. Leave Yonkers daily except Sunday, 8 00 a. m. Due in New York 9 30 a. m.

17 Yonkers, N. Y. Ben. Franklin Freight Barge Line leaves Franklin St. daily except Sunday 3 00 p. m. Freight received to 2 45 p. m. Leave Yonkers 12 00 noon. Time to New York about 4 hours.

NOTICE.—Steamboat Saugerties leaves Franklin St. Monday, Wednesday and Friday, 6 00 p. m. Fare $1 00. Exc. Fare $1 50. Freight received same days to 5 45 p. m. Leaves Saugerties Tuesday, Thursday, Saturday, 7 00 p. m. Stopping at Tivoli, 7 15 p. m., Ulster Landing, 7 45 p. m., Barrytown, 8 00 p. m., Rhinebeck, 8 50 p. m. Due in New York 5 00 a. m.

STEAMBOATS FROM NEW YORK TO LANDINGS *NOT* ON THE HUDSON.

MLS.
6 Astoria, L. I. Steamboat Morrisania leaves Pier 24 East River, daily, except Sunday, 11 30 a. m., 5 30 p. m. Fare 10c. Freight received to 5 15 p. m. Leave Astoria, daily, except Sunday, 7 55 a. m. Time to New York 25 minutes.

5 Bay Ridge, L. I. A steamboat leaves Whitehall St. daily, except Sunday, 8 00 a. m., 9 05 a. m., 10 10 a. m., 3 45 p. m., 4 50 p. m., 5 55 p. m. Fare 10c. Leave Bay Ridge daily, except Sunday, 7 35 a. m., 8 40 a. m., 9 45 a. m.; 3 15 p. m., 4 15 p. m., 5 25 p. m. Time to New York, 20 minutes (*may change.*)

Bedloe's Island. A steamboat leaves Whitehall St. every day, hourly. from 9 00 a. m. to 5 00 p. m. Fare 25c. Leave Bedloe's Island every day, hourly, from 9 30 a. m. to 4 30 p. m., then 5 45 p. m. Time to New York, 10 minutes.

7 Bergen Point, N. J. Steamboat Chancellor leaves Rector St. daily, except Sunday, 11 00 a. m., 5 00 p. m. Fare 10c. Freight received to 4 45 p. m. Leaves Bergen Point, 8 25 a. m., 2 25 p. m. Time to New York 45 minutes.

230 Boston, Mass. Fall River Line. Leave Murray St. 5 00 p. m. Pilgrim, Sunday, Monday, Wednesday, Friday; Old Colony, Tuesdays, Thursdays, Saturdays. Fare, $3.00; Stateroom, $1.00. Freight received to 4 45 p. m. Due at Boston, 6 50 a. m. Leave Boston daily, except Sunday, 6 00 p. m.; Sunday, 7 00 p. m. by the Old Colony R. R. Due in New York, 7 30 a. m.

240 Boston, Mass. Norwich Line. Leave Watts St. 5 00 p. m. City of New York, Monday, Wednesday, Friday. City of Worcester, Tuesday, Thursday, Saturday. Fare, $3.00; Stateroom, $1 00. Freight received to 4 45 p. m. Due at Boston, 8 00 a. m. Leave Boston daily, except Sunday, 6 00 p. m., by New York and New England R. R. Due in New York, 7 00 a. m.

211 Boston, Mass. Stonington Line. Leave Spring St., 5 00 p. m., Rhode Island, Monday, Wednesday, Friday. Stonington, Tuesday, Thursday, Saturday. Fare, $3.00. Freight received to 4 45 p. m. Due at Boston, 6 00 a. m. Leave Boston daily, except Sunday, 6 30 p. m., by Providence Division of Old Colony R. R. Due in New York, 6 00 a. m.

225 Boston, Mass. Providence Line. Propeller Nashua and Pequot (no passengers carried). Leave Warren St. daily, except Sunday, 5 00 p. m. Freight received to 5 00 p. m. Leave Boston for New York during the night.

Boston, Mass. Metropolitan Steamship Co. (*Outside Line*). Leave Carlisle St., Tuesday, Thursday, Saturday, 5 p.m. (No passengers carried.) Freight received daily to 6 00 p. m. Leave Boston, Monday, Wednesday, Saturday, 5 00 p. m. Time to New York about 20 hours.

35 Branchport, N. J. Steamboat Elberon, leave Franklin St. Tuesday, Wednesday, Thursday and Friday, 9 00 a. m. On Tuesday, 10 a. m. Fare 40c.; Exc. Fare 60c. Freight received up to 15 minutes before departure. Leave Branchport on Monday, 11 00 a. m., Wednesday, Thursday and Friday at 2 30 p. m. Time to New York 4 hours.

65 Bridgeport, Conn. Bridgeport Steamboat Company. Steamboat Waterbury leaves Catharine St. daily, except Sunday, 11 00 a. m. Fare, 50c.; Exc. Fare 75c. Freight received to 6 00 p. m. Leave Bridgeport daily, except Saturday, 11 00 a. m. Time to New York, 4 hours.

STEAMBOATS TO LANDINGS *NOT* ON THE HUDSON.—Continued.

MLS.
65 Bridgeport, Conn. People's Steamboat Co. Rosedale leaves Peck Slip daily, except Saturday and Sunday, at 3 00 p. m., on Saturday, 2 30 p. m. Fare, 50c.; Exc. Fare, 75c. (*Stopping at East 31st St. 15 minutes later.*) Freight received at Peck's Slip to 5 00 p. m. Leave Bridgeport daily, except Sunday, 7 30 a. m. Time to New York, 3½ hours.

65 Bridgeport, Conn. Propeller City of Bridgeport leaves Catharine St. Tuesday, Thursday, Saturday, 4 30 p. m. (*No Passengers carried.*) Freight received same days to 1 15 p. m. Leave Bridgeport Monday, Wednesday, Friday, 9 00 p. m. Time to New York, 4 hours.

Brockway's Landing, Conn. Hartford Line. Leave Peck Slip. City of Springfield, Monday, Wednesday, Friday, 5 00 p. m.; City of Richmond, Tuesday, Thursday, Saturday, 5 00 p. m. Fare, $1.50; Exc. Fare, $2.25. Freight received to 6 00 p. m. Leave Brockway's daily, except Sunday, 9 30 p. m. Due in New York at 6 00 a. m.

31 Brown Dock, N. J. Steamboat Sea Bird, leaves Franklin St. daily except Sunday, about 3 00 p. m. Fare 50c.; Exc. Fare 80c. Freight received up to 15 minutes before departure. Leave Brown's Dock daily except Sunday, about 7 20 a. m. Time to New York 2 hours 40 minutes.

18 Chelsea. Steamboat New Brunswick leaves Vesey St. Tuesday, Thursday, Saturday 3 00 p. m. Fare 20c.; Exc. fare 30c. Freight received same days to 2 45 p. m. Leaves Chelsea Tuesday, Thursday, Saturday, 9 10 a. m. Due in New York 10 20 a. m.

Cholera Banks. Steamboat Schuyler, on Tuesday, Thursday and Sunday. Leaves East 21st St. 7:30 a. m., Peck Slip 8 00 a. m., Franklin St. N. R., 8 30 a. m. Exc. Fare 60 cts. Due in New York, 5 30 p. m.

19 City Island, N. Y. Propeller Captain John, leaves Pike St. Tuesday, Thursday, Saturday, 12 noon. Fare 25c. Freight received same days to 11 45 a. m. Leaves City Island Monday, Wednesday, Friday, 8 00. Time to New York 2 hours 30 minutes.

19 City Island, N. Y. Propeller Baltimore leaves Pier 27 E. R. Monday, Wednesday, Friday, 2 00 p. m. Fare 25c. Freight received same days to 1 45 p. m. Leaves City Island Tuesday, Thursday, Saturday, 10 00 a. m. Time to New York, 1 hour 30 minutes.

9 Clifton, Staten Island. By Ferry from Whitehall St. to St. George, Staten Island and thence by Staten Island Rapid Transit R. R. (see page 91 for time table). Fare 10c.

35 Cold Spring, L. I. Propeller Baltimore leaves Pier 27 E. R. Monday, Wednesday, Friday 2 00 p. m. Fare 50c.; Exc. Fare 75c. Freight received same days to 1 45 p. m. Leave Cold Spring Tuesday, Thursday, Saturday 7 00 a. m. Time to New York 4½ hours.

5 College Point, L. I. New York and Long Island Ferry Co. Leaves E. 99th St. daily except Sundays, 5 00 a. m., 7 00 a. m., 9 00 a. m., 11 00 a. m., 1 00 p. m., 3 00 p. m., 5 00 p. m., 7 00 p. m. *Sundays*, 9 00 a. m., 11 00 a. m., 1 00 p. m., 3 00 p. m., 5 00 p. m., 7 00 p. m. Fare 10c. Leaves College Point daily except Sundays, 6 00 a. m., 8 00 a. m., 10 00 a. m., 12 noon, 2 00 p. m., 4 00 p. m., 6 00 p. m. *Sundays*, 8 00 a. m., 10 00 a. m., 12 noon, 2 00 p. m., 4 00 p. m., 6 p. m. Time to New York 35 minutes.

7 College Point. Boyer's freight Propeller leaves Pier 27 E. R. daily except Sunday 2 00 p. m. Freight received to 5 00 p. m. Leaves College Point daily except Sunday about 7 15 a. m. Time to New York 1 hour.

Coney Island. Via Bay Ridge and Sea Beach R. R. Boats leave Whitehall St. every day (*if weather permits*) about hourly to 6 p. m. Leave Coney Island about hourly to 6 10 p. m.

6 Constable Hook. Steamboat Chancellor leaves Rector St. daily except Sunday, 11 00 a. m., 5 00 p. m. Fare 10c. Freight received to 4 45 p. m. Leaves Constable Hook daily except Sunday, 8 35 a. m., 2 35 p. m. Time to New York 35 minutes.

140 Cromwell, Conn. Hartford Line. Leaves Peck Slip, City of Springfield, Monday, Wednesday, Friday, 5 00 p. m.; City of Richmond, Tuesday, Thursday, Saturday, 5 p. m. Fare $1.50; Exc. fare $2.25. Freight received to 6 00 p. m. Leaves Cromwell daily except Sunday, 9 35 p. m. Due in New York 6 a. m.

22 David's Island. U. S. Government boat leaves Gansevoort St. Tuesday, Thursday, Saturday, 9 00 a. m. (*by pass*). Leaves David's Island Tuesday, Thursday, Saturday, 2 00 p. m.

100 Deep River, Conn. Hartford Line. Leaves Peck Slip, City of Springfield, Monday, Wednesday, Friday, 5 00 p. m.; City of Richmond, Tuesday, Thursday, Saturday, 5 00 p. m. Fare $1.50; Exc. fare $2.25. Freight received to 6 00 p. m. Leave Deep River daily except Sunday, 9 35 p. m. Due in New York 6 00 a. m.

73 Derby, Conn. Naugatuck Valley Steamboat Co. Leaves Pier 39 E. R., between Market and Pike Sts., daily except Sunday, 6 00 p. m. Fare $1.00. Freight received to 6 00 p. m. Leave Derby daily except Sunday, 6 00 p. m. Time to New York 13 hours.

11 Elizabethport, N. J. Steamboat Chancellor leaves Rector St. daily except Sunday, 11 00 a. m., 5 00 p. m. Fare 15c. Freight received to 4 45 p. m. Leaves Elizabethport daily, except Sunday, 8 00 a. m., 2 00 p. m. Time to New York, 1 hour 10 minutes.

14 Elizabethport, N. J. Singer Mfg. Co.'s Propeller, E. Clark, leaves Dey St. daily, except Sunday, 2 00 p. m. Special freight received to 1 45 p. m. Leaves Elizabethport about 7 00 a. m. Time to New York, 1¼ hours.

106 Essex, Conn. Hartford Line. Leaves Peck Slip, City of Springfield, Monday, Wednesday, Friday, 5 00 p. m., City of Richmond, Tuesday, Thursday, Saturday, 5 00 p. m. Fare, $1.50; Exc. fare, $2.25. Freight received to 6 00 p. m. Leaves Essex daily, except Sunday, 10 15 p. m. Due in New York, 6 00 a. m.

31 Fairhaven, N. J. Steamboat Sea Bird leaves Franklin St. daily except Sunday, 3 00 p. m. Fare 50c.; Exc. Fare 80c. Freight received up to 15 minutes of departure. Leave Fairhaven about 7 15 a. m. Time to New York 2 hours 45 minutes.

170 Fall River Mass. Fall River Line. Leaves Murray st. every day 5 00 p. m. Boats of this line at present are running direct to Newport, connecting there with the Old Colony R. R. for Fall River. Fare, $2.

170 Fall River, Mass. Fall River Line, Boston, for freight only. Leave Murray St. about 5 00 p. m. (*no passengers carried*). Leave Fall River about 7 00 p. m. Due in New York, 9 00 p. m.

Fishing Banks. Steamboat Angler. On Tuesday, Thursday and Sunday. Leaves East 21st st. 6 30 a. m. Beekman St., 7 00 a. m. Pier 6, N. R., 7 30 a. m. Exc. Fare 75c. Due in New York about 5 30 p. m.

8 Flushing, L. I. Boyer's Freight Propeller leaves Pier 27, E. R., daily, except Sunday, 2 00 p. m. Freight received to 5 00 p. m. Leaves Flushing daily, except Sunday, about 7 00 a. m. Time to New York, 1 hour 30 minutes.

Fort Schuyler. U. S. Government Boat leaves Gansevoort St. Tuesday, Thursday, Saturday, 9 00 a. m. (*by pass*). Leaves Fort Schuyler, Tuesday, Thursday, Saturday, 2 00 p. m. Time to New York, 2 hours.

142 Gildersleeve's, Conn. Hartford Line. Leaves Peck Slip, City of Springfield, Monday, Wednesday, Friday, 5 00 p. m., City of Richmond, Tuesday, Thursday, Saturday, 5 00 p. m. Fare, $1.50; Exc. Fare, $2.25. Freight received to 6 00 p. m. Leaves Gildersleeve's daily, except Sunday, 6 10 p. m. Due in New York, 6 00 a. m.

152 Glastonbury, Conn. Hartford Line. Leaves Peck Slip, City of Richmond. Monday, Wednesday, Friday, 5 00 p. m.; City of Richmond, Tuesday, Thursday, Saturday, 5 00 p. m. Fare, $1.50; Exc. Fare, $2.25. Freight received to 6 00 p. m. Leaves Glastonbury daily, except Sunday, 5 30 p. m. Due in New York, 6 00 a. m.

28 Glen Cove, L. I. Steamboat Idlewild leaves Peck Slip daily, except Sunday, 4 00 p. m., East 31st St., 4 15 p. m. Fare, 35c.; Exc. Fare, 50c. Freight received at Peck Slip to 3 45 p. m. Leaves Glen Cove daily, except Sunday, 7 12 a. m. Due in New York, 9 15 a. m.

33 Glenwood, L. I. (*Townsend Dock*). Steamboat Idlewild leaves Peck Slip daily, except Sunday, 4 00 p. m., East 31st St., 4 15 p. m. Fare, 35c.; Exc. Fare, 50c. Freight received at Peck Slip to 3 45 p. m. Leaves Glenwood daily, except Sunday, 6 40 a. m. Due in New York, 9 15 a. m.

114 Goodspeed's, Conn. Hartford Line. Leave Peck Slip, City of Springfield, Monday, Wednesday, Friday, 5 00 p. m., City of Richmond, Tuesday, Thursday, Saturday, 5 00 p. m. Fare, $1.50; Exc. Fare, $2.25. Freight received to 6 00 p. m. Leave Goodspeed's daily, except Sunday, 9 00 p. m. Due in New York, 6 00 a. m.

STEAMBOATS TO LANDINGS *NOT* ON THE HUDSON.—Continued.

MLS.

Governor's Island. U. S. Government Boat Atlantic leaves Whitehall St. every day 7 00 a. m., 7 45 a. m., 8 00 a. m. 9 00 a. m., 9 30 a. m., 10 30 a. m., 11 30 a. m., 12 45 p. m., 1 15 p. m., 1 45 p. m., 2 30 p. m., 3 30 p. m., 4 15 p. m., 4 45 p. m., 5 15 p. m., 5 45 p. m., 6 15 p. m., 7 30 p. m., 8 30 p. m., 10 30 p. m., 12 night. The 7 00 a. m., 7 15 a. m., 12 night trips are omitted on Sunday (*by pass*). Leaves Governor's Island every day, 6 15 a. m.; 7 30 a. m., 8 00 a. m., 8 30 a. m., 9 15 a. m., 10 00 a. m., 11 00 a. m., 12 30 p. m., 1 00 p. m., 1 30 p. m., 2 00 p. m., 3 00 p. m., 4 00 p. m., 4 30 p. m., 5 00 p. m., 5 30 p. m., 6 00 p. m., 7 15 p. m., 8 00 p. m., 10 p. m., 11 30 p. m. The 6 15 a. m., 7 30 a. m., 8 00 a. m. trips are omitted on Sundays.

Governor's Island. U. S. Government boat leaves Gansevoort St. Monday, Wednesday, Friday, 9 00 a. m., 1 00 p. m., 4 00 p. m., Tuesday, Thursday, Saturday, 9 00 a. m. (*by pass*).

18 **Great Neck, L. I.** Steamboat Idlewild leaves Peck Slip daily, except Sunday at 4 00 p. m., E. 31st St., 4 15 p. m. Fare, 35c.; Exc. fare, 50c. Freight received at Peck Slip to 3 45 p. m. Leaves Great Neck daily, except Sunday, 8 05 a. m. Due in New York, 9 45 a. m.

30 **Greenwich, Conn.** Steamboat Maid of Kent leaves Pike St., Monday, Wednesday, Friday, 2 00 p. m. Fare, 25c. Freight received same days to 1 45 p. m. Leaves Greenwich, Tuesday, Thursday, Saturday, 2 00 p. m. Time to New York, 3 hours.

125 **Greenport, L. I.** Montauk Steamboat Co. Steamboat Shelter Island leaves Pier 24, E. R., Beekman St., Tuesday, Thursday, Saturday, 5 00 p. m. Fare, $1.25. Freight received same days. 4 45 p. m. Leaves Greenport, Monday, Wednesday, Friday, 6 00 p. m. Time to New York, 11 hours.

54 **Griggstown, N. J.** Merchants' Transportation Co. via Delaware and Raritan Canal. Propellers leave Vestry St. daily, except Sunday, 3 00 p. m. Freight received to 6 p. m. (*No passengers carried.*) Leaves Griggstown during the night. Due in New York about 3 p. m.

112 **Hadlyme, Conn.** Hartford Line. Leaves Peck Slip, City of Springfield, Monday, Wednesday, Friday, 5 00 p. m., City of Richmond, Tuesday, Thursday, Saturday, 5 00 p. m. Fare, $1.50; Exc. fare, $2.25. Freight received to 6 00 p. m. Leaves Hadlyme daily, except Sunday, 9 20 p. m. Due in New York, 6 00 a. m.

9 **Harlem (130th St.)** Steamboat Morrisania leaves Pier 24, E. R., daily, except Sunday, 11 30 a. m., 5 30 p. m. Freight received to 5 15 p. m. Fare, 10c. Leaves Harlem daily, except Sunday, 2 00 p. m. Time to New York, 40 minutes.

156 **Hartford, Conn.** Hartford Line. Leaves Peck Slip, City of Springfield, Monday, Wednesday, Friday, 5 00 p. m., City of Richmond, Tuesday, Thursday, Saturday, 5 p. m. Fare, $1.50; Exc. fare, $2.25. Freight received to 6 00 p. m. Leaves Hartford daily, except Sunday, 5 00 p. m. Due in New York, 6 00 a. m.

26 **Highlands, N. J.** Steamboat Elberon leaves Franklin St. Tuesday, Wednesday, Thursday and Friday 9 00 a. m.; on Saturday 10 a. m. Fare 10c.; Exc. Fare 60c. Freight received up to 15 minutes before departure. Leave Highlands on Monday on Signal 12 m. and Tuesday, Wednesday, Thursday and Friday on signal 3 30 p. m. Time to New York 3 hours.

26 **Highlands, N. J.** Steamboat Sea Bird leaves Franklin St. daily except Sunday, 3 00 p. m. Fare 50c.; Exc. Fare 80c. Freight received up to 15 minutes of departure. Leave Highlands daily except Sundays about 8 00 a. m. Time to New York 2 hours.

40 **Huntington, L. I.** Propeller Huntington leaves Pike St. Tuesday and Thursday, 4 00 p. m. Fare, 50c. Freight received same days to 3 45 p. m. Leaves Huntington Monday and Wednesday, 2 00 p. m. Time to New York, 3½ hours.

27 **Keyport, N. J.** Steamboat Minnie Cornell leaves Vesey St. daily, except Sunday, 4 00 p. m. Fare, 30c.; Exc. fare, 50c. Freight received to 3 45 p. m. Leaves Keyport daily, except Sunday, 7 00 a. m. Time to New York 1 hour 30 minutes.

59 **Kingston, N. J.** Merchants' Transportation Co., via Delaware and Raritan Canal. Propeller leaves Vestry St. daily, except Sundays, 3 p. m. (*No passengers carried.*) Freight received to 6 p. m. Leaves Kingston during the night. Due in New York about 3 00 p. m.

19 **Linoleumville.** Steamboat New Brunswick leaves Vesey St. daily, except Sunday, 3 00 p. m. Fare, 20c.; Exc. fare, 30c. Freight received to 5 00 p. m. Leaves Linoleumville daily, except Sunday, 9 a. m. Time to New York, 1 hour 20 minutes.

25 **Lloyd's Dock, L. I.** Propeller Baltimore leaves Pier 27, E. R., Monday, Wednesday, Friday, 2 p. m. Fare, 50c.; Exc. fare, 75c. Freight received same days to 1 45 p. m. Leaves Lloyd's Dock, Tuesday, Thursday, Saturday, 7 45 a. m. Time to New York, 3 hours 45 minutes.

30 **Locust Point, N. J.** Steamboat Sea Bird leaves Franklin St. daily except Sunday, 3 00 p. m. Fare 50c.; Exc. Fare 80c. Freight received up to 15 minutes of departure. Leave Locust Point daily except Sundays about 7 25 a. m. Time to New York 2 hours 35 minutes.

102 **Lyme, Conn.** Hartford Line. Leaves Peck Slip, City of Springfield, Monday, Wednesday, Friday, 5 00 p. m.; City of Richmond, Tuesday, Thursday, Saturday, 5 00 p. m. Fare, $1.50; Exc. fare, $2.25. Freight received to 6 00 p. m. Does not stop at this landing on return trip to New York.

24 **Mamaroneck, N. Y.** Propeller Mary E. Gordon leaves Pike St. Tuesday, Thursday, Saturday, 2 00 p. m. Fare, 25c. Freight received same days to 1 45 p. m. Leaves Mamaroneck, Monday, Wednesday, Friday, 2 00 p. m. Time to New York, 2½ hours.

11 **Mariner's Harbor.** Steamboat Chancellor leaves Rector St. daily, except Sunday, 11 00 a. m., 5 00 p. m. Fare 10c. Freight received to 4 45 p. m. Leaves Mariner's Harbor daily, except Sunday, 8 10 a. m., 2 10 p. m. Time to New York, 1 hour.

130 **Middle Haddam, Conn.** Hartford Line. Leaves Peck Slip, City of Springfield, Monday, Wednesday, Friday, 5 00 p. m. City of Richmond, Tuesday, Thursday, Saturday 5 00 p. m. Fare. $1.50 ; Exc. Fare, $2.25. Freight received to 6 00 p. m. Leaves Middle Haddam daily, except Sunday, 7 15 p. m. Due in New York, 6 00 a. m.

136 **Middletown, Conn.** Hartford Line. Leaves Peck Slip, City of Springfield, Monday, Wednesday, Friday, 5 00 p. m., City of Richmond, Tuesday, Thursday, Saturday, 5 00 p. m. Fare, $1.50; Exc. Fare, $2.25. Freight received to 6 00 p. m. Leave Middletown daily, except Sunday, 7 15 p. m. Due in New York, 6 00 a. m.

48 **Millstone, N. J.** Merchant's Transportation Co., via Delaware and Raritan Canal. Propeller leaves Vestry St. daily, except Sundays, 3 00 p. m. (*No passengers carried.*) Freight received to 6 00 p. m. Leaves Millstone during the night. Due in New York about 3 00 p. m.

Newark, N. J. Stephens & Condit's Freight Boats leave Jay St. daily, except Sunday, 11 00 a. m., 5 00 p. m. Freight received to 5 p. m. (*No passengers carried.*) Leaves Newark daily, Sunday, 6 00 a. m., 4 00 p. m. Time to New York, 2 hours.

187 **New Bedford, Mass.** Propeller City of Fitchburg leaves Pier 39, E. R., between Market and Pike Sts., Tuesday, Thursday, Saturday, 4 00 p. m. Freight received to 6 00 p. m. (*No passengers carried.*) Leave New Bedford, Monday, Wednesday, Friday, 4 00 p. m. Time to New York, 14 hours.

35 **New Brunswick, N. J.** Steamboat New Brunswick leaves Vesey St. daily, except Sunday, 3 00 p. m. Fare, 50c. Exc. Fare, 80c. Freight received to 5 00 p. m. Leaves New Brunswick daily, except Sunday, 6 30 a. m. Time to New York, 3 hours and 30 minutes.

35 **New Brunswick, N. J.** Merchant's Transportation Co. via *Delaware and Raritan Canal*. Propellers leave Vestry St. daily, except Sundays, 3 p. m. (*No passengers carried.*) Freight received to 6 p. m. Leaves New Brunswick during the night. Due in New York about 3 00 p. m.

76 **New Haven, Conn. The New Haven Steamboat Line** leaves Peck Slip daily, except Sundays. C. H. Northam, 3 00 p. m., Continental, 11 00 p. m., *on Saturdays*, 12 00 night. Fare, 75c.; Exc. fare, $1.25; Stateroom, $1.00. Freight received to 6 p. m. Leaves New Haven daily, except Sundays, 10 15 a. m., 12 00 night. *On Sundays*, 10 30 p. m. Time to New York, 5 hours.

76 **New Haven, Conn.** Starin's Line leaves Cortlandt St., Steamboat John H. Starin, Monday, Wednesday, Friday, 9 00 p. m. Propeller Erastus Corning, Tuesday, Thursday, Sunday, 9 00 p. m. Fare, 75c.; Exc. Fare, $1.25; Stateroom, $1.00. Freight received to 6 00 p. m. Leaves New Haven daily, except Saturday, 10 15 p. m. Time to New York, 6 hours.

STEAMBOATS TO LANDINGS *NOT* ON THE HUDSON.—Continued.

MLS.
- 130 **New London, Conn.** Norwich Line. Leave Watts St., 5 00 p. m., Steamboat City of New York, Monday, Wednesday, Friday, Steamboat City of Worcester, Tuesday, Thursday, Saturday, Fare, $1.10. Freight received to 4 45 p. m. Leaves New London daily, except Sunday. 10 45 p. m. Due in New York, 7 00 a. m.
- 120 **New London, Conn.** Central Vermont R. R. and Propeller Line. Leaves Market St. daily, except Sunday, 5 00 p. m. Freight received to 3 00 p. m. (*No passengers carried.*) Leave New London daily, except Sunday, 6 00 p. m. Time to New York, 11 hours.
- 170 **Newport, R. I.** Fall River Line. Leave Murray St., 5 00 p. m. Pilgrim, Sunday, Monday, Wednesday, Friday, Old Colony, Tuesday, Thursday, Saturday. Fare, $2.00. Freight received to 4 45 p. m. Due at Newport, 3 00 a. m. Leaves Newport daily except Sunday, 9 00 p. m., on Sundays. 10 00 p. m. Due in New York, 7 30 a. m.
- 23 **New Rochelle, N. Y.** Propeller Captain John. Leaves Pike St., Tuesday, Thursday, Saturday, 12 noon. Fare, 25c. Freight received on same days to 11 45 a. m. Leaves New Rochelle, Monday, Wednesday, Friday, 7 30 a. m. Time to New York, 3 hours.
- 50 **Northport, L. I.** Propeller Portchester leaves Pike st, E. R' Tuesday, Thursday, Saturday, 2 00 p. m. Fare, 75c. Freight received same days to 1 45 p. m. Leaves Northport, Monday, Wednesday, Friday, 2 00 p. m. Time to New York, 5 hours.
- 50 **Norwalk, Conn.** Norwalk Line. Propeller leaves Beekman St. daily, except Saturday and Sunday, 5 00 p. m., on Saturday, 1 00 p. m. Freight received up to time of departure (*no passengers carried*). Leave Norwalk during the night.
- 133 **Norwich, Conn.** Norwich Line. Leave Watts St, 5 00 p. m. daily, except Sunday, for New London, connecting there by railroad for Norwich.
- 133 **Norwich, Conn.** Steamboat City of Norwich leaves Watts St., Monday, Wednesday, Friday, 6 00 p. m. Freight received to 5 45 p. m. (*no passengers carried*). Leaves Norwich, Tuesday, Thursday, Saturday, 6 00 p. m. Due in New York, 7 00 a. m.
- 28 **Oceanic, N. J.** Steamboat Sea Bird leaves Franklin St. daily except Sunday 3 00 p. m., Fare 50c.; Exc. Fare 80c. Freight received up to 15 minutes of departure. Leave Oceanic daily except Sunday about 8 30 a. m. Time to New York, 1 hour, 30 minutes.
- 120 **Orient, L. I.** Montauk Steamboat Co. Steamboat Shelter Island leaves Pier 23 E. R., Beekman St., Tuesday, Thursday, Saturday, 5 00 p. m. Fare, $1.25. Freight received same days, 4 15 p. m. Leave Orient, Monday, Wednesday, Friday, 7 30 p. m. Time to New York, 9 hours 30 minutes.
- 49 **Oyster Bay, L. I.** Propeller Baltimore leaves Pier 27, E. R., Monday, Wednesday, Friday, 2 00 p. m. Fare, 50c.; Exc. Fare, 75c. Freight received same days, 1 45 p. m. Leaves Oyster Bay, Tuesday, Thursday, Saturday, 7 30 a. m. Time to New York, 4 hours.
- (25 **Perth Amboy, N. J.** Steamboat New Brunswick leaves Vesey St daily, except Sunday, 3 00 p. m. Fare, 25c.; Exc. Fare, 40 c. Freight received to 5 00 p. m. Leaves Perth Amboy daily, except Sunday, 8 00 a. m. Time to New York, 2 hours 20 minutes.
- 31 **Pleasure Bay, N. J.** Steamboat Elberon leaves Franklin St. Tuesday, Wednesday, Thursday and Friday 9 00 a. m. On Saturday 10 00 a. m. Fare 40c.; Exc. Fare 60c. Freight received up to 15 minutes before departure. Leave Pleasure Bay on Monday, 11 05 a. m. and Tuesday, Wednesday, Thursday and Friday at 2 35 p. m. Time to New York 3 hours 55 minutes.
- 137 **Portland, Conn.** Hartford Line leaves Peck Slip. City of Springfield, Monday, Wednesday, Friday, 5 00 p. m. City of Richmond, Tuesday, Thursday, Saturday, 5 00 p. m. Fare, $1.50; Exc. Fare, $2.25. Freight received to 6 00 p. m. Does not stop at this landing on return trip to New York.
- **Portland, Maine.** Maine Steamship Co. Steamer Eleanor or Winthrop leaves Pier 38 E. R., Market St., Wednesday and Saturday, 5 00 p. m. Fare $5.00; Exc. Fare, $8.00. Freight received daily to 6 00 p. m. Leaves Portland, Wednesday and Saturday, 5 00 p. m. Time to New York, 36 hours.
- 27 **Port Chester, N. Y.** Port Chester Transportation Line leaves Pike St. Monday, Wednesday, Friday, 2 00 p. m. Fare, 25c. Freight received same days to 1 45 p. m. Leaves Port Chester, Tuesday, Thursday, Sunday, about 2 00 p. m. Time to New York, 3 hours.
- 180 **Providence, R. I.** Stonington Line leaves Spring St., 5 00 p. m. daily, except Sunday, for Stonington, connecting there with New York, Providence and Boston R. R. for Providence. Fare, $2.25; Staterooms, $1.00. Due at Providence, 4 30 a. m. Leave Providence by Railroad, daily, Sundays excepted, 7 50 p. m. Due in New York, 6 00 a. m.
- 130 **Providence, R. I.** Providence Line. Propellers Nashau and Pequot, leaves Warren St. daily, except Sunday, 5 00 p. m. *No passengers carried.* Freight received to 4 45 p. m. Leave Providence daily, except Sunday, 7 30 p. m. Due in New York, 6 00 a. m.
- 180 **Providence, R. I.** Merchant's Freight Line. Propellor Amos C. Barstow leaves Pier 11 E. R., Saturday, 2 00 p. m. *No passengers carried.* Freight received same day to 1 45 p. m. Rackett & Bro., Agents, 52 South St.
- 5 **Randall's Island.** Steamboat Morrisania leaves Pier 24 E. R. daily, except Sunday, 11 30 a m. Fare 10c. Freight received to 11 15 a. m. Does not stop on return trip to New York.
- 25 **Redbank, N. J.** Steamboat Sea Bird leave Franklin St. daily except Sundays 3 00 p. m. Fare 50c. Exc. Fare 80c. Freight received up to 15 minutes of departure. Leave Red Bank daily except Sunday about 7 a.m. Time to New York 3 hours.
- 37 **Rocky Hill, N. J.** Merchants' Transportation Co., *via Delaware and Raritan Canal.* Propellers leave Vestry St. daily, except Sundays, 3 00 p. m. *No passengers carried.* Freight received to 6 00 p. m. Leaves Rocky Hill during the night. Due in New York about 3 00 p. m.
- 120 **Rock Landing, Conn.** Hartford Line leaves Peck Slip. City of Springfield, Monday, Wednesday, Friday 5 00 p. m.; City of Richmond, Tuesday, Thursday, Saturday, 5 00 p. m. Fare, $1.50; Exc. Fare, $2.25. Freight received to 6 00 p. m. Leaves Rock Landing daily, except Sunday, 8 30 p. m. Due in New York 6 00 a. m.
- 35 **Roslyn, L. I.** Steamboat Idlewild leaves Peck Slip daily, except Sunday. 1 00 p. m., East 31st St., 1 15 p. m. Fare, 35 c.; Exc. Fare, 50 c. Freight received Peck Slip 3 45 p. m. Leaves Roslyn daily, except Sunday, 6 25 a. m. Due in New York 9 15 a. m.
- 21 **Rossville, S. I.** Steamboat New Brunswick leave Vesey St. daily, except Sunday, 3 00 p. m. Fare, 25 c.; Exc. Fare, 40 c. Freight received to 5 00 p. m. Leave Rossville daily, except Sunday, 8 40 a. m. Time to New York, 1 hour, 40 minutes.
- 140 **Sag Harbor, L. I.** Montauk Steamboat Co., Steamboat Shelter Island leaves Pier 23 E. R., Beekman St., Tuesday, Thursday, Saturday, 5 00 p. m. Fare, $1.25. Freight received same days to 4 15 p. m. Leaves Sag Harbor Monday, Wednesday, Friday, 1 30 p. m. Time to New York 12 hours 30 minutes.
- 24 **Sands Point, L. I.** Steamboat Idlewild leaves Peck Slip daily except Sunday 1 00 p. m., East 31st St., 4 15 p. m. Fare 35 c.; Exc. Fare, 50 c. Freight received Peck Slip 3 45 p. m. Leaves Sands Point daily, except Sunday, 7 40 a. m. Due in New York 9 15.
- 100 **Saybrook, Conn.** Hartford Line leaves Peck Slip. City of Springfield, Monday Wednesday, Friday, 5 00 p. m. City of Richmond, Tuesday, Thursday, Saturday, 5 00 p. m. Fare, $1.50; Exc. Fare, $2.25. Freight received to 6 00 p. m. Leave Saybrook daily, except Sunday, 10 30 p. m. Due in New York 6 00 a. m.
- 33 **Sayreville, N. J.** Steamboat New Brunswick leaves Vesey St. daily, except Sunday, 3 00 p. m. Fare, 40 c.; Exc. Fare 60c. Freight received to 5 00 p. m. Leaves Sayreville daily, except Sunday, 7 00 a. m. Time to New York 3 hours 20 minutes.
- 30 **Seabright, N. J.** Steamboat Elberon leaves Franklin St. Tuesday, Wednesday, Thursday and Friday 9 00 a. m. on Saturday 10 00 a. m. Fare 40c.; Exc. Fare 60c. Freight received up to 15 minutes before departure. Leave Seabright on Monday 11 30 a. m. and Tuesday, Wednesday, Thursday and Friday 3 00 p. m. Time to New York 3 hours 30 minutes.
- 29 **Sea Cliff, L. I.** Steamboat Idlewild leaves Peck Slip daily, except Sunday, 1 00 p. m. East 31st St. 4.15 p. m. Fare, 35 c.; Exc. Fare, 50 c. Freight received Peck Slip 3 45 p. m. Leaves Sea Cliff daily, except Sunday, 7 00 a. m. Due in New York 9 15 a. m.

STEAMBOATS TO LANDINGS *NOT* ON THE HUDSON.—Continued.

MLS.

23 **Seawaren, N. J.** Steamboat New Brunswick leave Vesey St. daily, except Sunday, 3.00 p. m. Fare, 25 c.; Exc. Fare, 40 c. Freight received to 5.00 p. m. Leave Seawaren daily, except Sunday, 8.25 a. m. Time to New York 1 hour 35 minutes.

130 **Shelter Island (Prospect).** Montauk Steamboat Co. Steamboat Shelter Island leaves Pier 24 E. R., Beekman St., Tuesday, Thursday, Saturday, 5.00 p. m. Fare, $1.25. Freight received same days to 1.45 p. m. Leaves Shelter Island (Prospect) Monday, Wednesday, Friday, 5.45 p. m. Time to New York. 11 hours 15 minutes.

74 **Shelton, Conn.** Naugatuck Valley Steamboat Co. Leaves Pier 39 E. R., between Market and Pike Sts. daily, except Sunday, 6.00 p. m. Fare, $1.00. Freight received to 6.00 p. m. Leaves Shelton daily, except Sunday, 6.15 p. m. Time to New York, 12 hours 45 minutes.

27 **South Amboy, N. J.** Steamboat New Brunswick leaves Vesey St. daily, except Sunday, 3.00 p. m. Fare, 30 c.; Exc. Fare, 50 c. Freight received to 5.00 p. m. Leaves South Amboy daily, except Sunday, 7.45 a. m. Time to New York, 2 hours 35 minutes.

148 **South Glastonbury, Conn.** Hartford Line leaves Peck Slip. City of Springfield, Monday, Wednesday, Friday, 5.00 p. m. City of Richmond, Tuesday, Thursday, Saturday 5.00 p. m. Fare, $1.50; Exc. Fare, $2.50. Freight received to 6.00 p m. Leaves South Glastonbury daily, except Sunday, 5.30 p. m. Due in New York 6.00 a. m.

South Glenwood, L. I. Steamboat Idlewild leaves Peck Slip daily, except Sunday, 4.00 p. m., East 31st St., 4.15 p. m. Fare, 35 c.; Exc. 50 c. Freight received Peck Slip to 3.45 p. m. Leaves South Glenwood, tide permitting, 6.30 a. m. Due in New York 9.15 a. m.

48 **South Norwalk, Conn.** Norwalk Line leaves Beekman St. daily, except Saturday and Sunday, 5.00 p. m., on Saturday 1 p. m. Freight received up to time departure. *No passengers carried.* Leave South Norwalk during the night.

136 **Southold, L. I.** Montauk Steamboat Co. Steamboat Shelter Island leaves Pier 24 E. R., Beekman St., Tuesdays, Thursdays, Saturdays, 5.00 p. m. Fare, $1.25. Freight received same days to 1.45 p. m. Leaves Southold, Monday, Wednesday, Friday, 5.15 p. m. Time to New York, 11 hours, 45 minutes.

35 **Stamford, Conn.** Steamboat Sundy Side leaves Pike St. daily, except Sunday, 2.55 p. m., East 31st St., 3.10 p. m. Fare, 37c.; Exc. Fare, 50 c. Freight received at Pike St. to 2.45 p. m. Leave Stamford daily, except Sunday, 7.40 a. m. Time to New York 2¼ hours.

90 **Star Landing, N. J.** Steamboat New Brunswick leaves Vesey St. Monday, Wednesday, Friday, 3.00 p. m. Fare, 25 c.; Exc. Fare 40 c. Freight received same days 2.45 p. m. Leaves Star Landing, Monday, Wednesday, Friday, 8.45 a. m. Time to New York 1 hour 35 minutes.

6 **Stapleton, S. I.** By Ferry from Whitehall St. to St. George, and then by Staten Island Rapid Transit R. R. (See page 91 for time table.

5 **St. George, Staten Island.** Staten Island Ferry. Boat leaves foot Whitehall St. daily, except Sundays, 5.30 a. m., 6.00 a. m., 6.30 a. m., 7.30 a. m., 7.50 a. m., 8.10 a. m., 8.30 a. m., 9.00 a. m., 9.30 a. m., 10.00 a. m., 10.30 a. m., 11.00 a. m., 11.30 a. m., 12.00 noon, 12.30 p. m., 1.00 p. m., 1.30 p. m., 2.00 p. m., 2.30 p. m., 3.00 p. m., 3.30 p. m., 4.00 p. m., 4.30 p. m., 4.50 p. m., 5.10 p. m., 5.30 p. m., 5.50 p. m., 6.10 p. m., 7.00 p. m., 7.40 p. m., 8.20 p. m., 9.00 p. m., 10.00 p. m., 11.00 p. m., 11.30 p. m., 12.15 night. *On Sundays* 6.00 a. m., 7.30 a. m., 8.00 a. m., 9.00 a. m., 9.30 a. m., 10.00 a. m., 10.30 a. m., 11.00 a. m., 11.30 a. m., 12 noon, 12.30 p. m., 1.00 p. m., 1.30 p. m., 2.00 p. m., 2.30 p. m., 3.00 p. m., 3.30 p. m., 4.00 p. m., 4.30 p. m., 5.00 p. m., 5.30 p. m., 6.00 p. m., 6.30 p. m., 7.00 p. m., 7.30 p. m., 8.30 p. m., 9 p. m., 9.40 p. m., 10.20 p. m., 11.00 p. m., 11.30 p. m. Fare, 10c. **Leave St. George** daily, except Sundays, 5.20 a. m., 5.50 a. m., 6.15 a. m., 6.50 a. m., 7.20 a. m., 7.40 a. m., 8.00 a. m., 8.20 a. m., 8.40 m., 9.00 a. m., 9.20 a. m., 9.50 a. m., 10.20 a. m., 10.50 a. m., 11.20 a. m., 11.50 a. m., 12.20 p. m., 12.50 p. m., 1.20 p. m., 1.50 p. m., 2.20 p. m., 2.50 p. m., 3.20 p. m., 3.50 p. m., 4.10 p. m., 4.30 p. m., 4.50 p. m., 5.10 p. m., 5.30 p. m., 5.50 p. m., 6.20 p. m., 6.50 p. m., 7.30 p. m., 8.10 p. m., 8.50 p. m., 9.30 p. m., 10.30 p. m., 11.30 p. m. *On Sundays* 6.20 a. m., 7.20 a. m., 8.20 a. m., 8.50 a. m., 9.20 a. m., 9.45 a. m., 10.15 a. m., 10.45 a. m., 11.15 a. m., 11.45 a. m., 12.15 p. m., 12.45 p. m., 1.15 p. m., 1.45 p. m., 2.15 p. m., 2.45 p. m., 3.15 p. m., 3.45 p. m., 4.15 p. m., 4.45 p. m., 5.15 p. m., 5.45 p. m., 6.15 p. m., 6.45 p. m., 7.15 p. m., 7.45 p. m., 8.15 p. m., 9.00 p. m., 9.40 p. m., 10.20 p. m., 11.00 p. m. Time to New York 25 minutes. Fare, 10c.

120 **Stonington, Conn. Stonington** Line, leave Spring St. 5.00 p. m. Rhode Island, Monday, Wednesday, Friday; Stonington, Tuesday, Thursday, Saturday. Fare, $1.35; Stateroom, $1.00. Due at Stonington 3.00 a. m., leave Stonington 9.20 p. m. Due in New York 6.00 a. m.

6 **Tompkinsville, S. I.** By Ferry from Whitehall St. to St. George, and then by Staten Island Rapid Transit R. R. See page 91 for time table. Fare, 10c.

25 **Tottenville, S. I.** Steamboat New Brunswick leaves Vesey St. daily, except Sunday, 3.00 p. m. Fare, 25c.; Exc. Fare, 40c. Freight received to 5.00 p. m., Leaves Tottenville daily, except Sunday, 8.10 a. m. Time to New York 2 hours 10 minutes.

73 **Trenton, N. J.** Merchants' Transportation Co., *via Delaware and Raritan Canal.* Propellers leave Vestry St. daily, except Sundays, 3.00 p. m. (*No passengers carried.*) Freight received to 6.00 p. m., leaves Trenton daily, except Sunday, 5.00 p. m. Due in New York 8.00 p. m.

3 **Willet's Point, Conn.** U. S. Government Boat leaves Gansevoort St. Tuesday, Thursday, Saturday, 9.00 a. m. *By Pass.* Leaves Willet's Point Tuesday, Thursday, Saturday, 2.00 p. m. Time to New York 4½ hours.

45 **Wilson Point, Conn.** A Steamboat leaves Pier 49, E. R. daily, except Sunday, 5.00 p. m. Freight received to 5.00 p. m. Leaves Wilson Point during the night.

23 **Woodbridge, N. J.** Steamboat New Brunswick leaves Vesey St. daily, except Sunday, 3.00 p. m. Fare. 25c.; Exc. Fare, 40c. Freight received to 5.00 p. m. Leave Woodbridge, daily, except Sunday, 8.25 a. m. Time to New York 1 hour 35 minutes.

PORT JERVIS, MONTICELLO AND NEW YORK R. R.

Summitville Division.

Stations, and fares from New York (single and excursion) via N. Y., Ontario & W. R. R.
Summitville, Wurtsboro, $2.14, $3.60; Westbrookville, $2.32, $3.60; Port Orange, $2.33, $4.00; Cuddebackville, $2.33, $3.60; Godeffroy's, Huguenot Junction, $2.33, $3.60; Port Jervis, $2.33, $3.60.

Leave foot of Jay St., 3.55 p. m. (leave **foot W. 42d St.,** 4.10) for **Summitville, Port Jervis** and intermediate stations. Arrive Summitville, 7.58 p. m.; arrive Port Jervis, 8.50 p. m. Additional train leaves Summitville for Port Jervis and intermediate stations, 8.45 a. m. Arrive Port Jervis, 9.45 a. m.

Trains to New York.

Leave Port Jervis for Summitville and **New York.** 6.20 a. m., 2.30 p. m.; leave Huguenot Junction, 6.30 a. m., 2.42 p. m.; leave Godeffroy's, 6.36 a. m., 2.50 p. m.; leave Cuddebackville, 6.42 a. m., 3.00 p. m.; leave Port Orange, 6.46 a. m., 3.04 p. m.; leave Westbrookville, 6.52 a. m., 3.10 p. m.; leave Wurtsboro, 7.00 a. m., 3.30 p. m.; leave Summitville, 7.25 a. m., 3.58 p. m. **Arrive New York** (Jay and W. 42d St.), 10.45 a. m., 7.10 p. m.

MONTICELLO DIVISION.

Stations and fares from New York via N. Y., Lake Erie & Western R. R.:
Port Jervis, $2.70; Huguenot Junction, $2.90; Spring House, $2.90; Port Clinton, $2.95; Rose Point, $2.95; Paradise, $3.05; Oakland, $3.10; Hartwood, $3.20; Gilmans, $3.30; Barnum's, $3.35; Monticello, $3.45. excursion, $5.00.

Leave foot of Chambers St. (leave foot of West 23d St. 5 to 15 minutes earlier).

For **Port Jervis, Monticello,** and intermediate stations, 9.00 a. m. and on Wednesday and Saturday 3.30 p. m. Arrive Port Jervis, 12.35 p. m., 6.45 p. m.; arrive Monticello, 2.05 p. m., and on Wednesday and Saturday, 7.45 p. m.

Trains to New York.

Leave **Monticello,** 7.40 a. m., and on Wednesday and Saturday 3.50 p. m.; leave Gilmans', 8.00 a. m., and on Wednesday and Saturday, 4.05 p. m.; leave Oakland, 8.22 a. m., and on Wednesday and Saturday, 4.22 p. m.; leave Paradise, 8.26 a. m., and on Wednesday and Saturday, 4.26 p. m. Arrive Port Jervis, 9.00 a. m., and on Wednesday and Saturday 5.00 p. m. **Arrive New York** (Chambers and W. 23d Sts.), 12.07 p. m. and on Wednesday and Saturday, 10.32 p. m.

TRANSPORTATION LINES.
INCLUDING RAILROAD FREIGHT, FAST FREIGHT AND OTHER LINES.
For Canal Lines see Page 109.

Adirondack R'y. Ship by People's Line via Albany, foot of Canal St., until 5.45 p. m., Citizen's Line via Troy, foot of Christopher St., until 5.45 p.m., also by Hudson River R. R., Pier 4, E. R., St. John's Park, or cor. 11th Av. and 33d St., or by West Shore R. R., Pier 5, N. R., or foot of West 35th St., or foot of North 6th St. Brooklyn, E. D.

Anchor Line, Lake and Rail via Erie, Pa. Mark " Anchor Line," Ship at Pier 4, N. R. or foot of Laight St., and foot of North 4th St., Brooklyn, E. D., and foot of Pearl St., Brooklyn, until 4.00 p. m. H. S. Nichols, Agent, 76 Wall St., 381 Broadway.

Associated Railways of North and South Carolina and Virginia, including "Atlantic Coast Line," "Piedmont Air Line," "Sea Board Air Line." Ship packages by Old Dominion Steamship Co., foot of Beach St. H. P. Clark, Eastern Agent, 229 Broadway.

Atchison, Topeka & Santa Fe R. R. Freight Line from Chicago. Atchison, Kansas City or Halstead. For places on the Pacific Coast ship by any Line going to Chicago. C. D. Simonson, General Eastern Agent, 261 Broadway.

Atlantic Coast Dispatch. Mark "A. C. D." ship by Penn. R. R., foot of Hubert St., or foot of North 4th St., Brooklyn, E. D. George T. Smith, Agent, 435 Broadway. Bills of Lading signed 76 Wall St., 1 Astor House, 435 Broadway.

Atlantic Coast Line of Railways. Jonah H. White, Eastern Agent, 229 Broadway.

Baltimore and Ohio R. R. Freight for all points on this road, including Continental Line, B. & O. Kankakee Dispatch, is received at Pier 27 E. R. foot of Dover St., or Pier 20, N. R., foot of Day St., or foot of East 37th St., until 4.00 p. m. Also at foot of South 5th St., Brooklyn, E. D., until 3.30 p. m. Inward bound freight delivered at Pier 27, E. R., and Pier 20, N. R. A. C. Rose, General Agent, 415 Broadway.

Bay Line. H. V. Thompson, General Passenger Agent, 287 Broadway.

Bee Line, Comprising the Cleveland, Columbus, Cincinnati and Indianapolis Railway, Indianapolis & St. Louis Railway, and Dayton Union R. R. Thomas S. Timpson, General Eastern Agent, 287 Broadway.

Bennington & Rutland R'y. Freight received for all points on this road by New York Central and Hudson R. R. R. Pier 4, E. R., St. John's Park, 11th Av. and 33d St., and foot of North 6th St., Brooklyn, E. D.

Bitner Fast Freight Line for Lancaster, Pa. (Daily Line). Freight received at Pier 12, N. R., until 5.00 p. m. Office on Pier.

Blue Line and Canada Southern Line (Bonded Line). Mark goods " Blue Line." Freight received by N. Y. C. & Hudson River R. R., St. John's Park, Pier 5, E. R., foot of Barclay St., 33d St. and 11th Av., and foot of North 6th St., Brooklyn, E. D. W. Bond, Agent, 413 Broadway.

Brooklyn & Brighton Beach R'y. Freight received until 4.00 p. m. for points on this road, at Prospect Park Station, Flatbush Av. and Malbone St., Brooklyn.

Brooklyn, Canarsie & Rockaway Beach R. R. No freight received at present. Ship by Andrea's or Quinlan's Express, 66 Beekman St., 21 Church St. and 312 Canal St.

Brooklyn, Bath & West End R. R. Freight and Express Packages received for all points on this road by the Brooklyn, Bath and West End Express offices 30th St. Ferry Depot foot of Whitehall St., 313 Canal St. and 31 Hudson St.

Camden & Atlantic R. R. Freight for all points on this road received by Pennsylvania R.R., Pier 1, N. R., foot West St., or foot North 4th St., Brooklyn, E. D.

Canada Atlantic Line via Canada, Atlantic and Canadian Pacific Railways and their connections, taking freight for St. Paul, Minneapolis and other points in the Northwest. Freight received at Pier 36, E. R. Bills of Lading at 6 Coenties slip. Fred H. Goble, Agent, 6 Coenties Slip.

Canada Southern Line (West Shore R. R.) to all points in West, Northwest and Southwest. Mark packages "C. S. L." via West Shore and ship Pier 5, N. R., foot of West 35th St., until 4.00 p. m., or Wythe Av. and North 5th St., Brooklyn, E. D., 5 p. m. H. F. Lydecker, Agent, 363 Broadway.

Canadian Pacific R'y. Freight and Passenger office, 353 Broadway. E. V. Skinner, General Eastern Agent, 353 Broadway.

Carolina Central Despatch. For North and South Carolinas, etc., etc. Mark packages "C. C. D." and ship by Wilmington Steamer. Pier 26, E. R. W. P. Clyde & Co., General Agents, 5 Bowling Green.

Catskill Mountain R'y and Cairo R. R. Freight received for points on this road by Catskill Boats foot of Jay St., until 4.55 p. m., also, by West Shore R. R., Pier 5, N. R., foot of West 35 St., until 4.00 p. m., and Wythe Av. and North 5th St., Brooklyn, E. D., until 5.00 p. m.

Central Pacific R. R. Mark goods via " Union Pacific R'y," and ship by any line running to Omaha. R. Tenbroeck, General Eastern Agent, 287 Broadway.

Central R. R. of New Jersey. Freight for all local points on this road, including High Bridge and South Branches, is received at Pier 14, N. R., until 5 p. m., except Communipaw, Claremont, Greenville, Panrapo, Bayonne and Centerville, do not receive for these points. Inward and Philipsburg freight received at Pier 13, N. R. until 5.00 p. m. Freight for points on New Jersey Southern Division received at Pier 8, N. R., foot of Rector St., until 5.00 p.m. Inward bound freight delivered at Pier 8, N. R. Lehigh & Susquehanna Division. Freight for all points on this division received at Pier 12, N. R., until 5.00 p. m. Philadelphia New Line. Freight for all points on this division, received at Pier 13, N. R., until 6 p. m.

Elizabethport & Perth Amboy Branch. Freight for all points on this Branch received at Pier 8, N. R., foot of Rector St. Benzine, explosives and naptha received only at Jersey City. H. J. Billings, Agent, on Pier 8, N. R., George G. Moore, Agent, Pier 13, N. R. P. H. Wyckoff. General Freight Agent, 119 Liberty St.

Central Vermont Rail and Lake Line. Mark goods " C. V. Lake Line " and ship Pier 36, E. R. Orson Breed, Agent, 6 Coenties Slip.

Central Vermont R. R. Local and through freight for all points is received at Pier 36, E. R., until 5.00 p. m. W. M. Bassett, Freight Agent, Pier 36, E. R.

Chesapeake & Ohio R'y. Mark goods via " C. & O." and ship by Old Dominion Line Steamers at foot of Beach St. William Plummer, General Eastern Agent, 302 Broadway.

Chicago & Alton R. R. A. M. Wilkinson, Contracting Agent. William J. Bogert, General Eastern Freight Agent. 261 Broadway.

Chicago & Atlantic R'y. B. F. Popple. General Eastern Passenger Agent, 317 Broadway.

Chicago, Burlington & Quincy R. R. Mark goods, care " C. B. Q. R. R." and ship via any line to Chicago or East St. Louis. E. J. Swords, General Eastern Agent, 317 Broadway.

Chicago, Milwaukee & St. Paul R'y. Mark goods care of " C. M. & St. P. R'y," and ship by any line to Chicago.

Chicago & Northwestern R'y. Mark goods care of " C. & N. W. R'y" and ship by any line to Chicago. A. H. Pride, General Eastern Agent, 109 Broadway.

Chicago, Rock Island & Pacific R'y. Mark goods " C. R. I. & P. R'y.," ship by any line to Chicago. L. C. Ivory, Contracting Agent. F. B. Morlok. General Eastern Freight Agent.

Chicago, St. Paul & Kansas City R'y., formerly Minn. & Northwestern R. R. Mark goods " C. St. P. K. C. Ry." Ship by any line to Chicago. P. C. Stohr, General Eastern Agent, 323 Broadway.

Chicago, Santa Fe & California R'y., " Santa Fe Route " leased by Atchison, Topeka & Santa Fe R. R. Co., between Chicago and Kansas City. Ship freight by any line to Chicago. C. D. Simonson, General Eastern Agent, 261 Broadway.

TRANSPORTATION LINES.—Continued.

Cincinnati, New Orleans and Texas Pacific R'y. "Queen and Crescent Route" between Cincinnati and New Orleans. W. S. St. George, General Eastern Agent, 319 Broadway.

Cleveland, Columbus, Cincinnati & Indianapolis R'y. "Bee Line." T. S. Timpson, General Eastern Agent, 287 Broadway.

Commercial Express Line To West, Northwest, and Southwest freight received by the N. Y. & Lake Erie & Western R. R., at Pier 8 E. R. Foot Chambers St., foot W. 23d St., foot W. 40th St., until 4 00 p. m., and foot of North 5th St., Brooklyn, E. D., until 5 00 p. m. J. D. Abram, Agent. 101 Broadway. Bills of Lading, 120 Front St.

Connecticut River Railway Line. Freight received for all points on this road by New York, New Haven and Hartford R. R. Pier 50, E. R., until 4 30 p. m., or by New Haven Steamboat Co., Pier 25, E. R., Peck Slip, until 5 00 p.m., or Hartford boats, Pier 24, E. R., until 5 00 p. m.

Continental Line. For the West mark goods; "Continental Line." Ship at Pier 27, E. R., foot Dover, St., foot Dey St., or foot East 37th St., until 4 p. m., or foot South 5th St., Brooklyn, E. D., until 3 30 p. m. A. C. Rose, General Agent, 415 Broadway.

Cromwell-Pacific Through Line. "El Paso Route." Ship by Cromwell Steamship Co., Pier 9, N. R. Samuel E. Stohr, General Eastern Agent, 409 Broadway.

Danbury & Norwalk R. R. Ship freight at Pier 49, E. R., until 5 00 p. m. A. M. Smith, Agent, Pier 49, E. R.

Delaware, Lackawanna & Western R. R. Freight for **Morris & Essex Division** and **Branches** received at foot of Leroy St., until 5 00 p. m. Freight for all other Divisions and Branches received at Bulkhead, Pier 18, N. R., until 5 00 p. m. on Saturday to 4 00 p. m. Freight for Buffalo received at Bulkhead of Pier 19, N. R., and foot of Leroy St. until 4 00 p. m. Freight for all points received also at foot South 9th St., Brooklyn, E. D., until 4 p. m. Through freight for the West mark "via D. L. & W." or "Great Eastern Line," or "Lackawanna Line," and ship foot Dey St., foot of Leroy St., until 4 00 p. m. Also foot South 9th St., Brooklyn, E. D., and at Hoboken, N. J. Horses and Carriages received at Hoboken Station after one day's notice. Inward bound freight delivered at Pier 18, N. R., and foot of Leroy St. William S. Sloan, General Freight Agent, Room 11, 26 Exchange Place. H. S. Robertson, General Eastern Freight Agent, 129 Broadway and 93 Wall St.

Denver & Rio Grande R. R. Mark goods via "D. & R. G. R. R." Ship by any Freight Line to Chicago. T. W. Becker, General Eastern Agent, 317 Broadway.

Eastern Carolina Despatch. Mark Goods "E. C. D.," and ship by Pennsylvania R. R., foot of Hubert St., until 5 00 p. m., or foot of Pearl St., or foot North 4th St., Brooklyn, E. D. Geo. T. Smith, Agent. 435 Broadway.

East Tennessee, Virginia & Georgia R'y. Ship by " Va. Tenn. Georgia Air Line," at Old Dominion Steamship Co. foot of Beach St. Office, 303 Broadway.

Empire Line. To all points West mark goods "Empire Line." Ship at Pier 4, N. R., or foot of Laight St., or foot West 35th St., or Pearl St. and North 4th St. Brooklyn. William A. Jones, Agent, 381 Broadway. Bills of Lading, 76 Wall St., 381 Broadway.

Empire & New England Transportation Line. For the transportation of Coal between New York and Norwich and points on Long Island Sound. G. B. Martin, General Manager, Room 132, 1 Broadway.

Erie Despatch. (Bonded Line). For all points West, Northwest and Southwest. Ship foot Duane St., Pier 8, E. R., foot West 23d St., or foot of West 40th St., until 4 00 p. m., and foot of North 5th St., Brooklyn, E. D., until 5 00 p. m. M. W. DeWolf, Agent. 401 Broadway. Bills of Lading, 401 Broadway, 128 Front St.

Florida Despatch Freight Line via Savannah, Georgia and Savannah, Florida & Western R'y. Mark goods via "Florida Despatch," and ship freight by Savannah Steamers, foot of Spring St. J. D. Hashagen. Eastern Agent, 261 Broadway.

Fonda, Johnstown & Gloversville R. R. Ship freight by New York Central and Hudson River R. R. At foot of Barclay St., Pier 4, E. R., and corner 11th Ave. and 33d St., or foot North 6th St., Brooklyn, E. D., until 4 00 p. m.

Freehold & New York R. R. Freight received by Keyport boat foot of Vesey St., until 3 45 p. m. Saturday 1 45 p. m., and by Central R. R. of N. J., Pier 8, N. R. until 5 00 p. m.

Geneva, Ithaca & Sayre R. R. Freight received by Lehigh Valley R. R., Pier 2, N. R., until 5 00 p. m.

Grand Trunk Railway and Maine Steamship Co. Express Freight Line, via Portland, for Montreal, Quebec and Toronto, and other points in Canada, and to Western and Northwestern States. Ship by Portland steamers, Wednesday and Saturday, Pier 38, E. R., until 5 00 p. m. E. P. Beach, Genl. Agent, G. T. R'y., 271 Broadway.

Great Eastern Fast Freight Line, via Delaware Lackawanna & Western R. R., to all points in the Northwest and Southwest. Mark packages "Great Eastern Line," and ship foot of Dey St., foot of Leroy St., and foot of South 9th St. Brooklyn, E. D., and at Hoboken, N. J., until 4 p. m. W. Townsend Agent, and Bills of Lading offices 93 Wall St. and 429 Broadway.

Great Southern Despatch. Mark packages "Great Son. Des.." and ship by Pennsylvania R. R. at foot of Vestry St, until 4 p. m., at Pier 1, N. R., or foot West 35th St., or foot North 4th St., Brooklyn, E. D., or foot of Pearl St., Brooklyn, until 5 00 p. m. Geo. T. Smith, Agent, 435 Broadway, Bills of Lading, 76 Wall, 1 Astor House, 435 Broadway.

Great Southern Freight and Passenger Line, via Charleston. Mark packages, care " S. C. Ry.," and ship by Charleston steamers, 29 E. R. Wm. P. Clyde & Co., General Agents, 5 Bowling Green, Bills of Lading, Pier 29 E. R., and 53 Broadway.

Gulf Colorado & Santa Fe R'y, "Santa Fe Route." Ship by Mallory's Line, Pier 20, E. R. James N. Fuller, General Eastern Agent, 319 Broadway.

Hartford & Connecticut Western R. R. Ship freight for station between Rhinecliff and State Line by steamboat Ansonia, daily, except Saturday, to 5 45 p. m. and Saturday to 2 45 p. m., foot of Franklin St., or by N. Y. Central & Hudson River R. R., St. John's Park or cor. 11th ave and 33d St., Stations between State Line, Junction and Canaan, foot of Barclay St., 11th ave. and 33d St., between State Line and Hartford by New York, New Haven & Hartford R. R. at Pier 50, E. R., and Housatonic Line, Pier 49, E. R., until 5 p. m.

Housatonic Line, for all points on Housatonic R. R. Ship at Pier 49, E. R., until 5 00 p. m. A. M. Smith, Agent, Pier 49, E. R. The Danbury & Norwalk R. R., New York & New England R. R., Meriden, Waterbury & Conn. River R. R. New Haven & Derby R. R., Shepaug, Litchfield & Northern R. R., Hartford & Conn. Western R. R., Boston & Albany R. R.

Housatonic R. R., See Housatonic Line.

Housatonic & Texas Central R'y. E. Bawley, General Eastern Agent, 343 Broadway.

Illinois Central R. R. Mark goods, via "I. C. R. R.," and ship by any freight line to Chicago. John J. Sproull, General Eastern Passenger and Freight Agent, 343 Broadway.

Indianapolis & St. Louis Railway, "Bee Line." Thomas S. Timpson, General Eastern Agent, 287 Broadway.

Inland Transportation Company, Canal and Rail, and Canal and Lake, to all points in the West, Northwest, Southwest, Buffalo and Canada. Mark goods "I. T. Line," ship at Pier 3, E. R. George Stillwell, Manager 111 Broad St.

International & Great Northern R. R., "International Route." Mark packages, care "I. G. N. R. R.," and ship by Mallory's Line, Pier 20, E. R.

Inter-State Despatch, for all points in the West, Southwest and Northwest. Ship by N. Y., Lake Erie & Western R. R., Pier 8, E. R., foot of Duane St., foot of West 23d St., and foot of North 5th St., Brooklyn, E. D., until 4 p. m. Chas. F. Case, General Eastern Agent, 317 Broadway.

Kaaterskill R. R. Ship by Rondout boats, foot Harrison St., until 3 45 p. m., on Saturday until 12 45 p. m., and by West Shore R. R., Pier 5, N. R., foot West 35th St. and Wythe ave. and North 5th St. Brooklyn, E. D., until 4 p. m.

Kanawha Despatch, via Chesapeake & Ohio R. R., to West and Southwest. Mark goods, "Kanawha Despatch," and ship by Old Dominion Steamship Co., foot of Beach St. Wm. Plummer, General Eastern Agent, 343 Broadway.

Lackawanna Line, to all points West, Northwest and Southwest. Mark goods, "Lackawanna Linne," and ship by Delaware, Lack. & West. R. R., at foot of Dey St., or foot of Leroy St., foot of South 9th St., Brooklyn, E. D., until 4 p.m., and at Hoboken, N. J.

TRANSPORTATION LINES.—Continued.

Lake Shore & Michigan Southern R'y. General Offices of Company, Grand Central Depot, 42d St. and 4th ave.

Lebanon Springs R'y. Ship freight by New York & Harlem R. R., foot of Barclay St. and cor. Lexington ave & 47th St.,

Lehigh & Hudson River R'y. Ship freight by New York, Lake Erie & Western R. R., foot of Chambers St.

Lehigh and Susquehanna Division Central R. R. of N. J. Freight received at Pier 12, N. R., until 5 00 p. m.

Lehigh Valley & Wabash Despatch, Fast freight line to the West, Southwest and Northwest. Mark packages "L. V. W. Despatch," and ship by Lehigh Valley R. R., at Pier 2, N. R., until 4 p. m. R. F. Stobo, Contracting Agent, W. H. Burgess, Agent, 245 Broadway.

Lehigh Valley R. R. Freight received for all points on this road at Pier 2 N. R. until 5 p. m. Inward bound freight delivered at Pier 2, N. R. Through freight for the West, Southwest and Northwest, ship by "Lehigh Valley and Wabash Despatch" or "Traders Despatch," at Pier 2, N. R., until 4 p. m.

Long Island R. R. Freight received for all points on this road, except Atlantic Ave. Division, at Pier 32, E. R., until 4 00 p. m., also at Hunter's Point (Long Island City), until 5 00 p. m. Freight received for all points on road except North Side Division, at Flatbush Ave. Depot, Fort Greene Place, between Atlantic Ave. and Hanson, Brooklyn, until 5 00 p. m. Freight also received at Bushwick ave. Depot for all points on road, except North Side Division and Atlantic Ave. Division, until 5 00 p. m. Inward bound freight delivered at Pier 32, E. R., Long Island City Depot, Flatbush Ave. Depot, or Bushwick Depot, as packages are marked. H. M. Smith, Traffic Manager, Long Island City.

Louisville & Nashville R.R., "L. & N. Route," Cincinnatti. Louisville & New Orleans Line. S. B. Jones, General Eastern Agent. W. McGibney, Eastern Passenger Agent, 381 Broadway.

Merchant's Despatch Transportation Co. from New York, Philadelphia, Boston, Albany, Montreal and New England to the West, Northwest and Southwest. Mark packages "Merchant's Despatch" and ship by N. Y. C. H. R. R. R. Pier 5, E. R., foot of Barclay St. St. Johns Park, 33d St. and 11th ave, foot of North 5th St. Brooklyn, E. D. B. W. Southwick, Contracting Agent; W. Geagen, General Freight agent, 335 Broadway.

Merchant's Transportation Co. (Bonded Line) to all points West, Southwest and via Oswego and Rouses Point to Canada. H. N. Holt, Agent. Room 83, 1 Broadway.

Merchant's Transportation Co, for Trenton, New Brunswick, etc. Ship goods foot Vestry St. until 5 00 p. m. H. B. Hitchcock, Agent on pier foot of Vestry St.

Midland Line, Mark goods "Midland Line" and ship until 4 p. m. at St. John's Park, Pier 5 E. R., foot of Barclay St. cor. 33d St. and 11th ave. and foot North 6th St. Brooklyn, E. D., foot Washington St., Brooklyn. M. A. Zell, Agent, 413 Broadway.

Milwaukee and Michigan Line, Mark goods "M. & M." Ship by N. Y. C. & H. R. R. R. at Pier 5 E. R., foot of Barclay St., St. John's Park cor. 11th Ave. and 33d St. until 4 00 p. m. and foot North 6th St., Brooklyn, E. D., and foot Washington St. Brooklyn. W. J. Jennings, Agent, 413 Broadway.

Missouri Pacific Railway System operating the Missouri, Kansas & Texas Ry., St. Louis, Iron Mountain and So. R'y, International and Great Northern R'y, Central Branch, U. P. R. R., Fort Scott, Wichita and Western R. R. and Little Rock and Fort Smith Ry. Mark goods "Mo. Pac. Ry." Ship by any Freight Line to St. Louis, Mo. W. E. Hoyt, General Eastern Passenger Agent and H. C. Logan, General Eastern Freight Agent, 391 Broadway.

Morris & Essex Division of Delaware, Lackawanna & Western R. R. Freight received for this road and Branches foot Leroy St., until 5 00 p. m. W. S. Sloan, General Freight Agent, 26 Exchange Pl.

National Despatch (Bonded Line). For Montreal and all points in Canada and through to Detroit, Chicago, Milwaukee, St. Paul, Minneapolis, St. Louis, Kansas City, Louisville etc. Mark packages "National Despatch" and ship via Central Vermont R.R. at Pier 36, E. R. until 5 00 p. m. F. H. Goble, Contracting Agent; Orson Breed, Agent, 6 Cornties Slip.

Naugatuck R. R, Freight received for this road by Bridgeport Boats, Pier 35 E. R. until 5 p. m., also by N. Y. and New Haven R. R. at Pier 50 E. R.

Newark & New York R. R. Freight received at Bulkhead of Pier 13 N. R. and 14 N. R. until 5 30 p. m. George O. More, Agent on Pier 13 N. R.

Newburg, Dutchess & Conn. R. R. Ship by Homer Ramsdell Transportation Co., foot of Franklin St. until 5 p. m.

New Canaan R. R, Ship Freight by N. Y. N. H. Hartford R. R. at Pier 50 E. R.

New Haven & Derby R. R. Ship Freight by Housatonic Line, Pier 49 E. R. until 5 00 p. m.

New Haven & Northampton R. R, Ship freight by New Haven Boats, Pier 25 E. R. until 5 00 p. m.

New Jersey & New York R. R, Ship freight foot of Chambers until 4 00 p. m. Inward bound freight if so ordered delivered at foot of Chambers St.

New London Northern R. R. Ship freight by Central Vermont R. R. Steamers Pier 36 E. R.

New York & Baltimore Transportation Co, Ship Freight at Pier 7, N. R. until 5 p. m. H. C. Foster, Agent, Pier 7, N. R.

New York & Greenwood Lake R'y. Freight received at Foot of Chambers until 4 00 p. m.

New York & Harlem R. R. Ship Freight for this road at foot of Barclay St. cor. 47th St. and Lexington Ave. until 4 00 p. m. Inward bound freight delivered foot of Barclay St.

New York & Long Branch R. R. Freight received by Central R. R. of N. J., Pier 8, N. R. until 5 00 p. m., also by Pennsylvania R. R., Pier 1 or 16 N. R., foot West 35th and foot North 4th st. Brooklyn, E. D., until 5 00 p. m.

New York & Manhattan Beach R. R. See Long Island R. R.

New York & Massachusetts R'y, Ship by Propellers Hasbrouck and D. S. Miller at foot of Franklin St. until 6 00 p. m.

New York & Montreal Transportation Co, W. R. Moe & Co. Agents. 9 South St.

New York & Saugerties Transportation Co, Steamers Ansonia and Saugerties from foot Franklin St. daily except Saturday 6 00 p. m. and Saturdays 3 00 p. m. M. Freligh, Agent foot of Franklin St.

New York & New England R. R, Ship Freight for Melrose Branch, Rockville Extension and places between Hartford and Willimantic by New Haven Boats, Pier 25, E. R. or by New York and Northern R'y, Pier 40 E. R. or by Housatonic Line, Pier 49 E. R. until 5 00 p. m. Springfield Division ship by Hartford Boats Pier 24, E. R. or N. Y. & Northern R. R., Pier 40 E. R. Western Division ship by N. Y. & Northern R'y, Pier 40 E. R., and by Housatonic Line, Pier 49, E. R. For all other parts of the road ship by Norwich Line foot of Watts until 5 00 p. m.

New York & Northern R. R. Ship freight for all places on this road at Pier 40, E. R. until 4 30 p. m.

New York & Philadelphia New Line, See Central R. R. of N. J.

New York and Rockaway Beach R. R, Freight received at Pier 32. E. R. or at Flatbush Avenue Depot, Fort Greene Place between Atlantic Ave., and Hanson Place, until 4 00 p. m.

New York and Sea Beach R. R, Freight received for points on this road foot of Whitehall St., from 8 00 a. m. to 5 00 p. m. On Saturday to 12 noon.

New York Central & Hudson River R. R. Ship freight for points on Hudson River Division and connections, and for Albany, Troy, and railroads connecting at Albany and Troy, at St. John's Park and cor. 11th Ave. and 33d St., until 4 00 p. m. For Albany and Troy and railroads connecting at those points ship also Pier 4, E. R., until 4 00 p. m. For places west of Albany in New York State, Ship at foot of Barclay St., Pier 4, E. R., and cor. 11th Ave. and 33d St., until 4 00 p. m. Ship freight for places west of New York State and in Ontario, at foot of Barclay St., St. John Park, Pier 4, E. R., cor. 11th Ave. and 33d St., until 4 p. m. Bill of Lading signed at 16, 413 Broadway. E. Clark, Jr., General Freight Agent; Samuel Goodman Asst. General Freight Agent, Grand Central Depot. 4th Ave. and 42d St. Freight for all parts of this road received North 6th St., Brooklyn, E. D., and foot of Washington St., Brooklyn.

TRANSPORTATION LINES.—Continued.

New York, Lake Erie & Western R. R. Ship Freight for all points on Main Line and Branches at foot of Chambers St., foot of West 23d St., and foot of West 40th St., until 4 00 p. m., and foot of North 5th St., Brooklyn, E. D., until 5 00 p. m. The following places are also received at Pier 8, E. R.; Batavia, Buffalo, Clymer, Ithaca, Jamestown, Niagara Falls, Oswego, Panama, Rochester, Salamanca, Suspension Bridge, Syracuse, Stafford. Through Western Freight ships at Pier 8, E. R., foot Duane, foot West 23d St., foot of West 40th St., or foot North 5th St., Brooklyn, E. D. Inward bound freight from all parts of the road and Branches delivered at foot of Duane St. M. E. Staples, General Agent, 187 West St.

New York, New Haven & Hartford R. R. ship freight for all parts of this road and Eastern connections, at Pier 50, E. R., and Harlem River Station, until 4 30 p. m. Freight for Hartford and Northampton Divisions received also by Newhaven boats at Pier 25, E. R. Freight for Naugatuck Division received also by Bridgeport boats, Pier 35, E. R. Freight for Valley Division received also by Hartford boats, Pier 24, E. R. Charles Rockwell, General Freight Agent, New Haven, Conn.

New York, Ontario & Western Ry. ship freight for all places on this road at Pier 5, N. R., and foot of West 35th St., until 4 00 p. m., also at Wythe Ave. and North 5th St., Brooklyn, E. D., until 4 00 p. m. Through Western Freight ship by "Ontario Despatch," or "Soo Line," at Pier 5, N. R., foot of West 35th St. and Wythe Ave. and North 5th St., Brooklyn, E. D., until 4 00 p. m. J. C. Anderson, General Freight and Passenger Agent, 16 and 18 Exchange Place.

New York, Philadelphia & Norfolk R. R. ship by Pennsylvania R. R., foot of Hubert St. or foot of West 35th St., or foot of North 4th St., Brooklyn, E. D., until 4 00 p. m.

New York, Providence & Boston R. R. Ship freight by Stonington Line, foot of Spring St., until 5 00 p. m.

New York, Susquehanna & Western R. R. Ship freight at Pier 16, N. R., until 5 00 p. m. Coarse freight in bulk received only at Jersey City Depot. I. I. Demarest, General Freight Agent, 15 Cortlandt St.

Nickel Plate Line, Mark goods, "Nickel Plate Line," and ship at Pier 5, N. R., foot West 35th St., until 4 00 p. m., and Wythe Ave. and North 5th St., Brooklyn, E. D., until 3 00 p. m.

Northern Express Freight Line, via Albany and Troy, and railroads to all ports on Lake Champlain, Montreal and Canada, mark goods, "N. E. F. Line," and ship by "People's Line," foot of Canal St., until 6 00 p. m., and by "Citizen's Line," foot of Christopher St., until 6 00 p. m.

Northern R. R. of N. J. ships freight for places on this road, at Pier 20 N. R., foot of Chambers St., until 4 00 p. m.

Northern Pacific R. R. George Fitch, General Eastern Agent, 319 Broadway.

Ohio & Mississippi Ry. H. A. Wells, Eastern Passenger Agent, 415 Broadway.

Ontario Despatch to all points West, Southwest, Northwest and Canada, mark goods, "Ontario Despatch," and ship at Pier 5, N. R., foot West 35th St., N. R., and Wythe Ave. and North 5th St., Brooklyn, E. D., until 4 00 p. m. C. W. Perveil, Agent, 307 Broadway. Bills of Lading. 16 Beaver st. and 307 Broadway.

Oregon Short Line, Mark goods via "Union Pacific Ry.," and ship by any Freight Line to Chicago. R. Tenbroeck, Agent, 287 Broadway.

Paint Rock Line. Ship goods by Old Dominion Steamship Co., foot of Beach St.; office 229 Broadway.

Palmetto Freight Line, via Steamers to Charleston and Charleston and Savannah Ry. to the South and Southwest. Mark goods "Palmetto Line," and ship by Charleston Steamers Pier 29. E. R., foot of Roosevelt St. J. D. Harbagen, Eastern Agent, 261 Broadway.

Passaic & Delaware R. R. Ship by Delaware, Luckawanna & Western R. R., foot of Leroy St., until 5 00 p. m.

Pennsylvania R. R. Ship freight for places on the New York Division, Millstone Branch, Perth Amboy Branch, Rocky Hill Branch, Philadelphia, Germantown and Chestnut Hill Branch, at Pier 16, N. R., and foot of West 35th St., until 4 00 p. m. Ship freight for places on the Freehold & Jamesburg Branch, Philadelphia & Long Branch R. R., and Trenton, at Pier 1, N. R., or 16 N. R., and foot of West 35th St., until 4 00 p. m. Ship freight for places on the Amboy Division and Branches and Belvidere Division, at Pier 1, N. R., and at foot West 35th St., until 4 00 p. m. Ship freight for Baltimore City and Philadelphia at Pier 1, N. R., or 16 N. R., and foot of Vestry St., and foot of West 35th St., until 4 00 p. m. Ship freight for Washington City at Pier 1, N. R., and foot of Vestry St., and foot West 35th St., until 4 00 p. m. Ship freight for Richmond, Va., and all points South, at foot Hubert St., until 1 00 p. m. Ship freight for Pittsburgh, Pa., by "Star Union Line," at Pier 4, N. R., and foot of Laight St., and foot of West 35th St., until 4 00 p. m. Ship freight for Pennsylvania, Schuylkill Valley Branch, at Pier 16, N. R., until 4 00 p. m. Ship freight for Main Line & Northern Central R. R., and other points not named in lists, at Pier 1, N. R., and foot of Vestry St., and foot of West 35th St., until 4 00 p. m. Ship freight to all points on the Pennsylvania R. R. and connections at foot of North 4th St., Brooklyn, E. D., and foot of Pearl St., Brooklyn, and at Freight Station in Jersey City. George B. Raymond, freight agent, Pier 1 N. R., N. Y. Douglass freight agent, foot of Vestry St., J. T. Robb, freight agent, Pier 16 N. R., J. S. Boden, freight agent, Pier 4 North River, M. Townsend, freight agent, foot of Laight St., J. Mifflin, freight agent, foot of West 35th St.

Peoples Line, Express Freight Line for Albany and all points on the N. Y. Central R. R. and Delaware & Hudson Canal Co. R. R., and Ogdensburgh, Lake & Champlaine R. R., and all connecting points. Ship by Peoples Line, foot of Canal St. F. C. Earle, Asst. General Freight Agent, foot Canal St.

Phelpher's Daily Line to Harrisburg, Lewisburg and Sunbury, and intermediate points on Northern Central R. R. Mark goods "Phelpher's Line." Ship at Pier 18, N. R., foot of Cortlandt St., until 5 00 p. m.; on Saturday 4 00 p. m. Office on Pier.

Philadelphia & Reading R. R. Ship freight for all places on this road at Pier 12, N. R., until 5 00 p. m.

Philadelphia New Line. Ship freight for all places on this road, at Pier 13. N. R., until 6 00 p. m.

Piedmont Air Line, G. M. Huntington, Eastern Passenger Agent, 229 Broadway. H. P. Clark, General Eastern Passenger Agent, Tickets, &c., 1 Astor House, 229, 435, 819 and 944 Broadway.

Port Jervis, Monticello & N. Y, R. R. Ship freight at foot of Chambers St., until 4 00 p. m.

Port Royal Line, Mark Goods via "Port Royal Line," and ship by Mallory's Line, at Pier 21, E. R. Bills of Lading signed at Pier 20, E. R. C. B. Crowell, Agent, 234 Broadway.

Poughkeepsie Transportation Co. Homer Ramsdell, President. Foot of Franklin St., N. R., Main Office, Poughkeepsie, N. Y.

Prospect Park & Coney Island R. R Ship freight cor. 9th Ave. and 19th St., Brooklyn, until 5 00 p. m.

Providence & Worcester R. R. Ship freight by Providence Boats foot of Warren St., until 5 00 p. m.

Queen & Crescent Route, Embracing the Cincinnati, New Orleans & Texas Pacific Railway, Alabama, & Great Southern Railway, New Orleans & Northeastern R. R., Vicksburg, Meriden, Vicksburg, Shreveport & Pacific R. R. W. S. St. George, General Eastern Agent, 319 Broadway.

Red Line Transit Co. Mark Goods "Red Line," and ship at St. John's Park, Pier 5, E. R., foot of Barclay St., 33d St., and 11th Ave., until 4 00 p. m., and foot North 6th St., Brooklyn, E. D., and foot of Washington St., Brooklyn. W. A. Zell, Agent, 413 Broadway.

Richelieu & Ontario Navigation Co. Steamers between Niagara Falls, Toronto, Kingston, Montreal, Quebec, Murray Bay, Riviere du Loup, Tadousac, and Ha! Ha! Bay. Office, 271 Broadway. J. B. Labelle, General Manager, Montreal, Canada.

Richmond & Danville Despatch. Mark Packages "R. D. Despatch," and ship by Pennsylvania R. R., foot of Hubert or foot of North 4th St., Brooklyn, E. D., or foot of Pearl St., Brooklyn. Geo. T. Smith, Agent, 435 Broadway. Bills of Lading signed at 1 Astor House, 76 Wall st., 435 Broadway.

Rome, Watertown & Ogdensburg R. R. Ship freight by N. Y. Central & Hudson River R. R., foot of Barclay St., Pier 4, E. R., cor. 11th Ave. and 33d St., and also at Pier 5, N. R., until 4 00 p. m.

San Antonio & Arkansas Pass R'y. W. H. Kelley, General Eastern Agent, 353 Broadway.

Santa Fe Route, Same as Atchinson, Topeka & Santa Fe R. R. C. D. Simonson, General Eastern Agent, 261 Broadway.

TRANSPORTATION LINES.—Continued.

Savannah Fast Freight & Passenger Line, For all points in South and Southwest via Savannah & Central Railroad of Georgia, Mark packages "Central R. R. of Georgia, agent Savannah," and ship at Savannah Steamers foot of Spring St. R. L. Walker, Agent. office on Pier foot of Spring St., and W. H. Rhett, General Agent, Office 317 Broadway. Bills of Lading at both offices.

Savannah, Florida & Western R'y, Ship by Savannah Steamers, foot of Spring St. J. D. Hashagen, Eastern Agent, 261 Broadway.

Sea Board Dispatch, Mark "Seaboard Des." and ship until 4 p. m. by Pennsylvania R. R., foot of Hubert St. or foot of North 4th St., Brooklyn, E. D., or foot of Pearl St., Brooklyn. George T. Smith, Agent, 135 Broadway. Bills of lading, 1 Astor House, 76 Wall St., 435 Broadway.

Shenandoah Valley Route, For the South. J. E. Prindle, Passenger Agency, 303 Broadway.

Shepaug, Litchfield & Northern R. R., Ship by the Housatonic Line, Pier 49. E. R., until 5 p. m.

Soo Line, Mark packages "Soo Line," and ship by N. Y., Ontario & Western Railway, Pier 5, N. R., foot of West 25th St., until 4 p. m., foot of Washington St., Brooklyn, or Wythe Ave. and North 5th St. Brooklyn, E. D., and Weehawken, N. J., T. Fletcraft, Agent, 307 Broadway.

Southern Pacific Co., "Sunset Route," Mark packages "Sunset Route," Ship by Morgan's Line of steamers, foot of North Moore St. E. Hawley, Agent. 343 Broadway, 6 Bowling Green.

Star Union Line (bonded line) by Pennsylvania R. R. Mark Goods "Star Union Line," Ship at Pier 4, N. R., foot of Laight St., foot of West 35th St., foot of Pearl St., Brooklyn, or foot North 4th St., Brooklyn, E. D. Geo. T. Smith, Agent, 435 Broadway. Bills of Lading signed at 76 Wall St., 1 Astor House, 435 Broadway.

Staten Island R. R. Ship freight for all points on this road at foot of Whitehall St., until 5 p. m., Saturday until 12 noon. R. W. Pollock, General Traffic Agent, foot of Whitehall St.

Stony Clove and Catskill Mountain R. R. Ship freight by Rondout boats, foot of Harrison Street, until 3 45 p. m., on Saturday to 12 15 p. m.; and by West Shore R. R., Pier 5, N. R., foot West 35th St., and Wythe Ave. and North 5th st., Brooklyn, E. D., until 4 p. m.

St. Louis & San Francisco Ry. Mark packages care "St. L. & S. F. Ry." St. Louis," and ship by any freight line to St. Louis. W. L. Van Nest, General Eastern Agent, 353 Broadway.

St. Paul, Minneapolis and Manitoba Ry, for Watertown, Aberdeen, Ellendale and Sioux Falls, Fargo, Grand Forks, Grafton, Helena, and all principle points in Montana, Dakota, and Minnesota. Mark packages care "St. P. M. & M. R." St. Paul, Minn., and ship by any freight line to St. Paul, Minn. S. L. Warren, General Eastern Agent, 287 Broadway.

Sunset Route, Mark packages "Sunset Route" and ship by Morgan's Line steamers foot of North Moore St. E. Hawley, Agent. 343 Broadway and 6 Bowling Green.

Sussex R. R., Ship to all points on this road at Pier foot of Leroy St., until 5 00 p. m.

Texas & Pacific R'y, For points in Texas and Pacific on Coast. Mark goods "T. & P. R'y," and ship by any freight to St. Louis. Samuel E. Stohr, General Eastern Agent, 169 Broadway.

Traders' Despatch via Lehigh Valley R. R. New York, Chicago and St. Louis R. R., and connections for points West, Northwest, Southwest. Mark packages "Traders' Despatch," and ship at Pier 2 N. R. until 4 00 p. m. J. H. Gilbert, Contracting Agent, F. C. Hovey, Agent, 285 Broadway.

Tuckerton R. R, Ship for any point on this road at Pier 8, N. R., until 5 00 p. m.

Ulster & Delaware R. R. Ship freight for all points on this road, at Rondout boats foot of Harrison St., until 3 30 p. m., on Saturday, 12 30 p. m. Also, ship freight by West Shore R. R., Pier 5, N. R., foot West 35th St. and Wythe Av. and North 5th St., Brooklyn, E. D.

Union Pacific Railway, Oregon Railway & Navigation Co. (Oregon Short Line Co. Lessee). Mark packages "via Union Pac. R'y," and ship by any freight line to Chicago or St. Louis. R. Tenbroeck, General Eastern Agent, 287 Broadway.

Virginia, Tennessee & Georgia Air Line, Mark packages "V. T. & G. Air Line;" and ship by Old Dominion Line, foot of Beach St. Thomas Pinckney, General Eastern Agent, 303 Broadway.

Wabash Lake Line, (Wabash, St. Louis & Pacific Railway Lake Line) to the West by Rail, Lake and Rail. Mark packages care of "Wabash Lake Line," and ship by any freight line to to Buffalo, N. Y. F. W. Smith, Agent, 328 Broadway.

Wabash Western Railway Co. and Wabash Railway, Mark packages "Via Wabash," and ship by any freight line running to Chicago or St. Louis. H. B. McClellan, General Eastern Agent, 323 Broadway.

Walkill Valley R. R. Ship goods for all points on this road at Pier 5, N. R. foot of West 35th St., and cor. Wythe Ave. and North 5th St., Brooklyn, E. D.

Ward's Detroit and Lake Superior Line, A line of steamers from Buffalo, for Cleveland, Detroit and Duluth. Mark packages "Care Ward's Line, Buffalo," and ship by D. L. & W. R. R., at foot of Dey St., foot of Leroy St., foot of South 9th St., Brooklyn, E. D., and at Hoboken, N. J., until 4 00 p. m. Bills of Lading at 429 Broadway, 93 Wall St.

Western Express, Fast Freight Line by N. Y. Central and Hudson River Railroad and the Western Transit Co's. Steamers (the Western Transit Co., proprietors). Mark packages "Western Express" and ship at St. John Park, Pier 5, East River, foot of Barclay St., 33d St. cor. 11th Ave., foot of Washington St., Brooklyn, and foot of North 4th St., Brooklyn, E. D.

West Jersey, R. R. Ship freight by Pennsylvania R. R. at Pier 1, N. R. or foot of West 35th St., or foot of Pearl St., Brooklyn, or foot of North 4th st., Brooklyn, E. D.

West Shore, R. R, Ship freight for all points on this road and divisions at Pier 5, N. R., foot of West 35th St., until 4 00 p. m.; also at Wythe Ave. and North 5th St., Brooklyn, E. D., until 5 00, p. m. All inward bound freight delivered at Pier 1 & 5, N. R., at foot West 35th St., and also at Wythe Ave. & North 5th St., Brooklyn, E. D. F. P. Finch, Freight Agent, Pier 5, N. R. J. E. Brewington, Agent, foot of West 35th st., N. R.

West Shore Line, "Bonded Line." Mark goods "West Shore Line," and ship same Piers as West Shore R. R. See above.

White Line, Central Transit Co, Mark packages "White Line." Ship at foot of Barclay St., St. Johns Park, 33rd St., and 11th Ave., Pier 5, E. R., until 4 p. m., foot of Washington St., Brooklyn, and foot North 6th St., Brooklyn, E. D. W. A. Zell. Agent. 113 Broadway.

Wilson Transit Co, A line of steamers from Buffalo to Duluth. Mark packages "Care Wilson Transit Co." Ship by the Delaware, Lackawanna & Western R. R., foot of Dey St., foot of Leroy St., until 4 00 p. m., Hoboken, N. J., or foot of South 9th St., Brooklyn, E. D.

Wisconsin Central Line, Ship freight by any line to Chicago. W. F. Bemis, General Eastern Agent, 319 Broadway.

INTERNAL REVENUE DISTRICTS AND OFFICERS.

New York.—Second District, J. A. Sullivan, Collector Internal Revenue and Collector in charge of exports and drawbacks for Port of New York. Office 2 Beekman St. **Third District,** Leonard A. Giegerich, Collector. Office, 153 Fourth Ave.

Brooklyn.—First District Embracing all of Long Island and Staten Island, Kings, Queens, Suffolk, and Richmond Counties. Robert Black, Collector. Offices. 38 Court St., Brooklyn.

SOCIETIES.

In the following list we have dropped the prefix American, National and New York from the names of the Societies, as we believe these prefixes confusing to persons seeking information concerning these societies. American Chemical Society will be found under C ; National Horse Show Association under H ; New York Juvenile Guardian Society under J.

Academy of Sciences, 41 E. 49th.
Actors' Fund of America, 145 5th Ave.
Albion, 50 Union Pl.
Amateur Athletes of America, P. O. Box 3478.
Amateur Photographers, 122 W. 36th.
American Artists, 51 W. 10th.
American Institute, 19 Astor Pl.
Architects' Institute, 18 Broadway.
Architectural League, 10 W. 23d.
Art Students' League, 143 E. 23d.
Aryan Theosophical, 144 Madison Ave.
Associated Press, 195 Broadway.
Bar of the City of N. Y., 7 W. 29th.
Beethoven Maennerchor, 210 Fifth St.
Chemical, 1 University Building.
 ildren's Aid Society, office 24 St. Mark's Pl.
Choir Exchange, 701 6th Ave.
Christian Philosophy Institute, 4 Winthrop Pl.
Civil Engineers, 127 E. 23d.
Civil Service Reform Association, 35 Liberty.
Clinical Society Post Graduate Medical School, 226 E. 20th.
College of City of N. Y. Alumni, 17 Lexington Ave.
Cooper Union, Advancement of Science & Art, 8th st. c. 4th av.
Cremation Society, 140 Nassau.
Decorative Art, 28 E. 21st.
Dorcas Society, 29th cor. 5th Ave.
Dramatic Fund Association, 1267 Broadway.
Elks, 117 W. 23d.
Ethnological, 35 Pine.
Exchange for Women's Work, 329 5th Ave.
Flower and Fruit Mission, 243 4th Ave., meets Monday and Thursday from May to October.
Free Trade League, 39 Nassau.
Gaelic, 17 W. 28th.
Geographical, 11 West 29th.
Genealogical and Biographical, 64 Madison Ave.
German, 13 Broadway.
Gotham Art Students, 607 Broadway.
Grant Monument, 146 Broadway.
Horse Show Association of America, 48 Broad.
Hospital Saturday & Sunday Collection Association, 79 4th Av.
Improving the Condition of the Poor, 79 4th Ave.
Industrial Education Association, 9 University Pl.
Irish Emigrant Society, 51 Chambers.
Jewelers' Security Alliance, 170 Broadway.
Juvenile Guardian Society, 185 Bleecker.
King's Daughters, 17 W. 22d St.
Ladies' Art, 23 E. 14th.
Ladies' Christian Union, 27 Washington Sq.
Ladies' Depository, 27 E. 18th.
Liederkranz, 115 E. 58th.
Mardi Gras, 440 6th Ave.
Marine, 51 Wall.
Martin Luther, 12 W. 31st.
Mechanical Engineers, 280 Broadway.
Mechanics' and Tradesmen's, 18 E. 16th.
Medico Historical, 130 E. 30th.
Mercantile Library Association, 19 Astor Pl.
Methodist Book Concern, 805 Broadway.
Meteorological, 40th, n. Madison Ave.
Microscopical, 64 Madison Ave.
Mining Engineers' Institute, 13 Burling St.
Mount Sinai Training School for Nurses, 851 Lexington Ave.
National Prohibition Bureau, 32 E. 14th.
National Rifle Association, 5 Beekman.
National Temperance Society & Publication House, 58 Reade.

New England, L. P. Hubbard, Secretary, 74 Wall.
N. Y. Chapter, American Institute of Architects, 18 B'way.
N. Y. County Medical, 338 E. 26th.
N. Y. Historical, 170 2d Ave.
N. Y. State Society of the Cincinnati, 67 University Pl.
N. Y. State Veterinary, 141 W. 54th.
Neurological, 12 W. 31st.
Numismatic and Archæological, 25 University Building.
Obstetrical, 12 W. 31st.
Ohio Society, 530 5th Ave.
Old Guard, 84 5th Ave.
Oratorio, 40th, cor. 7th Ave.
Pathological, 214 E. 30th.
Philharmonic, A. Roebbelen, Sec., Metropolitan Opera House.
Phrenology Institute, 775 Broadway.
Police Endowment and Relief Fund, 300 Mulberry.
Prevention of Cruelty to Animals, 100 E. 22d.
Prevention of Cruelty to Children, 100 E. 23d.
Prevention of Cruelty to Sailors, 32 Broadway.
Prevention of Crime, 110 E. 19th and 17 Warren.
Prison Association of N. Y. 135 E. 15th.
Protective Tariff League, 23 W. 23d.
Promotion and Encouragement of Art, 6 E. 23d.
St. Andrews, 287 E. Broadway.
St. Davids, 21 University Pl.
St. George's, 7 Battery Pl.
St. John's Guild, 21 University Pl.
St. Johnland, 220 E. 23d.
St. Martha, 31 W. 22d.
St. Nicholas, C. A. schermerhorn, Treas., 1273 Broadway.
St. Vincent de Paul, 29 Reade.
Schillerbund, 64 E. 4th.
Schoolmasters' Association, meets 2d Saturday in each month at Columbia College.
School of Mines Alumni, 41 E. 49th.
Seamen's Friend, 74 Wall.
Sisters of the Stranger, 4 Winthrop Pl.
Societe de l'Amitie, 440 6th Ave.
State Charities Aid, 21 University Pl.
State Charities Hospital Books and Newspaper Committee, 21 University Pl.
Suppression of Vice, 150 Nassau.
Symphony, 40th, cor. 7th Ave.
Tammany, 143 E. 14th st.
Tammany Central, 207 E. 32d.
Training School for Nurses, 426 E. 26th.
Trustees of N. Y. Universal Relief Fund, 26 Exchange place.
Typographical, 19 Park Pl.
Typothetae, 19 Park Pl.
United Hebrew Charities, 58 St. Mark's Pl.
U. S. Trade Mark, 137 Broadway.
Verein Freundschaft, Park Ave. and 73d st.
Water Color, 51 W. 10th.
West Side, 86th, cor. 10th ave.
William's College Alumni, A. H. Masten, Sec., 146 B'way.
Women's Prison Association, 110 2nd Ave.
Yale Alumni, W. B. Anderson, 43 William.
Young Men's Christian Association, General Office, 40 E. 23d st.; Branches as follows: Bowery, 243 Bowery; German, 142 2d Ave.; Harlem, 5 W. 125 st.; 23d St., cor. 4th Ave.; Yorkville, 153 E. 86th; Young Men's Institute, 222 Bowery. For Railroad Men: 361 Madison Ave., 470 W. 30th. 861 11th Ave., and Weehawken and New Durham, N. J.
Young Men's Hebrew Association, 721 Lexington Ave.; Down-town Branch, 206 E. Broadway.
Young Women's Christian Association, 7 E. 15th St.

POST OFFICE DOMESTIC MONEY ORDER RATES.

Payable at Money Order Post Offices o' s

$5 or less, 5 cents. $15 to 30, 15 cents. $50 to 60, 30 cents. $70 to 80, 40 cents.
$5 to 10, 8 cents. $30 to 40, 20 cents. $60 to 70, 35 cents. $80 to 100, 45 cents.
$10 to 15, 10 cents. $40 to 50, 25 cents.

Postal notes, for less than $5, are issued and will be paid to the bearer either at the office designated for payment on the note, or at the office where issued, within 3 months from date of issue, rate 3 cents.

FOREIGN MONEY ORDER RATES.

$10 or less, 10 cents. $20 to 30, 30 cents. $40 to 50, 50 cents.
$10 to 20, 20 cents. $30 to 40, 40 cents.

EXPRESS MONEY ORDER RATES.

Money Orders payable in the United States or Canada, are issued by the American, United States, and Wells, Fargo & Co. Express. Rates as follows:

$5 or less, 5 cents.   Over $10 to 20, 10 cents.   Over $30 to 40, 15 cents.
Over $5 to 10, 8 cents.   "   20 to 30, 12 cents.   "   40 to 50, 20 cents.

The American Express Co. issues Money Orders payable in Europe also, at following rates: Not over $10, 10c. $10 to 20, 18c. $20 to 30, 25c. $30 to 40, 35c. $40 to 50, 45c.

HORSE CAR LINES.

1st & 2d Ave. Line. From Fulton Ferry, via Fulton, Water, Peck Slip (to South and Oliver), Pearl, Park Row, Bowery, Grand, Forsyth, E. Houston, Second Ave. to Harlem River. Return via Second Ave., 23d St., First Ave., Houston St., etc., to Fulton Ferry; also via Second Ave., Chrystie St., Grand St., Bowery, Park Row, Pearl St., Peck Slip, South St. to Fulton Ferry.
Also from 86th St. and Second Ave. to Astoria Ferry, foot of E. 93d St. Also from Park Row, via Worth, to Broadway, First Ave. Line; from Broadway and Astor Place, via Stuyvesant, Second Ave., 59th St., First Ave. to Harlem. Return over same route.

3d Ave. Line. From Post Office, via Park Row, Bowery, Third Ave., to Harlem. Return over same route.

4th Ave. Line. From Post Office, via Park Row, Centre, Grand, Bowery, Fourth Ave. to Grand Central Depot, thence via Madison Ave. to E. 134th St. Return over same route to Broome, Centre, Park Row to Post Office. Also from E. 32d, via Lexington Ave., E. 34th to Hunter's Point Ferry; also from Madison Ave. and 86th St., via E. 86th. Ave. A, E. 93d to Astoria Ferry. Return over same route.

5th Ave. Stage Line. From Bleecker St., via South Fifth Ave. and Fifth Ave., to 89th St. Transfer at 82d St. for Riverside Drive. Stages do not run on Sundays.

6th Ave. Line. From Vesey St. and Broadway, via Church, Chambers, W. Broadway, Canal, Varick, Carmine, Sixth Ave. to W. 59th St. Return over same route to W. Broadway, College Place, Vesey to Broadway; also from Canal and Broadway, via Canal, Varick, Carmine, Sixth Ave. to W. 59th St.

7th Ave. Line.—From Seventh Ave. and W. 59th St., via Greenwich Ave., Clinton Place, Macdougal, W. 4th St., Thompson, Canal, W. Broadway, College Place, Park Place to Broadway. Return via Park Place, Church, Canal, Sullivan, W. 3d St., Macdougal, Clinton Place, Greenwich Ave., Seventh Ave. to W. 59th St.

8th Ave. Line. From Vesey and Broadway, via Church, Chambers, W. Broadway, Canal, Hudson, 8th Ave. to 59th St. and Central Park, and 155th St. Return over same route.

9th Ave. Line. From Fulton St. and Broadway, via Greenwich St., 9th Ave., 64th St., Boulevard, 10th Ave. to 120th St., connecting with Cable road. Return over same route to Gansevoort, Washington, Fulton and Broadway.

10th Ave. & 125th St. Cable Line. From foot of 125th St., E. River, via E. 125th, W. 125th, Manhattan, to North River. Also from foot E. 125th, via E. 125th, W. 125th, Manhattan, 10th Ave. to W. 187th.

14th St. & Union Sq. Line. From Christopher St. Ferry, N. R., via Greenwich, 9th Ave., 14th St., to Fourth Ave. Return via 14th St., Ninth Ave., Washington, Christopher, to Ferry depot. Transfer at 14th St. and Ninth Ave. for Hoboken Ferry, foot W. 14th St.

23d St. Line. From foot W. 23d St. to foot E. 23d St. Also via 23d St., 2d Ave., 28th St., First Ave. to E. 34th St. Ferry. Returning via First Ave., E. 29th St., Second Ave., to foot W. 23d St. (Erie Ferry).

42d and Grand St. Line. From Grand St. Ferry, via Grand, Goerck, Houston, Second, Ave. A, 11th Ave., Fourth Ave., 23d St., Broadway, 34th St., 10th Ave. to foot W. 42d St. (Weehawken Ferry). Return over same route to Cannon St., thence via Grand to Ferry depot.

42d St. Manhattanville and St. Nicholas Ave. Line. From foot E. 34th St. via First Ave., E. 42d St. to foot W. 42d St. Return over same route. Also from foot E. 34th St., via First Ave., etc. to Seventh Ave., thence via Broadway to W. 59th St., Boulevard, Manhattan to foot W. 130th St. (Fort Lee Ferry). Return over same route.

Ave. C Line. From Erie Depot, foot of Chambers St., N. R., via West, Charlton, Prince, Bowery, Stanton, Pitt, Ave. C, 18th St., Ave. A, 23d St., First Ave., 35th St., Lex. Ave. to E. 42d St. and Park Ave. Return, via E. 42d St., Lex. Ave., 36th St., First Ave., 23d St., Ave. A, 17th St., Ave. C, Third St., First Ave., Houston St., West, to Chambers. Also via West, Charlton, Prince, Bowery, Pitt, Ave. C, to E. 10th St. Ferry.

Bleecker St. and Fulton Ferry Line.—From foot W. 23d St., via Ninth Ave., Hudson, Bleecker, Broadway, Park Row, Beekman, South, to Fulton Ferry. Return via Fulton, William, Ann, Broadway, Bleecker, Macdougal, W. 4th St., W. 12th St., Hudson, Ninth Ave. to foot W. 23d St. Also from foot W. 23d St. via Ninth Ave., Hudson, Bleecker, Broadway, Canal, Elm, Reade, Centre, to Brooklyn Bridge. Return via Centre, Leonard, Elm, Canal, Broadway, Bleecker, Macdougal, W. 4th St., W. 12th St., Hudson, Ninth Ave. to foot W. 23d St.

Broadway and Seventh Ave. Line. From Seventh Ave. and Broadway, via University Place, Clinton Place, Greene, Church, Barclay to Broadway. Return via Barclay, College Place, W. Broadway, Canal, Wooster, University Place, Broadway to Seventh Ave. and W. 59th St. Also from Seventh Ave. & W. 59th St. via Seventh Ave., Broadway to Bowling Green and South Ferry. Return over same route.

Central Cross Town Line. From foot E. 23d St. via Ave. A, 18th St., Broadway, 14th St., Seventh Ave., W. 11th St., West, to Christopher St. Ferry. Return over same route to 17th St. via Ave. A to foot E. 23d St.

Central Park N. and E. River Belt Line. East side Section, from foot Whitehall St., via Water, Old Slip, South, Montgomery, South, Jackson, Monroe, Grand, Goerck, E. Houston, Ave. D, E. 14th St., Ave. A, E. 23d St., First Ave., E. 59th St., Tenth Ave. to W. 59d St. West side Section from foot Whitehall St. via Battery Place, West, Tenth Ave., W. 59th to Fifth Ave.

Chamber St. and Grand St. Ferry Line. From Grand St. Ferry, E. R., via East, Cherry, Jackson, Madison, New Chambers, Chambers to Ferry depot, foot Chambers St., N. R. Also from foot Chambers St., N. R., via New Chambers, James Slip, South, to Roosevelt St. Ferry, E. R.

City Hall, Ave. B. and 34th St. Line.—From Post Office, via Park Row, E. Broadway, Clinton, Ave. B, 14th, First Av. to E.34th St. Ferry. Returns over same route to 2d St., thence via Av. A, Essex, E.B'dway, Park Row to Post Office.

Christopher and Tenth St. Line. From Christopher St. Ferry depot, via Greenwich, Eighth St., Ave. A, E. 10th to E. 10th St. Ferry depot. Return via E. 10th, Ave. A, E. 9th, Stuyvesant place, Eighth St., Sixth Ave., Greenwich Ave., W. 10th, to Christopher St. Ferry.

Desbrosses, Vestry and Grand St. Line.—From Grand St. Ferry, via Sullivan, Vestry, Greenwich, Desbrosses, to Ferry depot foot Desbrosses St. Return via Desbrosses, Washington, Vestry, Sullivan, Grand St. to Ferry depot.

Dry Dock and East Broadway Line.—From Post Office, via E. Broadway, Grand, Columbia, Ave. D, 11th, Ave. C, to E. 23d St. Ferry. Return via Ave. A, 11th St., Ave. B, Tenth, Ave. D, Eighth, Lewis, Grand, E. Broadway, Park Row to Post Office. Also from Grand St. Ferry via E. Broadway, Canal, Walker, North Moore, Washington to Cortlandt St. Ferry. Return via Cortlandt, Greenwich, Beach, Lispenard, Canal to Grand St. Ferry.

Harlem Bridge, Melrose and West Farms Line.—From E. 129th St. and Third Ave., via Third Ave., Mott Haven, Melrose, Boston Road, thence to West Farms.

Harlem Bridge, Fordham and Port Morris Line.—From 129th St., via Third Ave., Mott Haven, Melrose, Morrisania, Tremont to Fordham. Also from 129th St., via Third Ave., 138th St. to Port Morris.

Madison Ave. Line. See "4th Ave. Line."

110th St. and St. Nicholas Ave. Line.—From First Ave. & 110th St., via 110th St., St. Nicholas Ave., Manhattan to North River.

Suburban Rapid Transit.—From Second Ave. and 129th St. to Third Ave. and 170th St.

FERRIES FROM NEW YORK.

Trips are also made on Sundays if not otherwise stated.

Astoria, from E. 92d st., 5 30, 6 00, 6 40, 7 00 a. m., then every 15 min. to 6 10 p. m., then every 20 min. to 8 p. m., then every 30 min. to midnight. Fare 3 cents.
Bay Ridge, from Whit-hall st. For Time Table, see Index for Steamboats.
Blackwell's Island, from E. 26th st., 10 30 a. m., 1 30 p. m. except Sundays. Fare, 20 cents.
Blackwell's Island, from E. 52d st., every hour from 6 a. m. to noon; then every half hour to 7 p. m. On Sundays hourly from 10 a. m. to 7 p. m. Fare, 25 cents.
Blackwell's Island, from E. 76th st., hourly from 7 a. m. to 7 p. m.; then 9 p. m., 10 p. m. Frequently on Sundays. Pass required.
Bedloe's Island, from Whitehall st., every hour from 9 a. m. to 5 p. m. Excursion fare, 25 cents.
Brooklyn, from Catherine st. to Main st., every 10 min. from 5 a. m. to 9 p. m.; then every 20 min. to 5 a. m.
Brooklyn, from Fulton st. E. R. to Fulton st., about every 5 min. from 4 a. m. to 7 p. m., then about every 10 min. to 4 a. m.
Brooklyn, from Wall st. to Montague st., about every 10 min. from 6 a. m. to 7 p. m., then every 20 min. to 9 p. m. except Sundays.
Brooklyn, South Ferry, from Whitehall st. to Atlantic st., about every 10 min. from 5 a. m. to midnight, then every 30 min. to 5 a. m.
Brooklyn, from Whitehall st. to Hamilton av., about every 10 min. from 4 a. m. to midnight, then every 30 min. to 4 a. m.
Brooklyn, from Whitehall st. to 39th st., South Brooklyn, every half hour from 6 30 a. m. to 10 30 p. m. On Sundays every half hour from 6 30 a. m. to 10 30 p. m. Fare, 5 cents.
Brooklyn, E. D., from E. 23d st. to Broadway, about every 12 min. from 5 12 a. m. to 12 12 night, then occasionally to 5 12 a. m. Fare, 3 cents.
Brooklyn, E. D., from E. Houston st. to Grand st., about every 12 min. from 5 a. m. to midnight, then every 30 min. to 5 a. m.
Brooklyn, E. D., from Grand st. to Grand st., every 12 minutes from 5 a. m. to midnight, then every half hour to 5 a. m.
Brooklyn, E. D., from Grand st. to Broadway, every 8 min. from 7 a. m. to midnight, then every 20 min. to 7 a. m.
Brooklyn, E. D., from Roosevelt st. to Broadway, about every 4 min. from 7 a. m. to 8 20 p. m., then every 20 min. to 7 a. m.
College Point, L. I., from E. 99th st. For Time Table, see Index for Steamboats.
Communipaw Ferry, see below at Jersey City.
Fort Lee, N. J., from Canal & W. 130th sts. For Time Table, see Index for Steamboats.
Greenpoint, from E. 10th st. to Greenpoint av., about every 12 min. from 6 00 a. m. to 10 p. m., then every 20 min. to midnight. Fare, 3 cents.
Greenpoint, from E. 23d st. to Greenpoint av., every 12 min. from 5 a. m. to 9 p. m., then every 20 min. to midnight, then half hourly to 5 a. m.
Hart's Island, from E. 26th st., at 11 a. m. except Sunday. Fare, 40 cents.
Hoboken, from W. 14th st. to 11th st., every 15 min. from 6 a. m. to 8 p. m., then half hourly to 10 30 p. m., then 10 50 p. m., and about every half hour to 6 a. m. Fare, 3 cents.
Hoboken, from Christopher st. to Ferry st., about every 10 min. from 6 a. m. to 10 30 p. m., then about every 20 min. to 6 a. m. Fare, 3 cents.
Hoboken, from Barclay st. to Ferry st., every 10 min. from 6 30 a. m. to 11 p. m., then about every 30 min. to 4 15 a. m., then on 15 minute interval to 6 30 a. m.
Hunter's Point, see below at Long Island City.
Jersey City, from W. 23d st. to Pavonia av. (Erie R. R. Dock), every 15 min. from 5 55 a. m. to 6 55 p. m., then half hourly to 11 55 p. m., then hourly to 5 55 a. m. On Sundays hourly from 12 55 a. m. to 6 55 a. m., then every 30 min. to 11 55 p. m.
Jersey City, Chambers st., week days, 6 a. m. to 11 a. m. every 40 min.; 11 a. m. to 3 p. m. every 15 min.; 3 p. m. to 7 p. m. every 10 min.; 7 p. m. to 12 midnight every 15 min.; 12 midnight to 3 a. m. every 30 min.; 3 a. m. to 6 a. m. every 15 min. Sundays, 12 midnight to 3 30 a. m. every 30 min., then 4 15, 4 45, 5 30, 6, 6 30 a. m., and thereafter every 15 min. to 12 midnight.
Jersey City, from Cortlandt & Desbrosses sts. to Montgomery st., every 15 min. from 4 a. m. to 6 a. m., then every 10 min. to 8 p. m., every 15 min. to midnight, every 30 min. to 4 a. m., on Sundays half hourly to 6 a. m., then on 15 min. intervals to midnight.
Jersey City, from Liberty st. to Communipaw (C. R. R. of N. J. Dock), 12 15, 12 30, 12 45, 1 00, then every 30 min. to 5 30 a.m., then every 15 min. to 7 45 a. m., every 7 min. to 10 a. m., about every 15 min. to 8 15 p. m., every 7 min. to 6 30 p. m., every 15 min. to 12 night. On Sundays 12 15, 12 45, 1 30, 3 30, 4 00, 5 00, 6 00, 7 15, 8, 8 15, 9, 9 30, 10, 10 30, 11, 11 30 a. m., 12, 12 15, 12 40, 1, 1 30, 1 45, 2, 2 15, 3, 3 45, 4, 5, 5 30, 5 45, 6, 6 30, 6 45, 7 45, 8, 8 30, 9, 9 30, 10, 10 30, 10 45, 11 p. m., 12 night.
Long Island City, from E. 34th st. to Borden av.—Winter Service—Leave E. 34th st. 12 30 a. m., then every 30 min. to 4 30 a. m., then every 20 min. to 5 30 a. m., then every 10 min. to 9 10 p. m., then every 20 min. to 10 40 p. m., then every 20 min. to 12 10 a. m. Sundays 12 10, 12 30 a. m., then every 30 min. to 5 30 a. m., then 5 50 a. m., then every 10 min. to 10 20 p. m., then every 20 min. to 11 10 p. m. Summer Service—Leave E. 34th st., 12 30 a. m., then every 30 min. to 4 30 a. m., then every 20 min. to 5 30 a. m., then every 10 min. to 11 10 p. m., then 12 10 a. m. Sundays 12 10, 12 30 a. m., then every 30 min. to 5 30 a. m., then every 10 min. to 11 10 p. m., then 12 night.
Long Island City, from James Slip to Borden av., every 30 min. from 6 30 a. m. to 6 30 p. m. except Sundays. Fare, 6 cents.
Randall's Island, from E. 26th st., 10 30 a. m. except Sundays. Fare, 30 cents.
Randall's Island, from E. 120th st., occasionally between 7 a. m. and 10 p. m. Pass required.
Randall's Island, from E. 122d st., rowboat service only.
Staten Island, for Time Table to St. George, see Index for Steamboats.
Ward's Island, from E. 26th st., 10 30 a. m., 3 30 p. m. except Sundays. Fare. 30 cents.
Ward's Island, from E. 115th st., rowboat service only. Pass required.
Weehawken, from W. 42d st. to West Shore R. R. Dock, 12 15, 12 45, 1 15, 1 45, 2 30, 3 15, 3 45, 4 30, 5 30, 6 15, 6 40, 6 55, 7 15, 7 50, 8 25, 8 45, 9 15, 9 55, 10 15, 10 50, 11 30 a. m., 12 15, 12 45, 1 15, 1 45, 2 20, 2 50, 3 20, 3 40, 4, 4 10, 4 50, 5 15, 6, 6 25, 7, 7 15, 7 40, 8 15, 8 45, 9 15, 9 40, 10 05, 10 45, 11 15, 11 45 p. m.
Weehawken, from W. 42d st. to Old Slip, 6, 6 30, 7, 8, 8 50, 9 20, 10, 10 35, 11 15 a. m., 12, 12 35, 1 20, 2, 2 40, 3 25, 4 05, 4 40, 5 20, 6 05, 6 40, 7 20, 8, 8 35 p. m. Extra trip on Sunday 10 10 p. m.; on Saturday 9 20 p. m.
Weehawken, from Jay st. to West Shore R.R. Dock, 12 30, 1, 1 30, 2, 3, 3 30, 4, 5, 6, 6 30, 7, 7 35, 8 10, 8 30, 9, 9 40, 10 20, 11 15, 11 30 a. m., 12 30, 1 30, 2 30, 3, 3 45, 3 55, 4 35, 5, 5 10, 6 10, 6 40, 7 30, 8, 8 30, 9, 9 40, 10 20, 11, 11 30 p. m., 12 night.

OFFICE BUILDINGS.

Alburtis, 33 Liberty.	Evening Post, Broadway & Fulton.	Produce Exchange, Broadway & Beaver.
Aldrich, 32 Warren.	Exchange, 78 Broadway.	Real Estate Exchange, 59 Liberty.
Aldrich Court, 45 Broadway.	Exchange Court, 52 Broadway.	Schermerhorn, 96 B'way, 6 Wall, 3 Pine.
Armitage, 87 Pearl.	Guernsey, 160 Broadway.	Smith, 13 Cortlandt.
Astor, 10 Wall.	Hemenway, 35 Broadway.	Standard Oil, 26 Broadway.
Bank of America, 46 Wall.	Kemble, 15 Whitehall.	Staats Zeitung, Park Row & Centre.
Bennett, 93 Nassau.	Kemp, 68 William.	Stewart, Broadway & Chambers.
Bible House, 8th st. & 4th av.	Knickerbocker, 2 West 14th.	Stone, 28 36 Liberty.
Boreel, 115 Broadway.	Lackawanna, 26 Exchange Place.	Telephone, 16 Cortlandt.
Bryant, 57 Liberty.	Liverpool, London & Globe, 45 William.	Temple Court, 5 Beekman.
Central, Broadway & Beaver.	Manhattan Company, 42 Wall.	Times, Park Row & Nassau.
Central Trust, 56 Wall.	Mercantile Exchange, 6 Harrison.	Tontine, 88 Wall.
Cheesbrough, 21 State.	Merchants, 2 Stone.	Tower, 50 Broadway, 41 New.
Coal & Iron Exchange, 19 Cortlandt.	Metropolitan, Park Place & Church.	Tribune, Nassau & Spruce.
Commercial, 40 Broadway.	Mills, 15 Broad.	Trinity, 111 Broadway.
Continental, 100 Broadway.	Modlat, 385 Broadway.	Union, 51 William.
Cooper Union, 3d ave. & 8th st.	Munro, 15 Rose.	United Bank, Broadway & Wall.
Corbin, Broadway & John.	Morse, 138 Nassau.	United States Trust, 47 Wall.
Cotton Exchange, Beaver & William.	Mortimer, 11 Wall.	University, Waverly Pl. & E. Wash. Sq.
Drexel, Broad & Wall.	Mutual Life, 28 Nassau.	Vanderbilt, 132 Nassau.
Duncan, 11 Pine.	National, 57 Broadway.	Waltham, 1 Bond.
Eagle, Wall & Pearl.	New York Life, 318 Broadway.	Washington, 1 Broadway.
Empire, 69 Broadway.	Orient, 43 Wall.	Welles, 14 Broadway.
Equitable, 120 Broadway.	Post, 18 Exchange Place.	Wemple, 83 Nassau.
	Potter, 35 Park Row.	Western Union, 195 Broadway.

IMPORTANT STEAMSHIP SERVICE FROM VARIOUS PORTS.
LONDON, STRAITS, CHINA AND JAPAN.
Mail Service as performed by the Peninsular & Oriental Steam Navigation Co.

Mails Leave London	Leave Brindisi	Leave Port Said	Arrive Aden	Arrive Bombay	Arrive Colombo	Arrive Calcutta	Arrive Penang	Arrive Singapore	Arrive Hong Kong	Arrive Shanghai	Arrive Yokohama
April 12	April 15	April 17	April 23	April 29	April 30	May 6	May 6	May 8	May 14	May 18	
April 19	April 22	April 25	April 30	May 6							
April 26	April 29	May 1	May 7	May 13	May 14	May 20	May 20	May 22	May 28	June 1	
May 3	May 6	May 9	May 14	May 20							
May 10	May 13	May 15	May 21	May 27	May 28	June 3	June 3	June 5	June 11	June 15	
May 17	May 20	May 23	May 28	June 3							
May 24	May 27	May 29	June 4	June 10	June 11	June 17	June 17	June 19	June 25	June 29	
May 31	June 3	June 6	June 11	June 17							
June 7	June 10	June 12	June 18	June 24	June 25	July 1	July 1	July 3	July 9	July 13	
June 14	June 17	June 20	June 25	July 1							
June 21	June 24	June 26	July 2	July 8	July 9	July 15	July 15	July 17	July 23	July 27	
June 28	July 1	July 4	July 9	July 15							
July 5	July 8	July 10	July 16	July 22	July 23	July 29	July 29	July 31	Aug. 6	Aug. 10	
July 12	July 15	July 18	July 23	July 29							
July 19	July 22	July 24	July 30	Aug. 5	Aug. 6	Aug. 12	Aug. 12	Aug. 14	Aug. 20	Aug. 24	
July 26	July 29	Aug. 1	Aug. 6	Aug. 12							
Aug. 2	Aug. 5	Aug. 7	Aug. 14	Aug. 19	Aug. 20	Aug. 26	Aug. 26	Aug. 28	Sept. 3	Sept. 7	
Aug. 9	Aug. 12	Aug. 15	Aug. 20	Aug. 26							
Aug. 16	Aug. 19	Aug. 21	Aug. 27	Sept. 2	Sept. 3	Sept. 9	Sept. 9	Sept. 11	Sept. 17	Sept. 21	
Aug. 23	Aug. 26	Aug. 29	Sept. 3	Sept. 9							
Aug. 30	Sept. 2	Sept. 4	Sept. 10	Sept. 16	Sept. 17	Sept. 23	Sept. 23	Sept. 25	Oct. 2	Oct. 7	
Sept. 6	Sept. 9	Sept. 12	Sept. 17	Sept. 23							
Sept. 13	Sept. 16	Sept. 18	Sept. 24	Sept. 30	Oct. 1	Oct. 7	Oct. 7	Oct. 9	Oct. 16	Oct. 21	
Sept. 20	Sept. 23	Sept. 26	Oct. 1	Oct. 7							
Sept. 27	Sept. 30	Oct. 2	Oct. 8	Oct. 14	Oct. 15	Oct. 21	Oct. 21	Oct. 23	Oct. 30	Nov. 4	
Oct. 4	Oct. 7	Oct. 10	Oct. 15	Oct. 21							
Oct. 11	Oct. 14	Oct. 16	Oct. 22	Oct. 28	Oct. 29	Nov. 4	Nov. 4	Nov. 6	Nov. 13	Nov. 18	
Oct. 18	Oct. 21	Oct. 24	Oct. 29	Nov. 4							
Oct. 25	Oct. 28	Oct. 30	Nov. 5	Nov. 11	Nov. 12	Nov. 18	Nov. 18	Nov. 20	Nov. 27	Dec. 2	
Nov. 1	Nov. 4	Nov. 7	Nov. 12	Nov. 18							
Nov. 8	Nov. 11	Nov. 13	Nov. 19	Nov. 25	Nov. 26	Dec. 2	Dec. 2	Dec. 4	Dec. 11	Dec. 16	
Nov. 15	Nov. 18	Nov. 21	Nov. 26	Dec. 2							
Nov. 22	Nov. 25	Nov. 27	Dec. 3	Dec. 9	Dec. 10	Dec. 16	Dec. 16	Dec. 18	Dec. 25	Dec. 30	
Nov. 29	Dec. 2	Dec. 5	Dec. 10	Dec. 16							
Dec. 6	Dec. 9	Dec. 11	Dec. 17	Dec. 23	Dec. 24	Dec. 30	Dec. 30	Jan. 1	Jan. 8	Jan. 13	
Dec. 13	Dec. 16	Dec. 19	Dec. 24	Dec. 30							
Dec. 20	Dec. 23	Dec. 25	Dec. 31	Jan. 6	Jan. 7	Jan. 13	Jan. 13	Jan. 15	Jan. 22	Jan. 27	
Dec. 27	Dec. 30	Jan. 2	Jan. 7	Jan. 13							
Jan. 3	Jan. 6	Jan. 8	Jan. 14	Jan. 20	Jan. 21	Jan. 27	Jan. 27	Jan. 29	Feb. 5	Feb. 10	

The Time Table for this Service is not yet completed, being arranged by the Company's Superintendent at Hong Kong.

Connecting Steamer leaves Hong Kong every two weeks for Yokohama.

MARSEILLES, INDIA, CHINA, JAPAN.
The Messageries Maritimes Company's Service.

Leave Marseilles	Arrive Port Said	Arrive Aden	Arrive Colombo	Arrive Singapore	Arrive Hong Kong	Arrive Shanghai	Arrive Kobe	Arrive Yokohama
April 21	April 26	May 2	May 9	May 15	May 22	May 26	May 29	May 31
May 5	May 10	May 16	May 22	May 29	June 5	June 9	June 12	June 14
May 19	May 24	May 30	June 6	June 12	June 19	June 23	June 26	June 28
June 2	June 7	June 13	June 20	June 26	July 3	July 7	July 10	July 12
June 16	June 21	June 27	July 4	July 10	July 17	July 21	July 24	July 26
June 30	July 5	July 11	July 18	July 24	July 31	Aug. 4	Aug. 7	Aug. 9
July 14	July 19	July 25	Aug. 1	Aug. 7	Aug. 14	Aug. 18	Aug. 21	Aug. 23
July 28	Aug. 2	Aug. 8	Aug. 15	Aug. 21	Aug. 28	Sept. 1	Sept. 4	Sept. 6
Aug. 11	Aug. 16	Aug. 22	Aug. 29	Sept. 4	Sept. 11	Sept. 15	Sept. 18	Sept. 20
Aug. 25	Aug. 30	Sept. 5	Sept. 12	Sept. 18	Sept. 25	Sept. 29	Oct. 2	Oct. 4
Sept. 8	Sept. 13	Sept. 19	Sept. 26	Oct. 3	Oct. 11	Oct. 15	Oct. 18	Oct. 20
Sept. 22	Sept. 27	Oct. 3	Oct. 11	Oct. 17	Oct. 25	Oct. 29	Nov. 1	Nov. 3
Oct. 6	Oct. 11	Oct. 17	Oct. 25	Oct. 31	Nov. 8	Nov. 12	Nov. 15	Nov. 17
Oct. 20	Oct. 25	Oct. 31	Nov. 8	Nov. 14	Nov. 22	Nov. 26	Nov. 29	Dec. 1
Nov. 3	Nov. 8	Nov. 14	Nov. 22	Nov. 28	Dec. 6	Dec. 10	Dec. 13	Dec. 15
Nov. 17	Nov. 22	Nov. 28	Dec. 6	Dec. 12	Dec. 20	Dec. 24	Dec. 27	Dec. 29
Dec. 1	Dec. 6	Dec. 12	Dec. 20	Dec. 26	Jan. 3	Jan. 7	Jan. 10	Jan. 12
Dec. 15	Dec. 20	Dec. 26	Jan. 3	Jan. 9	Jan. 17	Jan. 21	Jan. 24	Jan. 26
Dec. 29	Jan. 3	Jan. 9	Jan. 17	Jan. 23	Jan. 31	Feb. 4	Feb. 7	Feb. 9

SAN FRANCISCO, JAPAN & CHINA.
Joint Schedule Pacific Mail S. S. Co., and Occidental & Oriental S. S. Co.

Dates with attached are Pacific Mail Steamers.*

Leave San Francisco	Arrive Yokohama	Arrive Hong Kong	Leave Hong Kong	Leave Yokohama	Arrive San Francisco
			April 9	April 17	May 12
			April 16	April 25	*May 10
			April 24	May 3	May 18
			May 2	May 11	*May 26
April 6	April 26	May 4	May 11	May 19	June 3
*April 15	May 5	May 13	May 19	*May 24	*June 12
April 24	May 13	May 22	May 28	June 4	June 21
*May 2	May 22	May 30	June 6	*June 15	*June 30
May 11	May 31	June 8	June 15	June 23	July 9
*May 25	June 11	June 22	June 30	*July 5	July 24
*June 4	June 23	July 1	July 9	*July 18	*Aug. 2
June 14	July 1	July 9	July 16	July 25	Aug. 9
*June 29	July 19	July 27	Aug. 3	*Aug. 14	*Aug. 26
*July 14	July 27	Aug. 5	Aug. 12	*Sept. 5	Sept. 1

And at corresponding intervals thereafter.

Train Service—London to Marseilles.

Leave London	8.20 a. m.	11.00 a. m.	8.00 p. m.
Leave Paris	7.15 p. m.	9.25 p. m.	11.15 a. m
Arrive Marseilles	10.42 a. m.	3.23 p. m.	5.48 a. m

SAN FRANCISCO TO AUSTRALIA, NEW ZEALAND AND SANDWICH ISLANDS.
via Oceanic Steamship Company.

Leave San Francisco	Arrive Honolulu	Arrive Auckland	Arrive Sydney	Leave Sydney	Leave Auckland	Leave Honolulu	Arrive San Francisco
April 6	April 13	April 27	May 2	April 17	April 22	May 4	May 11
May 4	May 11	May 25	May 30	May 15	May 20	June 1	June 8
June 1	June 8	June 22	June 27	June 12	June 17	June 29	July 6
June 29	July 6	July 20	July 25	July 10	July 15	July 27	Aug. 3
July 27	Aug. 3	Aug. 17	Aug. 22	Aug. 7	Aug. 12	Aug. 24	Aug. 31
Aug. 24	Aug. 31	Sept. 14	Sept. 19	Sept. 4	Sept. 9	Sept. 21	Sept. 28
Sept. 21	Sept. 28	Oct. 12	Oct. 17	Oct. 2	Oct. 7	Oct. 19	Oct. 26
Oct. 19	Oct. 26	Nov. 9	Nov. 14	Oct. 30	Nov. 4	Nov. 16	Nov. 23
Nov. 16	Nov. 23	Dec. 7	Dec. 12	Nov. 27	Dec. 2	Dec. 14	Dec. 21
Dec. 14	Dec. 21	Jan. 4	Jan. 9	Dec. 25	Dec. 30	Jan. 11	Jan. 18

GENERAL POST OFFICE.

(For Stations, see 3d page from this.)

The District encompassed by the General Office is as follows:—The Battery, East River, Catherine St., Chatham Square, Bowery, Canal St., West Broadway, Franklin St., North River to Battery. Station P, in the Produce Exchange building, affords mailing facilities for the Produce Exchange and vicinity.

The following arrangement in alphabetical order of the various departments will greatly facilitate the finding of any desired information concerning the mailing of letters, etc.:

Boxes are rented at 4 dollars quarterly, payable in advance.

Carriers leave Post Office for first delivery at 7.30 a. m. Last delivery at 1.40 p. m. On holidays at 8 a. m. only. No delivery by carrier on Sundays, but mail will be delivered from Carriers' Department to applicants on Sundays from 9 to 11 a. m. at Section 17, Park Row side.

Circulars when mailed in quantities should be made up in bundles and deposited at the window designated for the reception of such matter on Broadway side of ground floor. For conditions as to mailing circulars *unsealed*, see under "3d Class Matter."

Collections from Street Boxes are made frequently between the hours of 5.30 a. m. and 11.15 p. m.; on holidays a few collections are made between 7.30 a. m. and 8.30 p. m.; on Sundays at 2, 5, 6.45 p. m.

General Delivery, at Section 5, Park Row side, begins at 7 a. m. and ends at midnight; on holidays during the appointed hours of business; on Sundays from 8 a. m. to 6 p. m.

Missing Mail Matter.—Inquiries concerning missing letters, etc., should be made at Room 14, 2d floor, from 9 a. m. to 4 p. m.

Ladies' Window is at Section 9, Park Row side, for the obtaining of letters, stamps, etc.

Money Order Department, on 2d floor, Broadway side, is open from 10 a. m. to 6 p. m., excepting Sundays and holidays. See Index for "Money Order Rates."

Postage Stamps, Stamped Envelopes, etc., are sold at all hours on week days and Sundays on ground floor, Broadway side. For sums exceeding one dollar not after 5 p. m. and not on Sundays or holidays. Stamped envelopes or wrappers spoiled in addressing will be redeemed if not mutilated.

Registry Department, at head of stairs at main entrance, Broadway side. Open for receiving mail from 8 a. m. to 6.30 p. m.; for delivery of mail from 9 a. m. to 5 p. m.; on holidays during the appointed hours of business; on Sundays from 10 to 11 a. m. Registered mail must be prepaid with an additional 10 cents postage and name and address of the sender must be endorsed on the envelope. A receipt from the person to whom sent will be furnished by the postmaster to the sender, excepting letters addressed to foreign countries, when a written request for receipt must be endorsed on the address side of the envelope.

Ship Letters are received at Window 28, Park Row side, from 9 a. m. to 5 p. m.

Special Delivery is made at all Post Offices, and the official 10 cent stamp must be affixed in addition to the regular postage. Mail of any description (Merchandise, etc., and Registered Mail) will be received for Special Delivery if properly stamped. Special Delivery Mail will be delivered from 7 a. m. to 11 p. m. at Letter Carrier offices, and from 7 a. m. to 9 p. m. at other offices. No delivery on Sunday.

Supplementary Mail must be prepaid with double the ordinary postage.

RATES OF POSTAGE AND POSTAL REGULATIONS APPLYING TO MAIL MATTER WITHIN THE UNITED STATES.

(For Rates to Canada and Mexico, see "Foreign Countries" 2d page from this.)

Mail matter must be addressed to Post Offices only and not to villages or railroad stations not designated as a Post Office. It frequently happens, however, that the same locality bears two distinct names, for instance: Lake George, N. Y.; the rail road station name is "Caldwell," the Post Office name is "Lake George." Mail intended for this place should be addressed to Lake George. Mail for places other than Post Offices will be forwarded to the nearest Post Office if properly marked. Martha's Vineyard, Mass., is not a Post Office, but if marked "Martha's Vineyard, Mass., via Cottage City P. O.," it will be sent to Cottage City Post Office for delivery.

First Class Mail Matter.

Mailable matter of the first class includes letters, postal cards, and all matter wholly or partly in writing, except as hereinafter provided.

On mailable matter of the first class (except postal cards, but including New York City letters), the rate of postage is TWO CENTS FOR EACH OUNCE OR FRACTION THEREOF; matter produced by type-writer is included in the first class.

POSTAL CARD.—The Postage of one cent each is paid by the stamp impressed on these cards, and no further payment is required. No cards are "postal cards" except such as are issued by the Post Office Department.

In using postal cards, nothing should be written or printed on the side to be used for the address except what is necessary to secure their delivery. It is not permitted to paste, gum, or attach anything to them, except a label bearing the address of destination. They are unmailable as postal cards when these conditions are disregarded. Spoiled postal cards cannot be exchanged.

First class rate is charged on all matter not admitting of examination by postal clerks without injury to envelope or wrapper.

Letters exceeding one ounce in weight, and bearing but a single postage, will be forwarded to destination and the additional postage collected thereat. If entirely unpaid, or if exceeding one ounce and having less than a single postage, they will be returned to the sender if address be known, or the addressee will be notified of the deficiency in postage.

Letters delivered at wrong address may be re-directed from the place where first delivered to the proper address, and when dropped in the Mail Boxes they will be forwarded without extra postage. When a change of address either in residence or office occurs, a notice to that effect should be sent to the postmaster by correspondents.

Second Class Mail Matter.

This class embraces newspapers, magazines, and other periodicals issued at stated intervals not exceeding three months, dated and numbered, having a list of legitimate subscribers, and not designed primarily for advertising purposes, nor for circulation free, or at nominal subscription rates. When sent by the publishers or news agents, the rate of postage is ONE CENT PER POUND, payable in currency; and when sent by other persons, ONE CENT FOR EACH FOUR OUNCES, payable by postage stamps.

Third Class Mail Matter.

This class includes printed books, pamphlets, cards, circulars, handbills, engravings, lithographs, photographs, proof-sheets and manuscript accompanying the same, transient newspapers and periodicals (except those belonging in the second class), and all matter of the same general character. Circulars produced by hektograph or similar process, or by electric pen, belong in the third class.

Upon matter of this class, or on its wrapper, the sender may write his own name preceded by the word "from"; may make marks (other than by written or printed words) to call attention to any word or passage in the text, and may correct any typographical errors. There may also be placed upon the blank leaves or cover of any book or other matter of this class a simple manuscript dedication or inscription not in the nature of personal correspondence. There may also be placed upon the envelope, wrapper, tag or label of matter of this class any printing that is not in its character unmailable as third class matter, provided there be kept sufficient space for a legible superscription and the necessary postage stamps.

THE RATE OF POSTAGE ON MAIL MATTER OF THE THIRD CLASS IS ONE CENT FOR EACH TWO OUNCES OR FRACTION THEREOF. The limit of weight for mail matter of the third class is four pounds, except in the case of single books exceeding that weight.

Matter of this class must be so wrapped or enveloped that the contents may be readily examined without destroying the wrapper.

Fourth Class Mail Matter.

Fourth class matter includes all matter not embraced in the first, second, or third class, which is not in its form or nature liable to destroy, deface, or otherwise damage the contents of the mail bag, or harm the person of any one engaged in the postal service.

All matter of the fourth class is subject to postage at the rate of ONE CENT AN OUNCE OR FRACTION THEREOF.—☞ Except Seeds, Cuttings, Bulbs, Roots, Cions and Plants, the postage on which is ONE CENT FOR EACH TWO OUNCES or fraction thereof.

Upon any package of matter of the fourth class the sender may write or print his name and address, preceded by the word "from"; also any marks, numbers, names, or letters for purpose of description, and may also print upon the same anything that is not unmailable as printed matter, and that is not in the nature of personal correspondence, provided there be left sufficient space for a legible superscription and the necessary postage stamps.

Continued on next page.

POSTAL INFORMATION—Continued.

All packages of matter of the fourth class must be so wrapped or enveloped that their contents may be readily and thoroughly examined, without destroying the wrappers, and may weigh not exceeding four pounds.

Articles which, from their form or nature, might, unless properly secured, destroy, deface or otherwise damage the contents of the mail bag, or harm the person of any one engaged in the postal service, must, to be transmitted in the mails, be placed in a bag, box or removable envelope or wrapping, made of paper, cloth or parchment, and such bag, box, envelope or wrapping must again be placed in a box or tube made of metal or some hard wood, with sliding clasp or screw lid. In case of such articles liable to break, the inside box, bag, envelope or wrapping must be surrounded by sawdust, cotton or other elastic substance.

Poisons, explosives, perishable fruits and vegetables, articles exhaling a bad odor, and ardent, vinous, spirituous or malt liquids, are UNMAILABLE. (For information as to conditions on which other liquids are admitted, see below.)

Liquids, Etc., in the Mails.

The following Regulations of the Post Office Department relate to articles absolutely excluded from the mails, and to the manner in which liquids and other articles liable, unless properly protected, to injure other mail matter, must be packed before they can be admitted to the mails.

Liquids, except as hereinafter provided, poisons, explosive or inflammable articles, live or dead (and not stuffed) animals, insects or reptiles (except as prescribed in the next section), fruit or vegetable matter liable to decomposition, comb honey, guano, or any article exhaling a bad odor must not, under any circumstances, be admitted to the mails ; but liquids, not ardent, vinous, spirituous or malt, and not liable to explosion or spontaneous combustion or ignition by shock or jar (and not inflammable, such as kerosene oil, naphtha, benzine, turpentine and of like character, soft soap, pastes or confections, ointments, salves, and articles of similar consistency, may be admitted to the mails for transmission, with in the United States and territories, when enclosed in packages in conformity with the conditions prescribed in the next section. The provisions of these regulations do not apply to packages or parcels addressed to foreign countries, now prohibited from transmission by the Acts of the Universal Postal Union, or any postal convention or arrangement with any foreign postal administration.

Articles of the fourth class, not absolutely excluded from the mails, but which, from their form or nature, might, unless properly secured, destroy, deface or otherwise damage the contents of the mail bag, or harm the person of any one engaged in the postal service, may be transmitted in the mails when they conform to the following conditions :

1st. When not liquid, or liquefiable, they must be placed in a bag, box or removable envelope or wrapping, made of paper, cloth or parchment.

2d. Such bag, box, envelope or wrapping must again be placed in a box or tube made of metal or some hard wood, with sliding clasp or screw-lid.

3d. In case of articles liable to break, the inside box, bag, envelope or wrapping must be surrounded by sawdust, cotton or other elastic substance.

4th. Admissible liquids and oils (not exceeding 4 ounces liquid measure), pastes, salves or articles easily liquefiable, must conform to the following conditions : When in glass bottles or vials, such bottles or vials must be strong enough to stand the shock of handling in the mails, and must be enclosed in a wooden or papier-mache block or tube not less than three-sixteenths of an inch thick in the thinnest part, strong enough to support the weight of mails piled in bags and resist rough handling; and there must be provided between the bottle and its wooden base, a cushion of cork-crumbs, cotton, felt, asbestos, or some other absorbent, sufficient to protect the glass from shock in handling ; the block or tube to be closed by a tightly fitting screw-lid of wood or metal, with a rubber or other pad so adjusted as to make the block or tube water tight and to prevent the leakage of the contents in case of breaking of the glass. When enclosed in a tin cylinder, metal case or tube, such cylinder, case or tube should have a screw-lid with a rubber or cork cushion inside in order to make the same water-tight, and must be securely fastened in a wooden or papier-mache block (open only at one end) and not less in thickness and strength than above prescribed. Manufacturers or dealers, intending to transmit articles or samples in considerable quantities should submit a sample package, showing their mode of packing, to the postmaster at the mailing office, who will see that the conditions of this section are carefully observed.

5th. In case of sharp pointed instruments, the points must be capped or encased so that they may not by any means be liable to cut through their enclosure ; and where they have blades, such blades must be bound with wire so that they shall remain firmly attached to each other, and within their handles or sockets. Needles must be enclosed in metal or wooden cases so that they cannot by any means prick through or pass out of their enclosure.

6th. Seeds, or other articles not prohibited, which are liable, from their form or nature to loss or damage, unless specially protected, may be put up in sealed envelopes, if such envelopes are made of material sufficiently transparent to show the contents clearly without opening.

7th. Ink powders, pepper, snuff or other powders not explosive, or any pulverized dry substances, not poisonous (excepting flour, may be sent in the mails when enclosed in the manner prescribed herein for liquids, or when enclosed in metal, wooden or papier-mache cases in such secure manner as to render the escape of any particles of dust from the package by ordinary handling impossible, and of such strength as to bear the weight and handling of the mails without breaking ; the method of packing to be subject to the approval of the General Superintendent of Railway Mail Service.

8th. Queen bees and their attendant bees, and dried insects, may be sent in the mails when properly put up so as not to injure the persons of those handling the mails, nor soil the mail bags or their contents.

9th. Hard candies, or confectionery, yeast cakes, soap in hard cakes, when wrapped in strong paper boxes or heavy paper wrappers, adequate to prevent all injury to other mail matter in the same mail bag, are admissible in the domestic mails.

10th. Pistols or revolvers, in detached parts, may be sent in the mails ; but the mailing postmaster will carefully examine such packages and will receive them only when sure they are harmless.

11th. No specific mode of packing is prescribed for samples of flour ; but they should be put up in such a manner as to certainly avoid risk of the package breaking or cracking, or the flour being scattered in the mails ; and if this be not done, the sample should be excluded.

POSTAGE RATES TO FOREIGN COUNTRIES.

To the countries and colonies (EXCEPT CANADA AND MEXICO) which comprise the Universal Postal Union, the rates of postage are as follows :—

Letters, per 15 grams (1-2 ounce), prepayment optional	5 cents.
Postal cards each	2 cents.
Newspapers and other printed matter, per 2 ounces	1 cent.
Commercial papers. Packets not in excess of 10 ounces	5 cents.
Packets in excess of 10 ounces, for each 2 ounces or fraction thereof	1 cent.
Samples of merchandise. Packets not in excess of 4 ounces	2 cents.
Packets in excess of 4 ounces, for each 2 ounces, or fraction thereof	1 cent.
Registration fee on letters or other articles	10 cents.

Ordinary letters will be forwarded, whether any postage is prepaid on them or not, *double* rates being collected on delivery if unpaid or short paid.

All correspondence other than letters must be prepaid at least partially.

The maximum weight of printed matter is fixed at 4 lb. 6 oz. ; and the maximum size is 18 inches in any one direction, *except* that *rolls* of printed matter which could be inclosed in a cube of 45 centimeters may be forwarded by mail even if they exceed 18 inches in length. Commercial papers must be forwarded under band or in an open envelope. The maximum weight of commercial papers is fixed at 4 lb. 6 oz. ; and the maximum size at 18 inches. Samples of merchandise must conform to the following conditions: (1st) they must be placed in bags, boxes, or removable envelopes in such a manner as to admit of easy inspection; (2d) they must not have any salable value, nor bear any manuscript other then the name or profession of the sender, the address of the addressee, a manufacturer's or trade mark, numbers, prices and the weight or size of the quantity to be disposed of, and words which are necessary to precisely indicate the origin and nature of the merchandise; (3d) they must not exceed in weight 8-34 ounces, or the following dimensions; 8 inches in length, 4 inches in breadth, and 2 inches in depth (see exceptions below). Packets of printed matter, commercial papers, and samples must not contain any letter or manuscript note having the character of an actual and personal correspondence, and must be made up in such manner as to admit of being easily examined. "Commercial Papers" include instruments or documents wholly or partly in writing, such as deeds, invoices, insurance papers, etc., not having the character of personal correspondence, and manuscripts of works for publication. It is permitted to inclose in the same packet, samples of merchandise, printed matter, and commercial papers, provided the packet does not exceed 4 lbs. 6 oz. in weight and is prepaid at least 5 cents.

Exceptions. By special agreement between the United States and France, Great Britain, Belgium, Switzerland, and the Argentine Republic, packets of samples of merchandise are admissible in the mails between the two countries, up to 12 ounces in weight, and the following dimensions: 12 inches in length, 8 inches in width, and 4 inches in depth. Packets of books and other printed matter in mails to Germany and Great Britain are limited to 2 feet in length and 1 foot in each other dimension.

POSTAL INFORMATION—Continued.

Samples of liquids, fatty substances, and powders, whether coloring or not (except such as are dangerous, inflammable, explosive, or exhale a bad odor), are admitted to the mails exchanged between the United States and Germany, Argentine Republic, Austria, Hungary, Belgium, Chili, Curacoa, Denmark, Dutch Guiana, Egypt, Spain, France, French Colonies, Greece, Hawaii, Hayti, British India, Italy, Japan, Luxemburg, Norway, Netherlands, Dutch East Indies, Peru, Portugal, Roumania, Salvador, Servia, Siam, Sweden, Switzerland and Turkey, provided said samples conform to the following conditions, viz.: They must be placed in thick glass bottles, hermetically sealed; the bottles must be placed in a wooden box containing sufficient spongy matter to absorb the contents if the bottles should break; the whole to be inclosed in an outside metal case bearing the address; the wooden box and outside case must be closed so that they may be easily opened for examination of the contents; and the whole package must not exceed in weight 8 3-4 ounces, nor in size 8 x 4 x 4 inches, except those addressed to the Argentine Republic, Belgium, France, or Switzerland, which may weigh not to exceed 12 ounces, and measure not to exceed 12 x 8 x 4 inches.

Articles not specifically enumerated in postal conventions or in the United States postal laws and regulations as transmissible in the mails to foreign countries, or which are not homogeneous with those therein enumerated, are not entitled to be sent at the reduced rates of postage fixed for correspondence other than letters, but may be transmitted at letter rates of postage, fully prepaid, provided they are not absolutely excluded from the mails by the provisions of postal conventions, or by the laws and regulations.

Packages Excluded from Mails in Foreign Countries. Packages containing articles of salable value, or dutiable goods, or exceeding the prescribed limit of weight or size, are frequently deposited in Post Offices in Europe and elsewhere addressed to the United States, notwithstanding they are excluded from admission to Postal Union mails at less than letter rates by the terms of the Universal Postal Union convention. When their character is known, or they are not fully prepaid at letter rates, they are not forwarded from the post offices where posted, and this leads to complaint here by the addressees. It should be understood that the non-receipt of such packages is usually to be explained by their detention, for the reasons stated above, at the office of mailing, and inquiry concerning them should be addressed there. When such unmailable packages are deposited in a post office in Germany, they are given in charge of an express company for transportation to the United States outside the mails, and are delivered to New York agents of the express company, and by them to the addressees, with express and customs charges payable thereon.

Postage Rates to Foreign Countries Not in the Postal Union.

The following are the Postage Rates to the principal foreign countries which are not in the Universal Postal Union. All correspondence to these countries must be fully prepaid.

Australia (except New South Wales, Queensland and Victoria): Letters, 5 cents per half ounce; newspapers, 2 cents per copy; other printed matter, 2 cents for each 2 ounces. Samples not admitted.

New South Wales, Victoria, Queensland, New Zealand and Tasmania: Letters, 12 cents per half ounce; newspapers, 2 cents a copy; other printed matter and samples of merchandise, 4 cents for each 1 ounce s.

Cape Colony, Natal, Orange Free State, St. Helena and Ascension: Letters, 15 cents per half ounce; newspapers, 4 cents for each 4 ounces; other printed matter and samples of merchandise, 5 cents for each 2 ounces. **Transvaal:** Letters, 21 cents per half ounce; newspapers, 5 cents per 4 ounces; other printed matter and samples, 7 cents per 2 ounces.

China (in British Mail via Brindisi): Letters, 13 cents per half ounce; newspapers, 5 cents for each 4 ounces; other printed matter and samples of merchandise, 4 cents for each 2 ounces. **To Shanghai,** via San Francisco: Letters, 5 cents per half ounce; newspapers and other printed matter, and samples of merchandise, 1 cent per 2 ounces; postal cards, 2 cents.

Fiji Islands: Letters, 5 cents per half ounce; newspapers, 2 cents per copy; other printed matter, 2 cents for each 2 ounces. Samples not admitted.

Madagascar (except St. Marys and Tamatave): Letters, 13 cents per half ounce; newspapers, 6 cents for each 4 ounces; other printed matter and samples of merchandise, 4 cents for each 2 ounces.

Morocco (except Spanish possessions on West Coast): Letters, 15 cents per half ounce; newspapers and other printed matter, and samples of merchandise, 2 cents for each 2 ounces.

Dutiable Articles Received in Foreign Mails.

Customs officers are assigned to duty at the New York Post Office for the seizure of dutiable articles arriving in the mails from foreign countries. All unsealed packages containing such articles are seized by them, and when letters, sealed packages, or packages the wrappers of which cannot be removed without destroying them, are received in the United States from a foreign country, and there is reason to believe they contain articles liable to customs duties, the customs officers are notified of the receipt of such letters or packages, and their several addresses; and if any letter or package of this character be addressed to a person residing within the delivery of this office, the addressee thereof is notified that such letter or package has been received, and is believed to contain articles liable to customs duties, and that he must appear at the office of the customs examiners in the post office building within a time not exceeding twenty days from the day of said notice, and receive and open said letter or package in their presence.

All books received here from foreign countries addressed for delivery at any point within the United States are, under instructions of the Treasury and Post Office Departments, placed in the custody of customs officers for examination and appraisement, and are forwarded by them by mail, charged with duties (when found to be dutiable) to be collected by the Postmaster at the office of delivery. Books are decided by the Secretary " to include such as are bound in stiff covers, and also such as are usually so bound." Printed matter, in small quantities for personal use, and not for sale as merchandise (embracing magazines, periodicals, etc., in pamphlet form, and newspapers, photographs, lithographs, engravings and music), is free of duty when received by mail. Complaints of supposed overcharges or of any other irregularity in connection with customs duties should be addressed to the Secretary of the Treasury, Washington, D. C., AND NOT TO THE POSTMASTER, who has no authority to review or amend the action of the customs officers. All books, when returned to this office by the customs examiners, are promptly forwarded to their respective destinations. The packages will be found to bear two postmarks—one indicating the date of original receipt here, and the other the date on which they were returned by the customs officers for mailing.

Special Postage Rates to Canada and Mexico.

Letters (in their usual and ordinary form) two cents per ounce or fraction thereof.

Postal Cards.—One cent each.

Books, and other printed matter—one cent for each two ounces.

Newspapers and Periodicals, regularly issued not less frequently than four times a year and admitted to the mails in the United States as " Second Class Matter "—one cent per pound when mailed by the Publisher or a News Agent and one cent for each four ounces when mailed by others than the Publisher or a News Agent.

Merchandise.—(No merchandise other than bona fide trade samples may be sent to Mexico, except by Parcels Post). Bona fide trade samples to Mexico are rated as follows: Packets not in excess of 4 ounces, 2 cents. Packets in excess of 4 ounces, for each 2 ounces, or fraction thereof, 1 cent. To Canada, Merchandise and Samples of Merchandise, and in general all articles not included above—one cent per ounce, or fraction thereof (except Seeds, Cuttings, Bulbs, Roots, Cions and Plants, which are 1 cent per two ounces); but liquids, poisons, explosive or inflammable substances, fatty substances (or those which easily liquefy, live or dead (not dried) animals, insects and reptiles, confections, pastes, fruits and vegetables which quickly decompose, and substances which exhale a bad odor —together with other articles which may destroy or damage the mails, or injure persons handling the mails—are absolutely excluded from transmission in the mails to Canada and Mexico.

[Lottery tickets or circulars, publications which violate the copyright laws of Canada or Mexico, and all obscene or immoral articles, are also absolutely excluded.]

Articles other than Letters in their usual and ordinary form, must be so wrapped or enclosed as to permit their contents to be easily examined by postmasters or customs officers. Sealed packages which, from their form or general appearance evidently are not letters, are not mailable to Canada or Mexico, even though prepaid at letter rates.

No package of any kind (except single volumes of printed books, and except packages of second-class matter to Canada) can be transmitted by mail to Canada or Mexico if exceeding four pounds six ounces in weight.

All articles (except letters in their usual and ordinary form) will be inspected by customs officers, on arrival in Canada or Mexico, and if found to be dutiable under the laws of the country of destination, the proper customs duties will be charged and collected before delivery.

Parcels Post.

Parcels Post Conventions have been concluded between the United States and Jamaica, Barbadoes, Bahamas, British Honduras, U. S. of Colombia, Mexico and Hawaiian Kingdom, under the following provisions which apply in the United States to parcels of merchandise (other than samples) and all other articles not prohibited, which are exchanged between the United States and the countries above named:

POSTAL INFORMATION—Continued.

POSTAGE.

For a parcel not exceeding 1 pound in weight - - - - - - - - - - - - - 12 cents.
For every additional pound or fraction of a pound - - - - - - - - - - - - 12 cents.
 The postage must, in all cases, be prepaid, and by means of postage stamps which must be affixed by the sender; and no parcel will be accepted for transmission which is not sufficiently prepaid.

DIMENSIONS AND WEIGHT.

The dimensions allowed are:
 Greatest length - - - - - - - - - - - - - - - - - - 3 feet 6 inches
 (To Mexico and U. S. of Columbia, 2 feet by 4 feet.)
 Greatest length and girth combined - - - - - - - - - - - - - - 6 feet.
The maximum weight - - - - - - - - - - - - - - - - - 11 pounds.
 Parcels must be securely and substantially packed, so they can be safely transmitted in the open mail of the country of destination, but must be so wrapped or enclosed as to permit their contents to be easily examined by postmasters and customs officers.
 Any articles admitted to the Domestic mails of the United States may be sent in parcels post, except letters or communications of the nature of a correspondence, and except publications which violate the copyright laws of the country of destination; poisons and explosive or inflammable substances; liquids and those which easily liquefy; confections and pastes; live or dead animals, except dead insects and reptiles, when thoroughly dried; fruits and vegetables, and substances which exhale a bad odor; lottery tickets, lottery advertisements or lottery circulars; all obscene or immoral articles; articles which in any way damage or destroy the mails or injure the persons handling them.
 Each parcel must bear the words "Parcels Post," in the upper left hand corner, and the name and address of the sender.
 A parcel must not be posted in the letter-box, but must be taken into the post office, and presented at the counter to the postmaster or person in charge, between the hours of 9 a. m. and 5 p. m.
 The sender will, at the time of mailing the parcel, receive a certificate of mailing from the post office.
 All parcels may be liable to customs duties, and the sender of each parcel will therefore be required to make a customs declaration, giving a general description of the parcel, an accurate statement of the contents and value, date of mailing, and the sender's signature and residence, and the place of address. This declaration must be pasted upon or attached to every parcel, upon a special form which will be furnished on application at the post office.
 On the delivery of a parcel to the addressee, a charge of five cents must be collected on each single parcel of whatever weight; and if the weight exceed one pound, a charge of one cent for each four ounces of weight, or fraction thereof, will be collected.

DUTIABLE ARTICLES.

Dutiable articles received in the United States in parcels from the above countries, under these conventions, will be rated and charged with the proper amount of customs duty at New York, and these duties will be collected on delivery of the parcel.

POST OFFICE STATIONS.

Business is transacted at all stations from 7 a. m. to 8 p. m.; on Sundays, from 9 to 11 a. m.; on holidays, from 7 to 10 a. m. Money orders are issued and paid from 10 a. m. to 6 p. m., excepting Sundays and holidays.

STATIONS.

A 21 East Houston,
B 380 Grand,
C 65 Bank, near Hudson,
D E. 9th street, cor. Stuyvesant,
E 322 Seventh avenue,
F— 401 Third avenue.

G 1661 Broadway,
H 156 E. 51th,
J 1236 street, cor. 8th avenue,
K 231 E. 86th,
L 117 E. 125th,
M 155th street, cor. 10th avenue.

P Produce Exchange Building,
R Cor. 3d avenue and 150th street,
S— Kingsbridge, near N. Y. Central R. R. Station,
T Tremont, 710 Tremont avenue.

ART EXHIBITION AND SALE GALLERIES.

Associated Artists, 115 E. 23d.
Avery's, 368 5th Av.
Bing, Messrs, 220 5th Av.
Blakeslee & Co., 318 5th Av.
Bonaventure, E. F., 332 5th Av.
Fifth Av. Art Galleries, 366 5th Av.
First Japanese Mfg. & Trading Co., 865 Broadway.

Fishel, Adler & Schwartz, 94 Fulton.
Greey, Edward, 20 E. 17th.
Hirsch, Wm. H. & Co., 327 5th Av.
Jacoby, Max, cor. John & William.
Keppel, Fred. & Co., 23 E. 16th.
Klackner, C., 17 E. 17th.
Knoedler, M. & Co. (Goupil Galleries). 170 5th Av.

Kohn's, 166 5th Av.
Montross, N. E., 1380 Broadway.
Ortgies & Co., 366 5th Av.
Pate, Wm. & Co., William, n. Fulton.
Reichard & Co., 226 5th Av.
Schaus, William, 204 5th Av.
Tiffany Glass Co., 335 4th Av.
Wunderlich, H., 868 Broadway.

OTHER ART EXHIBITION GALLERIES AS FOLLOWS:

American Art Galleries, 6 E. 23d St.
Metropolitan Museum of Art, 5th Av. & 83d St. Admission free, except Mondays and Tuesdays, when 25 cents is charged.
Lenox Library, 70th St. & 5th Av. Closed on Mondays.

National Academy of Design, 4th Av. & 23d St.
New York Historical Society, 2d Av. & E. 11th St.
Salmagundi Sketch Club, 123 5th Av.
Yandell Gallery, 5th Av. & 19th St.

PROMINENT STUDIOS AND STUDIO BUILDINGS.

Association (Y. M. C. A.), 52 E. 23d.
Benedick, 80 E. Washington Square.
Buildings Nos. 4 & 6 W. 14th.
Buildings Nos. 11, 30, 32, 42 E. 14th.
Chelsea, 222 W. 23d.

Fourth Av. Studios, 387 Fourth Av.
Holbein (North), 139, 145 W. 55th.
Holbein (South), 146-152 W. 55th.
Knickerbocker, 4 & 6 W. 14th St.
Madison Av. Studios, 80 Madison Av.

Mendelssohn, 104 W. 55th.
Rembrandt, 152 W. 57th.
Sherwood Studios, 58 W. 57th.
Tenth Street Studios, 51 W. 10th.
University, E. Washington Square.

PRINCIPAL ART SCHOOLS.

Art Students' League, 143 E. 23d.
Charcoal Club, 14 W. 14th.
Columbia College, Madison Av. & 50th.
Cooper Union, 4th Av. & 7th.
Gorham Art Students (gentlemen only), 695 Broadway.

Hecker's, Carl, 6 W. 14th.
Kit Kat Club, 23 E. 14th.
Ladies' Art Association, 24 W. 14th.
Metropolitan Museum of Art, 214 E.34th.
National Academy Schools, 4th Av. &23d.

New York Trade Schools, 1st Av.&67th.
New York Turnverein Schools, 64 E.4th.
School of Industrial Art & Technical Design for Women, 120 W. 16th.

MISCELLANEOUS ART SOCIETIES.

American Artists, 152 W. 57th. | American Water-color, 51 W. 10th. | Decorative Art, 28 E. 21st.

CONSERVATORIES OF MUSIC.

Beethoven, 16 W. 23d.
College of Music, 103 E. 70th.

Conservatory of Music, 5 E. 14th.
German, 7 W. 42d.

Grand, 46 W. 23d.
Knickerbocker, 44 W. 14th.

DANCING ACADEMIES.

Cartier's, 80 5th Av.
Dodworth, Allen, 681 5th Av.
Dumar's, 312 W. 35th.
Fernando's, 162 E. 55th.

Knickerbocker Conservatory, 44 W.14th.
Macgregor, Alexander, 108 W. 55th.
Marwig, Carl, 911 7th Av. & 131 E. 58th.
Our Own, 68 W. 23d.

Trenor's, B'way near 33d.
Wallace, Geo. W., 20 W. 59th. & 129th & Park Av.

CHURCHES.

Prominent Churches bearing names that do not imply their denomination, and churches of the various denominations bearing the same name, we have arranged in alphabetical order in the following list, so as to facilitate the finding of any desired church. We have also inserted the names of prominent clergymen with their church address; this will further assist the inquirer; for example, a person wishing to go to the Fifth Avenue Presbyterian Church may know it only as "Dr. Hall's church"; both appellations are here given. *All other churches will be found under the denominations they represent.*

Church Days.

Ember Days: On Wednesday, Friday and Saturday, June 12, 14, 15, September 18, 20, 21, December 18, 20, 21.

Palm Sunday..............April 14	Ascension Day—HolyThursday.May 30	Michaelmas Day..............Sept. 29
Good Friday................April 19	Pentecost—Whit Sunday......June 9	St. Andrew..................Nov. 30
Easter Sunday..............April 21	Trinity Sunday..............June 16	First Sunday in Advent......Dec. 1
Low Sunday.................April 28	Corpus Christi..............June 20	Christmas Day...............Dec. 25
Rogation Sunday............May 26	St. John Baptist............June 24	

All Angels, P. E., West End Ave. & 81st St.
All Saints, P. E., 246 Henry.
All Saints, R. C., Madison Ave. & E. 129th.
All Souls, P. E., 139 W. 48th.
All Souls, Unit., 245 4th Ave.
Annunciation, P. E., 142 W. 14th.
Ascension, Bapt., 527 E. 110th.
Ascension, P. E., 36 5th Ave.
Beloved Disciple, P. E., 89th St., near Madison Ave.
Brick Church, Pres., 5th Ave. & 37th.
Broadway Tabernacle, Cong., Broadway & 34th.
Calvary, Bapt., 57th St., near 6th Ave.
Calvary, Pres., 113th St., cor. Madison Ave.
Calvary, P. E., 273 4th Ave.
Christ, Luth., 404 E. 19th.
Christ, P. E., 5th Ave. & 35th.
Christ, P. E., Riverdale.
Collegiate, D. R., 5th Ave. & 29th & 48th, 14 Lafayette Pl.
Covenant, Pres., Park Ave. & 35th.
Disciples of Christ, 56th St., near 8th Ave.
Divine Paternity, Univ., 5th Ave. & 45th.
Du St. Esprit, P. E., 30 W. 22d.
Epiphany, Bapt., Madison Ave. & 64th.
Epiphany, P. E., 47th St., near Lexington Ave.
Epiphany, R. C., 373 2d Ave.
Fifth Avenue, Bapt., 6 W. 46th.
Fifth Avenue, D. R., 5th Ave., cor. 29th.
Fifth Avenue, Pres., 708 5th Ave.
Fourth Avenue, Pres., 286 4th Ave.
Grace, Bapt., 1529 3d Ave.
Grace, D. R., 845 7th Ave.
Grace, M. E., 131 W. 104th.
Grace, P. E., 800 Broadway.
Grace, P. E., 219 E. 110th.
Grace, P. E., Vyse, near Tremont Ave.
Heavenly Rest, P. E., 551 5th Ave.
Holy Apostles, P. E., 300 9th Ave.
Holy Comforter, P. E., 343 W. Houston.
Holy Communion, P. E., 324 6th Ave.
Holy Faith, P. E., 166th, near Boston Road.
Holy Innocents, P. E., 128th St., near 7th Ave.
Holy Innocents, R. C., 129 W. 37th.
Holy Martyrs, P. E., 39 Forsyth.
Holy Sepulchre, P. E., 74th St., near Park Ave.
Holy Spirit, P. E., Madison Ave. & 66th.
Holy Trinity, P. E., Madison Ave. & 42d.
Holy Trinity, P. E., 5 W. 125th.
Incarnation, P. E., Madison Ave. & 35th.
Intercession, P. E., 158th St., cor. 11th Ave.
Little Church Around the Corner, P. E., 5 E. 29th.
Madison Avenue, Bapt., Madison Ave., cor. 31st.
Madison Avenue, D. R., Madison Ave., cor. 57th.
Madison Avenue, M. E., 659 Madison Ave.
Madison Avenue, Pres., 506 Madison Ave.
Mediator, P. E., 2057 Church St., King's Bridge.
Messiah, Unit., 34th St., cor. Park Ave.
Nativity, P. E., 70 Ave. C.
Nativity, R. C., 48 2d Ave.
Pilgrim, Cong., Madison Ave. & 121st.
Puritans, Pres., 15 W. 130th.
Reconciliation, P. E., 212 E. 31st.
Redeemer, Bapt., 131st St., near 7th Ave.
Redeemer, P. E., Park Ave. & 82d.
Reformation, P. E., 130 Stanton.
St. Ambrose, P. E., 117 Thompson.
St. Andrews, M. E., 71st St., near 9th Ave.
St. Andrews, P. E., 127th St., near Park Ave.
St. Andrews, R. C., Duane St. & City Hall Place.
St. Anns, P. E., 7 W. 18th.
St. Anns, P. E., St. Anns Ave. & E. 140th.
St. Anns, R. C., 112 E. 12th.
St. Augustines Chapel, P. E., 107 E. Houston.
St. Barnabas Chapel, P. E., 306 Mulberry.
St. Bartholomews, P. E., Madison Ave. & 44th.
St. Chrysostoms Chapel, P. E., 201 W. 39th.
St. Georges, P. E., 7 Rutherford Place.
St. Ignatius, P. E., 56 W. 40th.
St. James, Luth., Madison Ave. & 126th.
St. James, M. E., Madison Ave. & 126th.
St. James, P. E., Madison Ave. & 71st.
St. James, P. E., Jerome Ave, cor. St. James.
St. James, R. C., 32 James St.
St. Johns, Luth., 81 Christopher, 217 E. 119th, 801 E. 169th.
St. Johns, M. E., 231 W. 53d.
St. Johns, P. E., 46 Varick.
St. Johns, R. C., 2911 Church St., King's Bridge.
St. John the Baptist, P. E., 259 Lexington Ave.
St. John the Baptist, R. C., 200 W. 30th.

St. John the Evangelist, P. E., 222 W. 11th.
St. John the Evangelist, R. C., 355 E. 55th.
St. Lukes, Luth., 233 W. 42d.
St. Lukes, M. E., 119 W. 41st.
St. Lukes, P. E., 483 Hudson.
St. Marks, Luth., 323 6th St.
St. Marks, M. E., 65 W. 35th.
St. Marks, P. E., 2d Ave. & 10th.
St. Marys, P. E., Alexander Ave. & E. 142d.
St. Marys, P. E., Lawrence St., near 10th Ave.
St. Marys, R. C., 438 Grand.
St. Mary the Virgin, P. E., 228 W. 45th.
St. Matthews, Luth., 354 Broome.
St. Matthews, P. E., 1849 8th Ave.
St. Michaels, P. E., 10th Ave., near 99th.
St. Michaels, R. C., 408 W. 32d.
St. Patricks Cathedral, R. C., 5th Ave. & 50th.
St. Pauls, A. M. E., 158th St., near Elton Ave.
St. Pauls, D. R., 3d Ave. & 116th.
St. Pauls, Luth., 226 6th Ave.
St. Pauls, Luth., 149 W. 123d.
St. Pauls, M. E., 4th Ave. & 22d.
St. Pauls, P. E., Broadway & Vesey.
St. Pauls, P. E., 3d Ave., near 170th.
St. Pauls, R. C., 121 E. 117th.
St. Peters, Luth., 474 Lexington Ave.
St. Peters, P. E., 342 W. 20th.
St. Peters, R. C., 22 Barclay.
St. Phillips, P. E., 161 W. 25th.
St. Stephens, M. E., Kingsbridge Road & Broadway.
St. Stephens, P. E., W. 46th, near 5th Avenue.
St. Stephens, R. C., 149 E. 28th.
St. Thomas, P. E., 5th Ave. & 53d.
St. Timothy's, P. E., 332 W. 57th.
Strangers, Mercer St., near 8th Ave.
Tabernacle, Bapt., 166 2d Ave.
Transfiguration, P. E., 5 E. 29th.
Transfiguration, R. C., 25 Mott.
Trinity, Bapt., 141 E. 55th.
Trinity, Cong., Washington Ave. & E. 176th.
Trinity, Luth., 139 Ave. B.
Trinity, M. E., 323 E. 118th.
Trinity, P. E., Broadway & Wall.
Trinity, P. E., 3d Ave., near 163d.
Trinity Chapel, P. E., 15 W. 25th.
University Place, Pres., University Pl. & 10th.
Westminster, Pres., 151 W. 22d.
Zion, A. M. E., 351 Bleecker.
Zion, Bapt., 128 W. 24th.
Zion, Pres., 135 E. 40th.
Zion, P. E., Madison Ave. & 38th.

Prominent Clergymen and their Church address.

Armitage, Dr., 6 W. 46th.
Brooks, Arthur, Madison Ave. & 35th.
Brown, J. W., 5th Ave. & 53d.
Brown, P. A. H., 16 Varick.
Collyer, Robert, 34th St. & Park Ave.
Corrigan, Michael A., Archbishop, 5th Ave. & 50th.
Crosby, Howard, 4th Ave. & 22d.
Deems, Dr. Chas. F., Mercer St., near 8th Ave.
Deems, Edward M., 151 W. 22d.
Dix, Morgan, Broadway & Wall.
Donald, E. Winchester, 36 5th Ave.
Eaton, Chas. H., 5th Ave. & 45th.
Gallaudet, Thomas, 7 W. 18th.
Guilbert, Edmund, Madison Ave. & 66th.
Hall, Dr. John, 708 5th Ave.
Houghton, Dr. Geo. H., 5 E. 29th.
Huntington, Dr. Wm. R., 800 Broadway.
Morgan, D. Parker, 551 5th Ave.
Mulcahey, James, Broadway & Vesey.
Newton, R. Heber, 48th, near 6th Ave.
Parkhurst, Chas. H., 9 Madison Ave.
Potter, Henry C., Bishop, residence, 160 W. 59th.
Rainsford, Wm. S., 7 Rutherford Place.
Ritchie, Arthur, 56 W. 40th.
Rylance, J. H., 2d Ave. & 10th.
Satterlee, Henry Y., 273 4th Ave.
Shipman, J. S., 5th Ave. & 35th.
Taylor, Wm. M., Broadway & 34th.
Thompson, John Rhey, 4th St., near 6th Ave.
Tiffany, C. C., Madison Ave. & 38th St.
Tiffany, O. H., Madison Ave. & 126th St.
Tyler, B. B., 56th St., near 9th Ave.
Van DeWater, Geo. R., Park Ave. & 127th.
Van Dyke, Henry, 5th Ave. & 37th.
Warren, E. Walpole, Madison Ave. & 42d St.

Continued on next page.

AFRICAN METHODIST EPISCOPAL.

Bethel, 214 Sullivan.
First African Union, 124 W. 25th.
Little Zion, 236 E. 117th.
St. Paul's, E. 158th St. near Elton Av.
Union American, 230 E. 85th.
Zion, 351 Bleecker.

BAPTIST.

Abyssinian, 166 Waverly Pl.
Amity, 310 W. 54th.
Ascension, 527 E. 160th.
Berean, 33 Bedford.
Calvary, 57th, near 6th Av.
Carmel, 121st, near 2d Av.
Central, 220 W. 42d.
Central Park, 285 E. 83d.
Colgate Chapel, 342 E. 20th.
East, 323 Madison Av.
Ebenezer, 154 W. 36th.
Emmanuel, 17 Suffolk.
Epiphany, Madison Av. cor. 64th.
Fifth Avenue, 6 W. 46th.
First, E. 39th St. cor. Park Av.
First German, 336 E. 14th.
First German, 102 E. 112th.
First Swedish, 332 E. 20th.
Free, 285 W. 25th.
Grace, 1529 3d Av.
Laight Street, Laight cor. Varick.
Lexington Av., E.114 c. Lexington Av.
Macdougal Street, 22 Macdougal.
Madison Avenue, cor. E. 31st.
Mariners', 12 Oliver.
Mt. Morris, 5th Av. near W. 126th.
Mt. Olivet, 161 W. 53d.
North, 231 W. 11th.
North N. Y., Alexander Av.cor.E.141st.
People's, 365 W. 18th.
Redeemer, 131st, near 7th Av.
Riverside, 93d cor. 10th Av.
Second German, 151 W. 45th.
Sixth Street, 614 6th St.
Sixteenth, 257 W. 16th.
Tabernacle, 166 2d Av.
3d German, Washington Av. n. E.160th.
Thirty-third St., 327 W. 33d.
Tremont, 815 Washington Av.
Twenty-third St., 129 E. 23d.
Trinity, 141 E. 55th.
Zion, 158 W. 21th.

CONGREGATIONAL.

Bethany, 10th Av. near 35th.
Broadway Tabernacle, 5x2 6th Av.
Central, 309 W. 57th.
First, 1053 Washington Av.
Pilgrim, Madison Av. cor. 121st.
Smyrna, Welsh, 296 E. 11th.
Trinity, Washington Av. cor. E. 156th.

DUTCH REFORMED.

Bloomingdale, Boulevard cor. W. 68th.
Collegiate, 5th Av. cor. W. 48th.
Collegiate, 14 Lafayette Place.
Collegiate Missions, 113 Fulton, DeWitt Chapel, 160 W. 29th.
Collegiate of Harlem, First Church, 191 E. 121st.
Collegiate of Harlem, Second Church, 267 Lenox Av.
Fifth Avenue, 454 W. 29th.
Fordham, King's Bridge Road near Aqueduct Av.
Fourth, German, 214 W. 40th.
German Ev. Mission, 141 E. Houston.
German R-f. Prot., 131 Norfolk.
Grace, 415 7th Av.
Hamilton Grange, W. 145th & Convent Av.
High Bridge, Ogden Av. near Birch.
Holland, 279 W. 44th.
Madison Av. Reformed, cor. 57th.
Manhattan, 71 Av. B.
Melrose, Elton Av. cor. E. 156th.
Prospect Hill, 151 E. 86th.
St. Paul's, 3d Av. cor. 116th.
South, 5th Av.cor.21st. Manor Chapel, 318 W. 26th.
Thirty-fourth St., 307 W. 34th.
Union, 25 6th Av.
West Farms, Boston Road cor. Clover.

EVANGELICAL.

Dingeldein Memorial, Ger., 429 E. 77th.
1st Church of the Evangelical Assn., 214 W. 35th.
2d Church of the Evangelical Assn., 342 W. 53d.

FRIENDS.

East Fifteenth St., cor. Rutherford Pl.
Twentieth Street, 144 E. 20th.

JEWISH.

Adareth El, 135 E. 29th.
Adas Israel, Wilkowishker, 49 E.B'way.
Adath Israel, 350 E. 57th.
Ahawath Chesed, 652 Lexington Av.
Ansche Sfard, 99 Attorney.
Beth Hamedrash Hagodal, 54 Norfolk.
Beth Hamedrash Shualtel Torah, 24 Chrystie.
Beth Israel Emmanuel, 214 E. 108th.
Beth Israel Bikor Cholem, E. 72d cor. Lexington Av.
Beth-El, 817 Lexington Av.
Bnai Ames Mariampoler, 44 E. B'way.
Bnai Israel, 289 E. 4th.
Bnai Jeshurun, Madison Av. cor. 65th.
Bnai Sholom, 630 5th St.
Bnai Sholom, 2061 Lexington Av.
Chefra Kadischa Talmud Thora,022 5th.
Chebra Kadusha Bnay Rappaport, 66 Essex.
Darech Amuno, 7 7th Av.
Gates of Hope, 113 E. 88th.
Kahal Adath Jeshurun, 14 Eldridge.
Meshkan Israel Anshei Suvalk, 56 Chrystie.
Montefiore Home,Boulevard &W.138th.
Mount Sinai, 165 E. 112th.
Ohab Zedek, 146 Norfolk.
Olavay Sholom, 31 E. Broadway.
Orach Chaim, 804 First Av.
Rodolph Sholom, 8 Clinton.
Shauer Hashamoim, 91 Rivington.
Shaarai Beracho, 240 E. 15th.
Shaarai Tephilla, 127 W. 44th.
Shaarai Zedeck, 38 Henry.
Shearith Israel, 98 Av. C.
Shearith Israel, 5 W. 19th.
Sons of Israel, 15 Pike.
Talmud Torah, 38 Hester.
Temple Emanu-El, 521 5th Av.
Temple Israel of Harlem,5th Av.c.125th.
Thifereth Israel Meropln, 10 Norfolk.
Zichron Osher, 80th St. & 10th Av.

LUTHERAN.

Christ, 404 E. 19th.
Emigrant House Chapel, 26 State.
Evangelical of the Epiphany,72 E.128th.
Evangelical of Holy Trinity, 47 W.21st.
Gustavus Adolphus, 151 E. 22d.
Immanuel, 215 E. 83d.
Immanuel, 88th St. cor. Lexington Av.
St. James, 216 E. 15th.
St. John's, 81 Christopher.
St. John's, 217 E. 119th.
St. John's, 801 E. 129th.
St. Luke's, 233 W. 42d.
St. Mark's, 323 6th.
St. Matthew's, 354 Broome.
St. Matthew's, German, Cortlandt Av. near E. 154th.
St. Paul's, 226 6th Av.
St. Paul's, 149 W. 123d.
St. Paulus German Evangel.,928 E.150th.
St. Peter's, 471 Lexington Av.
Trinity, 189 Av. B.

METHODIST EPISCOPAL.

Allen Street, 126 Allen.
Asbury, 82 Washington Sq. E.
Bedford Street, 28 Morton.
Beekman Hill, 319 E. 50th.
Bethany Chapel, 1230, near 1st Av.
Centenary, Washington Av. c. E.166th.
Central, 58 7th Av.
Cornell Memorial, E. 78th, near 2d Av.
Duane, 291 Hudson.
Eighteenth St., 307 W. 18th.
Eleventh St. Chapel, 545 E. 11th.
Fifty-sixth St., 440 W. 56th.
First German, 253 2d St.
Fordham, 2079 Marion Av.
Forsyth St., 10 Forsyth.
Forty-fourth St., 253 W. 44th.
Franklin St., 176 Franklin.
German, Elton Av. cor. E. 158th.
German, 316 W. 19th.
German Emmanuel, 170 E. 114th.
German Mission House, 27 State.
Grace, 131 W. 40th.
Redding, 337 E. 17th.
Jane Street, 13 Jane.
John Street, 44 John.
Ladies' Five Points Home Mis., 63 Park.
Madison Avenue, 659 Madison Av.
Mott Avenue, Mott Av. cor. E. 150th.
New York, Willis Av. c. E.141st.
Park Avenue, 1533 Park Av.
Perry St., 122 Perry.
Rose Hill, 221 E. 27th.

Continued on next page.

St. Andrew's, 71st, near 9th Av.
St. James, Madison Av. cor. 126th.
St. John's, 231 W. 53d.
St. Luke's, 110 W. 41st.
St. Mark's, 65 W. 45th.
St. Paul's, 4th Av. cor. 22d St.
St. Paul's, German, 208 E. 55th.
St. Stephen's, King's Bridge Road cor. Broadway.
Saviour, 109th, near Madison Av.
Second St., 276 2d.
Seventh St., 24 7th.
Sixty-first St., 229 E. 61st.
Swedish, Lexington Av. cor. E. 52d.
Thirtieth Street, 331 W. 30th.
Thirty-fifth St., 160 W. 35th.
Thirty-seventh St., 225 E. 37th.
Tremont, Washington Av. cor. E.178th.
Trinity, 328 E. 118th.
Twenty-fourth St., 359 W. 24th.
Washington Heights, 10th Av. cor. 153d.
Washington Square, 137 W. 4th.
Wesley Chapel, 87 Attorney.
West Farms, 1251 Tremont Av.
West Harlem, 7th Av. cor. 129th.
Willett Street, 9 Willett.
Woodlawn, Woodlawn.

PRESBYTERIAN.

Adams Memorial, 211 E. 30th.
Alexander Chapel, 7 King.
Bethany, E. 187th, near Willis Av.
Brick, 410 5th Av.
Calvary, 113th, cor. Madison Av.
Canal Street, 17 Greene.
Central, 220 W. 57th.
Chinese Mission, 15 University Place.
Covenant, 28 Park Av. Memorial Chapel, 310 E. 42d.
East Harlem, 236 E. 116th.
Faith, 423 W. 46th.
Fifth Avenue, 708 5th Av. Chapel, 131 7th Av. Romeyn Chapel, 430 E. 14th.
First, 51 5th Av.
First, Washington Av. near E. 174th.
First of Morrisania, Washington Av. near E. 167th.
First Union, 147 E. 86th.
Fourth, 121 W. 34th. West Side Chapel, 529 W. 39d.
Fourth Av., 286 4th Av. Hope Chapel, 314 E. 4th. Grace Chapel, 310 E.42d.
Fourteenth Street, 225 2d Av.
French Evangelical, 126 W. 16th.
German, 292 Madison St.
Harlem, 171 E. 125th.
Knox, 252 E. 73d.
Madison Avenue, 506 Madison Av.
Madison Square, 9 Madison Av.
Mount Washington, Inwood.
New York, 7th Av. cor. 128th.
North, 371 Ninth Av.
Park, 10th Av. cor. 86th.
Phillips, Madison Av. cor. 73d.
Puritans', 15 W. 130th.
Riverdale, Riverdale.
Scotch, 53 W. 14th. Salem Mission, 185 Spring.
Sea & Land, 19 Market.
Second German, 435 E. Houston.
Seventh, 138 Broome.
Shiloh, 107 W. 26th.
Spring Street, 216 Spring.
Thirteenth Street, 219 W. 13th.
Twenty-third St., 219 W. 23d.
University Place, cor.10th. Missions,226 Thompson; Bethlehem, 189 Wooster; Emmanuel Chapel, 735 6th.
Washington Heights, 10th Av. cor.155th.
Welsh, 225 E. 13th.
West, 31 W. 42d.
West Farms, 1243 Samuel.
W. Fifty-first St., 359 W. 51st.
Westminster, 151 W. 22d.
Zion, German, 185 E. 40th.

REFORMED PRESBY-TERIAN.

First, 30 W. 119th.
First, 123 W. 12th.
Fourth, 365 W. 48th.
Second, 227 W. 39th.
Third, 228 W. 23d.

UNITED PRESBYTERIAN.

Harlem, 202 E. 119th.
Seventh Avenue, 29 7th Av.
Third, 41 Charles.
Forty-fourth St., 423 W. 44th.
W. Twenty-fifth St., 303 W. 23d.

PROTESTANT EPISCOPAL

Rt. Rev. Henry C. Potter, Bishop, h. 160 W. 59th.
All Angels', W. 81st, cor. West End Av.
All Saints, 286 Henry.
All Souls' Church, 139 W. 48th.
Anglo-American Free Church of St. George the Martyr, 222 W. 11th.
Annunciation, 112 W. 14th.
Ascension, 36 5th Av.
Beloved Disciple, 89th, n. Madison Av.
Calvary, 273 4th Av. Chapel, 220 E. 23d.
Galilee Mission, 310 E. 23d.
Chapel of the Comforter, 814 Greenwich.
Christ, 369 5th Av.
Christ, Riverdale.
Du St. Esprit, 30 W. 22d.
Epiphany, 47th, near Lexington Av.
Grace, 800 Broadway.
Grace, 212 E. 116th.
Grace, West Farms, Vyse n. Tremont Av.
Grace Chapel, 132 E. 14th.
Heavenly Rest, 551 5th Av.
Holy Apostles, 300 9th Av.
Holy Comforter, 349 W. Houston.
Holy Communion, 324 6th Av.
Holy Cross Mission, 43 Av. C.
Holy Faith, E. 106th. near Boston Road.
Holy Innocents', 136th, near 7th Av.
Holy Martyrs, 49 Forsyth.
Holy Sepulchre, E. 74th, near Park Av.
Holy Spirit, 66th, near Madison Av.
Holy Trinity, 5 W. 125th. Chapel, 307 E. 118th.
Holy Trinity, 319 Madison Av. Chapel, 46 E. 43d.
Holy Trinity, 1221 8'. & Lenox Av.
Incarnation, 205 Madison Av.
Intercession, 158th, cor. Eleventh Av.
Mediator, 2937 Church.
Memorial Chapel of the Ascension, 330 W. 43d.
Nativity, 70 Av. C.
Our Saviour, foot Pike. Seamen's Mission, 34 Pike.
Reconciliation, 242 E. 31st.
Redeemer, Park Av. cor. E. 82d.
Reformation, 150 Stanton.
St. Ambrose, 117 Thompson.
St. Andrew's, E. 127th near Park Av.
St. Ann's, St. Ann's Av. near E. 110th.
St. Ann's, 7 W. 18th.
St. Augustine's Chapel, 107 E. Houston.
St. Barnabas' Chapel, 306 Mulberry.
St. Bartholomew's, 318 Madison Av.
St. Chrysostom's Chapel, 201 W. 39th.
St. Clement's, 108 W. 3d. Mission, 173 Macdougal.
St. Edward the Martyr, 109th. n.5th Av.
St. George's, 7 Rutherford Place.
St. Ignatius, 56 W. 40th.
St. James', 71st, cor. Madison Av.
St. James', Fordham, Jerome Av. cor. St. James.
St. John the Baptist, 253 Lexington Av.
St. John the Evangelist, 222 W. 11th.
St. John's, 46 Varick.
St. Luke's, 483 Hudson.
St. Mark's, 2d Av. & 10th St. Memorial Chapel, 284 E. 10th.
St. Mary the Virgin, 228 W. 45th.
St. Mary's, Alexander Av. cor. E. 142d.
St. Mary's, Lawrence, near 10th Ave.
St. Matthew's, 18-9 9th Av.
St. Michael's, 10th Av. near 99th.
St. Paul's, Broadway cor. Vesey.
St. Paul's, 3d Av. near 170th.
St. Peter's, 312 W. 20th.
St. Philip's, 161 W. 25th.
St. Sauveur's, 5734 W. 16th.
St. Thomas's, 5th Av. cor. 53d. Chapel, 230 E. 60th.
St. Timothy's, 332 W. 57th.
Santiago, 273 4th Av.
San Salvatore, 309 Mulberry.
Transfiguration, 5 E. 29th. Chapel, W. 69th near Boulevard.
Trinity, Broadway & Wall.
Trinity, 3d Av. near 169th.
Trinity Chapel, 15 W. 25th.
Zion, 245 Madison Av. Zion Chapel, 418 W. 41st.

REFORMED EPISCOPAL

First, Madison Av. cor. 55th.

ROMAN CATHOLIC

All Saints, Madison Av. cor. 129th.
Annunciation, B. V. M., B'way c. 131st.
Assumption, 427 W. 49th.
Blessed Sacrament, W. 71st n. Boulevard.
Epiphany, 373 2d Av.
Guardian Angel, 519 W. 23d.
Holy Cross, 335 W. 42d.
Holy Rosary, 142 E 119th.
Holy Innocents, 126 W. 37th.
Holy Name of Jesus, 10th Av. cor. 97th.
Immaculate Conception, 505 E. 14th.
Immaculate Conception, German, 151st near 3d Av.
Mary Star of the Sea, 7 State.
Mission of the Infant Saviour, 285 E. 11th.
Most Holy Redeemer, 165 3d Av.
Nativity, 48 2d Av.
Our Lady of Good Counsel, 236 E. 90th.
Our Lady of Mercy, Fordham.
Our Lady of Mount Carmel, 110 E. 115th.
Our Lady of Perpetual Succor, 321 E. 61st.
Our Lady of Sorrows, 105 Pitt.
Our Lady of the Angels, 228 E. 113th.
Sacred Heart, Anderson Av. near Birch.
Sacred Heart of Jesus, 117 W. 51st.
St. Agnes, 143 E. 43d.
St. Alphonsus, 240 S. 5th Av.
St. Andrew's, Duane cor. City Hall Pl.
St. Ann's, 112 E. 12th.
St. Anthony, 153 Sullivan.
St. Augustine's, 867 Jefferson.
St. Benedict the Moor, 210 Bleecker.
St. Bernard's, 332 W. 14th.
St. Boniface, 882 2d Av.
St. Brigid's, 123 Av. B.
St. Catharine of Genoa, W. 153d St. near Boulevard.
St. Cecilia, E. 106th near Lexington Av.
St. Charles Borromeo, 2660 8th Av.
St. Columbus, 339 W. 25th.
St. Elizabeth, King's Bridge Rd. n. 187th.
St. Francis of Assisi, 139 W. 31st.
St. Francis Xavier, 36 W. 16th.
St. Gabriel's, 310 E. 37th.
St. James, 32 James.
St. Jean Baptiste, 159 E. 76th.
St. Jerome, Alexander Av. cor. E. 137th.
St. John Baptist, 209 W. 30th.
St. John Evangelist, 358 E. 55th.
St. John's, 2911 Church.
St. Joseph's, 59 6th Av.; 1850 Washington Av., 408 E. 87th, 125th, c. 9th Av.
St. Lawrence, Park Av. cor. E. 84th.
St. Leo's, 11 E. 28th.
St. Mary Magdalen's, 527 E. 17th.
St. Mary's, 438 Grand.
St. Michael's, 408 W. 32d.
St. Monica's, 403 E. 79th.
St. Nicholas', 125 2d St.
St. Patrick's, Mott cor. Prince.
St. Patrick's Cathedral, 5th Av. c. 50th.
St. Paul's, 121 E. 117th.
St. Peter's, 22 Barclay.
St. Raphael's, 509 W. 40th.
St. Rose of Lima, 42 Cannon.
St. Stanislaus', 13 Stanton.
St. Stephen's, 149 E. 28th.
St. Teresa, Rutgers cor. Henry.
St. Thomas Aquinas's, 1271 Tremont Av.
St. Veronica's, 636 Washington.
St. Vincent de Paul, 127 W. 23d.
St. Vincent Ferrer, 871 Lexington Av.
Transfiguration, 25 Mott.

UNITARIAN

All Souls, 245 4th Av.
Messiah, 6 E. 84th.
Unity Congregational Soc. 331 Lenox Av.

UNIVERSALIST

Second, 121 E. 127th.
Third, 133 W. 11th.
Fourth, 538 5th Av.

MISCELLANEOUS CHURCHES

Annex Hall Mission, 11 Fourth Av.
Battery Park Mission, 27 State.
Bowery Mission, 36 Bowery.
Broome Street Tabernacle, 395 Broome.
Camp Chapel, 126 Elizabeth.
Catholic Apostolic, 417 W. 57th.
Chinese Sunday School Un., 52 E. 23d.
Christian Israelites Sanctuary, 308 First.
Church Mission to Deaf Mutes, 220 E. 13th.
City Temple, 325 E. 86th.
Colored Mission, 135 W. 30th.
Cremorne Mission, 104 W. 32d.
DeWitt Memorial, 280 Rivington.
East s'de Chapel, 101 E. 15th.
German Evangelical Refmd., 97 Suffolk.
Gospel Chapel, 305 W. 30th.
Gospel Tabernacle, Madison Av. c. 45th.
Hebrew-Christian Church, 17 St. Marks pl
Italian Mission, 153 Worth.
Manhattan Chapel, 422 E. 26th.
Mariners, 46 Catharine.
Martha Memorial Refmd., German, 419 W. 52d.
Medical Mission, 81 Roosevelt.
Memorial Chapel, 133 Av. A.
New Jerusalem, Swedenbgn., 114 E. 35th.
N. Y. Christian Mission, 258 W. 18th.
Olivet, 63 Second.
People's, 97 Varick.
Reformed Catholic, 79 W. 23d.
St. Paul Evangelical, 250 W. 34th.
Seaman's Mission, 7 Coenties slip.
Second Church of Disciples of Christ, E. 169th near Franklin Av.
Sixth Av. Gospel Mission, 160 6th Av.
Strachan Margaret, Chapel, 103 W. 27th.
True Dutch Reformed, 58 Perry.
Union Tabernacle, 149 W. 85th.
United Brethren, English Moravian, 151 Lexington Av.
United Brethren, Ger. Moravian, 636 6th.

CEMETERIES

Calvary, office 266 Mulberry; located in Newtown, L.I., 1 mile from 10th St. Ferry, Greenpoint. Reached also from Long Island City by horse cars and by Long Island R. R. From Williamsburg by Grand St. cars.
Cypress Hills, office 124 Bowery; located on the Jamaica Plank and Myrtle Av. roads, 5 miles from ferry depots, Williamsburg; cars direct to cemetery. Also reached by Long Island R. R.
Evergreens, office at cemetery; located on Broadway, Brooklyn, E. D., 4 miles from ferry depots, Williamsburg; cars direct to cemetery. Also reached by Long Island R. R.
Greenwood, office 1 Broadway; located in Brooklyn, 4 miles from Hamilton Av. Ferry, and 4 miles from Fulton Ferry or Bridge depots; cars direct to cemetery. Also reached by the Franklin Av. line from Williamsburg ferry depots, and by horse cars from Wall st. and South Ferry depots. The northern or main entrance is on 5th Av. and 25th St.; the western entrance is on 4th Av., near 34th St.; the southern entrance is on 37th St., below 8th Av.; the eastern or Franklin Av. entrance is on Fort Hamilton Av. west of Gravesend Av.; the northeastern entrance is on 20th St., between 8 h and 9th Avs., and on 20th St., between 9th and 10th Avs.
Holy Cross, office in St. James Cathedral, Jay St., Brooklyn; located in Flatbush, 5 miles from Fulton ferry and Bridge depots; cars direct to cemetery. Also reached by No-trand Av. line from Williamsburg ferry depots.
Lutheran, office 263 Broadway; located on Jamaica Turnpike road, near Middle Village, L.I. 4 miles from ferry depots, Williamsburg; cars direct to cemetery.
Machpelah, office 215 W. 17th; located in New Durham, N. J., 2 miles from ferry depots, Weehawken, and 4 miles from Hoboken ferry depots. Reached by Nor. R. of N. J., and by N. Y., Susq. & Western R. R.
Maple Grove, office 1274 Broadway; located in Maple Grove, L.I., 6 miles from ferry depots in Hunter's Point. Reached by Long Island R. R.
Mount Olivet, office 27 E. 14th; located in Maspeth, L.I., 3½ miles from ferry depots, Williamsb'g; cars direct to cemetery.
Potter's Field, office 66 3d Av.; located on Hart's Island. Reached by boat from foot E. 26th St.
Rockland, office 69 Liberty; located in Sparkill, Rockland Co., N. Y. Reached by Nor. R. R. of N. J.
Washington, office 291 Broadway; located near Parkville, L. I. Reached by Prospect Park & Coney Island R. R., cor. 9th Av. and 36th St., Brooklyn.
Woodlawn, office 48 E. 23d; located in the 24th Ward, 12 miles from Grand Central depot. Reached by N. Y. & Harlem R. R. to Woodlawn station. Entrance at Central Av., near R. R. station; also at Central and Jerome Avs.

COLLEGES AND SEMINARIES.

Academy of the Holy Cross, 343 W. 49d.
Academy of the Sacred Heart, 49 W. 17th.
College for the Training of Teachers, 9 University pl.
College of Archaeology and Æsthetics, 120 E. 105th.
College of City of New York, Lexington ave. and 23d.
Columbia College, 11 E. 49th.
De La Salle Institute, 106 W. 59th.
Free Night School of Science and Art, Cooper Union.
General Theological Seminary of Prot. Epis. Church, 20th st. and 9th av.
Hebrew Technical Institute, 36 Stuyvesant.
La Salle Academy, 1st Second.
Manhattan College, Boulevard and W. 131st.
Missionary Training College, 245 W. 55th.

Normal College, Park av. and E. 68th.
Rutgers Female College, 56 W. 55th.
School of Art for Women, Cooper Union.
School for Phonography and Typewriting for Women, Cooper Union.
Science and Art, Free Night School, Cooper Union.
St. Francis Xavier, 30 W. 15th.
St. Johns College, Fordham.
St. Louis R. C. College, 15 W. 43d.
University of City of New York, Washington Square.
Union Theological Seminary, 1200 Park av.
Ursuline Academy, Westchester av. n. Eagle.
Workingmen's School, 109 W. 54th.

MEDICAL COLLEGES, ETC.

Academy of Medicine, 12 W. 31st.
American Veterinary, 141 W. 54th.
Bellevue, foot E. 26th.
Carnegie Laboratory of Bellevue Hospital, 338 E. 26th.
Columbia College of Midwifery, 154 W. 35th.
Columbian Institute for Preservation of Health and Cure of Chronic Diseases, 142 E. 34th.
Dentistry, 245 E. 23d.
Eclectic, 1 Livingston place.
First District Dental Soc. 1260 Broadway.
Homœopathic, 201 E. 23d.
Homœopathic Med. Soc. of Co. of N. Y., 201 E. 23d.
International Med. Missionary Training Institution, 118 E. 45th; Ladies' Branch, 110 Lexington av.

Magnolias, 30 E. 14th.
Medical College and Hospital for Women, 213 W. 54th.
Medical Society of Co. of New York, 12 W. 31st.
Midwifery, 247 W. 49th.
Odontological Society, 12 W. 31st.
Pathological Society, 435 W. 59th.
Pharmacy, 209 E. 23d.
Physicians and Surgeons, 437 W. 59th.
Post Graduate School and Hospital, 226 E. 20th.
University, 410 E. 26th.
United States, 12th st. near University pl.
Veterinary Surgeons, 392 E. 27th.
Women's, N. Y. Infirmary, 128 Second av.
Women's, Free, 51 St. Marks pl.

BOARD OF EDUCATION—1889.

Office, 146 Grand.

J. Edward Simmons, President. Arthur McMullin, Clerk.

Member.	Residence.	Office Address.	Term Expires.	Member.	Residence.	Office Address.	Term Expires.
Mrs. Mary N. Agnew	266 Madison Av		1890	Mrs. Sarah H. Powell	324 W. 58th St		1892
William A. Cole	62 W. 48th St		1892	Samuel M. Purdy	West Farms	West Farms	1890
Fred. W. Devoe	Fordham	101 Fulton St	1891	Adolph L. Sanger	50 E. 63d St	115 Broadway	1892
Miss Grace H. Dodge	262 Madison Av		1890	Henry Schmitt	20 Vandam St	229 Broadway	1890
Robert M. Gallaway	68 E. 55th st	71 Broadway	1891	DeWitt J. Seligman	328 W. 58th St	30 Union Square	1891
R. Guggenheimer	16 E. 81st St	55th St., c. 3d Av	1890	J. Edward Simmons	28 W. 52d St		1891
Charles L. Holt	117 W. 130th St	188 Front St	1891	Henry L. Sprague	330 W. 23d St	140 Broadway	1890
John L. N. Hunt	207 W. 68th St	137 Broadway	1892	Ferdinand Traud	137 Franklin Av		1891
Frederick Kuhne	785 Madison Av	5 So. William St	1892	Jacob D. Vermilye	4 W. 51st St	42 Wall St	1891
Miles M. O'Brien	135 E. 71st St	224 Church st	1892	H. Walter Webb	15 W. 47th St	Vanderbilt Ave	1890
Edward H. Peaslee	20 Madison Av	20 Madison Av	1892				

SCHOOLS.

College of the City of New York, 17 Lexington Av. Normal College, Park Av., cor. E. 68th St. Nautical School, Ship "St. Mary's," foot E. 31st

Public Schools.

No. 1. 32 Vandewater.
" 2. 187 Cherry.
" 3. 490 Hudson.
" 4. 293 Rivington.
" 5. 222 Mott.
" 6. Randall's Island.
" 7. 60 Chrystie.
" 8. 29 King.
" 9. 267 W. 82d.
" 10. 180 Wooster.
" 11. 314 W. 17th.
" 12. 374 Madison.
" 13. 239 E. Houston.
" 14. 220 E. 27th.
" 15. 729 5th.
" 16. 212 W. 13th.
" 17. 333 W. 47th.
" 18. 121 E. 51st.
" 19. 314 E. 14th.
" 20. 100 Chrystie.
" 21. 55 Marion.
" 22. 110 Sheriff.
" 23. 36 City Hall Pl.
" 24. 68 Elm.
" 25. 328 5th.
" 26. 124 W. 30th.
" 27. 208 E. 43d.
" 28. 255 W. 40th.
" 29. 97 Greenwich.
" 30. 143 Baxter.
" 31. 198 Monroe.
" 32. 357 W. 35th.
" 33. 418 W. 28th.
" 34. 108 Broome.
" 35. 60 W. 13th.
" 36. 710 E. 9th.
" 37. 113 E. 87th.
" 38. 8 Clark.
" 39. 235 E. 125th.
" 40. 227 E. 23d.
" 41. 40 Greenwich Av.
" 42. 30 Allen.
" 43. 10th Av. cor. 129th.
" 44. 12 N. Moore.
" 45. 227 W. 24th.
" 46. 150th e. St. Nicholas Av.
" 47. 30 E. 12th.
" 48. 122 W. 28th.
" 49. 239 E. 37th.
" 50. 213 E. 20th.
" 51. 519 W. 44th.
" 52. W. 206th cor. Kings Bridge Road.
" 53. 209 E. 79th.
" 54. 10th Av. cor. 104th.
" 55. 140 W. 20th.
" 56. 349 W. 18th.
" 57. 176 E. 115th.
" 58. 321 W. 52d.
" 59. 228 E. 57th.
" 60. College Av. n. E. 145th.
" 61. 3d Av. near 169th.
" 62. 3d Av. near 158th.
" 63. E. 173d c. Fordham Av.
" 64. 2436 Webster Av.
" 65. Tremont Av. c. Oosdorp Av.
" 66. King's Bridge Road, near Broadway.
" 67. 225 W. 41st.
" 68. 116 W. 128th.
" 69. 127 W. 54th.
" 70. 307 E. 75th.
" 71. 186 7th St.
" 72. 103d c. Lexington Av.
" 73. 203 E. 16th.
" 74. 220 E. 63d.
" 75. 23 Norfolk.
" 76. 68th c. Lexington Av.
" 77. 1st Av. cor. 85th.
" 78. Pleasant Av. c. E. 119th.
" 79. 40 1st. St.
" 80. 252 W. 42d.
" 81. 128 W. 17th.
" 82. 1st Av. cor. E. 70th.
" 83. 216 E. 110th.
" 84. 50th, near 9th Av.

Primary Schools.

No. 1. 105 Ludlow.
" 2. 101 Bayard.
" 3. 100 Cannon.
" 4. 418 E. 16th.
" 5. 339 E. 9th.
" 6. 13 3d St.
" 7. 43 W. 10th.
" 8. 63 Mott.

" No. 10. 32 Cannon.
" 11. 33 Vestry.
" 12. 85 Roosevelt.
" 13. 9 Downing.
" 14. 73 Oliver.
" 15. 68 Pearl.
" 16. 211 E. 32d.
" 19. 135th near 8th Av.
" 20. 187 Broome.
" 22. 150 1st Av.
" 23. 263 W. 124th.
" 24. 29 Horatio.
" 25. 530 Greenwich.
" 26. 558 E. 12th.
" 27. 517 W. 47th.
" 28. 324 E. 50th.
" 29. 449 E. 19th.
" 31. 272 2d St.
" 32. W. 182d near Kings Bridge Road.
" 34. 263 Pearl.
" 35. 996 1st Av.
" 36. 68 Monroe.
" 37. 67 Warren.
" 40. 104 Norfolk.
" 41. 464 W. 58th.
" 42. 234 E. 68th.
" 43. Ogden Avenue, Highbridgeville.
" 44. Concord Av. c. E. 145th.
" 45. 1787 Weeks.
" 46. Spuyten Duyvil.
" 47. Mosholu.

Kenny's Guide should be in every home. Its arrangement of time tables, postal information and other useful matter is so simple that the inexperienced can readily understand it.

POLICE STATIONS.

Central Office, 300 Mulberry. Bureau of Elections, 300 Mulberry. House for Detention of Witnesses, 203 Mulberry.

Station Houses.

Precinct and Location.	Precinct and Location.	Precinct and Location.
1st. Old Slip & Front.	13th. Union Market, E. Houston St.	24th. Pier A. N. R., Steamboat Patrol.
2d. Liberty & New Church Sts.	14th. 81 First Av.	25th. 155 E. 67th.
3d. City Hall.	15th. 221 Mercer.	26th. 134 W. 100th.
4th. 9 Oak.	16th. 230 W. 20th.	27th. 432 E. 88th.
5th. 19 Leonard.	17th. 34 E. 29th.	28th. Pier A. N. R.
6th. 19 Elizabeth.	18th. 327 E. 22d.	29th. 148 E. 126th.
7th. 247 Madison.	19th. 137 W. 30th.	30th. 126th St. & 8th Av.
8th. 128 Prince.	20th. 430 W. 37th.	31st. High Bridge.
9th. 94 Charles.	21st. 120 E. 35th.	32d. 10th Av. cor. 152d St.
10th. 205 Mulberry.	22d. 345 W. 47th.	33d. Town Hall, Morrisania.
11th. 105 Eldridge.	23d. 163 E. 51st.	34th. Bathgate Av. & 177th St.
12th. Cor. Attorney & Ridge.	23d. (Sub.) Grand Central Depot.	35th. 6 King's Bridge Road.

ASYLUMS AND HOMES.

All Saints', for Men & Boys. 521 E. 120th.
Assn. for Befriending Children & Young Girls, 138 2d Ave.
Assn. for Improving Condition of Poor, Bible House.
Assn. for Improved Instruction of Deaf Mutes, Lexington Ave. cor. E. 67th.
Assn. for Relief of Respectable Aged Indigent Females, 10th Ave. cor. W. 104th.
Babies' Shelter, 118 W. 21st.
Baptist Home for Aged, E. 68th & Park Ave.
Baptist Ministers' Home, 2020 Vyse.
Berachah Mission. 163 W. 33d.
Berachah Orphanage, 161st, near 10th Ave.
Bethlehem Day Nursery of Church of Incarnation, 248 E. 31st.
Bloomingdale Insane Asylum, Boulevard cor. W. 117th.
Board of United Charities, 9 E. 35th.
Chapin Home for Aged & Infirm, E. 66th n. Lexington Av.
Children's Aid Society, 19 E. 4th.
Children's Fold, Boulevard cor. W. 93d.
Christian Home for Intemperate Men, 1175 Madison Ave.
Christian Home for Women, 314 E. 15th.
Christian Workers. 129 E. 10th.
Colored Home & Hospital, 1st Ave. cor. 65th.
Colored Orphan Asylum, Boulevard near W. 143d.
Convalescents', 433 E. 118th.
Day Nursery, 309 Mulberry.
Deaf & Dumb Institution, foot W. 162d.
Dominican Convent of Our Lady of the Rosary, 329 E. 63d.
East Side Boys' Lodging House, 287 E. Broadway.
Eighth Ward Mission. 9 Ludlow Place.
Emigrants' Refuge & Hospital, Ward's Island : Ferry from foot of E. 110th. Apply at Castle Garden.
Five Points House of Industry, 155 Worth.
Five Points Mission, 63 Park.
Foundling Asylum, 68th St. near 3d Ave.
Florence Night Mission. 21 Bleecker.
Free Dormitory for Women, 54 W. 3d.
Free Home for Destitute Young Girls, 23 E. 11th.
Free Training School for Women, 47 E. 10th.
Friends' Employment Society, Meeting House, Rutherford Pl.
German Odd Fellows' Home, 1½ 2d Ave.
Girls' Lodging House, 27 St. Mark's Place.
Good Shepherd, foot E. 90th.
Guild of St. Catharine, 262 Bowery.
Hebrew Benevolent & Orphan Asylum, 10th Ave. near 136th.
Hebrew Orphan Asylum, 3d Ave. near 77th.
Hebrew Sheltering Guardian Society, Boulevard cor. W. 150th; Girls' Branch 87th St. n. Ave. A
Home for Aged & Infirm Hebrews, 105th St. n. 9th Ave.
Home for Aged Women, 3 Morris.
Home for Friendless Girls, 7th Ave. cor. 13th.
Home for Incurables, Fordham Ave. cor. E. 182d.
Home for Self Supporting Women, 170 W. 22d.
Home for Sailors' Children, Staten Island.
Home for Aged, 207 E. 70th and 105th St. n. 9th Ave.
Home for Friendless, for Females & Children, 32 E. 30th.
Home for Relief of Destitute Blind, 10th Ave. near 104th.
Home for Old Men & Aged Couples, 187 Hudson.
Home for Young Women, 27 Washington Sq.; for Young Girls, 72 7th Ave.
Home of Industry for Discharged Convicts. 10 E. Houston.
House & School of Industry, females only, 120 W. 16th.
House of Mercy, Prot. Epis., foot W. 86th.
House of Refuge, Randall's Island : Ferry foot of E. 26th & E. 129th Sts.
House of Rest for Consumptives, 1831 Anthony Ave.
House of the Good Shepherd, foot E. 90th.
House of the Holy Comforter, 355 W. 23d.
House of the Holy Family, 128 2d Ave.
Howard Mission, 40 New Bowery.
Howard Mission & Home for Little Wanderers, 201 5th St.
Infant Asylum, 10th Ave. cor. 61st.
Insane Asylum, Randall's Island : Ferry from E. 26th & 120th.
Institute for Relief of Ruptured and Crippled, 42d St. & Lexington Ave.
Institution for the Deaf & Dumb, foot W. 162d.
Isaac T. Hopper Home, 110 2d Ave.
Juvenile Asylum, 176th n. 10th Av.; Reception Room, 61 W. 13th.
Ladies' Union Relief Assn., 5th Ave. & 23d.
Ladies' Deborah Nursery & Child's Protectory, 95 & 103 E. Broadway and 415 & 423 E. 89d.

Leake & Watts' Orphan House, 110th near 9th Ave.
Lutheran Emigrant House, 16 State.
Lying-in Asylum for Destitute Females, 139 2d Ave.
McAuley's Water Street Mission, 316 Water.
Magdalen Benevolent Society, 7 E. 88th.
Masonic Board of Relief, 6th Ave. c. 23d.
Medical Missionary Home & Institute, 118 E. 45th ; Ladies' Branch 140 Lexington Ave.
Memorial Day Nursery. 375 E. Broadway.
Messiah Home for Children, 4 Rutherford Place.
Methodist Episcopal Home, 10th Ave. cor. 92d.
Midnight Mission, 260 Greene.
Mission of Our Lady of the Rosary. 7 State.
Montefiore Home for Chronic Invalids, Boulevard & W. 138th.
Mothers' Home, 106 W. 132d.
New Sailors' Home, 338 Pearl.
Newsboys' Lodging House, 9 Duane.
Old Gentlemen's Unsectarian Home, 175th St. c. 10th Ave.
Orphan Asylum, Riverside Ave. cor. W. 73d.
Orphan Asylum of St. Vincent de Paul, 211 W. 39th.
Orphanage, Church of the Holy Trinity, 400 E. 50th.
Orphan Home & Asylum of P. E. Church, 49th St. n. Park Av.
Peabody Home, 33d St. & Lexington Ave.
Peabody Home for Aged Women, 2061 Boston Road.
Presbyterian Home for Aged Women, 73d St. n. Madison Av.
Primrose House, 330 W. 33d.
Protestant Half Orphan Asylum, 65 W. 10th.
Riverside Rest Association, 310 E. 26th.
Roman Catholic Orphan Asylum, for Girls, Madison Ave. & 51st ; for Boys, 647 5th Ave.
Roman Catholic Protectory, Fordham.
Sailors' Home, 190 Cherry.
Sailors' Snug Harbor, Staten Island : Ferry from Whitehall St. to St. George ; office 74 Wall.
St. Agatha's Home for Children, 306 W. 15th.
St. Ann's Home for Children, 90th St. & Ave. A.
St. Augustine's Guild, 261 Bowery.
St. Barnabas' House, 304 Mulberry.
St. Benedict's Home for Colored Children, 120 Macdougal.
St. Christopher's Home for Children & Young Girls, Riverside Ave. cor. W. 112th.
St. James' Home, 21 Oliver.
St. John Baptist House, 233 E. 17th.
St. John's Guild, 52 Varick.
St. Joseph's Home for the Aged, 209 W. 15th.
St. Joseph's Industrial Home, 65 E. 81st.
St. Joseph's Institute for Improved Instruction of Deaf Mutes, 772 E. 188th.
St. Joseph's Night Refuge for Destitute Women, 143 W. 14th.
St. Joseph's Orphan Asylum, 89th St. cor. Ave. A.
St. Luke's Home for Indigent Christian Females, 89th St. & Madison Ave.
St. Mary's Lodging House for Girls. 143 W. 14th.
St. Philip's Parish Home, 127 W. 30th.
St. Stephen's Guild, 9 Livingston Place.
St. Vincent's Home for Friendless Boys, 53 Warren.
Samaritan Home for the Aged, 414 W. 22d.
Seaman's Fund & Retreat. 12 Old Slip.
Shelter for Respectable Girls and Domestic Training School, 87 7th Ave.
Sheltering Arms, 504 W. 126th.
Shepherd's Fold, 88th St. cor. 9th Ave.
Sick Children's Mission, 287 E. Broadway.
Society for Prevention of Cruelty to Children ; office 860 B'way.
Sunnyside Day Nursery, 51 Prospect Place.
Swiss Home, 108 2d Ave.
Temporary Home for Women, 84 2d Ave.
Trinity Chapel Home for Aged Women, 207 W. 27th.
Trinity Mission House, 209 Fulton.
Veteran Fireman's Home for Indigent Firemen, 53 E. 10th.
Virginia Day Nursery, 632 5th St.
Water Street Mission & Home for Women, 273 Water.
Welcome Lodging House for Women, 234 W. 4th.
West Side Boys' Lodging House, 400 7th Ave.
West Side Day Nursery & Industrial School, 266 W. 10th.
Wetmore Home for Friendless Girls, 49 Washington Sq.
Wilson Industrial School for Girls, 125 St. Mark's Place.
Women's Aid Soc. & Home for Training Young Girls, 41 7th Av.
Young Women's Home, 27 Washington Sq.
Zion Home for the Aged, 211 W. 10th.

DISPENSARIES.

Bellevue Bureau of Relief for Out-door Poor, foot E. 26th. Open 9 a. m to 5 p. m.
Bloomingdale, 157 W. 99th. Open 11 a. m. to 2 p. m.
Bloomingdale Dispensary for Urinary Diseases, 134 W. 35th. Open 12 m. to 3 p. m.
Demilt, 301 2d Ave. Open 8 a. m. to 5, p. m.
Dental Infirmary, 215 E. 23d. Open 9 a. m. to noon.
Dispensary for Children, 409 W. 34th. Open 1 to 2 p. m.
Eastern, 57 Essex. Open 9 a. m. to 5 p. m.
Eastern of Harlem, 241 E. 111th. Open 2 to 4 p. m.
Eclectic, 1 Livingston Place. Open 1.30 to 4 p. m.
Eye & Ear Infirmary, 218 2d Ave. Open 12 m. to 3 p. m.
Five Points House of Industry, 155 Worth.
German, 137 2d Ave. Open 2 to 5 p. m.
German, 111 W. 28th. Open 2 to 4 p. m.
German Poliklinik, 111 6th Ave. Open 1 to 5 p. m.
Gouverneur Hospital, Gouverneur Slip cor. Front. Open 10 a. m. to 12 noon ; 2 to 4 p. m.
Harlem, 160 E. 126th St. Open 1 to 3 p. m.
Harlem Dispensary for Women and Children, 2341 2d Ave. Open 1 to 3 p. m.
Harlem Eye & Throat Infirmary, 80 E. 125th. 2 to 3 p.m.
Homœopathic Medical College,201 E.23d. Open 10a.m.to4p.m.
Infirmary for Women & Children, 128 2d Av. Open 9 to 11 a.m.
International Medical Missionary Society ; Dispensary No. 1, 81 Roosevelt, open Tues., Thurs. & Sat. ; No. 2, 39 Pitt; No. 3, 143 Bleecker ; No. 4, 310 W. 54th ; No. 5, 2201 3d Ave.; No. 6, 163 W. 32d. All excepting No. 1 are open Mon., Wed. & Fri. only.
Manhattan, 301 E. 70th. Open 2 to 4 p. m.
Manhattan, 131st St. cor. 10th Ave. Open 2 to 4 p. m.
Manhattan Eye & Ear Ho-pital,103 ParkAv. Open 2 to 3.30 p.m.
Medical College & Hospital for Women, 213 W. 54th. Open 10 a. m. to 12 m. ; 2 to 4 p. m.
Metropolitan, 247 W. 40th. Open 1 to 3 p. m.
Metropolitan Throat, 351 W. 34th. Open 2 to 4 p. m.
Mt. Sinai Hospital,cor.66th & Lexington Av. Open 1.15 to 4p.m.
New York, 137 Centre. Open 9 a. m. to 5 p. m.
New York Hospital, 7 W. 15th. Open 2 to 4 p. m.
North Eastern, 222 E. 59th. Open 9 a. m. to 5 p. m.
Northern, cor. Waverley Pl. & Christopher. Open 8a.m. to5p.m.
North Western, 461 W. 36th. Open 9 a. m. to 4 p. m.
Ophthalmic & Aural Institute, 46 E. 12th. Open 2 to 3 p. m.
Orthopædic, 126 E. 59th. Open 1 to 3 p. m.
Polyclinic, 214 E. 34th. Open 9 a. m. to 5 p. m.
Post Graduate, 226 E. 20th. Open 9 a. m. to 7 p. m.
St. Chrysostom's, 550 7th Av. Open Mon. Wed. Fri.Sat,3 to 4p.m.
Sixth Street, 614 Sixth. Open 2 to 4 p. m.
Skin & Cancer, 243 E. 34th. Open 2 to 4 p. m.
Tompkins Square Homœopathic. 264 E. 4th. Open 1 to 3 p.m.
Trinity, 209 Fulton. Open 9 to 11 a. m.
Twenty-five Cent Providence, 80 E. 10th. Open 5 to 7 p. m.
Twenty-third & Twenty-fourth Wards, 702 Westchester Ave. Open 10 a. m. to 4 p. m.
University Medical College, 408 E. 26th. Open 10 a.m. to 4 p.m.
Vanderbilt Clinic, cor. 10th Ave. & 60th. Open 9 a.m. to 4 p.m.
Western, 301 W. 38th. Open 9.30 a. m. to 12 m. ; 2 to 4 p. m.
Wilson Mission, 134 Ave. A. Open 10 a. m. to 12 m.
Woman's Hospital Clinic, 50th St. & Park Av. Open 2to 4 p.m.
Yorkville, 1307 Lexington Ave. Open 3 to 4 p. m.

HOSPITALS.

American Veterinary, 141 W. 54th.
Bellevue, foot E. 26th.
Blackwell's Island; Ferry from E. 26th, 52d & 76th Sts.
Bloomingdale Reception, 157 W. 99th.
Cancer, 2 W. 106th.
Colored Home & Hospital, 65th n. 1st Ave.
College of Veterinary Surgeons, 382 E. 27th.
Emergency for Women, 223 E. 26th.
Emigrants' Refuge & Hospital, Ward's Island ; Ferry from E. 110th St. For admission apply at Castle Garden.
Eye & Ear Infirmary, 218 2d Ave.
French Benevolent Society, 131 W. 14th.
German, Park Ave. & E. 77th.
Gouverneur, Gouverneur Slip & Front.
Hahnemann, Park Ave. & E. 67th.
Harlem, foot E. 120th.
Hart's Island ; Ferry from foot E. 26th.
House of the Good Samaritan, 201 W. 38th.
Laura Franklin Hospital for Children, 17 E. 111th.
Lodge & Association, 66 St. Mark's Place.
Manhattan, 131st, near 10th Ave.
Manhattan Eye & Ear, 103 Park Ave.
Medical College & Hospital for Women, 12th, cor. 2d Ave.
Metropolitan Throat, 351 W. 34th.
Mount Sinai, Lexington Ave. & E. 66th.
New York, 7 W. 15th.
Infirmary for Women & Children, 5 Livingstone Place.
Nursery & Child's Hospital, 571 Lexington Ave.
Ophthalmic, 201 E. 23d.
Ophthalmic & Aural Institute, 46 E. 12th.
Post Graduate, 226 E. 20th.
Presbyterian, E. 70th, n. Park Ave.
Randall's Island Hospital ; Ferry from E. 26th & 122d Sts.
River Side, North Brother Island.
River Side, foot E. 16th.
Roosevelt, 50th St. & 9th Ave.
Skin & Cancer, 243 E. 34th. and Fordham Heights.
Society for the Relief of the Ruptured and Crippled. 42d St. & Lexington Ave.
St. Andrew's Convalescent for Women, 206 E. 16th.
St. Elizabeth's, 225 W. 31st.
St. Francis, 609 5th Street.
St. Joseph's, 328 E. 109th.
St. Joseph's Infirmary, 82d & Madison Ave.
St. Luke's, 17 W. 54th.
St. Mary's For Children, 407 W. 34th.
St. Vincent's, 153 W. 11th.
Sloane Maternity, 59th, cor. 10th Ave.
Trinity, 50 Varick.
United States Marine; office, foot Whitehall St.
Ward's Island ; Ferry from E. 26th & 115th Sts. Office. Castle Garden.
Willard Parker, foot E. 16th.
Women's, 50th, near Park Ave.
Women's Infirmary & Maternity Home, 247 W. 49th.

LIBRARIES.

Academy of Medicine, 12 W. 31st, free. Open 10 a. m. to 10 p. m, except Sundays & holidays.
Aguilar Free Library, 721 Lexington Ave. & 206 E. Broadway. Open 10 a.m. to 10 p.m.; on Saturdays 7 to 10 p.m. only.
American Institute, 19 Astor Place. Open in summer 9 a. m. to 4 p. m ; in winter 9 a. m. to 9 p. m.; $5 per annum.
Apprentices, 18 E. 16th, free. Open 8 a. m. to 6 p. m. except Sundays & holidays.
Astor, free, 34 Lafayette Pl. Open, except Sundays and holidays, in summer 9 a.m. to 5 p.m.; in winter 9 a. m. to 4 p.m.
Broome St., free, 391 Broome. Open Tues. Wed & Fri 4 to 9 p.m.
City, 12 City Hall, free. Open 10 a. m. to 4 p. m.
Columbia College, 11 E. 49th.
Cooper Union, 7th St. & 4th Ave. Open 8 a. m. to 10 p. m.
Five Points Mission, free, 63 Park. Open 6 to 9 p. m.
Free Circulating, 49 Bond, 135 Second Av., 251 W.13th, 226 W. 42d. Open 9 a. m. to 9 p. m., and Sundays from 1 to 9 p.m.
Free Library for the Blind, 206 9th Ave.
Free Library of St. Mark's Memorial Chapel, 288 E.10th. Open 7.30 to 9 p m. except Saturdays & Sundays.
Harlem, 2238 3d Ave. Open 9 a. m. to 9 p. m.; $3 per annum.
Historical Society, 170 2d Ave. Open from 9 a. m. to 6 p. m.
Law Institute, 116 P. O. Building. Open 9 a. m. to 5 p. m.; free, except to the profession.
Law Library of Equitable Life Assur. Soc., 120 Broadway.
Lenox, 895 5th Ave. Open 10 a. m. to 4 p. m. except Sundays and Mondays.
Library of American Museum of Natural History, 77th St. & 8th Ave. Open 10 a. m. to 5 p. m.
Lorraine, 41 W. 31st. Open 8 a. m. to 6 p. m. except Sundays and holidays.
Maimonides, 908 3d Ave. Open 9 a. m. to 9 p. m. except Saturdays, and on Sundays 9 a. m. to 1 p. m.
Masonic, 75 W. 23d. Open 3.30 to 5.30 p.m., and 7 to 10.30 p.m except Sundays.
Mercantile, 19 Astor Place, 426 5th Ave & 35 Liberty. Open 8 a. m. to 8 p.m. Rates; clerks, $1 per annum; others, $5.
Mott Memorial Free Medical, 64 Madison Av. Open 2 to 6 p.m.
N. Y. Hospital, 8 W. 16th. 10 a. m. to 5 p. m. except Sundays and holidays.
N.Y. Port Soc., 46 Catharine. 8 a.m. to 10 p.m.; for seamen only.
N. Y. Society, 67 University Place. Open 8 a. m. to 6 p. m. $15 per annum.
Odd Fellows', 2371 Park Ave.
Produce Exchange, Produce Exch. Open 9 a. m. to 4 p. m.
Printers', 3 Chambers, free. Open Saturday p. m. only.
Prot. Epis. Church Mis. Soc. for Seamen, 7 Coenties' Slip. Open 9 a. m. to 7 p. m. except Sundays & holidays.
St. Barnabas', 38 Bleecker, free. Open 7 to 10 p. m.
Seamen's, 34 Pike, free. Open 3 to 10 p. m.
University Law, 41 University Building.
Washington Heights, free, 10th Ave. near 156th, Open 9 a.m. to 12 m. and 1.30 to 9 p. m. except Sundays & holidays.
Woman's Library, 19 Clinton Pl. Open 9 a. m. to 4 p. m. $1.50 per annum.
Woman's Free Reading Room & Library, 16 Clinton Pl. Open 10 a. m. to 10 p. m.
Young Men's Christian Assn., 52 E. 23d, 243 Bowery, 142 2d Ave., 153 E. 86th, 470 W. 30th, 5 W. 125th & 361 Madison Ave. Open 8 a. m. to 10 p. m. and on Sundays from 1.30 to 10 p. m. $5 per annum.
Young Men's Institute, 222 Bowery. $1 per annum.
Young Women's Christian Assn., 7 E. 15th. Open 9 a. m. to 5 p. m. except Sundays, and every day 7 to 9.15 p. m.

Kenny's Guide should be in every Library. It is a neat and comprehensive work. Our Weekly Supplement, issued every Monday, contains all changes in time tables, etc.

APARTMENT AND "FLAT" HOUSES.

Abbotsford, 934 9th Av.
Adelaide, 120 W. 47th.
Adelphi, 203 W. 52d.
Adelwait, 211 17th Av.
Albany, 1065 Broadway.
Albert, 42 E. 11th.
Aldine, 358 W. 51st.
Alexandria, 901 6th Av.
Allerton, 100 E. 124th.
Allston, 47 E. 38th.
Alpine, 55 W. 33d.
Alvine, 101 E. 123d.
Amsterdam, 9th Av. & 40th St.
Angelena, 60 s. Washington Sq
Ariston, 1772 Broadway.
Arlington, 150 E. 49th.
Arvesta, 216 E. 70th.
Ashfield, 905 W. 55th.
Ashton, 611 Lexington Av.
Astor, 21 W. 128th.
Atlantic, 110 E. 91st.
Auburn, 807 Park Av.
Auburn, 101 E. 123d.
Bailey, 3464 7th Av.
Baltimore 138 E. 10th.
Bancroft, 421 W. 57th.
Barcelona, 165 W. 58th.
Barrington, 42 E. 25th.
Beaconsfield, 1211 Broadway.
Beaufort, 756 7th Av.
Bedford, 10th Av. & 82d St.
Beckman, 226 E. 52d.
Belair, 411 W. 61st.
Belgravia, 40th St. & 5th Av
Bella, 4th Av. cor. 96th.
Belport, 331 W. 56th.
Benedict, 80 E. Washington Sq
Berkeley, 30 Fifth Av.
Berkshire, 2322 8th Av.
Berkshire, 502 Madison Av.
Berlin, 218 W. 128th.
Berwick, 65 W. 131st.
Beverly, 6th Av. cor. 125th.
Black Building, 28th, c. 5th Av.
Blackburn, 100 W. 61st.
Bluebell, 108 E. 88th.
Boston, 30 W. 59th.
Brandon, 1279 Park Av.
Brighton, 214 W. 56th.
Bristol, 15 E. 11th.
Broadway, 1125 Broadway.
Bryn Mawr, 101 E. 90th.
Burlington, 12 W. 30th.
Cardinal, 141 W. 56th.
Carlton, 121 W. 36th.
Carlyle, 22 W. 60th.
Carteret, 201 W. 54th.
Cedarhurst, 41 E. 50th.
Central, 18, Fifth Av.
Central Park, 59th, u. 7th Av.
Chelsea, 216 W. 23d.
Chelsea, 338 W. 18th.
Chesterfield, 16 E. 53d.
Clarence, 138 W. 46th.
Claxton, 122 W. 37th.
Clermont, 1708 Broadway.
Cleveland, 128 E. 24th.
Cogshall, 9th Av. cor. 58th.
Coleman, 98 Madison Av.
Columbia, 136 E. 49th.
Columbia, 71 E. 125th.
Columbia, 40 E. 51st.
Cordova, 170 W. 59th.
Crescent, 138 5th Av.
Croisic, 5 W. 26th.
Crystal, 104 W. 46th.
Cumberland, 173 5th Av.
Dakota, 8th Av. cor. 72d.
Dalhousie, 10 W. 59th.
Dakota, 1931 Madison Av.
Delmonico, E. 79th, n. 2d Av.
Douglas, 103 E. 16th.
Drew, 24 E. 17th.
Dudley, 225 E. 14th.
Dundonald, 371 W. 83d.
East Minster, 230 E. 50th.
Edinboro, 10th Av. & 103d.
Edinburgh, 8 W. 28th.
Edrington, 4342 7th Av.
Ellingham, 355 W. 58th.
Eighty Madison Av.
Eisleben, 2091 6th Av.

Elberon, 62 W. 51st.
Elenora, 221 E. 127th.
Elise, 352 8th Av.
Elizabeth, 139 E. 16th.
Elmore, 240 W. 34th.
Elmwood, 779 9th Av.
Elsworth, 10th Av. & 52d.
Emerson, 212 E. 70th.
Emmet, 973 8th Av.
Empire City, 127 E. 125th.
Emporium, 25 W. 14th.
Englewood, 1187 Lexing'n Av.
Essex, 61e, cor. 9th Av.
Evangeline, 302 W. 124th.
Evelyn, 101 W. 78th.
Fairmount, 141 W. 57th.
Fennemore, 116 W. 57th.
Florence, 221 E. 124th.
Florence, 4th Av., cor. 18th.
Florida, 343 2d Av.
Folsom, 330 E. 17th.
Four Seasons, 117 W. 41st.
Franklin, 997 6th Av.
Franklyn, 55 E. 11th.
Fulton, 128 W. 83d.
Galaxy, Lexington Av., n. 88th
Garfield, 336 W. 56th.
Gerlach, 55 W. 27th.
Gilford, 155 E. 15th.
Girard, 101 Park Av.
Girard, 123 E. 84th.
Gladstone, 441 5th Av.
Glencoe, 854 7th Av.
Glenida, 152 E. 89th.
Glenwood, 203 E. 124th.
Gorham, 15 E. 19th.
Grace, 107 E. 48th.
Gramercy, 151 W. 20th.
Gramercy, 31 Gramercy Park.
Granada, 160 W. 50th.
Grant, 307 W. 55th.
Grenoble, 200 W. 57th.
Greenville, 227 E. 14th.
Greenwich, 93 Greenwich Av.
Greycourt, 2037 7th Ave.
Grosvenor, 37 5th Av.
Grove, 86 Grove.
Hamilton, 501 5th Av.
Hamilton, 1138 3d Av.
Hamilton, 136 W. 126th.
Hampshire, 28 W. 9th.
Hampton, 69 W. 131st.
Hanover, 2 E. 45th.
Hanover, 525 W. 83d.
Hart, 110 W. 40th.
Havemeyer, 318 W. 19th.
Havemeyer, 311 W. 89th.
Hawthorne, 41 W. 29th.
Heathwood, 315 W. 58th.
Heidelberg, 103 W. 62d.
Helena, 102 E. 31st.
Helene, 102 E. 124th.
Herbert, 101 E. 81st.
Hetherington, 1071 Park Av.
Hoffman Arms, 640 Madis'n Av
Home, 118 E. 86th.
Howard, 124th, c. Madison Av.
Hubert, 23 W. 59th.
Hudson, 311 W. 124.
Russell, 419 W. 71st.
Hyacinthe, 110 E. 89th.
Idaho, 153 E. 48th.
Imperial, 57 E. 76th.
Interlaken, 1380 Broadway.
Inwood, 227 W. 46th.
Iroquois, 150 E. 50th.
Irving, 433 W. 57th.
Irvington, Broadway & 53d.
Jackson, 232 W. 19th.
Jansen, 13 Waverly Place.
Jardine, 305 W. 56th.
Jeannette, 150 W. 125th.
Jefferson, 4th Av., cor. 78th.
Kenilworth, 411 W. 51st.
Kenilworth, 103 E. 10th.
Kenmore, 353 W. 37th.
Kensington, 309 Park Av.
Kenwood, 254 W. 37th.
Kimberly, 58 E. 130.
Kings, Lexington Av. & 30th.
Kingston, 129 E. 74th.
Knickerbocker, 217 5th Av.

Lafayette, 207 E. 60th.
Lafayette, 912 8th Av.
Lafayette, 9 Waverly Place.
Larchmont, 401st, near 9th Av.
Ledyate, 222 W. 128 n.
Lenox Hill, 987 Madison Av.
Lexington, 165 E. 19th.
Lexington, 675 9th Av.
Lexington, 165 E. 112th.
Lincoln, 911 8th Av.
Lincoln, 432 E. 89th.
Lincoln, 261 W. 47th.
Lisbon, 175 W. 58th.
Lispenard, 51 E. 86th.
Livingston, 49 W. 31st.
Livingston, 126 E. 19th.
Lonsdale, 4th Av., near 62d St.
Lorena, 302 East 27th.
Lorimer, 30 W. 59th.
Loring, W. 7th & Boulevard
Lorne, 131 S. 18th.
Lorne, 888 9th Av.
Lyceum, 33 E Grove.
Lyndon, 103 E. 123d.
Madeline, 79 E. 125th.
Madison, 40 E. 25th.
Madison Park, 4 E. 23d.
Madrid, 180 W. 59th.
Maine, 174 E. 94th.
Manhattan, 2d Ave., cor. 86th.
Manhattan, 141 E. 52d.
Manhattan Sq., 78th, c. 9th Av.
Marguerite, 118 W. 125th.
Marlborough, 355 W. 58th.
Maryland, 339 E. 79th.
Mason, 6 East 38th.
Massachusetts, 160 E. 94th.
Massasoit, 120 W. 139th.
Maxwell, 139 W. 127th.
Melville, 163 E. 111th.
Milden, 659 Lexington Av.
Millburne, 834 7th Ave.
Milton, 20 West 60th.
Montana 155 E. 18th.
Montgomery, 230 E. 86th.
Morris, 81 E. 125th.
Morton, 246 W. 3rd.
Mount Morris, 10 E. 120th.
Murray Hill, 150 E. 40th.
Mystic, 39th St., near 6th Av.
Napier, 114 W. 22d.
Narragansett, 435 W. 43d.
Nassau, 182 E. 76th.
Navarro, 59th St., near 7th Av.
New Hampshire, 170 E. 91th.
Newport, 200 W. 52d.
Newton, 218 W. 14 th St.
Niagara, Park Av., cor. 87th.
Noble, 7th Av., near 57th.
Norfolk, 241 E. 85th.
Norfolk, 45 W. 30th.
North Hamilton, 166 E. 67th.
Northumberland, 672 Lex. Av.
Norwood, 109 W. 82d
Oakhurst, 2 39 7th Av.
Oakland, 152 W. 19th.
Ogden, 41 E. 79th.
Onslow, 245 W. 124th.
Oxford, 200 W. 55th.
Opera, 217 W. 40th.
Oradel, 111 W. 124th.
Oriental, 316 E. 57th.
Orienta, 155 E. 73d.
Orleans, 975 8th Av.
Osborne, 661 5th Av.
Osborne, 57th St., cor. 7th Av.
Oxford, 137 W. 56th.
Pacific, 108 E. 91st.
Palermo, 125 E. 57th.
Palisade, 325 W. 56th.
Paris, 339 W. 23d.
Park Hill, 1429 Park Av.
Parkhurst, 2085 7th Av.
Park View, 51 Wash. Sq. S.
Park View, 249 W. 59th.
Peabody, 102 Waverly Pl.
Pearl, 318 E. 96th.
Pelham, 245 E. 85th.
Percival, 224 W. 42d.
Perfection, 150 E. 86th.
Phillips, 187 W. 49th.
Portsmouth, 38 W. 91th.

Princeton, 322 W. 57th.
Providence, 112 E. 53d.
Randall, 12 W. 16th.
Rodman, 19 W. 125th.
Rembrandt, 152 W. 57th.
Rensselaer, 1271 Broadway.
Rhode Island, 136 E. 91th.
Richfield, 215 W. 43d.
Richmond, 3 Bank St.
Riverside, 10th Av., near 74th.
River View, 517 W. 51st.
Rockingham, 1738 Broadway.
Rockland, 23 W. 53d.
Roosevelt, 334 W. 59th.
Rosedale, 252 W. 124th.
Rothsay, 136 E. 18th.
Rutland, 252 W. 57th.
Salamanca, 155 W. 58th.
Santa Rosa, 120 E. 88th.
Saratoga, 340 E. 70th.
St. Albans, 349 W. 58th.
St. Augustine, 261 W. 57th.
St. Catharine, 507 Madison av.
St. George, 223 E. 17th.
St. Germaine, 1438 Lex. Av.
St. James, 956 8th Av.
St. John, 1118 Broadway.
St. John, 401 W. 57th.
St. Monica, 161 E. 79th.
St. Nicholas, 39 E. 18th.
St. Nicholas, 124th, o. St. Nicholas Av.
St. Thomas, 71 W. 53d.
Scofield, 367 W. 23d.
Seneca, 215 E. 89th.
Seward, 175 E. 93d.
Shelbourne, 256 W. 55th.
Sherman, 157 W. 48th.
Sherwood, 539 5th Av.
Sirmount, 331 E. 86th.
Sloane, 39 W. 33d.
Smithsonian, 118 E. 36th.
Somerset, 1250 7th Av.
Soncy, 19 W. 57th.
South Hamilton, 165 E. 66th.
South Kensington, 881 4th Av.
Stanahan, 254 W. 124th.
Stanhope, 229 W. 14th.
Stanhope, 101 E. 124th.
Strathmore, 1071 Broadway.
Stuyvesant, 142 E. 18th.
Stuyvesant, 238 E. 13th.
Sutherland, 709 Madison Av.
Tacoma, 1185 Lexington Av.
Tennyson, 131 E. 43d.
Tenterden, 263 W. 125th.
Todd, 131 W. 41st.
Toloss, 145 W. 55th.
Trenton, Park Av., near 91st.
Union, 109 W. 56th.
Valencia, 150 W. 59th.
Vancorlear, 200 W. 56th.
Vanderbilt, 399 Lexington Av
Venice, 402 W. 57th.
Vermont, 166 E. 94th.
Vernon, 107 E. 123d.
Vienna, 1180 3d Ave.
Vienna, 341 W. 28d.
Virginia, 208 E. 88th.
Waldine, 163 W. 128th.
Warwick, 186 W. 10th.
Washington, 940 8th Av.
Washington, 7th Av., e. 122d.
Washin'tn, 28 Washin'tn Sq. W.
Wave Crest, 39 E. 50th.
Webster, 774 9th Av.
Wellington, 364 Madison Av.
Wellington, 118 W. 23d.
West End, 172 W. 128th.
West End, 779 8th Av.
Westerly, 103 W. 54th.
Westminster, 115 E. 16th.
Westmoreland, 166 E. 17th.
Winchester, 1211 Broadway.
Windemere, 400 W. 57th.
Windsor, 1760 Broadway.
Winfield, 207 W. 53th.
Winthrop, 7th Av., cor. 125th.
Witherbee, 111 W. 125th.
Wyoming, 7th Av., near 55th.

Don't leave your home or office to obtain information concerning the various routes to your point of destination. **Consult this Guide** or address your inquiry to this office and complete information will be gladly furnished.

The postal information contained in this Guide is complete. No confusing reference marks to trace out in order to obtain the information you need. Every line contains information.

HOTELS IN NEW YORK CITY AND THEIR RATES.

At Hotels conducted on the European plan we have given the *lowest* rate; for example, the rate given at Astor House is $1.00, but the rates at this hotel range from $1.00 up. When on both plans [a and e], the rate shown includes either plan. For Hotels not found in alphabetical order, see under "Hotel Albert," etc.

a–American plan. e–European plan. ae–American and European plan.

Plan.   Hotel and rate per day.

- e Aberdeen, Broadway & 21st, $1.00 to $2.00.
- e Albemarle, Broadway & 24th, $2.00.
- ae Allman House, 67 E. 10th, 50c. to $3.00.
- ae Arno, 1170 Broadway, $1.00 to $3.00.
- ae Ashland, 4th Ave., & 24th, $1.00 to $3.00.
- e Astor House, 221 Broadway, $1.00.
- e Bancroft House, Broadway & 21st, 50c.
- e Barrett House, Broadway & 13d, $1.50.
- e Belmont, 144 Fulton, 50c. to $1.00.
- e Belvedere, 4th Ave., & 18th, $1.00 to $2.00.
- a Berkeley (private), 20 5th Ave.
- e Brevoort House, 11 5th Ave., rate refused.
- ae Bradford, 65 11th St., 75c. to $2.00.
- ae Bristol, 17 E. 11th, $1.00 to $2.50.
- e Broadway, 834 Broadway, 75c. to $2.00.
- e Brower House, 24 W. 28th, $1.00.
- ae Bryant Park, 660 6th Ave., 50c. to $2.00.
- e Buckingham, 5th Ave., & 50th, $3.00 to $5.00.
- a Canda House, 17 Lafayette Place, $1.50 to $2.00.
- e Carleton, cor. Frankfort & William, 25c. to $1.00.
- e Centennial, 8th Ave. & 51st, 50c. to $1.00.
- e Central, 453 Canal, 50c. to $1.50.
- e Central Park, 7th Ave., & 59th, $2.00.
- ae Clarendon, 4th Ave., & 18th, $2.00 to $4.50.
- e Coleman House, Broadway & 27th, $1.00.
- e Colonnade, 726 Broadway, $1.00 to $3.50.
- e Continental, 904 Broadway, $1.00.
- e Cooper Union, 19 3d Ave., $1.00 to $2.00.
- e Cosmopolitan, Chambers & West B'way, $1.00.
- e Dey Street, 58 Dey, 50c. to $1.50.
- e Earles, Canal, cor. Centre, $2.00.
- ae Eastern, 62 Whitehall, $2.00.
- e Everett House, 4th Ave. & 17th, $1.50.
- e Everett, 104 Vesey, 50c. to $1.00.
- a Fifth Avenue, 5th Ave. & 23d, $5.00.
- e Fulton Ferry, 2 Fulton, 50c. to $1.00.
- e Gedney House, Broadway & 40th, $1.00.
- a Germania, 137 Grand, $1.00.
- e Gilsey House, Broadway & 29th, $2.00.
- ae Gladstone, 59th St. & 6th Ave., $1.00 to $3.50.
- a Gramercy Park, E. 20th, b't 3d & 4th Avs., $2.00.
- e Grand, Broadway & 31st, $1.50.
- ae Grand Central, 673 Broadway, $2.50 to $3.50
- e Grand Union, 4th Ave. & 42d, $1.00.
- e Halls, Duane & Park Row, 50c. to $1.00.
- e Hamilton, 125th & 8th Ave., $1.00.
- e Hansfields, 622 Grand, 50c.
- e Hoffman House, 1144 Broadway, $2.00.
- e Hotel Albert, 11th st. n. Broadway, $1.50 to $2.00.
- ae Hotel America, Irving pl. & 15th, $1.00 to $2.00.
- e Hotel Bartholdi, Broadway & 23d, $2.00.
- a Hotel Bristol, 5th Ave. & 42d, $7.50 per week.
- ae Hotel Brunswick, 225 5th Ave., e plan, $2.00, a plan $4.50
- e Hotel Dam, 104 E. 15th, $2.00.
- e Hotel Devonshire, 120 near Madison Ave., $1.00.
- ae Hotel Espanol Hispano, 116 W. 14th, $1.00 to $4.00.
- e Hotel Everett, 174 Park Row, 50c. to $1.00.
- e Hotel Glenham, 155 5th Ave., $1.00 to $3.00.
- a Hotel Hamilton, 5th Ave. & 43d, $5.00.
- a Hotel Marlborough, Broadway & 36th, $4.00.
- e Hotel Martin, 21 University place, $1.00 to $5.00.
- ae Hotel Monico, 7 E. 18th, $2.00 to $2.50.
- e Hotel Normandie, Broadway & 38th, $2.00.
- e Hotel Royal, 6th Ave. & 40th, $1.00.

- a Hotel St. George, 825 Broadway, $2.50.
- ae Hotel St. Marc, 492 5th Ave., $1.50 to $4.00.
- e Hotel St. Stephen, 46 E. 11th, $1.00 to $2.00.
- e Hotel Vanderbilt, Vanderbilt Ave. & 4th, $1.00 to $3.00.
- a Hotel Vendome, Broadway & 41st, $1.00.
- ae Hotel Wellington, 43d & Madison Ave., $3.00.
- ae Hygienic, 15 Laight, $1.00.
- e International, 17 Park Row, 75c. to $2.00.
- e Lafayette House, 7 Lafayette place, $1.00.
- a Langham, 5th Ave. & 52d, $50.00 per week.
- e Leggetts, 76 Park Row, 50c. to $1.00.
- ae Lenox, 72 5th Ave., $2.50.
- e Madison Avenue, Madison Ave. & 58th, $3.00.
- e Manor House, 26th & Broadway, $1.00 to $5.00.
- e Mercantile, 762 Broadway, 75c.
- e Merchants, 39 Cortlandt, 50c.
- ae Metropole, Broadway near 42d, $1.00 to $3.50.
- a Metropolitan, Broadway & Prince, $3.00.
- e Millers, 37 W. 26th, $2.50 to $5.00.
- e Mitchell House, Broadway & 42d, $1.00.
- e Morton House, Broadway & 14th, $1.00.
- e Mount Morris, 3d Ave. & 130th, 50c. to $1.00.
- e Mount St. Vincent, 10th Ave. and 18th.
- ae Murray Hill, Park Ave. & 40th, $4.00.
- e New England, 70 Bowery, 50c to $1.00.
- a New Sailors Home, 338 Pearl, $1.00.
- e New York, 721 Broadway, $1.00 to $3.00.
- e N. Y. & Brooklyn Bridge, 80 Park Row, 50c. to $2.00.
- e North River, 118 West, 50c. to $1.00.
- e Occidental, Broome St. & Bowery, 50c. to $3.00.
- e Oriental, Broadway & 39th, $2.00.
- ae Orlando, 115 E. 14th, $3.50.
- e Parker House, Broadway & 34th, $1.50 to $2.50.
- e Park Avenue, Park Ave. & 32d, $3.50.
- e Putnam, 360 4th Ave., 50c. to $2.00.
- e Revere, 606 Broadway, 50c. to $2.00.
- e Rochester, 114 Bleecker, 50c. to $2.50.
- a Sailors Home, 190 Cherry, $1.00.
- e St. Charles, 648 Broadway, 50c. to $2.00.
- e St. Cloud, Broadway & 42d, $1.00.
- e St. Denis, Broadway & 11th, $1.00 to $5.00.
- e St. James, Broadway & 26th, $2.00.
- ae St. Nicholas, Broadway & Washington pl., $1.00 to $4.
- e St. Omer, 6th Ave. & 23d, 75c.
- e Sheridan Square, 159 Canal, 50c. to $1.00.
- a Sherwood, 5th Ave. & 44th, $1.00.
- e Sinclair House, 754 Broadway, $1.00.
- e Smith & McNells, 197 Washington, 50c. to $1.00.
- e Spingler House, University pl. & 11th, $1.00.
- e Stevens House, 23 Broadway, $1.00.
- ae Sturtevant, 1186 Broadway, $1.00 to $4.00.
- e Summit, Canal & Bowery, 50c. to $3.00.
- e Sweeneys, 23 Duane, 50c. to $1.00.
- e Sweets, 4 Fulton, 50c. to 75c.
- e Tremont, 663 Broadway, $1.00.
- e Union Square, 16 Union Square, $1.00.
- e United States, Fulton & Water, 75c. to $3.00.
- ae Victoria, 5th Ave. & 27th, $2.00 to $3.00.
- ae Western Union, 91 Cortlandt, $1.10.
- a Westminster, Irving place & 16th, $3.50.
- e West Side, 227 6th Ave., $2.00 to $3.00.
- a Wilton, 15 W. 27th, $2.00.
- a Windsor, 5th Ave. & 46th, $5.00.
- e Worth House, [Hoffman Annex], B'way & 25th, $2.00.

BALTIMORE.

- e Albion, $1.00.
- a Barnum's, $2.50 to $4.00.
- ae Carrollton, $1.25 to $4.00.
- e Eutaw House, $2.50 to $3.50.
- e Mount Vernon, $1.50.
- e Rennert, $1.50.
- e St. James, $1.50.

BOSTON.

- e Adams House, rate refused.
- ae American House, $1.00 to $3.00.
- a Brunswick, $5.00.
- e Crawford House, $1.00 to $5.00.
- ae International, $1.00 to $5.00.
- a Langham, $3.00.
- ae New Marlboro, 75c. to $2.50.
- e Parker House, $1.00.
- e Revere House, $1.00.
- e Thorndyke, $1.00.
- a Tremont House, $3.00 to $4.00.
- ae United States, $1.00 to $3.50.
- e Vendome, $5.00.
- e Victoria, $1.50.
- e Vieth's, $1.00.
- e Young's, $2.00 to $4.00.

PHILADELPHIA.

- a Aldine, $3.50 to $5.00.
- a Bingham House, $2.50.
- a Colonnade, $3.50 to $4.50.
- a Continental, $3.00 to $4.00.
- a Girard House, $3.00.
- ae Lafayette, $1.00 to $4.00.
- e Stratford, $2.00.
- a Washington, $2.50.
- e West End, $2.50.

WASHINGTON.

- a Arlington, $1.00 to $5.00.
- a Arno, $1.00 to $6.00.
- a Congressional, $2.00 to $4.00.
- a Ebbitt, $4.00.
- a Hamilton, $4.00.
- a Harris House, $2.50 to $3.00.
- a Maltby, $3.00 to $5.00.
- a Metropolitan, $3.00 to $4.00.
- a National, $2.50 to $4.00.
- ae Normandie, $2.00 to $5.00.
- a Riggs House, $4.00 to $5.00.
- e St. James, $1.00.
- ae Tremont, $2.50.
- a Welcker's, $2.00.
- a Willard's, $4.50.
- a Wormley's, $4.00 to $5.00.

NEW YORK CENTRAL AND HUDSON RIVER R. R.

From Grand Central Depot, 42d St. & 4th Ave.

Tickets, etc., can be obtained at the following offices: 1 Battery Place, 12 Park Place, 413, 785, 942 Broadway, 62 W. 125th St., 138th Street Station, 125th Street Station, and at Grand Central Station, 42d Street, Brooklyn: 333 Washington Street, 730 Fulton Street, and 79 Fourth Street, Eastern District.

For Drawing-Room and Sleeping Car Rates, see at end of this Table.

* Daily. † Daily, except Sunday. § On Sundays, will run only from Poughkeepsie. ‡ Daily, except Saturday. E Does not leave Albany for Syracuse Sunday nights. s Stops on Sundays only.

LOCAL TIME TABLE FROM NEW YORK.

STATIONS	Fare	23 A.M.	1 A.M.	3 A.M.	25 A.M.	103 P.M.	27 P.M.	5 P.M.	29 P.M.	11 P.M.	9 P.M.	37 N'GT	
New York (G.C. Station) [Leave		*8 00	*9 50	*10 30	*11 30	*3 30	*3 58	*6 00	*6 30	*9 00	*10 00	†12 00	**For Additional Local Trains,**
" (138th St Station)		8 11		10 41	11 47			6 03	6 40		10 10		
Yonkers	$ 30	8 31			12 01							12 38	**New York**
Tarrytown	50	8 50			12 20		4 41						**to Pough-**
Sing Sing	60	9 02			12 32		4 51		7 28		11 00	1 13	**keepsie, see**
Peekskill	82	9 22			12 53		5 13		7 48		11 20	1 35	**below.**
Garrisons	98	9 39			1 10	1 46	5 28		8 05				
Dutchess Junction	1 14	9 52					5 41						
Fishkill	1 16	9 57		12 11	1 30	5 02	5 50		8 30		11 35	2 18	
Poughkeepsie [Arrive	1 40	10 20		12 34	1 58	5 25	6 20		7 55	8 15	12 16	2 50	
Poughkeepsie [Leave	1 40	10 30		12 44	2 08	5 35	6 30	8 05	9 05		12 26	3 00	
Rhinebeck	1 76	11 02		1 00	2 30	5 59	7 02		9 36				
Tivoli	1 96	11 22			2 58		7 21		9 56				
Catskill Station	2 18	11 41			3 20	6 32	7 46						
Hudson	2 28	11 52		1 48	3 30	6 42	7 57		10 25			4 43	
Coxsackie Station	2 42	12 05			3 41		8 11						
Castleton	2 66	12 26			4 00		8 30						
East Albany [Arrive	3 00	12 43		2 32	4 30	7 25	8 55		11 30			5 30	
Albany	3 10	12 50	1 10	2 35	4 35	7 30	9 00	9 50	11 35		2 35	5 55	
Troy	3 15	12 57			4 50	7 45			11 40			6 55	
Troy [Leave	3 15	12 20		2 50	4 40			E.				*7 50	
Albany	3 10	1 23	1 15	3 00	5 00	7 45		10 00	11 35		2 55	*8 25	
Schenectady	3 44	2 00		3 35	5 40	8 20		10 32	12 14			9 00	
Amsterdam	3 76	2 31		4 02	6 15	8 53			12 47			9 31	
Fonda	3 98	2 52		4 18	6 38	9 15			1 07		4 23	9 52	
Palatine Bridge	4 20	3 15		4 37	7 03	9 38			1 30		4 44	10 15	
Fort Plain	4 28	3 20			7 10	9 45			1 36			10 21	
St. Johnsville	4 38	3 30			7 22	9 50			1 48			10 33	
Little Falls	4 58	3 50			7 37	10 10			2 05		5 17	10 53	
Herkimer	4 72	4 03			7 50	10 31			2 20			11 07	
Ilion	4 78	4 08			8 03	10 36			2 26			11 12	
Frankfort	4 82				8 10	10 41			2 30				
Utica	5 00	4 35	3 35	5 15	8 35	11 00		12 30	2 55		5 57	11 40	
Rome	5 30	5 00		6 08	9 20				3 33		6 22	12 10	
Oneida	5 54	5 28			9 37				3 43		6 45	12 35	
Canastota	5 61	5 38			9 49				3 52			12 46	
Chittenango	5 78	5 49			10 02							12 58	
Dewitt					10 25								
Syracuse [Arrive	6 00	6 20	4 32	7 15	10 40		2 05		4 35		7 40	1 30	
Syracuse [Leave	6 06			*7 15				*6 00			*9 30	*2 05	
Auburn	6 58							7 05			10 40	4 15	
Geneva	7 10				10 05			7 30			11 55	4 15	
Canandaigua	7 54				11 10						1 15	5 18	
Syracuse [Leave	6 00	*6 40	*4 55	*7 10				*6 00			*8 00	*1 50	
Weedsport	6 50	7 20									8 43	2 30	
Port Byron	6 59	7 28										2 45	
Savannah												3 05	
Clyde	6 82	7 52									9 15	3 15	
Lyons	6 96	8 12			8 53						9 35	3 35	
Newark	7 08	8 22										3 45	
Palmyra	7 22	8 37										4 00	
Rochester [Arrive	7 08	9 25	6 50	9 50				4 15			7 40	10 35	4 50
Rochester [Leave	7 08			10 05							*10 50	*5 25	
Spencerport				10 25							11 12	5 25	
Brockport	8 02			10 30							11 25	5 51	
Holley				10 46							11 37	6 05	
Albion	8 30			11 05							12 00	6 17	
Medina	8 48			11 25							12 20	6 38	
Gasport				11 45							12 40	6 57	
Lockport				12 00							12 52	7 10	
Suspension Bridge	9 25			12 40				7 25			1 30	7 45	
Niagara Falls [Arrive	9 25			12 50							1 55	8 03	
Rochester [Leave	7 08			6 50	10 00			4 20			7 45	10 45	5 00
Batavia	8 30							5 20			11 55	6 14	
Buffalo [Arrive	9 25			8 35	12 15			6 15			9 35	1 00	7 30
		P.M.	P.M.	A.M.	A.M.			P.M.			A.M.	P.M.	

ADDITIONAL LOCAL TRAINS FROM NEW YORK.

Leave **Grand Central Depot for High Bridge, Morris Dock, Kings Bridge and Spuyten Duyvil,** 6 40, 8 10, *9 10, *10 45, 11 50 a. m., 12 58, 2 10, *2 55, †3 10, 4 10, *4 15, 5 10, §5 40, 6 10, ±6 40, *7 10, 8 10, *9 10, *10 40, 11 40 p. m. Sundays only, 8 10 a. m., 1 30, 9 10 p. m.; due at Spuyten Duyvil in 25 minutes. §Stops at High Bridge on Sundays only. +Express train, stops at Spuyten Duyvil only. ‡Stops at Kings Bridge and Spuyten Duyvil only. *Daily.

For **Riverdale, Mt. St. Vincent, Ludlow and Yonkers,** 6 40, †7 15, *8 00, 8 10, 9 10, *10 45, †11 30, 11 50 a. m., 12 58, 2 10, †2 30, *2 55, 3 40, 4 10, ±4 25, §4 45, *4 58, 5 10, ±5 28, *5 40, 6 10, 6 40, *7 10, 8 10, 9 10, *10 40, 11 40 p. m., 12 night. Sundays only, 8 10, *9 00 a. m., 1 30, 9 40 p. m.; due at Yonkers in 30 minutes. *Daily. +Express train, make no stops between New York City and Yonkers. ‡Does not stop at Riverdale. §Does not stop at Mt. St. Vincent or Ludlow.

For **Tarrytown, Sing Sing, Croton** and intermediate stations, 6 40, †7 15, †8 00, 8 10, 9 10, *10 45, †11 30, 11 50 a. m., 12 58, 2 10, †2 30, *2 55, 3 40, *±3 58, 4 10, §4 25, *4 58, 5 10, ±5 28, *5 40, 6 10 (for Sing Sing only), 6 40, *7 10, 8 10, §9 10 (10 00 p. m., for Sing Sing only) *10 40, 11 40 p. m. (12 night for Sing Sing only). Sundays only, 8 40, 9 00 a. m., 1 30, 9 40 p. m.; due at Tarrytown in 50 minutes, at Sing Sing in 1 hour, 5 minutes, at Croton in 1 hour, 40 minutes. *Daily. ‡Stops only at Tarrytown and Sing Sing. §Does not stop at Glenwood. +Makes no stop between Yonkers and Tarrytown. ±Does not stop at Glenwood, Hastings or Irvington. §§Does not stop at Glenwood or Scarborough.

For **Peekskill** and intermediate stations, 7 15, *8 00, 9 10, †11 30 a. m., 12 58, †2 30, *±3 58, 4 15, 4 58, 5 28, *±6 30, 9 10, *±10 40 p. m., 12 night; Sundays, 9 00 a. m., 1 30 p. m.; due at Peekskill in 1 hour, 25 minutes. +Express train, makes no stop between Sing Sing and Peekskill. ‡Stops at Oscawana on Sundays only. ±Does not stop between Croton and Peekskill. §Does not stop at Cragers or Montrose. *Daily.

For **Poughkeepsie** and intermediate stations, 7 15 a. m., 2 30, 4 58 p.m.; Sunday, 9 00 a. m.; due at Poughkeepsie, 10 00 a. m., 4 55, 7 30 p. m.; Sunday, 11 45 a. m.

NEW YORK CENTRAL & HUDSON RIVER R. R.—Continued.
LOCAL TIME TABLE TO NEW YORK.

STATIONS.	28	2	14	100	32	6	4	30	18	8	26	21	10	12
	A.M.	A.M.			A.M.	A.M.	A.M.	P.M.		P.M.			P.M.	P.M.
Buffalo............[Leave		11 50	....	....	*6 05	*7 30	*8 50	....	....	*4 00	....	....	*6 10	*9 45
Batavia..................		5 55	....	....	7 25	8 25	....	....	....	5 05	....	....	7 12	10 50
Rochester........[Arrive	....	6 50	....	....	8 30	9 15	10 30	....	....	6 00	....	....	*8 00	11 45
Niagara Falls....[Leave		*3 55	....	....	*6 10	*6 28	7 16	....	....	*2 16	....	....	*8 15	*8 23
Suspension Bridge.......		4 00	....	....	6 20	6 20	7 40	....	....	2 10	....	....	4 00	8 15
Lockport...............		4 10	....	....	7 00	....	....	....	....	....	....	....	4 43	
Gasport................		4 52	....	....	7 12	....	....	....	....	....	....	....	4 55	
Medina................		5 14	....	....	7 33	....	....	....	....	....	....	....	5 17	
Albion................		5 37	....	....	7 55								5 40	
Holley................		6 00	....	....	8 17	Via Buffalo.	Via Buffalo.			Via Buffalo.			6 08	Via Buffalo.
Brockport.............		6 13	....	....	8 28								6 17	
Spencerport...........		6 28	....	....	8 45								6 30	
Rochester........[Arrive		6 50	....	....	9 10			P.M.					6 50	
Rochester........[Leave		7 00	....	....	*8 40	*9 20	*10 30			*5 50	*6 10		*8 05	*11 50
Palmyra..............		7 36	....	....	9 25	....	....	....	....	6 30	....	....	....	....
Newark...............		....	....	....	9 40	....	....	....	....	6 42	....	....	....	....
Lyons................		8 05	....	....	9 55	10 30	....	....	....	7 10	7 10	....	9 05	12 55
Clyde................		8 17	....	....	10 08	....	....	....	....	7 22	7 20	....	....	....
Savannah.............		....	....	....	10 21	....	....	....	....	7 32	....	....	....	....
Port Byron...........		....	....	....	10 35	....	....	....	....	7 45	....	....	....	....
Weedsport............		8 47	....	....	10 44	....	....	....	....	....	....	....	....	....
Syracuse.........[Arrive		9 30	....	....	11 25	11 35	12 25	....	....	8 32	8 30	....	10 15	2 15
Canandaigua.....[Leave		*6 05	....	....	....	18 45	....	....	....	*5 00	....	....	....	10 35
Geneva...............		7 00	....	....	....	9 35	....	....	....	6 05	....	....	....	10 35
Auburn...............		8 05	....	....	....	10 10	....	....	....	7 05	....	....	....	11 35
Syracuse.........[Arrive	A.M.	9 15	....	....	....	11 30	....	....	....	8 15	....	....	....	12 10
Syracuse.........[Leave	*7 30	*9 50	....	....	*12 10	*11 55	*12 30	....	....	*8 40	....	....	*10 25	*2 20
DeWitt...............	7 45	....	....	....	....	....	....	....	....	....	....	....	....	....
Chittenango..........	8 05	....	....	....	1 15	....	....	....	....	9 15	....	....	....	....
Canastota............	8 19	....	....	....	1 26	12 38	....	....	....	9 27	....	....	....	....
Oneida...............	8 31	10 37	....	....	1 36	12 49	....	....	....	9 40	....	....	....	....
Rome.................	8 57	10 58	A.M.	A.M.	2 00	1 8	....	....	....	10 05	....	....	....	....
Utica................	9 30	11 20	*5 45	*6 20	2 30	1 35	1 30	....	....	10 35	....	....	11 57	3 51
Frankfort............	9 48	....	....	6 40	2 46	....	....	....	....	....	....	....	....	....
Ilion.................	9 51	....	....	6 15	2 53	....	....	....	....	11 00	....	....	....	....
Herkimer............	9 59	11 55	....	6 59	2 57	2 12	....	....	....	11 05	....	....	....	....
Little Falls..........	10 14	12 07	....	7 05	3 10	2 25	....	....	....	11 20	....	....	....	....
St. Johnsville........	10 25	....	....	7 26	3 28	....	....	....	....	11 40	....	....	....	....
Fort Plain...........	10 40	12 23	....	7 38	3 45	....	....	....	....	11 52	....	....	....	....
Palatine Bridge......	10 51	12 28	....	8 13	3 51	2 51	....	....	....	12 00	....	....	....	5 15
Fonda...............	11 18	....	....	8 19	4 05	3 16	....	....	....	12 22	....	....	....	....
Amsterdam...........	11 42	1 10	....	8 31	4 26	3 36	....	....	....	12 46	....	....	....	5 45
Schenectady.........	12 15	1 43	....	9 05	4 50	3 55	....	....	....	1 20	....	....	1 57	6 15
Albany...........[Arrive	12 50	2 20	*8 05	9 15	5 30	4 30	1 00	....	....	1 55	....	....	2 30	6 55
Troy.............[Arrive		2 30	....	10 05	....	....	....	....	....	....	....	....	....	7 45
Troy.............[Leave		12 25	....	9 15	....	....	*2 10	....	110 00	*5 10	....	....	....	....
Albany...............	1 30	2 30	*8 15	9 55	6 00	*4 50	*4 45	1 15	....	*2 20	10 20	6 00	*2 55	*7 15
East Albany..........	1 33	....	....	10 00	6 05	....	....	1 18	2 35	....	10 30	6 08	....	....
Castleton............	1 49	....	....	....	6 21	....	....	1 34	....	....	10 46	6 19	....	....
Coxsackie Station....	2 12	....	....	....	6 48	....	....	1 56	....	....	11 12	6 41	....	....
Hudson..............	2 30	3 25	....	10 45	7 00	5 30	5 30	2 23	3 21	3 11	11 30	6 56	....	*8 32
Catskill Station.....	2 39	....	....	11 01	7 09	....	....	3 22	....	....	11 40	7 05	....	....
Tivoli...............	3 04	....	....	....	7 32	....	....	3 41	....	....	12 01	7 28	....	....
Rhinebeck...........	3 19	....	....	11 35	7 50	....	....	3 02	....	....	12 15	7 47	....	*8 12
Poughkeepsie....[Arrive	3 47	4 40	10 40	12 00	8 20	6 10	....	3 30	4 35	4 25	12 55	8 15	5 00	9 05
Poughkeepsie.....Leave	*3 57	4 50	10 15	12 10	8 30	6 55	....	3 40	4 15	4 35	10 05	8 25	5 10	9 15
Fishkill.............	4 25	5 15	....	12 34	8 57	....	....	3 29	....	....	1 31	8 52	....	....
Dutchess Junction...	4 28	....	....	....	....	....	....	3 32	....	....	....	8 55	....	....
Garrisons............	4 45	5 30	....	12 47	9 16	....	....	3 48	....	....	1 52	9 11	....	....
Peekskill............	5 02	5 45	....	....	9 31	....	....	4 05	....	....	2 10	9 24	6 10	....
Sing Sing...........	5 27	6 02	....	....	9 55	....	....	4 28	....	....	2 36	9 46	....	....
Tarrytown...........	5 38	....	....	....	10 06	....	....	4 35	....	....	2 47	9 57	....	....
Yonkers.............	5 58	....	....	....	10 28	....	....	4 51	6 05	....	3 05	10 15	....	....
New York (138th St. St'n).[Ar	6 19	6 19	....	....	10 49	8 10	....	5 15	6 19	6 33	3 15	10 36	7 00	11 06
" (G. C. Station).[Ar	6 30	7 00	12 00	2 12	11 00	*8 50	*7 30	9 25	7 00	6 45	3 25	10 45	7 20	11 15
	P.M.	P.M.	N'N.	P.M.	P.M.	P.M.	P.M.	P.M.	A.M.	A.M.	P.M.	A.M.	A.M.	A.M.

For Additional Trains from Poughkeepsie to New York, see below.

Additional Local Trains to New York.

Leave **Poughkeepsie**, stopping at intermediate stations, 6 25, 7 15 a. m.; leave **Fishkill**, 6 54, 7 41 a. m.; due in New York, 9 00, 9 30 a. m.

Leave **Peekskill**, **6 10, 7 00, §7 31, +8 15, 8 35, *9 28, 11 30 a. m., *2 10, 3 00, *5 02, +5 45, ++8 05, +*9 34, +10 80 p. m.; Sundays only 3 30 p. m.; due in New York—express trains, 1 hour, 40 minutes; accommodation trains in 1¼ hours. *Daily. † Does not stop at Montrose, Crugers, Oscawana. §Does not stop of Crugers or Oscawana.

Leave **Croton**, 5 25, 6 00, 6 30, 7 00, 7 16, 7 30, 7 45, 8 00, 8 30, *8 52, *10 35, 11 46 a. m., *1 30 *2 30, 3 15, 4 00, *5 00, *5 18, 6 15, *7 00, 8 00, *8 35, 10 00, 11 02 p. m.; Sundays only, 3 15 p. m. *Daily. Due in New York in 1¼ hours.

Leave **Sing Sing** (Scarboro 4 minutes later), 5 31, 6 06, 6 35, 7 06, 7 22, 7 36, 7 52, 8 06, 8 31, 8 36, *9 00, *9 16, *10 41, 11 54 a. m., *1 36, 2 26, *2 36, 3 25, 1 06, *5 06, *5 22, 6 03, 6 20, *7 06, 8 05, *8 23, *9 01, *9 55, 10 06, 1108 p. m.; Sundays, 3 55 p. m. *Daily. Due in New York in 1 hour, 10 minutes.

Leave **Tarrytown**, stopping at intermediate stations, 5 42, 6 17, 6 46, 7 17, 7 37, 7 47, 8 01, 8 17, 8 46, *9 12, **9 37, *10 52 a. m., 12 06, *1 17, *2 37, *2 47, 3 37, 4 17, *5 17, *5 38, 6 31, *7 17, 8 16, **8 35, *9 12, **10 07, 10 17, 11 19 p. m.; Sundays only 4 07 p. m. *Daily. †Stop only at Yonkers.

Leave **Yonkers**, stopping at intermediate stations, 6 03, **6 38, 6 38, 7 07, 7 38, **8 00, 8 08, **8 50, 8 39, 9 07, *9 37, *+10 15, *11 13 a. m., 12 30, *2 08, 12 55, *3 08, 4 01, 4 38, *5 38, **5 58, 6 50, *7 38, 8 87, **8 54, *9 33, **+10 28, 10 38, *11 43 p. m.; Sundays only, 4 31 p. m. †Stops at no intermediate stations. *Daily.

30TH STREET BRANCH.

Fare from 30th street: Manhattan, 12c.; 152d street, 14c.; Fort Washington, 16c.; Inwood, 20c.; Spuyten Duyvil, 22c.

Leave **30th Street & 10th Avenue** at 6 20, 7 15, 8 00, 9 35 a. m., 12 50, 4 00, 5 00, *5 55, 8 45 p. m.; Sundays, 1 15 p. m.; due at Spuyten Duyvil in 30 minutes. *Daily.

To New York.

Leave **Spuyten Duyvil**, 6 55, 7 50, 8 20, *10 10 a. m., 1 35, 5 00, 6 00, *7 00, 9 45 p. m.; Sundays, 2 20 p. m.; leave Inwood 3 minutes later; leave Fort Washington 7 minutes later; arrive in New York in 30 minutes.

NEW YORK CENTRAL & HUDSON RIVER R. R.—Continued.

Via Delaware & Hudson Railroad.
SHARON SPRINGS, COOPERSTOWN, RICHFIELD SPRINGS AND OSWEGO.

STATIONS.		1	3	5	9	37
New York (G. C. Station)	Leave	*9 30 a. m.	*10 30 a. m.	*6 00 p. m.	*10 10 p. m.	†12 00 night
(138th St. Station)		....	10 41 "	6 09 "	10 40 "	....
Albany	Arrive	1 10 p.m.	2 35 p. m.	9 30 "	2 55 a. m.	5 55 a. m.
Utica		3 35 "	5 45 "	....	5 57 "	10 55 "
Syracuse		4 52 "	7 15 "	....	7 10 "	1 00 p. m.
Albany	Leave	†1 25 p.m.	4 00 p. m.	*10 30 p. m.	....	†8 35 a. m.
Howe's Cave	Arrive	2 56 "	5 27 "	....	....	10 11 "
Cobleskill		3 08 "	5 40 "	12 25 a. m.	....	10 25 "
Sharon Springs	Arrive	....	6 26 p. m.	....	....	11 32 a. m.
Cherry Valley		....	6 55 "	....	....	12 00 m.
Cooperstown	Arrive	5 10 p. m.	7 25 p. m.	....	....	12 27 p. m.
Utica	Leave	....	6 15 p. m.	....	....	....
Richfield Springs		....	7 15 "	....	....	....
Syracuse, via D. L. & W. R. R.	Leave	*6 10 p. m.	10 00 p. m.	....	*10 35 a. m.	*2 60 p. m.
Oswego	Arrive	7 30 "	10 10 "	....	11 50 "	3 40 "

No. 1. Drawing-Room Car New York to Utica and Syracuse. Dining Car New York to Utica and Syracuse. Buffet Smoking Car New York to Utica and Syracuse. **No. 3.** Drawing-Room Cars New York to Albany and Syracuse. **No. 25.** Drawing-Room Cars New York to Troy. **No. 5.** Drawing-Room Cars New York to Albany. Dining Car New York to Albany. **No. 9.** Sleeping Cars New York to Utica and Syracuse. **No. 37.** Sleeping Cars New York to Albany.

SARATOGA, LAKE GEORGE, THE ADIRONDACKS AND MONTREAL.

STATIONS.		No. 23. Montreal Express.	No. 25. Northern Express.	No. 29. Montreal Express.	No. 37. Albany Express.
New York (G. C. Station)	Leave	*8 00 a. m.	*11 30 a. m.	*6 30 p. m.	†12 00 night
(138th St. Station)		8 11 "	11 40 "	6 40 "	....
Albany	Arrive	12 30 p. m.	4 35 p. m.	11 25 "	5 55 a. m.
Troy		12 57 "	4 50 "	11 40 "	6 55 "
Albany	Leave	*1 05 p. m.	....	*11 15 p. m.	....
Troy		1 05 "	*5 05 p. m.	11 50 "	*8 25 a. m.
Ballston	Arrive	2 07 "	6 10 "	12 50 a. m.	9 31 "
Saratoga		2 20 "	6 35 "	1 05 "	9 45 "
Saratoga	Lv	....	....	....	10 10 a. m.
Jessup's Landing	Adirondack	....	....	....	10 58 "
Hadley (Luzerne)	Railway.	....	....	....	11 13 "
Riverside		....	....	....	12 31 "
North Creek	Ar	....	....	....	12 54 p. m.
Fort Edward	Arrive	3 05 p. m.	7 10 p. m.	1 40 a. m.	10 35 a. m.
Glens Falls	Arrive	3 30 p. m.	7 35 p. m.	....	10 05 a. m.
Caldwell (Lake George)		....	8 10 "	....	11 15 "
Whitehall	Arrive	3 45 p. m.	8 00 p. m.	2 20 a. m.	11 20 a. m.
Rutland	Arrive	4 15 p. m.	9 00 p. m.	....	12 20 p. m.
Crown Point	Arrive	5 10 p. m.	....	3 31 a. m.	....
Port Henry		5 25 "	....	3 48 "	....
Westport		5 50 "	....	4 12 "	....
Essex		6 12 "	....	4 30 "	....
Port Kent		6 55 "	....	5 10 "	....
Plattsburgh		7 20 "	....	5 35 "	....
Loon Lake House	Chateaugay R. R.	Ar	....	*9 56 a. m.	....
Paul Smith's		....	....	10 47 "	....
Saranac Lake		....	....	11 35 "	....
Rouse's Point	Arrive	8 30 p. m.	....	*6 35 a. m.	....
Montreal		10 25 "	....	8 25 "	....
Rouse's Point	Lv	....	....	7 10 a. m.	....
Moira	Northern	....	....	9 35 "	....
Paul Smith's	Adirondack	Ar	....	11 35 "	....

No. 23.—Drawing-Room Cars New York to Albany. Drawing-Room Cars Albany to Montreal. **No. 25.**—Drawing-Room Cars New York to Troy. **No. 29.** Sleeping Cars New York to Saratoga, Plattsburgh and Montreal daily. **No. 37.**—Sleeping Cars New York to Albany.

NIAGARA FALLS.

STATIONS.	No. 3. Chicago Express.	No. 5. Fast Express.	No. 9. Night Express.
N.Y. (G.C.St'n)	Lv	†10.30 a.m	*6.00 p.m	*10.00 p.m
(138th St.St'n)	10.41 "	6.09 "	10.10 "
Poughkeepsie	12.41 p.m	8.05 "	12.38 a.m
Albany	3.00 "	10.00 "	2.55 "
Utica	5.45 "	12.30 a.m	5.57 "
Rome	6.08 "	....	6.22 "
Syracuse	7.10 "	2.10 a.m	8.00 "
Rochester	9.55 "	4.20 "	10.85 "
Buffalo	Arrive	12.15 a.m	6.15 "	1.00 p.m
Suspension Bridge	12.50 "	7.28 "	1.30 "
Niagara Falls	Ar	12.40 "	7.20 "	1.40 "

No. 3 runs daily, except Sunday. Drawing-Room Car New York to Syracuse. Sleeping Car Syracuse to Niagara Falls. **No. 5** runs daily, including Sunday. Drawing-Room Car New York to Albany. Dining Car New York to Albany. Sleeping Cars New York to Niagara Falls. **No. 9** runs daily, including Sunday. Sleeping Cars New York to Niagara Falls.

NIAGARA RIVER ROUTE.
Connecting train leaves Niagara Falls for Lewiston, to connect with steamer for Toronto, during season of navigation.

CAYUGA, GENEVA, CLIFTON SPRINGS & CANANDAIGUA.

STATIONS.	No. 3. Chicago Express.	No. 29. Canandaigua Exp.	No. 9. Pacific Express.	No. 37. Night Express.
N.Y. (G.C.St'n)	Lv	†10.30 a.m	*6.30 p.m	*10.00 p.m	†12.00 n'ht
(138th St.St'n)	10.41 "	6.40 "	10.10 "	....
Syracuse	Arrive	7.15 p.m	4.35 a.m	7.40 a.m	1.30 p.m
Syracuse	Leave	*7.15 "	*6.00 "	*9.50 "	*2.05 "
Auburn	Arrive	8.50 "	6.55 "	10.40 "	3.15 "
Cayuga	9.20 "	7.20 "	11.15 "	3.42 "
Seneca Falls	9.35 "	7.33 "	11.30 "	3.52 "
Geneva	10.05 "	7.55 "	11.55 "	4.15 "
Clifton Springs	10.35 "	8.31 "	12.32 p.m	4.45 "
Canandaigua	11.00 "	9.05 "	1.15 "	5.12 "

No. 3 runs daily, except Sunday. Drawing-Room Cars New York to Canandaigua. **No. 29** runs daily. Sleeping Car New York to Canandaigua, daily, except Sunday. **No. 9** runs daily, including Sunday. Sleeping Cars New York to Canandaigua on Sundays only. **No. 37** runs daily, except Sunday. Sleeping Cars New York to Albany.

NEW YORK CENTRAL & HUDSON RIVER R. R.—Continued.

TRENTON FALLS, CLAYTON, CAPE VINCENT, OSWEGO, THOUSAND ISLANDS AND THE ADIRONDACKS, Via Rome, Watertown & Ogdensburgh R. R.

STATIONS.	No. 1. Limited.	No. 3. Chicago Express.	No. 9. Night Express.	No. 37. Albany Express.
N.Y.(G.C.St'n)..[Lv	*9.50 a.m	†10.30 a.m	*10.00 p.m	†2.00 p'ht
" (138th St. St'n)		10.41 "	10.10 "	
Poughkeepsie		12.14 p.m	12.26 a.m	3.00 a.m
Albany	1.15 p.m	3.00 "	2.55 "	*7.15 "
Utica......[Arrive		5.45 "	5.57 "	10.55 "
Rome		6.08 "	6.22 "	11.28 "
Syracuse	4.52 p.m	7.15 "	7.10 "	1.00 p.m
Utica.....[Leave		*5.50 p.m	*6.35 a.m	*1.00 p.m
Trenton Falls...[Ar				
Carthage		8.50 p.m	9.35 a.m	4.00 p.m
Watertown..[Arrive		9.35 p.m	10.10 a.m	4.40 p.m
Philadelphia [Arrive			10.15 a.m	4.40 p.m
Rome......[Leave		†6.15 p.m	†6.35 a.m	†2.50 p.m
Watertown..[Arrive		9.10 "	9.30 "	4.00 "
Philadelphia		9.55 "	10.15 "	4.40 "
Watertown....[Leave				*4.00 p.m
Sackett's Harb'r.[Ar				5.20 "
Watertown...[Leave			10.15 a.m	4.10 p.m
Cape Vincent....[Ar			11.15 "	5.00 "
Clayton......[Arrive			*11.15 a.m	*5.25 p.m
Philadelphia.[Leave			10.15 a.m	*4.40 p.m
Morristown			11.38 a.m	6.00 "
Ogdensburgh....[Ar			12.25 p.m	6.30 "
Philadelphia.[Leave		*9.55 p.m	10.15 a.m	4.40 p.m
DeKalb Junction		11.15 "	11.35 "	5.50 "
Ogdensburgh			12.00 n'n	6.40 "
Norwood		12.15 a.m	12.35 p.m	6.45 "
Paul Smith's [Arrive				
Massena Springs [Ar			*1.00 p.m	7.15 p.m
Syracuse.....[Leave	*5.25 p.m	†7.45 p.m	†7.50 a.m	†1.40 p.m
Oswego....[Arrive	6.35 "	9.05 "	9.05 "	3.05 "

Connecting Steamers leave Cape Vincent and Clayton for 1,000 Islands and Alexandria Bay during season of navigation. **No. 1.**—Drawing-Car New York to Syracuse. Dining Car New York to Syracuse. Buffet Smoking Car New York to Syracuse. **No. 3.**—Drawing-Room Car New York to Utica, Rome and Syracuse. **No. 9.** Sleeping Car New York to Watertown, via Utica, daily except Saturday. Sleeping Car New York to Rome and Syracuse. **No. 37.**—Sleeping Car New York to Albany.

☞ *Are you going to the theatre to-night? If so, select your seat from our diagrams, and avoid posts.*

DETROIT, JACKSON AND CHICAGO. Via Michigan Central R. R.

STATIONS.	No. 3. Chicago Express.	No. 5. Fast West. Ex.	No. 9. Night Express.
New York (G.C. Station)..Lv	*10.30 a.m	*6.60 p.m	*10.00 p.m
" (138th St. Station).. "	10.41 "	6.09 "	10.10 "
Buffalo (Eastern Time)...Ar	12.15 "	6.15 "	1.00 "
Buffalo (Central Time)....Lv	*11.30 p.m	*5.35 a.m	*12.30 p.m
Niagara Falls	12.44 a.m	6.44 "	1.34 "
Falls View.......[Arrive		6.46 "	1.38 "
Welland	1.08 a.m	7.14 "	2.05 "
St. Thomas	1.20 "	9.55 "	11.35 "
Windsor	7.35 "	12.40 p.m	9.05 "
Detroit	8.05 "	1.05 "	9.40 "
Detroit, via M. C. R. R....Lv	*8.35 a.m	*6.40 p.m	*11.00 p.m
Lapeer......[Arrive	11.00 "	9.01 "	2.50 a.m
Vassar	12.01 p.m	9.56 "	3.50 "
East Saginaw......[Arrive	†2.35 p.m	†10.40 p.m	*5.05 a.m
Bay City	*1.25 p.m	*10.40 p.m	6.15 a.m
Mackinaw City....[Arrive	*9.05 p.m	*6.30 a.m	
Detroit......[Leave	*9.10 a.m	*1.20 p.m	*10.15 p.m
Wayne Junction..[Arrive	9.50 "		10.55 "
Ypsilanti	10.17 "	2.12 p.m	11.18 "
Ann Arbor	10.35 "	2.24 "	11.35 "
Jackson	11.42 "	3.25 "	12.49 a.m
Grand Rapids....[Arrive	†3.15 p.m	†10.45 p.m	*6.00 a.m
Albion.......[Arrive	*12.14 p.m	*4.00 p.m	*4.30 a.m
Marshall	12.35 "	4.18 "	1.50 "
Battle Creek	1.16 "	4.38 "	2.15 "
Kalamazoo	1.55 "	5.15 "	3.07 "
Niles	3.30 "	6.27 "	4.32 "
New Buffalo	4.07 "		
Michigan City	4.32 "	7.26 p.m	5.40 a.m
Lake	5.13 "		
Kensington	5.55 "	8.50 p.m	7.00 a.m
Hyde Park	6.18 "	9.13 "	7.21 "
Chicago......[Arrive	6.40 p.m	9.30 p.m	7.45 "

Central time is one hour slower than Eastern time.

No. 3 runs daily, except Sunday, but Saturday train runs to Detroit only. Drawing-Room Cars New York to Syracuse. Drawing-Room Cars New York to Rochester. Sleeping Car Syracuse to Detroit and Chicago. Drawing-Room Cars Detroit to Bay City and Mackinaw. Drawing-Room Cars Detroit to Chicago. **No. 5** runs every day. Drawing-Room Car New York to Albany. Vestibuled Sleeping Car New York to Buffalo. Vestibuled Sleeping Car New York to Detroit. Vestibuled Sleeping Car New York to Chicago. Drawing-Room Cars Detroit to Grand Rapids. Dining Car New York to Albany. Dining Car Buffalo to St. Thomas. Dining Car Kalamazoo to Chicago. **No. 9** runs every day. Sleeping Cars New York to Detroit and Chicago. Sleeping Cars Detroit to Grand Rapids and Bay City. Dining Car Rochester to Detroit.

CLEVELAND, TOLEDO AND CHICAGO, Via Lake Shore Route.

STATIONS.	No. 1. Vestibule Limited.	No. 3. Chicago Express.	No. 5. Fast Western Express.	No. 11. Special Mail Limited.	No. 9. Night Express.
New York (Grand Central Station).......Leave	*9.50 a.m.	†10.30 a.m.	*6.00 p.m.	*9.00 p.m.	*10.00 p.m.
" (138th Street)		10.41 "	6.09 "		10.10 "
Buffalo (Eastern Time)	8.35 p.m.	12.15 "	6.15 a.m.	9.35 a.m.	1.00 "
Buffalo (C'en. Time 1 hour slower than E. Time).Leave	*7.45 p.m.	*11.45 p.m.	*5.40 a.m.	*8.45 a.m.	*12.30 p.m.
Dunkirk......[Arrive		12.56 a.m.	6.48 "	9.41 "	1.46 "
Brocton			7.00 "		2.03 "
Erie	9.55 p.m.	2.26 a.m.	8.05 "	10.56 a.m.	3.15 "
Girard					3.19 "
Ashtabula		3.46 a.m.	9.14 a.m.	12.01 p.m.	4.35 "
Painesville		4.31 "	9.57 "		5.21 "
Cleveland......[Arrive	12.15 a.m.	5.30 "	10.50 "	1.25 p.m.	6.25 "
Cleveland......[Leave	*12.15 a.m.	*5.45 a.m.	*10.57 a.m.		*6.50 p.m.
Elyria......[Arrive		6.41 "	11.41 "		7.32 "
Sandusky		7.52 "	12.15 p.m.		
Clyde		8.22 "			9.38 a.m.
Fremont		8.40 "			9.55 "
Toledo......[Arrive	3.25 a.m.	9.40 "	2.10 p.m.		10.55 "
Toledo......[Leave	3.25 a.m.	10.00 a.m.	2.20 p.m.		11.05 p.m.
Butler......[Arrive		12.23 p.m.	4.10 "		1.37 a.m.
Kendallville		1.17 "	4.44 "		2.17 "
Goshen		2.24 "	5.38 "		3.20 "
Elkhart	6.15 a.m.	2.45 "	5.55 "		3.40 "
South Bend		3.31 "	6.39 "		4.16 "
La Porte		4.25 "	7.20 "		5.10 "
Otis		4.47 "			5.31 "
Chicago......[Arrive	9.50 a.m.	6.45 "	9.30 p.m.		7.35 "

No. 1 runs every day. Vestibuled Drawing-Room Cars New York to Albany and Buffalo. Vestibuled Buffet Smoking Car New York to Chicago. Vestibuled Sleeping Cars New York to Chicago. Vestibuled Dining Car New York to Buffalo. Vestibuled Dining Car Elkhart to Chicago. **No. 3** runs daily, except Sunday, but Saturday train does not run beyond Cleveland. Drawing-Room Car New York to Syracuse. Sleeping Cars Syracuse to Cleveland, Toledo and Chicago. **No. 5** runs every day. Drawing-Room Car New York to Albany. Vestibuled Sleeping Cars New York to Cleveland, Toledo and Chicago. Vestibuled Dining Car New York to Albany. Dining Car Buffalo to Cleveland. **No. 11** runs every day. Sleeping Car New York to Cleveland. **No. 9** runs every day. Sleeping Cars New York to Cleveland, Toledo and Chicago.

NEW YORK CENTRAL & HUDSON RIVER R. R.—Continued.
GREEN MOUNTAIN RESORTS, BURLINGTON AND MONTREAL, FITCHBURG AND CENTRAL VERMONT RAILROADS.

STATIONS.		No. 23. Montreal Express.	No. 3. Chicago Express.	No. 25. Northern Express.	No. 27. Express.	No. 29. Montreal Express.	No. 37. Albany Express.
New York (G. C. Station)....Leave		8 00 a. m.	*10 30 a. m.	*11 30 a. m.	*3 58 p. m.	*6 30 p. m.	*12 00 night
" (138th St. Station)......		8 11 "	10 41 "	11 40 "		6 40 "	
East Albany................		12 43 "	2 25 p. m.	4 30 p. m.	8 55 "	11 20 "	5 50 a. m.
Albany....................		12 50 p. m.	2 30 "	4 35 "	9 00 "	11 25 "	5 55 "
Troy.................Arrive		12 57 "	2 55 "	4 50 "	9 55 "	11 40 "	6 55 "
Troy................[Lv		*1 20 p. m.	*3 15 p. m.	*5 00 p. m.	*10 30 p. m.	*11 50 p. m.	*6 00 a. m.
East Schaghticoke	[Ar	1 46 "		5 29 "	11 00 "		8 20 "
Valley Falls.....	Fitchburg	1 52 "	3 40 "	5 34 "	11 04 "		8 34 "
Johnsonville....	R. R.	1 58 "	3 46 "	5 41 "	11 11 "		8 41 "
Eagle Bridge....	"Hoosac	2 12 "	4 01 "	5 55 "	11 27 "		8 58 "
White Creek.....	Tunnel	2 22 "		6 24 "		1 03 a. m.	9 25 "
Petersburg Junc.	Route."	2 43 p. m.	4 22 p. m.	6 25 p. m.	11 50 p. m.		10 00 "
Williamstown....		3 03 "	4 42 "	6 46 "	12 16 a. m.		10 06 "
North Adams.....		3 22 "		7 00 "	12 40 "		10 25 "
White Creek.....	[Lv	*2 42 p. m.		*6 24 p. m.		*1 03 a. m.	*9 25 a. m.
North Bennington	[Ar	2 46 "		6 28 "		1 06 "	9 29 "
Bennington......		3 05 "		6 38 "			9 45 "
Arlington........	Benning-	3 13 "		6 52 "		1 29 a. m.	9 51 "
Manchester......	ton & Rut-	3 34 "		7 12 "		1 48 "	10 15 "
Wallingford.....	land R'y.	4 22 "		8 04 "		2 24 "	11 00 "
Rutland..........	[Ar	4 45 "		8 25 "		2 40 "	11 20 "
Rutland..........[Leave		*5 10 p. m.				*2 40 a. m.	*2 15 p. m.
Proctor..........[Arrive		5 27 "				2 53 "	2 29 "
Brandon		5 52 "				3 13 "	2 54 "
Leicester Junction......		6 04 "				3 26 "	3 04 "
Salisbury		6 17 "				3 35 "	3 12 "
Middlebury......		6 32 "				3 47 "	3 26 "
Vergennes.......		7 03 "				4 15 "	3 54 "
Shelburne........		7 30 "				4 47 "	4 26 "
Burlington.......		7 55 "				5 00 "	4 40 "
Essex Junction..		8 28 "				5 30 "	5 05 "
Milton...........		8 52 "				5 40 "	5 40 "
St. Albans.......		9 15 "				6 05 "	6 05 "
Waterbury, for Stowe, Mt. Mansfield.		12 30 a. m.				8 15 a. m.	6 30 p. m.
Montpelier..........[Arrive		1 02 a. m.				9 15 a. m.	6 55 p. m.
Barre..............[Arrive						10 40 a. m.	8 05 p. m.
Williamstown......						11 30 "	
Ottawa.............[Arrive						*11 50 a. m.	
Rouse's Point......[Arrive						*7 10 a. m.	
Champlain.........						7 21 "	
Chateaugay........						8 53 "	
Malone............						9 20 "	
Moira.............						9 47 "	
Norwood...........						10 35 "	
Ogdensburgh.......						11 30 a. m.	
St. John's..........[Arrive		10 55 p. m.				*7 45 a. m.	7 45 p. m.
Montreal...........		11 45 "				8 35 "	8 40 "

No. 23.—Drawing-Room Car New York to East Albany. Passengers are transferred at that point to Drawing-Room Car running through to St. Albans. **No. 3.**—Drawing-Room Cars New York to Troy. **No. 25.**—Drawing-Room Cars New York to Troy. **No. 27.**—Drawing-Room Cars New York to Albany. **No. 29.**—Sleeping Cars New York to Montreal daily. **No. 37.**—Sleeping Cars New York to Albany.

FT. WAYNE, DECATUR AND ST. LOUIS, Via "Wabash."

STATIONS.	No. 3. Chicago Express.	No. 5. Fast St. Louis Express.	No. 9. Night Express.
N.Y.(G.C.St'n).[Lv	*10.30 a.m	*6.00 p.m	*10.00 p.m
" (138th St. St'n)	10.41 "	6.09 "	10.10 "
Buffalo E. Time [Ar	12.15 "	6.15 a.m	1.00 "
Suspension Bridge.	12.40 "	7.28 "	1.30 "
Buffalo C. Time [Lv	*11.10 p.m	*5.10 a.m	*1.00 p.m
Toledo.....[Arrive	9.55 a.m	2.10 p.m	11.15 "
Toledo.....[Leave	*10.20 a.m	*5.30 p.m	*12.10 a.m
Fort Wayne [Arrive	1.25 p.m	8.12 "	4.50 "
Peru.............	3.30 "	10.00 "	7.15 "
Lafayette........	4.52 "	11.35 "	9 15 "
Danville.........	6.35 "	1.20 a.m	11.30 "
Decatur...[Arrive	9.00 "	3.50 "	2.30 p.m
St. Louis..[Arrive		*7.15 a.m	*6.15 p.m
Susp. Bridge...[Lv	*12.50 a.m	7.45 a.m	2.00 p.m
Detroit....[Arrive	8.30 "	2.05 p.m	9.40 "
Detroit....[Leave	*9.00 a.m	2.00 p.m	9.50 p.m
Adrian............	10.57 "	3.35 "	11.36 "
Butler............	12.15 p.m	5.00 "	1.12 a.m
Chicago....[Arrive			10.15 m	7.15 "

No. 3 runs daily, except Sunday, but Saturday train does not run beyond Cleveland. Dining Car Cleveland to Toledo. Drawing-Room Cars New York to Syracuse and Rochester, Sleeping Cars Syracuse to Toledo. **No. 5** runs every day, Dining Car New York to Albany. Sleeping Cars New York to Toledo. **No. 9.**—Sleeping Cars New York to Toledo. Sleeping Car Buffalo to St. Louis. Drawing Room Car Syracuse to Cleveland.

HAMILTON, TORONTO, LONDON, DETROIT AND CHICAGO
Via Grand Trunk and Chicago & Grand Trunk Railroads.

STATIONS.	No. 3. Chicago Express.	No. 5. Fast Wes. Express.	No. 9. Night Express.
New York (G. C. Station). [Lv	*10.30 a.m	*6.00 p.m	*10.00 p.m
" (138th St. Station).	10.41 "	6.09 "	10.10 "
Suspension Bridge... [Arrive	12.40 "	7.28 a.m	1.30 "
Susp'n Bridge (E. Time). [Lv	*12.50 a.m	*7.45 a.m	*2.25 p.m
St. Catharines.......[Arrive	1.35 "	8.29 "	3.05 "
Hamilton.............[Arrive	2.30 "	9.30 "	4.00 "
Toronto..............[Arrive	*8.10 a.m	*11.30 a.m	*8.30 p.m
London...............[Arrive	5.10 a.m	*11.30 a.m	*6.50 p.m
Chatham..............[Arrive	7.20 a.m	1.30 p.m	8.50 p.m
Windsor..............	8.15 "	2.30 "	10.05 "
Detroit (Central Time)...[Ar	8.20 "	2.05 "	9.40 "
London (Central Time)....[Lv	5.30 a.m		7.10 p.m
Port Huron...........[Arrive			
Port Huron...........[Leave	7.15 a.m		7.55 p.m
Lansing..............[Arrive	10.20 "		11.53 "
Chicago (Central Time)...[Ar	6.25 p.m		8.10 a.m

No. 3 runs daily, except Sunday. Drawing-Room Cars New York to Rochester. Sleeping Car Rochester to Detroit. **No. 5** runs every day. Dining Car New York to Albany. Drawing-Room Car New York to Albany. Sleeping Car New York to Buffalo. **No. 9.**—Sleeping Car New York to Buffalo.

Kenny's Guide Map of New York City is official, and shows the exact location of all important places in the City.

NEW YORK CENTRAL & HUDSON RIVER R. R.—Continued.

COLUMBUS, DAYTON, CINCINNATI, INDIANAPOLIS & ST. LOUIS, Via "Bee Line."

STATIONS.	No. 1. Vestibule Limited.	No. 3. Day Express.	No. 5. Fast West. Ex.	No. 9. Night Express.
N.Y.(G.C.St'n)|Lv	*9.50a.m	*10.30a.m	*6.00p.m	*10.00p.m
" (138th St. St'n)	....	10.11 "	6.06 "	10.10 "
Buffalo E.Time|Ar	8.35p.m	12.15 "	6.15a.m	1.00 "
Buffalo C.Time|Lv	*7.45p.m	*11.15p.m	*5.40a.m	*1.00p.m
Cleveland |Arrive	12.15a.m	5.30a.m	10.50 "	6.55 "
Cleveland....Leave	*12.25a.m	*7.15a.m	10.51a.m	*7.30p.m
Grafton....|Arrive	1.23 "	8.10 "	11.45 "	8.32 "
Crestline........	2.55 "	10.17 "	1.10p.m	10.25 "
Galion...........	3.05 "	10.23 "	1.30 "	10.35 "
Delaware........	5.40 "	11.35 "	2.20 "	12.00p.m
Columbus..|Arrive	6.35a.m	12.15p.m	3.20 "	1.00a.m
Cleveland....Leave	*12.25a.m	*7.15a.m	*10.51a.m	*7.30p.m
Springfield.|Arrive	7.35 "	1.30p.m	4.10p.m	2.25a.m
Dayton..........	8.35 "	2.20 "	4.56 "	3.50 "
Cincinnati.|Arrive	10.05 "	4.25 "	6.55 "	6.35 "
Cleveland...Leave	*12.25a.m	*6.45a.m	*11.20a.m	*7.30p.m
Galion.....|Arrive	3.05 "	9.35 "	2.35p.m	10.35 "
Marion..........	4.05 "	10.28 "	3.25 "	11.28 "
Bellefontaine....	5.45 "	11.51 "	4.57 "	12.55a.m
Union City	8.15 "	1.55p.m	7.20 "	3.15 "
Muncie..........	9.45 "	3.07 "	8.43 "	4.32 "
Indianapolis.....	11.35 "	5.15 "	10.35 "	6.50 "
Terre Haute.....	2.00p.m	8.15 "	1.32a.m	10.38 "
Mattoon..........	3.40 "	10.30 "	3.05 "	12.30p.m
Panu.............	4.17 "	....	4.48 "	2.00 "
St. Louis..|Arrive	7.40 "	....	7.30 "	6.40 "

Central time is one hour slower than Eastern time.

No. 1 runs every day. Vestibuled Drawing-Room Car New York to Buffalo. Vestibuled Sleeping Car Buffalo to St. Louis. Vestibuled Sleeping Car New York to Cleveland. Vestibuled Sleeping Car Cleveland to Cincinnati. Vestibuled Dining Car New York to Buffalo. Vestibuled Buffet Smoking and Library Car New York to Cleveland. **No. 3** runs daily except Sunday, but Saturday train does not run beyond Cleveland. Drawing-Room Car New York to Syracuse. Drawing-Room Car New York to Rochester. Sleeping Cars Syracuse to Cleveland. **No. 5** runs every day. Sleeping Car New York to Cincinnati. Sleeping Car New York to Indianapolis and St. Louis. Dining Car New York to Albany. Dining Car Buffalo to Cleveland. **No. 9** runs every day. Sleeping Car New York to Buffalo. Sleeping Car Cleveland to Cincinnati. Sleeping Cars Cleveland to Columbus. Sleeping Cars Cleveland to Indianapolis.

DRAWING-ROOM & SLEEP'G CAR RATES

In effect on all trains except the New York, Chicago & St. Louis Limited; on the latter train a slight extra fare is charged.

Between NEW YORK and	Seat.	Berth.	Section.	Stateroom.
Albany or Troy......	$1 00	$1 25	$2 50	$5 00
Saratoga............	1 50	1 50	3 00	6 00
Lake George.........	1 75			
North Creek.........		2 00	4 00	7 00
Plattsburg...........	2 00	2 00	4 00	7 00
Burlington...........	2 00	2 00	4 00	7 00
Montreal............	2 00	2 00	4 00	7 00
Utica...............	1 50	1 50	3 00	
Clayton.............		2 00	4 00	7 00
Paul Smith's........		2 50	5 00	9 00
Richfield............	2 00			
Syracuse............	1 75	1 75	3 00	6 00
Rochester...........	2 00	2 00	4 00	7 00
Niagara Falls or Buffalo.	2 00	2 00	4 00	7 00
Detroit..............		3 50	7 00	12 00
Toledo..............		4 00	8 00	14 00
Cleveland...........		3 00	5 00	10 00
Chicago.............		5 00	10 00	18 00
Cincinnati...........		4 00	8 00	14 00
Indianapolis.........		5 00	10 00	18 00
Fort Wayne.........		4 00	8 00	14 00
St. Louis............		6 00	12 00	22 00

For Fares to every place in United States, see Index.

Kenny's Guide is issued weekly, on Mondays. Adapted to the Counting House or Home. Complete information as to Coupons, Elections, etc., Mails and Steamships.

Any information desired by the lady at home will be found in this Guide, and can be understood by all.

☞ Our Weekly Supplement contains all changes in time tables, etc.

ELEVATED RAILROADS.

Fare, 5 cents at all hours. Children under five years, free.

THIRD AVENUE LINE.

Between South Ferry and 129th St., trains run daily at intervals of 3 to 5 minutes, from 4.45 a.m. to 12 night; then every 15 minutes to 4.45 a.m.

Between City Hall and 129th St., trains run daily at intervals of 3 to 5 minutes, from 5.30 a.m. to 12.30 night; then every 15 minutes to 5.30 a.m.

On Grand Central Depot Branch, trains run daily every 3 to 5 minutes from 6 a.m. to 12 night.

On East 34th St. Ferry Branch, trains run daily every 3 to 5 minutes from 5.30 a.m. to 12 night.

Time between South Ferry and 129th St. 43 minutes ; between City Hall and 129th St. 38 minutes.

Stations.

South Ferry, Hanover Square, Fulton, Franklin Square, Chatham Square—change here for 2d Ave. Line; Canal, Grand, Houston, 9th, 14th, 18th, 23d, 28th, 34th—change here for E. 34th St. Ferry; 42d, change here for Grand Central Depot; 47th, 53d, 59th, 67th, 76th, 84th, 89th, 98th, 106th, 116th, 125th, 129th.

SECOND AVENUE LINE.

Between South Ferry and 129th St., trains run daily at intervals of 3 to 5 minutes, from 4.45 a.m. to 12 night. Through time, 43 minutes.

Stations.

South Ferry, Hanover Square, Fulton, Franklin Square, Chatham Square—change here for 3d Ave. Line; Canal, Grand, Rivington, 1st, 8th, 14th, 19th, 23d and 31st Ave., 34th—change here for 34th St. Ferry; 42d, 50th, 57th, 65th, 70th, 75th, 80th, 86th, 92d, 105th, 111th, 116th, 120th, 127th, 129th—connects here with suburban rapid transit trains to 170th St. and 3d Ave.

SIXTH AVENUE LINE.

Between South Ferry and 155th St. & 8th Avenue, trains run on week days at intervals of 2 to 5 minutes from 5.30 a.m. to 12 night, then every 20 minutes to 5.30 a.m. ; alternately to 58th St. & 6th Ave. and 155th St. & 8th Ave. Sunday trains run at intervals of 4 minutes from 6.30 a.m. to 12 night, then every 20 minutes.

Time from South Ferry to 58th St. is 28 minutes ; to 155th St., 52 minutes. Cross-town cars leave Grand Central Depot for 42d St. Station of this line, and for Weehawken Ferry, foot of W. 42d St.

Stations.

South Ferry, Battery Place, Rector, Cortlandt, Park Place, Chambers, Franklin, Grand, Bleecker, Sch. 4th, 18th, 23d, 28th, 33d, 42d, 50th, 58d, branch to 8th Ave., 58th, 59th—change here for 9th Ave. Line free of charge; 72d, 81st, 104th, 116th, 125th, 135th, 145th, 155th and 8th Ave—connects here with N. Y. & Northern R. R.

NINTH AVENUE LINE.

Between South Ferry and 59th St., trains run daily from 5.30 a.m. to 8 p.m., at intervals of 5 minutes. Through time, 26 minutes.

Stations.

South Ferry, Rector, Cortlandt, Barclay, Warren, Franklin, Desbrosses, Houston, Christopher, 14th, 23d, 30th, 34th, 42d, 50th, 59th—change here for 6th Ave. Line without extra charge.

NEW YORK, LAKE ERIE & WESTERN R. R.

Depot, foot of Chambers and West 23d Sts.

Ticket Offices—1, 317, 401, 711, 957 Broadway; 153 Bowery; foot of Chambers and West 23d Sts., N. Y.; 331 Fulton St., 107 Broadway, Brooklyn.

Excursion tickets are good for 30 days from day of issue.

MAIN LINE.

M.	Stations.	Fare. Single, Ex.	M.	Stations.	Fare. Single, Ex.	M.	Stations.	Fare. Single, Ex.	M.	Stations.	Fare. Single, Ex.	M.	Stations.	Fare. Single, Ex.
	Jersey City		15	Lake View	50c 70c	28	Ramsey's	85c–$1.15	44	Arden	$1.08 $1.85	67	Main St.	
6	Secaucus	15c—25c	17	Paterson	50c 70c	30	Mahwah	95c $1.25	46	Newburg Junc.		67	Middletown	1.68 2.75
10	Rutherford	30c–40c	18	River St.	55c–75c	32	Suffern	$1.00–$1.35	47	Turner's	$1.08 $1.95	71	Howell's	$1.78 $2.90
11	Carlton Hill	35c–50c	19	Hawthorne	60c–85c	33	Hillburn	$1.05–$1.40	50	Monroe	$1.18 $2.05	76	Otisville	$1.93 $3.10
11	Passaic Bdg.	35c—55c	22	Ridgewood	70c–95c	34	Ramapo	$1.05 $1.40	52	Oxford	$1.23 $2.15	80	Guymard	$2.08 $3.30
12	Prospect St.			Undercliff.		35	Sterlington	1.08 $1.45	54	Greycourt	$1.28 $2.25	88	P't Jervis	$2.33 $3.60
13	Passaic	40c 55c	24	Hohokus	75c–$1.00	36	Sloatsburg	1.08 $1.45	55	Chester	$1.33 $2.30			
13	Harrison St., Passaic		25	Waldwick	80c $1.05	38	Tuxedo	$1.08 $1.60	60	Goshen	$1.43 $2.50			
13	Clifton	45c 65c	26	Allendale	80c $1.10	42	Southfields	1.08 $1.75	64	Hampton	$1.58 $2.60			

To **Passaic, Paterson, Suffern, Turners, Middletown** and **Port Jervis,** stopping at intermediate stations.

Leave foot of Chambers St. (Leave foot of W. 23d St. 5 to 15 minutes earlier). *Trains marked * leave W. 23d St. at 3.55 a.m.*

For **Passaic** and **Paterson** (see also Newark Branch below), 1.00, *4.45, 6.10, 7.00, 7.50, 9.30, 10.30 a. m., 12, 1.00, 1.45, 3.00, †3.30, 3.40, †4.00, 4.10, †4.30, 4.40, 5.00, 5.10, 5.30, 5.50, 6.10, 6.30, 7.00, 7.30, 8.30, 9.00, 10.30 p. m., 12 night. Sundays, *4.45, 8.30, 10.30 a. m., 12, 1.45, 3.00, 4.00, 5.00, 6.30, 7.30, 8.30, 9.00, 10.30 p. m., 12 night. Time to Passaic about 35 minutes; to Paterson 40 to 50 minutes. *Trains marked † are express trains and make no stops between Jersey City and Paterson.*

For **Suffern,** 4.00, *4.45, 7.50, 9.30, 10.30 a. m., 1.00, 3.00, 3.30, 4.00, 5.00, 5.30, 6.10, 6.30, 7.00, 9.00, 10.30 p. m., 12 night. Sundays, *4.45, 8.30, 10.30 a. m., 1.45, 4.00, 6.30 p. m., 12 night. Time to Suffern, about 1 hour, 10 minutes.

For **Turners,** *4.45, 7.50, 9.00, 10.30 a. m., 1.00, 3.30, 4.30, 5.00, 5.30, 7.00, 8.30 p. m. Sundays, *4.45, 8.40, 10.30 a. m., 5.00, 6.30, 8.30 p. m. Time to Turners, 2 to 2½ hours.

For **Middletown,** *4.45, 7.50, 9.00, 10.30 a. m., 3.30, 4.30, 5.00, 5.30, 7.00, 8.30 p. m. Sundays, *4.45, 8.30 a. m., 5.00, 6.30, 8.30 p. m. Time to Middletown about 2½ hours.

For **Port Jervis,** *4.45, 7.50, 9.00, 10.30 a. m., 3.30, 4.30, 5.00, 7.00, 8.30 p. m. Sundays, *4.45, 8.30 a. m., 5.00, 6.30, 8.30 p. m. Time to Port Jervis about 3¾ hours.

Trains to New York.

Stopping at intermediate stations.

Leave **Port Jervis,** 4.50, 6.30, 7.42, 9.25 a. m., 12.15, 2.18, 4.11, 8.15 p. m. Sundays, 1.50, 9.25 a. m., 12.15, 4.35, 8.15 p. m. Due in New York in about 3¾ hours.

Leave **Middletown,** 5.32, 6.00, 7.10, 8.19, 10.01 a. m., 12.50, 2.55, 4.56, 8.55 p. m. Sundays, 5.32, 10.01 a. m., 12.50, 5.21, 8.55 p. m. Due in New York in about 2½ hours.

Leave **Turners,** 6.44, 7.57, 10.41 a. m., 1.50, 3.36, 4.27, 5.43, 9.35 p. m. Sundays, 10.41 a. m., 1.00, 1.50, 6.11, 9.35 p. m. Due in New York in 2 to 2½ hours.

Leave **Suffern,** 4.58, 6.25, 6.55, 7.18, 7.36, 7.59, 8.45, 9.27, 10.28 a. m., 12.30, 2.21, 4.57, 6.13, 10.45 p. m. Sundays, 7.17, 8.41 a. m., 1.30, 2.21, 6.50, 10.45 p. m. Due in New York in about 1¼ hours.

Leave **Paterson,** 5.20, 5.58, 6.40, 6.58, 7.09, 7.20, 7.46, 7.57, 8.10, 8.32, 8.48, 9.20, 9.55, 10.00, 11.02, 11.28 a. m., 12.02, 1.03, 2.05, 2.57, 3.02, 4.00, 4.26, 5.04, 5.30, 6.05, 6.55, 7.40, 9.05, 10.05, 10.26, 11.20 p. m. Sundays, 7.09, 7.15, 7.50, 9.19, 10.33, 11.28 a. m., 2.05, 2.57, 3.02, 4.00, 6.40, 7.35, 9.05, 10.26, 11.20 p. m. (Leave **Passaic,** 8 minutes later). Due in New York about 40 minutes after leaving Paterson.

NEWARK BRANCH.

§ *Leave West 23d Street, 4.55 a. m.*

M.	Stations.	Fare. Single, Ex.	M.	Stations.	Fare. Single, Ex.	M.	Stations.	Fare. Single, Ex.	M.	Stations.	Fare. Single, Ex.	M.	Stations.	Fare. Single, Ex.
	Jersey City.		8	Grant Ave.	15c–25c	11	Belleville	20c—30c	14	Franklin	35c–50c	20	Paterson	50c—70c
3	West End.		9	Newark	15c–25c	12	Essex	25c 40c	15	Peru	40c—60c			
5	Pontiac.		10	Riverside	20c–25c	13	Avondale	30c–45c	17	Athenia	45c—65c			
8	Harrison	15c 25c	10	Woodside	20c—25c	13	Nutley	35c 50c	19	S. Paterson	50c 70c			

Leave foot of Chambers St. (Leave foot of West 23d St. 5 to 10 minutes earlier), for **Newark** and **Paterson,** and intermediate stations, §5.45, 6.50, 8.00, 8.30, 10.00, 11.30 a. m., 2.00, 3.30, 4.20, 4.50, 5.20, 5.50, 6.20, 7.30, 10.00 p. m., 12.00 night. Sundays, 9.00 a. m., 3.30, 6.30, 10.00 p. m. Due at Newark in 35 minutes; Paterson, 1 hour, 5 minutes.

Leave **Paterson** for New York, 5.50, 6.33, 6.58, 7.30, 7.57, 9.25, 10.07, 11.30 a. m., 1.30, 2.25, 3.27, 4.55, 5.57, 7.35, 10.07 p. m. Sundays, 8.35 a. m., 1.34, 5.30, 10.07 p. m.

Leave **Newark** for New York, 6.17, 7.00, 7.26, 7.58, 8.29, 9.55, 10.36 a. m., 12.03, 1.53, 2.56, 3.56, 5.26, 6.26, 8.06, 10.34 p. m. Sundays, 9.08 a. m., 2.07, 6.05, 10.34 p. m.

BERGEN COUNTY R. R.

Stations.	Miles.	M.	Stations.	Fare. Single, Ex.	Stations.	Miles.	M.	Stations.	Fare. Single, Ex.	M.	Stations.	Fare. Single, Ex.
Saddle River	12	12	Garfield	40c–55c	Dundee	14	18	Fair Lawn	55c–75c	20	Ridgewood	70c–95c
Rutherford	10		Spring Tank		Warren Point	16	19	Paramus	65c–85c			

Leave foot of Chambers St. (Leave foot of West 23d St. 5 minutes earlier), for **Ridgewood,** stopping at intermediate stations, 8.30 a. m., 5.20, 6.00 p. m. Time to Ridgewood, 1 hour.

Leave **Ridgewood,** 7.15, 8.18 a. m. (Dundee, 5.15 p. m.), Garfield, 7.20, 8.32 a. m., 5.25 p. m. Due in New York, 8.07, 9.07 a. m., 6.07 p. m.

HONESDALE BRANCH.

M.	Stations.	Fare—Single, Ex.	M.	Stations.	Fare—Single, Ex.	M.	Stations.	Fare—Single, Ex.
111	Lackawaxen	$2.98—$5.00	123	Kimbles	$3.38—$5.35	131	White Mills	$3.68—$5.60
115	Rowlands	$3.13 $5.15	127	Hawley	$3.48—$5.50	135	Honesdale	$3.83—$5.75
119	Glen Eyre	$3.28—$5.25	127	West Hawley	$3.53—$5.50			

Leave foot of Chambers St. (Leave foot of West 23d St. 5 minutes earlier), for **Honesdale** and intermediate stations, 9.00 a. m., 3.30, 8.30 p. m. Due at Honesdale, 2.15, 8.30 p. m., 10.15 a. m.

Leave **Honesdale** for New York, 7.10, 10.40 a. m., 5.55 p. m. Leave **Lackawaxen,** 8.29 a. m., 1.11, 7.17 p. m. Due in New York, 12.07, 5.07, 11.07 p. m.

JEFFERSON BRANCH.

Stations.	Miles.	Stations.	Miles.	Stations.	Miles.	Stations.	Miles.	Stations.	Miles.
Susquehanna.		Brandts	1	Thompson	14	Herrick Centre	26	Carbondale	39
Lanesboro	2	Stevens Point	5	Ararat Summit	19	Uniondale	28		
Jefferson Junction	4	Starrucca	10	Cotrill's Switch	22	Forest City	33		

Leave foot of Chambers St. (Leave foot of West 23d St. 5 minutes earlier), for **Carbondale** and intermediate stations, 9.00 a. m., 8.30 p. m. Due at Carbondale, 7.30 p. m., 9.35 a. m.

Leave **Carbondale** for New York, 10.30 a. m., 5.55 p. m. Due at 11.07 p. m., 7.57 a. m.

☞ **For Express Trains to the West, see second page following this.**

FOR FARES TO EVERY PLACE IN THE UNITED STATES, SEE INDEX.

NEW YORK, LAKE ERIE AND WESTERN R. R.—Continued.

MIDDLETOWN AND CRAWFORD BRANCH.

M.	Stations.	Fare-Single, Ex.
67	Middletown.	
70	Crawford Junc.	$1.78-$2.90
72	Circleville	$1.84-$3.00
74	Bullville	$1.91 $3.10
77	Thompson Ridge	$1.98-$3.20
79	Van Keurens	$2.07-$3.25
80	Pine Bush	$2.08-$3.30

Leave foot of Chambers St. (West 23d St. 5 minutes earlier), for **Pine Bush** and intermediate stations, 9.00 a. m., 4.30 p. m. Sundays, 8.30 a. m. Due at Pine Bush, 12.38, 7.50 p. m. Sundays, 12.38 p. m.

Leave **Pine Bush** for New York, 7.24 a. m., 5.15 p. m. Sundays, 8.50 a. m., 5.15 p. m. Due in New York, 10.37 a. m., 11.07 p. m. Sundays, 12.07 noon, 11.07 p. m.

MONTGOMERY BRANCH.

M.	Stations.	Fare—Single & Exc.
60	Goshen.	
62	Kipps	$1.52-$2.55
65	Campbell Hall	$1.56-$2.55
67	Neely Town	$1.67-$2.55
69	Beaver Dam	$1.70-$2.55
70	Montgomery	$1.71—$2.80

Leave foot of Chambers St. (Leave foot of West 23d St. 5 minutes earlier), for **Montgomery** and intermediate stations, 9.00 a. m., 3.30, 4.30 p. m. Sundays, 8.30 a. m. Time to Montgomery, 2½ hours.

Leave **Montgomery,** 8.06 a. m., 4.23, 6.06, 7.20 p. m. Sundays, 4 55, 7.20 p. m. Due in New York, 10.27 a. m., 7.25, 11.07 p. m. Sundays, 8.37, 11.07 p. m.

NEWBURG SHORT CUT.

M.	Stations.	Fare-Single, Ex.
46	Newburg Junc.	
49	Central Valley	$1.08-$2.00
50	Highland Mills	$1.08 $2.00
51	Woodbury	$1.08 $2.00
51	Houghton Farm	$1.08-$2.00
55	Mountainville	$1.08 $2.00
57	Cornwall	$1.08 $2.00
59	Vail's Gate Junc.	$1.16—$2.25
61	New Windsor	$1.16-$2.25
62	West Newburg.	
64	Newburg	$1.16-$2.25

Leave foot of Chambers St. (Leave foot of West 23d St. 5 to 10 minutes earlier), for **Cornwall** and **Newburg,** stopping at intermediate stations, 7.50, 9.00 a. m., 3.30, 4.00, 4.30, 5.00 p. m. Sundays, 8.30 a. m., 1.45, 5.00 p. m. Due at Cornwall in 2¼ hours, due at Newburg in 2½ hours.

Leave **Newburg** for New York and intermediate stations, 5.50, 7.40, 8.15 a. m., 2.42, 3.50, 5.38 p. m. Sundays, 7.26, 9.45 a. m., 5.05 p. m. Due in New York, 8.27, 9.37, 10.37 a. m., 5.07, 7.25, 11.07 p. m. Sundays, 10.07 a. m., 12.07, 8.37 p. m.

PINE ISLAND BRANCH.

M.	Stations.	Fare—Single & Exc.
60	Goshen.	
64	Orange Farm	$1.53-$2.65
66	Florida	$1.61-$2.80
68	Big Island	$1.68 $2.85
72	Pine Island	$1.78 $3.00

Leave foot of Chambers St. (Leave foot of West 23d St. 5 minutes earlier), for **Pine Island** and intermediate stations, 9.00 a. m., 5.30 p. m. Sundays, 8.30 a. m., 5.30 p. m. Due at Pine Island, 12.28, 8.30 p. m. Sundays, 12.28, 8.30 p. m.

Leave **Pine Island** for New York, 6.40 a. m., 4.45 p. m. Sundays, 9.35 a. m., 4.45 p. m. Due in New York, 9.27 a. m., 11.07 p. m. Sundays, 12.07 noon, 11.07 p. m.

THROUGH COACH ARRANGEMENT.—Trains to the West.

For Time Table see following page.

Train 1.—Every day (Sundays, 8.30 a.m.). To Buffalo.—Smoking and Day Coaches and Pullman Buffet Drawing-Room Coaches.

Train 5.—Every day. To Chicago.—Smoking Coach, Day Coach and Pullman Buffet Sleeping Coach. A Solid Pullman Train from New York, via Salamanca, Marion and the Chicago & Atlantic Railway. To Cleveland.—Pullman Buffet Sleeping Coach from New York. To St. Louis. Pullman Buffet Sleeping Coach from New York, via Salamanca, Cincinnati and the Ohio & Mississippi Railway. To Buffalo.—Smoking Coach and Day Coach from New York. To Suspension Bridge.—Pullman Buffet Sleeping Coach from New York via Buffalo.

Train 3.—Every day. To Chicago. Pullman Sleeping Coach, Smoking Coach and Day Coach from New York via the Chicago & Atlantic Railway and Salamanca. To Cleveland. Pullman Parlor Car from Buffalo. To Cincinnati.—Pullman Sleeping Coach from Youngstown. To Buffalo. Day Coach and Pullman Buffet Sleeping Coach from New York. To Rochester.—Pullman Buffet Sleeping Coach from New York.

Train 11.—Daily, except Sunday. To Hornellsville. Pullman Buffet Parlor Coach.

NEW YORK AND GREENWOOD LAKE RY.

From Erie Depot, Foot of Chambers and W. 23d St.

M.	Stations.	Fare Single and Exc.
...	Jersey City	20c-30c.
8	Arlington	20c 30c.
8½	Kearney	20c 30c.
9	North Newark	20c 30c.
9½	Orange Br.: Forest Hill	
10	Orange Br.: Silver Lake	25c 40c.
11	Orange Br.: Bloomfield Ave	28c 45c.
11½	Orange Br.: Watsessing Junc.	28c 45c.
11¾	Orange Br.: Prospect Street.	28c 45c.
12	Orange Br.: Brighton Ave	28c-45c.
12¾	Orange Br.: Washington St.	30c 50c.
13¼	Orange Br.: Llewellyn	30c 50c.
13½	Orange Br.: Orange (Main St.)	30c 50c.
10	Soho	28c 45c.
11½	Bloomfield	30c-50c.
12½	Chestnut Hill.	32c 55c.
13	Montclair	35c 60c.
14	Watchung	40c 65c.
15	Upper Montclair	45c 70c.
16	Montclair Heights	50c 75c.
17½	Great Notch	55c 80c.
18½	Cedar Grove	60c 80c.
20	Little Falls	65c 80c.
20¾	Singac	68c 90c.
23	Mountain View	70c 90c.
23½	Wayne	75c $1 00
25	Pequannock	80c 1 10
26½	Pompton Plains	85c 1 20
28	Riverdale	90c 1 30
28¾	Pompton	95c 1 40
29	Pompton Junction	$1 00 $1 50
32	Wanaque	1 10- 1 60
32½	Midvale	1 15- 1 60
35½	Ringwood Junction	1 25- 1 60
36½	Erskine	1 25 1 60
38	Ringwood	1 30- 1 60
40	Monks	1 30 1 75
40½	Hewitt	1 40 1 75
43	Cooper (Fuller House)	1 40- 1 75
45	Sterling Forest	1 40- 1 75
...	Greenwood Lake	1 50- 1 85
46	Warwick Woodlands	1 50- 1 85
47	Club House	
48	Brandon House	
49	Windermere House	

Leave **Foot of Chambers St.** (W. 23d St. 5 to 15 minutes earlier), for **Orange** (Main St.) and intermediate stations, 6 00, 8.50, 10 50 a. m., 12 00, 1 15, 3 10, 3 40, 4 30, 5 00, 5 30, 6 00, 6 20, 7 00, 8 30, 11 30 p. m. Sundays, 10 00 a. m., 1 30, 6 00, 9 30 p. m., due at Orange in 45 minutes.

For **Montclair Heights,** 6 00, 8 20, 9 00 a. m., 12 m., 1 45, 3 40, 4 30, 5 10, 5 40, 6 20, 7 00, 8 00, 10 00 p. m., 12 night. Sunday, 9 00 a. m., 8 00 p. m., due at Montclair Heights in 1 hour.

For **Little Falls,** 6 10, 8 20 a. m., 12 m., 3 40, 4 30, 5 10, 5 40, 6 20, 7 00 p. m., 12 00 night. Sundays, 9 00 a. m., 8 00 p. m., due at Little Falls in 1 hour, 10 minutes.

For **Pompton** and **Pompton Junc.,** 8 20 a. m., 3 40, 5 10, 5 40 p. m. Sundays, 9 00 a. m., due at Pompton in 1½ hours.

For **Ringwood,** 3 40 p. m., due at 6 08 p. m.

For **Cooper** (Greenwood Lake), 8 20 a. m., on Saturdays and Mondays 5 10 p. m. also, due at Greenwood Lake in 2¾ hours.

Trains For New York.

Leave **Cooper** (Greenwood Lake), stopping at intermediate Stations, 1 15 p. m., on Saturdays and Mondays, 6 45 a. m. also, due in New York 4 47 p. m., Saturdays and Mondays, 8 57 a. m. also.

Leave **Ringwood,** 5 50 a. m., due in New York 8 27 a. m.

Leave **Pompton Junction,** 5 52, 7 01, 7 30 a. m., 2 34 p. m. Sundays, 6 25 p. m., due in New York 7 27, 8 27, 8 57 a. m., 4 47 p. m. Sundays, 8 07 p. m.

Leave **Little Falls,** 5 10, 6 18, 6 55, 7 28, 7 58, 8 31, 10 04 a. m., 1 20, 3 14, 5 52 p. m. Sundays, 7 28 a. m., 6 54 p. m., due in New York in 1 hour.

Leave **Montclair Heights,** 5 21, 6 30, 7 07, 7 39, 8 09, 8 41, 10 15 a. m., 1 29, 3 09, 3 47, 6 10, 9 12, 11 16 p. m. Sundays, 7 39 a. m., 7 06 p. m., due in New York in 1 hour.

Leave **Orange** (Main St.), 5 23, 6 37, 7 07, 7 35, 7 57, 8 27, 9 09, 10 20 a. m., 12 25, 1 35, 3 12, 4 10, 5 50, 6 50, 10 25 p. m. Sundays, 8 45 a. m., 12 15, 4 45, 7 45 p. m., due in New York in 40 minutes.

NEW YORK, LAKE ERIE & WESTERN R. R.—Continued.

WESTWARD.

☞ Train 1 leaves New York at 8.30 a.m. on Sundays.

STATIONS.	Miles.	1 Ev'y Day.	11 Daily ex. Sun.	5 Ev'y Day.	29 Daily ex. Sun.	3 Ev'y Day.
		A.M.	A.M.	P.M.	P.M.	P.M.
23d Street........[Leave		*8.55	10.25	4.55	6.55	8.25
CHAMBERS ST.		9.00	10.30	5.00	7.00	8.30
Jersey City.............	1	9.20	10.43	5.18	7.15	8.50
		Noon	P.M.			Night.
Port Jervis......[Leave	88	12.25	2.05	8.06	p12.30	11.50
Lackawaxen...........	111	1.05	2.58	....	p1.33	12.30
Narrowsburg..........	128	1.24	3.15	....	p2.10	....
Susquehanna..........	193	3.34	a6.05	1.29	a6.05	3.05
Binghamton....[Arrive	215	4.11	6.56	12.06	6.46	3.45
Owego.................	237	4.45	7.51	12.35	7.29	4.30
Waverly...............	256	5.15	8.41	1.10	8.22	5.15
Elmira.................	274	5.41	9.24	1.39	9.00	5.46
Corning...............	291	6.18	10.08	2.17	9.49	6.27
Hornellsville..........	332	7.27	12.40	3.30	11.30	7.45
		P.M.	Night.	P.M.		A.M.
Portage........[Arrive	362	8.36	....	4.28	4.44	9.01
Attica.................	393	9.35	....	5.30	6.10	10.03
Buffalo................	423	10.30	....	6.25	7.15	11.00
Niagara Falls..........	443	12.11	....	7.11	....	12.56
Suspension Bridge.....	445	12.19	....	7.50	....	1.04
Olean............[Arrive	395	10.06	....	5.83	3.22	10.33
Carrollton.............	408	10.33	....	....	3.49	11.00
Salamanca.............	414	10.45	....	6.10	4.00	11.13
Roch.,B.R.&P.Ry...[Lv		5.40	....	....	....	7.45
Sal'a,B.R.&P.Ry...[Ar		9.45	....	....	....	11.20
Dunkirk.........[Arrive	460	P.M.	....	....	6.00	1.10
		P.M.		P.M.	P.M.	
Elmira..........[Leave	274	6.10	....	1.40	....	6.50
Corning...............	291	6.43	....	2.15	....	7.23
Bath..................	311	7.29	....	3.01	....	8.10
Avon............[Arrive	367	9.24	....	5.00	....	10.10
Caledonia........[Arrive	374	....	....	5.34	....	b10.33
Le Roy...............	381	....	....	5.48	....	b10.48
Batavia...............	391	....	....	6.09	....	b11.07
				P.M.		A.M.
Rochester.......[Arrive	385	10.05	....	5.55	....	p9.40
Buffalo..........[Leave		7.30	....	7.30	....	8.45
Jamestown......[Arrive		4.00	....	4.01	....	11.20
		P.M.		A.M.		A.M.
(Central Time.)						
Salamanca......[Leave	413	....	....	5.15	....	10.25
Jamestown......[Arrive	447	....	....	6.15	....	11.25
Corry.................	474	....	....	7.0	....	12.25
Meadville.............	516	....	....	8.15	....	2.10
Youngstown...........	571	....	....	11.00	....	4.15
Leavittsburg..........	578	....	....	10.20	....	5.05
Cleveland.............	626	....	....	12.50	....	6.55
Kent..................	665	....	....	11.20	....	6.25
Chicago, C. & A. R'y..	986	....	....	11.25	....	8.25
Springfield............	781	P.M.	....	5.11	....	2.25
Indianapolis,O.I.& W.	820	3.15	....	10.30	....	7 a m
Bloomington...........	1086	9.40	....	5.25	....	2.05
Peoria................	1132	11.40	....	7.20	....	4.10
Cincinnati,C.C.C.&T.	861	....	....	7.55	....	6 a m
St. Louis,O.&M.R'y.	1199	....	....	7.45	....	6.50
Grand Trunk R'y		P.M.		A.M.	Noon	
Buffalo........[Lv East'n	424	10.50	....	6.40	12.00	....
Hamilton..Time.|	487	2.30	....	9.30	4.10	....
Toronto.[Ar	525	8.10	....	11.30	5.30	....
Detroit...............	673	8.20	....	2.05	9.40	....
Chicago,C.& G.T.R'y.	975	6.25	....	P.M.	8.10	....
Chic'o,N.F.S.Line..[Ar		....	....	10.15	7.20	....
Mich. Cent. R. R.		P.M.		P.M.		P.M.
Buffalo..........[Leave	424	11.30	....	5.35	9.00	1.00
St. Thomas...........	554	4.25	....	10.00	1.10	5.50
Detroit..........[Arrive	674	8.05	....	1.05	5.20	9.40
Toledo................	734	10.15	....	4.15	9.30	11.52
East Saginaw.........	781	12.45	....	....	10.40	5.05
Jackson...............	770	11.12	....	3.25	10.50	12.40
Grand Rapids.........	844	8.15	....	10.15	6.00	6.00
Kalamazoo............	848	2.04	....	5.35	1.15	3.07
Chicago.........[Arrive	130	6.30	....	9.30	7.00	7.45
L. S. & M. S. R'y.		A.M.	A.M.	P.M.	P.M.	P.M.
Buffalo..........[Leave	424	5.40	1.00	7.45	7.51	11.45
Dunkirk...............	464	6.48	2.17	....	9.15	12.56
Erie...................	512	8.03	3.55	9.55	10.55	2.31
Ashtabula............	553	9.14	5.08	....	12.20	3.45
Cleveland.............	707	10.55	7.15	12.15	2.15	65.45
Toledo................	720	2.20	11.25	3.25	A.M.	b10.00
Elkhart...............	863	6.15	4.15	6.45	....	b8.05
Chicago.........[Arrive	960	9.30	7.50	9.30	....	b6.45
		P.M.		P.M.	A.M.	P.M.

EASTWARD.

☞ For "Fares to all Places," see Index.

STATIONS. (Central Time.)	12 Ev'y Day.	4 Ev'y Day.	10 Daily ex. Sun.	8 Ev'y Day.
Grand Trunk Ry.	P.M.			A.M.
Chicago, N.F.S. Line..[Lv	....	9.00	....	9.05
Chicago, C. & G. T. Ry....	3.25	....	....	8.15
Detroit....................	12.05	12.00	....	6.25
Toronto...................	3.55	11.00	....	12.30
Hamilton -E. Time	6.40	7.00	....	1.55
Buffalo................[Ar	9.20	9.35	....	1.50
Mich. Central R. R.	A.M.	P.M.		P.M.
Chicago.............[Leave	9.00	3.10	10.10	9.10
Kalamazoo.................	1.33	6.58	3.35	2.27
Grand Rapids..............	1.10	5.10	10.45	6.45
Jackson...................	1.15	8.19	6.15	4.50
East Saginaw..............	2.06	3.30	11.30	7.00
Toledo.....................	1.30	9.10 A.M.	7.50	6.00
Detroit....................	7.15	10.55	6.40	9.50 12.95
St. Thomas................	11.10	2.05	10.15	12.50 3.30
Buffalo...............[Arrive	3.35	6.15	2.30	1.15 6.05
L. S. & M. S. Ry.	A.M.	P.M.	P.M.	P.M.
Chicago.............[Leave	8.50	5.30	8.00	11.80
Elkhart...................	12.45	8.25	11.55	3 30
Toledo....................	5.30	11.50	7.60	4.25 10.10
Cleveland.................	10.00	2.55	11.50	8.50 3.00
Ashtabula.................	11.32	....	1.13	10.22 4.30
Erie.......................	12.50	5.18	2.18	11.57 5.41
Dunkirk...................	2.04	....	3.35	1.21 6.50
Buffalo...............[Arrive	3.30	7.40	4.50	2.50 8.15
	A.M.	A.M.	P.M.	P.M.
St. Louis, O. & M. R'y.|Leave	8 a m	....	....	....
Cincinnati, C. C. C.& I. R'y	10 p m	....	....	5.45
Peoria, O.I. & W. Ry.......	11.50	7.30	....	2.30
Bloomington, O.I. & W....	2.05	9.28	....	4.25
Indianapolis, O.I. & W.....	9.00	4.10	....	11.00
Springfield................	1.47	A.M.	....	8.35
Chicago, C. & A. Ry.......	8.10	....	....	2.30
Kent......................	9.25	....	....	2.25
Cleveland.................	8.30	....	....	10.50
Leavittsburg..............	10.35	....	....	3.28
Youngstown...............	11.10	....	....	2.40
Meadville..................	1.40	....	....	5.30
Corry.....................	3.05	....	....	6.35
Jamestown................	3.55	....	....	7.35
Salamanca...........[Arrive	4.55	....	....	8.35
	P.M.			A.M.
(Eastern Time.)				
Jamestown.........[Leave	5 30	....	....	9.15
Buffalo.............[Arrive	8.09	....	....	11.45
Rochester..........[Leave	7 00	....	....	9.45
Batavia...................	b1.15	....	....	b9.25
Le Roy...................	b1.37	....	....	b9.45
Caledonia.................	b1.52	....	....	b10.00
Avon......................	7.33	....	....	10.26
Bath......................	9.20	....	....	12.19
Corning...................	10.21	....	....	1.39
Elmira...............[Arrive	10.55	....	....	2.06
	P.M.			P.M.
Dunkirk.............[Leave	3.40	....	....	7 a m
Salamanca................	6.00	....	....	9.40
Sal'a, B. R. & P. Ry..|Leave	....	....	....	10 a m
Roch.,B.R.&P.Ry..|Arrive	....	....	....	2 p m
Carrollton...........[Leave	6.12	....	....	9.51
Olean.....................	6.35	....	....	10.12
	P.M.			A.M.
Suspension Bridge..[Leave	4.00	5.11	....	8.35
Niagara Falls.............	4.10	8.27	....	8.43
Buffalo...................	5.30	10.00	....	9.15
Attica.....................	6.36	12.04	....	10.40
Portage...................	....	....	....	11.32
	P.M.	A.M.	A.M.	Noon
Hornellsville........[Leave	9.00	2.00	6.00	12.30
Corning...................	10.21	3.09	7.17	1.89
Elmira....................	11.00	3.43	7.55	2.09
Waverly...................	11.29	4.11	8.30	2.36
Owego.....................	12.03	4.43	9.08	3.12
Binghamton...............	12.41	5.30	9.49	3.58
Susquehanna........[Leave	1.25	6.02	10.40	1.15
Narrowsburg..............	3.48	....	12.52	....
Lackawaxen...............	4.06	8.29	1.11	7.17
Port Jervis................	4.50	9.25	2.18	8.15
Jersey City................	7.40	11.55	4.55	10.55
CHAMBERS ST.	7.57	12.07	5 07	11.07
New York, 23d Street.....	8.00	12.15	5.15	11.15
[Arrive	A.M.	Noon	P.M.	P.M.

a Daily. b Daily, except Sundays. p Daily, except Mondays. * Stops to take on passengers for Buffalo, Salamanca and points beyond. *On Sundays leave New York 8 30 a.m. **For Ticket Offices, Sleeping Cars, etc.**, see preceding page.

NEW YORK, NEW HAVEN & HARTFORD R. R.

From Grand Central Depot, 4th Ave. and 42d St.

For "Fares to all Places," see Index.

NEW YORK & HARTFORD DIVISION

Stations and Distances.

M. New York,
10 Williams Bridge,
13 Mount Vernon,
15 Pelhamville,
16 New Rochelle,
18 Larchmont Manor,
20 Mamaroneck,
22 Harrison,
24 Rye,
25 Port Chester,
28 Greenwich,
29 Cos Cob,
30 Riverside,
31 Sound Beach,
33 Stamford,
35 Glenbrook,
36 Noroton,
38 Darien,
39 Five Mile River,
41 South Norwalk,
42 East Norwalk,
44 Westport & Saugatuck
47 Green's Farms,
49 Southport,
50 Fairfield,
55 Bridgeport,
59 Stratford,
60 Naugatuck Junction,
63 Milford,
67 Woodmont,
70 West Haven,
73 New Haven,
77 Quinnipiack,
80 North Haven,
85 Wallingford,
88 Yalesville,
91 Meriden,
99 Berlin,
104 Newington,
109 Hartford,
112 Wilson's,
116 Windsor,
118 Hayden's,
121 Windsor Locks,
124 Warehouse Point,
125 Enfield Bridge,
127 Thompsonville,
131 Longmeadow,
133 Pecowsic,
135 Springfield.

Time from Grand Central Depot to New Rochelle, 30 minutes; to Port Chester, 50 minutes; to Stamford, 1 hour to 1 hour 20 minutes.

Local Trains Leave Grand Central Depot.

For **Mount Vernon**—5 01, 6 01, 7 01, 9 02, 10 02, 11 02 a. m.; 12 02, 1 02, 2 02, 2 30, 3 01, 4 06, 4 32, 5 01, 5 32, 6 07, 6 30, 7 01, 8 01, 9 30, 11 35 p. m. Sundays, 6 01, 7 30, 9 00 a. m.; 5 00, 10 00 p. m.

For **Pelhamville**—5 01, 6 01, 7 01, 9 02, 10 02, 11 02 a. m.; 12 02, 1 02, 2 02, 3 01, 4 06, 4 32, 5 01, 5 32, 6 07, 6 30, 7 01, 8 01, 11 35 p. m. Sundays, 6 01, 7 30, 9 00 a. m.; 5 00, 10 00 p. m.

For **New Rochelle** 5 01, 6 01, 7 01, 8 00, 9 02, 10 02, 11 02 a. m.; 12 02, 1 02, 2 02, 2 30, 3 01, 4 06, 4 32, 5 01, 5 32, 6 07, 6 30, 7 01, 8 01, 9 30, 11 35 p. m. Sundays, 6 01, 7 30, 9 00 a. m.; 5 00, 10 00 p. m.

For **Larchmont Manor** 6 01, 7 01, 9 02, 10 02, 11 02 a. m.; 12 02, 1 02, 2 02, 3 01, 4 06, 4 32, 5 01, 5 32, 6 07, 6 30, 7 01, 8 01, 9 30, 11 35 p. m. Sundays, 6 01, 7 30, 9 00 a. m.; 5 00, 10 00 p. m.

For **Mamaroneck** 5 01, 6 01, 7 01, 9 02, 10 02, 11 02 a. m.; 12 02, 1 02, 2 02, 2 30, 3 01, 4 06, 4 32, 5 01, 5 30, 5 32, 6 07, 6 30, 7 01, 8 01, 9 30, 11 35 p. m. Sundays, 6 01, 7 30, 9 00 a. m.; 5 00, 10 00 p. m.

For **Harrison**—6 01, 7 01, 9 02, 10 02, 11 02 a. m.; 12 02, 1 02, 2 02, 3 01, 4 06, 4 32, 5 01, 5 30, 5 32, 6 07, 6 30, 7 01, 8 01, 9 30, 11 35 p. m. Sundays, 6 01, 7 30, 9 00 a. m.; 5 00, 10 00 p. m.

For **Rye** 5 01, 6 01, 7 01, 9 02, 10 02, 11 02 a. m.; 12 02, 1 02, 2 02, 2 30, 3 01, 4 05, 4 32, 5 01, 5 30, 5 32, 6 07, 6 30, 7 01, 8 01, 9 30, 11 35 p. m. Sundays, 6 01, 7 30, 9 00 a. m.; 5 00, 10 00 p. m.

For **Port Chester** 5 01, 6 01, 7 01, 9 02, 10 02, 11 02 a. m.; 12 02, 1 02, 2 02, 2 30, 3 01, 3 30, 4 01, 4 06, 4 30, 4 32, 5 02, 5 01, 5 30, 5 32, 6 04, 6 07, 6 30, 7 01, 8 01, 9 30, 11 35, p. m. Sundays, 6 01, 7 30, 9 00 a. m.; 5 00, 10 00 p. m.

For **Greenwich** 5 01, 6 01, 7 01, 9 02, 10 02, 11 02 a. m.; 12 02, 1 02, 2 02, 2 30, 3 01, 3 30, 4 01, 4 05, 4 30, 5 02, 5 01, 5 30, 6 07, 6 30, 7 01, 8 01, 9 30, 11 35 p. m. Sundays, 6 01, 7 30, 9 00 a. m.; 5 00, 10 00 p. m.

For **Cos Cob** 5 01, 6 01, 7 01, 9 02, 10 02, 11 02 a. m.; 12 02, 1 02, 2 02, 3 01, 4 06, 4 30, 5 01, 5 30, 6 07, 6 30, 7 01, 8 01, 9 30, 11 35 p. m. Sundays, 6 01, 7 30, 9 00 a. m.; 5 00, 10 00 p. m.

For **Riverside**—6 01, 7 01, 9 02, 10 02, 11 02 a. m.; 12 02, 1 02, 2 02, 2 30, 3 30, 4 05, 4 30, 5 01, 5 30, 6 07, 6 30, 7 01, 8 01, 11 35 p. m. Sundays, 6 01, 7 30, 9 00 a. m.; 5 00, 10 00 p. m.

For **Sound Beach** 5 01, 6 01, 7 01, 10 02, 11 02 a. m.; 12 02, 1 02, 2 02, 3 01, 4 05, 5 01, 5 30, 6 07, 6 30, 7 01, 8 01, 11 35 p. m. Sundays, 6 01, 7 30 a. m.; 5 00, 10 00 p. m.

For **Stamford**—5 01, 6 01, 7 01, 8 00, 9 00, 9 02, 10 02, 11 00, 11 02 a. m.; 12 02, 1 02, 2 00, 2 02, 2 30, 3 02, 3 01, 3 30, 4 01, 4 06, 4 30, 5 02, 5 01, 5 30, 6 03, 6 07, 6 30, 7 01, 8 01, 9 0, 11 30, 11 35 p. m. Sundays, 6 01, 7 30, 9 00 a. m.; 5 00, 10 00, 11 30 p. m.

Local Trains to New York Leave

Stamford—5 05, (5 35 except Mondays), 6 04, 6 10, 6 33, 6 40, 6 50, 7 00, 7 16, 7 45, 7 50, 8 12, 8 15, 8 42, 8 50, 9 19, 9 56, 10 28 a. m.; 12 05, 12 15, 1 15, 1 40, 3 08, 4 20, 5 02, 5 35, 5 40, 6 10, 7 05, 7 10, 8 32, 10 34 p. m. Sundays, 5 35, 6 01, 9 37, a. m.; 4 30, 6 35, 6 40, 8 10, 9 23 p. m.

Sound Beach—6 14, 7 04, 7 21, 7 55, 8 19, 10 01 a. m.; 12 19, 1 11, 3 12, 4 25, 5 15, 6 13, 7 15, 8 37, 10 38 p. m. Sundays, 9 11 a. m.; 4 35, 6 11, 8 15, 9 28 p. m.

Riverside 5 11, 6 17, 6 17, 6 57, 7 08, 7 25, 7 59, 8 22, 10 05 a. m.; 12 22, 1 18, 3 16, 4 28, 5 19, 6 16, 7 19, 8 41, 10 40 p. m. Sundays, 9 45 a. m.; 4 38, 6 48, 8 19, 9 31 p. m.

Cos Cob 5 13, 6 19, 6 49, 6 59, 7 10, 7 27, 8 01, 8 24, 10 07 a. m.; 12 24, 1 50, 3 18, 4 50, 5 51, 6 18, 7 21, 8 43 p. m. Sundays, 9 47 a. m.; 4 40, 6 50, 8 21, 9 34 p. m.

Greenwich 5 16, 6 23, 6 44, 6 54, 7 03, 7 14, 7 31, 8 05, 8 23, 8 28, 9 01, 10 11 a. m.; 12 28, 1 54, 3 22, 4 34, 5 55, 6 21, 7 25, 8 47, 10 45 p. m. Sundays, 9 52 a. m.; 4 44, 6 54, 8 25, 9 37 p. m.

Port Chester 5 22, 5 55, 6 30, 6 50, 6 59, 7 10, 7 20, 7 37, 7 45, 8 11, 8 35, 9 07, 9 31, 10 17 a. m.; 12 35, 2 00, 3 28, 4 40, 6 01, 6 27, 7 31, 8 53, 10 51 p. m. Sundays, 10 00 a. m.; 4 50, 7 02, 8 31, 9 43 p. m.

Rye 5 26, 6 00, 6 35, 7 01, 7 15, 7 25, 7 50, 8 15, 8 40, 9 12, 10 22 a. m.; 12 40, 2 05, 3 32, 4 45, 6 04, 6 31, 7 36, 8 58, 10 56 p. m. Sundays, 10 06 a. m.; 4 55, 7 09, 8 36, 9 48 p. m.

Harrison 5 30, 6 05, 6 40, 7 09, 7 20, 7 30, 7 55, 8 45, 10 27 a. m.; 12 45, 2 10, 3 37, 4 49, 6 11, 6 36, 7 41, 9 03, 11 01 p. m. Sundays, 10 13 a. m.; 5 00, 7 17, 8 42, 9 53 p. m.

Mamaroneck 5 34, 6 10, 6 45, 7 14, 7 25, 7 35, 8 00, 8 22, 8 50, 9 20, 10 32 a. m.; 12 50, 2 15, 3 41, 4 54, 6 16, 6 40, 7 46, 9 08, 11 06 p. m. Sundays, 10 19 a. m.; 5 05, 7 23, 8 48, 9 58 p. m.

Larchmont Manor 5 38, 6 15, 6 50, 7 19, 7 30, 7 39, 8 05, 8 55, 10 37 a. m.; 12 55, 2 19, 3 45, 4 59, 6 21, 6 44, 7 51, 9 13, 11 10 p. m. Sundays, 10 24 a. m.; 5 10, 7 29, 8 54, 10 03 p. m.

New Rochelle 5 42, 6 20, 6 55, 7 24, 7 35, 7 44, 8 10, 8 30, 9 00, 9 19, 10 42 a. m.; 1 00, 2 24, 3 50, 5 04, 6 26, 6 49, 7 56, 9 18, 11 15 p. m. Sundays, 10 31 a. m.; 5 15, 7 37, 9 00, 10 08 p. m.

Pelhamville 5 46, 6 25, 7 00, 7 28, 7 40, 7 48, 8 15, 8 34, 9 05, 10 46 a. m.; 1 05, 2 29, 3 54, 5 08, 6 30, 6 51, 8 00, 9 2?, 11 20 p. m. Sundays, 10 37 a. m.; 5 19, 7 43, 9 06, 10 13 p. m.

Mount Vernon 5 50, 6 30, 7 05, 7 33, 7 45, 7 53, 8 20, 8 39, 9 10, 9 32, 10 51 a. m.; 1 10, 2 34, 3 58, 5 12, 6 35, 6 59, 8 05, 9 28, 11 25 p. m. Sundays, 6 09, 10 43 a. m.; 5 24, 7 51, 9 12, 10 18 p. m.

Leave Grand Central Depot

For **South Norwalk** and intermediate stations, 5 01, 6 01, 7 01, †8 00, 9 02, †11 00, 11 02 a. m.; †12 00 m.; 12 02, †2 00, †3 02, 3 02, 3 30, †4 02, 4 01, 5 02, †6 03, 6 03, 7 01, 8 01, 9 30, *†11 30 p. m. Sundays, 7 30 a. m.; 5 00 p. m. *Trains marked † are express trains, making but few intermediate stops.* **Daily.* Express trains arrive in South Norwalk in 1 hour 10 minutes; accommodation trains in 1½ to 1¾ hours.

For **Bridgeport** and intermediate stations, 5 01, 6 01, 7 01, †8 00, †9 00, 9 02, †10 00, †11 00 a. m.; †12 00 m.; 12 02, †1 00, †2 00, †3 02, 3 02, †4 02, 4 02, †5 00, 5 02, †6 03, 6 03, 7 01, 8 01, †9 30, *†11 00, *†11 30 p. m. Sundays, 7 30 a. m.; †3 00, 5 00 p. m. *Trains marked † are express trains, making but few intermediate stops.* **Daily.* Express trains arrive in Bridgeport in 1½ hours; accommodation trains in 2 to 2¾ hours.

For **New Haven** and intermediate stations, 5 01, *6 01, 7 01, †8 00, †9 00, 9 02, †10 00, †11 00 a. m.; †12 00 m.; 12 02, †1 00, †2 00, †*3 00, 3 02, †*4 00, 4 02, †5 00, †6 03, 7 01, 8 01, 9 30, †*11 00, †*11 30 p. m. Sundays, 7 30 a. m.; 5 00 p. m. *Trains marked † are express trains, making but few intermediate stops.* **Daily.* Express trains arrive in New Haven in 2 hours; accommodation trains in 2 hours 10 minutes.

For **Berlin**, 5 01, 8 00, 9 02 a. m.; 12 00 m.; 12 02, 3 00, 4 02, 6 03, 7 01 p. m.; due in Berlin, 9 01, 11 17 a. m.; 1 09, 2 48, 4 13, 5 56, 7 15, 9 12, 11 01 p. m.

For **Meriden** and **Hartford** and intermediate Stations, 5 01, †8 00, †9 00, 9 02, †11 00 a. am., †12 00 noon, 12 02, 3 00, *†4 00, 4 02, 6 03, 7 01, 9 30, *†11 00 p. m. *Trains marked † are express trains, making but few intermediate stops.* **Daily.* Express trains arrive in Meriden in 2½ to 3 hours; accommodation trains in 3¾ hours. Arrive in Hartford, express trains, in 3 to 3½ hours; accommodation trains in 4½ hours.

For **Windsor Locks** and intermediate Stations, 5 01, 8 00, 9 02 a.m., 12 02, 3 00, 6 03, 7 01 p.m., due in Windsor Locks, 9 53 a. m., 12 02, 2 03, 5 07, 6 46, 9 59, 11 52 p. m.

For **Springfield** and intermediate Stations, 5 01, †8 00, †9 00, 9 02, †11 00 a. m., 12 02, 3 00, †4 00, 6 03, 7 01, 9 30, *†11 00 p. m. *Trains marked † are Express trains, making but few intermediate stops.* **Daily.*

Due in **Springfield** at 10 25 a. m., 12 27, 12 45, 2 38, 3 02, 5 42, 7 16, *7 27, 10 30 p. m., 12 25, 2 35, *3 02 night.

NEW YORK, NEW HAVEN & HARTFORD R. R.—Continued.

Trains to New York.
*Express trains, making but few intermediate stops. *Daily.*

Leave Springfield *†*1.58 (12.08, except Monday), 5.45, 7.00, *7.50, 9.25, *11.15, 11.50 a. m., 1.58, 3.25, 1.30, *†6.33, 6.10 p. m.
Arrive in New York, *6.00 (*6.35, except Monday), 10.30, 11.10, *11.10 a. m., 2.15, *3.30, 4.30, 6.00, 8.00, 9.00, *†10.00, 11.00 p. m.

Leave Windsor Locks, 6.16, 7.33, 9.58 a. m., 12.25, 3.50, 5.01, 7.11 p. m., due in New York, 10.30, 11.10 a. m., 2.15, 4.30, 8.00, 9.00, 11.00 p. m.

Leave Hartford, *†2.40 (*3.00, except Monday), 6.15, 8.05, *8.29, 10.30 a. m., *12.24, 12.55, *2.10, *3.25, 4.30, 5.35, *†7.10, 7.10 p. m.
Arrive in New York, *6.00 (*6.35, except Monday), 10.30, 11.10, *11.10 a. m., 2.15, *3.30, 4.30, *6.00, *6.30, 8.00, 9.00, *†10.00, 11.00 p. m.

Leave Berlin, 7.05, 8.25, 10.59 a. m., 12.42, 1.16, 3.43, 4.54, 5.55, 8.00 p. m., due in New York, 10.29, 11.10 a. m., 2.15, 3.30, 4.30, 6.30, 8.00, 9.00, 11.00 p. m.

Leave Meriden, *3.12, *3.36 except Monday, 7.29, 8.10, 9.01, 11.06 a. m., 12.56, 1.43, 3.12, 3.57, 5.08, 6.09, *7.37, 8.16 p. m.
Arrive in New York, *6.00 (6.35 except Monday) 10.30, 11.10, 11.40 a. m., 2.15, 3.30, 4.30, 6.00, 6.30, 8.00, 9.00, *10.00, 11.00 p. m.

Leave New Haven, stopping at intermediate stations, *†3.50 (†4.20 except Monday) *†* 4.50, 6.15, *7.05, *7.30, *8.10, 8.30, *9.35, 10.10, *11.50 a. m., *†1.30, *†2.30, *3.50, 4.00 †4.30, 5.01, 5.30, *6.00, 6.30, *†7.05, *8.08, 8.15, *9.05, 9.10 p. m. Sundays— 8.00 a. m., 5.00, 6.20, 7.30 p. m. *Express trains, making but few intermediate stops. *Daily.* Express trains arrive at New York in 2 to 2½ hours. Accommodation trains in 2½ hours.

Leave Bridgeport, *†4.20, *†5.51 except Monday) *†5.21, 5.10, 6.25, 6.53, *7.30, *8.00, *8.37, 9.04, 10.50, 10.05, 11.14 a. m., 12.27, *1.57, 2.11, *2.57, *4.20, 4.31, *4.57, 6.01, *6.30, *7.31, 7.30, *7.31, 9.44, p. m. Sundays— 8.10 a. m., 5.10, 6.55, 8.10 p. m. *Express trains, making but few intermediate stops. *Daily.* Express trains arrive at New York in 1¾ to 1⅞ hours. Accommodation trains in two hours.

Leave South Norwalk, *5.16 except Monday, *†*5.48, 6.12, 6.56, 7.23, *7.56, *8.26, 8.30, 9.03, 9.36, *10.13, 11.15 a. m., *12.50, 1.20, 2.14, *4.46, 5.06, *5.20, 6.36, 8.11, 10.15 p. m. Sundays— 9.15 a. m., 6.14, 7.28, 8.59 p. m. *Express trains, making but few intermediate stops. *Daily.* Express trains arrive in New York in 1 hour, 12 minutes. Accommodation trains in 1¾ hours.

HARLEM RIVER BRANCH.

Stations and Distances—

Harlem River		Hunter's Point	2	Westchester	6	Pelham Manor	10
Port Morris	1	West Farms	4	Baychester	7	W. New Rochelle	
Casanova	2	Van Nest	5	Bartow	8	New Rochelle	12

Leave Harlem River (East 130th St.) for **New Rochelle** and intermediate stations 6.10, 7.50, 9.00, 10.00 a. m., 12 m., 2.00, 4.00, 4.40, 5.40, 6.10, 6.40, 8.00, 10.30 p. m., 12.10 night. Sundays— 12.10, 9.00 a. m., 12 m., 5.00, 9.30 p. m., due at Rochelle in 35 minutes.
Leave New Rochelle for **Harlem River** and intermediate stations 5.55, 6.58, 7.10, 8.45, 10.00, 10.50 a. m., 12.70, 3.05, 3.45, 4.45, 5.45, 6.55, 8.15, 10.10 p. m. Sundays— 9.00 a. m., 3.15, 5.30, 9.45 p. m., due at Harlem River in 35 minutes.

NEW CANAAN BRANCH.

Stations.—Stamford, Glenbrook, Springdale, Talmadge Hill, New Canaan.

Leave Grand Central Depot for **New Canaan** and intermediate stations, 5.01, 8.00 a. m., 2.00, 4.01, 5.02, 6.03 p. m., due at New Canaan at 7.03, 9.55 a. m., 3.43, 5.33, 6.28, 7.28 p. m.
Leave New Canaan, stopping at intermediate stations, 6.10, 7.20, 8.20, 11.35 a. m., 4.45, 6.35 p. m. Due in **New York** at 7.35, 8.50, 9.30 a. m., 1.05, 6.00, 8.00 p. m.

NEW BRITAIN BRANCH.

Leave Berlin for **New Britain**, 7.06, 7.45, 8.26, 9.02, 11.18 a. m., 12.43, 2.10, 4.44, 4.52, 5.57, 7.16, 9.30 p. m., due at New Britain in 10 minutes.
Leave New Britain for **Berlin**, 6.52, 7.30, 8.12, *8.47, 10.38 a. m., 12.30, 2.35, 3.30, 4.38, 5.12, 7.02, 9.00 p. m., due at Berlin in ten minutes.

MIDDLETOWN BRANCH.

Stations.—Berlin, Beckley's, East Berlin, Westfield, Newfield, Middletown.

Leave Berlin for **Middletown** and intermediate stations, 7.45, 9.02, 11.18 a. m., 12.43, 4.44, 5.57, 7.16 p. m., due at Middletown in 25 minutes.
Leave Middletown for **Berlin**, 6.25, 7.55, 10.12, 10.59 a. m., 12.10, 3.15, 4.45, 6.15 p. m., due at Berlin in 25 minutes.

SUFFIELD BRANCH.

Leave Windsor Locks for **Suffield**, 8.15, 10.12 a. m., 2.04, 5.08, 6.48 p. m., due at Suffield in 15 minutes.
Leave Suffield for **Windsor Locks**, 7.40, 9.30 a. m., 1.40, 4.50, 6.10 p. m., due at Windsor Locks in 15 minutes.

VALLEY DIVISION.

Stations and Distances.

M. Hartford,	9 Rocky Hill.	22 Maromas.	31 Goodspeed's,	39 Essex,
1 State St. Depot,	13 North Cromwell.	25 Higganum,	34 Hadlyme,	43 Saybrook Junction,
5 Wethersfield,	14 Cromwell,	28 Haddam,	35 Chester,	45 Saybrook Point,
7 South Wethersfield.	16 Middletown.	28 Arnold's,	36 Deep River,	46 Fenwick.

Leave Hartford for **Saybrook Point** and intermediate stations, 6.44, 10.30, 11.00 a. m., 2.00, 4.30, 1.45 p. m. (3.55 p. m. for Middletown).
Due at **Middletown**, 7.17, 11.12 a. m., 1.15, 2.42, 5.11, 6.37, 6.35 p. m.
Due at **Saybrook Junction**, 8.15 a. m., 12.10, 3.31, 5.51, 6.45, 8.15 p. m.
Due at **Saybrook Point**, 8.20 a. m., 12.15, 3.40, 3.55, 6.35, 8.50 p. m.
Leave Saybrook Point for **Hartford**, 3.20, 8.05, 8.50 a. m., 12.00, 3.45, 6.20 p. m. Leave **Saybrook Junction**, 3.30, 8.25, 9.18 a. m., 12.10, 3.51, 6.30 p. m.
Due at **Hartford**, 7.25, 10.00 a. m., 1.40, 1.55, 5.10, 8.23 p. m.
Leave Middletown for **Hartford**, 6.10, 7.17, 9.20 a. m., 12.15, 1.45, 7.11 p. m. Due at Hartford, 7.25, 7.55, 10.00 a. m., 1.40, 1.55, 5.40, 8.23 p. m.

AIR LINE DIVISION.

Stations and Distances.

M. New Haven,	18 Middlefield,	25 Portland,	39 Westchester,	54 Willimantic.
4 Montowese,	19 Middlefield Center,	29 Cobalt & Mid. Had.,	44 Turnerville,	
7 Northford,	20 Rockfall,	33 East Hampton,	46 Leonard's Bridge,	
12 East Wallingford,	21 Middletown.	36 Lyman Viaduct,	49 Chestnut Hill,	

Leave Grand Central Depot, via New Haven, for **Middletown, Turnerville** and **Willimantic** and intermediate stations, 5.01, 11.00 a. m., *†3.40, 4.00 p. m. Due at **Middletown**, 8.58 a. m., 2.15, *5.10, 7.24 p. m. Due at **Turnerville**, 9.38 a. m., 3.00, 8.11 p. m. Due at **Willimantic**, 10.02 a. m., 3.23, *6.37, 8.40 p. m. *Express trains, stop only at Middletown. *Daily.*

To New Haven and New York.

Leave Willimantic, 7.15, 11.30 a. m., *†5.20, 6.58 p. m. *Express train, stops only at Middletown. *Daily.*
Leave Turnerville, 7.38, 11.51 a. m., 7.19 p. m.
Leave Middletown, 8.24 a. m., 12.35, *6.17, 8.04 p. m., due in New Haven, 9.15 a. m., 1.22, *6.58, 8.53 p. m.
Arrive New York, 11.10 a. m., 3.30, *9.00, 11.00 p. m.

NEW YORK, NEW HAVEN & HARTFORD R. R.—Continued.

COLCHESTER BRANCH—AIR LINE DIVISION.

Leave **Turnerville** for **Colchester**, 7.45, 9.15, 11.35 a. m., 3.10, 7.25, 8.20 p. m., due at Colchester in 10 minutes.
Leave **Colchester**, 7.30, 9.20, 11.35 a. m., 2.45, 7.00, 8.00 p. m., due at Turnerville in 10 minutes.

NAUGATUCK DIVISION.
Stations and Distances.

M. Bridgeport,	15 Ansonia,	27 Naugatuck,	41 Thomaston,	57 Burrville,
3 Stratford,	19 Seymour,	27 Union City,	46 Campville,	61 Winsted.
4 Naugatuck Junc.,	23 Beacon Falls,	32 Waterbury,	49 Litchfield,	
14 Derby,	— High Rock Grove,	31 Waterville,	52 Torrington.	

Leave **Grand Central Depot**, via Bridgeport, for **Derby, Ansonia, Waterbury, Winsted** and intermediate stations, 5.01, 8.00 a. m., 1.00, 4.02 (6.03 to Waterbury) p. m., Sunday, 6.01 a. m. Arrive **Derby**, 7.16, 10.22 a. m., 3.03, 6.02, 8.11 p. m., Sundays, 8.11 a. m. Arrive **Ansonia**, 7.51, 10.29 a. m., 3.10, 6.09, 8.20 p. m., Sundays, 8.46 a. m. Arrive **Waterbury**, 8.18, 11.17 a. m., 3.58, 6.56, 9.00 p. m., Sundays, 9.25 a. m. Arrive **Winsted**, 10.02 a. m., 12.30, 5.12, 8.10 p. m., Sundays, 10.30 a. m.

To Bridgeport and New York.

Leave **Winsted**, 7.10, 9.10 a. m., 1.20, 4.50 p. m., Sundays, 3.00 p. m.; due in New York, 11.25 a. m., 2.15, 6.00, 9.00 p. m. Sundays, 7.35 p. m.
Leave **Waterbury**, 6.05, 8.26, 10.51 a. m., 2.42, 6.07 p. m., Sundays, 4.15 p. m. Leave **Ansonia**, 6.17, 9.10, 11.10 a. m., 3.28, 6.40 p. m., Sundays, 4.54 p. m. Leave **Derby**, 6.53, 9.16, 11.16 a. m., 3.35, 6.55 p. m., Sundays, 5.01 p. m.
Arrive in New York, 9.10, 11.25 a. m., 2.15, 6.00, 9.00 p. m., Sundays, 7.35 p. m.

WATERTOWN BRANCH—NAUGATUCK DIVISION.

Leave **Waterbury** for Oakville and **Watertown**, 6.50, 8.53, 11.22 a. m., 4.03, 6.10, 7.01 p. m., Saturdays only 9.15 p. m., due at Oakville in 12 minutes; at Watertown in 19 minutes.
Leave **Watertown** for Oakville and Waterbury at 6.30, 7.55, 10.15 a. m., 2.40, 4.50, 6.30 p. m., Saturdays only 7.50 p. m. Due at Waterbury in 19 minutes.

NORTHAMPTON DIVISION.
Stations and Distances.

M. New Haven,	19 Hitchcock's,	37 Avon,	54 Southwick,	87 South Deerfield,
5 Centreville,	21 Plantsville,	39 Weatogue,	60 Westfield,	92 Conway,
8 Mt. Carmel,	22 Southington,	41 Simsbury,	67 Southampton,	100 Shelburne Falls.
11 Brooksvale,	27 Plainville,	46 Granby,	71 Easthampton,	
15 Cheshire,	30 Farmington,	Congamond,	76 Northampton,	

Leave **Grand Central Depot**, via New Haven, for **Farmington, Westfield, Northampton** and **Shelburne Falls**, stopping at intermediate Stations, 5.01, 9.00 a. m., 2.00 p. m. (4.00 p. m. to Northampton only and intermediate Stations); due at **Farmington**, 8.38 a. m., 12.09, 4.59, 7.16 p. m.; due at **Westfield** at 9.47 a. m., 1.05, 5.48, 8.15 p. m.; due at **Northampton**, 10.31 a. m., 1.45, 6.17, 8.50 p. m.; due at **Shelburne Falls** at 11.29 a. m., 2.35, 7.01 p. m.

To New Haven and New York.

Leave **Shelburne Falls**, 9.45 a. m., 1.00, 5.30 p. m.; due in New Haven, 1.18, 4.21, 8.55 p. m. **Arrive New York**, 3.30, 6.50, 11.00 p. m.
Leave **Northampton**, 6.35, 10.34 a. m., 1.45, 6.17 p. m.; leave **Westfield**, 7.10, 11.07 a. m., 2.18, 6.54 p. m.; leave **Farmington**, 8.07 a. m., 12.00, 3.18, 7.55 p. m.; due in New Haven, 9.25 a. m., 1.18, 4.21, 8.55 p. m. **Arrive New York**, 11.10 a. m., 3.30, 6.50, 11.00 p. m.

NEW HARTFORD BRANCH.

Leave **Farmington** for **Unionville, Burlington, Collinsville, Pine Meadow** and **New Hartford**, 8.52 a. m., 12.10, 5.01, 7.18 p. m.; due at New Hartford in 30 minutes.
Leave **New Hartford**, stopping at intermediate stations, 7.30, 11.25 a. m., 2.31, 6.30 p. m.; due at Farmington in 30 minutes.

HOLYOKE BRANCH.

Leave **Westfield** for **Ingleside** and **Holyoke**, 9.55 a. m., 1.08, 5.55 p. m.; due at Holyoke in 24 minutes.
Leave **Holyoke**, 6.45, 10.48 a. m., 5.15 p. m.; due at Westfield in 23 minutes.

WILLIAMSBURGH BRANCH.

Leave **Northampton** for **Florence, Leeds, Haydenville** and **Williamsburg**, 10.45 a. m., 1.50, 6.32, 8.52 p. m.; due at Williamsburg in 30 minutes.
Leave **Williamsburg**, 6.15, 10.40 a. m., 1.15, 5.15 p. m.; due at Northampton in 30 minutes.

TURNERS FALLS BRANCH.

Leave **South Deerfield** for **Deerfield, Cheapside** and **Turners Falls**, 11.00 a. m., 2.42, 6.37 p. m.; due at Turners Falls in 20 minutes.
Leave **Turners Falls**, 9.42 a. m., 1.00, 5.30 p. m.; due at South Deerfield in 20 minutes.

SHORE LINE DIVISION.
(For trains to and from Boston see following page.)

Stations and Distances.

M. New Haven,	11 Stony Creek,	20 Madison,	31 Conn. River,	43 Crescent Beach,
2 Fair Haven,	13 Leete's Island,	23 Clinton,	33 Lyme,	44 E. Lyme & Niantic,
5 East Haven,	Sachem's Head,	Grove Beach,	35 Black Hall,	47 Waterford,
8 Branford,	15 Guilford,	28 Westbrook,	39 South Lyme,	50 New London.
10 Pine Orchard,	18 East River,	32 Saybrook Junction,	Black Point,	

Leave **Grand Central Depot** for **Guilford** and intermediate Stations, 5.01, 9.00 a. m., 1.00, 4.00 (8.01) p. m., Wednesdays and Saturdays only, ‡‡11.30 p. m.; due at Guilford, 8.41, 11.36 a. m., 3.31, 5.56, 7.00 p. m., ‡‡11.50 p. m., Wednesdays and Saturdays only; *2.23 a. m. *Express train, stops at no stations between New Haven and Guilford. °Daily.

For **Saybrook Junction** and intermediate stations, 5.01, 9.00, *10.00 a. m., ‡1.00, 3.00, ‡5.00, **11.30 p. m.; due at Saybrook Junction, 9.16 a. m., 12.10, *12.51, ‡3.51 (accommodation train due at 4.26 p. m.), 6.30, *7.41 p. m., *‡2.51 a. m. ‡Express train, making no intermediate stops. ‡Boston Express; change at New Haven for accommodation train to all stations. *Daily.

For **New London** and intermediate Stations, 5.01, 9.00, *10.00 a. m., ‡1.00, 3.00, ‡5.00, **‡11.30 p. m.; due at New London, 10.01 a. m., 12.55, *1.25, ‡4.25 (accommodation train due at 5.15 p. m.), ‡8.10 p. m., *‡3.40 a. m. ‡Express train, stopping only at Saybrook Junction. ‡Boston Express; change at New Haven or Saybrook Junction for accommodation train to all Stations. *Daily.

To New Haven and New York.

Leave **New London**, **‡3.05, 7.30, 11.25 a. m., *‡1.05, 3.05, *‡4.35, ‡5.45, *7.50 p. m.; due in New Haven, **‡4.35, 9.25 a. m., 1.30, *2.25, 5.00, *5.55, 7.45, ‡3.05 p. m. ‡Express trains stop only at Saybrook Junction. *Daily.
Arrive New York, *‡7.00, 11.10 a. m., 3.30, *4.30, 8.00, *8.00, 10.00, ‡11.00 p. m.
Leave **Saybrook Junction**, *‡3.40, *‡15 a. m., 12.10, *1.40, 3.51, *5.10, 6.30, *8.20 p. m.; due in New Haven, **‡4.35, 9.25 a. m., 1.30, *2.25, 5.00, *5.55, 7.45, *‡9.05 p. m.
Arrive New York, *‡7.00, 11.40 a. m., 3.30, *4.30, 8.00, *8.00, 10.00, ‡11.00 p. m. ‡Express trains, make no intermediate stops. *Daily.
Leave **Guilford**, stopping at intermediate stations, **‡1.05, 6.00, 8.50 a. m., 12.45, 4.25, 7.05 p. m., due at New Haven **‡4.35, 6.40, 9.25 a. m., 1.20, 5.00, 7.45 p. m. **Arrive New York**, *‡7.00, 9.10, 11.40 a. m., 3.30, 8.00, 10.00 p. m. *Daily
‡Express train, makes no intermediate stops.

NEW YORK, NEW HAVEN & HARTFORD R. R.—Continued.
BOSTON AND THE EAST.

NEW YORK, NEW HAVEN, HARTFORD, SPRINGFIELD AND BOSTON,
Via Springfield Line.—Boston & Albany R. R.

Dist. from N. York	STATIONS.	84. A.M.	50. A.M.	60. P.M.	2. P.M.
0	N. Y., 42d St. & 4th Av..[Lv	*9.00	*11.00	*4.00	*11.00
34	Stamford.............	9.55	11.57	....	....
56	Bridgeport............	10.32	12.39	....	12.40
71	New Haven............	11.05	1.10	5.55	1.16
92	Meriden..............	11.35	1.48	6.22	1.48
110	Hartford.............	12.05	2.20	6.50	2.20
136	Springfield....[Leave	12.49	3.06	7.31	3.20
151	Palmer..........[Arrive	....	3.32	....	....
191	Worcester............	2.17	4.42	8.51	4.56
213	South Framingham....	....	5.32	9.29	5.37
234	Boston.........[Arrive	3.30	6.00	10.00	6.15
		P.M.	P.M.	P.M.	A.M.

* Daily.   † Except Sunday.

Parlor and Sleeping Car Service.

No. 84.—Drawing-Room Buffet Cars New York to Boston. No. 50.—Drawing-Room Cars New York to Boston. Dining Car New Haven to Worcester. No. 60.—Drawing-Room Cars New York to Boston. Dining Car New Haven to Worcester. No. 2.—Sleeping Cars New York to Boston.

BOSTON, SPRINGFIELD, HARTFORD, NEW HAVEN AND NEW YORK,
Via Springfield Line.—Boston & Albany R. R.

STATIONS.	83. A.M.	19. A.M.	75. P.M.	63. P.M.
Boston...............[Leave	*9.00	*11.00	*1.00	*11.00
South Framingham...	....	....	....	11.38
Worcester............	10.13	12.20	5.08	12.10
Palmer...............	....	1.29	....	1.29
Springfield........[Arrive	11.11	1.51	6.29	1.54
Hartford.............	12.24	2.40	7.10	2.40
Meriden..............	12.56	3.17	7.37	3.12
New Haven...........	1.24	3.42	8.03	3.42
Bridgeport............	1.57	4.20	....	4.20
Stamford.............	....	5.02	....	....
N. Y. (G. C. Station)...[Arrive	3.30	6.00	10.00	6.00
	P.M.	P.M.	P.M.	A.M.

* Daily.   † Except Sunday.

No. 83.—Drawing-Room Buffet Cars Boston to New York. No. 19.—Drawing-Room Cars Boston to New York. Dining Car Worcester to New Haven. No. 75.—Drawing-Room Cars Boston New York. Dining Car Worcester to New Haven. No. 63.—Sleeping Cars Boston to New York.

VIA AIR LINE AND NEW YORK AND NEW ENGLAND R. R.

Trains from New York to Boston.

STATIONS.	W'k Days A.M.	W'k Days NO'N	W'k Days A.M.	Daily P.M.
N. Y., 42d St. & 4th Av....[Lv	5.01	12.00	11.00	3.00
Bridgeport............	7.03	1.31	12.39	x
New Haven.........[Arrive	7.40	2.00	1.10	4.55
New Haven (via Air Line)..[Lv	8.03	....	1.25	5.00
Middletown............	8.58	....	2.15	5.40
Willimantic........[Arrive	10.02	....	3.24	6.37
New Haven (via H'rt'f'd Line)[Lv	....	2.05	....	....
Berlin................	....	2.48	....	....
Hartford.............	....	3.05	....	....
Hartford (via N. Y. & N. E.)..[Lv	3.10	....	....	....
Willimantic........[Arrive	....	4.09	....	....
Willimantic........[Leave	10.15	4.09	3.25	6.40
Putnam...............	11.00	4.49	4.10	....
Blackstone............	11.48	5.28	5.00	....
Franklin..............	12.06	5.43	5.21	....
Boston............[Arrive	1.00	6.30	6.10	9.00
(x Stops at Bridgeport Sundays)	P.M.	P.M.	P.M.	P.M.

Trains from Boston to New York.

STATIONS.	W'k Days A.M.	W'k Days NO'N	Daily P.M.	W'k Days P.M.
Boston (via N.Y. & N.E.)..[Lv	8.30	12.00	3.00	3.30
Franklin..............	9.25	12.42	....	4.29
Blackstone............	9.48	12.55	....	5.00
Putnam...............	10.45	1.37	....	5.53
Willimantic........[Arrive	11.25	2.17	5.15	6.45
Willimantic (via Air Line)..Lv	11.30	....	5.20	6.58
Middletown............	12.35	....	6.17	8.06
New Haven........[Arrive	1.22	....	6.58	8.53
Willimantic (N. Y. & N. E.).Lv	....	2.17	....	....
Hartford.........[Arrive	....	3.15	....	....
Hartford..........[Leave	....	3.25	....	....
Berlin................	....	3.43	....	....
New Haven........[Arrive	....	4.25	....	....
New Haven..........[Leave	1.30	4.30	7.05	9.05
Bridgeport............	1.57	4.57	7.31	9.31
New York........[Arrive	3.30	6.30	9.00	11.00
	P.M.	P.M.	P.M.	P.M.

SHORE LINE ROUTE.
NEW YORK, PROVIDENCE AND BOSTON R. R.

STATIONS.	A.M.	A.M.	A.M.	P.M.	P.M.	P.M.
N Y 42d St & 4th av[Lv	....	5.00	10.00	1.00	5.00	*11.30
New London....[Leave	7.15	10.05	1.25	4.30	8.15	3.35
Mystic...........[Arrive	7.43	10.31	....	5.01	....	....
Stonington............	7.55	10.39	....	5.08	....	....
Westerly..............	8.03	10.18	2.07	5.18	....	4.18
Kingston..............	8.30	11.18	2.32	....	....	4.47
Narragansett Pier.....	....	....	3.30	....	....	....
Wickford Junc........	8.43	11.36	2.45	6.05	....	....
Newport.............	9.55	1.00	....	7.20	....	....
East Greenwich.......	8.53	11.46	....	6.14	....	....
Providence............	9.15	12.15	3.15	6.40	9.55	5.25
Worcester.............	....	2.15	6.00	9.10	....	8.02
Taunton..............	10.5	3.12	6.04	7.55	....	7.15
New Bedford..........	1.10	3.58	6.10	8.35	....	8.08
Cottage City...........	4.00	....	....	....	....	....
Attleboro..............	9.42	1.06	3.41	7.09	....	....
Mansfield..............	9.55	1.16	....	7.21	....	6.14
Canton Junction......	10.11	2.56	....	....	....	....
Boston.........[Arrive	10.35	1.55	4.30	8.00	11.50	*7.00
	A.M.	P.M.	P.M.	P.M.	P.M.	A.M.

STATIONS.	A.M.	A.M.	A.M.	P.M.	P.M.	P.M.
Boston..........[Leave	7.45	10.00	1.00	2.00	5.00	*11.30
Mansfield.............	8.30	....	1.41	2.50	....	12.11
Attleboro.............	8.42	10.11	1.54	3.04	....	12.24
Cottage City..........	....	7.30	7.30	....	....	....
New Bedford..........	7.25	8.45	10.55	1.30	3.40	5.55
Taunton..............	8.05	9.31	11.38	2.10	4.35	6.48
Worcester.............	7.00	7.30	11.45	....	4.00	*7.35
Providence............	9.10	11.10	2.20	3.35	6.00	*12.55
East Greenwich.......	9.38	....	2.43	3.55	....	1.17
Wickford Junction....	9.48	11.40	2.55	4.05	6.38	....
Newport.............	7.30	10.20	....	....	4.15	....
Narragansett Pier.....	9.00	....	2.00	4.00	....	....
Kingston..............	10.02	....	3.08	4.17	....	1.42
Westerly..............	10.36	12.12	3.35	4.42	....	2.09
Stonington............	10.45	....	3.45	4.51	....	....
Mystic................	10.53	....	3.51	4.78	....	....
New London....[Arrive	11.20	1.05	4.20	5.25	7.15	2.55
New York........[Arrive	3.30	4.30	8.00	10.00	11.00	*7.00
	A.M.	P.M.	P.M.	P.M.	P.M.	A.M.

Through Cars.—The *11.30 p. m. train from New York run daily Sleeping Cars for Providence and Boston attached. Drawing Room Buffet Cars on 10.00 a. m., 1.00, 5.00 p. m. trains from New York. Dining Car attached to 5.00 p. m. train from New York, at New London, 8.15 p. m. *Daily. ‡Sundays only.

Additional trains **leave New London for Providence** and intermediate stations at 6.30, 7.15 a. m., 3.05, 5.25 p. m. Arrive at Providence at 8.55, 9.15 a. m., 5.35, 7.50 p. m.

☛ *If you want the time of departure of Train, Steamer or Steamship, send to Kenny's Guide, 83 Nassau St., and your inquiry will be answered.*

Through Cars. The *11.30 p. m. train from Boston, and 12.55 a. m. train from Providence, run daily and have Sleeping Cars attached. Drawing-Room Cars on 10 a. m., 1 and 5 p. m. trains from Boston; 11.10 a. m., 2.20 a d 6 p. m. from Providence. Dining Car between Boston and New London on train leaving Boston at 5.00 p. m. *Daily. ‡Except Sunday.

Additional trains **leave Providence for New London** and intermediate stations at 6.10 a. m., 12.30 p. m., arriving at New London at 8.55 a. m., 2.55 p. m., connecting with New London Northern R. R. for Norwich and Willimantic. The 6.10 a. m. train from Providence connects at New London with Steamer Manhanset for Greenport, Shelter Island and Sag Harbor.

NEW YORK, PROVIDENCE & BOSTON R. R.—Continued.

Leave Providence for Pawtuxet, Oakland Beach, Buttonwoods and intermediate stations, 6.25, 9.30 a. m., 2.30, 4.00, 6.25 p. m., on Saturdays 11.10 p. m., due at Buttonwoods 7.20, 10.35 a. m., 3.30, 4.15, 7.10 p. m., Saturdays 11.55 p. m.

Leave Providence for Hope and intermediate stations 7.05, 9.25, 11.55 a. m., 2.10, 4.00, 6.25 p. m., Saturdays 11.30 p. m., due at Hope 7.45, 10.05 a. m., 12.43, 3.24, 4.50, 7.10 p. m., Saturdays 11.55 p. m.

Leave Providence for Olneyville, Elmwood and **Auburn** 6.25, 6.40, 7.05, 8.00, 9.10, 9.25, 9.50, 11.30, 11.55 a.m., 12.30, 2.30, 2.40, 4.00, 4.10, 5.20, 6.15, 6.25, 7.20, 9.15, 11.00 p.m.

PROVIDENCE AND WORCESTER R. R.

Leave Providence for Woodlawn, Pawtucket, Central Falls, Valley Falls and Lonsdale. 6.30, 9.30, 10.30 a. m., 12.00 m., 1.00, 1.30, 2.30, 3.30, 4.30, 5.00, 5.30, 6.10, 6.30, 8.10, 9.00, 10.20 p.m., Saturdays 11.00 p. m., Sundays 9 p. m., due at Lonsdale in 20 minutes.

Leave Providence for Woonsocket 6.15, 7.30, 8.05, 9.40, 11.30 a. m., 12.30, 2.10, 4.00, 4.20, 5.45, 7.45, 11.25 p. m., Sundays 8.30 a. m., 12.15, 4.15, 6.30 p. m., due at Woonsocket in 35 minutes.

Leave Providence for Uxbridge, Worcester and intermediate stations, 7.30, 9.40 a. m., 12.30, 2.10, 4.20, 5.45, 7.45 p. m., Sundays 8.30 a. m., 6.30 p. m., due at **Uxbridge** in 1 hour, at Worcester in 1½ hours.

Leave Worcester for Providence 7.00, 7.30, 10.00, 11.45 a. m., 2.30, 4.00, 6.05, 7.35 p. m., Sundays 8.20 a. m., 5.40 p. m., due at Providence in 1¼ hours.

TO PLACES EAST OF BOSTON,
Via Boston and Maine R. R.
For "Fares to all Places," see Index.

Leave Boston (Haymarket Sq.) for **Haverhill, Exeter, Kennebunk** and **Portland**, stopping at intermediate stations, 7.30, 8.30 a. m., 1.00, 3.15, 5.00 p. m. Sundays, 6.00 p. m. **Arrive Portland**, 12.10, 12.20, 5.00, 8.05, 11.00 p. m. Sundays, 1.00 p. m.

Leave Portland, stopping at intermediate stations, 6.25, 8.35 a. m., 12.10, 3.20 p. m. Sundays, 1.00, 1.15 p. m. **Arrive Boston**, 10.15 a. m., 1.15, 4.45, 8.00 p. m. Sundays, 5.30, 8.48 p. m.

Leave Boston (Causeway St.) for **Lynn, Gloucester, Newburyport, Portsmouth** and **Portland**, stopping at intermediate stations, 7.30, 9.00 a. m., 12.30, 7.00 p. m. Sundays, 7.00 p. m. **Arrive Portland**, 12.10, 12.25, 4.40, 11.00 p. m. Sundays, 11.00 p. m.

Leave Portland, 2.00, 9.00 a. m., 1.00, 6.00 p. m. Sundays, 2.00 a. m. **Arrive Boston**, 6.20 a. m., 1.15, 4.45, 9.30 p. m. Sundays, 6.20 a. m.

Leave Boston (Causeway St.), for **Brunswick, Bath, Augusta** and **Waterville**, 9.00 a. m., †12.30, *†7.00 p. m. Due at Brunswick, 2.25, 6.30 p. m., *12.25 night; due at Bath, 2.50, 6.35 p. m., †12.50 Saturday nights; due at Augusta, 3.47, 7.35 p. m., *2.20 a. m.; due at Waterville, 4.30, 8.20 p. m. Saturdays only, *3.17 a. m. ‡*Daily. ‡To Waterville on Saturdays only. ‡To Bath on Saturdays only.*

For **Bangor, Bar Harbor** and **Vanceboro**, 9.00 a. m., *7.00 p. m. Due at Bangor, 6.35 p. m., *5.40 a. m.; due at Bar Harbor, 9.35 p. m., *10.15 a. m.; due at Vanceboro, 12.30 night, *11.30 a. m. *Daily.

For **Lewiston**, 7.30 a. m., 12.30, 7.00 p. m. Due at Lewiston, 2.33, 6.24 p. m., 1.10 night. Daily.

BOSTON AND THE PROVINCES.

Leave Boston (Haymarket Sq.), for **St. Stephen, St. Andrews, Fredericton, St. John, Annapolis** and **Halifax**, 8.30 a. m., 5.00 p. m. Due at St. Stephen, 1.00 a. m., 2.40 p. m.; due at St. Andrews, 3.30 p. m.; due at **Fredericton**, 11.25 a. m., 2.40 p. m.; due at **St. John**, 5.15 a. m., 4.40 p. m.; due at **Halifax**, 7.50 p. m., 12.05 noon.

Steamer leaves St. John for Annapolis Monday, Wednesday and Saturday, at 7.00 a. m., connecting at Annapolis with express train for Halifax, arriving at 7.20 p. m., and leaves Annapolis for St. John Monday, Thursday and Saturday.

NORTHERN R. R. OF NEW JERSEY.

From Erie Depot, foot of Chambers and W. 23d Sts.

M.	STATIONS	FARES Sgl	Ex	M.	STATIONS	FARES Sgl	Ex	M.	STATIONS	FARES Sgl	Ex	M.	STATIONS	FARES Sgl	Ex
	Jersey City			14	Nordhoff	30c	50c	24	Tappan	55c	1.00	32	Nanuet	70c	1.10
5	Tyler Park	15c	25c	15	Englewood	35c	40c	25	Sparkill	55c	1.00	33	Nanuet Junc.		
6	Homestead	15c	25c	16	Highwood	40c	70c	26	Piermont-on-Hill	55c	1.00	34	Spring Valley	80c	1.20
7	New Durham	15c	25c	17	Tenafly	40c	70c	27	Grand View	55c	1.00	35	Monsey	80c	1.30
8	Granton	20c	30c	18	Cresskill	45c	80c	28	Broadway			36	Tallmans	90c	1.40
9	Fair View	25c	40c	19	Demarest	45c	90c	29	South Nyack	60c	1.00	41	Suffern		
10	Ridgefield	25c	40c	20	Closter	50c	90c	29	Nyack	60c	1.00				
12	Palisades Park	30c	50c	22	Norwood	50c	90c	30	Orangeburg	55c	1.00				
14	Leonia	30c	50c	24	Northvale	55c	90c	27	Blauveltville	60c	1.00				

Leave **foot of Chambers St.**, leave foot of W. 23d St. 10 to 20 minutes earlier for **Cresskill** and intermediate stations, 5.30, 7.00, 8.20, 9.10, 10.00, 11.30 a. m., 1.15, 2.30, 4.00, 5.10, 6.10, 6.40, 8.00, 10.30 p. m., 12 night. Sundays, 7.00, 9.30 a. m., 1.00, 7.15 p. m., due at Cresskill in 50 minutes.

For **Nyack** and intermediate stations, 5.30, 7.00, 8.20, 10.00, 11.30 a. m., 1.15, 3.30, 4.00, 4.50, 5.40, 5.40, 6.10, 6.40, 8.00, 10.30 p. m., 12 night. Sundays, 7.00, 9.30 a. m., 1.00, 7.15 p. m., due at Nyack in 1¼ hours.

For **Suffern** and intermediate stations, 7.00, 10.00 a. m., 4.50, 6.40 p. m. Sundays, 9.30 a. m., 7.15 p. m.; due at Suffern, 10.00, 11.55 a. m., 6.30, 8.40 p. m. Sundays, 11.31 a. m., 9.45 p. m.

Trains to New York.

Leave **Suffern**, stopping at intermediate stations, 7.20, 10.20 a. m., 2.25, 6.40 p.m. Sundays, 7.30 a.m., 5.22 p.m.; due in New York 8.55 a. m., 12.07, 5.27, 9.52 p. m. Sundays, 9.22 a. m., 7.37 p. m.

Leave **Nyack**, stopping at intermediate stations, 5.05, 6.12, 6.54, 7.27, 7.45, 8.05, 8.48, 9.23, 10.55 a. m., 1.12, 3.15, 4.14, 5.35, 7.05, 8.25, 10.40 p.m. Sundays, 8.05 a. m., 1.12, 6.16, 8.40 p. m.; due in New York in 1 hour, 20 minutes.

Leave **Cresskill**, 5.32, 6.46, 7.22, 8.31, 9.53, 11.27, 11.41 a. m., 1.43, 3.15, 4.18, 4.44, 6.08, 7.35, 8.55, 11.10 p. m. Sundays, 8.34 a. m., 1.14, 6.40, 8.31 p. m.; due in New York in 50 minutes.

LOCATION OF MARKETS.

Catharine, foot of Catharine St., E. R.
Centre, Grand & Centre Sts.
Clinton, Canal & West Sts.
Essex, Grand & Essex Sts.
Farmer's, West & Gansevoort Sts.
Fulton, Fulton & South Sts.
Fulton Fish, foot of Fulton St., E. R.

Gouverneur, Water & Gouverneur Sts.
Jefferson, 6th & Greenwich Avs.
Tompkins, 3d Av. & 7th Sts.
Union, Columbia & Houston Sts.
Washington, Fulton & West Sts.
West Washington, 13th Av. & Gansevoort St.

PUBLIC BUILDINGS.

Assay Office, 30 Wall St.
Barge Office, foot of Whitehall.
Castle Garden, Battery Park.
City Hall, City Hall Park.
County Court House, Chambers near Broadway.
Custom House, Wall & William.
Jefferson Market Court, 6th Av. & 10th.

Ludlow Street Jail, near Grand St.
Navy Yard, Wallabout Bay, Brooklyn.
Post Office, Broadway & Park Row.
State Arsenal, 7th Av. & 35th.
Sub-Treasury, Wall & Nassau.
Tombs, Centre & Franklin Sts.
U. S. Army Building, Whitehall & Pearl.

LONG ISLAND R. R.

Depots at Long Island City, and Flatbush Avenue, Brooklyn. Leave New York for Long Island City by James Slip Ferry or E. 34th St. Ferry, as stated below.

For "Fares to all Places," see Index. ☞ For Stage Connections to places on Long Island, see 3d page from this.

Ferry Connections from New York City. Leave New York: East 34th St. (daily, except Sundays), every 10 minutes from 6 00 a. m., until 9 00 p. m., until at 10 03, 11 10 p. m, and 12 10 night. Sundays, every 10 minutes from 6 00 a. m. until 10 20 p. m. James Slip, foot New Chambers St., E. R. (daily, except Sundays), every 30 minutes from 6 30 a. m. until 7 00 p. m.

Ticket offices: James Slip Ferry: Foot of E. 34th St., 71, 115, 681, 942, 1140, 1314 Broadway, 246 Canal, 112 14th St., 112 West, 62 W. 125th St. Brooklyn: L. I. R. R. Station, cor. Flatbush and Atlantic Aves., 333 Fulton, 10 Broadway and L. I. City Depot.

JAMAICA TRAINS.
No connection via James Slip Ferry.

Leave **Foot of E. 34th St.** (leave James Slip Ferry 20 minutes earlier, except Sundays), *6 30, *7 40, 7 50, 8 20, 8 50, *10 40, 10 50 a. m., *12 10, 12 50, 1 50, *3 10, 3 20, *4 10, 4 20, 5 20, 5 50, 6 20, 6 50, *7 50, *10 01 p. m., *12 10 night. Sundays, *8 10, *8 50, *9 20, *9 50, *10 50 a. m., *1 50, *6 20 p. m. Arrive at Jamaica in 40 minutes.

Leave **Jamaica**, 6 02, 6 31, 7 03, 7 30, 7 38, 8 05, 8 08, 8 10, 8 32, 8 31, 8 40, 8 43, 10 06, 10 10, *10 12, 10 34, 10 37, 11 30 a. m., 9 12 58, 12 58, 1 35, 2 58, 3 39, 3 44, 4 20, 5 06, 5 09, 5 31, 6 05, *7 05, *7 10, *9 26, *11 36 p. m. Sundays, *7 30, *8 02, *8 05, *10 23 a. m., *3 12, *5 19, *5 23, *5 31, *7 08, *7 11, *8 37 p. m. Arrive in New York via 34th St. Ferry in 30 minutes, via James Slip Ferry in 50 minutes.

Leave **Cor. Flatbush and Atlantic Avenues, Brooklyn**, 6 15, 7 20, 8 00, 8 30, 8 52, 9 15, 10 20, 10 57 a. m., 12 56, 2 00, 3 22, 4 22, 5 22, 6 00, 6 30, 6 55, 7 54, 10 05 p. m., 12 15 night. Sundays, 8 15, 8 55, 9 30, 11 09 a. m., 2 00, 4 27, 6 30, 8 00, 10 04 p. m., arrive at Jamaica in 30 to 40 minutes.

Leave **Jamaica**, 6 02, 6 31, 7 03, 7 30, 7 38, 8 05, 8 08, 8 10, 8 32, 8 31, 8 40, 8 43, 10 06, 10 10, 10 31, 10 37 a. m., 12 53, 12 58, 2 58, 3 39, 3 44, 5 06, 5 09, 5 31, 6 05, 7 05, 7 10, 9 26, 11 36 p. m. Sundays, 7 30, 8 02, 8 05, 8 52, 10 22 a. m., 1 08, 3 12, 5 19, 5 24, 5 31, 7 08, 7 11, 8 37 p. m. Arrive in Brooklyn in 27 to 35 minutes.

MAIN LINE TRAINS FROM NEW YORK AND BROOKLYN.
No connection via James Slip Ferry. ‡Does not stop at Glendale. ‖Does not stop at Hollis. §Does not stop at Waverly or Baiting Hollow.

Stations.

Long Island City.	Hollis.	Westbury.	Central Islip.	Riverhead.
Bushwick.	Queens.	Hicksville.	Ronkonkoma.	Jamesport.
Fresh Pond.	East Hinsdale.	Central Park.	Waverly.	Mattituck.
Glendale.	Garden City.	Farmingdale.	Medford.	Cutchogue.
Richmond Hill.	Hempstead.	West Deer Park.	Yaphank.	Peconic.
Maple Grove.	Hyde Park.	Deer Park.	Manor.	Southold.
Brooklyn.	Mineola.	Brentwood.	Baiting Hollow.	Greenport.
Jamaica.				

Jamaica, Garden City, Hempstead, Roslyn, Glen Cove, Huntington, Ronkonkoma, Riverhead, Greenport.

Leave **Foot of E. 34th St.** (leave James Slip Ferry 20 minutes earlier, except Sundays):

For **Glendale** and **Richmond Hill**, ‡6 30, *7 10, 8 50, *10 40 a. m., *12 10, 1 50, *3 10, *4 10, ‡4 20, 5 20, 5 30, 6 20, 6 50, *7 50, *10 00 p. m., *12 10 night. Sundays, 8 10, ‡9 20, ‡10 50 a. m., 6 20 p. m.
Leave **Flatbush Avenue**, 6 45, 7 20, 8 52 a. m., 2 00, ‡4 22, 5 22, 6 00, 6 30, 6 55, 7 54, 10 05 p. m., 12 15 night. Sundays, 8 15, ‡9 30, 11 00 a. m., 6 30 p. m.
Arrive Glendale in 25 minutes from foot of E. 34th St.; in 20 minutes from Flatbush Ave., Brooklyn.

For **Hollis, Queens** and **East Hinsdale**, *6 30, ‖8 20, 8 50, 10 50 a. m., 1 50, 3 20, 4 20, 5 20, 6 20, 6 50, *7 50, *10 00 p. m., ‖12 10 night. Sundays, 9 20 a. m., 1 50, 6 20 p. m.
Leave **Flatbush Avenue**, 6 45, ‖8 30, 8 52, 10 57 a. m., 2 00, 3 22, 4 22, 5 22, 6 30, 6 55, 7 54, 10 05 p. m., ‖12 15 night. Sundays, 9 30 a. m., 2 00, 6 30 p. m.
Arrive East Hinsdale in 50 minutes from foot E. 34th St.; in 45 minutes from Flatbush Avenue.

For **Garden City** and **Hempstead**, *6 30, 8 20, 10 50 a. m., 1 50, 3 20, 4 20, 5 20, 6 20, 6 50, *7 50, *10 00 p. m., *12 10 night. Sundays, 8 50 a. m. (9 20 a. m. to Garden City only), 1 50, 6 20 p. m.
Leave **Flatbush Avenue**, 6 45, 8 30, 10 57 a. m., 2 00, 3 22, 5 22, 6 30, 6 55, 7 54, 10 05 p. m., 12 15 night. Sundays, 8 55 a. m. (9 30 a. m. to Garden City only), 2 00, 6 30 p. m.
Arrive Garden City in 1 hour from foot E. 34th St.; in 50 minutes from Flatbush Avenue; arrive Hempstead 5 minutes later.

For **Hyde Park**, 8 50 a. m.; 1 20, 5 20, 6 20, 6 50 p. m. Sundays, 8 50, 9 59 a. m., 6 20 p. m.
Leave **Flatbush Avenue**, 8 52 a. m., 1 22, 5 22, 6 30, 6 55 p. m. Sundays, 8 55 a. m., 6 30 p. m.
Arrive Hyde Park in 55 minutes from E. 34th St.; in 50 minutes from Flatbush Ave.

For **Mineola**, 8 20, 8 50, 10 50 a. m., 1 50, 3 20, 4 20, 5 20, 6 20, 6 50 p. m. Sundays, 8 50, 9 20, 9 50 a. m., 6 20 p. m.
Leave **Flatbush Avenue**, 8 30, 8 52, 10 57 a. m., 2 00, 3 22, 4 22, 5 22, 6 30, 6 55 p. m., 12 15 night. Sundays, 8 55, 9 30 a. m., 6 30 p. m.
Arrive Mineola, 1 hour from E. 34th St.; in 55 minutes from Flatbush Avenue.

For **Westbury** and **Hicksville**, 8 20, 8 50 a. m., 4 20, 5 20, 6 20, 6 50 p. m., (on Saturdays only, *12 10 night). Sundays, 9 50, 9 50 a. m., 6 20 p. m.
Leave **Flatbush Avenue**, 8 30, 8 52 a. m., 3 22, 4 22, 5 22, 6 30, 6 55 p. m., (on Saturdays only, 12 15 night). Sundays, 8 55, 9 30 a. m., 6 30 p. m.
Arrive at Westbury in about 1 hour from E. 34th St. and Flatbush Avenue; arrive Hicksville 7 minutes later.

For **Central Park, Farmingdale, West Deer Park** and **Deer Park**, 8 20 a. m., 3 20, 5 20, 6 50 p. m. (on Saturday only, *12 10 night to West Deer Park). Sunday, 8 50 a. m.
Leave **Flatbush Avenue**, 8 30 a.m., 3 22, 5 22, 6 55 p.m. (on Saturdays only, 12 15 night, to West Deer Park). Sundays, 8 55 a. m.
Arrive at Deer Park in 1¼ hours from E. 34th St. and Flatbush Avenue.

For **Brentwood, Yaphank, Riverhead, Greenport** and intermediate stations, 8 20 a. m., 3 20 p. m. Sundays, §8 50 a. m.
Leave **Flatbush Avenue**, 8 30 a. m., 3 22 p. m. Sundays, §8 55 a. m.
Arrive Yaphank in 2½ hours from E. 34th St. and Flatbush Avenue; arrive Riverhead in 3 hours; arrive Greenport in 3¼ hours.

To Brooklyn and New York.
Trains to New York arrive via James Slip Ferry 20 minutes later than E. 34th St. time.

Leave **Greenport**, stopping at intermediate stations, 7 30 a. m., 1 27, 2 52 p. m. Sundays, 4 17 p. m.
Arrive foot of E. 34th St., 11 07 a. m., 5 37, 6 37 p. m. Sundays, 7 37 p. m.
Arrive Flatbush Avenue, 11 03 a. m., 5 40, 6 32 p. m. Sundays, 7 38 p. m.

Leave **Riverhead**, stopping at intermediate stations, 8 16 a. m., 2 11, 3 38 p. m. Sundays, 5 03 p. m.
Arrive foot E. 34th St., 11 07 a. m., 5 37, 6 37 p. m. Sundays, *7 37 p. m.
Arrive Flatbush Avenue, 11 03 a. m., 5 40, 6 32 p. m. Sundays, 7 38 p. m.

Leave **Deer Park**, stopping at intermediate stations, 5 28, 6 00, 9 29 a. m., 5 00 p. m. (10 31 p. m. from W. Deer Park on Saturdays only), 6 17 p. m.
Arrive foot of E. 34th St., 7 07, 7 37, 11 07 a. m., 6 37 p. m., Saturdays only *12 07 night. Sundays, *7 37 p. m.
Arrive Flatbush Avenue, 7 02, 7 33, 11 03 a. m., 6 32 p. m., Saturdays only 12 04 night. Sundays, 7 38 p. m.

LONG ISLAND R. R.—Continued.

MAIN LINE TRAINS Continued.

Leave **Hicksville** (stopping at Westbury 5 minutes later) 5 54, 6 23, 7 00, 8 13, 9 56 a. m., 4 32, 5 20 p. m., on Saturdays only 10 53 p. m. Sundays, 7 31 a. m., 1 18, 7 05 p. m.
Arrive foot of E. 34th St., 7 07, 7 37, 8 07, 9 07, 11 07 a. m., 5 37, 6 37 p. m., Saturdays only *12 07 night. Sundays, *8 37 a. m., *5 57, *9 17 p. m.
Arrive Flatbush Avenue, 7 02, 7 33, 8 05, 9 11, 11 03 a. m., 5 10, 6 32 p. m., Saturdays only 12 01 night. Sundays, 8 33 a m., 5 55, 9 15 p. m.

Leave **Mineola**, 5 26, 6 40, 6 37, 7 15, 7 42, 10 12 a. m., 12 22, 3 10, 1 48, 5 10, 5 43, *6 34, *11 08 p. m. Sundays, *7 37, *7 15, *9 57 a. m. *1 17, *5 02, *8 05 p. m.
Arrive foot of E. 34th St. in 45 to 60 minutes; at Flatbush Avenue in 1 hour.

Leave **Hyde Park**, 6 15, 7 20, 7 48, 10 17 a. m., 5 18 p. m. Sundays, 7 50, 10 03 a. m., 5 07, 8 13 p. m.
Arrive at E. 34th St. in about 50 minutes; at Flatbush Avenue in 1 hour.

Leave **Hempstead** (leave **Garden City** 5 minutes later) 5 25, 5 57, 6 10, 7 02, 7 50, 8 04, 8 20, 10 02 a. m., 12 23, 3 10, 5 00, *6 35, *8 59, *11 00 p. m. Sundays, 7 35 a. m., 12 41, 3 11, 1 18, 6 10 p. m.
Arrive foot E. 34th St. in 1 hour; arrive Flatbush Avenue in 55 minutes.

Leave **East Hinsdale** (leave Queens 4 minutes later; Hollis, 7 minutes later), *5 16, 6 18, 6 51, 7 51, 8 15, 10 15 a. m., 12 38, 3 24, *6 51, *6 50, *9 11, *11 22 p. m. Sundays, 7 48, 10 06 a. m., 3 26, 5 03, 8 17 p. m. Extra trains from Queens at 7 27 a. m., 4 58 p. m.; from Hollis, 1 02 p. m. Sundays.
Arrive foot of E. 34th St. and Flatbush Avenue in 46 minutes from East Hinsdale.

Leave **Maple Grove**, Sundays, 8 47 p. m.; arrive at E. 34th St. and Flatbush Avenue in 20 minutes.

Leave **Richmond Hill** (Glendale, 5 minutes later; Fresh Pond, 9 minutes later), 6 06, 6 37, *7 06, 7 35, *8 10, *8 38, 10 17, 11 35 a. m., *12 57 (1 10 to New York only), *3 48 (4 27 to New York only), *5 36, *7 15, *9 30, *11 10 p. m. Sundays, 7 35 a. m., 5 23, *8 13 p. m.
Arrive foot E. 34th St. and Flatbush Av. in 30 minutes from Richmond Hill.

GLEN COVE BRANCH.
Stations—Mineola, East Williston, Albertson's, Roslyn, Glen Head, Sea Cliff, Glen Cove, Locust Valley.
**No connection via James Slip Ferry. †Does not stop at East Williston or Albertson's. ‡Does not stop at Albertson's.*
Leave **foot of E. 34th St.** (leave via James Slip Ferry 20 minutes earlier except Sundays) for **Locust Valley** and intermediate stations, 8 50, 10 50 a. m., 1 50, 3 20, ‡4 20, ‡5 20, 6 20, 6 50 p. m., *‡12 10 night. Sundays, 9 20, 9 50 a. m., 6 20 p. m.
Leave **Flatbush Avenue** at 8 52, 10 57 a.m., 2 00, 3 22, ‡4 22, ‡5 22, 6 30, 6 55 p.m., ‡12 15 night. Sundays, 9 30 a.m., 6 30 p.m.
Arrive at Locust Valley in 1½ hours.

To Brooklyn and New York.
Leave **Locust Valley**, stopping at intermediate stations, 5 10, 6 15, 7 16, ‡7 53, 9 10, 11 50 a. m., 2 40, 4 14, 6 03 p. m., on Wednesday and Saturday only 10 39 p. m. Sundays, 7 10, 9 27 a. m., 4 17, 7 00 p. m.
Arrive foot of E. 34th St. and Flatbush Avenue in 1½ hours.

PORT JEFFERSON BRANCH.
Stations.

Hicksville,	Huntington,	East Northport,	St. James,	Port Jefferson.
Syosset,	Greenlawn,	St. Johnland,	Stony Brook,	
Cold Springs	Northport,	Smithtown,	Setauket,	

**No connection via James Slip Ferry. †Does not stop at Northport.*
Leave **foot of E. 34th St.** (leave James Slip Ferry 20 minutes earlier except Sundays) for **Port Jefferson** and intermediate stations, *8 50 a.m., *4 20 p.m. (6 20 p.m. to Northport). Sundays, *8 50 a.m. (9 50 a.m., 6 20 p.m. to Northport).
Leave **Flatbush Avenue**, *8 52 a. m., *4 22 p. m. (6 30 p. m. to Northport). Sundays, *8 55 a.m. (9 30 a.m., 6 30 p.m., to Northport.)
Arrive at Northport in 2 hours; at Port Jefferson 2½ hours.

To Brooklyn and New York.
Leave **Port Jefferson**, stopping at intermediate stations, *6 55 a. m., *3 10 p. m. Sundays, *3 24 p.m.
Leave **Northport**, stopping at intermediate stations, 6 20 a. m. Sundays, 6 32 a. m., 6 04 p. m.
Arrive foot of E. 34th St. and Flatbush Avenue in 2¼ hours from Port Jefferson; in 1¾ hours from Northport.

MONTAUK DIVISION.
Stations.

Long Island City,	Ocean Point,	Bellmore,	Sayville,	West Hampton,
Bushwick,	Lawrence,	Ridgewood,	Bayport,	Quogue,
Brooklyn,	Far Rockaway,	South Oyster Bay,	Patchogue,	Good Ground,
Jamaica,	Pearsall's (East Rockaway),	Amityville,	Bellport,	Shinnecock Hills,
Locust Avenue,	Rockville Centre,	Breslau,	Brookhaven,	Southampton,
Springfield,	Baldwin's,	Babylon,	Forge,	Water Mills,
Valley Stream,	Freeport,	Bayshore,	Moriches,	Bridgehampton,
Hewletts,	Merrick,	Islip,	Eastport,	Sag Harbor.
Woodburgh,		Oakdale,	Speonk,	

**No connection via James Slip Ferry. †Does not stop at Bellmore. ‡Does not stop at Merrick, Bellmore, Ridgewood or Breslau. §Does not stop at Bayport.*

Leave **foot of E. 34th St.** (leave James Slip Ferry 20 minutes earlier, except Sunday):
For **Springfield** and **Valley Stream**, *6 30, 7 50, 10 50 a. m., 12 50, 3 20, 4 20, 5 20, 5 50, 6 54, *7 50, *10 00 p. m., *12 10 night. Sundays, 8 10, 10 50 a. m., 1 50, 6 20 p. m.
Leave **Flatbush Avenue**, 6 15, 8 00, 10 57 a. m., 12 56, 3 22, 4 22, 5 22, 6 00, 6 55, 7 54, 10 05 p. m., 12 15 night. Sundays, 8 15, 11 00 a. m., 2 00, 6 30 p. m.
Arrive **Valley Stream** in 50 minutes.

For **Babylon** and intermediate stations, *6 30, 7 50 (8 20 to Babylon only), 10 50 a. m., 12 50, †3 20, 4 20, ‡5 20, 5 50, 6 50 p. m. (*12 10 night on Wed. and Sat. only). Sundays, 8 10 a. m. (8 50 a. m. to Babylon only), 6 20 p. m.
Leave **Flatbush Avenue**, 6 15, 8 00 (8 30 to Babylon only). 10 57 a.m., 12 56, †3 22, 4 22, ‡5 22 6 00, 6 55 p.m. (12 15 night on Wed. and Sat. only). Sundays, 8 15 a. m., 8 55 a. m. to Babylon only), 6 30 p. m.
Arrive at Babylon in 1¾ hours.

For **Patchogue** and intermediate stations, 8 20, 10 50 a. m., 3 20, 4 20, 5 20 p. m. Sundays, 8 50 a. m.
Leave **Flatbush Avenue**, 8 30, 10 57 a. m., 3 22, 4 22, 5 22 p.m. Sundays, *8 55 a.m.
Arrive at Patchogue in 2¼ hours.

For **Bellport, The Hamptons, Sag Harbor** and intermediate stations, 8 20 a. m., 3 20 p. m. Sundays. 8 50 a. m.
Leave **Flatbush Avenue**, *8 30 a. m., 3 22 p.m. Sundays, 8 55 a. m.
Arrive at West Hampton in 3 hours; at Sag Harbor in 4 hours.

To Brooklyn and New York.
Leave **Sag Harbor**, stopping at intermediate stations, 7 05 a. m., 1 57 p. m. Sundays, 3 58 a. m.; leave **West Hampton**, 7 56 a. m., 2 49 p. m. Sundays, 4 50 p.m. Arrive foot of E. 34th St., 10 37 a. m., 5 37 p. m. Sundays, 7 37 p.m.
Arrive Flatbush Avenue, 10 35 a. m., 5 40 p. m. Sundays, 7 38 p. m.
Leave **Patchogue**, stopping at intermediate stations, 6 30, 7 15, 18 40 a. m., 1 40, 3 54 p. m. Sundays, 5 36 p.m. Arrive at E. 34th St., *8 37, 9 10, 10 37 a. m. (17, 5 37 p.m. Sundays, 7 37 p.m. Arrive at Flatbush Avenue, 8 35, 9 11, 10 35 a. m., 4 15, 5 40 p. m. Sundays, 7 38 p. m.

(Continued on next page.)

LONG ISLAND R. R.—Continued.

MONTAUK DIVISION—Continued.

Leave **Babylon**, stopping at intermediate stations, 5 27, 6 25, 27 13, 7 25, *9 00, 9 26 Express 9 28, 11 52 a. m., 2 31, 4 15 Express 4 21, 6 07 p m ; on Wednesday and Saturday only, 10 30 p. m. Sundays. 6 25 a. m., 4 16 p. m. 6 1* p. m. Express.
Arrive Foot of East 34th street, 7 07, *6 07, *8 37, *5 57 (9 10, 10 37 Express) 11 07 a. m.; 1 27, 4 17 (5 27 Express), 6 07, *7 37 p. m.. on Wednesday and Saturday, *12 07 night. Sundays, *0 6 a. m., 6 06 p. m. (7 37 p. m. Express).
Arrive Flatbush Avenue 7 02, *6 05, *8 35, 9 02, 9 11, 10 35 Express, 11 03 a. m., 1 26, 4 15, (5 10 Express), 6 02, 7 10 p. m.; on Wednesday and Saturday, 12 04 night. Sundays, 7 57 a. m., 6 05 p. m., (7 3* p. m. Express).
Leave **Valley Stream**, (Leave Springfield 6 minutes later) 5 41, 6 15, 7 14, 7 54, *9 14, 9 50, 10 19 a. m., 12 13, 2, 4 14, 3 25, 5 13, 6 47, 9 12, 11 21 p. m. Arrive foot of East 34th street and Flatbush avenue in 50 minutes.

FAR ROCKAWAY BRANCH.
Does not connect via James Slip Ferry.

Stations. Valley Stream, Hewletts, Woodburgh, Ocean Point, Lawrence, Far Rockaway.
Leave **foot of East 34th street**, (leave via James Slip Ferry 20 minutes earlier, except Sundays) for **Far Rockaway**, and intermediate stations, *6 30, 7 50, 10 50 a. m., 12 50, 3 30, 4 30, 5 30, 5 50, 6 50, *7 50, *10 00 p. m., *12 10 night. Sundays, *9 10, 10 50 a. m., 1 50, 6 30 p. m.
Leave **Flatbush Avenue**, 6 45, *9 01, 10 57 a. m., 12 36, 3 22, 4 22, 5 24, 6 00, 6 55, 7 54, 10 05 p.m., 12 15 night. Sundays, *5 15, 11 00 a. m., 2 00, 6 30 p. m.
Arrive at Far Rockaway in one hour, 10 minutes.

To Brooklyn and New York.
Leave **Far Rockaway**, stopping at intermediate stations, 5 27, 6 00, 6 58, 7 37, *9 10, 9 34 a. m.; 12 26, 2 28, 4 52, 6 32, 9 05, 11 07 p. m. Sundays, 6 59, 9 50 a. m ; 3 10, 4 55 p. m. Arrive foot of East 34th street and Flatbush avenue in one hour.

NORTH SIDE DIVISION.
Time from Long Island City to Corona, 10 minutes ; to Whitestone, 32 minutes ; to Great Neck, 40 minutes.
Leave **Long Island City**.
For **Woodside, Winfield, Newtown, Corona, Flushing, College Point, Whitestone and Whitestone Landing**, 6 10, 6 35, 7 10, 7 35, *8 10, 8 45, 10 05, 11 05 a. m... 12 05, 1 00, 2 00, 3 05, 3 30, 4 00, 4 30, 5 00, 5 30, 6 00 6 30, 7 00, 7 30, *8 10, 9 10, 10 10, 11 10 p. m., 12 20 night. Sundays only, *8 35, 9 35, 11 35 a. m... 12 05, 1 35, 2 35, 3 35, 5 35, 6 10, 6 55, 7 35, *8 15, 9 25, 10 30 p. m.
For **Broadway, Bayside, Douglaston, Little Neck and Great Neck**, 6 35, *7 35, *8 45, 11 05 a. m., 1 00, 2 00, 3 30, 4 30, 5 00, 5 30, 6 00, 6 30, 7 00, *8 10, 9 10, 10 10, 11 10 p. m., 12 20 night. Sundays only, *8 35, 9 35 a. m., 12 05, 3 35, 6 10, *8 45 p. m.
Trains marked thus § do not run to College Point, Whitestone or Whitestone Landing. Trains marked thus ‡ do not stop at Douglaston or Little Neck.

To Long Island City and New York.
Leave **Great Neck**, 5 40, 6 10, 6 40, 7 12, 7 53, *8 25, 9 40 a. m... 12 25, 1 54, 2 56, 4 25, 5 31, 6 33, 7 05, 9 05, 10 05, 11 10. p. m. Sundays, *9 10, 9 37, 10 40 a. m., 4 30, 5 10, 7 10 p. m.
Leave **Little Neck**, 5 43, 6 14, 6 43, 7 16, 7 56, *8 28, 9 43 a. m., 12 28, 15*, 3 00, 4 28, 5 30, 6 38, 7 11, 9 03, 10 03, 11 13 p. m. Sundays, *9 14, 9 41, 10 44 a. m., 4 33, 5 14, 7 14 p. m.
Leave **Douglaston**, 5 46, 6 17, 6 46, 7 19, 7 58, *8 30, 9 46 a. m., 12 31, 2 01, 3 03, 4 41, 5 42, 6 41, 7 14, 9 06, 10 05, 11 16 p. m. Sundays, *9 17, 9 45, 10 47 a. m., 4 36, 5 47, 7 47 p. m.
Leave **Bayside**, 5 50, 6 21, 6 50, 7 23, *8 02, *8 34, 9 50 a. m., 12 34, 2 04, 3 07, 4 45, 5 05, 6 44, 7 17, 9 10, 10 10, 11 20 p. m. Sundays, *9 49, 10 51 a. m., 4 40, 5 51, 7 51 p. m.
Leave **Broadway**, 5 54, 6 25, 6 54, 7 27, *8 06, *8 38, 9 54 a. m... 12 38, 2 08, 3 11, 4 50, 5 51, 6 48, 7 21, 9 14, 10 14, 11 24 p. m. Sundays, *9 24, 9 55, 10 55 a. m., 4 44, 5 55, 7 55 p. m.
Leave **Flushing**, *5 33, 6 00, 6 30, 7 00, *7 34, *7 48, *8 01, *8 03, *8* 12, *8 33, *8 45, 9 30, 10 00, 11 02 a. m., 12 42, 12 48, 2 12, *3 02, *3 16, *3 58, *4 36, 4 55, *5 26, *5 56, 6 52, 7 26, *8 35, 9 17, 10 17, 11 27 p. m. Sundays, *8 01, *9 30, 10 00, 11 00 a. m., 12 30, 1 30, 2 20, *4 31, *4 50, 5 20, *6 46, *8 10, *8 36 p. m.
Leave **Whitestone Landing**, 5 22, 5 49, 6 21, 6 49, 7 20, 7 52, *8 22, 9 19, 9 50, 10 51, 11 51 a. m., 12 36, 2 04, 2 59, 4 14, 4 45, 5 15, 6 40, 7 14, *8 23, 9 05, 10 05, 11 15 p. m. Sundays, 7 50, *8 20, 10 47, 10 47 a. m., 12 17, 1 30, 2 30, 4 25, 5 05, 7 46, *8 22, 9 25 p. m.
Leave **Whitestone**, 5 25, 5 52, 6 21, 6 52, 7 34, 7 55, *8 25, 9 22, 9 53, 10 54, 11 54 a. m., 12 40, 2 01, 2 54, 4 17, 4 48, 5 18, 6 14, 7 17, *8 26, 9 08, 10 08, 11 1* p. m. Sundays, 7 53, *8 23, 9 51, 10 51 a. m., 12 21, 1 23, 2 23, 4 23, 5 50, 6 38, 7 50, *8 26, 9 28 p. m.
Leave **College Point**, 5 29, 5 56, 6 25, 6 56, 7 38, 7 59, *8 29, 9 26, 9 57, 10 58, 11 58 a. m., 12 44, 2 05, 2 58, 4 21, 4 52, 5 22, 6 19, 7 21, *8 30, 9 13, 10 13, 11 23 p. m. Sundays, 7 57, *8 27, 9 55, 10 55 a. m., 12 25, 1 27, 2 27, 4 27, 5 54, 6 42, 7 55, *8 30, 9 32 p. m.
Leave **Corona**, 5 39, 6 08, 6 39, 7 08, 7 38, 8 09, *8 39, 9 38, 10 09, 11 09 a. m... 12 09, 12 57, 2 21, 3 09, 3 32, 4 05, 4 32, 5 04, 5 32, 6 02, 7 00, 7 31, *8 42, 9 26, 10 26, 11 36 p. m. Sundays, *8 07, *8 39, 10 07, 11 07 a. m., 12 37, 1 37, 2 37, 4 37, 4 57, 6 08, 6 53, *8 08, *8 41, 9 42 p. m.
Leave **Newtown**, 5 42, 6 11, 6 42, 7 11, 7 41, 8 12, *8 42, 9 41, 10 12, 11 12 a. m... 12 12, 1 01, 2 26, 3 12, 3 37, 4 08, 4 35, 5 07, 5 35, 6 05, 7 03, 7 37, *8 45, 9 30, 10 30, 11 40 p. m. Sundays, *8 10, *8 42, 10 10, 11 10 a. m., 12 40, 1 40, 2 40, 4 40, 5 00, 6 11, 6 56, *8 11, *8 44, 9 45 p. m.
Leave **Winfield**, 5 45, 6 14, 6 45, 7 14, 7 44, *8 15, *8 45, 9 44, 10 15, 11 15 a. m... 12 15, 1 04, 2 30, 3 15, 3 30, 4 11, 4 38, 5 10, 5 38, 6 08, 7 06, 7 40, *8 48, 9 33, 10 33, 11 43 p. m. Sundays, *8 13, *8 45, 10 13, 11 13 a. m... 12 43, 1 43, 2 43, 4 43, 5 03, 6 14, 6 59, *8 14, *8 47, 9 48 p. m.
Leave **Woodside**, 5 48, 6 18, 6 48, 7 18, 7 48, *8 18, *8 48, 9 48, 10 18, 11 18 a. m., 12 18, 1 08, 2 31, 3 18, 3 34, 4 15, 4 41, 5 13, 5 41, 6 11, 7 09, 7 43, *8 51, 9 36, 10 36, 11 46 p. m. Sundays, *8 17, *8 48, 10 17, 11 16 a. m., 12 46, 1 46, 2 46, 4 47, 5 07, 6 18, 7 03, *8 18, *8 51, 9 52 p. m.
Trains marked thus * leave Main St. only. Trains marked thus + leave Bridge St. only.

MANHATTAN BEACH DIVISION.
Stations.
Long Island City, Bushwick Av. (Evergreens Cemetery), Flatlands,
Penny Bridge (Calvary Cemetery), Brooklyn, South Greenfield,
Bushwick Junc. (Lutheran Cemetery), East New York, King's Highway,
Ridgewood (Cypress Avenue), New Lots, Sheepshead Bay,
Cooper Avenue, Kowenhovens, Manhattan Beach.

Leave **Long Island City** for **East New York** and intermediate stations, 6 30, 7 30, *8 11, *9 40, *11 20 a. m., *12 30, *2 0*, *3 10, *5 39, *6 40, *7 35 p. m.; due at East New York in 32 minutes. *Daily.*
For **Sheepshead Bay and Manhattan Beach**, stopping at intermediate stations, 6 30, *8 41, 11 30, a. m., 3 10, 5 39, p. m.; Sundays, *8 41 a. m., 12 30, 2 08 p. m.; due at Manhattan Beach in 50 minutes.

To Long Island City and New York.
Leave **Manhattan Beach** (Sheepshead Bay 4 minutes later), 6 33, 7 33, 9 40 a. m... 12 38, 4 10, 6 35 p. m.; Sundays., 9 40 a. m., 5 40 p. m.; due at Long Island City in 47 minutes.
Leave **East New York**, 6 00, 6 59, *7 59, *9 07, *10 07, *11 50 a. m., *1 05, *2 35, *4 35, *6 05, *7 00 p. m.; due at Long Island City in 22 minutes.

BROOKLYN TO SHEEPSHEAD BAY AND MANHATTAN BEACH.
Leave **Flatbush Avenue**, 6 40, 8 11 30 a. m., 3 20, 5 45 p. m. on Wednesday and Saturday nights, 11 30 p. m.; Sundays, *8 50 a. m., 12 37, 2 20, 4 00 p. m.; due at Manhattan Beach in 40 minutes.

Manhattan Beach to Brooklyn.
Leave **Manhattan Beach** (Sheepshead Bay 4 minutes later), 6 33, 7 33, 9 40 a. m., 12 38, 4 10 p. m.; on Wednesdays and Saturdays, 6 35 p. m.; Sundays, 9 40 a. m., 1 27, 3 10, 5 40 p. m.; due at Flatbush Avenue in 40 minutes.

LONG ISLAND R. R.—Continued.

RAPID TRANSIT TRAINS.

Brooklyn, Woodhaven, Morris Park, Jamaica.

Stopping at Vanderbilt, Grand, Franklin, Nostrand, Brooklyn, Kingston, Troy, Utica, Ralph, Saratoga, and Rockaway Avenues; and in East New York, at Manhattan Beach R. R. crossing, Howard House, Pennsylvania and Van Sicklen Avenues, Linwood Street and Morse Avenue, and at Cypress Avenue, Adamsville, Union Course, Clarenceville and Van Wyck Avenue.

Daily Except Sundays.

Leave Flatbush Avenue Station for Woodhaven Junction at 6.01 a. m., and from 6.15 a. m. every 10 minutes to 6.45 a. m.; from 6.45 a. m. every 7 minutes to 9.00 a. m.; from 9.00 a. m. every 10 minutes to 5.00 p. m.; from 5.00 p. m. every 7 minutes to 7.00 p. m.; from 7.00 p. m. every 15 minutes to 11.00 p. m.; and at 11.00, 11.30 and 12.00 night.

Leave Woodhaven Junction for Flatbush Avenue at 5.19 a. m. 6.30 a. m. for East New York only), 5.38, 5.48, 5.59, 6.05, 6.11, 6.22, 6.29, 6.35, 6.52, 6.59, 7.05, 7.11 a. m.; from 7.11 a. m. every 7 minutes to 8.29 a. m.; from 8.29 a. m. about every 10 minutes to 4.22 p. m.; from 4.22 p. m. about every 7 minutes to 6.22 p. m.; from 6.22 p. m. every 15 minutes to 10.22 p. m., and at 10.22, 10.52, and 11.22 p. m.

Sundays only.

Leave Flatbush Avenue Station for Woodhaven Junction at 7.00, 7.30 and 8.00 a. m. (and from 8 a. m. every 15 minutes to 12.30 p. m.; from 12.30 p. m. every 10 minutes to 9.00 p. m.; from 9.00 p. m. every 15 minutes to 11.00 p. m., and at 11.00, 11.30 and 12.00 night.

Leave Woodhaven Junction for Flatbush Avenue at 6.22, 6.52, 7.22, 7.40, 7.52, 8.08 and at 8.22 a. m., and from 8.22 a. m. every 14 minutes to 11.52 a. m.; from 11.52 a. m. every 10 minutes to 8.22 p. m.; from 8.22 p. m. about every 14 minutes to 10.22 p. m., and at 10.22, 10.51 and 11.22 p. m.

JAMAICA AND MORRIS PARK TRAINS.

Daily, except Sundays.

Leave Flatbush Avenue for Morris Park and Jamaica at 6.00, 6.25, 7.00, 7.30, 8.00, 8.30, 9.30, 10.30, 11.30 a. m., 12.30, 1.30, 2.30, 3.30, 4.30, 5.30, 5.30, 6.00, 6.30, 7.00 and 11.30 p. m.

Leave Jamaica for Flatbush Avenue at 5.12, 5.40, 6.15, 6.45, 7.15, 7.45, 8.15, 8.55, 9.25, 10.15, 11.15 a. m., 12.15, 1.15, 2.15, 3.15, 4.15, 5.15, 5.45, 6.15, 6.45 p. m. Leave Morris Park 1 minutes later.

Sundays only.

Leave Flatbush Avenue for Morris Park and Jamaica at 9.30, 10.30, 11.30 a. m., 12.30, 1.30, 2.30, 3.30, 4.30, 5.30, 6.30, 7.30 and 11.30 p. m.

Leave Jamaica for Flatbush Avenue at 7.15, 8.15, 10.30, 11.30, a. m., 12.05, 12.35, 1.35, 2.35, 3.35, 4.35, 5.35 and 6.35 p. m. Leave Morris Park 4 minutes later.

BOAT AND STAGE CONNECTIONS.

For Shelter Island.—Ferry at Greenport.
For Orient. Stages connect at Greenport with train leaving Long Island City at 8.35 a. m.
For East Hampton, Amagansett and Springs.—Stages connect at Bridgehampton and Sag Harbor (daily, except Sundays).
For Cold Spring Harbor. Stages connect at Cold Spring station with trains from Long Island City.
For Oyster Bay.—Stages connect at Syosset with trains leaving Long Island City at 9.00 a. m. and 4.35 p. m., and at Locust Valley with trains leaving Long Island City at 9.00 a. m. and 4.35 p. m. (daily, except Sundays).
For New Suffolk and Robbins Island. Stages connect at Cutchogue.
For Atlanticville.—Stages connect at Quogue.
For Lake Ronkonkoma and Lake Grove. Stages connect at Ronkonkoma.
For Selden and Coram.—Stages connect at Medford.
For Wading River.—Stages connect at Manor.
For Northville, Aquebogue and Flanders.—Stages connect at Riverhead.
For Mastic.—Stages connect at Forge.
For Blue Point.—Stages connect at Bayport.
For East Rockaway.—Stages connect at Pearsall's.

The steamer "Manhansett," for New London, Conn., leaves Greenport at 1.30 p. m. daily (except Sundays).

LOCATION OF PIERS.

Unless otherwise stated the numbers given are "old" numbers.

NORTH RIVER.

Pier No.	Street.
A & 1	Battery Pl.
2, 3	Battery Pl. & Morris.
1	Morris.
5, 6, 7	Morris & Rector.
	Rector.
9, 10	Rector & Carlisle.
11	Carlisle.
12	Albany.
13	Albany & Cedar.
14	Cedar.
15	Liberty.
16	Liberty & Cortlandt.
17, 18	Cortlandt.
19	Cortlandt & Dey.
20	Dey.
New 20	Chambers.
21	Fulton.
New 21	Duane.
22	Fulton & Vesey.
23	Vesey.
24	Vesey & Barclay.
New 24	Franklin & N. Moore.
25	Barclay.
26	Barclay & Park Pl.
New 26	Beach.
27	Park Place.
New 27	Hubert.
28	Murray.
New 28	Laight.
32	Duane & Jay.
33	Jay.

Pier No.	Street.
34	Harrison.
New 34	Canal.
35	Franklin.
New 35	Spring.
36	N. Moore.
New 36	Spring & Charlton.
New 37	Charlton.
New 38	King.
39	Vestry & Desbrosses.
New 39	W. Houston.
40	Watts.
New 40	Clarkson.
41	12 Canal.
New 41	Leroy.
New 42	Morton.
New 43	Barrow.
New 44	Christopher.
46, 47	W. 10th.
New 48	W. 11th.
51	Perry.
New 51	W. 49th.
New 55	W. 25th.
56	Bethune.
New 56	W. 26th.
57	Bogart.
New 57	W. 27th.
58	Bloomfield.
59	Little 12th.
New 59	W. 49th.

EAST RIVER.

Pier No.	Street.
1, 2	Whitehall.
3	Moore.
4	Moore & Broad.
5	Broad & Coenties Sl.
6, 7, 8	Coenties Slip.
9, 10	Coenties & Old Slip.
11, 12	Old Slip.
13	Old Slip & Gouverneur Lane.
14	Jones Lane.
15, 16	Wall.
17	Pine.
18	Maiden Lane.
19	Fletcher.
20, 21	Burling Slip.
22	Fulton.
23	Beekman.
24	Beekman & Peck Sl.
25, 26	Peck Slip.
27	Dover.
28	Dover & Roosevelt.
29	Roosevelt.
30	Roosevelt & James Sl.
31, 32	James Slip.
33	Oliver.
34, 35	Catherine.
36	Catherine & Market.
37, 38	Market.
39	Market & Pike.
40, 41	Pike.

Pier No.	Street.
42	Pike & Rutgers.
43, 44	Rutgers.
45	Rutgers & Jefferson.
46	Jefferson.
47	Jefferson & Clinton.
48	Clinton.
49	Clinton & Montgomery.
50	Montgomery.
51, 52	Gouverneur Slip.
53	Jackson.
54	Corlears.
55	Cherry.
56, 57	Broome.
58, 59	Delancey.
60	Rivington.
61	Rivington & Stanton.
62	Stanton.
63	Third.
64	Fifth.
65	Sixth.
66	Seventh.
67	Eighth.
68	E. 9th.
69	E. 10th.
70	E. 11th.
71	E. 12th.
72	E. 13th.
73	E. 14th.

FOREIGN CONSULS IN NEW YORK.

Argentine Republic—Carlos Carranza, C. G.; A. G, Calvo, C.; F. L. de Castro, V. C., 60 Wall.
Austria-Hungary—T. A. Havemeyer, C. G.; Herr Palitzchek, C.; O. F. Eberhard, A. C., 33 Broadway.
Belgium—J. Rouleaux, C. G., 236 5th av.; C. Mali, C.; P. Mali, V. C., 329 Broadway.
Bolivia—Melechor Obarrio, C. G., 178 Broadway.
Brazil—S. de Mendonca, C. G., 22 State; G. H. Gossler, V. C., 18 Pearl.
Chili—F. A. Bechan, C. G., 102 West 131st; J. R. de la Espriella, C., 59 Liberty.
China—Yee Shaw How, C.; Lew Yuk Lin, V. C., 26 W. 9th.
Colombia—C. Calderon, C. G., 16 Beaver.
Costa Rica—J. M. Munoz, C. G., 59 Liberty; J. M. Ceballos, V. C., 80 Wall.
Denmark—H. M. Braem, C.; Thomas Schmidt, V. C., 69 Wall.
Dominican Republic—Leonico Julia, C. 31 Broadway.
Ecuador—D. L. Ruiz, C. G., 51 Liberty.
France—Paul d'Abzac, C. G.; A. Bonnefons, C.; A. Daussing, V. C., 4 Bowling Green.
German Empire—A. Feigel, C. G.; C. B. Marheinecke, C.; C. Ferle, V. C., 2 Bowling Green.
Great Britain—W. L. Booker, C. G.; W. R. Hoare, C., 24 State; G. Fraser, 1st V. C., 2 Morris; H. D. Nugent, 2d V. C., 24 State.
Greece—D. N. Botassi, C. G., 115 Pearl.
Guatemala—J. Baiz, C. G., 102 Front.
Hawaiian Islands—E. H. Allen, C. G., 51 Leonard.
Hayti—Nourmil Deslandes, C. G.; C. Singleton, V. C., 24 State.
Honduras—J. Baiz, C. G., 102 Front; F. Spies, V. C., 36 B'way.
Italy—J. P. Riva, C. G.; A. Monaco, 1st V. C.; G. Markazzi, 2d V. C., 24 State.
Japan—K. Kawakami, C., 7 Warren.
Korea—E. Frazar, C. G., 124 Water.
Liberia—J. W. Yates, C., 19 William st.
Mexico—J. N. Navarro, C. G.; R. V. Williams, Chancellor, 35 Broadway.
Monaco—A. Daussing, C., 4 Bowling Green.
Netherlands—J. R. Planten, C. G.; W. M. B. Gravenhorst, V. C., 17 Broad.
Nicaragua—A. I. Cotheal, C.G.; Gerardo Canton, C., 76 Beaver.
Norway—C. Bors, C.; C. Ravn, V. C., 11 Broad.
Orange Free State, South Africa—C. D. Pierce, C., 80 Beaver.
Peru—Hernandez & Tracy, 39 Broad.
Portugal—Barnod'Almeirim, C. G.; G. Amsinck, C., 118 Pearl.
Russia—Baron Rosen, C. G.; C. G. Petersen, V. C., 24 State.
Salvador—J. A. P. Ronalde, C.G.; S. P. Triana, V.C., 16 Beaver.
Siam—T. T. Smith, C. G., 135 Broadway.
Spain—M. S. Guanes, C. G.; M. de la Cueva, V. C., 30 B'way.
Sweden—C. Bors, C.; C. Ravn, V. C., 11 Broad.
Switzerland—J. Bertschmann, C., 69 Beaver; J. E. Robert, V. C., 30 Maiden Lane.
Turkey—Ballazzi Effendi, C. G., 16 East 40th st.
Uruguay—E. M. Estranulas, C. G., 120 Front.
Venezuela—Pedro Vicente Mijares, C. G., 18 Broadway.

GRAND ARMY OF THE REPUBLIC.
Posts in New York City. Meeting Place, etc.

Anderson, Robt., No. 58, 190 8th av.—2d and 4th Wednesday.
Andrew, John A., No. 234, 835 B'way.—1st and 3d Thursday.
Aspinwall, L., No. 600, 156th st. & 10th av.—Every 2d Thursday.
Bendix, John E., No. 404, W. Boulevard & 74th st.—2d and 4th Tuesday.
Cameron, No. 79, 64 E. 4th.—2d and 4th Thursday.
Claflin, Horace B., No. 578, cor. 4th av. & 129th.—1st and 3d Mondays.
Cooper, Peter, No. 582, cor. Grand & Ludlow.—Every Thursday.
Corcoran, Geo. M., No. 427, 189 Bowery.—1st & 3d Wednesday.
Dahlgren, No. 113, 52 Orchard.—Every Tuesday.
Dix, John A., No. 135, 38 Union Sq.—1st and 3d Tuesday.
Ellsworth, No. 67, 1501 2d av.—1st and 3d Monday.
Farnham, N. L., No. 458, Broadway & 49th st.—2d and 4th Wednesday.
Farragut, No. 75, W. 74th st. & Boulevard.—Every 2d Monday.
Gilsa, No. 264, 207 E. 56th st.—2d and 4th Tuesday.
Goss, Adam, No. 330, 63 Ludlow.—Every Tuesday.
Greeley, Horace, No. 577, 52 Union sq.—Every 3d Sunday.
Hamilton, Alex., No. 182, 331 Lenox av.—1st, 3d and 5th Thursday.
Hancock, W. S., No. 259, cor. 8th av. & 25th st.—2d and 4th Tuesday.
Hecker, Fred., No. 408, 260 W. 41st st.—1st and 3d Thursday.
Hooker, Joe, No. 128, 263 Bowery.—2d and 4th Friday.
Jackson, Andrew, No. 300, 52 Union sq.—1st and 3d Monday.
Kearney, Phil., No. 8, 389 6th av.—1st and 3d Thursday.
Kennedy, Wm. D., No. 42, cor. Bowery & 2d st.—2d and 4th Wednesday.
Kilpatrick, Judson, No. 143, 124th st. & 3d av.—2d and 4th Monday.
Kimball, E. A., No. 100, 54 Union sq.—1st and 3d Saturdays.
Koltes, No. 33, 291 Bowery.—1st and 3d Fridays.
Lafayette, No. 140, Masonic Temple, 6th av. & 23d.—1st and 3d Friday.
Lincoln, Abraham, No. 13, 54 Union sq.—2d & 4th Wednesday.
McClellan, Geo. B., No. 552, cor. Bleecker & Morton.—1st and 3d Wednesday.
M'Quade, Gen. Jas., No. 557, 234 Spring.—Every Wednesday.
Meade, George G., No. 39, 501 Hudson.—Every Friday.
Meagher, Gen. Thos. F., No. 567, 1501 2d av.—1st & 3d Sunday.
Mitchell, Wm. G., No. 559, 52 Union sq.—1st & 3d Wednesday.
Monroe, James, No. 607, 22d Reg't Armory, 14th st.—1st Saturday and 3d Friday.
Morgan, E. D., No. 307, Grand Opera House, 23d st. & 8th av.—1st and 3d Thursday.
Musicians, No. 452, 61 E. 4th st.—Every 4th Thursday, 2 p. m.
Naval, No. 316, 189 Bowery—2d, 4th and 5th Monday.
Powell, Hans, No. 658, 225 Grand—2d and 4th Saturday.
Rawlins, John A., No. 80, 52 Union sq.—2d and 4th Tuesdays.
Reno, No. 44, 151 E. 51th st.—2d and 4th Tuesday.
Rice, James C., No. 29, cor. 8th av. & 25th st.—3d & 4th Friday.
Riker, J. L., No. 62, 263 Bowery—2d and 4th Monday.
Sedgwick, No. 186, 289 Bleecker—2d and 4th Wednesday.
Sheridan, Phil., No. 233, 2009 3d av.—1st and 3d Monday.
Shields, James, No. 69, 20 2d av.—2d and 4th Tuesday.
Steinwehr, No. 192, 314 5th st.—1st and 3d Wednesday.
Stevens, Thad., No. 255, 89 6th av.—2d and 4th Wednesday.
Sumner, No. 24, 341 W. 17th.—2d and 4th Monday.
Tilden, Oliver, No. 96, 3d av. & 105th st.—2d and 4th Tuesday.
Vanderbilt, No. 139, cor. 86th st. & 3d av.—2d and 4th Tuesday.
Veteran, No. 436, 54 Union sq.—2d and 4th Thursday.
Volunteer, No. 459, 276 Spring—1st, 3d and 5th Monday.
Wade, Edw. H., No. 539, 278 Bleecker—2d and 4th Wednesday.
Wadsworth, No. 77, 630 9th av.—2d and 4th Monday.
Washington, Geo., No. 103, Hotel Brunswick—Once a month.
Williams, A. S., No. 394, 147 W. 32d.—2d and 4th Monday.

Posts in Kings County.

Barbara Freitchie, No. 11, 116 Culyer—2d and 4th Wednesday.
Beecher, H. W., No. 620, 416 Adelphi.—2d and 4th Monday.
Cushing, No. 231, 476 5th av.—1st and 3d Monday.
Dakin, T. S., No. 206, 136 Broadway—2d and 4th Tuesday.
Devin, No. 148, 153 Pierrepont—1st and 3d Friday.
Doane, Chas. B., No. 499, cor. Dekalb & Bedford avs.—1st & 3d Thursday.
Dupont, S. F., No. 187, 98 Graham av.—2d and 4th Wednesday.
Ford, N. S., No. 161, Leuken's Assembly Rooms, Canarsie—1st and 3d Saturday.
Garrison, Wm. Lloyd, No. 207, 61 Henry—1st and 3d Monday.
Germain, Metternich, No. 122, 54 Graham av.—2d & 4th Friday.
Grant, U. S., No. 327, cor. Nevins St. & Flatbush av.—2d & 4th Tuesday.
Hamilton, L. M., No. 152, Schielleins Hall, East N. Y.—2d & 4th Tuesday.
Head, Frank, No. 67, cor. Court & Harrison—2d & 4th Thursday.
Kerswell, No. 149, Schoonmaker's Hall, Flatbush—2d and 4th Tuesday.
Lee, Harry, No. 21, Amphion Academy, W'msburg—2d & 4th Thursday.
Mackenzie, C. D., No. 369, 315 Washington—1st & 3d Tuesday.
Mallery, No. 84, cor. Fulton & Flatbush avs.—Every 3d Wed.
Mansfield, No. 45, Bedford av. & N. 2d st.—1st 3d & 5th Tuesday.
Middleton, B. F., No. 509, 654 Gates av.—1st and 3d Saturday.
M'Pherson, Geo., No. 614, 142 Flatbush av.—1st & 3d Thursday.
Odell, Moses F., No. 443, 153 Pierrepont—2d & 4th Thursday.
Perry, James B., No. 89, Stella Hall, Bedford near Myrtle—1st, 3d and 5th Wednesday.
Rankin, No. 10, cor. Court & Schermerhorn—1st & 3d Friday.
Ricard, Geo., No. 392, Bedford av. & S. 2d st.—1st & 3 I Thursday.
Smith, Abel, No. 435, cor. Bedford av. & S. 2d st.—2d & 4th Monday.
Strong, Geo. C., Gates & Nostrand avs.—2d and 4th Tuesday.
Tefft, Erastus T., No. 355, 153 Pierrepont—2d & 4th Saturday.
Thatford, No. 3, cor. 5th av. & 19th st.—1st and 3d Tuesday.
Wall, Michael W., No. 628, 572 Wythe av.—1st & 3d Thursday.
Warren, G. K., No. 286, c. Troy & Fulton av.—1st & 3d Monday.
Winchester, Salmon, No. 197, cor. Bedford & Fulton avs.—1st and 3d Thursday.

This is the only Guide designed to answer the perplexing questions that arise in our homes. "What train (or boat) will you take?" "When does the Mail close?" "When is the Steamer due?" These questions are all answered in Kenny's Guide.

TELEGRAPH RATES

TO ALL IMPORTANT POINTS IN THE UNITED STATES, CANADA AND MEXICO.

Western Union Telegraph Co.

The Rate given is explained thus: For a message to Birmingham, Ala., containing ten words, the charge is 50 cents, and 3 cents for each additional word.

Alabama.
Birmingham	50–3
Blount Springs	50–3
Decatur	50–3
Huntsville	50–3
Mobile	50–3
Montgomery	50–3
Tuscaloosa	50–3

Arizona.
Benson	1.00–7
Prescott	1.00–10
Tucson	1.00–7
Willcox	1.00–7
Yuma	1.00–7

Arkansas.
Arkansas City	60–4
Batesville	60–4
Benton	60–4
Camden	60–4
Eureka Springs	60–4
Fayetteville	60–4
Fort Smith	60–4
Helena	60–4
Hope	60–4
Hot Springs	50–3
Little Rock	50–3
Mammoth Springs	60–4
Morrilton	60–4
Newport	60–4
Pine Bluff	50–3
Plummerville	60–4
Searcy	60–4
Texarkana	50–3

British Columbia.
Donald	1.85–13
Kamloops	1.85–13
Lytton	1.60–11
Nanaimo	1.60–11
Vancouver	1.60–11
Victoria	1.60–11

California.
Alameda	1.00–7
Eureka	1.00–7
Los Angeles	1.00–7
Mendocino	1.00–7
Merced	1.00–7
Napa	1.00–7
National City	1.00–7
Oakland	1.00–7
Port Harford	1.00–7
Sacramento	1.00–7
San Bernardino	1.00–7
San Diego	1.00–7
San Francisco	1.00–7
San Mateo	1.00–7
Santa Cruz	1.00–7
Soledad	1.00–7
Yosemite	1.00–7

Colorado.
Canon City	75–5
Colorado Springs	75–5
Denver	75–5
Durango	75–5
Georgetown	75–5
Glenwood Springs	75–5
Grand Junction	75–5
Gunnison	75–5
Idaho Springs	75–5
Las Animas	75–5
Leadville	75–5
Pitkin	75–5
Pueblo	75–5
Silverton	75–5
Trinidad	75–5

Connecticut.
Ansonia	25–2
Beacon Falls	25–2
Berlin	25–2
Bethel	25–2
Birmingham	25–2
Bridgeport	25–2
Bristol	25–2
Canaan	25–2
Clinton	25–2
Cobalt	25–2
Colchester	25–2
Collinsville	25–2
Cornwall Bridge	25–2
Cos Cob	25–2
Danbury	25–2
Darien	25–2
Derby	25–2
East Berlin	25–2
East Canaan	25–2
East Haven	50–4
Essex	50–4
Fairfield	25–2
Fair Haven	25–2
Farmington	25–2
Greenwich	25–2
Groton	25–2
Guilford	25–2
Haddam	50
Hadlyme	25–2
Hartford	25–2
Hawleyville	25–2
Kent	25–2
Lime Rock	25–2
Litchfield	25–2
Lyme	25–2
Manchester	25–2
Meriden	25–2
Merwinsville	25–2
Middlefield	25–2
Middletown	25–2
Milford	25–2
Mystic	25–2
Naugatuck	25–2
New Britain	25–2
New Canaan	25–2
New Haven	25–2
New London	25–2
New Milford	25–2
Newtown	25–2
Noroton	25–2
Norwalk	25–2
Norwich	25–2
Plainfield	25–2
Putnam	25–2
Roxbury	25–2
Saybrook	25–2
Southington	25–2
South Norwalk	25–2
Southport	25–2
Stamford	25–2
Stepney	25–2
Stonington	25–2
Stratford	25–2
Suffield	25–2
Tolland	25–2
Torrington	25–2
Union City	50
Unionville	25–2
Vernon	25–2
Wallingford	25–2
Waterbury	25–2
Westbrook	25–2
West Haven	25–2
Westport	25–2
Willimantic	25–2
Wilton	25–2
Windsor	25–2
Windsor Locks	25–2
Winnipauk	25–2
Winsted	25–2
Woodbury	25–2

Dakota.
Bismarck	75–5
Brookings	75–5
Buffalo Gap	75–5
Cooperstown	75–5
Deadwood	75–5
Dickinson	75–5
Elkhdale	75–5
Fargo	75–5
Flandreau	75–5
Grand Forks	75–5
Howard	75–5
Jamestown	75–5
Lead City	75–5
Mandan	75–5
Medora	75–5
Milnor	75–5
Minnewaukan	75–5
Pembina	75–5
Pierre	75–5
Plankinton	75–5
Rapid City	75–5
Running Water	75–5
Tower City	75–5

Delaware.
Delaware Breakwater	25–2
Delaware City	25–2
Delmar	25–2
Georgetown	25–2
Lewes	25–2
Newark	1.00
New Castle	25–2
Rehoboth	25–2
Smyrna	25–2
Wilmington	25–2

District of Columbia.
Georgetown	25–2
Washington	25–2

Florida.
Astor	1.10–7
Brooksville	1.10–7
Cedar Keys	1.10–7
Cleveland	1.10–7
Daytona	1.00–7
Fernandina	60–4
Gainesville	85–6
Jacksonville	60–4
Key West	2.10–14
Leesburg	1.00–7
Marianna	60–4
New Smyrna	1.85–9
Ocala	1.00–7
Palatka	85–6
Pensacola	60–4
Ponce de Leon	60–4
St. Augustine	85–6
Tampa	1.50–10
Titusville	1.10–7

Georgia.
Athens	50–3
Atlanta	50–3
Augusta	50–3
Brunswick	50–3
Columbus	50–3
Forsyth	50–3
Fort Gaines	50–3
Fort Valley	50–3
Gainesville	50–3
Macon	50–3
Quitman	50–3
Rome	50–3
Savannah	50–3
Thomasville	50–3
Way Cross	50–3

Idaho.
American Falls	1.00–7
Boise City	1.00–7
Coeur d'Alene City	1.05–7

Illinois.
Altamont	50–3
Alton	50–3
Amboy	50–3
Aurora	50–3
Batavia	50–3
Belvidere	50–3
Bloomington	50–3
Buda	50–3
Cairo	50–3
Carrollton	50–3
Champaign	50–3
Chicago	40–3
Clay City	50–3
Decatur	50–3
Du Quoin	50–3
East St. Louis	50–3
Edwardsville	50–3
Elgin	50–3
Elvaston	50–3
Galena	50–3
Galesburg	50–3
Havana	50–3
Jacksonville	50–3
Jerseyville	50–3
Joliet	50–3
Lanark	50–3
La Salle	50–3
Litchfield	50–3
Mason City	50–3
Mattoon	50–3
McLeansboro	50–3
Mendota	50–3
Odin	50–3
O'Fallon	50–3
Paris	50–3
Pekin	50–3
Peoria	50–3
Princeton	50–3
Pulaski	50–3
Quincy	50–3
Rockford	50–3
Rockport	50–3
Sangamon	50–3
Savanna	50–3
Shawneetown	50–3
Shelbyville	50–3
Shumway	50–3
Springfield	50–3
Strawn	50–3
Streator	50–3
Tamaroa	50–3
Urbana	50–3
Vienna	50–3
Virden	50–3
Waggoner	50–3
Washington	50–3
Winnebago	50–3

Indiana.
Albany	50–3
Auburn	50–3
Brazil	50–3
Cambridge City	50–3
Clay City	50–3
Decatur	50–3
De Pauw	50–3
Elkhart	50–3
Evansville	50–3
Fort Wayne	40–3
Goshen	50–3
Indianapolis	40–3
Laketon	50–3
La Porte	50–3
Logansport	40–3
Michigan City	50–3
Muncie	50–3
New Albany	50–3
Oakland City	50–3
Peru	50–3
Poseyville	50–3
Richmond	40–3
Rushville	50–3
South Bend	50–3
Switz City	50–3
Terre Haute	50–3
Union City	40–3
Valparaiso	50–3
Vincennes	50–3

Indian Territory.
Gibson	75–5
McAllister	75–5
Muskogee	75–5
Savanna	75–5

Iowa.
Ackley	60–4
Adair	60–4
Albia	60–4
Anamosa	60–4
Audubon	60–4
Belle Plaine	60–4
Calmar	60–4
Cedar Falls	60–4
Cedar Rapids	60–4
Clarinda	60–4
Correctionville	60–4
Council Bluffs	60–4
Crawfordsville	60–4
Dakota City	60–4
Davenport	50–3
Davis City	60–4
Des Moines	50–3
Dubuque	50–3
Dysart	60–4
Farmington	60–4
Forest City	60–4
Harlan	60–4
Hawarden	60–4
Homestown	60–4
Independence	60–4
Iowa City	60–4
Judd	60–4
Keokuk	50–3
Linn	60–4
Malvern	60–4
Marshalltown	60–4

TELEGRAPH RATES—Continued.

Place	Rate
Mason City	.60-4
McGregor	.60-4
Missouri Valley	.60-4
Montezuma	.60-4
Ottumwa	.60
Palo	.60-4
Plano	.60-4
Pulaski	.60-4
Ruthven	.60-4
Sac City	.60-4
Shellsburg	.60-4
Sioux City	.60
Sioux Rapids	.90-4
Spirit Lake	.60-4
Story City	.60-4
Tama	.60-4
Wadena	.60
Wapello	.60
Waukon	.60-4
What Cheer	.60-4
Winterset	.60-4

Kansas.

Place	Rate
Abilene	.60-4
Anthony	.60-4
Arkansas City	.60-4
Atchison	.50-3
Burlingame	.60-4
Cherryvale	.60-4
Concordia	.60-4
Dodge City	.60-4
El Dorado	.60-4
Emporia	.60-4
Fort Leavenworth	.60
Fort Scott	.60
Fredonia	.60-4
Garden City	.60-4
Greeley	.60-4
Harper	.60-4
Hutchinson	.60-4
Larned	.60-4
Leavenworth	.50-3
Meade Centre	.60-4
Olathe	.60-4
Osage City	.60-4
Rush Centre	.85-6
Salina	.60-4
Springfield	.60
Wabaunsee	.60-4
Wichita	.60
Wyandotte	.60-4

Kentucky.

Place	Rate
Bowling Green	.50-3
Burnside	.50-3
Covington	.40-3
Frankfort	.50-3
Georgetown	.50-3
Glasgow Junction	.50-3
Hartodsburg	.50-3
King's Mountain	.50-3
Lebanon	.50-3
Lexington	.50-3
Louisville	.40-3
Newport	.40-3
Owensboro	.50-3
Paducah	.50-3
Paris	.50-3
Springfield	.50-3
Woodbine	.50-3

Louisiana.

Place	Rate
Baton Rouge	.60-4
Donaldsonville	.60
Morgan Chy	.60
New Orleans	.60-4
Shreveport	.60-4

Maine.

Place	Rate
Augusta	.25-2
Bangor	.25
Bar Harbor	.25-2
Bath	.25-2
Belfast	.25-2
Booth Bay	.25-2
Bridgton	.25-2
Calais	.25-2
Camden	.25-2
Damariscotta	.25-2
Deering	.25-2
Dexter	.25
Eastport	.25
Ellsworth	.25-2
Farmington	.25-2
Fryeburg	.25-2
Gardiner	.25-2
Kennebunkport	.25-2
Lewiston	.25-2
Machias	.25-2
Portland	.25-2
Presque Isle	.25-2

Place	Rate
Richmond	.25-2
Rockland	.25-2
Rockport	.25-2
Saco	.25-2
Searsport	.25-2
Sebago Lake	.25-2
South West Harbor	.45-4
Thomaston	.25-2
Vanceboro	.25-2
Winterport	.25-2
Wiscasset	.25-2

Manitoba.

Place	Rate
Brandon	.75-5
Winnipeg	.75-5

Maryland.

Place	Rate
Annapolis	.25-2
Baltimore	.25-2
Bel Air	.40-3
Canton	.25-2
Catonsville	.25-2
Chesapeake City	.25-2
Crisfield	.40-3
Cumberland	.25-2
Emmitsburg	.40-3
Hagerstown	.25-2
Havre de Grace	.25-2
Port Deposit	.25-2

Massachusetts.

Place	Rate
Athol	.25-2
Belchertown	.25-2
Beverly	.25-2
Brockton	.25-2
Brookline	.25-2
Buzzards Bay	.25-2
Chelsea	.25-2
Chicopee Falls	.25-2
Cohasset	.25-2
Danvers	.25-2
Deerfield	.25-2
Dorchester	.25-2
Duxbury	.25-2
Easthampton	.25-2
Fitchburg	.25-2
Great Barrington	.25-2
Harwich	.25-2
Hingham	.25-2
Holyoke	.25-2
Hyannis	.25-2
Jamaica Plain	.25-2
Lee	.25-2
Lenox	.25-2
Lynn	.25-2
Manchester	.25-2
Marblehead	.25-2
Marshfield	.25-2
Martha's Vineyard	.50-2½
Medford	.25-2
Middleboro	.25-2
Myrick's	.25-2
Nantasket Beach	.25-2
New Bedford	.25-2
Newburyport	.25-2
Newton	.25-2
Norfolk	.25-2
Northampton	.25-2
Northfield	.25-2
Peabody	.25-2
Pittsfield	.25-2
Provincetown	.25-2
Quincy	.25-2
Salem	.25-2
Scituate	.25-2
Shelburne Falls	.25-2
South Acton	.25-2
Southbridge	.25-2
South Lee	.25-2
Springfield	.25-2
Stoughton	.25-2
Taunton	.25-2
Walpole	.25-2
Wellesley	.25-2
Westboro	.25-2
Westfield	.25-2
Weymouth	.25-2
Williamstown	.25-2
Woods Holl	.25-2
Worcester	.25-2

Mexico.

Except to Tampico, Vera Cruz and City of Mexico, all messages to Mexico via Galveston must be prepaid.

Place	Rate
Campeche, v. Galveston	3.50-30
Frontera, "	3.30-30
Merida, "	3.50-30
Mexico, "	3.00-25
Progreso, "	3.50-30
Puebla, via Galveston	3.50-30
Tampico, "	3.00-25
Tuxpan, "	3.50-30
Vera Cruz, "	3.00-25

Michigan.

Place	Rate
Allegan	.50-3
Alpena	.50-3
Ann Arbor	.40-3
Bad Axe	.50-3
Battle Creek	.50-3
Bay City	.40-3
Big Rapids	.50-3
Cass City	.50-3
Detroit	.40-3
Eagle Harbor	1.15-8
East Saginaw	.40-3
Grand Haven	.50-3
Grand Rapids	.50-3
Houghton	.60-4
Jackson	.40-3
Kalamazoo	.50-3
Kent City	.50-3
Kinde	.50-3
Ludington	.50-3
Mackinaw City	.50-3
Marquette	.60-4
Monroe	.50-3
Muskegon	.50-3
Newaygo	.50-3
Oscoda	.50-3
Pentwater	.50-3
Pontiac	.50-3
Port Sanilac	.50-3
Richland	.50-3
Saginaw City	.40-3
St. Clair	.50-3
St. Louis	.50-3
Tawas City	.50-3
Traverse City	.50-3
Wyandotte	.50-3
Ypsilanti	.40-3

Minnesota.

Place	Rate
Albert Lea	.60-4
Anoka	.60-4
Austin	.60-4
Blue Earth City	.60-4
Brainerd	.60-4
Breckenridge	.60-4
Cauby	.60-4
Chaska	.60-4
Clear Lake	.60-4
Crookston	.60-4
Dakota	.60-4
Duluth	.50-3
Faribault	.60-4
Fond du Lac	.60-4
Frazee City	.60-4
Freeport	.60
Jackson	.60-4
Kandiyohi	.60-4
Le Sueur	.60-4
Mankato	.60-4
Minneapolis	.50-3
Minnesota City	.60-4
New Ulm	.60-4
Red Wing	.50-3
Renville	.60-4
St. Paul	.50-3
Sauk Centre	.60-4
Sleepy Eye	.60-4
Stillwater	.50-3
Wabasha	.50-3
Waseca	.60-4
Winnebago City	.60-4
Zumbrota	.60-4

Mississippi.

Place	Rate
Aberdeen	.50-3
Biloxi	.50-3
Brandon	.50-3
Byhalia	.50-3
Columbus	.50-3
Holly Springs	.50-3
Jackson	.50-3
Natchez	.50-3
Starkville	.50-3
Vicksburg	.50-3
West Point	.50-3
Winona	.50-3
Yazoo City	.50-3

Missouri.

Place	Rate
Camden	.60
Clayton	.50-3
Hannibal	.60-4
Hunnewell	.60-4
Independence	.60
Ironton	.60-4
Jefferson Barracks	.60-4

Place	Rate
Jefferson City	.50-3
Joplin	.60-4
Kansas City	.50-3
Minden	.60-4
Mound City	.60-4
Nodaway	.60-4
Ozark	.60-4
Richland	.60-4
Rushville	.60-4
St. Joseph	.50-3
St. Louis	.40-3
Sedalia	.50-3
Springfield	.60-4
West Plains	.60-4
Wright City	.60-4

Montana.

Place	Rate
Billings	.75-5
Butte City	.75-5
Gallatin	.75-5
Glendive	.75-5
Helena	.75-5
Jefferson	.75-5
Miles City	.75-5
Missoula	.75-5
Stillwater	.75-5
Townsend	.75-5
Wickes	.75-5

Nebraska.

Place	Rate
Ainsworth	.60-4
Arapahoe	.60-4
Aurora	.60-4
Beatrice	.60-4
Broken Bow	.60-4
Cedar Rapids	.60-4
Chadron	.60-4
Creighton	.60-4
Crete	.60-4
Dakota City	.60-4
Falls City	.60-4
Fort Robinson	.60-4
Fremont	.60-4
Greeley Centre	.60-4
Haigler	.60-4
Hastings	.60-4
Hebron	.60-4
Holdrege	.60-4
Indianola	.60-4
Kearney	.60-4
La Platte	.60-4
Long Pine	.60-4
Loup City	.60-4
Nantasket	.60-4
Nebraska City	.60-4
Neligh	.60-4
Nemaha City	.60-4
Norfolk	.60-4
North Bend	.60-4
North Loup	.60-4
Ogallala	.60-4
Omaha	.50-3
O'Neill	.60-4
Osceola	.60-4
Pawnee City	.60-4
Petersbargh	.60-4
Platte Centre	.60-4
Plattsmouth	.60-4
Republican City	.60-4
Rockville	.60-4
Rushville	.60-4
St. Paul, Howard Co.	.60-4
Scotia	.60-4
South Auburn	.60-4
Springfield	.60-4
Steele City	.60-4
Strang	.60-4
Syracuse	.60-4
Thayer	.60-4
Utica	.60-4
Valentine	.60-4
Wahoo	.60-4
Weeping Water	.60-4
Wymore	.60-4
Wyoming	.60-4

Nevada.

Place	Rate
Austin	1.00-7
Carson City	1.00-7
Eureka	1.00-7
Hawthorne	1.00-7
Humboldt	1.00-7
Reno	1.00-7
Virginia City	1.00-7
Winnemucca	1.00-7

New Brunswick.

Place	Rate
Campbellton	.50-3
Dalhousie	.50-3
Edmunston	.50-3
Millville	.50-3

TELEGRAPH RATES--Continued.

Place	Rate		Place	Rate		Place	Rate		Place	Rate	
Perth	.50	3	Centreville, Hudson Co.	.25	2	Plainfield	.25	2	Amenia	.25	2
St. Andrews	.50	3	Charlotteburg	.25	2	Point Pleasant	.25	2	Amityville, L. I.	.25	2
St. George	.50	3	Clayton	.25	2	Pompton	.25	2	Amsterdam	.25	2
St. John	.50	3	Clifton	.25	2	Port Oram	.25	2	Ancram	.25	2
St. Stephens	.50	3	Closter	.25	2	Princeton	.25	2	Andover	.25	2
Woodstock	.50	3	Collingswood	.25	2	Rahway	.25	2	Angelica	.25	2
Newfoundland and Miquelon Island.			Cooper	.25	2	Redbank	.25	2	Annandale	.25	2
			Cranford	.25	2	Ridgefield	.25	2	Antwerp	.25	2
St. John's	1.25	11	Cresskill			Riegelsville	.5	2	Arcade	.25	2
St. Pierre, M. I.	1.25	11	Dayton	.25	2	Ringwood	.25	2	Ardsley	.25	2
New Hampshire.			Deal Beach	.25	2	Rio Grande	.25	2	Arkport	.25	2
			Dean			River Edge	.25	2	Ashland	.25	2
Alton Bay	.25	2	Demarest	.25	2	Rockaway	.25	2	Astoria, L. I	.20	1
Bethlehem (Summer)	.25	2	Denville	.25	2	Roselle	.25	2	Athens	.25	2
Canaan	.25	2	Dover	.25	2	Rutherford	.25	2	Attica	.25	2
Claremont	.25	2	Drakeville	.25	2	Salem	.25	2	Auburn	.25	2
Concord	.25	2	Dunellen	.25	2	Sandy Hook	.25	2	Auriesville	.25	2
Contoocook	.25	2	East Newark	.25	2	Schooley's Mountain	.25	2	Au Sable Chasm	.25	2
Crawford House (Summer)	.25	2	East Orange	.20	1	Schraalenburg	.25	2	Avoca	.25	2
			Eatontown	.25	2	Sea Bright	.25	2	Avon	.25	2
Derry Depot	.25	2	Egg Harbor City	.25	2	Sea Girt	.75	2	Babylon, L. I.	.25	2
Dover	.25	2	Elizabeth	.20	1	Seaville	.25	2	Baldwin Place	.25	2
Durham	.25	2	Englewood	.25	2	Sewaren	.25	2	Baldwin's, L. I	.25	2
Exeter	.25	2	Faunton	.25	2	Shamong	.25	2	Ballston	.25	2
Fabyan House (Summer)	.25	2	Farmingdale	.25	2	Short Hills	.25	2	Bangall	.25	2
Fabyans	.25	2	Findene	.25	2	Somer's Point	.25	2	Barrytown	.25	2
Farmington Depot	.25	2	Flemington	.25	2	South Amboy	.25	2	Barton	.25	2
Franklin	.25	2	Fort Lee	.25	2	South Orange	.20	1	Bartow	.25	2
Glen Station	.25	2	Franklin	.25	2	South Plainfield	.25	2	Batavia	.25	2
Grafton	.25	2	Freehold	.25	2	Sparta	.25	2	Bath	.25	2
Groveton	.25	2	Frenchtown	.25	2	Spotswood	.25	2	Bath Beach, L. I	.25	2
Haverhill	.25	2	Glassboro	.25	2	Spring Lake	.25	2	Bayport, L. I.	.25	2
Hooksett	.25	2	Glen Gardner	.25	2	Stanhope	.25	2	Bay Ridge, L. I.	.25	2
Jefferson	.25	2	Glen Ridge	.20	1	Stelton	.25	2	Bay Shore, L. I.	.25	2
Keene	.25	2	Gloucester City	.25	2	Stillwater	.25	2	Bayside, L. I.	.25	2
Littleton	.25	2	Grovestend	.25	2	Stirling	.25	2	Beaverdams,Schuyler Co	.25	2
Manchester	.25	2	Hackensack	.25	2	Stockholm	.25	2	Bedford Station	.25	2
Meredith Village	.25	2	Hackettstown	.25	2	Stockton	.25	2	Beekman	.25	2
Mt. Washington (Summer)	.25	2	Haddonfield	.25	2	Summit, Union Co.	.25	2	Belfast	.25	2
			Hamburgh	.25	2	Swedesboro	.25	2	Bellona	.25	2
Nashua	.25	2	Hammonton	.25	2	Tea Neck	.25	2	Belport, L. I.	.25	2
Northfield Depot	.25	2	Harrison (East Newark)	.25	2	Tenafly	.25	2	Belmont	.25	2
Peacock	.25	2	High Bridge	.25	2	Tremley	.25	2	Belvidere	.25	2
Peterboro	.25	2	Highlands	.25	2	Trenton	.25	2	Bergen	.25	2
Pittsfield	.25	2	Hightstown	.25	2	Tuckerton	.25	2	Berlin	.25	2
Profile House (Summer)	.25	2	Hillsdale	.25	2	Vincentown	.25	2	Bernhard's Bay	.25	2
Rochester	.25	2	Hoboken	.20	1	Vineland	.25	2	Big Indian	.25	2
Rumney Depot	.25	2	Hopewell	.25	2	Washington	.25	2	Binghamton	.25	2
Salem Depot	.25	2	Hudson City	.25	2	Waterloo	.25	2	Binnewater	.25	2
Seabrook Depot	.25	2	Iselin	.25	2	Weehawken	.20	1	Blauveltville	.25	2
Suncook	.25	2	Janesburg	.25	2	Wenonah	.25	2	Bliss	.25	2
Twin Mt. House (Summer)	.25	2	Jersey City	.20	1	West Creek	.25	2	Blodgett's Mills	.25	2
			Jutland	.25	2	West Englewood	.25	2	Bloods	.25	2
Walpole	.25	2	Keyport	.25	2	Westfield, Union Co.	.25	2	Bloomingburg Station	.25	2
Weirs	.25	2	Kinkora	.25	2	Weston	.25	2	Blue Mountain Lake	.50	4
Wentworth	.25	2	Kirkwood	.25	2	Westwood	.25	2	Bolivar	.25	2
Westmoreland Depot	.25	2	Lake Hopatcong	.25	2	White House	.25	2	Bolton	.50	4
Wilton	.25	2	Lakewood	.25	2	Whitings	.25	2	Bomoville	.25	2
Wing Road	.25	2	Lambertville	.25	2	Wilburtha	.25	2	Boston	.25	2
Woodsville	.25	2	Landsdown	.25	2	Winslow	.25	2	Boston Corners	.25	2
New Jersey.			Lewistown	.25	2	Winslow Junction	.25	2	Bouckville	.25	2
			Little Falls	.25	2	Woodbridge	.25	2	Bowmansville	.25	2
Absecon	.25	2	Long Branch	.25	2	Woodbury	.25	2	Brainard	.25	2
Andover	.25	2	Manasquan	.25	2	Woodstown	.25	2	Brasher Falls	.25	2
Asbury	.25	2	Mantoloking	.25	2	Wortendyke	.25	2	Breesport	.25	2
Asbury Park	.25	2	Manunuskin	.25	2	Wyckoff	.25	2	Brentwood, L. I	.25	2
Atco	.25	2	Marlton	.25	2	**New Mexico.**			Breslau, L. I	.25	2
Athenia	.25	2	Matawan	.25	2				Brewster's	.25	2
Atlantic City	.25	2	Medford	.25	2	Albuquerque	.75	5	Bridgehampton	.25	2
Atlantic Highlands	.25	2	Merchantville	.25	2	Bernal	.75	5	Brighton	.25	2
Barnegat	.25	2	Metuchen	.25	2	Bernalillo	.75	5	Brighton Beach	.50	2
Barnegat City	.25	2	Middletown	.25	2	Deming	.75	5	Brinkerhoff	.25	2
Basking Ridge	.25	2	Milburn	.25	2	Fort Wingate	.75	5	Brisbin	.25	2
Beach Haven	.25	2	Milford	.25	2	Grant	.75	5	Broadalbin	.25	2
Belleville	.25	2	Montclair	.25	2	Las Vegas	.75	5	Brockport	.25	2
Belvidere, not Sundays	.25	2	Moorestown	.25	2	Lordsburg	.75	5	Brocton	.25	2
Bergen Fields	.25	2	Morristown	.25	2	Rincon	.75	5	Brookhaven, L. I.	.25	2
Bergen Point	.25	2	Mountain Station	.20	1	Santa Fe	.75	5	Brooklyn	.20	1
Bernardsville	.25	2	Mount Holly	.25	2	Wingate	.75	5	Brookton	.25	2
Blairstown	.25	2	Neshanic	.25	2	**New York.**			Brown's Station	.25	2
Bloomfield	.20	1	Newark	.20	1				Brownville	.25	2
Bloomingdale (or Butler)	.25	2	New Brunswick	.25	2	Acra	.25	2	Buffalo	.25	2
Boonton	.25	2	Newfoundland	.25	2	Addison	.25	2	Bull's Head, S. I.	.25	2
Bordentown	.25	2	North Branch	.25	2	Adrian	.25	2	Bullville	.25	2
Bound Brook	.25	2	North Vineland	.50	2	Afton	.25	2	Burns	.25	2
Branchport	.25	2	Norwood	.25	2	Akron	.25	2	Burnside	.25	2
Brick Church (Orange)	.25	2	Ocean Beach	.25	2	Alabama	.25	2	Buskirks	.25	2
Bridgeton	.25	2	Ocean Grove	.25	2	Albany	.25	2	Byron	.25	2
Broadway, Warren Co.	.25	2	Ogdensburg	.25	2	Albion	.25	2	Cadosia Summit	.25	2
Budds Lake	.25	2	Oradell	.25	2	Alder Creek	.25	2	Cairo	.25	2
Burlington	.25	2	Orange	.25	2	Alexandria Bay	.25	2	Caldwell	.25	2
Buttsville	.25	2	Orange Valley	.20	1	Allegany	.25	2	Caledonia	.25	2
Caldwell	.25	2	Oxford	.25	2	Allentown	.25	2	Callicoon	.25	2
Califon	.25	2	Palmyra	.25	2	Almond	.25	2	Cambridge	.25	2
Camden	.25	2	Passaic	.20	1	Altamont	.25	2	Camden	.25	2
Cape May City	.25	2	Passaic Bridge	.25	2	Alton	.25	2	Cameron	.25	2
Carlstadt	.20	1	Paterson	.20	1	Altona	.25	2	Camillus	.25	2
Carteret	.25	2	Pemberton	.25	2	Amagansett, L. I.	.40	4	Campbell Hall	.25	2
Centreville, Bergen Co.	.20	1	Perth Amboy	.25	2	Amawalk	.25	2	Campville	.25	2
Camden Co.	.25	2	Phillipsburg	.25	2	Amboy	.25	2	Canaan Four Corners	.25	2

TELEGRAPH RATES—New York Continued.

Place	Rate	Place	Rate	Place	Rate	Place	Rate
Canajoharie	25-2	Dobbs Ferry	25-2	High Falls	25-2	Melleuville	25-2
Canandaigua	25-2	Douglaston, L. I	25-2	Highlands	25-2	Melrose, N. Y. County	25-2
Canaseraie, L. I	25-2	Dover Plains	25-2	Highland Falls	25-2	Melrose, Rensselaer Co	25-2
Canaseraga	25-2	Dresden, Yates Co	25-2	Hollsdale	25-2	Memphis	25-2
Canastota	25-2	Dryden	25-2	Hmrods	25-2	Merrick, L. I	25-2
Candor	25-2	Duanesburg	25-2	Hinsdale	25-2	Merrifield	25-2
Castelro	25-2	Dundee	25-2	Hobart	25-2	Merritt's Corners	25-2
Cape Vincent	25-2	Dunkirk	25-2	Holland	25-2	Mexico, Oswego Co	25-2
Carlton Station	25-2	Durham	25-2	Holland Patent	25-2	Middle Granville	25-2
Carmel	25-2	Earlville	25-2	Hollis, L. I	25-2	Middleport	25-2
Caroline	25-2	East Albany	10-2	Homer	25-2	Milford	25-2
Carrollton	25-2	East Durham	25-2	Honeoye Falls	25-2	Millbrook	25-2
Carthage	25-2	East Hampton, L. I	25-2	Hoosick	25-2	Millerton	25-2
Cassadaga	25-2	East Hinsdale, L. I	25-2	Hopewell Junction	25-2	Milton	25-2
Castile	25-2	Eastport, L. I	25-2	Hornellsville Junction	25-2	Mindenville	25-2
Castleton	25-2	East View	25-2	Horseheads	25-2	Mineola	25-2
Cato	25-2	Eaton Station	25-2	Hotel Kaaterskill	25-2	Mohawk	25-2
Catskill	25-2	Edmeston	25-2	Houghton	25-2	Moira	25-2
Catskill Mountain House	25-2	Ellenburg Depot	25-2	Howe's Cave	25-2	Monroe	25-2
Catskill Station	25-2	Ellenville	25-2	Hudson	25-2	Montezuma	25-2
Cattaraugus	25-2	Elmira	25-2	Hulett's Landing	25-2	Monticello	25-2
Cayuga	25-2	Elmsford	25-2	Hunter	25-2	Moravia	25-2
Cazenovia	25-2	Erieville	25-2	Hunter's Point, L. I	20-1	Morris Dock	20-1
Cedarville	25	Esopus, Ulster Co	25-2	Huntington, L. I	25-2	Morris Park, L. I	25-2
Central Bridge	25	Esperance	25	Hurleyville	25-2	Mountain Dale	25-2
Central Islip, L. I	25-2	Fairhaven	25-2	Hyde Park	25-2	Mountainville	25-2
Central Square	25-2	Fairport, Monroe Co	25-2	Ilion	25-2	Mount Kisco	25-2
Central Valley	25-2	Falconer	25-2	Irving	25-2	Mount McGregor	25-2
Centre Village	25-2	Fallsburg	25-2	Islip, L. I	25-2	Mount Morris	25-2
Centreville	25-2	Farmingdale, L. I	25-2	Ithaca	25-2	Nanuet	25-2
Ceres	25-2	Fayetteville	25-2	Jamaica, L. I	25-2	Narrowsburg	25-2
Chaffee	25-2	Fillmore	25-2	Jamesport, L. I	25-2	Newark	25-2
Champlain	25-2	Fire Island	25-2	Jamestown	25-2	New Baltimore	25-2
Chapinville	25-2	Fishkill	25-2	Java Centre	25-2	New Berlin	25-2
Chappaqua	25-2	Fishkill Village	25-2	Jeffersonville	25-2	New Brighton	25-2
Chateaugay	25-2	Flatbush, L. I	20-1	Jewett	25-2	Newburgh	25-2
Chatham	25-2	Flushing, L. I	25-2	Johnsonville	25-2	New Dorp, S. I	25-2
Chautauqua	25-2	Fonda	25-2	Johnstown	25-2	Newfane	25-2
Chazy	25-2	Fordham Heights	20-1	Jordan	25-2	New Paltz	25-2
Chemung	25-2	Forge, L. I	25-2	Kanona	25-2	New Rochelle	25-2
Chenango Bridge	25-2	Fort Ann	25-2	Kasoag	25-2	Newtown, L. I	25-2
Cherry Valley	25-2	Fort Edward	25-2	Katonah	25-2	New Utrecht	25-2
Chichester	25-2	Fort Montgomery	25-2	Keeneville	25-2	New Windsor	25-2
Chili Station	25-2	Fort Plain	25-2	Kinderhook	25-2	New York City	20-1
Chittenango	25-2	Frankfort	25-2	Kingsbridge	20-1	Niagara Falls	25-2
Churchville	25-2	Fredonia	25-2	Kingston	25-2	Nineveh	25-2
Circleville	25-2	Freehold	25-2	Knowlesville	25-2	Northport, L. I	25-2
City Island	25-2	Freeport, L. I	20-1	La Fargeville	25-2	Norwich	25-2
Claverack	25-2	Fulton, Oswego Co	25-2	Lake George (Caldwell)	25-2	Norwood	25-2
Clay	25-2	Fultonville	25-2	Lake Mahopac	25-2	Nunda	25-2
Clayton	25-2	Gainesville	25-2	Lake Mohonk Mountain House	30-2	Nyack	25-2
Clifton, S. I	10-2	Gansevoort	25-2			Ogdensburgh	25-2
Clifton Springs	25-2	Garden City	25-2	Lake Placid	50-4	Olean	25-2
Clinton	25-2	Garneville	25-2	Lake View	25-2	Oneida	25-2
Clintonville	25-2	Garrison's	25-2	Lansingburg	25-2	Oneonta	25-2
Clyde	25-2	Gasport	25-2	Larchmont	25-2	Oriskany	25-2
Cobleskill	25-2	Genesco	25-2	La Salle	25-2	Orleans	25-2
Cochecton	25-2	Geneva	25-2	Lebanon	25-2	Oswego	25
Coeymans	25-2	Genoa	25-2	Leeds	25-2	Otego	25-2
Cohocton	25-2	Germantown	25-2	Le Roy, Genesee Co	25-2	Otisville	25-2
Cohoes	25-2	Gilboa	25-2	Lewiston	25-2	Ovid	25-2
Co den	25-2	Glen Cove, L. I	25-2	Liberty, Sullivan Co	25-2	Owego	25-2
Cold Water	25-2	Glendale, Lewis Co	25-2	Liberty Falls	25-2	Oyster Bay, L. I	25-2
College Point	25-2	Glenham	25-2	Lima	25-2	Palenville	25-2
Community	25-2	Glen Head, L. I	25-2	Linden	25-2	Palmyra	25-2
Conesus	25-2	Glen Island	25-2	Lisle	25-2	Patchogue, L. I	25-2
Conewango	25-2	Glens Falls, Warren Co	25-2	Little Falls	25-2	Paul Smith's (Summer)	50-4
Coney Island	25-2	Gloversville	25-2	Little Valley	25-2	Pawling	25-2
Constantia	25-2	Good Ground, L. I	25-2	Liverpool	25-2	Pearsalls, L. I	25-2
Cooperstown	25-2	Goshen	25-2	Livingston Manor	25-2	Peconic, L. I	25-2
Copake	25-2	Governor's Island	20-1	Lockport	25-2	Peekskill	25-2
Copenhagen	25-2	Gowanda	25-2	Lockwood	25-2	Pelhamville	25-2
Corning	25-2	Grand Gorge	25-2	Locust Valley, L. I	25-2	Pendleton Centre	25-2
Cornwall	25-2	Granville	25-2	Long Beach, L. I	25-2	Penn Yan	25-2
Corona, L. I	25-2	Great Neck, L. I	25-2	Long Eddy	25-2	Peru (Clinton Co)	25-2
Cortland	25-2	Great Valley	25-2	Long Island City	20-1	Phoenicia	25-2
Coventry Station	25-2	Greece	25-2	Looneyville	25-2	Piermont	25-2
Coxsackie	25-2	Green Island	25-2	Lordville	25-2	Pikeville	25-2
Coxsackie Station	25-2	Greenport, L. I	25-2	Lowville	25-2	Pine Hill	25-2
Craigville	25-2	Greenville	25-2	Lyndonville	25-2	Pittsford	25-2
Cranston's Station	25-2	Greenwich	25-2	Lyons	25-2	Plattsburg	25-2
Craryville	25-2	Greenwood Lake	25-2	Macedon	25-2	Pleasant Valley	25-2
Croton Falls	25-2	Griffin's Corners	25-2	Machias	25-2	Pleasantville	25-2
Croton Lake	25-2	Guilderland Centre	25-2	Mallory	25-2	Poolville	25-2
Crown Point	25-2	Haines Falls	25-2	Malone	25-2	Port Byron	25-2
Cuba	25-2	Hamburg	25-2	Mamaroneck	25-2	Port Chester	25-2
Cutchogue, L. I	25-2	Hamilton	25-2	Manlius Centre	25	Port Jefferson, L. I	25-2
Cuyler	25-2	Hamlin	25-2	Manlius Station	25-2	Port Jervis	25-2
Cuylerville	25-2	Hammondsport	25-2	Manor, L. I	25-2	Poughkeepsie	25-2
Dannemora	25-2	Hancock	25-2	Marcellus	25-2	Prattsville	25-2
Dansville	25-2	Hannibal	25-2	Marilla	25-2	Putnam	25-2
Darien	25-2	Hastings, Oswego Co	25-2	Marlboro	25-2	Queens, L. I	25-2
Dayton	25-2	Havana	25-2	Martindale	25-2	Quogue, L. I	25-2
Dennsville	25-2	Haverstraw	25-2	Massena	25-2	Randolph	25-2
De Kalb	25-2	Hayt's Corners	25-2	Mattewan	25-2	Ravenswood, L. I	20-1
Delhi	25-2	Hempstead, L. I	25-2	Mattituck	25-2	Red Creek	25-2
Depuit	25-2	Herkimer	25-2	Mayville	25-2	Rhinebeck	25-2
Deposit	25-2	Hewlett's, L. I	25-2	Mechanicstown	25-2	Richburg	25-2
De Ruyter	25-2	Hicksville, L. I	25-2	Medford, L. I	25-2	Richfield Springs	25-2
De Witt	25-2	High Bridge	20-1	Medina	25-2	Richmond Hill	25-2

TELEGRAPH RATES—Continued.

Place	Rate
Richmondville	25-2
Ridgewood, L. I.	25-2
Rivensburg	35-2
Riverdale	20-1
Riverhead, L. I.	25-2
Rochester	25-2
Rockland	25-2
Rome	25-5
Rondout	25-2
Ronkonkoma, L. I.	25-2
Roslyn, L. I.	25-2
Rouse's Point	25-2
Roxbury	25-2
Rush	25-2
Rye	25-2
Sackett's Harbor	25-2
Sag Harbor, L. I.	25-2
St. George, S. I.	25-2
St. James, L. I.	25-2
St. Johnland, L. I.	25-2
Salamanca	25-2
Sandusky	25-2
Saranac	50-2
Saranac Lake	50-4
Saratoga	25-2
Saugerties	25-2
Savannah	25-2
Sayville, L. I.	25-2
Schenevus	25-2
Schroon Lake	50-4
Schuylerville	25-2
Scottsville	25-2
Sea Cliff, L. I.	25-2
Setauket, L. I.	25-2
Shandaken	25-2
Sharon Springs	25-2
Sheepshead Bay, L. I.	25-2
Shelter Island	25-2
Sherburne	25-2
Shushan	25-2
Sing Sing	25-2
Skaneateles	25-2
Slingerland's	25-2
Smith's Basin	25-2
Smithtown, L. I.	25-2
Smyrna	25-2
Sodus	25-2
Somers' Centre	25-2
Southampton, L. I.	25-2
Southold, L. I.	25-2
Sparkill	25-2
Spencer	25-2
Speonk, L. I.	25-2
Sprakers	25-2
Springfield Centre	25-2
Spuyten Duyvil	20-1
Stamsburg	25-2
Stapleton, S. I.	25-2
Sterlington	25-2
Stissing	25-2
Stockport Station	25-2
Stony Brook, L. I.	25-2
Stuyvesant	25-2
Suffern	25-2
Summitville	25-2
Suspension Bridge	25-2
Syosset, L. I.	25-2
Syracuse	25-2
Tannersville	25-2
Tarrytown	25-2
Thiells	25-2
1000 Island House	25-2
Ticonderoga	25-2
Tioga Centre	25-2
Tivoli	25-2
Tompkins Cove	25-2
Tompkinsville, S. I.	25-2
Tottenville, S. I.	25-2
Trenton	25-2
Trenton Falls	25-2
Troy	25-2
Trumansburg	25-2
Turner's	25-2
Tuxedo Park	25-2
Ulster Park	25-2
Unionville, Kings Co.	25-2
Unionville, Orange Co.	25-2
Unionville, W'stchester Co.	25-2
Utica	25-2
Valley Cottage	25-2
Valley Stream, L. I.	25-2
Van Cortlandt	20-1
Vernon	25-2
Verona Depot	25-2
Voorheesville	25-2
Walden	25-2
Walkill	25-2
Warrensburg	25-2
Warsaw	25-2
Water Mill, L. I.	25-2
Watertown	25-2
Watkins	25-2
Waverly	25-2
Wayland	25-2
Webster	25-2
Weedsport	25-2
Wellsville	25-2
Westbury, L. I.	25-2
West Camp	25-2
West Falls	25-2
West Hampton, L. I.	25-2
Westmoreland	25-2
W. New Brighton, S. I.	40-2
Whitehall	25-2
White Plains	25-2
Whitestone, L. I.	25-2
William's Bridge	20-1
Williamson	25-2
Windham	25-2
Windsor	25-2
Woodhaven, L. I.	25-2
Woodlawn	20-1
Woodbourne, L. I.	25-2
Woodside, L. I.	25-2
Woodstock	25-2
Wurtsboro	25-2
Yaphank, L. I.	25-2
Yonkers	20-1

North Carolina.

Place	Rate
Asheville	50-3
Burgaw	50-3
Burlington	50-3
Chadbourn	50-3
Charlotte	50-3
Durham	50-3
Enfield	50-3
Fayetteville	50-3
Goldsboro	50-3
Halifax	50-3
Hot Springs	50-3
Kings Mountain	50-3
Kingston	50-3
Kittrell	50-3
Lenoir	50-3
Lilesville	50-3
Lincolnton	50-3
Magnolia	50-3
Marion	50-3
Morehead City	50-3
Mount Holly	50-3
New Berne	50-3
Ore Hill	50-3
Pineville	50-3
Polecat	50-3
Raleigh	50-3
Reidsville	50-3
Rockingham	50-3
Rocky Mount	50-3
Roxobel	50-3
Salisbury	50-3
Scotland Neck	50-3
Shelby	50-3
Smithfield	50-3
Statesville	50-3
Tarboro	50-3
Thomasville	50-3
Wadesboro	50-3
Warrenton	50-3
Washington	50-3
Waynesville	50-3
Weldon	50-3
Williamston	50-3
Wilmington	50-3
Winston	50-3

Nova Scotia.

Place	Rate
Amherst	50-3
Annapolis	50-3
Antigonish	50-3
Canning	50-3
Digby	50-3
Guysboro	50-3
Halifax	50-3
Liverpool	50-3
Lunenburg	50-3
Maitland	50-3
New Glasgow	50-3
Parrsboro	50-3
Picton	50-3
Port Hastings	50-3
Port Mulgrave	50-3
Shelburne	50-3
Sherbrooke	50-3
Shubenacadie	50-3
Sydney	50-3
Tracadie	50-3
Truro	50-3
Wentworth	50-3
Weymouth	50-3
Windsor	50-3

Place	Rate
Wolfville	50-3
Yarmouth	50-3

Ohio.

Place	Rate
Akron	40-3
Alliance	40-3
Ashland	40-3
Ashtabula	40-3
Athens	40-3
Aurora	40-3
Barnesville	40-3
Batavia	40-3
Bellaire	35-2
Bellefontaine	40-3
Bellevue	40-3
Berea Station	40-3
Berwick	40-3
Bowerston	40-3
Bridgeport	35-2
Brooklyn	40-3
Bucyrus	40-3
Burgoon	40-3
Cadiz	40-3
Cambridge	40-3
Canal Dover	40-3
Canal Fulton	40-3
Canton	40-3
Carthage	40-3
Chauncey	40-3
Chicago Junction	40-3
Chillicothe	40-3
Cincinnati	40-3
Circleville	40-3
Cleveland	40-3
Clyde	40-3
Columbus	40-3
Conneaut	40-3
Continental	40-3
Corning	40-3
Cuba	40-3
Cuyahoga Falls	40-3
Dawson	40-3
Dayton	40-3
Defiance	40-3
Delaware	40-3
Delphos	40-3
Deshler	40-3
Dresden	40-3
East Liverpool	40-3
Elyria	40-3
Euclid	40-3
Fairview	40-3
Fayette	40-3
Findlay	40-3
Fostoria	40-3
Freedom	40-3
Fultonham	40-3
Galion	40-3
Gatlin	40-3
Gallipolis	40-3
Garrettsville	40-3
Geneva	40-3
Genoa	40-3
Girard	40-3
Glenville	40-3
Grafton	40-3
Granville	40-3
Guernsey	40-3
Hamilton	40-3
Hartwell	40-3
Haydenville	40-3
Hebron	40-3
Hicksville	40-3
Hillsboro	40-3
Hollandsburg	40-3
Iberia	40-3
Independence	40-3
Ironton	40-3
Jackson	40-3
Jeffersonville	40-3
Jewell	40-3
Kensington	40-3
Kent	40-3
Killbuck	40-3
Kinnickinnick	40-3
Kirkwood	40-3
Lancaster	40-3
Leavittsburg	40-3
Leetonia	40-3
Le Moyne	40-3
Lexington	40-3
Lima	40-3
Lorain	40-3
Loudenville	40-3
Louisville	40-3
Lucas	40-3
Madison	40-3
Mahoning	40-3
Marietta	40-3
Marion	40-3

Place	Rate
Mason	40-3
Martin's Ferry	35-2
Massillon	40-3
Maumee	40-3
Medina	40-3
Mentor	40-3
Mercer	40-3
Miamisburg	40-3
Middlefield	40-3
Middleport	40-3
Milan	40-3
Milledgeville	40-3
Miller's City	40-3
Minerva	40-3
Mingo	40-3
Monroeville	40-3
Morrow	40-3
Mount Gilead	40-3
Mount Vernon	40-3
Moxahala	40-3
Myersville	40-3
Navarre	40-3
Nevada	40-3
Newark	40-3
New Bremen	40-3
New Comerstown	40-3
New Lisbon	40-3
New London	40-3
Newton Falls	40-3
Newtown	40-3
Niles	40-3
North Bend	40-3
Norwalk	40-3
Norwich	40-3
Oberlin	40-3
Ontario	40-3
Ottawa	40-3
Painesville	40-3
Phalanx	40-3
Picton	40-3
Piqua	40-3
Plain City	40-3
Plymouth	40-3
Portage	40-3
Portsmouth	40-3
Put-in-Bay	65-5
Ravenna	40-3
Republic	40-3
Richwood	40-3
Rockport	40-3
Rushsylvania	40-3
Rushville	40-3
Sabina	40-3
St. Clairsville	40-3
Sandusky	40-3
Sardinia	40-3
Scio	40-3
Sciotoville	40-3
Shanesville	40-3
Shelby	40-3
Sherrodsville	40-3
Somerset	40-3
Sparta	40-3
Springfield	40-3
Steubenville	40-3
Stoutsville	40-3
Struther's	40-3
Tallmadge	40-3
Tiffin	40-3
Toledo	40-3
Trimble	40-3
Tuscarawas	40-3
Urichsville	40-3
Upper Sandusky	40-3
Urbana	40-3
Utica	40-3
Van Wert	40-3
Versailles	40-3
Vinton	40-3
Washington C. H.	40-3
Washingtonville	40-3
Wellington	40-3
Wellsville	40-3
Westminster	40-3
Wilmington	40-3
Winchester	40-3
Wooster	40-3
Xenia	40-3
Youngstown	40-3
Zanesville	40-3

Ontario.

Place	Rate
Bath	40-3
Caledonia	40-3
Cobourg	40-3
Collingwood	40-3
Durham	40-3
Gananoque	40-3
Glencoe	40-3
Gravenhurst	40-3

TELEGRAPH RATES—Continued.

Place	Rate		Place	Rate		Place	Rate	
Hamilton	.40	3	Chestnut Hill	.25	2	Mercer	.25	2	Uniontown	.25	2
Hastings	.40	3	Clarion	.25	2	Middleport	.25	2	Venango	.25	2
Kincardine	.40	3	Claysville	.25	2	Minard	.25	2	Wampum	.25	2
Kinmount	.40	3	Clearfield	.25	2	Minooka	.25	2	Waymart	.25	2
Lanark	.40	3	Clermont	.25	2	Monocacy	.25	2	Wayne	.25	2
Lyndhurst	.40	3	Clintonville	.25	2	Monongahela City	.25	2	Waynesboro	.25	2
Monckton	.40	3	Coatesville	.25	2	Monroeton	.25	2	Welsport	.25	2
Napanee	.40	3	Concordville	.25	2	Montoursville	.25	2	Wernersville	.25	2
Niagara	.40	3	Conneautville	.25	2	Montrose	.25	2	West Chester	.25	2
Niagara Falls	.40	3	Coushohocken	.25	2	Mount Airy, Phila. Co.	.25	2	Westfield	.25	2
Norwood	.40	3	Cooperstown	.25	2	Mount Carmel	.25	2	Westport	.25	2
Pembroke Station	.40	3	Coplay	.25	2	Mount Jewett	.25	2	Westtown	.25	2
Perth	.40	3	Corry	.25	2	Mount Moriah	.25	2	White Haven	.25	2
Peterboro	.40	3	Corydon	.25	2	Moyer	.25	2	Wilcox	.25	2
Port Dalhousie	.40	3	Coudersport	.25	2	Muncy	.25	2	Williwanna	.25	2
Port Hope	.40	3	Cresson	.25	2	Nanticoke	.25	2	Willmore	.25	2
Port Lambton	.40	3	Curwensville	.25	2	Natrona	.25	2	Wind Gap	.25	2
Prescott	.40	3	Dallas	.25	2	Nesquehoning	.25	2	Womelsdorf	.25	2
Renfrew	.40	3	Danville	.25	2	Newport	.25	2	Woodlawn	.25	2
Ruthven	.40	3	Dauphin	.25	2	Nicetown	.25	2	Wurtemburg	.25	2
Sarnia	.40	3	Delano	.25	2	Niles Valley	.25	2	Wyalusing	.25	2
Sault Ste Marie	.90	6	Dillsburg	.25	2	Northumberland	.25	2	Wysox	.25	2
Selkirk	.40	3	Downingtown	.25	2	Nottingham	.25	2	York	.25	2
Simcoe	.40	3	Drifton	.25	2	Ogontz	.25	2			
Stratford	.40	3	Duncannon	.25	2	Oil City	.25	2	**Prince Edward I.**		
Tilsonburg	.40	3	Dunmore (not Sunday)	.25	2	Oleopolis	.25	2	Charlottetown	1.00	7
Toronto	.40	3	Dushore	.25	2	Olyphant	.25	2	Summerside	1.00	7
Uxbridge	.40	3	East Brady	.25	2	Packerton	.25	2	Wellington	1.00	7
Wallacetown	.40	3	Easton	.25	2	Paoli	.25	2			
Waterford	.40	3	Ebensburg	.25	2	Parkesburg	.25	2	**Quebec.**		
Whitby	.40	3	Emaus	.25	2	Pen Argyl	.25	2	Arthabaska	.40	3
Wiarton	.40	3	Emporium	.25	2	Penfield	.25	2	Aylmer	.40	3
Windsor	.40	3	Fairchance	.25	2	Petrolia	.25	2	Beauharnois	.40	3
Woodstock	.40	3	Fall Brook	.25	2	Philadelphia	.20	1	Berthier	.40	3
York	.40	3	Fallston	.25	2	Phillipsburg	.25	2	Bonaventure	.40	3
			Fayette City	.25	2	Phillipson	.25	2	Chateauguay	.40	3
Oregon.			Fernwood	.25	2	Phoenixville	.25	2	Georgeville	.40	3
Astoria	1.00	7	Fort Loudon	.25	2	Pittsburgh	.25	2	Granby	.40	3
Baker City	1.00	7	Frackville	.25	2	Pittsfield	.25	2	Lachine	.40	3
Corvallis	1.00	7	Frazer	.25	2	Pittston	.25	2	Magog	.40	3
Dalles (or The Dalles)	1.00	7	Freemansburg	.25	2	Plymouth	.25	2	Montreal	.40	3
Empire City	1.00	7	Gallitzin	.25	2	Pomeroy	.25	2	Percé	.40	3
Eugene City	1.00	7	Germantown	.25	2	Portage	.25	2	Quebec	.40	3
Huntington	1.00	7	Girard	.25	2	Port Carbon	.25	2	Rimouski	.40	3
Junction City	1.00	7	Girardville	.25	2	Port Clinton	.25	2	St. Johns	.40	3
Lafayette	1.00	7	Glen Carbon	.25	2	Portland	.25	2	Sherbrooke	.40	3
Oregon City	1.00	7	Glencoe	.25	2	Pottstown	.25	2	Stanstead	.40	3
Pendleton	1.00	7	Glen Moore	.25	2	Punxsutawney	.25	2	Thurso	.40	3
Portland	1.00	7	Greencastle	.25	2	Radnor	.25	2	Upton	.40	3
Salem	1.00	7	Greensboro	.25	2	Rasselas	.25	2	Yamaska	.40	3
			Greensburg	.25	2	Rathbun	.25	2			
Pennsylvania.			Hanover	.25	2	Reading	.25	2	**Rhode Island.**		
Addison	.25	2	Harmony	.25	2	Redington	.25	2	Apponaug	.25	2
Alburtis	.25	2	Harrisburg	.25	2	Reno	.25	2	Arnolds Mills	.25	2
Allegheny City	.25	2	Hauto	.25	2	Renovo	.25	2	Block Island	.30	2
Altoona	.25	2	Hawley	.25	2	Richmond Furnace	.25	2	Bristol	.25	2
Antrim	.25	2	Hazleton	.25	2	Ridgway	.25	2	Cranston	.25	2
Ararat Summit	.25	2	Hilliards	.25	2	Ridley Park	.25	2	Greene	.25	2
Archbald	.25	2	Honesdale	.25	2	Ringtown	.25	2	Narragansett Pier	.25	2
Atlantic	.25	2	Huntingdon	.25	2	Rochester	.25	2	Newport	.25	2
Audenreid	.25	2	Indiana	.25	2	Rockport	.25	2	Pascoag	.25	2
Bangor	.25	2	Irwin	.25	2	Royer's Ford	.25	2	Peacedale	.25	2
Bath	.25	2	Jamestown	.25	2	Sabula	.25	2	Providence	.25	2
Beach Haven	.25	2	Jenkintown	.25	2	Saegertown	.25	2	Tiverton	.25	2
Beaver Meadow	.25	2	Jersey Shore	.25	2	Sayre	.25	2	Wakefield	.25	2
Beaver Station	.25	2	Kane	.25	2	Schuylkill Haven	.25	2	Warren	.25	2
Bedford Springs (Sum'r)	.25	2	Karthaus	.25	2	Scottdale	.25	2	Watch Hill	.25	2
Beach Creek	.25	2	Kendall	.25	2	Scranton	.25	2	Westerly	.25	2
Bellefonte	.25	2	Kinzua	.25	2	Sewickley	.25	2	Wickford Junction	.25	2
Benezette	.25	2	Kittanning	.25	2	Sharpsville	.25	2	Woonsocket	.25	2
Berlin	.25	2	Kutztown	.25	2	Shenandoah	.25	2			
Bernice	.25	2	Lackawaxen	.25	2	Shickshinny	.25	2	**South Carolina.**		
Berwyn	.25	2	Lancaster	.25	2	Shippensville	.25	2	Beaufort	.60	4
Bethlehem	.25	2	Lansboro	.25	2	Shoholo	.25	2	Charleston	.50	3
Birdsboro	.25	2	Lansdale	.25	2	Slatington	.25	2	Cheraw	.60	4
Blairsville	.25	2	Latrobe	.25	2	Smethport	.25	2	Chester	.60	4
Blairsville Intersection	.25	2	Lawndale	.25	2	Snow Shoe	.25	2	Eutawville	.60	4
Blossburg	.25	2	Leaman Place	.25	2	Somerset	.25	2	Kingstree	.60	4
Boston	.25	2	Leesport	.25	2	Spartansburg	.25	2	Lancaster	.60	4
Braddock	.25	2	Leetsdale	.25	2	Springboro	.25	2	Lanes	.60	4
Bradford	.25	2	Lehighton	.25	2	Stenton	.25	2	Laurens	.60	4
Branchton	.25	2	Lenape	.25	2	Stoyestown	.25	2	Marion	.60	4
Bridgeport	.25	2	Lewisburg	.25	2	Stroudsburg	.25	2	Piedmont	.60	4
Bristol	.25	2	Lewistown	.25	2	Sugar Notch	.25	2	Society Hill	.60	4
Brockport	.25	2	Ligonier	.25	2	Sunbury	.25	2	Sumter	.50	3
Brookville	.25	2	Lititz	.25	2	Swarthmore	.25	2	Trenton	.60	4
Bryn Mawr	.25	2	Livermore	.25	2	Tacony	.25	2	Williamston	.60	4
Burgettstown	.25	2	Lock Haven	.25	2	Tamahend	.25	2	Yemassee	.60	4
Bustleton	.25	2	Lofty	.25	2	Tamaqua	.25	2			
Camelton	.25	2	Ludlow	.25	2	Tarport	.25	2	**Tennessee.**		
Carbondale	.25	2	Lykens	.25	2	Taylorstown	.25	2	Brownsville	.50	3
Carlisle	.25	2	Mahanoy Plane	.25	2	Tidioute	.25	2	Chattanooga	.50	3
Catasauqua	.25	2	Malvern	.25	2	Tionesta	.25	2	Chickamauga	.50	3
Catawissa	.25	2	Manayunk	.25	2	Titusville	.25	2	Clarksville	.40	3
Centralia	.25	2	Manorville	.25	2	Towanda	.25	2	Cleveland	.50	3
Center Hall	.25	2	Masontown	.25	2	Treichlers	.25	2	Dayton	.50	3
Chadd's Ford	.25	2	Mauch Chunk	.25	2	Trevorton	.25	2	Gallatin	.50	3
Chapman's Quarries	.25	2	McVeytown	.25	2	Tunkhannock	.25	2	Jellico	.50	3
Cheltenham	.25	2	Meadville	.25	2	Tyrone	.25	2	Johnson City	.50	3
Chester	.25	2	Media	.25	2	Union City	.25	2	Knoxville	.50	3
									Lenoir's	.50	3

TELEGRAPH RATES—Continued.

London... 60 4	Groton... 25–2	Lynchburg... 40 3	Ripon... 40 3
McNairy... 60–4	Highgate Springs... 25–2	Manassas... 40 3	Romney... 40–3
Memphis... 50–3	Leicester Junction... 25–2	Marion... 40 3	Salem... 40 3
Murfreesboro... 60 4	Ludlow... 25 2	Mattoax... 40 3	Sir John's Run... 40 3
Nashville... 40 3	Lyndon... 25 2	Meherrin... 40 3	Wellsburg... 40–3
Newport... 60 4	Lyndonville... 25 2	Natural Bridge... 40 3	Wheeling... 35–2
Paris... 60 4	Manchester... 25 2	New River Depot... 40 3	**Wisconsin.**
Rogersville... 85 6	Middlebury... 25 2	Norfolk... 35 2	Appleton, Outagamie Co. 50 3
Shelbyville... 60 4	Middlesex... 25 2	Nottoway... 40 3	Ashland, Ashland Co... 50 3
Sparta... 60 4	Montpelier... 25 2	Ocean View... 40 3	Baraboo... 50–3
Spring City... 60 4	Newfane... 25 2	Old Point Comfort... 40–3	Beloit... 50 3
Tracy City... 60 4	Newport... 25 2	Orange... 40 3	Blair... 50 3
Wartrace... 60–4	North Hartland... 25–2	Pearisburg... 40 3	Cable... 50 3
Texas.	Pascoumpsic... 25 2	Petersburg... 35–2	Colby... 50 3
Austin... 75 5	Pittsford... 25–2	Pittsylvania... 40 3	Custer... 50 3
Cisco... 75 5	Poultney... 25–2	Portsmouth... 35 2	Doylestown... 50 3
Cleburne... 75 5	Pownal... 25 2	Rapidan... 40 3	Eldorado... 50 3
Corpus Christi... 75–5	Proctorsville... 25 2	Richmond... 35 2	Fond du Lac... 50–3
Corsicana... 75–5	Putney Depot... 25 2	Salem... 40 3	Gratiot... 50 3
Dallas... 75 5	Readsboro... 25–2	Scottsburg... 40 3	Green Bay... 50–3
El Paso... 75 5	Richford... 25–2	Staunton... 35 2	Independence... 40–3
Fayetteville... 75 5	Roxbury... 25 2	Stuart... 40–3	Jackson... 50–3
Galveston... 75 5	Rutland... 25 2	Suffolk... 40–3	Jefferson... 50 3
Harrisburg... 75 5	St. Albans... 25 2	Tasley... 40 3	Kenosha... 50–3
Hico... 75 5	St. Johnsbury... 25 2	University of Virginia... 40–3	Madison... 50–3
Houston... 75 5	Sharon... 25 2	Warm Springs... 40 3	Marshfield, Wood Co... 50 3
Ingersoll... 75 5	Shelburne... 25 2	Waynesboro... 40 3	Menslon... 50 3
Leadbetter... 75 5	South Londonderry... 25 2	West Point... 40–3	Milwaukee... 50 3
Longview... 75 5	Springfield... 25 2	**Washington.**	Mineral Point... 50 3
Lufkin... 75 5	Sudbury... 25 2	Carbonado... 1.00 7	Monticello... 50 3
Marfa... 75–5	Swanton... 25 2	Chehalis... 1.00 7	Necedah... 50–3
McKinney... 75 5	Townshend... 25 2	Colfax... 1.00 7	Neenah... 50–3
Mineola... 75 5	Vergennes... 25 2	Dayton... 1.00 7	Oconomowoc... 50 3
Navasota... 75 5	Wallingford... 25 2	Hot Springs... 1.00–7	Oconto... 50 3
Nevada... 75 5	Waterbury... 25 2	Olympia... 1.00 7	Omalaska... 50 3
Paris... 75 5	Wells River... 25–2	Pomeroy... 1.00 7	Oshkosh... 50–3
Plano... 75 5	West Hartford... 25 2	Puyallup... 1.00 7	Peshtigo... 50 3
Reagan... 75 5	Westminster... 25 2	Riparia... 1.00 7	Plainfield... 50 3
Ross... 75 5	White River Junction... 25 2	Seattle... 1.00 7	Portage... 50–3
Rusk... 75 5	Windsor... 25 2	Spokane Falls... 1.00 7	Princeton... 50 3
San Antonio... 75 5	Woodstock... 25 2	Sprague... 1.00 7	Racine... 50 3
San Marcos... 75–5	**Virginia.**	Starbuck... 1.00 7	Rhinelander... 50 3
Sherman... 75 5	Abington... 40 3	Steilacoom... 1.00–7	Ripon... 50–3
Sulphur Springs... 75–5	Alexandria... 25–2	Tacoma... 1.00 7	Rush, Dunn Co... 50 3
Texarkana... 50 3	Amelia... 40 3	Tenino... 1.00 7	St. Croix Falls... 50 3
Tyler... 75–5	Amherst... 40 3	Vancouver... 1.00 7	Sauk City... 50–3
Waco... 75 5	Christiansburg... 40 3	Walla Walla... 1.00 7	Sheboygan... 50 3
Weatherford... 75 5	City Point... 40 3	**West Virginia.**	Shiocton... 50 3
Utah.	Clifton Forge... 40–3	Benwood... 40–3	Shullsburg... 50 3
Echo City... 75 5	Culpepper... 40 3	Buffalo... 40 3	Steven's Point... 50–3
Kelton... 75 5	Danville... 40 3	Charleston... 40–3	Stoughton... 50 3
Lehi... 75 5	Fortress Monroe (or Old	Charlestown... 40–3	Superior... 50 3
Ogden... 75 5	Point Comfort)... 40 3	Clarksburg... 40 3	Tomah... 50 3
Scofield... 75 5	Franklin, Accomac Co. 40–3	Colfax... 40 3	Trempeleau... 50 3
Uintah... 75 5	Franklin,Southampn Co. 40–3	Farmington... 40–3	Waukesha... 50 3
Wasatch, Salt Lake Co. 75 5	Fredericksburg... 25 2	Flemington... 40 3	Waupaca... 50 3
Vermont.	Gordonsville... 40 3	Grafton... 40 3	Wausau... 50 3
Alburgh... 25–2	Hampton... 40–3	Greenbrier White Sulphur	Wyocena... 50 3
Barre... 25 2	Hanover Court House... 40 3	Springs... 40 3	**Wyoming.**
Bellows Falls... 25–2	Harrisonburg... 40 3	Harper's Ferry... 40 3	Cheyenne... 75–5
Bennington... 25–2	Haymarket... 40 3	Huntington... 40 3	Evanston... 75 5
Brattleboro... 25 2	Hot Springs... 40 3	Ingleside... 40 3	Fort Steele... 75 5
Burlington... 25–2	Jarrett's... 40–3	Kanawha... 40 3	Green River... 75–5
Centre Rutland... 25 2	Lexington... 40 3	Keyser... 40 3	Laramie City... 75–5
Danby... 25 2	Lithia... 40 3	Morgantown... 40–3	Medicine Bow... 75 5
Enosburg Falls... 25 2	Louisa... 40 3	Parkersburg... 35–2	Rawlins... 75 5
	Luray... 40 3	Point Pleasant... 40 3	Yellowstone Nat. Park. 75 5

TUCKERTON R. R.
Stations, Distances and Fares. Single and Excursion.

M. New York	113 Barnegat... $2.35–$3.80	121 Barnegat City.	122 West Creek.
95 Whiting's... $1.85 $3.25	118 Manahawken.. 2.50–4.05	125 Penhala.	125 Tuckerton... $2.75–$4.50
100 Bamber.	122 Barnegat City Junc.	128 North Beach Haven.	
111 Waretown... 2.25 3.65	126 Harvey Cedars	129 Beach Haven. $2.95 $4.75	

VIA CENTRAL R. R. OF N. J.:
Leave **foot of Liberty St.** for **Tuckerton** and intermediate stations, (8:30 a. m., 4:00 p. m Arrive 11:10 a. m., 6:42 p.m.
Leave **Tuckerton**, 7:20 a. m., 3:18 p. m. Arrive New York, 1:00, 8:40 p. m.

VIA PENNSYLVANIA R. R.:
Leave **foot of Cortlandt** or **Desbrosses Sts.** for **Tuckerton** and intermediate stations, 4:00 p. m. Arrive 6:42 p. m.
Leave **Tuckerton**, 7:20 a. m., 3:18 p. m. Arrive New York 11:10 a. m., 7:20 p. m.

SHEPAUG, LITCHFIELD, AND NORTHERN R. R.
Via New York, New Haven and H. R. R., Grand Central Depot.
Stations, Distances and Fares from New York.

M. Stations. Fare.	M. Stations. Fare.	M. Stations. Fare.	M. Stations. Fare.
New York	15 Roxbury Falls... $2.15	26 New Preston... $2.65	35 Bantam... $2.85
Bethel... $1.50	18 Roxbury... 2.30	30 Romford... 2.75	36 Lake... 2.85
6 Hawleyville... 1.84	21 Judd's Bridge... 2.45	32 Morris... 2.80	38 Litchfield... 2.85
11 Shepaug... 1.95	25 Washington... 2.60		

Leave **Grand Central Depot** for **Hawleyville, Roxbury, New Preston, Litchfield** and intermediate stations, 5:01 a. m., 3:02 p. m. Arrive Roxbury, 11:00 a. m., 6:16 p. m. Arrive New Preston, 11:58 a. m., 6:41 p. m.; arrive Litchfield, 1:00, 7:15 p. m.

Trains to New York.
Leave **Litchfield**, stopping at intermediate stations, 7:25 a. m., 1:00 p. m.; Sundays, 3:40 p. m.; leave **New Preston**, 7:37 a. m., 2:45 p. m.; Sundays, 3:43 p. m.; leave **Roxbury**, 8:20 a. m., 3:30 p. m.; Sundays, 4:15 p. m. Arrive Hawleyville, 8:52 a. m., 4:35 p. m.; Sundays, 4:50 p. m. Arrive **New York**, 11:25 a. m., 9:00 p. m.; Sundays, 7:35 p. m.

OLD COLONY R. R.

Via Fall River Line, foot of Murray St.

NEW YORK, NEWPORT, FALL RIVER AND BOSTON.

Leave foot of Murray St., 5.00 p.m., via Newport, for **Boston.** Arrive Fall River, 5.25 a.m.; arrive Boston, 6.50 a.m.
Leave foot of Murray St., 5.00 p.m., via Fall River, for **Taunton.** Arrive Taunton (Central Station), 6.12 a.m. Connecting trains leave **Fall River,** 6.30, 6.15 a.m., for Middleboro, Bridgewater, Brockton, Taunton and **Boston.** Arrive Middleboro, 7.36 a.m., Bridgewater, 7.14 a.m., Brockton, 8.07 a.m., Taunton, 7.50 a.m., **Boston,** 8.50 a.m.

Trains to New York.

Leave **Boston,** 6.00 p.m.; leave Taunton (Central Station), 6.56 p.m.; leave Fall River, 7.15 p.m.; arrive Newport, 8.40 p.m. Arrive **foot of Murray St.,** 7.20 a.m.

NEWPORT TO BOSTON.

Leave **Newport** for **Taunton** and **Boston,** 6.50, 7.35, 10.20 a.m., 2.55, 5.15 p.m., Sundays, 1.45, 6.30 a.m., 6.30 p.m. Arrive Taunton, 8.03, 8.50, 11.42 a.m., 4.14, 6.34 p.m., Sundays, 5.57, 8.30 a.m., 7.35 p.m.; arrive Boston, 9.05, 10.00 a.m., 1.00, 5.40, 7.50 p.m., Sundays, 7.05, 9.35 a.m., 8.45 p.m.

BOSTON TO FALL RIVER AND NEWPORT.

Leave **Boston** for **Fall River,** 5.45, 8.15, 8.30, 9.30, 11.10 a.m., 12.00 m., 2.15, 3.40, 4.35, 6.00 p.m., Sundays, 4.15, 4.30 a.m., 5.45, 7.00 p.m. Arrive Fall River in 1½ hours.
For **Newport,** 5.45, 8.30, 11.40 a.m., 3.40 p.m., Sundays, 4.30 a.m. Arrive Newport, 8.55, 11.15 a.m., 2.20, 5.55 p.m., Sundays, 6.55 a.m.

FALL RIVER TO NEW BEDFORD.

Leave **Fall River,** 8.50 a.m., 12.40 m., 3.20, 6.35 p.m., (10.15 p.m. on Saturdays only). Arrive New Bedford in 35 minutes.
Leave **New Bedford,** 7.05, 10.00 a.m., 12.35, 5.15 p.m. (10.00 p.m. on Saturdays only). Arrive Fall River in 35 minutes.

FALL RIVER AND PROVIDENCE.

Leave **Fall River,** 6.50, 8.25 a.m., 12.25, 3.40, 5.55 p.m., Sundays, 9.00 a.m. Arrive Providence in 1 hour.
Leave **Providence,** 7.25, 9.35 a.m., 12.40, 4.15, 6.30 p.m., Sundays, 6.15 p.m. Arrive Fall River, 8.18, 10.38 a.m., 1.41, 5.19, 7.30 p.m., Sundays, 7.05 p.m.

BOSTON TO PLYMOUTH.

Leave **Boston,** 8.15 a.m., 2.30, 3.40, 3.50, 5.30 p.m., Sundays, 9.15 a.m. Arrive Plymouth in 1¾ hours.
Leave **Plymouth,** 6.30, 7.25, 7.50, 9.30, 11.45 a.m., 3.30, 4.25 p.m., Sundays, 4.05 p.m. Arrive Boston in 13¼ hours.

BOSTON AND PROVINCETOWN.

Leave **Boston** for **Yarmouth** and **Provincetown,** 8.55 a.m., 4.15 p.m. Arrive **Yarmouth,** 11.19 a.m., 6.46 p.m. Arrive Provincetown, 12.55, 8.30 p.m.
Leave **Provincetown,** 5.35 a.m., 2.05 p.m.; leave Yarmouth, 7.21 a.m., 3.58 p.m. Arrive Boston, 10.05 a.m., 7.05 p.m.

HOUSATONIC R. R.

Via New York, New Haven and Hartford R. R., Grand Central Depot, 4th Av. & 42d St.
Stations and Distances and Fares from New York.

Bridgeport............$1 15	29 Brookfield..........$2 02	65 Lime Rock..........$2 75	89 Housatonic..........$3 25
2 North Bridgeport.... 1 25	32 Lanesville & Still River	67 Falls Village........ 2 75	91 Glendale............ 3 35
5 Trumbull Church.... 1 33	35 New Milford........ 2 23	73 Canaan.............. 2 75	93 Stockbridge......... 3 40
8 Long Hill............ 1 42	42 Merwinsville........ 2 41	75 Ashley Falls........ 2 85	95 South Lee........... 3 40
10 Stepney............. 1 48	45 South Kent......... 2 50	79 Sheffield............ 2 93	99 Lee................. 3 40
15 Botsford............ 1 60	48 Kent................ 2 62	85 Great Barrington... 3 10	101 Lenox Furnace..... 3 40
19 Newtown............ 1 75	52 North Kent......... 2 63	87 Van Deusenville.... 3 20	102 Lenox.............. 3 40
23 Hawleyville......... 1 81	57 Cornwall Bridge.... 2 75	91 West Stockbridge... 3 20	106 Deweys............ 3 40
27 Brookfield Junction	61 West Cornwall...... 2 75	97 State Line.......... 3 20	110 Pittsfield.......... 3 40

Leave Grand Central Depot, via Bridgeport, for **Lenox, Pittsfield** and intermediate stations, 501, 8.00 a.m., 3.02 p.m. (4.02 p.m. to New Milford). Arrive Pittsfield, 11.05 a.m., 2.20, 8.55 p.m.
Leave Pittsfield, 8.10 a.m., 1.10, 5.00 p.m. Sundays, 2.00 p.m. Arrive Grand Central Depot, 2.15, 6.30, 11.00 p.m. Sundays, 9.00 p.m.
Leave New Milford, 8.25, 10.48 a.m., 3.12, 8.00 p.m. Sundays, 5.30 p.m. Arrive Grand Central Depot, 11.25 a.m., 2.15, 6.30, 11.00 p.m. Sundays, 9.00 p.m.
State Line Branch—Leave Bridgeport for Van Deusenville, West Stockbridge and **State Line.** 7.08, 10.05 a.m., 4.50 p.m. Arrive State Line 10.55 a.m., 1.26, 8.15 p.m.
Leave **State Line** 8.35 a.m., 12.00 noon, arrive Bridgeport 12.15, 4.50 p.m.

DANBURY AND NORWALK DIVISION.

* *Express train, makes but few stops.*

Stations and Distances and Fares from New York.

Wilson Point	6 Winnipauk.$1 00	12 Cannon....$1 17	20 Ridgefield.$1 41	24 Bethel....$1 50	27 Danbury..$1 60
3 So. Norwalk...85c.	8 So. Wilton.. 1 05	15 Georgetown 1 20		27 Hawleyville 1 08	33 Brookfield. 2 02
4 Norwalk.....90c.	11 Wilton...... 1 11	16 Branchville. 1 29	18 Sanford.... 1 35		
			20 Redding.... 1 38	25 E. Danbury	

Leave Grand Central Depot for Danbury and intermediate stations, 5.01, 8.00, 11.00 a.m., *1.02, 5.02 p.m. Sundays, 7.30 a.m., 5.00 p.m. Arrive at Danbury, 8.03, 10.22 a.m., 1.17, *6.02, 7.41 p.m. Sundays, 10.30 a.m., 7.57 p.m.
Leave Danbury, stopping at intermediate stations, 6.35, *7.36, 9.05 a.m., 12.01, 3.40 p.m. Sundays, 8.05 a.m., 5.05 p.m. Arrive Grand Central Depot, 9.10, 9.40, 11.25 a.m., 2.15, 6.00 p.m. Sundays, 11.12 a.m., 7.35 p.m.
Ridgefield Branch—Leave Grand Central Depot for **Branchville and Ridgefield,** 5.01, 8.00 a.m., 2.00, 4.02, 5.02 p.m. Arrive Ridgefield, 9.05, 10.11 a.m., 4.30, 5.57, 7.30 p.m.
Leave **Ridgefield,** stopping at Branchville, 6.45, 7.40, 9.18 a.m., 3.50, 6.30 p.m. Arrive New York, 9.10, 9.40, 11.25 a.m., 6.00, 9.55 p.m.
Hawleyville Branch—Leave **Grand Central Depot** for **Bethel** and **Hawleyville,** 5.01, 8.00, 11.00 a.m., 4.02 p.m. Arrive Hawleyville, 8.15, 10.35 a.m., 1.33, 6.13 p.m.
Leave **Hawleyville** (Bethel 10 minutes later), 8.55 a.m., 3.20, 6.42 p.m., Sundays, 4.52 p.m. Arrive New York, 11.25 a.m., 6.00, 9.55 p.m., Sundays, 7.35 p.m.
Brookfield Branch Leave **Danbury** for **Brookfield Junction,** 5.35, 7.45, 8.30, 10.15 a.m., 3.35, 5.15, 8.00 p.m. Arrive Brookfield Junction, 5.50, 8.00, 8.42, 10.58 a.m., 3.50, 5.30, 8.35 p.m.
Leave **Brookfield Junction** for **Danbury,** 6.00, 8.06, 8.47, 11.17 a.m., 4.00, 5.55, 8.25 p.m. Arrive, 6.15, 8.20, 9.02, 11.32 a.m., 4.15, 6.10, 8.40 p.m.

NEW HAVEN AND DERBY R. R.

Stations.— New Haven, West Haven, Tyler City, Orange, Derby, Birmingham, Ansonia. Botsford Branch- Shelton, Botsford.
Leave New Haven for **Derby, Ansonia** and intermediate stations, 7.30, 9.30, 9.55 a.m., 1.00, 2.35, 4.10, 5.35, 7.35, 11.15 p.m. Sundays, 8.10 a.m., 8.40 p.m. Arrive at Derby in 25 minutes, at Ansonia in 30 minutes.
Leave New Haven for **Shelton** and **Botsford,** 9.30 a.m., 4.10 p.m. Arrive Shelton in 28 minutes, at Botsford in 1 hour, 10 minutes.
Leave Botsford (leave Shelton 42 minutes later), 11.15 a.m., 8.50 p.m. Arrive New Haven in 1 hour, 10 minutes.
Leave Ansonia (leave Derby 6 minutes later), 6.49, 9.08, 11.42 a.m., 12.30, 12.50, 3.25, 6.10, 6.51, 8.30 p.m. Sundays, 7.20 a.m., 5.00 p.m. Arrive New Haven in 35 minutes.

NEW YORK AND NEW ENGLAND R. R.

For "All Rail" Express Trains to and from Boston, see Index for "Boston."

For "Fares to all Places," see Index.

Leave foot of Watts St. (Norwich Line), 5.00 p.m., except Sundays, for **New London, Putnam, Worcester** and **Boston.** Arrive Putnam, 5.30 a. m.; Webster, 5.51 a. m.; Worcester, 6.25 a. m.; **Boston,** 8.00 a. m.
Leave **Boston,** 6.00 p. m.; Worcester, 6.50 p. m.; Webster, 7.30 p. m.; Putnam, 7.55 p. m. Arrive foot of Watts St., 7.00 a.m.

NEW YORK AND WORCESTER TRAINS.

Leave **Grand Central Depot** for **Putnam, Webster** and **Worcester,** 5.01, 11.00 a. m. Arrive Worcester 12.10, 5.29 p. m.
Leave **Worcester** 9.30 a. m., 4.45 p. m.; leave Webster 10.12 a. m., 5.25 p. m.; leave Putnam 10.45 a. m., 5.53 p. m. Arrive Grand Central Depot 3.30, 11.40 p. m.

NEW YORK AND PROVIDENCE TRAINS.

Leave **Grand Central Depot** for **Plainfield** and **Providence,** 5.01, 11.00 a.m., 3.00 p.m. Arrive Providence, 12.50, 5.50, 8.30 p. m.
Leave **Providence,** 9.15 a. m., 3.30, 4.30 p. m.; leave **Plainfield,** 10.35 a. m., 4.25, 5.55 p. m. Arrive Grand Central Depot, 3.30, 9.00, 11.00 p. m.

TRAINS GOING EAST.

Fishkill-on-Hudson, Danbury, Waterbury, New Britain, Hartford, Willimantic, Putnam, Blackstone, Franklin and **Boston.**
Leave **Fishkill-on-Hudson** for **Boston,** *12.20 a. m. express train; 10.05 a.m. accommodation. Arrive Waterbury, *3.10 a. m., 12.50 p. m.; New Britain, *4.00 a. m., 1.55 p. m.; Hartford, *4.20 a. m., 2.10 p. m.; Willimantic, *5.23 a.m., 3.20 p. m.; Putnam, *6.10 a. m., 4.10 p. m.; Blackstone, 6.54 a. m., 5.01 p. m.; Franklin, *7.10 a. m., 5.21 p. m.; **Boston,** *8.00 a. m., 6.10 p. m. *Daily.*
Leave **Brewsters** for **Waterbury, Hartford** and intermediate stations, 7.30, 11.25 a. m., 6.30 p. m. Arrive Waterbury, 8.50 a. m., 12.50, 7.55 p. m.; arrive Hartford, 10.10 a. m., 2.10, 9.20 p. m. Additional train—leave **Waterbury** for **Hartford** and **Boston,** 7.30 a. m., 3.40 p. m. Arrive Hartford, 8.50 a. m., 5.00 p. m.; arrive **Boston,** 1.00, *9.00 p. m. *Daily.*
Leave **Hartford** for **Manchester, Vernon, Willimantic** and intermediate stations, 6.50, 9.00 a. m., 2.20, 5.10, 7.40 p. m. Arrive Willimantic in 1 hour, 10 minutes.
Leave **Willimantic** for **Boston,** *5.23, 6.30, 10.15 a. m., 3.25, 4.00, *6.40 p. m. Arrive Boston, *8.00, 9.46 a. m., 4.00, 6.10, *9.00 p. m. *Daily.*

TRAINS WESTWARD.

Leave **Boston** for **Fishkill-on-Hudson,** 8.30 a. m., *6.00 p. m. Arrive Willimantic, 11.25 a. m., *8.27 p. m.; Hartford, 12.30, *9.25 p. m.; Waterbury, 1.45, *10.42 p.m.; Fishkill-on-Hudson, 4.45 p. m., *1.20 a. m. *Daily.*
Additional trains leave **Boston** for **Willimantic** and **Hartford,** 12.00 noon, *3.00, 3.30 p. m. Arrive Willimantic, 2.17, *7.35, 6.45 p. m.; arrive Hartford, 3.15, 6.35, 8.05 p. m. *Daily.*
Leave **Hartford** for **Waterbury,** 6.35, 10.40 a. m., 12.35, 4.15, 6.40, *9.30 p. m. Arrive Waterbury in 1 hour, 30 minutes.
Leave **Waterbury** for **Danbury,** 8.00 a. m., 1.55, 5.38, *10.42 p. m. Arrive Danbury, in 1 hour, 10 minutes.
Leave **Waterbury** for **Fishkill-on-Hudson,** 8.00 a. m., 1.55, *10.42 p. m. Arrive Fishkill-on-Hudson, 11.00 a. m., 4.45 p. m., *1.20 night. *Daily.*

HARTFORD AND SPRINGFIELD TRAINS.

Leave **Hartford** for **Melrose** and **Springfield,** 10.25 a. m., 6.15 p. m. Arrive Melrose, 11.12 a. m., 7.02 p. m.; arrive Springfield, 11.50 a. m., 7.40 p. m.
Leave **Springfield** for **Hartford,** 7.30 a. m., 3.20 p. m. Arrive Hartford. 8.55 a. m., 4.45 p. m.

HARTFORD & CONNECTICUT WESTERN R. R.

Connect at Rhinebeck via N. Y. C. & H. R. R. R., at Millerton via Harlem Division.

Leave **Grand Central Depot** via N. Y. C. & H. R. R. R., at 8.00 a. m. for **Rhinebeck** and **Canaan,** stopping at intermediate stations. Arrive State Line 2.10 p. m., Canaan 1.25 p. m.
Leave **Grand Central Depot,** via Harlem Division, at 10.45 a. m., 3.25 p. m., Sundays, 9.45 a.m., for **Millerton, Canaan** and **West Winsted,** stopping at intermediate stations. Arrive Canaan 2.51, 6.15 p. m., Sundays, 5.31 p.m. Arrive West Winsted 3.38, 8 p. m., Sundays, 6.25 p. m.
Leave **Grand Central Depot,** via Harlem Division, at 10.35 a. m. for **Hartford** and intermediate stations. Arrive Hartford 5.04 p. m.

To New York.

Leave **Hartford,** stopping at intermediate stations, 10.15 a. m., 12.30 p. m. Arrive Grand Central Depot 5.26, 9.50 p. m.
Leave **Canaan,** stopping at intermediate stations, 7.30 a.m., 12.30, 3.40 p.m. Arrive Grand Central Depot 2.42, 5.26, 9.50 p.m.
Leave **Boston Corners** for **Rhinebeck** and intermediate stations, 8.30 a. m., 1.45 p. m. Arrive Grand Central Depot, 2.42, 9.25 p. m.

FONDA, JOHNSTOWN AND GLOVERSVILLE R. R.

From Grand Central Depot, via N. Y. C. & H. R. R. R.

Leave **Fonda** for **Johnstown** and **Gloversville,** 9.05 a. m., 12.37, 4.25, 6.43 p. m. Arrive Gloversville in 30 minutes.
Leave **Fonda** for Kingsboro, Mayfield, Cranberry Creek and **Northville,** 9.05 a. m., 4.25 p. m. Arrive Northville, 10.30 a. m., 5.45 p. m.
Leave **Northville** for **Fonda,** 6.22 a. m., 1.30 p. m. Arrive Fonda, 7.50 a. m., 2.58 p. m.
Leave **Gloversville,** stopping at Johnstown, 7.25, 10.40 a. m., 2.10, 5.35 p. m. Arrive Fonda in 28 minutes.

FREEHOLD AND NEW YORK R. R.

Via Central R. R. of New Jersey, foot of Liberty st.

Stations, Distances and Fare. Regular & Excursion from New York.

M. Keyport... 1 Mt. Pleasant 75c $1.35 | 8 Wickatunk...80c $1.45 11 Marlboro...90c $1.60 15 Freehold .$1.00-$1.75
2 Matawan...50c $1.25 6 Morganville.75c 1.35 | 9 Bradevelt...85c 1.50 13 E. Freehold95c 1.70
Leave foot of **Liberty St.** for **Matawan** and **Freehold,** stopping at intermediate stations, 4.30, 8.15, 11.15 a. m., 1.00, 4.30, 6.10 p. m. Leave **Matawan** 6.30, 8.30, 9.31 a. m., 12.26, 2.08, 5.30, 7.25 p. m. Arrive Freehold in 1½ to 2 hours from foot of Liberty St.
Leave **Freehold** for **Matawan** and **New York,** stopping at intermediate stations, 7.15, 8.10, 11.15 a. m., 1.35, 4.30, 6.30 p. m. Leave **Matawan** 7.43, 8.48, 11.45 a. m., 2.05, 5.00, 7.05 p. m.
Arrive foot of **Liberty St.,** *8.52, 9.37 a. m., 12.55, 3.30, 6.15, 8.10 p. m.

GENEVA, ITHACA & SAYRE R. R.

Via Lehigh Valley R. R., foot of Cortlandt and Desbrosses Sts.

Leave foot of **Cortlandt** or **Desbrosses Sts.,** for **Sayre, Ithaca, Geneva** and **Lyons,** stopping at intermediate stations, 8.00 a. m., 7.00 p. m., Sundays, 7.00 p. m. Arrive Ithaca 6.40 p. m., 6.00 a. m., Sundays, 6.00 a. m. Arrive Geneva 8.48 p. m., 8.40 a. m., Sundays, 8.40 a.m.
Leave **Lyons** 10.25 a. m., Sundays, 7.10 p. m.; leave **Geneva** 11.00 a. m., Sundays, 7.10 p. m.; leave **Ithaca** 12.35 p. m., Sundays, 9.12 p.m.; leave **Sayre** 2.57 p. m., Sundays, 10.55 p.m.
Arrive foot of **Cortlandt** or **Desbrosses Sts.,** 11.35 p. m., 7.50 a. m.

NEW YORK, SUSQUEHANNA & WESTERN R. R.

M. Stations.	Fare. Single. Ex.	M. Stations.	Fare. Single. Ex.	M. Stations.	Fare. Single. Ex.	M. Stations.	Fare. Single. Ex.
Jersey City.		21 Paterson	.50 .70	46 Newfoundland	$1.85 $2.15	58 So. Ogdensburg	$1.70 $2.75
7 Schuetzen Park	15c. 25c.	23 Riverside	.50 .70	48 Oak Ridge	1.10 2.30	61 Sparta	1.80 2.80
8 New Durham	15c. 25c.	24 Van Winkles	.70 .90	51 Stockholm	1.55 2.50	64 Sparta Junc.	1.85 2.85
12 Little Ferry	30c. 45c.	26 Midland Park	.70 .90	54 Two Bridges	1.65 2.60	— Branchville June. 1.95 3.00
13 Ridgefield Park	35c. 50c.	27 Wortendyke	.75 .95	58 Ogdensburgh	1.70 2.75	69 Washing'nville	2.05 3.10
14 Bogota	35c. 50c.	29 Wyckoff	.80 $1.00	60 Franklin	1.75 2.75	72 Swartswood	2.10 3.25
15 Hackensack	35c. 50c.	30 Campgaw	.90 1.10	63 Hamburgh	1.85 2.75	76 Stillwater	2.25 3.15
16 Maywood	35c. 50c.	31 Crystal Lake	.90 1.20	67 Deckertown	1.85 2.75	80 Marksboro	2.40 3.60
17 Rochelle Park	35c. 50c.	33 Oakland	.90 1.30	71 Quarryville	1.85 2.75	83 Paulina	2.40 3.60
18 Passaic Junction	35c. 50c.	34 Pompton	.95 1.40	73 Unionville	1.85 2.75	84 Blairstown	2.40 3.60
— Garfield	35c. 50c.	36 Pompton Junc.	$1.05 1.50	78 West Town	1.85 2.75	98 Del. Water Gap	2.55 3.80
21 Passaic	35c. 50c.	37 Bloomingdale	1.10 1.55	81 Johnsons	1.85 2.75	102 Stroudsburg	2.70 4.00
19 Dundee Lake	45c. 70c.	39 Butler	1.15 1.60	83 Slate Hill	1.85 2.75		
20 Vreeland Avenue	50c. 70c.	44 Charlottesburgh	1.30 2.00	89 Middletown	1.86 2.75		

LOCAL TRAINS TO PATERSON.

Schuetzen Park, New Durham, Little Ferry, Ridgefield Park, Bogota, Hackensack, Maywood, Rochelle Park, Garfield, Passaic, Dundee Lake, Paterson.

Leave foot of Cortlandt or Desbrosses Sts., for **Hackensack and Paterson**, and intermediate stations, 6 40. *8 10, *9.30, *10 30 a. m., 12 00 noon, *1 40, *3 30, *4 00, *4 30, *5 30, *5 40, *6 00, 6 40, 7 40, 10 00 p. m., 12 15 a. m., Sundays, 7 45, 10 30 a. m. 1 45, 7 15 p. m. Arrive Hackensack in 40 minutes; arrive Paterson in 1 hour. * *Express Trains.* *Connect for Passaic.*

To New York.

Leave **Paterson**, 5 37, 6 32, 7 00, 7 22, *8 00, *8 24, *8 58, *11 01, *11 13 a. m., 1 15, 3 00, 3 38, 5 01, 6 18, 7 18, *8 30, 10 52 p. m., Sundays, 9 05 a. m., 1 00, 6 05, *8 30 p. m.; leave **Hackensack**, 5 53, 6 50, 7 15, 7 40, *8 15, *8 41, *9 13, *10 16, *11 27 a. m., 1 33, *3 15, 3 57, 5 21, 6 38, 7 35, 9 10, 11 11 p. m., Sundays, 9 25 a. m., 1 15, 6 24, 9 10 p. m. Arrive New York in 50 minutes from Paterson; in 35 minutes from Hackensack. *Express Trains.*
Leave **Passaic**, *8 22, 9 55, 11 10 a. m., 1 15, 6 16 p. m. Arrive New York in 1 hour.
Leave **Rochelle Park**, 5 48, 6 45, *7 10, 7 34, *8 10, *8 85, 10 11 a. m., 1 27, *3 11, 3 51, 5 16, 6 32, *7 30, 11 05 p. m., Sundays, 9 16 a. m., 1 10, 6 18 p. m. Arrive New York in 40 to 50 minutes. *Express Trains.*

Riverside, Pompton, Blairstown, Delaware Water Gap, Middletown.

Leave foot of Cortlandt and Desbrosses Sts., for **Riverside**, *8 10, 10 30 a. m., 12 00 m., 3 30, 4 30, 5 00, 5 30, 6 00, 6 40, 10 00 p. m., 12 15 night, Sundays, 7 45, 10 30 a. m., 1 45 p. m. Arrive Riverside in 1 hour, 3 minutes.
For **Wortendyke** and intermediate stations, *8 10 a. m., 12 00 m., 4 00, 5 30, 6 00, 6 40 p. m., Sundays, 7 45 a. m. Arrive Wortendyke in 1½ hours.
For **Pompton, Butler** and intermediate stations. *8 10 a. m., 12 00 m., 4 00, 5 30 p. m., Sundays, 7 45 a. m. Arrive Butler in 1 hour, 50 minutes.
For **Two Bridges, Blairstown, Delaware Water Gap, Stroudsburg** and intermediate stations, *8 10 a. m., 4 00 p. m. Arrive Two Bridges, 11 15 a. m., 6 22 p. m.; arrive Blairstown, 1 27, 7 29 p. m.; arrive Stroudsburg, 1 35, 8 12 p. m.
For **Two Bridges, Ogdensburg, Franklin, Hamburg, Middletown** and intermediate stations, *8 10 a. m., 4 00 p. m., Sundays, 7 45 a. m. Arrive **Two Bridges**, 11 15 a. m., 6 22 p. m., Sundays, 10 50 a. m.; arrive Ogdensburg, 10 minutes later; Franklin, 20 minutes later; Hamburg, 30 minutes later; arrive **Middletown**, 1 35, 7 40 p. m., Sundays, 1 10 p. m.

To New York.
All Trains stop at intermediate stations.

Leave **Middletown**, 6 20 a. m., 4 25 p. m., Sundays, 4 25 p. m.; leave **Hamburg**, 7 12 a. m., 6 22 p. m., Sundays, 6 22 p. m.; leave **Two Bridges**, 7 40 a. m., 7 30 p. m., Sundays, 7 30 p. m. Arrive New York, 9 54 a. m., 10 05 p. m., Sundays, 10 05 p. m.
Leave **Stroudsburg**, 5 47 a. m., 2 4 p. m.; leave **Delaware Water Gap**, 5 55 a. m., 3 00 p. m.; leave **Sparta**, 7 17 a. m., 3 50 p. m. Arrive New York, 9 54 a. m., 10 05 p. m.
Leave **Butler**, 7 15, *8 16 a. m., 2 54, *8 04 p. m., Sundays, *8 04 p. m.; leave **Pompton**, 7 22, *8 24 a. m., 3 02, *8 12 p. m., Sundays, *8 12 p. m. Arrive New York, *9 30, 9 54 a. m., 4 40, 10 05 p. m., Sundays, 10 05 p. m.
Leave **Wortendyke**, 6 13, 6 40, 6 35 from Wyckoff, 7 40, *8 12 a. m., 3 21, *8 36 p. m., Sundays, *8 36 p. m. Arrive New York in 1 hour, 10 minutes.
Leave **Riverside**, 5 20, 6 25, 6 51, 7 13, 7 22, 9 51 a. m., 1 02, 3 32, 6 11 p. m., Sundays, *8 45 a. m., 12 58, 5 58 p. m. Arrive New York in 1 hour.

NEW JERSEY AND NEW YORK R. R.

M. Station.	Fare. Exc.	Station.	Fare. Exc.	Station.	Fare. Exc.	Station.	Fare. Exc.
New York.		17 River Ridge	45c. 75c.	26 Montvale	65c. $1 10	34 New Hempstead	80c. $1 20
10 Carlstadt	30c. 40c.	18 New Milford	45c. 75c.	27 Pearl River	65c. 1 10	34 Summit Park	1 20
11 Woodridge	35c. 50c.	19 Oradell	45c. 75c.	29 Nanuet	70c. 1 10	36 Pomona	80c. 1 20
12 Corona	35c. 50c.	20 Etna	50c. 85c.	30 Bardon's	75c. 1 15	37 Mount Ivy	80c. 1 20
13 Lodi Junction	35c. 50c.	21 Westwood	55c. 90c.	31 Germond's	75c. 1 15	39 Thiells	80c. 1 20
14 Hackensack	35c. 50c.	22 Hillsdale	55c. 90c.	33 New City	75c. 1 15	41 W. Haverstraw	80c. 1 20
15 Fairmount	40c. 65c.	24 Pascack	60c. $1 00	31 Spring Valley	80c. 1 20	42 Haverstraw	80c. 1 20
16 Cherry Hill	40c. 65c.	25 Park Ridge	65c. 1 10	32 Union	80c. 1 20		

Leave foot of Chambers St. (leave W. 23d St. 20 minutes earlier), for **Hillsdale** and intermediate stations, 7 50, 8 40, 9 50, 11 15 a. m., 1 00, 4 10, 5 20, 5 50, 6 30, *8 30 p. m., Saturday, 12 night, Sundays, *8 45, 11 15 a. m., *8 00, 9 30 p.m. Arrive Hillsdale in 1 hour, 10 minutes.
For **Nanuet, Spring Valley** and intermediate stations. 7 50, 9 50, 11 15 a. m., 1 00, 4 10, 5 50, 6 30 p. m. Arrive Nanuet in 1¼ hours, at Spring Valley in 1 hour, 40 minutes.
For **New City** (Branch) and intermediate stations. 9 50 a. m., 4 10, 5 50 p. m., Sundays, *8 45 a. m., *8 03 p. m. Arrive in 1 hour, 40 minutes.
For **Haverstraw** and intermediate stations. 7 50 a. m., 1 00, 4 10, 5 50 p. m., Sundays, *8 45 a. m., *8 00 p.m. Arrive Haverstraw in 2 hours.

Trains to New York.

Leave **Haverstraw**, 6 15, 7 31, 10 43 a. m., 3 30 p.m., Sundays, *8 13 a. m., 5 28 p. m. Arrive New York in 2 hours.
Leave **Spring Valley**, 6 02, 6 48, 7 38, 11 10 a. m., 1 38, 4 08 p.m., Sundays, *8 46 a. m., 6 11 p.m. Arrive New York in 1 hour. 35 minutes.
Leave **New City**, 5 53, 7 03 a. m., 3 54, 8 09 p.m., Sundays, *8 26 a.m., 6 02 p.m. Arrive New York in 1 hour. 40 minutes.
Leave **Nanuet**, stopping at intermediate stations, 6 00, 6 54, 7 17, 8 04, 11 23 a. m., 1 45, 4 10, 6 23 p. m., Sundays, *8 52 a. m., 6 18 p.m. Arrive New York in 1½ hours.
Leave **Hillsdale**, stopping at intermediate stations, 5 14, 6 29, 7 13, 7 36, *8 18, 10 30, 11 41 a. m., 2 01, 4 27, 7 07 p.m., Sundays, 7 25, 9 11 a. m., 6 39, *8 14 p. m. Arrive New York in 1 hour, 6 minutes.

NEW YORK, ONTARIO & WESTERN R. R.

Depots foot of Jay and W. 42d Sts.
Ticket Offices: 307 Broadway, and foot of Jay and W. 42d St.

M.	Stations.	Single.	Exc.	M.	Stations.	Single.	Exc.	M.	Stations.	Single.	Exc.	M.	Stations.	Single.	Exc.
	New York,			116	Liberty Falls..	$2.85	$5.00	219	So. New Berlin.	$5.15	$9.00	281	Rome	$5.50	$10.00
	Weehawken,			118	Liberty	2.91	5.21	226	New Berlin	5.70	9.00	250	Eaton	5.50	10.00
55	West Cornwall	$1.08	$2.00	123	Parksville	3.06	5.51	209	Guilford Centre	5.00	9.00	253	Morrisville	5.50	10.00
56	Orr's Mills	1.08	2.00	129	Livingn Manor	3.21	5.81	211	Guilford	5.00	9.00	255	Pratts	5.50	10.00
57	Meadow Brook	1.25	2.36	135	Rockland	3.42	6.23	218	Oxford	5.00	9.00	259	Munnsville	5.50	10.00
59	Dennistons	1.32	2.45	140	Cook's Falls	3.57	6.53	226	Norwich	5.00	9.00	260	Stockbridge	5.50	10.00
61	Geungs	1.35	2.30	144	Whirling Eddy	3.78	6.95	232	North Norwich	5.00	9.35	262	Valley Mills	5.50	10.00
64	Rock Tavern	1.46	2.35	148	Trout Brook	3.78	6.95	234	Sher. 4 Corners	5.00	9.55	265	Community	5.50	10.00
65	Burnside	1.59	2.40	150	East Branch	3.87	7.10	237	Smyrna	5.00	9.70	267	Oneida Castle	5.50	10.00
68	Campbell Hall	1.66	2.55	154	Fish's Eddy	3.96	7.10	241	Earlville	5.00	10.00	268	Oneida	5.50	10.00
70	Stony Ford	1.65	2.50	160	Hancock	4.14	7.40	245	Randall-ville	5.00	10.00	271	Durhamville	5.62	10.00
72	Crystal Run	1.65	2.50	167	Cadosia	4.35	7.50	248	Hamilton	5.00	10.00	273	State Bridge	5.68	10.00
74	Mechanicstown	1.68	2.75	171	Rock Rift	4.50	7.75	251	Pecksport	5.00	10.00	276	Sylvan	5.77	10.00
77	Middletown	1.68	2.75	179	Walton	4.71	8.15	253	Brookville	5.00	10.00	277	Sylvan Beach	5.77	10.00
83	Fair Oaks	1.83	2.75	188	Hamden	5.00	8.25	255	Solsville	5.00	10.00	279	North Bay	5.86	10.00
85	Winterton	1.92	3.00	195	Delhi	5.25	8.40	259	Oriskany Falls	5.00	10.00	282	West Vienna	5.95	10.00
88	Bloomingburg	1.98	3.00	191	Franklin	5.00	8.60	263	Deansville	5.00	10.00	286	Cleveland	6.07	10.00
89	Wurtsboro	2.04	3.47	194	Sidney Centre	5.00	8.75	264	Franklin I Wks	5.00	10.00	288	Bernhards Bay	6.16	10.00
93	Summitville	2.13	3.60	197	Young's	5.00	8.90	267	Clinton	5.00	10.00	292	Constantia	6.25	10.00
94	Phillipsport	2.19	3.77	202	Sidney	5.00	9.00	274	New Hartford	5.00	10.00	296	West Monroe	6.37	10.00
97	Homowack	2.25	3.80	204	New Berlin Junc	5.00	9.00	276	Utica	5.00	10.00	300	Central Square	6.50	10.00
100	Ellenville	2.37	4.13	207	Rockdale	5.00	9.00	270	Kirkland	5.06	10.00	303	Caughdenoy	6.50	10.00
101	Mountain Dale	2.35	4.33	211	Mt. Upton	5.21	9.00	272	Clark's Mills	5.00	10.00	306	Pennellville	6.50	10.00
104	Centreville	2.49	4.37	212	Rockwells Mills	5.27	9.00	273	Westmoreland	5.15	10.00	314	Fulton	6.50	10.00
108	Fallsburgh	2.58	4.55	215	White's Stores	5.33	9.00	275	Bartlett	5.24	10.00	326	Oswego	6.50	10.00
111	Hurleyville	2.67	4.73	217	Holmesville	5.39	9.00	278	Dix	5.30	10.00				

* Daily.   § Daily Express train making but few stops.

Leave foot of Jay St. (leave foot of W. 42d St. 15 minutes later), for Cornwall, for **Campbell Hall, Middletown, Summitville** and intermediate stations, *3.30, 7.35 a. m., 3.55, $6.10 p. m.   Arrive Campbell Hall, *7.50, 10.30 a. m., 6.11, 8.53 p. m.; arrive Middletown, *8.13, 10.40 a. m., 7.05, 9.15 p. m.; arrive Summitville, *11 30, 11.25 a. m., 7.53, 9.58 p. m.

For **Fallsburg, Liberty, Walton, Sidney** and intermediate stations, *3.30, 7.35 a. m., *6 40 p. m.   Arrive Fallsburg, *12 26, 12.02, 10.32 p. m.; arrive Liberty, *1.08, 12.25, *10.58 p. m.; arrive Walton, *4.50, 2.40 p. m., *1.10 a. m.; arrive Sidney, *6 10, 3.40 p. m., *2.07 a. m.

For **Norwich, Earlville, Randallsville, Oneida, Oswego** and intermediate stations, 7.35 a. m., *6.10 p. m.   Arrive Norwich, 4.35 p. m., *3.45 a. m.; arrive Earlville, 5.05 p. m., *3.49 a. m.; arrive Randallsville, 5.13 p. m., *3.50 a. m.; arrive Oneida, 6.20 p. m., *4.55 a. m.; arrive Oswego, 8.25 p. m., *6.55 a. m.

Trains to New York.

Trains stop at intermediate stations.

Leave **Oswego**, 7.00 a. m., *9.55 p. m.; leave **Oneida**, 9.06 a. m., *11.53 p. m.; leave **Earlville**, 10.43 a. m., *12.57 night; leave **Norwich**, 10.50 a. m., *1.30 a. m. Arrive New York, 7.10 p. m., *9.15 a. m.

Leave **Sidney**, *10.40, 11.15 a. m., *2.27 p. m.; leave **Walton**, *11.50 a. m., 12.55, *9.25 p. m.; leave **Liberty**, *3.38, 3.03 p. m., *5.45 a. m.   Arrive New York, *11.05, 7.10 p. m., *9.45 a. m.

Leave **Summitville**, *6.25, 7.25 a. m., 3.58, *5.28 p. m.; leave **Middletown**, *7.10, 8.10 a. m., 4.40, *7.05 p. m.; leave **Campbell Hall**, *7.30, 8.31 a. m., 4.59, *7.18 p. m.; leave **Cornwall**, *8.00, 9.05 a. m., 5.30, *9.00 p. m.   Arrive New York, *9.45, 10.45 a. m., 7.10, *11.05 p. m.

ELLENVILLE BRANCH.

Leave **Summitville** for **Phillipsport, Homowack** and **Ellenville**, 9.40, 11.30 a. m., 7.56 p. m.   Arrive Ellenville in 20 minutes.

Leave **Ellenville** for **Summitville**, 7.05, 10.45 a. m., 3.25 p. m.   Arrive in 20 minutes.

DELHI BRANCH.

Leave **Walton** for **Colchester, Hawley, Hamden, De Lancey** and **Delhi**, *8.00 a. m., 2.45, 9.00 p. m.   Arrive Delhi in 1 hour.

Leave **Delhi** for **Walton**, 7.00, 10.40 a. m., 5.30 p. m., Sundays, 10.00 a. m.   Arrive in 1 hour.

NEW BERLIN BRANCH.

Leave **Sidney** for **New Berlin, Edmeston** and intermediate stations, 11.45 a. m., 8.00 p. m. Sundays, 10.30 a. m.   Arrive New Berlin, 1.40, 9.45 p. m., Sundays, 11.45 a. m.; arrive Edmeston, 2.10, 9.40 p. m., Sunday, 12.10 p. m.

Leave **Edmeston** (leave New Berlin, 25 minutes later), 7.00 a. m., 4.45 p. m., Sundays, 7.30 a. m.   Arrive Sidney, 8.45 a. m., 7.15 p. m., Sundays, 9.30 a. m.

UTICA DIVISION.

Leave **Randallsville** for **Clinton, Utica** and intermediate stations, 6.45, 10.40 a. m., 2.00, 5.15 p. m.   Arrive Clinton, 8.10, 11.37 a. m., 5.01, 6.15 p. m.; arrive Utica, 8.50, 11.59 a. m., 5.40, 6.40 p. m.

Leave **Utica** for **Randallsville**, 8.15 a. m., 4.38, 11.15 p. m.; leave **Clinton**, 8.48 a. m., 5.03 p.m., 12.01 night.   Arrive Randallsville, 9.50 a. m., 5.54 p. m., 1.30 a. m.

WALLKILL VALLEY R. R.

Via West Shore and New York, Ontario & W. R. Rs., foot of Jay and W. 42d St.

Stations and Fare from Campbell Hall, Montgomery 15c., Walden 20c., Wallkill 30c., New Hurley 44c., Gardiner 53c., Forest Glen 61c., New Paltz 69c., Springtown 80c., Rosendale 90c., Binnewater 95c., Whiteport $1.04, Kingston $1.14.

Via New York, Ontario & Western R. R.

Leave foot of Jay St. (leave foot W. 42d St. 15 minutes later) for **Campbell Hall, Gardiner, Kingston** and intermediate stations, 7.35 a. m., 3.55 p.m.   Arrive Gardiner, 12.08, 7.19 p.m.; arrive Kingston, 12.57, 8.10 p.m.

Leave **Kingston**, 6.55 a. m., 3.05 p. m.; leave **Gardiner**, 7.12 a. m., 3.25 p. m.   Arrive New York, at 10.10 a. m., 7.15 p. m.

Via West Shore R. R.

Leave foot of Jay St. (leave foot W. 42d St. 15 minutes later) for **Kingston, Gardiner, Montgomery** and intermediate stations, 3.00, 7.00, 11.15 a. m., Sundays, 9.40 a. m.   Arrive Montgomery, 8.05 a. m., 1.45, 4.23 p. m., Sundays, 3.50 p. m.

To New York—Leave **Montgomery**, 9.40, 11.45 a. m., 4.00 p. m., Sundays, 4.05 p. m.

Leave **Gardiner**, 9.31 a. m., 12.08, 4.51 p. m., Sundays, 4.43 p. m.   Arrive Kingston, 10.20 a. m., 12.57, 6.00 p. m., Sundays, 5.55 p. m.; arrive New York, 2.50, 7.10, 10.00 p. m., Sundays, 10.00 p. m.

LEBANON SPRINGS R. R.

Leave Grand Central Depot, via Harlem R.R., for **Chatham, Lebanon Springs** and **Bennington**, stopping at intermediate stations, 10.35 a. m.   Arrive at Lebanon Springs, 5.05 p. m., at Bennington, 8.00 p. m.

Leave **Bennington** 9.00 a. m., leave **Lebanon Springs** 11.05 a. m.   Arrive Grand Central Depot, 5.20 p. m.

BUFFALO, ROCHESTER AND PITTSBURG R. R.

Connect from New York via N. Y. C. & H. R. R. R., West Shore R. R., or Erie R. R.

Leave Rochester for **Gainesville, Salamanca, Bradford** and intermediate stations, 7 20 a. m., 3 30, 5 15 p. m. Arrive Gainesville, 9 26 a. m., 5 48, 8 15 p. m.; arrive Salamanca, 11 20 a. m., 10 42 p. m.; arrive Bradford, 11 58 a. m., 11 00 p.m. Leave **Bradford** for **Ridgway, Punxsutawney, Walston** and intermediate stations, 7 00 a. m., 1 00 p. m. Arrive Punxsutawney, 12 01, 6 30 p. m.; arrive Walston, 6 40 p. m.

Trains to Rochester.

Leave **Walston**, 8 50 a. m.; leave **Du Bois**, 10 00 a. m., 3 00 p. m. Arrive Bradford, 2 15, 7 15 p. m.
Leave **Bradford**, 9 15 a. m., 2 35 p. m.; leave **Salamanca**, 10 05 a. m., 3 24 p. m. Arrive Rochester, 2 25, 7 30 p. m.
Leave **Ashford**, 10 15 a. m., 3 55 p. m.; arrive Rochester, 2 25, 7 30 p. m. Leave **Bliss**, stopping at Gainesville, Warsaw, and intermediate stations, 6 30, 11 52 a. m., 1 56 p. m.; arrive Rochester, 9 00 a. m., 2 25, 7 30 p. m.

BUFFALO DIVISION.

Leave **Buffalo** for **Ashford, Salamanca, Bradford** and intermediate stations, *8 10 a. m., 5 20 p. m. Arrive Bradford, *11 58 a. m., 8 40 p. m. *Daily.
Leave **Bradford**, 7 15 a. m., *2 35 p. m.; leave Salamanca, 7 55 a. m., *3 20 p. m.; leave Ashford, 8 25 a. m., *3 55 p. m. Arrive Buffalo, 10 25 a. m., *6 00 p. m. *Daily.

CONNECTICUT RIVER R. R.

Via New York, New Haven and Hartford R. R., Grand Central Depot.

Connecting trains leave **Grand Central Depot:**
For **Springfield** at 5 01, 8 00, 9 00, 9 02, 11 00 a. m., 12 02, 3 00, 4 00, 6 05, 7 01, 9 30, *11 00 p. m. *Daily.
Due **Springfield**, 10 25 a. m., 12 27, 12 15, 2 24, 3 02, 5 42, 7 16, *7 27, 10 30 p. m., 12 25, 2 35, *3 02 a. m.

Leave **Springfield** for **Chicopee Falls**, 6 40, 10 00, 11 45 a. m., 3 00, 5 05, 6 18, 8 45 p. m. Arrive in 20 minutes.
For **Holyoke**, 6 40, 7 15, 8 00, 9 10, 10 35 a. m., 12 00, 1 05, 1 30, 2 25, 3 15, 5 00, 5 45, 6 15, 6 45, 8 00, 9 10, 11 00 p. m. Arrive in 20 minutes.
For **Easthampton**, 8 00, 9 10 a. m., 12 m., 1 30, 3 15, 5 00, 6 45 p. m. Arrive in 40 minutes.
For **Northampton**, 7 15, 8 00, 9 10, 10 35 a.m., 12 00 m., 1 05, 1 30, 2 25, 4 15, 5 00, 6 15, 6 45, 8 00, 11 00 p.m. Arrive in 35 min.
For **South Deerfield, Greenfield, South Vernon, Brattleboro, Bellows Falls, Windsor** and intermediate stations, 8 00 a. m., 1 05, 3 15, 6 45, 8 00 p. m. Arrive South Deerfield, 1½ hours; at South Vernon in 2 hours; at Bellows Falls in 3½ hours; at Windsor in 4 hours.
For **Keene**, 8 00 a. m., 3 15 p. m. Arrive at Keene, 3½ hours.

Trains to Springfield.

Leave **Windsor**, 3 55 a.m. except Monday, 7 55 a.m., 12 55, 3 15 p.m.; leave **Bellows Falls**, 4 40 a.m. except Monday, 9 00 a. m., 2 00, 4 40 p. m.; leave **Brattleboro**, 5 25 except Monday, 9 08 a. m., 3 00, 4 40 p. m.; leave **South Vernon**, 5 43 except Monday, 10 25 a. m., 3 50, 5 00 p. m. Arrive **Springfield**, 7 10 a. m. except Monday, 12 30, 5 50, 6 27 p. m.
Leave **Keene**, 9 00 a. m., 2 50 p. m. Arrive Springfield 12 30, 5 50 p. m.
Leave **Greenfield**, 6 08 except Monday, 7 20, 11 00 a.m., 1 30, 5 25 p.m. Arrive Springfield in 1½ hours.
Leave **Northampton**, 6 00 (6 40 except Monday), 8 05, 9 23, 10 15, 11 20, 11 44 a.m., 12 35, 2 20, 4 30, 5 05, 5 55, 7 05, 11 10 p. m. Arrive Springfield in 45 minutes.
Leave **Easthampton**, 7 53, 10 06, 11 40 a. m., 1 50, 3 35, 5 00, 6 40 p. m. Arrive Springfield in 1 hour.
Leave **Holyoke**, 6 21 (6 56 except Monday), 7 20, 8 28, 9 45, 10 38, 11 42 a. m., 12 10, 1 13, 2 40, 4 15, 5 30, 6 13, 7 25, 10 25 11 58 p. m. Arrive Springfield in 20 minutes.
Leave **Chicopee Falls**, 6 20, 7 55, 10 30 a. m., 1 00, 3 35, 5 35, 6 42 p. m. Arrive Springfield in 20 minutes.

NEW YORK & ROCKAWAY BEACH R. R.

Stations and Fares from L. I. City - Single and Exc.—Woodhaven Junction, 20c., 30c., Ozone Park, 20c., 30c., Aqueduct, 25c., 35c., Goose Creek, 30c., 50c., The Raunt, 30c., 50c., Broad Channel, 30c., 50c., Beach Channel, 30c., 50c., Hammel's, Holland's, Seaside, Rockaway Beach, 30c., 50c., Atlantic Park, Arverne, 35c., 60c., Far Rockaway, 65c., $1 00*. *Between June 1st and Sept. 30th. excursion fare is 50 cents.

Leave **Long Island City** for **Rockaway Beach** and intermediate stations, 7 35, 10 10 a.m., 2 11, 4 27, 5 42, 6 45 p.m. (12 23 Wednesday night only). Sundays. 7 10, 9 10, 11 10 a.m., 2 05, 4 00, 6 45 p. m. Arrive Rockaway Beach in 45 minutes.

To Long Island City.

Leave **Rockaway Beach** (Hammel's 9 minutes later), stopping at intermediate stations, 6 30, 8 00, 11 10 a. m., 3 10, 4 30, 5 30 p. m. (11 00 p. m. Wednesdays only), Sundays, 8 00, 10 10 a. m., 12 30, 3 00, 5 30, 7 30 p. m. Arrive Long Island City in 45 minutes.

TRAINS FROM BROOKLYN.

Fare - Single and Exc.—Ozone Park, 20c., 30c., Aqueduct, 25c., 35c., Goose Creek, 25c., 45c., Broad Channel, 25c., 45c., Beach Channel, 25c., 45c., Rockaway Beach, 25c., 45c., Arverne, 35c., 60c., Far Rockaway, 65c., $1 00*. *Between June 1st and Sept. 30th excursion fare is 70 cents.

Leave **Flatbush Avenue** for **Rockaway Beach** and intermediate stations, 7 30, 10 00 a. m., 2 00, 4 23, 5 22, 6 30, p. m. (12 15 Wednesday night only), Sundays, 7 00, 9 20, 11 20 a.m., 1 40, 3 40, 6 05 p.m. Arrive Rockaway Beach in 1 hour.

To Brooklyn.

Leave **Rockaway Beach** (Hammel's 9 minutes later), 6 30, 8 00, 11 10 a. m., 3 10, 4 30, 5 30 p. m. (11 00 p. m. Wednesdays only), Sundays, 8 10, 10 20 a. m., 12 40, 3 00, 5 00, 7 30 p. m. Arrive Flatbush Avenue in 1 hour.

NEW LONDON NORTHERN R. R.

Via Norwich Line and New York, New Haven & Hartford R. R.

Stations and Distances.

M.	New London.	30	Willimantic	61	Monson	100	Miller's Falls
6	Montville	35	South Coventry	65	Palmer	109	Northfield
13	Norwich	39	Mansfield	68	Three Rivers	111	South Vernon
17	Yantic	44	Tolland	73	Belchertown	121	Brattleboro
26	South Windham	50	Stafford	85	Amherst		

Leave **Grand Central Depot**, via New London, for **Norwich, Willimantic** and intermediate stations, 5 00, 10 00 a. m., 1 00 p. m. Arrive Willimantic, 11 25 a. m., 3 48, 6 38 p.m.
For **Palmer** and **Brattleboro** and intermediate stations, 10 00 a.m. Arrive Palmer, 5 15 p.m.; arrive Brattleboro, 9 20 p.m.
Leave via Norwich Line, foot of **Watts St.**, 5 00 p.m. for **New London, Willimantic, Palmer, Brattleboro** and intermediate stations. Arrive at Willimantic, 6 07 a.m.; at Palmer, 7 25 a. m.; at Brattleboro, 10 37 a. m.

To New London and New York.

Leave **Brattleboro**, †6 30, 10 50 a.m., *3 15 p. m.; leave **Palmer**, 8 40 a.m., 2 05, 7 10 p. m.; trains marked † arrive Grand Central Depot, 3 30, 11 00 p.m.; trains marked * arrive foot of Watts St. 6 30 a. m. Extra train from Willimantic, 6 40 p. m.; arrive Grand Central Depot, 11 00 p.m.

Our Weekly Supplement, issued every Monday, contains all changes in Time Tables of Railroads, Steamboats, etc.

NEWSPAPER OFFICES.

Associated Press, 195 Broadway.

Commercial Advertiser, cor. Fulton and Nassau sts.
Daily News, 25 Park Row, 1258 Broadway.
Graphic, 39 Park Place, 1258 Broadway.
Herald, cor. Broadway and Ann st., cor. 5th ave. and 23d st.
Journal of Commerce, cor. Hanover and Beaver sts.
Mail and Express, 23 Park Row, 1258 Broadway.
Morning Journal, Nassau and Spruce sts.
Post, cor. Fulton and Broadway, 1258 Broadway.
Press, 26 North William, 1258 Broadway.
Star, cor. Broadway and Park Place.
Staats-Zeitung, cor. Tryon Row and Centre st.
Sun, cor. Nassau and Frankfort sts., 1265 Broadway.
Telegram, cor. Broadway and Ann st., 532 6th av.
Times, Park Row and Nassau st., 1269 Broadway.
Tribune, cor. Nassau and Spruce sts., 1258 Broadway.
World, 31 Park Row, 1297 Broadway.

NEW YORK AND MASSACHUSETTS R. R.

Via New York Central & Hudson River R. R.

Stations and Fares from Poughkeepsie, Van Wagner's 22c., Pleasant Valley 30c., Salt Point 45c., Clinton Corners 50c., Willow Brook 60c., Stanfordville 70c., McIntyre 70c., Stissing 75c., Pine Plains 80c., Ancram Lead Mines $1.05, Halstead's $1.10, Tanner's $1.15, Boston Corners $1.20.

Leave Grand Central Depot, via Poughkeepsie, for **Boston Corners** and intermediate stations, 8 00 a. m. and 3 30 p. m. Arrive Pine Plains 12 45, 6 57 p. m.; arrive Boston Corners 1 30, 7 28 p. m. Trains leave Poughkeepsie for Boston Corners, 8 00, 11 30 a. m., 5 15 p. m., Sundays, 9.30 a.m.

To New York.

Leave **Boston Corners**, stopping at intermediate stations, 7 02 a. m., 2 45 p. m., Sundays, 1 00 p.m. Arrive Poughkeepsie 8 47 a. m., 4 05 p. m., Sundays, 5 51 p.m.; arrive **New York**, 11 15 a. m., 7 00 p.m.; Sundays, 8 50 p.m.

NEW YORK & NORTHERN R. R.

YONKERS BRANCH.

Stations and Fares—Single and Excursion.

M. 155th St. & 8th Av.	3 Fordham Heights.. 10c. 20c.	6 Mosholu.......... 20c. 30c.	8 Yonkers (GettySq.)25c. 40c.
1 High Bridge....... 5c.	4 King's Bridge..... 10c. 20c.	7 Lowerre........... 20c. 35c.	
2 Morris Dock...... 10c. 20c.	5 Van Cortlandt..... 15c. 25c.	7 Park Hill.......... 25c. 40c.	

Leave 155th St. & 8th Avenue for **Yonkers** and intermediate stations, daily (except Sunday), 6 00, 6 30, 7 00, 7 30, 8 00, 8 30, 9 00, 9 30, 10 00, 11 05 a. m., 12 m., 1 00, 2 00, 3 00, 4 35, 5 12, 15 15 to Van Cortlandt), 5 40, 6 01, 6 30, 7 00, 8 00, 9 00, 10 00, 11 10 p. m., 12 30 night. *Sundays*, hourly from 8 00 a. m. to 9 00 p. m., then 10 30 p. m. Arrive Yonkers in 25 minutes.

Trains to New York 155th St. & 8th Avenue,

Leave **Yonkers** (daily except Sunday), 5 30, 6 30, 7 00, 7 42, 8 00, 8 30, (8 11 from Van Cortlandt), 9 00, 9 30, 10 00, 10 30, 11 30, a. m., 12 30, 1 30, 2 30, 3 30, 4 30, 5 00 (5 34 from Van Cortlandt), 5 40, 6 00, 6 30, 7 00, 7 30, 8 30, 9 30, 10 10, 11 45 p. m. *Sundays*, hourly from 7 30 a. m. to 8 30 p. m., then 9 15 p.m. Arrive 155th St. in 25 minutes.

MAIN LINE.

Stations and Fares—Single and Excursion.

M. 155th St. & 8th Av.	16 Aqueduct	32 Kitchawan.. 75c.$1.35	44 Dean House
4 Van Cortlandt.. 15c. 25c.	18 Elmsford... 15c. 75c.	33 Croton Lake.. 80c. 1.45	45 Lake Mahopac. $1.05 $1.90
8 Dunwoodie...... 25c. 40c.	20 East View... 45c. 85c.	36 Yorktown.... 90c. 1.65	47 Crafts............ 1.10 2.00
9 Bryn Mawr Park. 25c. 45c.	21 Tarrytown.... 15c. 80c.	37 Amawalk.... 95c. 1.75	49 Carmel.......... 1.15 2.00
10 Nepperhan..... 30c. 50c.	22 Sleepy Hollow. 15c. 80c.	40 West Somers. $1.05 1.90	51 Tilley Foster
11 Gray Oaks	23 Tarryt'n Heights. 15c. 80c.	42 Baldwin Place.. 1.05 1.90	Mines.......... 1.20 2.00
12 Mount Hope.... 35c. 60c.	27 Whitsons...... 60c.$1.05	44 Mahopac Falls.. 1.05 1.90	54 Brewster...... 1.20 2.05
14 Ardsley......... 40c. 65c.	28 Hammonds	46 Mahopac Mines.. 1.05 1.90	
15 Woodlands	30 Mertens........ 70c. 1.45	44 Thompson House	

Leave 155th St. & 8th Avenue :

For **Dunwoodie**, 7 00, 9 15, 11 15 a.m., 4 33, 5 14, 6 00, 7 30 p.m., Sundays 7 30, 9 10 a.m. Arrive Dunwoodie in 45 minutes.
For **Tarrytown Heights** and intermediate stations, 7 00, 9 15, 11 15 a. m., 4 33, 5 14, 6 00 p.m., Sundays, 7 30, 9 10 a. m. Arrive Tarrytown Heights in 1 hour.
For **Lake Mahopac, Brewster** and intermediate stations, 7 00, 9 15 a.m., 1 33, 5 14 p.m., Sundays, 7 30, 9 10 a.m. Arrive Lake Mahopac, 11 30, 11 02 a. m., 6 07, 7 10 p. m. Sundays, 11 00, 11 10 a. m. Arrive Brewster, 12 15 p. m., 11 25 a. m., 6 28, 7 30 p. m. Sundays, 11 15 a. m., 12 05 p. m.

To New York 155th Street and 8th Avenue.

Leave **Brewsters**, 6 55, 9 35 a. m., 3 25, 7 30 p. m., Sundays, 4 00, 7 30 p. m.; leave **Lake Mahopac**, 7 30, 9 55 a. m., 3 45, 8 20 p. m., Sundays, 4 22, 7 58 p. m.; leave **Croton Lake**, 7 46, 10 18 a. m., 4 33, 9 30 p. m., Sundays, 4 40, 8 20 p.m. Arrive **New York**, 9 00, 11 26 a. m., 5 35, 11 30 p. m., Sundays, 6 40, 10 55 p. m.
Leave **Tarrytown Heights**, 7 00, 8 40, 10 10 a. m., 1 25, 4 36, 9 45 p. m., Sundays, 5 44, 9 35 p. m. Arrive New York in 50 minutes.
Leave **Ardsley**, 7 21, 8 31, 10 58 a. m., 1 47, 5 00 p. m., Sundays, 5 36 p. m. Arrive New York in 35 minutes.
Leave **Dunwoodie**, 7 36, 8 46, 11 12 a. m., 2 01, 5 16, 8 00, 10 30 p. m., Sundays, 5 54, 10 25 p. m. Arrive New York in 25 minutes.

KINGS COUNTY ELEVATED R. R.

Fare 5 cents. Trains run daily. Running time 22 minutes.

STATIONS.—Fulton Ferry, Brooklyn Bridge, Clark St., Tillary St., Court St., Myrtle Ave., Bocrum Place, Elm Place, Duffield St., Flatbush Ave., Lafayette Ave., Cumberland St., Vanderbilt Ave., Grand Ave., Franklin Ave., Nostrand Ave., Brooklyn Ave., Tompkins Ave., Albany Ave., Utica Ave., Ralph Ave., Saratoga Ave., Rockaway Ave.

Leave **Fulton Ferry and Bridge Depots for Rockaway Avenue** and intermediate stations, 12 31, 1 00, 2 00, 3 00, 4 00, 5 00, 5 30 a. m., then every 3 to 6 minutes to 12 night.
Leave **Rockaway Avenue** for **Brooklyn Bridge and Fulton Ferry** every 3 to 6 minutes from 5 00 a. m. to 12 night. Night trains leave Saratoga Avenue, 12 25, 1 25, 2 25, 3 25, 4 25 a. m. 5 25 a. m. Sundays only.

BROOKLYN ELEVATED R. R.

Fare 5 cents. Trains run daily. Running time as follows: From Fulton Ferry to Van Sielen Avenue 32 minutes. From Sands and Washington Sts. (Bridge Depot) to Van Sielen Avenue 8 minutes. From Broadway Ferry, E. D., to Van Sielen Avenue 28 minutes.

Trains run every 2 to 8 minutes from 4 58 a. m. to 1 10 night on all branches.

Main Line Stations, (Fulton Ferry, York and Washington Sts.(Bridge), Bridge St., Navy St., Cumberland St., Washington Ave., Myrtle Ave., De Kalb Ave., Greene Ave., Franklin Ave., Nostrand Ave., Tompkins Ave., Summer Ave., Reid Ave., Gates Ave., Halsey St., Chauncey St., Manhattan Beach Crossing, Alabama Ave., Van Sielen Ave.

Myrtle Avenue Branch Stations, Sands and Washington Sts. (Brooklyn Bridge), Myrtle Ave. and Adams St., Bridge St., Navy St., Vanderbilt Ave., Washington Ave., De Kalb Ave. to Van Sielen Ave.

Broadway Branch Stations, Broadway Ferry, Driggs St., Marcy Ave., Hewes St., Lorimer St., Flushing Ave., Park Ave., Stuyvesant Ave., Kosciusko St., Gates Ave. to Van Sielen Ave.

RATES OF FARE TO ALL PLACES IN UNITED STATES.

Reached via the following Railroads:
New York Central & Hudson River.
West Shore.
New York, Ontario & Western.
New York, Lake Erie & Western.
Delaware, Lackawanna & Western.
Pennsylvania.
Baltimore & Ohio.

GENERAL INSTRUCTIONS.

Children under 5 years of age, Free. Between 5 and 12, Half Rate.
One hundred and fifty (150) pounds of baggage will be checked free on each full ticket and seventy-five (75) pounds on each half ticket of any class.
Where specific routes are not designated the unlimited rates apply via all roads shown at head of column in which quotations appear, and the limited rates (where same are quoted) apply also via the roads thus designated in the unlimited column.
The date of sale is always included as forming one day of the time-limit; for instance, a limited first or second-class ticket to Kansas City, for which the time-limit is 3 days, if sold on the 7th, would be punched as expiring on the 9th.

☞ *For Fare to places not in this list, see time tables.*

Destination. *Note.—Passengers holding Limited Tickets at Second-Class Rates, are entitled to use of Smoking Car only.*	1st Class Unlimited.		Limited Tickets.		Destination. *Note.—Passengers holding Limited Tickets at Second-Class Rates, are entitled to use of Smoking Car only.*	1st Class Unlimited.		Limited Tickets.	
	Via Pennsylvania or B. & O. Railroads.	Via N.Y.C. & H.R. West Shore, N.Y.O. & W.N. Y., L.E. & W., D.L. & W. Penna. via Metuchen.	Time Limit—Days. First Class.	Second Class. (See Note.)		Via Pennsylvania or B. & O. Railroads.	Via N.Y.C. & H.R. West Shore, N.Y.O. & W.N. Y., L.E. & W., D.L. & W. Penna. via Metuchen.	Time Limit—Days. First Class.	Second Class. (See Note.)
Abilene, Kan	$43 20	$40 15	4 $36 15	$33 15	Big Rapids, Mich	$25 95	$21 50	3 $20 00	$18 00
Adrian, Mich	20 75	17 80	2 16 75	15 50	Binghamton, N.Y. v.DL.W or E		6 15	1 5 00	
Aiken, S. C	27 30		3 23 00		" " Excursion			30 8 00	
Akron, Ohio		15 10	3 13 00	12 00	Birmingham, Ala...$30 25 to	36 15	35 60	4 26 80	23 80
Albany, Ga	33 35		4 28 20		Bismarck, Dak	53 10	49 85	6 46 60	37 00
Albany, N.Y. v.N.Y.C.orW.S.		3 10			Bloomington, Ill	28 80	26 55	3 22 65	20 65
" " Excursion			30 6 00		Boise City, Idaho	94 55	91 50	10 87 50	59 75
Albia, Iowa	35 65	32 40	3 29 15	26 35	Booneville, Iowa	37 10	33 85	3 30 60	28 60
Albion, Mich	22 40	18 95	3 17 90	16 25	Booneville, Mo	36 40	33 45	3 29 70	26 70
Albuquerque, N. Mex	69 80	66 75	7 62 25	54 25	Boulder, Col	57 15	53 90	6 49 90	46 90
Allegan, Mich	24 20	20 85	3 19 75	16 75	Bowerston, Ohio	15 20		2 13 20	12 10
Allen'n, Pa. v.D.L.W. or Penn		2 60			Bozeman, Mont	89 20	78 95	8 75 70	57 00
" Excur. via Penn			4 10		Bradford, Pa. (not B.&O.R.R.)	11 70	9 51	2 8 74	
Alliance, Ohio	15 00	15 25	2 13 00	12 00	Braidwood, Ill	28 40	25 45	3 21 90	19 90
Alton, Ill	31 15	29 80	3 24 00	21 00	Brazil, Ind	25 50	24 20	3' 20 70	18 70
Altoona, Pa., via Penn. R. R	9 45		2	8 00	Breckenridge, Minn	43 95	40 70	5 37 45	32 95
Amboy, Ill	29 35	26 10	3 22 85	20 58	Bridgeport, Ohio, via P. R. R	14 70		2 12 50	11 00
Americus, Ga	32 20		4 27 15		Bristol, Tenn	21 30		3 18 70	
Anamosa, Iowa	32 60	29 35	3 26 10	24 10	Brookfield, Mo	36 20	32 25	3 29 50	26 50
Ann Arbor, Mich	22 15	17 20	3 16 15	15 40	Brunswick, Ga	33 60		3 30 00	
Anniston, Ala	29 00		4 24 60	21 90	Bryan, Tex	54 55	53 25	5 44 80	36 15
Anoka, Minn	38 80	35 55	5 32 30	27 80	Bucyrus, Ohio	18 35	16 90	3 15 45	14 00
Anthony, Kan	48 80	45 00	4 39 25	36 25	Buena Vista, Col	62 95	59 90	7 55 90	52 90
Apple River, Ill	30 60	27 85	3 21 10	22 10	Buffalo, N. Y		9 25		
Appleton, Wis	32 00	28 75	4 25 60	23 50	Burlingame, Kan	41 10	38 05	4 34 05	31 05
Arcadia, Wis	35 45	32 20	4 28 95	26 05	Burlington, Iowa	32 65	29 40	3 26 15	23 25
Arcadia, Ohio		17 35	2 16 10	14 60	Burlington, Kan	41 80	38 75	4 34 75	31 75
Arkansas City, Kan	45 05	42 80	4 38 00	35 00	Bushnell, Ill	31 65	29 00	3 25 65	23 15
Asbury Park, N.J., via P.R.R	1 55		1 20		Butte City, Mont	86 90	83 65	8 80 40	59 50
Asheville, N. C	23 70		4 22 05	21 05	Cadillac, Mich	27 10	22 55	3 20 85	18 85
Ash Fork, Ariz	93 85	90 80	10 86 30	63 75	Cadiz, Ohio	15 00		2 13 00	12 00
Ashland, Neb	40 15	36 90	4 33 65	31 65	Cairo, Ill	32 05	30 75	4 25 25	23 25
Ashland, Ohio	18 20	16 50	3 14 50	13 50	Caldwell, Kan	46 00	43 35	4 38 95	35 95
Ashland, Wis	39 20	35 95	4 32 70	29 00	Caldwell, N.Y. v.N.Y.C.orW.S		5 55		
Ashtabula, Ohio	14 00	12 75	2 12 00	11 50	Calera, Ala	36 90	36 65	5 26 95	23 95
Aspen, Col	69 80	66 75	7 62 75	59 75	Calumet, Mich	39 90	36 65	4 33 40	31 40
Assinniboine, Mont	76 40	73 15	8 69 90	55 60	Calvert, Tex	54 10	52 80	5 44 80	36 15
Astor, Fla	39 00		6 34 00		Cambridge, Ohio	16 70		2 14 00	12 10
Atchison, Kan	38 80	35 75	3 31 75	28 75	Cambridge City, Ind	22 25	21 40	3 18 75	16 75
Athens, Ga	33 10		4 24 00		Camden, S. C	25 75		4 23 00	
Athens, Ohio, via P. R. R	19 45		2 15 35	12 85	Cameron, Mo	38 55	35 60	3 31 50	28 50
Atlanta, Ga....$27 45 to	37 30	31 30	4 24 00	21 00	Canal Dover, Ohio	15 75	16 75	3 13 75	12 65
Atlantic, Iowa	34 85	33 60	3 32 35	30 35	Canton, Ill	30 70	27 45	3 24 20	22 20
Attica, Ind	26 05	24 25	3 20 45	18 15	Canton, Miss....$39 35 to	42 65	41 70	5 32 30	28 00
Augusta, Ga....$25 30 to	32 15		3 23 00		Canton, Ohio	15 55	15 95	3 13 55	12 00
Aurora, Ill	28 10	24 85	3 21 60	19 60	Carbondale, Pa., v.D.L.W or E		4 55		
Austin, Minn	36 70	33 45	4 30 20	27 20	" Excursion			6 6 75	
Austin, Tex....$52 20 to	61 05	55 85	5 46 95	37 60	Carrollton, Mo	36 90		3 30 40	27 20
Baker City, Oreg	99 50	96 45	10 87 50	60 00	Catskill, N.Y., via West Shore		2 18		
Baltimore, Md	5 30				" " via N.Y.C		2 50		
Baraboo, Wis	31 55	28 30	4 25 05	23 05	Cedar Falls, Iowa	38 45	31 60	3 28 35	26 35
Batavia, Ill	28 10	24 85	3 21 60	19 60	Cedar Rapids, Iowa	33 25	30 00	3 20 75	24 75
Baton Rouge, La	47 40	47 25	5 31 60	29 00	Central City, Col	58 40	55 85	6 51 35	48 35
Battle Creek, Mich	23 85	19 70	3 18 65	16 75	Centralia, Ill	29 60	28 30	3 24 25	21 25
Bay City, Mich	24 40	19 30	4 17 70	16 05	Champaign, Ill	27 35	25 50	3 22 00	20 15
Beardstown, Ill	30 95	29 35	3 25 00	22 10	Chariton, Iowa	35 60	33 35	3 30 10	27 15
Beatrice, Neb	40 00	37 65	4 34 40	32 40	Charles City, Iowa	37 70	32 45	4 29 30	27 30
Beaufort, S.C	33 40		4 24(top)		Charleston, Ill	27 35	26 05	3 22 50	20 15
Beaver Dam, Wis	30 95	27 70	4 24 45	22 45	Charleston, S. C	24 35		3 23 00	
Bellaire, Ohio	14 75		2 12 50	11 00	Charleston, W. Va	20 20		3 18 00	15 10
Bellefontaine, Ohio	20 10	18 50	3 17 00	15 00	Charlotte, N. C....$18 60 to	21 25		3 18 60	
Bellevue, Ohio	18 50	16 25	2 15 00	14 00	Chattanooga, Tenn...25 95 to	31 55	31 30	3 23 00	20 00
Beloit, Wis	29 15	25 90	4 22 65	20 65	Cheyenne, Wyo	50 15	51 00	6 48 65	46 65
Belvidere, Ill	28 70	25 45	4 22 20	20 20	Chicago, Ill	26 50	23 25	3 20 00	18 00
Benson, Ariz	79 60	78 30	10 70 95	59 85	Chillicothe, Mo	37 10	34 15	3 30 15	27 15
Berlin, Wis	31 85	28 60	4 25 35	23 35	Chillicothe, Ohio....$18 35 to	19 50	19 90	3 16 25	14 00
Bethlehem, Pa., v.D.L.W.or Pa		2 45			Chippewa Falls, Wis	35 85	32 60	4 28 35	27 00
" Exc. via Penn			5 3 85		Cincinnati, Ohio	21 50	21 25	3 18 00	16 00

FARES TO ALL PLACES—Continued.

DESTINATION. *Note.—Passengers holding Limited Tickets at Second-Class Rates, are entitled to use of Smoking Car only.*	Via Pennsylvania or B. & O. Railroads.	Via N.Y.C.& H.R. West Shore, N.Y., O. & W., N.Y., L.E.& W., D.L.& W. Penn. via Metuchen.	1st Class Unlimited.	Time Limit—Days.	First Class.	Second Class. (See Note.)	Limited Tickets.
Circleville, Ohio	$18 90	$19 30		3	$16 25	$14 00	
Clarinda, Iowa	39 00	35 75		3	32 50	30 50	
Clarksburg, W. Va	11 35			2	12 50	11 00	
Clarksville, Tenn	30 10	29 85		4	25 85	24 65	
Cleveland, Ohio	16 50	14 25		2	13 00	12 00	
Clifton Forge, Va...$12 90 to	18 80			3	12 90		
Clinton, Ill	28 55	26 70		3	22 85	20 50	
Clinton, Iowa	30 75	27 50		3	24 25	22 25	
Clyde, Ohio	18 70	16 45		2	15 25	14 30	
Coldwater, Mich	22 35	19 60		3	18 45	16 50	
Colorado Springs, Col	58 70	55 65		6	49 90	46 90	
Columbia, Mo	35 65	32 10		3	28 60	25 60	
Columbia, S. C...$22 30 to	26 60			3	22 00		
Columbia City, Ind	22 65	20 80		3	17 30	15 75	
Columbus, Ga...$31 15 to	36 60			5	27 70		
Columbus, Ind	24 15	23 75		3	20 25	18 25	
Columbus, Miss...$36 15 to	40 90	39 30		5	29 90	26 25	
Columbus, Neb	11 85	38 50		4	35 35	33 35	
Columbus, Ohio	18 50	15 40		5	16 25	11 00	
Concordia, Kan	43 15	40 10		4	36 40	33 40	
Connellsville, Pa	12 50			2	10 50	10 00	
Conshohocken, Pa.v.Penn.R.R	2 85			1	2 68		
Cooperstown, N.Y.v.NYCorWS		6 15					
Corinth, Miss...$32 45 to	38 05	35 80		3	27 35	24 75	
Corning, N.Y., via Penn, D.L.& W. or Erie.		7 50		2	6 25		
" Excursion				30	10 90		
Curry, Pa	13 00			2	10 30		
Corsicana, Tex	52 05	50 75		5	13 40	35 10	
Cortland, N. Y., via N. Y. C. W. S. or D. L. & W		7 05		1	5 80		
Cortland, N.Y..Exc.v.D.L. & W				30	10 00		
Coshocton, Ohio	16 45			2	11 45	12 55	
Council Bluffs, Iowa	39 00	35 75		3	32 50	30 50	
Crawfordsville, Ind	25 10	23 40		3	20 30	18 30	
Crested Butte, Col	68 40	65 35		7	61 35	55 30	
Cresson, Pa., via Penn. R. R	9 90			2		4 40	
Crestline, Ohio	17 55	16 50		3	15 25	11 00	
Creston, Iowa	38 10	35 15		3	31 75	28 75	
Crete, Neb	40 90	37 65		1	34 40	32 40	
Cumberland, Md	10 80			2	10 50	10 00	
Custer, Mont	71 25	68 00		7	61 75	52 95	
Dallas, Tex...$50 85 to	56 85	50 20		5	42 85	31 80	
Dalton, Ga...$25 90 to	32 75	32 50		3	28 05	20 00	
Danville, Ill	26 85	24 50		3	21 00	18 85	
Danville, Va...$13 65 to	16 30			2	13 65		
Davenport, Iowa	31 70	28 45		3	25 30	23 20	
Dayton, Ohio	20 55	19 80		3	17 00	13 50	
Deadwood, Dak	60 60	57 35		10	54 10		
Decatur, Ala...$29 60 to	35 15	33 90		3	26 65	23 65	
Decatur, Ill	28 40	26 70		3	23 10	20 75	
Decorah, Iowa	31 95	31 70		4	28 45	21 45	
Deer Lodge, Mont	86 90	83 65		8	80 40	59 50	
Defiance, Ohio	20 25	19 00		3	16 50	15 00	
De Kalb, Ill	28 70	25 45		3	22 20	20 20	
Delaware, Ohio	19 35	17 65		3	16 25	11 00	
Delphos, Ohio	20 75	19 00		3	16 60	11 90	
Deming, N. Mex...$70 90 to	87 25	69 60		10	62 25	51 25	
Denison, Tex	50 25	47 80		5	41 90	38 75	
Dennison, Ohio	15 50			2	13 50	12 10	
Denver, Col	56 95	53 90		6	49 90	46 90	
Des Moines, Iowa	36 65	33 40		3	30 15	28 10	
Detroit, Mich	21 00	18 35		2	16 25	11 50	
Dodge City, Kan	48 45	45 40		4	41 40	38 40	
Dubuque, Iowa	31 90	28 65		3	25 10	23 40	
Duluth, Minn	42 55	39 30		5	35 55	30 00	
Dunkirk, N. Y		10 25		2	9 50		
Du Quoin, Ill	30 70	29 10		4	22 25	22 35	
East Liverpool, Ohio	13 80			2	11 80	11 00	
East Saginaw, Mich	24 00	19 60		3	17 55	16 00	
Eau Claire, Wis	35 85	32 60		4	29 35	27 00	
Effingham, Ill	28 00	26 70		3	23 40	20 75	
Elberon, N. J., via P. R. R	1 45			1	1 70		
Eldorado, Kan	14 10	41 30		4	37 05	30 05	
Elgin, Ill	28 10	24 15		3	21 60	19 60	
Elkhart, Ind	23 75	20 40		4	19 00	17 50	
Ellendale, Dak	17 10	14 15		6	40 30	36 10	
Elmira, N. Y., D.L.W., E. or P.		7 25		1	6 20		
" Excursion				30	10 25		
El Paso, Tex...$70 40 to	81 30	69 60		6	62 25	51 25	
Elyria, Ohio	17 30	15 05		2	13 80	12 80	
Emerson, Manitoba	49 75	46 50		5	43 25	37 00	
Emmettsburg, Iowa	38 75	35 50		4	32 25	30 25	
Emporia, Kan	42 15	39 10		4	35 10	32 10	
Erie, Pa		11 00		2	10 85		

DESTINATION. *Note.—Passengers holding Limited Tickets at Second-Class Rates, are entitled to use of Smoking Car only.*	Via Pennsylvania or B. & O. Railroads.	Via N.Y.C.& H.R. West Shore, N.Y., O. & W., N.Y., L.E.& W., D.L.& W. Penn. via Metuchen.	1st Class Unlimited.	Time Limit—Days.	First Class.	Second Class. (See Note.)	Limited Tickets.
Escanaba, Mich	$36 15	$32 90		4	$29 65	$27 65	
Eureka, Nev	102 25	99 20		10	95 20	71 75	
Evansville, Ind	28 85	27 55		3	21 05	22 05	
Fairbury, Ill	28 85	25 90		3	21 55	19 55	
Fairfield, Iowa	31 20	30 95		3	27 70	24 75	
Fargo, Dak	45 00	41 75		5	38 50	31 00	
Faribault, Minn	37 00	33 75		4	30 50	27 00	
Fayetteville, N. C...$15 80 to	20 60			4	15 80		
Fernandina, Fla...$36 15 to	40 75			6	31 83		
Flandreau, Dak	42 00	38 75		5	35 50	31 00	
Flint, Mich	23 00	18 00		3	16 85	15 20	
Fond du Lac, Wis	30 15	27 50		4	24 45	22 45	
Fort Benton, Mont	79 85	76 60		8	73 35	55 60	
Fort Dodge, Iowa	37 60	31 85		4	31 10	28 80	
Fort Howard, Wis	32 45	29 20		4	25 85	23 85	
Fort Madison, Iowa	33 05	30 80		3	26 25	23 25	
Fort Smith, Ark	43 75	42 45		5	36 70	32 85	
Fort Wayne, Ind	22 10	19 85		3	16 75	15 30	
Fort Worth, Tex...$51 05 to	58 25	51 15		5	43 80	35 35	
Fostoria, Ohio	19 10	17 15		3	15 90	11 40	
Frankfort, Ky	25 10	23 10		3	21 25	19 25	
Fredericksburg, Va	8 85			3	8 20		
Freeport, Ill	29 70	26 45		3	23 20	21 20	
Fremont, Neb	40 25	37 00		4	33 85	31 85	
Fremont, Ohio	18 95	16 70		2	15 15	11 40	
Gainesville, Fla	37 15			6	32 00		
Galena, Ill	31 25	28 00		3	24 75	22 75	
Galesburg, Ill	31 40	28 15		3	27 60	22 90	
Galion, Ohio	18 30	16 05		3	15 40	11 00	
Gallatin, Mont	83 65	80 40		7	75 15	58 45	
Gallipolis, Ohio...$17 85 to	21 85	21 85		2	17 85	14 75	
Galva, Ill	30 70	27 45		3	24 20	22 20	
Galveston, Tex...$55 90 to	61 90	55 90		6	46 30	37 65	
Geneseo, Ill	31 15	27 90		3	24 65	22 65	
Georgetown, Col	59 65	56 60		6	52 60	49 00	
Gettysburg, Pa	6 55			6 77		2	6 55
Girard, Ohio	11 70	11 25		2	12 50	11 50	
Glendive, Mont	62 45	59 40		8	56 15	44 85	
Glyndon, Minn	45 00	41 75		5	38 50	31 00	
Gogebic, Mich	37 15	31 40		4	30 55	28 55	
Golden, Col	56 95	53 90		6	49 90	46 90	
Goldsboro, N. C...$14 05 to	17 10			3	14 05		
Grafton, W. Va., via B. & O.	13 70			2	12 50	11 00	
Grand Forks, Dak	17 75	41 50		5	41 25	36 75	
Grand Haven, Mich	25 70	21 00		3	20 00	19 00	
Grand Island, Neb	42 30	39 05		4	36 70	34 70	
Grand Rapids, Mich	21 05	20 05		3	19 50	17 75	
Green Bay, Wis	32 45	29 20		4	25 85	23 85	
Greenfield, Ind	22 25	22 35		3	18 90	16 40	
Gunnison, Col	66 75	63 70		7	59 70	53 75	
Hamilton, Ohio	20 90	20 75		3	18 00	15 75	
Hammondsport, N.Y., via Pa., Erie, D. L. & W		7 05		2	6 95		
Hannibal, Mo	32 85	30 00		3	26 25	23 25	
Hastings, Mich	23 70	19 70		3	19 00	17 60	
Hastings, Neb	37 40	34 15		4	30 90	27 90	
Hastings, Neb	13 20	30 95		3	36 70	31 70	
Havana, Cuba						15 50	60 00
Havana, Ill	30 35	28 50		3	24 25	21 35	
Havana, N.Y., v. Erie, DLW, Pa.		7 60		2	6 35		
Helena, Ark	39 00	37 70		4	31 60	28 50	
Helena, Mont	90 15	83 65		8	80 40	59 50	
Hillsdale, Mich	21 75	18 80		3	17 75	16 50	
Holden, Mo	38 25	35 75		3	31 20	28 00	
Holland, Mich	25 70	20 85		3	20 00	18 00	
Hollidaysburg, Pa., via P. H. R.	9 08			2		8 20	
Hot Springs, Ark...$42 60 to	49 85	42 75		4	35 40	32 80	
Houghton, Mich	39 15	35 00		1	32 65	30 00	
Houston, Tex...$51 40 to	60 10	55 75		5	41 80	36 15	
Howard City, Mich	25 25	20 85		3	19 80	18 50	
Hudson, Wis	37 00	34 15		4	31 40	27 00	
Huntington, Ind., via P. R. R	24 85			3		18 50	7 15
Huntington, Ind	23 85	21 00		3	17 15	16 00	
Huntington, Oregon	97 10	91 55		10	87 50	60 00	
Huntington, W. Va...$18 95 to	21 85			3	16 15	14 65	
Huntsville, Ala		33 00		4	28 30	25 30	
Huron, Dak	45 50	42 25		5	39 00	33 85	
Independence, Iowa	34 00	30 75		4	27 50	25 50	
Independence, Kan	42 25	40 15		4	35 40	32 40	
Independence, Mo	36 75	32 50		3	29 25	26 25	
Indianapolis, Ind	26 85	22 55		3	19 65	17 60	
Indiana, Iowa	30 15	28 40		3	30 15	28 15	
Indianola, Neb	44 25	41 15		5	40 90	37 90	
Ionia, Mich	24 10	19 75		3	18 70	17 30	
Iowa City, Iowa	33 30	30 05		3	26 80	24 80	
Jackson, Mich	21 85	18 35		3	17 30	16 00	

FARES TO ALL PLACES Continued.

Destination.	Via Pennsylvania or B. & O. Railroads.	Via N.Y.C. & R.R. West Shore, N.Y.O. & W., N.Y., L.E. & W., B. & W. Penna. via Metuchen.	1st Class Unlimited. First Class.	Time Limit — Days.	Limited Tickets. Second class. (See Note.)	Destination.	Via Pennsylvania or B. & O. Railroads.	Via N.Y.C. & R.R. West Shore, N.Y.O. & W., N.Y., L.E. & W., B. & W. Penna. via Metuchen.	1st Class Unlimited. First Class.	Time Limit — Days.	Limited Tickets. Second class. (See Note.)
Note.—Passengers holding Limited Tickets at Second-Class Rates, are entitled to use of Smoking Car only.						*Note.—Passengers holding Limited Tickets at Second-Class Rates, are entitled to use of Smoking Car only.*					
Jackson, Miss......$37 70 to	$47 20	$41 90	5	$33 00	$28 00	Macon, Ga........$29 05 to	$37 25	$37 00	4	$25 00	$22 00
Jackson, Tenn...$34 25 to	35 40	34 00	1	27 35	24 75	Macon, Mo............	35 05	32 10	3	24 25	25 25
Jacksonville, Ill.........	30 60	28 60	3	21 25	21 35	Madison, Ind.........	24 00	23 75	3	18 50	18 75
Jacksonville, Fla...$30 25 to	41 05		6	27 75		Madison, Wis.........	30 40	27 15	4	23 10	21 90
Jamestown, Dak........	40 00	45 55	5	42 50	37 00	Manchester, Iowa...	33 30	30 05	4	26 80	24 80
Jamestown, N.Y.......	12 50	10 25	2	9 50		Manhattan, Kan......	41 85	38 80	4	34 80	31 80
Janesville, Wis........	29 25	26 00	1	22 75	20 75	Manistee, Mich.......	28 00	23 40	3	20 80	18 80
Jefferson, Tex.........	47 75	46 45	5	33 10	32 25	Manitowoc, Wis......	31 35	28 10	4	24 85	22 85
Jefferson, Wis.........	30 00	26 75	1	23 50	21 50	Mankato, Minn........	37 85	34 60	1	31 35	27 85
Jefferson City, Mo...	35 05	33 75	3	26 00	25 00	Mansfield, Ohio......	17 75	16 60	3	15 25	13 65
Jeffersonville, Ind...$24 75 to	26 15	24 50	3	21 25	18 75	Mapleton, Dak........	45 85	42 55	5	39 30	34 80
Jellico, Tenn...........	28 25	28 00	4	22 15	20 75	Maquoketa, Iowa.....	31 60	28 35	1	25 10	23 10
Jersey Shore, Pa., via P. R. R.	8 74		2	7 35		Marietta, Ohio....$15 75 to	18 00		2	14 25	12 10
Johnstown, Pa., via P. R. R.	10 61		1	10 50	9 00	Marinette, Wis........	33 00	30 05	4	27 40	25 40
Joliet, Ill...............	28 05	24 80	3	21 55	19 55	Marion, Iowa..........	33 10	29 85	4	26 60	24 60
Joplin, Mo.............	40 90	39 10	3	33 85	30 85	Marion, Ind...........	23 20	22 05	3	18 50	16 50
Junction City, Kan..	42 65	39 60	4	33 60	32 00	Marion, Kan..........	43 45	40 40	4	36 10	33 40
Kalamazoo, Mich.....	23 85	20 35	3	19 20	18 00	Marion, Ohio.........	18 80	17 25	3	15 90	14 00
Kandiyohi, Minn.......	40 80	37 65	5	34 40	29 90	Marquette, Mich.....	36 80	33 85	4	29 70	26 55
Kankakee, Ill..........	27 25	25 10	3	20 75	18 75	Marshall, Mich.......	22 80	19 30	3	18 25	16 50
Kansas City, Mo.....	38 80	35 75	3	31 75	28 75	Marshall, Mo.........	30 65	33 70	3	29 00	26 00
Kearney, Neb.........	44 35	41 10	4	37 85	35 85	Marshall, Tex....$46 85 to	52 45	46 95	5	39 60	32 55
Kendallville, Ind......	22 50	20 25	3	17 00	16 00	Marshalltown, Iowa..	35 20	31 90	1	28 70	26 70
Kenosha, Wis.........	28 55	25 30	3	22 05	20 05	Martin's Ferry, Ohio.	14 60		2	12 50	11 00
Kent, Ohio.............		14 85	2	13 00	12 00	Maryville, Mo........	38 80	35 75	3	31 75	28 75
Kenton, Ohio..........	19 55	18 00	3	16 25	14 35	Mason City, Iowa....	36 15	33 20	4	28 95	27 00
Keokuk, Iowa.........	33 10	30 00	3	26 35	23 35	Massillon, Ohio......	15 80	16 30	2	13 70	12 10
Kewanee, Ill..........	30 45	27 20	3	23 95	21 95	Mattoon, Ill..........	27 70	26 40	3	22 90	20 75
Keyser, W. Va.......	11 85		2	11 20	10 70	Mauch Chunk, Pa.v.DLW or Pa		8 45			
Key West, Fla........	58 90		10	42 50		" Excursion.....			5	5 55	
Kilbourn City, Wis...	32 05	28 80	4	25 55	23 55	Meadville, Pa.(not B.& O.R.R.)	14 75	18 20	2	11 10	
Kingston, N.Y., v. N.Y.C. or WS		1 76				Memphis, Tenn....$35 25 to	40 85	35 90	3	29 40	26 80
Kinsley, Kan..........	47 85	44 80	4	40 30	37 30	Menasha, Wis........	31 85	28 60	4	25 35	23 35
Kittanning, Pa., via Penn. R.R.	12 60		1	11 05		Mendota, Ill..........	29 00	25 75	3	22 50	20 50
Knoxville, Iowa.......	35 85	32 60	3	28 35	26 35	Menominee, Mich....	33 95	30 70	4	27 45	25 45
Knoxville, Tenn.......	25 85		3	22 05	19 50	Menomonee, Wis.....	36 60	33 35	4	30 10	27 00
Kokomo, Ind..........	24 30	22 18	3	19 00	17 00	Meridian, Miss...$34 45 to	44 30	40 10	5	30 65	26 65
La Crosse, Wis.......	34 35	31 10	4	27 85	25 85	Mexico City, Mex...$94 60 to	180 70	113 75	11	85 20	62 65
Lafayette, Ind.........	25 40	23 15	3	20 00	17 50	Mexico, Mo..........	34 60	31 55	3	27 55	24 55
Lake City, Minn......	36 45	33 20	4	29 95	27 00	Michigan City, Ind...	26 50	22 40	3	20 00	18 00
Lancaster, Ohio......	18 20		2	16 25	14 00	Midland City, Ohio..	21 05	21 25	3	17 10	15 60
Lansing, Mich.........	22 05	19 65	3	17 55	16 25	Miles City, Mont....	66 55	63 80	7	60 05	58 25
La Peer, Mich.........	23 35	16 25	3	16 25	14 60	Milledgeville, Ga.....	42 80		4	25 00	
La Porte, Ind..........	25 00	22 05	3	20 00	18 00	Milton, Pa., via Penn. R. R.	7 57		6	6 03	
Laramie City, Wyo..	58 00	54 75	5	51 50	49 50	Milwaukee, Wis......	29 05	25 80	1	22 55	20 55
Laredo, Tex......$62 90 to	75 60	62 40	7	53 05	41 75	Minneapolis, Minn...	38 00	34 75	4	31 50	27 80
La Salle, Ill............	29 35	26 10	3	22 85	20 85	Missouri Valley, Iowa.	39 00	35 75	3	32 50	30 50
Las Animas, Col.....	55 15	52 10	5	47 60	44 60	Mitchell, Dak.........	44 50	41 25	5	38 00	34 80
Las Vegas, N. Mex.	64 50	61 45	4	56 65	48 10	Mobile, Ala.......$34 10 to	51 25	43 95	5	32 00	27 25
Lawrence, Kan.......	39 80	36 75	4	32 75	29 75	Monmouth, Ill.......	31 85	29 55	3	25 30	23 05
Lawrenceburg, Ind...	22 15	21 90	3	18 65	16 65	Monroe, Mich........	20 50	17 15	3	16 10	14 50
Leadville, Col........	64 95	61 90	7	57 90	54 60	Monroe, Wis.........	30 25	27 00	4	23 75	21 75
Leavenworth, Kan...	38 80	35 75	3	31 75	28 75	Monroeville, Ohio...	18 35	16 00	2	14 75	13 65
Lebanon, Pa., via Penn. R. R.	5 84	4 30	2	4 05		Montgomery, Ala...$32 70 to	42 40	38 55	5	28 50	24 50
Lebanon, Ky..........	25 90	25 95	4	22 40	20 40	Montreal,Que.,v.N.Y.C. or WS		10 00			9 00
Lectonia, Ohio........	14 40	14 65	2	12 50	11 50	Mount Carmel, Ill...	28 05	26 75	4	23 25	21 25
Le Sueur, Minn......	38 00	34 75	4	31 50	27 85	Mt.Carmel, Pa.v.DLW or Penn.		4 92			
Lewisburg, Pa., v. Penn. R. R.	7 48		2	6 09		" Excursion v. Pa.RR			5	8 30	
Lexington, Ky........	23 90	23 45	3	18 55	16 55	Mount Vernon, Ohio.	17 75	17 70	3	15 25	13 65
Lexington, Mo........	38 25	35 10	3	31 20	28 20	Muncie, Ind..........	22 80	21 15	3	18 25	16 25
Lexington, Va....$13 39 to	17 85		2	12 35		Muscatine, Iowa.....	32 55	29 80	3	26 05	24 05
Lima, Ohio...........	20 30	18 65	3	16 50	14 25	Muskegon, Mich.....	30 60	26 10	4	23 25	21 25
Lincoln, Ill............	29 20	27 55	2	23 85	20 75	Nashville, Tenn......	30 50	30 25	4	25 05	23 05
Lincoln, Neb..........	44 30	37 05	4	34 40	32 40	Natchez, Miss.......	40 70	44 00	5	34 85	29 85
Litchfield, Ill..........	30 10	28 80	3	24 25	21 25	National City, Cal...	98 80	95 75	10	91 75	63 75
Little Rock, Ark..$40 15 to	45 75	40 45	5	34 80	30 40	Natural Bridge Station, Va...	14 65		3	12 50	
Livingston, Mont.....	79 70	76 45	7	73 20	57 00	Nebraska City, Neb..	39 25	36 00	3	32 75	30 75
Lock Haven, Pa., v. Pa. or DLW	9 11	8 75	2	7 57		Negaunee, Mich......	36 00	33 35	4	30 10	26 90
Logansport, Ind.......	24 30	22 50	3	19 00	17 25	New Albany, Ind.....	26 40	24 75	3	21 25	18 75
Loudon, Ohio.........	19 25	19 15	3	17 00	14 75	Newark, N.J.,v.Pa.,Erie,DLW		15		20	
Long Branch, N.J., v. Pa. R.R.	1 85		1	1 00		Newark, Ohio.........	17 50	18 45	3	15 25	13 65
Longview, Tex........	48 95		5	41 50	34 00	New Berne, N.C.....	19 50		3	16 45	
Lorain, Ohio..........		14 80	3	18 80	12 80	Newberry, S. C.......	23 85		3	23 55	
Los Angeles, Cal.....	68 80	95 75	9	91 75	63 75	New Brighton, Pa....	13 85		2	11 35	10 85
Louisiana, Mo........	32 55	30 05	2	18 80	12 80	New Brunswick,N.J.v.P.R.R.	90				
Louisville, Ky....$24 45 to	26 40	24 75	3	21 50	19 00	Newburg,N.Y., v. NYC, WS or E		1 16			
Loup City, Neb.......	44 75	41 50	4	38 25	36 25	" Excursion.....			30	2 25	
Ludington, Mich......	26 50	23 15	3	20 00	18 00	New Castle, Ind.....	22 60	22 00	3	18 75	11 25
Luray, Va............	10 55		3	10 05		New Castle, Pa......	14 85		2	12 25	11 80
Lynchburg, Va...$11 70 to	16 00		2	11 10		New Cumerstown, Ohio....	16 10		2	14 00	12 10
Lyons, Iowa..........	30 75	27 50	4	24 25	22 25	New Orleans, La...$42 35 to	55 50	40 00	3	34 00	29 00
McGregor, Iowa......	34 35	30 15	4	26 90	24 90	New Philadelphia, Ohio.....	15 80	16 85	3	13 85	12 70
McKeesport, Pa......	12 50		1	10 50	10 00	New Ulm, Minn......	38 75	35 50	4	32 25	28 75
McPherson, Kan.....	44 15	41 10	4	37 10	34 10	Niagara Falls, N.Y..		9 25			
Mackinaw City, Mich.	29 75	23 15	3	28 15		Niles, Mich..........	24 60	21 15	3	20 00	18 00

FARES TO ALL PLACES—Continued.

Destination.	1st Class Unlimited.		Limited Tickets.		Destination.	1st Class Unlimited.		Limited Tickets.	
	Via Penn. or B. & O. RR	Via NYC&HR, West Shore, NY O&W, V.L.&W, D.L.&W, Penn via Meturhen	First Class	Second Class (See Note)		Via Penn. or B. & O. RR	Via NYC&HR, West Shore, NY O&W, V.L.&W, D.L.&W, Penn via Meturhen	First Class	Second Class (See Note)
Niles, Ohio	$14 80	$13 95	$12 50	$11 50	Pontiac, Mich		$16 55	$15 80	$14 90
Norfolk, Va., v. Balt. or Delmar	8 50			6 50	Portage City, Wis	$31 50	28 25	25 00	23 00
" Excursion			16 00		Port Hope, Ont. (not Er. or PRR)		12 25		11 70
Norristown, Pa., v. Penn. R.R.	3 00		2 79		Port Huron, Mich		14 90		13 95
N. Adams, Mass., v. NYC or W.S.		4 47	3 73		Portland, Oregon	101 00	100 75	87 50	60 50
Northfield, Minn	37 00	33 75	30 50	27 00	Port Royal, S.C.	30 50		21 00	
North Platte, Neb	47 75	44 50	41 25	49 25	Portsmouth, Ohio	21 00	21 40	17 75	15 00
Northumberl'd, Pa. (not B.&O.)	7 26	5 71	5 71		" via B. & O.	19 05		16 25	14 75
" Exc. v. D.L.&W			9 25		Port Townsend, Wash	104 00	100 75	87 50	60 50
Norwalk, Ohio	18 15	15 90	14 65	13 65	Pottstown, Pa., via Penn. R.R.	3 70		3 47	
Norwich, N.Y., v. O.&W. or D.L.W		6 33	5 00		Pottsville, Pa., via Penn. R.R.	5 30		4 43	
" Excursion			9 00		" Excursion			7 36	
Oberlin, Ohio	17 50	15 25	14 00	13 00	Prairie du Chien, Wis	33 30	30 05	26 80	24 80
Oconomowoc, Wis	30 00	26 75	23 50	21 50	Princeton, Ill	20 65	26 10	23 15	21 15
Oconto, Wis	33 30	30 05	26 80	24 80	Princeton, N.J., v. Penn. R.R.	1 51			
Ogden, Utah	78 80	75 75	71 75	53 75	Princeton, Ind	28 05	26 75	23 25	21 25
Oil City, Pa. (not B. & O.)	14 11	13 85	11 40		Pueblo, Col	50 95	53 90	49 90	46 90
Old Point Comfort	8 50			6 50	Quebec, Q. v. NYC, WS or D&W		12 00		10 00
" v. Wash. & Rich.	14 00		12 00		Quincy, Ill	32 95	30 00	26 25	23 25
Olean, NY, v. D.L.W, Erie or Pa		9 10	8 15		Racine, Wis	28 85	25 60	22 35	20 35
" via N.Y.C. or W.S.		10 85	8 15		Raleigh, N.C.	17 75		14 70	
Olympia, Wash	104 00	100 75	77 50	55 50	Rapid City, Dak	57 30	54 05	50 80	48 80
Omaha, Neb	39 25	36 00	32 75	30 75	Ravenna, Ohio	15 60	14 65	13 00	12 00
O'Neill, Neb	41 95	41 70	38 45	36 45	Reading, Pa., v. D.L.W or Penn.	4 23		3 67	
Oneonta, N.Y., v. N.Y.C. or W.S		5 55			" Exc. v. Penn. R.R.			6 94	
" via O.&W. Ry		6 66	5 19		Red Oak, Iowa	39 00	35 75	32 85	30 35
Osage, Iowa	36 20	32 95	29 70	27 00	Red Wing, Minn	37 00	33 75	30 50	27 00
Osage City, Kan	41 35	38 30	34 30	31 30	Renovo, Pa., via Penn. R.R.	9 97		8 50	
Oshkosh, Wis	31 45	28 20	24 95	22 95	Richfield Springs, N.Y., Exc.,				
Oskaloosa, Iowa	35 10	31 85	28 60	26 40	via N.Y.C., W.S. or D.L.W			10 75	
Oswego, Kan	41 40	39 45	34 35	31 35	Richmond, Ind	21 80	20 95	18 40	16 50
Ottawa, Ill	28 90	25 65	22 40	20 40	Richmond, Va	10 50		10 35	
Ottawa, Kan	40 45	37 40	33 40	30 40	Roanoke, Va	31 45	28 20	24 95	22 95
Ottawa, Ont. v. NYC, WS or O&W		11 35			Roanoke, Va	13 85			
Ottumwa, Iowa	34 95	31 70	28 45	25 50	Rochester, Minn	36 55	33 30	30 05	27 00
Owatonna, Minn	37 00	33 75	30 50	27 00	Rochester, N.Y., v. NYC, W.S, Erie		7 68		
Owosso, Mich	23 45	18 45	17 40	16 05	Rockford, Ill	29 15	25 90	22 65	20 65
Paducah, Ky	31 60	31 35	25 00	22 25	Rock Island, Ill	31 65	28 40	25 15	23 15
Painesville, Ohio	15 65	13 50	12 75	12 00	Rome, Ga	27 15	33 45	24 00	20 00
" via B. & O.	16 50		13 00	12 00	Rondout, N.Y. v. N.Y.C or W.S		1 76		
Palatka, Fla $38 25 to	48 05		32 00		Rosendale, N.Y., via W.S.		2 00		
Palestine, Texas	51 25	49 35	42 60	34 65	" Excursion			3 03	
Palmyra, Mo	33 40	30 15	26 70	23 70	Rutland, Vt., v. N.Y.C. or W.S		5 64		
Pana, Ill	28 65	27 55	24 75	21 00	St. Albans, Vt. v. N.Y.C. or W.S.		8 50		
Paola, Kan	39 90	37 10	32 85	29 85	St. Augustine, Fla $37 75 to	42 55		29 25	
Paris, Ill	26 55	25 85	21 75	19 75	St. Clair, Pa. v. DLW or Pa.R.R.	5 40	4 41	4 77	
Paris, Ky	23 75	23 50	18 00	16 00	St. Cloud, Minn	40 25	37 00	33 75	29 25
Paris, Tex	48 75	47 45	40 10	32 85	St. Johns, Q. v. NYC, WS, O&W		9 25		9 00
Parkersburg, W. Va	17 25		14 25	12 10	St. Joseph, Mo	38 80	35 75	31 75	28 75
" v. B. & O. R.R.	15 30		12 50	11 00	St. Louis, Mo	31 30	30 00	23 50	21 25
Parsons, Kan	41 40	39 30	34 35	31 85	St. Paul, Minn	34 00	34 75	31 50	27 00
Peirce City, Mo	39 90	38 85	32 85	29 85	Sacramento, Cal	98 00	95 75	91 75	63 75
Pekin, Ill	29 85	27 25	23 35	21 35	Salamanca, N.Y., v. Erie or Pa.		9 25	8 50	
Pella, Iowa	35 60	32 35	29 10	26 70	Salem, N. J., via Penn. R.R.	3 50			
Pembina, Dak	49 70	46 45	43 20	37 00	Salem, Ohio, via Penn. R.R.	14 60		12 60	11 75
Pendleton, Oregon		100 75	87 50	60 00	Salina, Kan	43 85	40 80	36 80	33 80
PennYan, N.Y, v. N.Y.C or W.S		7 38	7 10		Salineville, Ohio	14 40		12 40	11 75
" v. DLW, Erie or Pa.		8 15	6 00		Salisbury, Md., v. Penn. R.R	6 36			
Pensacola, Fla $38 10 to	46 40	13 95	32 40	27 25	Salisbury, N. C	18 75		17 10	
Peoria, Ill	29 85	27 25	23 35	21 35	Salt Lake City, Utah	78 80	75 75	71 75	53 75
Peru, Ill	29 40	26 15	22 90	20 90	San Antonio, Tex $57 70 to	63 45	57 75	49 85	39 30
Peru, Ind	23 80	22 00	18 45	17 00	San Diego, Cal	98 80	95 75	91 75	63 75
Peshtigo, Wis	33 70	30 45	27 20	25 20	Sandusky, Ohio	18 30	16 05	14 80	13 80
Peterborough, Ont		12 80		12 40	" via B. & O. R.R.	19 65		15 25	13 80
Petersburg, Va	11 90		11 30		Sandy Hill, N.Y., v. NYC or W.S		4 70		
Petoskey, Mich	29 00	24 00	23 15	21 50	San Francisco, Cal	98 80	95 75	91 75	63 75
Philadelphia, Pa., v. Penn. R.R.	2 50				San Jose, Cal	98 80	95 75	91 75	63 75
Phillipsburg, N.J., v. DLW or Pa		2 05			Santa Fe, N. Mex	67 85	64 80	60 30	50 10
" Excursion			3 85		Saranac Lake, NY, v NYC or WS		11 35		
Phœnixville, Pa., v. Penn. R.R.	3 31		3 11		Saratoga, N.Y., v. N.Y.C. or W.S		4 90		
Piedmont, W. Va	11 50		11 35	10 85	Sarnia, Ont		14 87		24 95
Pierre, Dak	50 30	17 05	43 80	39 85	Sault Ste. Marie, Mich		26 60		
Pipestone City, Minn	41 45	38 20	34 95	31 45	Savannah, Ga $28 95 to	33 55		21 00	
Piqua, Ohio	21 65	19 50	17 00	15 50	Schuylkill Haven, Pa., via				
Pittsburg, Pa., via Penn. R.R.	12 50		10 50	10 00	Pa. or D. L. & W.	5 17		4 43	
" via B. & O.	12 80		10 50	10 00	Scranton, Pa., v. D.L.W. or Erie		4 55		
Pittsfield, Mass, v. NYC or Har.		3 28			" Excursion			6 75	
Pittston, Pa., Excur. v. D.L.W.			7 15		Sea Girt, N. J. via Penn. R.R.	4 49		1 35	
" Exc. v. Penn. R.R.			5 75		Seattle, Wash	104 00	100 75	87 50	60 50
Plattsburg, NY, v. N.Y.C. or W.S		8 00			Selma, Ala $33 60 to	42 30	38 55	35 50	27 40
Plattsmouth, Neb	39 25	36 00	32 75	30 75	Seymour, Ind	24 15	23 90	20 65	18 85
Pleasant Hill, Mo	38 40	35 75	31 35	28 55	Shakopee, Minn	38 00	34 75	31 50	27 00
Pt. Pleasant, N.J., v. Penn.R.R.	1 80		1 45		Sharon, Pa	14 00	13 50	12 50	11 50
Pomeroy, Ohio	22 45	22 35	18 25	15 25	Sharon Springs, N.Y., v. N.Y.C				
" via B. & O.	17 85		15 05	13 55	" or W.S.		4 90		

FARES TO ALL PLACES—Continued.

Note.—Passengers holding Limited Tickets at Second-Class Rates, are entitled to use of Smoking Car only.

Destination.	1st Class Unlimited. Via Pennsylvania or B. & O. Railroad.	Via N.Y.C. & H.R., West Shore, N.Y.C. & W., V., L. & W., D., L. & W., Penna. via Metuchen.	Limited Tickets. Time Limit—Days.	First Class.	Second Class. (See Note.)
Shawnee, Ohio	$18 45		3	$16 10	$14 00
Sheboygan, Wis	30 60	$27 85	4	24 10	23 10
Shelbyville, Ill	28 85	26 00	3	24 35	21 00
Shenandoah, Pa., v. D.L. W or Pa.	5 73		4	4 47	
" Exc.v.Penn.R.R.			5	7 41	
Sherman, Tex.....$49 25 to	51 85	48 10	5	41 90	33 85
Shippensburg, Pa., v. Pa. R.R.	6 77				
Shreveport, La.....$46 30 to	55 05	38 40	5	39 60	31 55
Sidney, Ohio	20 70	19 15	3	17 00	15 50
Sioux City, Iowa	41 20	37 95	4	34 70	31 10
Sioux Falls, Dak	42 10	38 85	5	35 60	31 00
South Bend, Ind	24 25	21 30	3	19 50	18 00
Sparta, Wis	33 65	30 40	4	27 75	25 15
Spartanburg, S.C	21 25		3	21 25	20 50
Spokane Falls, Wash	103 45	100 20	9	87 50	60 00
Springfield, Ill	29 60	28 00	3	24 75	20 75
Springfield, Mo	38 40	37 10	3	31 35	28 85
Springfield, Ohio	19 85	19 15	3	17 00	15 00
Stamford, Va.	11 15				
Sterling, Ill	29 80	26 55	3	23 20	21 20
Steubenville, Ohio, v. Pa. R.R.	14 00		2	12 00	11 00
Stevens Point, Wis	35 55	30 30	4	27 05	25 45
Stillwater, Minn	38 00	34 75	4	31 50	27 00
Stockton, Cal	98 80	95 75	10	91 75	63 75
Streator, Ill	29 05	25 80	3	22 55	20 55
Sturgis, Mich	23 80	20 15	3	18 45	16 75
Sunbury, Pa., via Penn. R.R.	7 20		2	5 66	
Suspension Bridge, N.Y.		9 25			
Syracuse, N.Y.v. N.Y.C or W.S.		6 06			
" Exc.v.D.L.&W.			30	10 00	
Tacoma, Wash	104 00	100 75	9	87 50	60 50
Tallahassee, Fla....$84 10 to	45 55		6	32 40	
Tama, Iowa	34 00	31 35	3	28 10	26 10
Tamaqua, Pa., via D.L.&W.		3 00			
Tampa, Fla	48 45			35 70	
Tarboro, N.C.	13 30				
Taylorsville, Ill	29 20	27 95	3	24 00	21 00
Tecumseh, Mich	20 85	17 70	3	16 15	15 60
Terre Haute, Ind	26 05	24 75	3	21 25	19 25
Texarkana, Ark	46 00	41 70	5	37 35	31 85
The Dalles, Oregon	101 00	100 75	10	87 50	60 50
Thomasville, Ga	35 10		4	29 95	
Three Rivers, Mich	24 15	20 45	3	19 40	18 00
Tiffin, Ohio	19 05	16 95	3	15 70	14 20
Titusville, Pa. (not B.&O.R.R.)	13 53	12 70	2	10 85	
Toledo, Ohio	19 75	17 50	2	16 25	14 50
Topeka, Kan	40 30	37 25	5	33 25	30 25
Toronto, Ont		11 85			
Towanda, Pa., v. Pa., Er., D.L.W.		6 95	1	5 75	
Traverse City, Mich	28 55	23 85	3	22 30	20 30
Trenton, Mo.	37 10	34 15	3	30 40	27 40
Trenton, N.J., via Penn. R.R.		3 15			
Trinidad, Col	59 15	56 10	6	49 90	46 15
Troy, N.Y.v. N.Y.C. or W.S.		3 15			
Tuckerton, N.J., via Pa. R.R.	8 90		1	2 75	
" Excursion.			30	4 50	
Tucson, Ariz	81 90	80 00	10	73 25	62 25
Two Rivers, Wis	31 60	28 85	4	25 10	24 10
Tyler, Tex	49 85	48 35	5	41 20	33 60
Tyrone, Pa., via Penn. R.R.	9 02		2		7 65
Uhrichsville, Ohio	15 50		2	13 50	12 10
Umatilla, Oregon	101 00	100 75	10	87 50	60 00
Union, Pa., via Penn. R.R.	13 10		2	10 60	
" via Erie Railway,		11 35	2	10 60	
Union City, Ind	21 60	20 20	3	18 00	16 25
Uniontown, Pa.	12 89		2	10 50	10 00
Upper Sandusky, Ohio	18 00	17 35	2	16 10	14 00
Urbana, Ill	27 25	25 80	3	22 00	20 15
Urbana, Ohio	19 90	18 70	3	17 00	15 00
Utica, N.Y.v. N.Y.C or W.S.		5 00			
Valparaiso, Ind.	25 25	22 70	3	20 00	18 00
Van Buren, Ark	46 00	42 30	5	38 55	32 85
Vancouver, B.C.,v. No. Pac.R.R.	104 00	100 75	10	87 50	60 50
" v.Can.Pac.R.R.	104 00	100 75	10	77 50	55 50
Vandalia, Ill	28 95	27 65	3	24 00	21 00
Van Wert, Ohio	21 15	19 45	3	16 75	15 00
Vicksburg, Miss....$39 00 to	50 25	48 70	5	34 00	29 00
Victoria, B.C., v. Nor.Pac.R.R.	104 00	$100 75	10	$87 50	$60 50
" v. Can. Pac.R.R.	104 00	101 75	10	77 50	55 50
Vincennes, Ind	27 30	26 00	3	22 50	20 50
Vineland, N.J., v. Penn. R.R.	3 25				
Vinton, Iowa	33 55	30 10	3	27 45	25 45
Virginia City, Nev	101 80	98 75	10	94 75	66 75
Wabash, Ind	23 35	21 55	3	18 00	16 25
Wabasha, Minn	36 00	32 80	4	29 55	27 00
Waco, Tex.....$32 85 to	58 25	52 15	5	44 80	36 15
Wa Keeney, Kan	48 10	45 05	5	41 05	39 05
Warren, Ohio	11 95	13 15	2	12 50	11 50
Warren, Pa			2	9 15	
Warsaw, Ill	33 10	30 40	3	26 25	24 25
Warsaw, Ind	23 30	21 50	3	17 95	16 50
Washington, D.C.	6 50				5 75
Washington, Iowa	33 65	30 10	3	27 15	24 75
Washington, Ohio	19 70		2	16 60	14 80
Washington, Pa., v. Penn. R.R.	13 50			11 50	11 00
" v. B.&O.R.R.	13 65		2	11 50	11 00
Waterbury, Ct., v. Harlem R.R.		9 27			
Waterloo, Iowa	34 70	31 45	4	28 20	26 20
Watertown, Dak	48 75	40 50	5	37 25	33 85
Watertown, N.Y. v. NYC or WS.		7 50			
Watertown, Wis	30 35	27 10	4	23 85	21 85
Watkins Glen, N.Y., v. D.L.W., Erie or Penn. R.R.		7 70	2	6 45	
Watkins Glen, N.Y., v. N.Y.C		7 85	2	7 10	
Waukegan, Ill	28 05	24 80	3	21 55	19 55
Waukesha, Wis	29 25	26 00	4	22 75	20 75
Waupaca, Wis.	32 70	29 15	4	26 30	24 30
Waupun, Wis	31 10	27 85	4	24 00	22 00
Wausau, Wis	34 45	31 20	4	27 95	25 95
Waverly, Iowa	35 20	31 95	4	24 70	26 70
Waverly, N.Y., via D.L.W., Erie or Penn. R.R.		6 95	1	5 75	
Waverly, N.Y., Excursion			30	9 60	
Webster City, Iowa	37 05	33 80	4	30 55	28 20
Weldon, N.C	14 35		3	11 30	
Wellington, Kan	45 35	42 70	4	38 30	35 30
Wellsboro, Ind	21 90			19 85	17 50
Wellsville, Ohio	13 95		2	11 95	11 00
West Chester, Pa., v. Penn. R.R.	3 30				
West End, N.Y., v. Pa. R.R.	1 35		1	1 00	
West Point or Cranston's, N.Y.		98			
West Point, Va.	7 50				
W. Rutland, Vt., v. N.Y.C or WS	11 50	5 55	2	12 50	11 00
Wheeling, W. Va			2	12 85	12 60
Whitby, Ont. (not Erie R'y).		5 30			
Whitehall, N.Y., v. NYC or WS		26 90	4	23 15	21 15
White Water, Wis	30 15	41 60	4	37 50	34 50
Wichita, Kan	14 65	5 00	4		
Wilkesbarre, Pa., v. DLW or Pa.			5	7 50	
" Excursion.			5	7 50	
Williamsport, Pa.,v. DLW or Pa.	8 30	6 85	2	6 85	
Williamstown, Mass., v.N.Y.C or W.S.		4 34	2	3 73	
Wilmington, Del	3 25				
Wilmington, N.C	20 00		3	16 95	
Wilmington, Ohio	20 85		2	17 50	15 45
Winfield, Kan	44 70	42 40	4	37 85	34 65
Wingate, N. Mex	78 55	75 50	8	71 00	60 00
Winnebago City, Minn	38 25	35 00	4	31 75	22 95
Winnipeg, Man	52 40	49 15	5	45 90	38 25
Winona, Minn	35 10	31 85	4	24 60	26 60
Winterset, Iowa	37 45	34 40	3	30 95	28 95
Woodstock, Ont		12 10			
Woonsocket, Dak	45 55	42 30	6	39 05	35 20
Wooster, Ohio	16 55	16 00	2	11 0	12 50
Worthington, Minn	40 55	37 30	5	34 05	30 35
Xenia, Ohio	20 10	19 75	3	17 00	15 25
Yankton, Dak	42 90	36 95	5	36 40	32 70
York, Pa., via Penn. R.R	5 40				
Youngstown, Ohio	14 55	13 95	2	12 50	11 50
Ypsilanti, Mich	21 25	16 95	2	15 90	15 15
Zanesville, Ohio	17 00		2	15 00	12 90
"		18 75	1	15 25	13 65
Zumbrota, Minn	37 35	34 10	4	30 85	27 75

This is the only Guide giving the fare to every place in the United States. The time tables in this work are so arranged that they can be readily understood. For Telegraph Rates to all Places, see Index.

NEW YORK, NEW HAVEN AND HARTFORD R. R.
RATES OF FARE FROM NEW YORK.

Stop-Over Regulations.—Passengers holding Unlimited First Class Tickets will be allowed to stop over at New Rochelle, Stamford, South Norwalk, Bridgeport, Ansonia, Waterbury, Litchfield, New Haven, Meriden, Berlin, Hartford, Windsor Locks, Plainville, Westfield, Northampton, South Deerfield, Guilford, Saybrook, Goodspeed's, Middletown or Turnerville. For Stop-Over at other stations, Conductor will, on application, furnish Stop-Over Check, except that no such Stop-Over Check will be issued between stations the regular fare between which is less than Ten Cents.
Children between four and twelve years of age half fare. 150 pounds of baggage allowed each passenger presenting a full ticket, and 75 pounds for a half ticket.

NEW YORK TO	Unlimited	1st Class Limited	NEW YORK TO	Unlimited	1st Class Limited
Alburgh Springs, Vt	$8 70		Burlington, Vt	$8 00	
" & Return			Burrville, Conn	2 60	
Altona, N. Y	9 30		Burke, Vt	9 85	
Amesbury, Mass	6 64		Bucksport, Me	12 75	12 00
Amherst, Mass., via Palmer	3 71		Cambridge, N. H. (See Upton, Me.)		
" " via Northampton	3 50		Campton Village, N. H	8 41	
Amherst, N. S	18 75	17 25	Campville, Conn	2 30	
Andover, N. B	18 00	15 85	Campbellton, N. B	21 00	19 50
Andover, Me. & Return			Canaan, Conn	2 75	
Ansonia, Conn	1 55		Cannon, Conn	1 17	
Aroostook, N. B	18 15	16 00	Canterbury, N. B	15 25	18 85
Ashley Falls, Mass	2 85		Caribou, Me	18 75	16 55
Ashland, Mass	1 45		Champlain, N. Y	8 85	
Ashuelot, N. H	4 55		Charlemont, Mass	3 85	3 11
Athol, Mass	3 85		Charlestown, N. H	5 85	
Attleboro, Mass	1 60		Charlton, Mass	3 70	
Auburn, Me	9 25	8 75	Chateaugay, N. Y	9 80	
Augusta, Me., via Boston	10 00	9 50	Cherubusco, N. Y	9 70	
" " via Worcester	9 10		Cheshire, Conn	1 90	
Avon, Conn	2 15		Chester, Conn., via A. L. Dir	2 00	
Ayer Junction, Mass	4 85		" " via Saybrook		
Baldwinsville, Mass., via Palmer	4 08		Chester, Vt	6 15	
" " via Worcester	4 90		Chicopee, Mass	2 85	
Baltic, Conn	3 11		Chicopee Falls, Mass	2 90	
Bangor, N. Y	9 95		Claremont Junc., N. H	6 30	
Bangor, Me., via Boston	12 25	11 50	Clinton, Conn	2 10	
" " via Worcester	11 10		Clinton, Mass	4 50	
Bantam, Conn	2 85		Cobalt (Middle Haddam), Conn	2 25	
Bar Harbor, Me., via Boston & B. & B. S. Co.	9 25		Colchester, Conn	2 70	
" " & Steamer Olivette			Coldbrook, Mass	3 72	
" " & Return			Collins, Mass	2 98	
" " Rail to Portland & Steamer			Collinsville, Conn	2 45	
" " & Return			Concord, N. H., via Palmer	6 10	
" " All Rail Route	13 50	12 00	" " via Worcester	6 10	
" " & Return			Conn. River, Conn	2 85	
Barnet, Vt	8 10		Conway, Mass	3 70	
Barre Plains, Mass	3 65		Cordaville, Mass	1 87	
Barre, Vt	7 85		Cornwall Bridge, Conn	2 75	
Barrett's Junction, Mass	3 16		Cos Cob, Conn	60	
Barton, Vt	8 85		Cottage City, (See Oak Bluffs)		
Bartow, N. Y	40		Crawford House, N. H., via C. P. Line	9 00	
Bath, Me	9 25	8 75	" " & Return		
Bath, N. H	8 05		" " via Boston	11 25	
" & Return			Dalhousie, N. B	20 75	19 25
Bath, N. B	17 35	15 35	Damariscotta, Me	10 00	9 00
Bathurst, N. B	20 00	18 50	Damariscotta Mills, Me	10 10	9 00
Bay Chester, N. Y	45		Danbury, Conn	1 60	
Beacon Falls, Conn	1 70		" & Return	2 90	
Belfast, Me., via Boston	12 00	10 50	Darien, Conn	80	
" " via Worcester	10 85		Dover Junc., N. B	16 25	14 50
Bellows Falls, Vt	5 55		Deep River, Conn., via A. L. Dir	2 60	
Belmont, Mass	4 81		" " via Saybrook	2 50	
Benton, N. B	15 85	14 10	Deerfield, Mass	3 05	
Bemis, Me., & Return, Rail to Phillips			Derby, Conn	1 50	
" " via Bry. P'd & Andover			Deweys, Mass	3 40	
Berlin, Conn	2 00		Dexter, Me	12 15	11 25
Bernardston, Mass	1 10		Dover, Me	13 00	12 25
Bethel, Conn	1 50		Dover, N. H	2 35	
" & Return	2 85		Dummerston, Vt	7 60	
Bethel, Vt	7 25		East Berlin, Conn	2 10	
Bethlehem, N. H			East Brookfield, Mass	3 51	
Bethlehem Junction, N. H	8 50		East Douglass, Mass	3 84	
" & Return			East Granville, Vt	7 10	
Biddeford, Me	8 18	8 00	East Greenwich, R. I	1 60	
Blackstone, Mass	4 09		East Hampton, Conn	2 35	
Block Island, Rail to and St'r from New London			Easthampton, Mass	3 15	
" & Return			East Haven, Conn	1 65	
Bondsville, Mass	3 18		East Lyme, Conn	2 60	
Boston, Mass	5 00		East Putney, Vt	5 15	
" via Shore Line	5 30	5 00	East River, Conn	1 95	
Botsford, Conn	1 60		East Wallingford, Conn	1 80	
Bradford, Vt	7 60		Edmundston, N. B	19 35	17 70
Braintree, Vt	7 85		Ellenburg, N. Y	9 30	
Branchville, Conn	1 20		Ellsworth, Me	13 25	12 00
Brandon, Vt	7 50		Enfield Bridge, Conn	2 50	
Branford, Conn	1 70		Enfield, Mass	3 30	
Brattleboro, Vt	4 55		Epping, N. H	6 42	
Brasher, N. Y	10 35		Essex, Conn., via A. L. Dir	2 70	
Brightwood, Mass	2 80		" " via Saybrook	2 45	
Bridgeport, Conn	1 15		Essex Junc., Vt	8 00	
Bristol, Conn	2 31		Exeter, N. H	6 83	
Brookfield, Conn	2 02		Fabyan's, N. H., via Conn. R. Line	8 70	
Brooks, Mass	4 35		" " & Return		
Brushton, N. Y	10 00		" " via Boston	11 50	
Brunswick, Me	9 25	8 75	Fairfield, Conn	1 05	
			Fair Haven, Conn	1 53	

NEW YORK, NEW HAVEN AND HARTFORD R. R.—Continued.

NEW YORK TO	Unlimited	1st Class Limited	NEW YORK TO	Unlimited	1st Class Limited
Fairlee, Vt	$7 45		Lenox Furnace, Mass	$3 40	
Falls Village, Conn	2 75		Lennoxville, P. Q	10 00	
Farmington, Conn	2 25		Lewiston, Me	9 25	8 75
Farmington, Me	10 75	10 50	Lime Rock, Conn	2 75	
Farnham, P. Q	9 25		Lincoln, Me	11 60	12 75
Fenwick, Conn			Lisbon, N. H	8 05	
Fitchburg, Mass	4 65		" & Return		
Five Mile River, Conn	80		Lisbon, N. Y	11 15	
Florence, Mass	3 35		Litchfield, Conn., via So. Norwalk or Bridgeport	2 85	
Florenceville, N. B	17 15	15 10	" via Naugatuck Division	2 10	
Forestville, Conn	2 25		Littleton, N. H	8 10	
Fort Fairfield, Me	18 85	16 15	" & Return		
Franklin, Mass	4 30		Long Hill, Conn	1 40	
Fredericton Junc., N. B	15 25	13 50	Long Meadow, Mass	2 65	
Fredericton, N. B	15 95	14 10	Lowell, Mass	5 20	
Gardiner, Me	9 75	9 25	Ludlow, Mass	2 90	
Gardner, Mass	4 75		Ludlow, Vt	6 70	
Gassets, Vt	6 80		Lyme, Conn	2 35	
Georgetown, Conn	1 20		Lyndonville, Vt	M 45	
" & Return	2 30		Lynn, Mass	5 70	
Gilbertville, Mass	3 47		Madison, Conn	2 00	
Glenbrook, Conn	70		Madrid, N. Y	10 90	
Glendale, Mass	3 85		Malone, N. Y	9 90	
Gloucester, Mass	6 25		Mamaroneck, N. Y	45	
Goodspeed's, Conn., via A. L. Div	2 50		Manchester, Conn	2 47	
" via Saybrook	2 65		Manchester, N. H	5 74	
Grand Falls, N. B	18 75	16 60	Mansfield, Mass	4 75	
Granby, Conn	2 65		Mattawamkeag, Me	14 50	13 10
Great Barrington, Mass	3 10		McAdam Junc., N. B	15 10	13 50
Great Falls, N. H	7 50		Meriden, Conn	1 85	
Greenfield, Mass	3 75		Merwinsville, Conn	2 14	
Green's Farms, Conn	95		Metapedia, N. B	21 20	19 70
Greenwich, Conn	60		Middlebury, Vt	7 65	
Groton, Mass	4 95		Middle Dam, Me. & Return, via Bethel		
Groveton Junc., N. H., via C. R. Line	9 25		" " Bryant's Pond		
Grouts, Vt	5 30		Middlefield, Conn	1 95	
Guilford, Conn	1 90		Middletown, Conn., via Berlin	2 25	
Guilford, Me	13 15	12 50	" via A. L. Division	2 10	
Haddam, Conn., via A. L. Div	2 40		Milford, Conn	1 30	
" via Saybrook	2 70		Milford, Mass	4 75	
Halifax, N. S	20 00	18 00	Millton, Vt	8 25	
Hallowell, Me	9 00	9 40	Moira, N. Y	10 00	
Harrison, N. Y	45		Moncton, N. B	17 65	16 15
Hartford, Conn	2 25		Montpelier, Vt	7 60	
Hartford, Vt	7 00		" & Return		
Hartland, Vt	6 60		Montreal, P. Q	10 00	
Hartland, N. B	16 80	14 85	" & Return		
Harvey, N. B	15 00	13 50	Morris, Conn	2 40	
Hatfield, Mass	3 85		Morrisville, Vt	9 00	
Hawleyville, Conn., via South Norwalk	1 68		Mooer's Junc., N. Y	9 90	
" via Bridgeport	1 84		Mooer's Forks, N. Y	9 10	
Hayden's, Conn	2 40		Mount Hermon, Mass	4 15	
Haydenville, Mass	3 45		Mount Kineo, Me., & Return		
Haverhill, Mass	6 35		Mount Toni, Mass	3 15	
Heywood's, Mass	4 75		Mount Vernon, N. Y., via Bethel	30	
Higganum, Conn., via A. L. Div	2 35		Mt. Carmel, Conn	1 75	
Highgate Springs, Vt	8 85		Mystic, Conn	3 03	
" & Return			Narragansett Pier, R. I	4 17	
Hinsdale, N. H	4 40		Nashua, N. H	5 40	
Hitchcock's, Conn	2 00		Natick, Mass	4 60	
Holden, Mass	4 23		Naugatuck, Conn	1 80	
Holyoke, Mass	3 00		New Bedford, Mass	5 40	
Hoosac Tunnel, Mass	3 85		New Britain, Conn	2 05	
Houlton, Me	16 50	14 50	New Castle, N. B	19 25	17 75
Housatonic, Mass	3 25		New Salem, Mass	3 65	
Hubbardston, Mass	4 55		Newbury, Vt	7 75	
Hudson, Mass	4 35		Newburyport, Mass	6 50	
Hyde Park, Vt	10 05		New Canaan, Conn	85	
Indian Rock & Ret., via Bethel and Cambridge			New Glasgow, N. S	20 00	18 00
" Bryant's P'd and Andover			New Hartford, Conn	2 60	
" Farmington and Phillips			New Haven, Conn	1 50	
Jefferson, N. H., via Conn. R. Line	9 25		Newington, Conn	2 15	
" & Return			New London, Conn	2 75	
Jefferson's, Mass	4 20		New Milford, Conn	2 29	
Judd's Bridge, Conn	2 45		Newport, R. I	4 50	
Keene, N. H	5 00		Newport, Vt	9 25	
Kennebunk, Me	7 07	7 85	" & Return		
Kennebunkport, Me	8 17	8 05	New Preston, Conn	2 65	
Kent, Conn	2 62		New Rochelle, N. Y	35	
Kingston, R. I	3 07		Newtown, Conn	1 75	
Knapps, N. Y	10 55		Nobleboro, Me	10 20	9 00
Laconia, N. H	7 36		Norfolk, Conn	3 08	
Lake Megantic, Canada			Noroton, Conn	75	
" & Return			Northampton, Mass	3 25	
Lake Village, N. H	7 41		North Adams, Mass., via New Haven	4 27	3 85
Lancaster, N. H	9 00		" " via Bridgeport	3 85	
" & Return			North Conway, N. H., via Worcester	8 75	
Larchmont Manor, N. Y	40		" " via Boston	9 43	
Lawrence, Mass	6 15		" " via Fabyan's	10 70	
Lawrence, N. Y	10 15		North Dana, Mass	3 61	
Lee, Mass	3 40		North Derby, Vt	9 40	
Leeds, Mass	3 40		North Grafton, Mass	4 13	
Loete's Island, Conn	1 85		Northfield, Vt	7 50	
Leicester Junc., Vt	7 80		North Hampton, N. H	6 81	
Lenox, Mass	3 40		North Hartland, Vt	6 75	

NEW YORK, NEW HAVEN AND HARTFORD R. R.—Continued.

NEW YORK TO	Unlimited	1st Class Limited	NEW YORK TO	Unlimited	1st Class Limited
North Hatfield, Mass	$3 45		Shelburne Falls, Mass., via Greenfield	$4 15	
North Haven, Conn	1 60		" " " via Northampton Div	3 85	
North Wilbraham, Mass	2 98		Shepaug, Conn	1 95	
North Woodstock, N. H	8 86		Sherbrooke, P. Q	10 00	
Norwich, Conn., via New London	3 15		" " & Return		
" " via Williamantic	3 35		Simsbury, Conn	2 55	
Norwich, Vt	7 10		Skowhegan, Me	11 50	11 00
Norwood, N. Y	10 65		Smith's Ferry, Mass	3 15	
Oak Bluffs, Mass			Sound Beach, Conn	65	
" " & Return			Southampton, Mass	3 05	
Oakdale, Mass	4 00		Southbridge, Mass	4 00	
Oakville, Conn	2 05		South Deerfield, Mass	3 55	
Ogdensburg, N. Y	11 25		South Framingham, Mass	1 50	
Old Furnace, Mass	3 50		Southington, Conn	2 05	
Old Orchard, Me	8 33	8 00	South Lee, Mass	3 40	
Oldtown, Me	12 65	11 90	South Lyme, Conn	2 50	
Orono, Me	12 50	11 75	South Manchester, Conn	2 57	
Otter River, Mass	4 86		South Norwalk, Conn	85	
Palmer, Mass	3 11		Southport, Conn	1 00	
Pawtucket, R. I	4 40		South Royalton, Vt	7 15	
Pecowsic, Mass	2 70		South Vernon, or West Northfield, Vt	4 20	
Pelham Manor, N. Y	90		Southwick, Mass	2 75	
Pelhamville, N. Y	90		South Wilbam, Conn	1 65	
Phillips, Me., & Return			South Windham, Conn	2 94	
Picton, N. S	20 00	18 00	South Spencer, Mass	3 50	
Pittsfield, Mass	3 10		Springfield, Mass	2 75	
Pittsfield, Me	11 50	10 80	Stafford, Conn., via New London	1 25	
Plainfield, Conn	3 43		" " via Springfield	3 50	
Plainville, Conn	2 20		Stamford, Conn	70	
Plantsville, Conn	2 05		Stanbridge, P. Q	9 25	
Plattsburgh, N. Y	9 42		Stanstead, P. Q	9 55	
Plymouth, N. H	8 26		State Line, Mass	3 30	
Point Levi, P. Q	12 00		Stepney, Conn	1 48	
Poland Springs & Return			Sterling June., Mass	1 36	
Pomfret, Conn	3 35		Stockbridge, Mass	3 40	
Port Chester, N. Y	55		Stonington, Conn	3 72	
Portland, Conn	2 15		Stony Creek, Conn	1 80	
Portland, Me., via Boston	8 50	8 00	Stratford, Conn	1 20	
" " via Worcester	8 10		Suffield, Conn	2 55	
Portsmouth, N. H	7 10		Swanton, Vt	8 70	
Presque Isle, Me	18 75	16 65	Swanzey, N. H	4 85	
Princeton, Mass	1 45		Taunton, Mass	1 80	
Providence, R. I., via Hartford and Wackstone	1 50		Templeton, Mass	3 99	
" " via H'fd and N. Y. & N. E	1 50		Terryville, Conn	2 41	
" " via Shore or Air Line	1 30		Thetford, Vt	7 30	
Profile House, N. H			Thomaston, Conn	2 20	
" " & Return			Thomaston, Me	10 40	9 00
Putnam, Conn	3 17		Thompson, Conn	3 57	
Putney, Vt	1 05		Thompsonville, Conn	2 55	
Quebec, P. Q	12 00		Thorndike, Mass	3 20	
" " & Return			Torrington, Conn	2 45	
Quinnipiac, Conn	1 55		Trumbull Church, Conn	1 33	
Randolph, Vt	7 30		Truro, N. S	20 00	18 00
" " & Return			Turner's Falls, Mass	3 80	
Redding, Conn	1 58		Turnerville, Conn	2 60	
" " & Return	2 65		Twin Mountain, N. H	8 60	
Richmond, Me	9 50	9 00	" " & Return		
Richmond, Vt	7 90		Union City, Conn	1 85	
Richmond, P. Q	10 00		Unionville, Conn	2 35	
Ridgefield, Conn	1 41		Upper Dam, Me., & Return, via Phillips		
" " & Return	2 65		" " " Bryant's Pond		
Riverside, Conn	60		" " " via Bethel		
Rochester, N. H., via Boston	7 05		Upton, Me., & Return		
" " via Worcester	6 80		Van Densenville, Mass	3 20	
Rockfall, Conn	2 05		Vanceboro, Me	15 00	13 50
Rockland, Me	10 50	9 00	Vergennes, Vt	7 55	
Rockville, Conn	2 67		Waldoboro, Me	10 25	9 00
Romford, Conn	2 75		Wallingford, Conn	1 75	
Rouse's Point, N. Y	8 70		Walpole, Mass	4 52	
Roxbury, Conn	2 30		Waltham, Mass	4 71	
Roxbury, Vt	7 45		Ware, Mass	3 38	
Roxbury Falls, Conn	2 15		Warehouse Point, Conn	2 50	
Royalston, Mass	5 05		Warren, Mass	3 96	
Royalton, Vt	7 20		Warren, Me	10 35	9 00
Rutland, Mass	7 80		Washington, Conn	2 60	
Rutland, Vt	7 80		Watch Hill, R. I., via New London and Steamer		
Rye, N. Y	50		" " " via Stonington		
Saco, Me	8 18	8 00	Waterbury, Conn	1 95	
St. Albans, Vt	8 50		Waterbury, Vt	7 70	
" " & Return			Waterloo, P. Q	9 25	
St. Alexandre, P. Q	9 25		Watertown, Conn	2 15	
St. Andrew's, N. B	15 50	13 50	Waterville, Conn	2 05	
St. John, N. B., via Boston	15 50	13 50	Waterville, Mass	4 19	
" " via Worcester	15 10		Waterville, Me	10 75	10 25
St. John's, P. Q	9 25		Wayland, Mass	4 57	
St. Johnsbury, Vt	8 30		Webster, Mass	3 72	
St. Leonard's, N. B	19 05	16 85	Weirs, N. H	7 56	
St. Stephen's, N. B	15 50	13 50	Wellesley, Mass	4 07	
Salem, Mass	5 85		Wells River, Vt	7 85	
Sanford, Conn	1 35		Wellsford, N. B	15 40	13 50
Saybrook, Conn	2 30		Wellsboro, Mass	4 90	
Seymour, Conn	1 65		West Boylston, Mass	4 11	
Sharon, Vt	7 10		Westbrook, Conn	2 20	
Shediac, N. B	18 00	16 50	West Brookfield, Mass	3 43	
Sheffield, Mass	2 93		West Burke, Vt	8 00	

NEW YORK, NEW HAVEN AND HARTFORD R. R.—Continued.

NEW YORK TO	Unlimited	1st Class Limited	NEW YORK TO	Unlimited	1st Class Limited
Westchester, Conn	$2 50		Willimantic, Conn., via A. L. Division	$2 85	
Westchester, N. Y	45		" " via Hartford	2 85	
West Cornwall, Conn	2 75		" " via New London	3 65	
Westerly, R. I.	3 20		Wilson's, Conn	2 30	
Westfield, Conn	2 15		Wilton, Conn	1 11	
Westfield, Mass	2 85		" " & Return	2 10	
Westfield, N. B.	15 50	13 50	Winchendon, Mass	4 24	
West Haven, Conn	1 45		" " via Worcester	5 00	
West Hartford, Vt	7 05		Winchester, N. H	1 60	
Westminster, Mass	5 35		Windsor, Conn	2 35	
West Northfield or South Vernon, Vt	4 25		Windsor, Vt	6 45	
Weston, Mass	4 05		Windsor Locks, Conn	2 45	
Westport, Conn	90		Winnepauk, Conn	1 00	
Westport, N. H	4 75		Winooski, Vt	8 00	
West Stockbridge, Mass	3 20		Winsted, Conn., via Hous. R. R.	3 10	
West Warren, Mass	3 30		" " via Naug. Division	2 70	
Whately, Mass	3 50		Winthrop, Me	9 75	9 50
Whitefield, N. H.	8 50		Wiscasset, Me	9 75	9 00
" " & Return			Woodmont, Conn	1 40	
White River June., Vt	6 95		Woodstock, N. B	16 50	14 50
Wickford Junc., R. I.	3 86		Woonsocket, R. I., via Blackstone	1 18	
Wickford Landing, R. I.	4 00		" " via Providence	1 70	
Williamsburgh, Mass	3 45		Wolfboro, N. H.	8 55	
Williamstown, Mass	4 42	3 98	Worcester, Mass	1 00	
Williamsville, Mass	3 88		Yalesville, Conn	1 80	
Williamsett, Mass	2 95				

LONG ISLAND R. R.
RATES OF FARE FROM LONG ISLAND CITY OR BROOKLYN.

Ten cents extra will be charged on all tickets sold on train. No Stop-Over allowed on any ticket.

	STATION.	Miles.	Single Ticket	Round Trip		STATION.	Miles.	Single Ticket	Round Trip
Atlantic Division	East New York	3	$ 10	$ 20	North Side Div.	Woodside	3	$ 10	$ 15
	Cypress Avenue	5	15	25		Winfield	4	15	25
	Union Course	6	15	25		Newtown	4	15	25
	Woodhaven	6	20	30		Corona	5	20	25
	Morris Park	8	25	40		Flushing	7	20	35
MAIN LINE	Maple Grove	8	25	40		College Point	9	25	45
	Jamaica	9	30	50		Whitestone	10	30	55
	Hollis	11	35	60		Whitestone Landing	11	35	65
	Queens	13	40	70		Broadway	9	25	45
	East Hinsdale	15	45	80		Bayside	11	30	55
	Hyde Park	16	50	90		Douglaston	12	35	65
	Mineola	19	55	1 00		Little Neck	12	35	65
	Garden City	18	55	1 00		Great Neck	14	40	70
	Hempstead	20	60	1 10	Rockaway Branch	Fresh Pond	3	10	15
	East Williston	20	55	1 00		Glendale	5	15	25
	Albertson	21	55	1 00		Richmond Hill (Morris Park)	8	25	45
	Roslyn	22	55	1 00		Locust Ave	11	35	65
	Glen Head	25	55	1 00		Springfield	13	40	70
	Sea Cliff	27	55	1 00		Valley Stream	16	50	90
	Glen Cove	27	55	1 00		Hewletts	17	55	1 00
	Locust Valley	29	60	1 10		Woodsburgh	18	55	1 00
	Westbury	21	65	1 15		Ocean Point	19	55	1 00
	Hicksville	25	75	1 35		Lawrence	20	60	1 00
	Syosset	29	90	1 60		Far Rockaway	21	65	1 00
	Cold Spring	31	95	1 70		Pearsalls	17	55	1 00
	Huntington	34	1 05	1 90	MONTAUK DIVISION	East Rockaway	18	55	1 00
	Greenlawn	37	1 15	2 05		Barnum's Island	21	65	1 20
	Northport	40	1 20	2 15		Long Beach	23	70	1 25
	St. Johnland	43	1 30	2 35		Point Lookout	27	80	1 45
	Smithtown	47	1 40	2 50		Rockville Centre	19	55	1 00
	St. James	50	1 50	2 70		Baldwins	21	65	1 15
	Stony Brook	53	1 60	2 90		Freeport	22	70	1 25
	Setauket	55	1 65	3 10		Merrick	24	75	1 35
	Port Jefferson	57	1 75	3 15		Bellmore	25	75	1 40
	Central Park	28	85	1 55		Ridgewood	26	80	1 45
	Farmingdale	30	90	1 60		South Oyster Bay	29	85	1 55
	West Deer Park	34	1 05	1 90		Amityville	31	95	1 70
	Deer Park	36	1 10	2 00		Breslau	33	1 00	1 80
	Brentwood	41	1 25	2 25		Babylon	36	1 10	2 00
	Central Islip	43	1 30	2 35		Bayshore	40	1 20	2 15
	Ronkonkoma	48	1 45	2 60		Islip	43	1 30	2 35
	Waverly	51	1 55	2 80		Oakdale	47	1 40	2 50
	Medford	54	1 65	2 95		Sayville	49	1 50	2 70
	Yaphank	58	1 75	3 15		Bayport	51	1 55	2 40
	Manor	65	1 95	3 50		Patchogue	53	1 60	2 90
	Baiting Hollow	69	2 05	3 70		Bellport	57	1 75	3 15
	Riverhead	73	2 20	3 95		Brookhaven	59	1 80	3 25
	Jamesport	78	2 35	4 25		Forge	63	1 90	3 40
	Mattituck	82	2 45	4 40		Moriches	66	2 00	3 60
	Cutchogue	85	2 55	4 60		Eastport	69	2 10	3 80
	Peconic	87	2 65	4 75		Speonk	71	2 15	3 85
	Southold	89	2 70	4 85		West Hampton	74	2 30	4 15
	Greenport	94	2 85	5 15		Quogue	81	2 45	4 40
						Good Ground	83	2 50	4 50
						Shinnecock Hills	85	2 55	4 60
						Southampton	88	2 65	4 80
						Water Mills	91	2 75	4 95
						Bridge Hampton	94	2 80	5 05
						Sag Harbor	98	2 95	5 30

The publisher will consider it a favor to be notified of any error discovered in this work. Such notices will enable him to make more correct subsequent reports.

CENTRAL RAILROAD CO. OF NEW JERSEY.
RATES OF FARE FROM NEW YORK.

Rates herein also apply to Jersey City. Children between 5 and 12 years of age will be charged half the regular trip rate. Where no time-limit appears opposite Excursion Rates, tickets will be good until used. The two day time-limit on single tickets includes day of issue.

Destination.	First Class Un-limited Rates.	Excursion Ticket Rates.	Time Limit days for Exc. Rates.	Destination.	First Class Un-limited Rates.	Excursion Ticket Rates.	Time Limit days for Exc. Rates.
Abington, Pa....	$2 32	$4 10	5	Chain Dam, Pa	$2 29	$3 50	
Akron, Pa., via Phillipsburg...	4 31	7 19	5	Chapel Hill, N. J.	1 00	1 50	
" via Bound Brook...	1 89	7 19	5	Chapman Quarries, Pa...	2 00	1 55	
Alburtis, Pa...	2 05	....		Chester, N. J	1 80	65	
Alden, Pa...	5 25	7 85		Chester Furnace, N. J	1 80	2 00	
Allentown, Pa...	2 00	4 10		Chestnut Hill, Pa	2 59	4 20	5
Allenwood, Pa., (Dewart), via Tamaqua...	6 23	10 14	15	Chickies, Pa	3 57	8 13	5
" via Bound Brook	7 66	11 15	15	" limited 2 days...	4 25	....	
" limited 2 days, via Bd. Bk.	6 23	....		Claremont, N. J...	08	14	
Annandale, N. J...	1 85	2 25		Clark's Summit, Pa...	4 60	....	
Apollonio, N. J	1 00	3 00		Clearfield, Pa...	9 85	....	
Asbury, N. J	1 65	2 70		Cliffwood, N. J...	70	1 25	
Asbury Park, N. J...	1 20	1 85		Clyde, Pa...	2 75	1 35	
Ashland, Pa., via Tamaqua...	4 55	7 60	10	Coaldale, Pa...	3 80	6 10	
" via Bound Brook...	6 03	8 79	10	Columbia, Pa...	5 01	7 75	5
" limited 2 days, via Bound Bk.	4 55	....		" limited 2 days...	4 00	....	
Ashley, Pa...	5 00	7 50		Communipaw, N. J...	08	14	
Atco, N. J	2 80	4 50		Como, N. J	1 30	2 05	
Athens, Pa...	6 95	....		Conshohocken, Pa...	2 67	4 31	5
Atlantic City, N. J., via Winslow June...	3 25	4 75	10	Considerable Hook, N. J., via steamboat...	10	....	
" via Bound Brook...	3 25	4 75	10	Council Ridge, Pa...	4 15	0 70	
Atlantic Highlands, N. J., via steamer...	60	1 00		Cranford, N. J	40	60	
" all rail...	1 00	1 50		Danville, Pa., via Tamaqua...	5 58	9 00	15
Atson, N. J...	2 60	1 00		" lim 2 days, via Bound Brook.	5 58	....	
Auderreid, Pa	4 23	6 80		Deal Beach, N. J...	1 10	1 75	
Bacon's Neck, N. J...	3 55	5 70		Denver, Pa., via Phillipsburg...	1 12	6 94	5
Banger, Pa...	3 25	4 70		" via Bound Brook...	1 70	6 94	5
Banger Junction, Pa...	3 25	1 70		Dividing Creek, N. J...	3 65	5 95	
Barnegat, N. J...	2 25	3 80		Dornsife, Pa., via Tamaqua	5 51	9 58	10
Barnegat Park, N. J. (Bayville)...	2 00	3 25		Douglassville, Pa., via Bound Brook...	3 60	5 78	5
Barnesville, Pa., via Tamaqua	4 05	6 60	10	Dover, N. J	2 10	3 10	
" via Bound Brook...	5 59	8 12	10	Doylestown, Pa., via Bound Brook...	2 97	5 40	5
Bartley, N. J...	1 80	2 65		Drakes Point, Pa	3 80	6 15	
Bath, Pa...	2 85	1 45		Drakesville, N. J	1 95	2 85	
Bayonne, Pa...	15	23		Drifton, Pa...	4 25	6 80	
Bay Side, N. J...	3 60	5 75		Drifton Junction, Pa...	4 05	6 55	
Bay View, N. J	1 00	1 50		Dryland, Pa...	2 30	3 60	
Bayway, N. J	30	50		Dunellen, N. J	70	1 15	
Beach Haven, N. J...	2 95	4 75		East Bridgeton, N. J...	3 35	5 40	
Beaver Meadow, Pa	4 10	6 60		East Freehold, N. J	95	1 70	
Beech Creek, Pa...	9 36	....		Easton, Pa...	2 10	3 30	
" limited 2 days...	7 82	....		Mahanoy Junction, Pa., via Tamaqua...	4 07	6 61	15
Belle Mead, N. J...	1 09	1 98	5	" via Bound Brook...	5 61	8 13	15
Beneert, Pa...	2 21	3 95	5	Eatontown, N. J	1 00	1 50	
Bergen Point, N. J., all rail...	20	30		Eckley, N. J...	4 25	6 70	
" by steamboat...	10	....		Egg Harbor, N. J	3 16	4 61	10
Bethayres, Pa...	2 14	3 81	5	Elberon, N. J	1 00	1 60	
Bethlehem, Pa...	2 45	3 85		Elizabeth, N. J...	25	40	10
Bigler, Pa...	11 18	....		Elizabeth Ave., N. J...	25	40	
" limited 2 days...	9 64	....		Elizabethport, N. J., all rail...	25	40	
Birdsboro, Pa...	3 97	5 96	5	" by steamboat...	15	....	
" limited 2 days...	3 67	....		Elm, N. J...	2 75	4 00	
Blackwell's, Pa., lim. 2 days, via Tamaqua...	7 50	....		El Mora, N. J...	25	40	
" lim. 2 days, via Bound Bk	8 40	....		Elwood, N. J...	3 03	4 42	10
Blandon, Pa...	3 43	....		Emaus, Pa...	2 70	....	
Bloomsburg, Pa...	5 35	....		Ephrata, Pa., via Bound Brook...	4 83	7 11	5
Bloomsbury, N. J...	1 80	2 90		" limited 2 days, via Bound Bk	4 25	....	
Bound Brook, N. J...	80	1 30		Evona, N. J...	65	1 10	
Bowentown, N. J...	3 35	5 40		Ewing, N. J	1 58	2 75	5
Bowman, N. J	3 25	5 20		Excelsior, Pa., via Tamaqua	4 98	8 46	10
Bradway, N. J	3 25	1 95		" via Bound Brook...	6 43	9 98	10
Bradevelt, N. J. (Hillsdale)...	85	1 50		Exeter, Pa...	4 06	6 07	5
Branchport, N. J...	1 00	1 50		" limited 2 days...	3 65	....	
Brandonville, Pa., via Tamaqua...	4 52	7 51	15	Fairton, N. J...	3 40	5 50	
" via Bound Brook...	6 06	8 75	15	Fanwood, N. J...	35	85	
Breaker No. 10, Pa...	3 85	6 20		Farmingdale, N. J	1 30	2 00	
Bridgeport, Pa...	2 70	4 58	5	Fern Rock, Pa...	2 38	4 01	5
Bridgeton, N. J...	3 25	5 25		Fifth Avenue, (Scranton) Pa...	5 30	8 25	
Brielle, N. J	1 40	2 25		Finderne, N. J...	85	1 40	
Brodhead, Pa...	2 65	4 20		Flagtown, N. J	1 05	1 75	
Califon, N. J	1 60	2 45		Flanders, N. J	1 85	2 75	
Camnal, Pa., limited 2 days, via Tamaqua...	7 50	....		Fleetwood, Pa...	3 83	....	
" lim. 2 days, via Bound Brook	7 90	....		Flemington, N. J...	1 35	2 20	
Carbondale, Pa...	5 30	....		Ford, N. J...	2 45	3 80	
Carteret, N. J...	42	70		Forked River, N. J...	2 20	3 45	
Carys, N. J	1 90	2 80		Ft. Washington, Pa...	2 42	4 30	5
Catasauqua, Pa...	2 70	4 30		Fox Chase, Pa...	2 39	4 06	5
Catawissa, Pa., via Tamaqua...	5 31	8 75	15	Frackville, Pa., via Tamaqua	4 50	7 08	
" via Bound Brook	6 85	9 80	15	" via Bound Brook...	5 56	7 84	
" lim. 2 days, via Bound Bk.	5 31	....		" lim. Bk. lim. 2 days...	4 50	....	
Cedar Creek, N. J...	2 10	3 35		Freehold, N. J...	85	1 35	
Cedar Lake, N. J...	3 00	4 40		Freemansburg, Pa...	2 35	3 75	
Cedar Run, Pa., lim. 2 days, via Tamaqua...	7 50	....		Galileo, N. J., via Sandy Hook...	90	1 45	
" lim. 2 days, via Bound Bk	7 25	....		" all rail...	1 00	1 50	
Cedarville, N. J...	3 50	5 65		Gazzam, Pa., via Tamaqua...	10 32	....	
Centreville, Cumberland Co., N. J...	3 85	6 25		" via Bound Brook...	11 86	....	
" Hudson Co., N. J...	17	23		" limited 2 days, via Bound Bk.	10 32	....	

FARES VIA CENTRAL R. R. OF NEW JERSEY—Continued.

Destination.	First Class Unlimited Rates.	Excursion Ticket Rates.	Time Limit days for Exc. Rates	Destination.	First Class Unlimited Rates.	Excursion Ticket Rates.	Time Limit days for Exc. Rates
Germania, N. J	$1 85	$3 00	...	Linfield, Pa	$3 32	$5 38	5
Germantown, Pa	2 50	4 00	5	Lititz, Pa	5 06	7 42	5
German Valley, N. J	1 75	2 45	...	" limited 2 days	4 18	...	...
Gilberton, Pa., via Tamaqua	4 35	7 20	10	Little Silver, N. J	1 00	1 50	...
" via Bound Brook	5 73	8 41	10	Lock Haven, Pa., via Tamaqua	7 57	12 50	15
Gillintown, Pa., via Tamaqua	8 82	...	...	" via Bound Brook	9 11	13 21	15
" via Bound Brook	10 36	...	...	" lim. 2 days, via Bound Bk	7 57	...	...
" lim. 2 days, via Bound Bk.	8 82	...	...	Lockport, Pa	3 00	4 80	...
Girard Manor, Pa., via Tamaqua	4 40	7 30	10	Locust Dale, Pa., via Tamaqua	4 71	7 98	10
" via Bound Brook	5 94	8 59	10	" via Bound Brook	5 23	9 05	10
Girardville, Pa., via Tamaqua	4 47	7 44	10	Locust Gap, Pa., via Tamaqua	4 85	8 20	10
" via Bound Brook	5 68	8 70	10	" via Bound Brook	6 28	9 19	10
" lim. 2 days, via Bound Bk.	4 47	...	...	Locust Summit, Pa., via Tamaqua	4 82	8 14	10
Glassboro, N. J	3 06	4 85	5	" via Bound Brook	6 28	9 15	10
Glen Gardner, N. J	1 50	2 45	...	Lofty, Pa., (Summit) via Tamaqua	4 26	7 02	15
Glenlake, Pa	1 84	3 21	5	" via Bound Brook	5 80	8 35	15
Glendon, Pa	2 25	3 40	...	Long Branch, N. J	1 00	1 50	...
Glen Onoko, Pa	3 55	5 70	...	Long Reach, N. J	3 95	6 30	...
Gordon, Pa., via Tamaqua	4 62	7 74	10	Look Out, Pa	4 25	6 95	...
" via Bound Brook	6 11	8 80	10	Lost Creek, Pa., via Tamaqua	4 47	7 44	10
Grant Avenue, N. J	60	1 05	...	" via Bound Brook	5 73	8 41	10
Greenville, N. J	11	17	...	Lower Catasauqua, Pa	2 70	4 25	...
Greenwich, N. J	3 50	5 60	...	Low Moor, N. J., via Sandy Hook	90	1 40	...
Halls, Pa., via Tamaqua	6 48	10 61	15	" all rail	1 00	1 50	...
" via Bound Brook	7 91	11 48	15	Mahanoy City, Pa	5 73	8 41	10
Hamburg, Pa., via Bound Brook	4 76	7 02	5	" limited 2 days	4 25	...	...
" lim. 2 days, via Bound Bk.	4 17	...	...	Mahanoy Plane, Pa., via Tamaqua	4 11	7 32	10
Hamilton, N. J	1 00	1 80	5	" via Bound Brook	5 73	8 41	10
Hammonton, N. J	2 88	4 15	10	" lim. 2 days, via Bd. Bk.	4 41	...	...
Hanover, Pa	5 15	7 75	...	Main Avenue, N. J	3 25	4 75	...
Harlingen, N. J	1 14	2 08	5	Mainville, Pa., via Tamaqua	5 12	8 75	15
Harris, Pa	2 35	3 95	...	" via Bound Brook	6 66	9 55	15
Harrisburg, Pa	5 05	9 00	5	Makefield, Pa	1 74	2 99	5
" limited 2 days	5 27	...	...	Manahawken, N. J	2 50	4 08	...
Hauto, Pa	3 75	6 00	...	Mamasquan, N. J	1 10	2 22	...
Hazard, Pa	3 20	5 15	...	Manayunk, Pa	2 50	4 00	5
Hazle St., Pa	5 00	7 50	...	Manchester, N. J	1 70	2 75	...
Hazlet, N. J	75	1 35	...	Manheim, Pa	5 20	7 60	5
Hazleton, Pa	4 29	6 80	...	" limited 2 days	4 55	...	...
Hecla, Pa., via Phillipsburg	4 58	7 56	5	Marlboro, N. J	90	1 00	...
" via Bound Brook	5 17	7 56	5	Matawan, N. J	70	1 25	...
Herndon, Pa., via Tamaqua	5 73	9 96	10	Mauch Chunk, Pa	3 45	5 55	...
" via Bound Brook	7 16	10 20	10	Maurers, N. J	57	95	...
High Bridge, N. J	1 45	2 30	...	Mauricetown, N. J	3 75	6 10	10
Highland Beach, N. J., via Sandy Hook	70	1 20	...	McAuley, Pa., via Tamaqua	5 04	8 58	15
" via all rail	1 00	1 50	...	" via Bound Brook	6 58	9 15	15
Hokendauqua, Pa	2 75	4 35	...	Middletown, N. J	85	1 50	...
Hopatcong Junction	2 05	3 00	...	Middle Valley, N. J	1 70	2 45	...
Hope, Pa	2 25	3 55	...	Mill Creek, Pa	3 00	7 05	...
Hopewell, N. J	1 32	2 44	5	Mill Hall, Pa	9 21	...	...
Hopping, N. J., all rail	1 00	1 50	...	" limited 2 days	7 67	...	...
Horn's Springs, Pa	3 10	1 70	...	Millway, Pa., via Phillipsburg	4 36	7 26	5
Hummelstown, Pa	5 58	8 11	5	" via Bound Brook	4 94	7 26	5
" limited 2 days	4 99	...	...	Milton, Pa., via Tamaqua	6 03	9 74	15
Hurd, N. J	2 35	3 15	...	" via Bound Brook	7 46	10 85	15
Jackson Ave., N. J	10	19	...	" limited 2 days, via Bound Bk.	6 03	...	...
Janney, Pa	1 95	3 41	5	Miner's Mills, Pa	5 00	7 65	...
Janesville, Pa	4 20	6 75	...	Minersville, Pa	5 40	7 86	5
Jeddo, Pa	4 20	6 75	...	" limited 2 days	4 66	...	...
Jenkintown, Pa	2 27	4 00	5	Minnisink, N. J	2 20	3 00	...
Jersey Shore, Pa	8 74	...	...	Minooka, Pa	5 20	8 10	...
" limited 2 days	7 20	...	...	Monmouth Beach, N. J., via Sandy Hook	90	1 45	...
Junction, N. J	1 55	2 50	...	" all rail	1 00	1 50	...
Katellen, Pa	3 05	1 70	...	Monocacy, Pa	3 90	5 87	5
Kenvil, N. J	1 95	2 90	...	" limited 2 days	3 07	...	...
Kerrmoor, Pa	11 83	...	...	Montgomery, Pa., via Tamaqua	6 30	10 40	15
" limited 2 days	10 29	...	...	" via Bound Brook	7 79	11 35	15
Key East, N. J	1 25	2 00	...	" lim. 2 days, via Bd. Bk.	6 36	...	...
Kutztown, Pa	3 21	...	...	Montoursville, Pa., via Tamaqua	6 79	11 28	15
Lafayette, N. J	10	16	...	" via Bound Brook	8 22	11 80	15
Latlin, Pa	5 00	7 75	...	Moores, N. J	1 80	2 58	5
Lake Hopatcong, N. J	2 25	3 00	...	Mooresburg, Pa., via Tamaqua	5 77	9 05	15
Lakewood, N. J	1 45	2 35	...	" via Bound Brook	7 33	10 45	15
Lancaster, Pa	5 52	7 75	5	Moosic, Pa	5 10	7 85	...
" limited 2 days	4 95	...	...	Moraine, N. J	4 15	6 70	...
Landisville, N. J	3 15	4 65	...	Morgan, N. J	70	...	...
Landisville, Pa., via Phillipsburg	4 76	7 75	5	" continuous passage	...	1 15	...
" via Bound Brook	5 34	7 75	5	Morganville, N. J	75	1 35	...
Langhorne, Pa	1 88	3 29	5	Morris Co. Junction	2 05	3 00	...
Lansford, Pa	3 75	6 05	...	Morrisdale Mines, Pa	11 01	...	...
Laurel Run, Pa	4 75	7 50	...	" limited 2 days	9 47	...	...
Laurys, Pa	2 90	1 60	...	Mountain Park, Pa	3 95	...	...
Lebanon, Pa	4 30	2 10	...	Mount Airy, N. J	2 55	4 10	5
Lebanon, Pa	5 08	7 44	5	Mount Carbon, Pa., via Phillipsburg	4 60	7 36	5
" limited 2 days	4 50	...	...	" via Bound Brook	5 28	7 36	5
Leemine, Pa	5 20	7 85	...	Mount Carmel, Pa., via Tamaqua	1 92	8 30	10
Lehigh Gap, Pa	3 15	5 05	...	" via Bound Brook	6 28	9 21	10
Lehighton, Pa	3 35	5 35	...	" lim. 2 days, via Bd. Bk.	4 92	...	...
Leslie Run, Pa	4 00	6 50	...	Mount Pleasant, N. J	75	1 35	...
Lewisburg, Pa., via Tamaqua	5 94	9 87	15	Muncy, Pa., via Tamaqua	6 48	10 64	15
" via Bound Brook	7 37	10 00	15	" via Bound Brook	7 91	11 45	15
" lim. 2 days, via Bound Bk.	5 94	...	...	" limited 2 days, via Bound Bk.	6 48	...	...
Linden, Pa	8 59	...	...	Munson's, Pa	10 89	...	...
" limited 2 days	6 99	...	...	" limited 2 days	9 35	...	...

FARES VIA CENTRAL R. R. OF NEW JERSEY—Continued.

Destination.	First Class Unlimited Rates.	Excursion Ticket Rates.	Time-limit days for Exc. Rates.	Destination.	First Class Unlimited Rates.	Excursion Ticket Rates.	Time-limit days for Exc. Rates.
Myerstown, Pa.	$4 88	$7 18	5	Reading, Pa., via Phillipsburg	$3 67	$6 24	
" limited 2 days	4 30			" via Bound Brook	4 25	6 21	5
Nanticoke, Pa.	5 25	7 85		" limited 2 days via Bound Bk.	3 67		
Naughright, N. J.	1 75	2 60		Red Bank, N. J.	1 00	1 50	
Navesink Beach, N. J., via Sandy Hook	80	1 25		Ricefield, N. J.	1 00	1 65	
" all rail	1 00	1 50		Ringtown, Pa., via Tamaqua	1 65	7 80	15
Nescopec Junction, Pa.	4 15	6 77		" via Bound Brook	6 19	8 95	15
Neshaminy Falls, Pa.	1 96	3 45	5	Rita, Pa.	4 50	7 05	
Neshanic, N. J.	1 15	1 85		Ritter, Pa.	2 00	1 10	
Nesquehoning, Pa.	3 60	5 80		Rittersville, Pa.	2 50	3 95	
Netherwood, N. J.	60	95		Robesonia, Pa.	4 61	6 82	5
Newark, N. J.	15	25	10	" limited 2 days	1 02		
New Columbia, Pa., via Tamaqua	6 10	9 90	15	Rockaway, N. J.	2 20	3 25	
" via Bound Brook	7 53	10 83	15	Rockport, Pa.	3 90	6 30	
New Millport, Pa.	11 82			Roselle, N. J.	30	50	
" limited 2 days	10 28			Rosenhayn, N. J.	5 15	5 29	
Newport, N. J.	3 60	5 85		Royer's Ford, Pa.	3 23	5 27	5
Newtown, Pa.	2 60	4 00	5	Rumson Beach, N. J., via Sandy Hook	80	1 25	
Nicetown, Pa.	2 46	4 00	5	" all rail	1 00	1 50	
Noble, Pa.	2 21	3 99	5	Rupert, Pa., via Tamaqua	5 35	8 75	15
Normandie, N. J. (Bellevue), via Sandy Bk	80	1 25		" via Bound Brook	6 91	9 85	15
" all rail	1 00	1 50		" limited 2 days, via Bound Bk.	5 35		
Norristown, Pa.	2 79	1 58	5	Sandy Hook, N. J., via steamer	60	1 00	
North Asbury Park, N. J.	1 20	1 85		" all rail	1 00	1 50	
North Branch, N. J.	1 05	1 75		Sandy Run, Pa.	1 80	7 70	
North Cedarville, N. J.	3 50	5 65		St. Clair, Pa., via Phillipsburg	4 77	7 48	5
North Hammonton, N. J. (Elm)	2 75	4 60		" via Bound Brook	5 30	7 48	5
N. Long Branch, N. J., via Sandy Hook	95	1 50		" via Tamaqua	4 41	7 32	5
" all rail	1 00	1 50		St. Nicholas, Pa., via Tamaqua	4 29	7 08	10
Northumberland, Pa., via Tamaqua	5 71	9 12	15	" via Bound Brook	5 73	8 11	10
" via Bound Brook	7 14	10 28	15	Schuylkill Haven, Pa., via Phillipsburg	4 58	7 36	5
" lim. 2 days via Bd.Bk.	5 71			" via Bound Brook	5 17	7 36	5
North Wales, Pa.	2 61	4 08	5	" lim. 2 days via Bd.B	4 43		
Ocean Beach, N. J.	1 25	2 00		Scranton, Pa.	5 30	8 25	
Ocean Grove, N. J.	1 20	1 85		Seabright, N. J., via Sandy Hook	85	1 35	
Oceanport, N. J.	1 00	1 50		" all rail	1 00	1 50	
Odenwelder, Pa.	2 15	3 10		Sea Girt, N. J.	1 35	2 15	
Ogden, N. J.	2 60	3 55		Sewaren, N. J.	52	85	
Ogontz	2 32	4 00	5	Shamokin, Pa., via Tamaqua	5 10	8 70	10
Olanta, Pa	11 55			" via Bound Brook	6 53	9 54	10
" limited 2 days	10 21			" lim. 2 days, via Bound Bk.	5 10		
Ostrom, N. J.	2 20	3 50		Shamong, N. J.	2 25	3 95	
Pamrapo, N. J.	19	20		Shark River, N. J.	1 30	1 80	
Parkdale, N. J.	2 70	4 00		Sheldon Pa.	5 00	7 65	
Parryville, Pa	3 30	5 25		Shenandoah, Pa., via Tamaqua	4 47	8 41	10
Parsons, Pa.	5 00	7 65		" via Bound Brook	5 73	8 41	10
Paul Brook, Pa	2 18	3 85	5	" lim. 2 days via Bound Bk.	4 47		
Paxinos, Pa., via Tamaqua	5 27	9 00	15	Sheppard's Mills, N. J.	3 15	5 55	
" via Bound Brook	6 69	9 75	15	Sheridan, Pa., via Phillipsburg	4 17	7 00	5
Peale, Pa.	9 43			" via Bound Brook	5 10	7 00	5
" limited 2 days	10 67			Shimer, Pa.	1 55	4 05	
Pen-Argyl, Pa.	2 20	4 70		Shrewsbury, N. J.	95	1 50	
Penn Haven, Pa.	3 65	5 90		Siegfried, Pa.	2 80	1 45	
Penn Haven Junc., Pa	3 65	5 90		Skillman, N. J.	1 22	2 24	5
Pennington, N. J.	1 46	2 72	5	Slatington, Pa.	3 05	4 80	
Penobscot, Pa.	1 60	7 15		Snow Shoe, Pa.	10 25		
Perth Amboy, N. J.	60	1 00		" limited 2 days	8 71		
Philadelphia, Pa.	2 50	4 00	5	Solomon's Gap, Pa.	1 60	7 50	
Phillipsburg, N. J.	2 05	3 25		Somerton, Pa.	2 05	3 63	5
Philipsburg, Pa.	10 91			Somerville, N. J.	1 00	1 50	
" limited 2 days	9 40			South Amboy, N. J.	70		
Philmont, Pa.	2 10	3 73	5	" continuous passage		1 10	
Phœnixville, Pa.	3 11	5 08	5	South Wilkesbarre, Pa.	5 00	7 50	
Pine Brook, N. J.	1 05	1 60		Spring Lake, N. J.	1 30	2 10	
Pine Grove, Pa	5 52	8 39	5	Spring St., N. J.	25	40	10
" limited 2 days	5 21			Springtown, N. J.	1 90	3 05	
Pittston, Pa.	5 00	7 75		Squankum, N. J.	1 35	2 05	
Plainfield, N. J.	60	1 00		Stemton, Pa.	2 75	4 40	
Pleasant Valley, Pa.	5 30	7 90		Steuben, Pa.	2 70	4 25	
Pleasantville, N. J. (Absecom)	3 25	1 75	10	Stockton, Pa.	4 30	6 70	
Point Phillipp, Pa	2 05	4 65		Stoutsburg, N. J.	1 27	2 34	5
Point Pleasant, N. J.	1 45	2 35		Sugar Notch, Pa.	5 05	7 60	
Pomona, N. J.	3 25	4 75	10	Sunbury, Pa., via Tamaqua	5 66	9 00	15
Pond Creek Junction, Pa.	4 30	7 00		" via Bound Brook	7 09	10 20	15
Port Carbon, Pa., via Phillipsburg	4 71	7 36	5	" limited 2 days	5 66		
" via Bound Brook	5 30	7 36	5	Switch Back, without stage		6 00	
" via Tamaqua	4 32	7 11	5	Tamanend, Pa., via Tamaqua	4 16	6 93	5
Port Clinton, Pa.	4 84	7 12	5	" via Bound Brook	5 70	8 27	15
" limited 2 days	4 25			Tamaqua, Pa.	3 90	6 30	
Port Monmouth, N. J.	1 00	1 50		Tannery, Pa.	4 15	6 70	
Port Norris, N. J.	3 80	6 25		Taylorville, Pa.	5 30	7 95	
Port Oram, N. J.	2 05	3 05		Three Bridges, N. J.	1 25	2 05	
Pottsgrove, Pa., via Tamaqua	5 92	9 70	15	Tioga, Pa.	2 47	4 00	5
" via Bound Brook	7 46	10 65	15	Tivoli, Pa.	6 73	10 10	15
Pottstown, Pa.	3 17	5 20	5	Toms River, N. J.	1 80	3 00	
Pottsville, Pa., via Bound Brook	5 30	7 36	5	Topton, Pa.	3 11	5 12	5
" lim. 2 days, via Bound Bk.	1 43			Tower City, Pa., via Phillipsburg	4 75	9 11	5
" via Tamaqua	4 43	7 36	5	" via Bound Brook	6 39	9 11	5
Prospect Rock, Pa	5 00	7 50		Township Line, Pa.	2 75	4 35	
Quakake, Pa., via Tamaqua	4 17	6 84	15	Treichler, Pa.	2 90	4 65	
" via Bound Brook	5 71	8 35	15	Tremley, N. J.	37	60	
Quakertown, Pa., via Bound Brook	3 15			Tremont, Pa.	6 02	8 70	5
" via Bethlehem Junc.	2 95			" limited 2 days	5 41		
Raritan, N. J.	95	1 60		Trenton, N. J.	1 70	2 75	5

FARES VIA CENTRAL R. R. OF NEW JERSEY.—Continued.

Destination.	First Class Unlimited Rates.	Excursion Ticket Rates.	Time Limit days for Exc. Rates.	Destination.	First Class Unlimited Rates.	Excursion Ticket Rates.	Time Limit days for Exc. Rates.
Trenton Junction, N. J.	$1 61	$2 75	5	West Milton, Pa., via Tamaqua	$6 03	$9 74	15
Trevorton, Pa., via Tamaqua	5 33	9 26	10	" via Bound Brook	7 46	10 85	15
" via Bound Brook	6 76	9 83	10	Weston, N. J.	92	1 64	5
Trevose, Pa.	2 00	3 54	5	Wheatland, N. J.	1 95	3 55	...
Tuckerton, N. J.	2 75	4 50	...	Wheat Road, N. J.	3 20	4 75	...
Tunnel, Pa.	4 35	7 05	...	White Deer, Pa., (Watsontown) v. Tamaqua	6 16	10 00	15
Upper Lehigh, Pa.	4 50	7 30	...	" lim. 2 days, v. B.B.	6 85	...	...
Valley, N. J.	1 75	2 75	...	White Haven, Pa.	4 20	6 75	...
Vernoy, N. J.	1 65	2 45	...	White House, N. J.	1 20	1 95	...
Vineland, N. J.	3 25	4 75	...	Whites, N. J.	1 65	2 55	...
Wallaceton, Pa.	11 14	...	...	Whitings, N. J.	1 85	3 25	...
" limited 2 days	9 60	...	...	Wickatunck, N. J.	80	1 45	...
Walnut Lane, Pa.	2 50	4 00	5	Wilkesbarre, Pa.	5 00	7 50	...
Walnutport, Pa.	3 05	4 90	5	William Penn, Pa., via Tamaqua	1 47	7 14	10
Wanamie, Pa.	5 25	7 85	...	" via Bound Brook	5 73	8 41	10
Warctown, N. J.	2 25	3 65	...	Williamsport, Pa., via Tamaqua	6 85	11 38	15
Warrior Run, Pa.	5 10	7 65	...	" via Bound Brook	8 28	12 00	15
Waterville, Pa., via Tamaqua	7 00	...	...	" lim. 2 days, via B'd Brook.	6 85	...	...
" lim. 2 days, via Tamaqua.	7 50	...	...	Williamstown, N. J.	3 06	4 85	5
" lim. 2 days, via B'd Brook	7 60	...	...	Wind Gap, Pa.	3 20	4 70	...
Wayne, Pa.	8 07	...	...	Winfield, Pa., via Tamaqua	5 82	9 84	15
" limited 2 days	7 43	...	...	" via Bound Brook	7 25	10 50	15
Wayne Junction, Pa.	2 14	4 00	5	Winslow, N. J.	2 85	4 10	...
Weissport, Pa.	3 35	5 35	...	Winslow Junction, N. J.	2 80	4 00	...
Weldon, N. J.	2 40	3 25	...	Womelsdorf, Pa., via Phillipsburg	4 09	6 91	5
Wernersville, Pa.	4 51	6 68	5	" via Bound Brook	4 66	6 91	5
" limited 2 days	3 92	...	...	Woodbourne, Pa.	1 81	3 13	5
West Bangor, Pa.	3 25	4 70	...	Woodfern, N. J.	1 20	1 95	...
West Bergen, N. J.	10	16	...	Woodland, Pa.	11 20	...	...
Westcotts, N. J.	3 45	5 60	...	" limited 2 days	9 60	...	...
West Creek, N. J.	1 65	4 30	...	Woodmansie, N. J.	2 05	3 70	...
West End, N. J.	1 00	1 50	...	Woodruffs, N. J.	3 25	5 25	...
Westfield, N. J.	50	75	...	Yardley, Pa.	1 68	2 87	5
West Falls, Pa.	2 50	4 00	5	Yatesville, Pa.	5 00	7 75	...

CLUBS.

☞ *We will consider it a favor if our patrons will notify us of any error or omission they may discover in this list.*

Aldine, 20 Lafayette pl.
American Athletic, 6th Av. cor. 112th.
American Jockey, 22 E. 27th.
American Kennel, 44 Broadway.
American Yacht, Milton Point, Rye, N.Y.
Anawanda, 345 Second Ave.
Arion, Park Ave., cor. E. 59th.
Arlington League, 242 W. 14th.
Atlanta Boat, 8th Ave., cor. W. 159th.
Atlantic Yacht, Bay Ridge, L. I
Authors', 19 W. 24th.
Balfe Musical, 263 Bowery.
Berkeley Athletic, 19 W. 44th.
Berkeley Lyceum, 14 W. 44th.
Bloomingdale Boat, 740 9th av. & ft. w. 83d.
Boys', 125 St. Mark's Pl.
Caledonian, 10 Horatio.
Calumet, 267 Fifth Ave.
Canadian, 12 E. 29th.
Canteen, 41 Liberty.
Catholic, 20 W. 27th.
Century, 109 E. 15th.
Cercle Francais de l'Harmonie, 38 Clinton Place.
Chess, 49 Bowery.
Citizens' Bicycle, 26 W. 60th.
City Reform, 35 Liberty.
Clergy, 29 Lafayette Place.
Collie of America, 44 Broadway.
Columbus, 52 Lexington Ave.
Columbia College Boat, at W. 150th St.
Columbia Working Girls, 245 W. 55th.
Columbia Yacht, foot W. 86th.
Coney Island Jockey, 173 Fifth Ave.
Congregational, 22 W. 23d.
Contra Bass, 70 E. 4th.
Cosmos, Washington sq., cor. Waverly pl.
Dauntless Rowing, 147th, cor. 6th Av.
Delta, 68 E. 49th.
Delta Kappa Epsilon, 435 Fifth Ave.
Delta Phi, 5 E. 47th.
Delta Upsilon, 8 E. 47th.
Deutscher Press Club, 9 Centre.
Down Town Association, 60 Pine.
Downtown (H. M. B. A.), 67 New.
Eagle Athletic, E. 134th, cor. Park Ave.
Eastern Boulevard, 519 E. 121st.
Eclipse Yacht, foot E. 102d.
Electric, 17 E. 22d.
Elks, 51 Union Place.
Equity, 225 Avenue C.
Etching, 51 W. 10th.
Falcon Boat & Athletic, ft. W. 77th.
Fanciers, 218 Fulton.
Federal, 629 Madison Ave.

Fellowcraft, 32 W. 28th.
Fidelio, 816 Fifth Ave.
Fordham, Creston Av., n. Welch.
Forty, 141 W. 42d.
Free Trade, 39 Nassau.
Friendship Boat, foot E. 132d.
Fulton, Bank Building, Fulton & Gold.
German, 13 W. 24th.
Girls' Endeavor, 59 Morton.
Gotham, 624 Madison Ave.
Graduate Asn. Alpha Delta Phi, 427 4th av
Gramercy Boat, E. 13th, cor. Park Ave.
Grolier, 64 Madison Ave.
Hamilton Republic, 211 W. 126th.
Hancock, 322 W. 59th.
Harlem, 2056 Fifth Ave.
Harlem Democratic, 15 E. 125th.
Harlem Republican, 24 E. 125th.
Harmonic, 45 W. 42d.
Harvard, 11 W. 22d.
Hide and Leather, 1 Ferry.
Hoffman, 16 W. 25th.
Home, 21 W. 24th.
Hoot, 16 University Building.
Hudson River Yacht, foot W. 74th.
Independent Walhalla Boat, 52 Orchard.
Jockey, 22 E. 27th.
Kennel, 44 Broadway.
Kindly, 19 E. 16th.
Kit Kat, 23 E. 14th.
Knickerbocker, 319 Fifth Ave.
Knickerbocker Canoe, ft. W. 152d.
Knickerbocker Yacht, Port Morris.
Lambs, 34 W. 26th.
Larchmont Yacht, 57 Madison Ave.
Lawyers', 120 Broadway.
Lincoln, 56 Clinton Place.
Long Island Jockey, 132 Nassau.
Lotos, 149 Fifth Ave.
Manhattan, 96 Fifth Ave.
Manhattan Athletic, Madison Av. & 45th
Manhattan Bicycle, 263 W. 70th.
Manhattan Chess, 22 E. 17th.
Manhattan Yacht, foot E. 89th.
Mendelssohn Glee, 108 W. 55th.
Merchants', 108 Leonard.
Metropolitan, 756 Fifth Ave.
Metropolitan Rowing, 133d. cor. Lex. Av.
Monmouth Park Assn., 22 E. 27th.
Morningside Park, Murray Hill Hotel.
Musical, Social, Cricket, 83 E. 4th.
Narragansett, 307 W. 54th.
Nassau Boat, foot E. 132d.
New Amsterdam, 11 W. 24th.
New Rochelle Yacht, Echo Island.

New York, 2 W. 35th.
N. Y. Athletic, 104 W. 55th; Boat house, Travers Island.
N. Y. Bicycle, 302 W. 58th.
N. Y. Republican, 450 Fifth Ave.
N. Y. Yacht, 67 Madison Ave.
N. Y. Whist, 20 E. 27th.
Nonpareil Rowing, 133d, cor. Park Av.
North Side Republican, 2,661 3d Av.
Olympic Athletic, 8th Av., cor. 86th.
Oriental, 443 Grand.
Owl, 806 Eighth Ave.
Pastime Athletic, foot E. 66th.
Phœnix, 146 Fifth Ave.
Players' Club, 16 Gramercy Park.
Press, 120 Nassau.
Progress, 110 E. 59th.
After Oct. '88, at 5th Ave. and 63d St.
Psi Upsilon, 33 E. 42d.
Racquet, 55 W. 26th.
Railroad, 113 Liberty.
Reform, 12 E. 33d.
Religious Press Club, 38 Park Row.
Republican, 450 Fifth Ave.
Riding, 7 E. 58th.
Riverside, 70 W. 104th.
Rockaway Steeplechase, 13 Park Row.
St. Anthony, 29 E. 28th.
St. Nicholas, 386 Fifth Ave.
Seawanhaka Corinthian Yacht, 7 E. 32d, and Stapleton, S. I.
Shanghai, 73 Eighth Ave.
Sigma Phi, 9 E. 27th.
Sorosis, 212 Fifth Ave.
Stuyvesant Democratic, 176 E. 106th.
Swiss, 73 E. Fourth.
Tennis, 21 W. 41st.
The Lambs, 34 W. 26th.
Thirteen, 6 W. 28th.
Torrey Botanical, E. 49th, n. Park Ave.
Union, 1 W. 21st.
Union Boat, E. 134th, cor. Park Ave.
Union League, 1 E. 39th
Union Square, 50 Union Square, E.
University, 32 E. 26th.
Veteran, 139 Grand.
Waverly Boat, foot W. 75th.
West Side Athletic, 329 W. 54th.
Wyanoke Boat, 192 3d Av. & ft. E. 132d.
Yorkville Yacht, foot E. 115th.
Young Men's Democratic, Hoffman H.
Young Men's Independent, 146 E. 59th.
Young Men's Prohibition, 107 W. 34th.
Zeta Psi, 8 W. 29th.

FOREIGN TELEGRAPH RATES.

☞ The publisher is indebted to the Western Union Telegraph Co. for the very complete telegraph information contained in this Guide.

ATLANTIC CABLES.

CENTRAL CABLE OFFICE, 16 BROAD STREET, NEW YORK.

Tariff from New York City to Great Britain, Ireland, France and Germany, 25 cents per word.

NOTE.—Messages to places beyond England and France are forwarded by the cheapest route, unless specially directed by any other. When there is more than one route to the same place at the same charge, and messages are not specially directed via any particular one, they are forwarded via the best one, at the discretion of the telegraph officials.

Senders can ensure their messages being forwarded by any particular route, such as "via Siberia," "via Santander," "via Teheran," etc., by inserting the indication of route in the "Check." The indication is transmitted free of charge.

Messages destined to places beyond the lines of telegraph must contain instructions from the sender as to the name of the place from which they are to be posted. The charge for postage is 37 cents.

Rules for Atlantic Cable Business.

1.—The maximum length of a chargeable word will be fixed at 10 letters. Should a word contain more than 10 letters, every 10, or fraction of 10 letters will be counted as a word.

2.—Code words must be composed of words in the English, French, German, Spanish, Italian, Dutch, Portuguese or Latin languages. Proper names (i. e., of persons and places), will not be allowed in the text of Code Messages, except in the manner they are used in ordinary private messages.

3.—Groups of figures or letters will be counted at the rate of three figures or letters to a word, plus one word for any excess.

AFRICA.

From New York, per word.

Algeria and **Tunisia**.	$ 33
do do via Eastern	52
Assab—(Secret language prohibited)	1 19
Benghazi—Messages can be posted at Malta.	
Egypt—Alexandria	58
Cairo, Port Said, Suez Canal Stations and L'r Egypt.	63
Suakin (by Red Sea Cable)	86
do via Brest or Marseilles	81
All other offices	68
Massowah—(Secret language prohibited)	1 21
Morocco—Tangiers	45
Messages for other places can be posted at Tangiers.	
Tripoli—(Secret language prohibited.)	
Tripoli	53
All other offices	50
South Africa—via Aden:	
Cape Colony	2 43
Delagoa Bay	2 41
Griqualand, West	2 43
Mozambique	2 41
Natal—Durban	2 39
All other offices	2 43
Orange Free State	2 43
Transvaal	2 43
Zanzibar	2 15

From New York, per word.

	via Cadiz and Canaries.	via Lisbon and St. Vincent.
West Coast of Africa—		
Accra	$2 21	$2 21
Bathurst	1 70	1 70
Bissao	2 19	2 46
Bolama	2 19	2 46
Bonny	2 02	2 02
Brass	2 62	2 62
Cape Coast Castle	2 25	2 25
Conakry	2 19	2 52
Elmina	2 25	2 25
Gaboon	3 07	3 27
Grand Bassam	2 39	2 94
Lagos	2 41	3 15
Loanda	2 78	3 68
Porto Novo	2 86	3 15
Principe	2 21	3 33
Salt Pond	2 25	2 25
San Thomas	3 01	3 19
Senegal	1 04	2 15
Sierra Leone	1 90	1 90
Whydah	2 25	2 25

EUROPE, ASIA, AUSTRALASIA, ETC.

Annam—via Eastern or Indo. (Secret language prohibited.)	
Thuan-an, Hué and all offices	$1 80
do do do via Northern (Siberia).	2 78
Arabia Aden and Perim Island	$1 17
Djedda, Mecca and all Hedjaz. (Secret language prohibited)	1 17
Muscat—Messages can be posted from Gwadur in Beloochistan. Insert before the address and charge for the words "Post Gwadur." Messages can also be sent by special boat from Jask, in Persia. Insert before the address and charge for the words "Boat paid Jask." Extra charge for boat hire, $13.72 in addition to the rate to Jask.	
Yemen—Messages can be sent by express from Aden. Insert "Express Aden," before the address. The express charges are collected from the addressee.	
Ascension Island—Messages can be posted at Madeira or Lisbon.	
Australia—via Eastern or Indo:	
New South Wales	$2 58
Queensland	2 64
South Australia, Victoria and Western Australia.	2 54
Tasmania	2 68
Do via Northern (Siberia):	
New South Wales	3 49
Queensland	3 56
South Australia, Victoria and Western Australia.	3 45
Tasmania	3 60
Austria (Hungary	36
Azores—Messages can be posted at Lisbon.	
Balearic Islands—Same as to Spain.	
Belgium	31
Beloochistan (South)—Gwadur and all offices on coast.	1 17
Gwadur and all offices on coast, via Bombay	1 41
Bocicieng, Bali Island	1 92
Bokhara	74
Borneo—Messages can be posted at Singapore.	
Bosnia—Herzegovina. (Secret language prohibited).	47
Bulgaria	49
Burmah (Upper and Lower)—via Eastern or Indo:	
Mandalay, Rangoon and all offices east of Chittagong	1 37
do do do via Penang.	1 94
Canary Islands—Teneriffe, Palma and Grand Canary	72
Cape Verde Islands—St. Vincent	96
St. Jago	1 19
Ceylon—via Eastern or Indo	1 37
Channel Islands—Same as to Great Britain.	
China—via Eastern, Indo or Northern (Siberia):	
Amoy, Foochow, Gutzlaff, Hong Kong and Shanghai.	1 70
Canton and Macao	2 09
All other offices, including Formosa and Pescadore Islands	2 39
Cochin China—via Eastern or Indo	1 64
Do via Northern (Siberia)	2 60

FOREIGN TELEGRAPH RATES.—Continued.

	Per Word.
Corea—*via* Northern (Siberia):	
Fusan (by cable from Japan)	$2 56
do (by land lines from China)	2 78
Seoul (by cable from Japan)	2 76
Seoul (by land lines from China)	2 56
All other offices (by land lines from China)	2 56
Corea—*via* Eastern or Indo:	
Fusan (by cable from Japan)	3 27
do (by land lines from China)	2 78
Seoul (by cable from Japan)	3 47
do (by land lines from China)	2 56
All other offices (by land lines from China)	2 56
Corfu	39
Corsica—Same as to France.	
Cyprus	58
Denmark	35
Falkland Islands—Messages can be posted at Monte Video.	
Formosa Islands—See China.	
Gibraltar	43
Greece and Islands	40
Heligoland Island	38
Herzegovina—(Secret language prohibited)	37
Holland	33
Hungary	36
Iceland—Messages can be posted at Leith (Scotland).	
India—*via* Eastern or Indo	1 31
Do *via* Northern (Siberia)	3 43
Italy, Sicily, Sardinia	34
Japan—*via* Northern (Siberia):	
Tsushima Island (by cable from Japan)	2 56
All other offices	2 21
Do *via* Eastern or Indo:	
Tsushima Island (by cable from Japan)	3 27
All other offices	2 86
Java—*via* Eastern or Indo	1 92
Do *via* Northern (Siberia)	2 90
Labuan Island—Messages can be posted at Singapore.	
Luxemburg	31
Macassar, Celebes Island	1 92
Madagascar—Messages can be posted at Aden.	
Madeira Island	50
Malay Peninsula—*via* Eastern or Indo:	
Malacca	1 78
Perak	1 66
Selangor	1 88
Sungie Ujong	1 88
Do.—*via* Northern (Siberia):	
Malacca	2 80
Perak	2 84
Malta	39
Mauritius Island—Messages can be posted at Aden or Durban.	
Montenegro—(Secret language prohibited)	37
New Caledonia—Messages can be posted at Sydney.	
New Hebrides—Messages can be posted at Sydney.	
New Zealand—*via* Eastern or Indo	2 82
Do *via* Northern (Siberia)	3 74
Norway	35
Penang—*via* Eastern or Indo	1 62
Do *via* Northern (Siberia)	2 90
Perim Island	1 17
Persia—Bushire (Persian Gulf)	86
Jask (Persian Gulf)	1 17
Jask, *via* Bombay (in case of interruption to Persian Gulf Cables)	1 41
All other offices	64
Bunder Abbas, Bassidore, Lingah.—Messages to these places can be sent by special boat from Jask. Insert before the address and charge for the words "Express paid Jask." Extra charge for boat hire in addition to rate to Jask: To Bunder Abbas, $7.84; Bassidore and Lingah, $11.76. Code and cipher may be accepted to Bushire, Chiraz, Ispahan, Kirkmanschah, Salmas, Tauris and Teheran. To all other places messages must be written in French and in plain language. They will be translated at Teheran and forwarded to their destination in Persian.	
Pescadore Islands—Makong. Same as to China.	
Philippine Islands—*via* Eastern, Indo or Northern (Siberia).	
Luzon, Manilla and all offices	2 46
Portugal	39
Reunion Island (Bourbon)—Messages can be posted at Aden or Durban.	
Rodriguez Island—Messages can be posted at Aden.	
Roumania—(Secret language prohibited.)	37
Russia, in Europe	45
Do Caucasus	50
Russia, in Asia (Siberia).	
1st region West of Werkbne Oudinsk	68
2d do East do do	90
St. Helena Island—Messages can be posted at Madeira.	
Sardinia—See Italy.	
Servia—(Secret language prohibited)	$ 37
Seychelle Islands—Messages can be posted at Aden.	
Siam—*via* Eastern or Indo:	
Bangkok and all offices *via* Moulmein	1 43
Do do *via* Saigon	1 76
Do—*via* Northern (Siberia)	2 72
Sicily—See Italy	
Singapore—*via* Eastern or Indo	1 82
Do *via* Northern (Siberia)	2 70
Spain—	
Barcelona, *via* France and Marseilles cable	39
All other offices *via* Eastern, direct Spanish, or Submarine	41
Sumatra—*via* Eastern or Indo	1 92
Do *via* Northern (Siberia)	2 90
Sweden	39
Switzerland	31
Tonquin—*via* Eastern or Indo. (Secret language prohibited.)	
Haiphong and all offices	1 90
Do do *via* Northern (Siberia)	2 04
Turkey in Europe. (Secret language prohibited).	39
Turkey in Asia and Islands—(Secret language prohibited)	49

SOUTH AMERICA.

Argentine Republic	1 97
Bolivia—La Paz	3 72
All other offices	2 13
Brazil—Pernambuco	1 72
Fortaleza, Maranham, Para and all offices between Pernambuco and Para (Région du Nord)	2 66
Rio de Janeiro and all offices between Rio and Pernambuco (Région du Centre)	1 92
All offices south of Rio de Janeiro (Région du Sud)	2 13
Chili	2 41
Colombia (United States of):	
Buenaventura	1 91
Colon	1 95
Panama	1 95
All other offices	1 95
Ecuador—St. Helena and Guayaquil	4 62
Paraguay	1 97
Peru—Arequipa, Islay, Mollendo and Puno	3 60
Callao, Lima and Chorillos	4 05
Payta	4 02
Uruguay—Montevideo, etc.	2 91

CENTRAL AMERICA.

Costa Rica	6 80
Guatemala	7 03
Honduras (Independent)	7 03
Nicaragua—San Juan del Sur	6 71
All other offices	6 80
San Salvador—La Libertad	6 97
All other offices	7 03

CUBA CABLES.

Cuba, The West Indies, Mexico, Central America and South America, via Key West.

RATES.

From New York City to Cuba, Havana, 50 cents per word.

Cuba, other places.

To the following named places in Cuba, charge the above given Havana rate *per word* for all words in the message; and add thereto forty cents for each ten or fraction of ten words, allowing five for free words in the address, "place to," and signature. (The Government lines beyond Havana make no charge for the address "place to," and signature, if comprised in five words, but all words over five and *all* the body words are counted and charged for.)

Aserradero.	Colon.
Aguada de Pasageros.	Consolacion del Sur.
Alfonso Doce.	Contramaestre.
Bahia Honda.	Corral Falso de Macuriges.
Baitiquira.	Corvalillo.
Baracoa.	Cristo.
Batabanó.	Dos Palmas.
Bayamo.	Fray Benito.
Bejucal.	Guaimaro.
Cabañas.	Guano.
Caibarien.	Guanabacoa.
Caimanera.	Guanajay.
Camajuani.	Guantanamo.*
Cardenas.	Guane.
Canto Abajo.	Guaracabulla.
Cauto Embarcadero.	Güines.
Cayo Damas.	Hato Nuevo.
Chambas.	Holguin.
Ciego de Avila.	Jaruco.
Cobre.	Jibara.

FOREIGN TELEGRAPH RATES.—Continued.

Cuba, other places.—Continued.

Jiguani.
Jovellanos.
Júcaro.
Jumento.
Las Cruces.
Los Abreus.
Macagua.
Mantua.
Manzanillo.*
Marianao.
Mariel.
Matanzas.
Mayari Abajo.
Minas de Principe.
Moron de Ciego.
Neuvetas.
Palmo Soriano.
Pinar del Rio.
Placetas.
Puerto Padre.
Puerto Principe.
Quemado de Güines.
Rancho Veloz.
Regla.
Remanganaguas.
Remedios.

Sabanilla de Songo.
Sagua de Tanamo.
Sagua la Grande.
San Augustin.
San Andres.
San Antonio de los Baños.
San Cristobal.
Sancti Spiritus.
San Geronimo.
San Juan y Martinez.
San Luis de Enramadas.
San Miguel de Neuvitas.
Santa Clara.
Santa Cruz del Sur.
Santa Isabel de Nipe.
Santo Domingo.
Sierra Morena.
Trinidad.
Tunas de Zaza.
Union de Reyes.
Veguita.
Victoria de las Tunas.
Yaguajay.
Yaguaramas.
Ysabela de Sagua.

* To Guantanamo and Manzanillo an additional charge of $3.00 for ten words, and 30 cents for each word over ten, should be made.

To the following named places in Cuba, charge the Havana rate per word, and add thereto sixty cents for each ten or fraction of ten words; allowing for five free words, in the address, " place to," and signature as in the case of messages to places named above :

Alquizar,
Artemisa,
Calabazar,
Cañas
Candelaria,
Gabriel,
Guira de Melena,
Herradura,

Jovellar,
Los Palacios,
Paso Real de San Diego,
Pinos,
Rincon,
Salud,
Santiago de las Vegas.
Taco Taco.

To Cienfuegos and Santiago in Cuba, and places in West Indies beyond Cuba.

Per Word.
†**Cienfuegos**.................................. $ 44
†**Santiago**..................................... 44
Hayti—Mole St. Nicholas................ 1 67
   Other places 25 cts., post Mole, St. Nicholas.
San Domingo................................ 2 17
Curacao....................................... 2 25
Venezuela.
   La Guayra................................... 2 42
   Other offices................................. 2 43
‡‡**Jamaica**—Kingston and Holland Bay.. 1 35
**Porto Rico—San Juan.................. 2 08
   Do   —Other places.
St. Thomas................................... 2 17
St. Croix...................................... 2 22
St. Christopher or St. Kitts............. 2 35
Antigua.. 2 41
Guadaloupe—Basse Terre................ 2 49
   Do   Point a Pitre........................ 2 51
Dominica...................................... 2 55
Martinique—Fort de France.............. 2 60
   Do   St. Pierre............................. 2 60
St. Lucia....................................... 2 66
St. Vincent................................... 2 73
Grenada....................................... 2 83
Barbadoes.................................... 2 84
Trinidad—Port of Spain.................... 2 94
   Do   Other places........................ 2 96

†To the word rate to Cienfuegos add $2.25, for ten words or less and 22 cents for each word over ten. To the word rate to Santiago add $3 for ten words or less, and 30 cents for each word over ten.

‡‡The name of " place to " and name of the Island must be given in address, and must be counted and charged for. For messages to all places in Jamaica other than Kingston and Holland Bay collect 25 cents for twenty words, and 6 cents for each additional five or part of five words in addition to the rates to Kingston.

**Charge rate to San Juan, and then add 6 cents per word for all words except five in the address, " place to," and signature, which five words are sent free over Government lines in Port Rico. The name of " place to " and name of Island must be given in the address.

CENTRAL AND SOUTH AMERICA.

South America :   Per Word.
Colon (Aspinwall)........................ $ 97
Panama...................................... 97
Demerara (English Guiana)........... 3 36
Berbice (English Guiana).............. 3 38
Georgetown (English Guiana)........ 3 36

To Central and South America *via* Galveston, Tex., from New York City *via* Central America and South American Cables.

Central America.

Salvador.
   La Libertad................................. $ 72
   Other offices in Salvador................ 77
Guatemala.
   All offices in Guatemala................. 77
Honduras.
   All offices in Honduras.................. 77
Nicaragua.
   San Juan del Sur.......................... 97
   Other offices in Nicaragua.............. 1 02
Costa Rica.
   All offices in Costa Rica................. 1 02

South America.

U. S. of Columbia.
   Colon (Aspinwall)......................... $ 97
   Panama...................................... 97
   Buenaventura.............................. 1 00
   Other Offices in U. S. of Col........... 1 14
Ecuador—St. Elena........................ $1 74
   Guayaquil.................................... 1 71
   Ballenita. Address messages " Ballenita St. Elena " 1 84
   Other offices in Ecuador................ 1 84
Peru—Arequipa............................. 2 66
   Callao... 1 83
   Chancay..................................... 1 83
   Chicla... 1 83
   Chorillos..................................... 1 72
   Chosica...................................... 1 83
   Huacho....................................... 1 83
   Islay.. 1 66
   Lima.. 1 72
   Matucana................................... 1 83
   Mollendo.................................... 2 44
   Payta... 1 89
   Piura (Code and cipher accepted subject to censorship).. 2 09
   Puno.. 2 66
   San Bartolome............................ 1 83
   San Mateo.................................. 1 83
   Santa Clara................................ 1 83
   Supe.. 1 83
   Surco... 1 83
Bolivia—All offices.......................... 2 09
Chili—All offices............................. 2 25
Argentine Republic—Buenos Ayres and all other stations.................................... 1 82
Uruguay—All offices........................ 2 00
Paraguay—Assumpcion and all other stations... 1 82
Brazil—Aracaju............................... 1 89
   Banis... 1 89
   Fortaleza (Ceara)......................... 2 59
   Maranham................................. 2 59
   Maroim...................................... 1 89
   Natal... 1 89
   Para... 2 59
   Parahyba................................... 1 89
   Pernambuco............................... 1 69
   Pelotas....................................... 2 09
   Rio de Janeiro............................. 2 09
   Rio Grande do Sul....................... 2 09
   Santa Catarina........................... 2 09
   Santos....................................... 2 09
   Other offices north of Rio Janeiro.... 1 89
   "   "   south...................... 2 09

Examine the Index and make yourself familiar with the Contents of this Guide. You will find it a valuable compendium of useful information.

CENTRAL R. R. OF NEW JERSEY.

Depot foot of Liberty St., North River.

For "Fares to all Places," see Index.

Tickets, etc., can be procured at the following offices: 71, 261, 415, 944, 1140, 1323 Broadway, 737 Sixth Avenue, 264 W. 125th St., 132 E. 125th St. In Brooklyn: at 4 Court St., 860 Fulton St.; 98 Broadway, Williamsburg.

Fare—New York to Philadelphia, $2.50, Exc., $4.00; Baltimore, $5.30, Exc., $8.00; to Washington, $6.50, Exc., $10.00.

New York to Philadelphia, Baltimore and Washington.

LEAVE	AM	AM	AM	AM	AM	PM	PM	PM	PM	PM	PM	PM	M'd't	SUNDAYS ONLY.		
														AM	PM	PM
New York, foot Liberty street	1 00	7 45	*8 30	9 30	11 00	*1 30	2 30	3 15	1 00	*4 45	5 30	7 30	12 00	9 30	2 30	6 30
Bound Brook	3 35	8 40	9 26	10 30	11 55	2 27	3 25	4 10	4 53	5 37	6 29	8 31	1 19	11 02	3 25	7 39
Trenton	Arrive 6 50	9 30	10 12	11 17	12 35	3 15	4 12	4 52	5 33	6 22	7 16	9 21	2 40	11 54	4 12	8 12
Germantown	8 30	10 00	11 23	12 25	1 34	3 59	5 02	5 30	6 08	7 25	8 16	10 11		1 21	5 40	10 10
Chestnut Hill	8 45	10 35	11 40	12 30	1 46	4 15	5 17	5 34	6 21	7 39	8 30	10 25		1 39	5 55	10 25
Manayunk	8 40	10 20	11 27	12 26	2 00	4 25	5 11	5 56	6 33	8 02	8 54	10 15	Sundays also	1 55	5 35	10 15
Conshohocken	8 55	10 42	11 41	12 42	2 15	4 45	5 27	6 11	6 50	8 17	9 10	10 31		2 11		10 31
Norristown	9 03	10 50	11 49	12 51	2 23	4 50	5 33	6 17	6 59	8 25	9 19	10 40		2 20		10 40
Wayne Junction	8 08	9 48	10 45	11 49	1 05	3 15	4 10	5 19	5 58	6 50	7 47	9 51	3 30	12 35	4 40	9 08
Columbia Avenue	8 15	9 54	10 55	11 55	1 15	3 55	4 50	5 25	6 04	7 00	7 53	9 59	3 40	12 42	4 50	9 15
Phila. { 3d & Berks st.	8 11	10 45			2 05	§1 37					8 07	10 30		1 05		
{ 9th & Green st	8 20	9 59	11 00	12 00	1 20	4 00	4 55	5 30	6 09	7 05	7 58	10 04	3 45	12 47	4 55	9 20
{ 24th & Chestnut st			11 15			1 35	4 15	5 10		7 20			4 00		5 10	
Baltimore			1 40			1 10	6 35	*7 45		10 00			7 00		7 45	
Washington			2 30			5 00	7 15	8 15		10 55			8 00		8 45	
	AM	AM	PM	M		PM	PM	PM	PM	PM	PM	PM	AM	PM	PM	PM

*Trains marked * run on Sunday also. ‡ Stop on Sunday only. § Does not stop on Sunday. † On Sundays leave Norristown, 6 00 p. m., Conshohocken, 6 08 p. m., Manayunk, 6 24 p. m., Chestnut Hill, 7 00 p. m., Germantown, 7 14 p. m. On Sundays leave Norristown, 10 55 p.m., Conshohocken, 11 03 p.m., Manayunk, 11 19 p.m., Chestnut Hill, 10 40 p.m., Germantown, 10 54 p.m.*

Parlor Cars on day express trains, and Sleeping Cars on midnight trains, to and from New York. Sleeping Cars can be occupied from 10.30 P. M. to 7.00 A. M.

WASHINGTON, BALTIMORE AND PHILADELPHIA TO NEW YORK.

LEAVE	PM	AM	AM	AM	AM	AM	A*	PM	PM	PM	PM	PM	M'd't	SUNDAYS ONLY.		
														AM	PM	PM
Washington	10 30				8 00	9 30	11 25		2 30	*4 15			*	9 30	2 30	
Baltimore	11 50			8 38	10 30	12 35		4 03						10 30	3 20	
		3 10			11 05	12 50	2 45		5 50	7 20				12 50	5 50	
Philadelphia { 24th & Ches	*		7 30	8 30	9 45	11 30	1 05	3 00	3 45	5 15	6 00	7 35	8 45	12 00		4 00
{ 9th & Green		5 50		8 20	9 05	10 30	12 55		3 30	5 00		*7 00	8 00	§11 40	8 30		5 30
{ 3d & Berks				8 35	8 35	9 50	11 25	1 10	3 05	3 50	5 20	6 05	7 40	8 51	12 00	9 05	1 00	6 10
Columbia Avenue			7 34	8 42	9 56	11 35	1 20	3 15	3 56	5 27	6 10	7 50	9 00	12 14	9 13	1 20	6 20
Wayne Junction	3 40		7 40													
Norristown		Sundays also	6 40	8 00	8 45	10 00	12 25		2 55	4 35	5 20	6 45	8 15	11 15	7 10		4 30
Conshohocken			6 49	8 06	8 51	10 07	12 32		3 04	4 41	5 26	6 51	8 24	*11 24	7 50		4 39
Manayunk			7 05	8 15	9 10	10 21	12 48		3 20	5 00	5 43	7 10	8 40	11 38	8 06		4 55
Chestnut Hill			7 15	8 10	9 21	10 45	1 00		2 10	3 15	4 85	5 20	7 00	7 45	11 52	8 30	12 05	5 04
Germantown			7 29	8 30	9 44	10 50	1 14	3 00	3 29	4 50	5 55	7 30	8 25	12 07	8 44	12 45	5 14
Trenton....Leave	4 25	7 00	8 00	9 00	10 21	12 06	1 15	3 16	4 21	5 35	6 52	8 05	10 00		9 30	1 48	6 50
Bound Brook	5 33	8 10	8 44	9 56	11 14	12 55	2 35	4 38	5 14	6 17	41	9 04	11 10	3 10	10 49	2 35	7 41
New York, foot Liberty st.	*6 55	9 30	9 30	10 50	12 10	1 50	3 30	*5 30	6 10	7 40	8 35	*9 55	12 37	4 50	12 00	3 30	8 35
	AM	AM	AM	PM	PM	PM	PM	PM	PM	PM	PM	PM	M'd't	AM	M	PM	PM

LAKEWOOD AND ATLANTIC CITY TRAINS.

Leave **Foot of Liberty St.** for **Lakewood** and **Manchester**, stopping at intermediate stations, 4 30, 8 15 a. m., 1 00, 2 30, 4 30 p. m., due at Lakewood, 7 30, 10 42 a. m., 3 19, 4 18, 6 18 p. m., due at Manchester 7 50, 10 58 a. m., 3 36, 4 35, 6 35 p. m.

For **Atlantic City**, 4 30 a. m., 1 00, 2 30 p. m., due at Atlantic City 10 15 a. m., 5 45, 6 15 p. m. None on Sundays.

To New York.

Leave **Atlantic City**, 8 05, 9 10 a. m., 4 00 p. m., due in New York 1 00, 1 00, 8 40 p. m.

Leave **Manchester** (Lakewood 13 minutes later), 7 30, 10 28, 11 00 a. m., 3 36, 6 16 p. m., due in New York 9 37 a. m., 1 00, 1 00, 6 15, 8 40 p. m.

Parlor Cars on trains leaving New York at 2 30, 4 30 p. m., Lakewood at 7 48, 11 13 a. m.

ELIZABETHPORT, SPRING ST., ELIZABETH, EL MORA, ROSELLE.

Time from New York to Elizabeth, 32 to 45 minutes, to Roselle 42 to 52 minutes.

Leave **foot of Liberty St.** for **Elizabeth**, 5 00, 6 00, 6 15, 6 45, 7 00, 7 15, 7 45, 8 30, 9 00, 9 30, 10 00, 10 15, 11 00, 11 15, a. m., 12 m., 12 45, 1 00, 1 30, 2 00, 2 30, 3 00, 3 30, 3 45, 4 00, 4 15, 4 30, 4 45, 5 00, 5 15, 5 30, 5 45, 6 00, 6 15, 6 30, 6 45, 7 00, 7 30, 8 00, 8 40, 9 15, 10 00, 10 45, 11 30 p. m., 12 00, 12 15 night. SUNDAYS.—5 00, 8 00, 9 00, 10 00 a. m., 12 00 m., 1 30, 3 00, 4 00, 5 30, 6 30, 8 00, 9 30, 10 30, p. m. 12 night.

For **El Mora**, 6 00, 6 15, 6 45, 7 15, 7 45, 8 30, 9 00, 9 30, 10 00, 10 15, 11 15 a. m., 12 m., 12 45, 2 00, 2 30, 3 00, 3 45, 4 15, 4 30, 4 45, 5 00, 5 15, 5 45, 6 00, 6 15, 7 00, 7 30, 8 00, 8 30, 9 15, 10 00, 10 45, 11 30 p. m., 12 00, 12 15 night. SUNDAYS.—8 00, 9 00, 11 00 a. m., 12 m., 1 30, 3 00, 4 00, 5 30, 8 00, 9 30, 10 30 p. m.

For **Roselle**, 4 00, 6 00, 6 15, 6 45, 7 00, 7 15, 7 45, 8 30, 9 00, 9 30, 10 00, 10 15, 11 15 a. m., 12 m., 12 45, 1 00, 2 00, 2 30, 3 00, 3 30, 3 45, 4 00, 4 15, 4 30, 4 45, 5 00, 5 15, 5 30, 5 45, 6 00, 6 15, 7 00, 7 30, 8 00, 8 30, 9 15, 10 00, 10 45, 11 30 p. m., 12 00, 12 15 night. SUNDAYS.—5 00, 8 00, 9 00, 11 00 a. m., 12 m., 1 30, 3 00, 4 00, 5 30, 6 30, 8 00, 9 30, 10 30 p. m., 12 night.

To New York.

Leave **Roselle**, 3 53, 4 58, 5 28, 6 03, 6 23, 6 53, 7 03, 7 23, 7 25, 7 53, 7 56, 8 23, 8 25, 8 40, 9 08, 9 13, 9 38, 9 58, 10 38, 11 15 a. m., 12 03, 12 53, 1 23, 1 43, 2 28, 3 13, 3 43, 4 23, 4 48, 5 15, 5 34, 6 03, 6 23, 6 30, 6 53, 7 24, 8 01, 8 48, 9 53, 5 38, 7 08, 7 52, 9 10, 9 50 p. m. SUNDAYS.—3 53, 8 23, 9 18, 10 08, 11 22, 11 32 a, m., 12 53, 1 47, 2 53, 3 53, 4 53, 5 38, 7 08, 7 52, 9 10, 9 50 p. m.

Leave **El Mora** 5 02, 5 32, 6 06, 6 27, 6 56, 7 06, 7 26, 7 28, 7 55, 8 00, 8 28, 8 43, 9 16, 9 41, 10 02, 10 41, 11 18 a. m., 12 06, 12 56, 1 26, 1 46, 2 31, 3 16, 3 46, 4 51, 5 21, 6 06, 6 33, 6 57, 7 27, 8 06, 9 21, 10 30, 11 52 p. m., 12 27 night. SUNDAYS—8 26, 9 21, 10 11, 11 35, a. m., 12 57, 1 50, 2 56, 3 56, 4 57, 5 41, 7 11, 7 55, 9 22 p. m.

Leave **Elizabeth** 4 00, 5 06, 5 35, 6 10, 6 30, 7 00, 7 10, 7 30, 7 32, 7 48, 8 00, 8 03, 8 20, 8 30, 8 32, 8 47, 8 57, 9 15, 9 20, 9 45, 10 05, 10 19, 10 45, 11 03, 11 22, 11 10 a. m., 12 10, 12 47, 1 00, 1 30, 1 50, 2 35, 3 20, 3 48, 3 15, 3 20, 4 29, 4 30, 4 55, 5 25, 5 39, 6 06, 6 10, 6 30, 6 37, 7 00, 7 09, 7 30, 8 10, 8 54, 9 13, 9 25, 10 40, 11 55, p. m. 12 30 night. SUNDAYS.—4 00, 8 30, 9 25, 10 15, 11 28, a. m. 12 m., 1 00, 1 55, 3 00, 4 00, 5 00, 5 45, 7 15, 7 89, 9 00, 9 45, 10 00 p. m.

CENTRAL R. R. OF NEW JERSEY—Continued.

CRANFORD, WESTFIELD, FANWOOD (Scotch Plains), NETHERWOOD, PLAINFIELD GRANT AVENUE, EVONA, DUNELLEN.

Time from New York to Cranford, about 50 minutes ; to Plainfield, about 1 hour.

Leave **foot of Liberty St. for Cranford** 4 00, 6 00, 7 00, 8 30, 9 00, 10 15 a. m., 1 00, 2 30, 3 30, 4 00, 4 30, 5 00, 5 15, 5 30, 6 00, 6 30, 7 00, 8 00, 8 30, 10 00, 11 30 p. m., 12 night. SUNDAYS.—5 00, 9 00, a. m., 12 m., 1 30, 4 00, 5 30, 6 30, 9 30 p. m. 12 night.

For **Westfield and Fanwood** 4 00, 6 00, 7 00, 8 30, 9 00, 10 15 a. m., 1 00, 2 30, 3 30, 4 00, 4 30, 5 00, 5 15, 5 30, 6 00, 6 30, 7 00, 8 00, 8 30, 10 00, 11 30 p. m., 12 night. SUNDAYS.—5 00, 9 00 a. m., 12 m., 1 30, 4 00, 5 30, 6 30, 9 30 p. m., 12 night.

For **Netherwood,** 6 00, 7 00, 9 00, 10 15 a. m., 1 00, 2 30, 3 30, 4 00, 4 30, 5 00, 5 30, 6 00, 6 30, 7 00, 8 00, 8 30, 10 00, 11 30 p. m., 12 night. SUNDAYS.—5 00, 9 00, a. m., 12 m., 1 30, 4 00, 5 30, 6 30, 9 30, p. m., 12 night.

For **Plainfield,** 4 00, 6 00, 7 00, 8 30, 9 00, 10 15, 11 00 a. m., 1 00, 2 30, 3 30, 4 15, 4 00, 4 30, 5 00, 5 15, 5 30, 5 45, 6 00, 6 30, 7 00, 7 30, 8 00, 8 30, 10 00, 11 30 p. m., 12 night. SUNDAYS.—5 00, 9 00, a. m., 12 m., 1 30, 4 00, 5 30, 6 30, 9 30 p. m., 12 night.

For **Grant Avenue,** 6 00, 7 00, 9 00, 10 15 a.m., 2 30, 3 30, 4 30, 5 00, 5 30, 6 00, 6 30, 7 00, 8 00, 8 30, 10 00, 11 30 p.m., 12 night. SUNDAYS.—9 00 a. m., 12 m., 1 30, 4 00, 6 30, 9 30 p. m., 12 night.

For **Evona,** 4 00, 6 00, 7 00, 9 00, 9 00 10 15 a. m., 2 30, 3 30, 4 00, 4 30, 5 00, 5 30, 6 00, 6 30, 7 00, 8 00, 8 30, 10 00, 11 30 p. m., 12 night. SUNDAYS. 5 00, 9 00 a. m., 12 m., 1 30, 4 00, 5 30, 6 30, 9 30 p. m., 12 night.

For **Dunellen,** 4 00, 6 00, 7 00, 8 30, 9 00, 10 15 a. m., 1 00, 2 30, 3 30, 4 00, 4 30, 5 00, 5 15, 5 30, 6 00, 6 30, 7 00, 8 00, 8 30, 10 00, 11 30 p. m., 12 night. SUNDAYS.—5 00, 9 00, a. m., 12 m., 1 30, 4 00, 5 30, 6 30, 9 30 p. m., 12 night.

To New York.

Leave **Dunellen,** 3 18, 5 35, 6 20, 6 50, 7 20, 7 50, 8 08, 8 23, 8 30, 9 20, 10 31, 11 34 a. m., 1 14, 2 19, 3 43, 5 24, 5 58, 6 25, 6 55, 8 39, 9 10, 11 22 p. m. SUNDAYS.—3 18, 7 53, 8 49, 10 57, 11 45 a m., 1 20, 3 23, 5 08, 7 30, 9 15 p. m.

Leave **Evona,** 5 38, 6 23, 6 58, 7 23, 7 53, 8 11, 8 26, 9 32, 11 36 a. m., 1 16, 3 46, 5 27, 6 27, 6 57, 8 42, 11 21 p. m. SUNDAYS.—7 56, 8 52, 11 28 a. m., 1 23, 3 26, 5 11, 7 23, 9 18 p. m.

Leave **Grant Avenue,** 5 40, 6 25, 6 55, 7 26, 7 56, 8 13, 8 29, 9 34, 11 38 a. m., 1 18, 3 48, 5 29, 6 29, 6 59, 11 26 p. m. SUNDAYS.—7 58, 8 54, 11 29 a. m., 1 24, 3 28, 5 13, 7 25 p. m.

Leave **Plainfield,** 3 27, 5 43, 6 29, 6 50, 7 26, 7 30, 7 58, 8 00, 8 17, 8 33, 8 37, 9 37, 10 37, 11 25, 11 42 a. m., 12 32, 1 21, 2 25, 2 57, 3 51, 5 24, 5 32, 6 05, 6 32, 6 54, 7 03, 8 47, 9 18, 11 28 p. m. SUNDAYS.—3 27, 8 01, 8 57, 11 03, 11 32 a. m., 1 27, 3 30, 5 16, 7 20, 7 28, 9 23 p. m.

Leave **Netherwood,** 3 30, 6 32, 7 02, 7 33, 8 01, 8 03, 8 20, 8 36, 9 40, 11 45 a. m., 1 24, 3 33, 5 35, 6 35, 7 06, 8 50, 9 22, 11 31 p. m. SUNDAYS.—3 30, 8 04, 9 01, 11 34 a. m., 1 29, 3 31, 5 19, 7 31, 9 27 p. m.

Leave **Fanwood,** 3 33, 5 48, 6 36, 7 06, 7 37, 8 07, 8 24, 8 43, 9 43, 10 43, 11 48 a. m., 1 28, 2 30, 3 56, 5 39, 6 40, 6 38, 7 09, 8 53, 9 26, 11 34 p. m. SUNDAYS.—3 33, 8 07, 9 03, 11 08, 11 37 a. m., 1 32, 3 37, 5 24, 5 27, 7 40, 9 31 p. m.

Leave **Westfield,** 3 40, 5 53, 6 41, 7 11, 7 42, 8 12, 8 29, 8 43, 8 52, 9 48, 10 48, 11 53 a. m., 1 33, 2 35, 4 01, 5 44, 6 45, 6 43, 7 14, 8 58, 9 32, 11 39 p. m. SUNDAYS.—3 40, 8 12, 9 08, 11 13, 11 42 a. m., 1 37, 3 42, 5 27, 7 40, 9 37 p. m.

Leave **Cranford,** 3 46, 5 58, 6 47, 7 17, 7 17, 8 17, 8 34, 9 00, 9 53, 10 53, 11 58 a. m., 1 38, 2 40, 4 07, 5 49, 6 20, 6 48, 7 19, 9 03, 9 38, 11 44 p. m. SUNDAYS.—3 46, 8 18, 9 13, 11 17, 11 47 a. m., 1 42, 3 48, 5 33, 7 45, 9 43 p. m.

NEWARK AND NEW YORK BRANCH.

Stations. Lafayette, Jackson Avenue, West Bergen, E. Ferry St., Ferry St., Broad St.

Time from New York to Broad St., Newark, 32 minutes.

Leave **foot of Liberty St.** for **Newark** at 5 00, 5 30, 6 00, 6 30, 7 00, 7 15, 7 45, 8 15, 8 20, 9 00, 9 15, 10 15, 10 15, 11 15 a. m.: 12 00 noon ; 12 45, 1 15, 2 00, 2 30, 3 00, 3 30, 4 00, 4 30, 5 00, 5 15, 5 30, 5 45, 6 00, 6 15, 6 30, 7 00, 7 30, 8 15, 9 00, 9 45, 10 30, 11 15 p. m.; 12 00 night. SUNDAY : 8 00, 9 00, 10 00, 11 00 a. m.; 12 00 noon ; 1 00, 2 00, 3 00, 4 00, 5 00, 6 30, 8 00, 9 00, 10 00, 11 00 p. m.; 12 00 night.

Leave **Broad St.** (Newark), for **New York** at 4 40, 5 20, 5 50, 6 25, 6 50, 7 05, 7 35, 7 52, 8 10, 8 40, 9 03, 9 22, 9 45, 10 05, 10 35, 11 05, 11 35 a. m.; 12 20, 1 05, 1 35, 2 01, 2 45, 3 20, 3 50, 4 20, 4 50, 5 20, 5 48, 6 05, 6 35, 6 55, 7 20, 7 50, 8 25, 9 10, 9 55, 10 50, 11 20 p. m.; 12 05, 12 40 night. SUNDAY : 8 00, 9 00, 10 00, 11 00 a. m.; 12 00 m.; 1 00, 2 00, 3 00, 4 00, 5 00, 6 00, 7 00, 8 00, 9 00, 10 00, 11 00 p. m.

COMMUNIPAW, CLAREMONT, GREENVILLE, PAMRAPO, BAYONNE, CENTREVILLE, BERGEN POINT.

Time from New York to Bergen Point, 26 to 32 minutes.

Leave **foot of Liberty St.**

For **Bergen Point** only, 7 00 a. m.; 3 30, 4 00, 4 30, 5 00, 5 30 p. m.

For **Bergen Point** and all stations excepting Claremont, 6 00 a. m.; 2 30, 3 45, 8 00, 8 30 p. m.; Sundays, 12 00 night.

For **Bergen Point and all Stations,** 6 15, 6 45, 7 15, 7 45, 8 30, 9 00, 9 30, 10 00, 10 15, 10 30, 11 15 a. m.; 12 00 m.; 12 45, 2 00, 3 00, 4 15, 4 45, 5 15, 5 30, 5 45, 6 00, 6 15, 6 30, 7 30, 9 15, 10 00, 10 15, 11 30 p. m.; 12 15 night. Sundays; 8 00, 9 00, 11 00 a. m.; 12 00 m.; 1 30, 3 00, 4 00, 5 30, 6 30, 8 00, 9 30, 10 30 p. m.

For **Communipaw, Greenville, Bayonne** and **Bergen Point** only, 1 00 a.m.; Sundays, 5 00 a. m.

For **Greenville** and **Bergen Point** only, 7 00 p. m.

To New York.

Time from Bergen Point to New York, about 30 minutes.

Leave **Bergen Point,** 4 15, 5 20, 5 48, 6 23, 6 48, 7 12, 7 23, 7 45, 7 47, 8 16, 8 27, 8 45, 8 59, 9 29, 9 33, 9 57, 10 17, 10 58, 11 36 a. m.; 12 23, 1 13, 1 18, 2 02, 2 48, 3 33, 4 32, 4 43, 5 08, 5 38, 6 12, 6 28, 6 42, 6 50, 7 11, 7 42, 8 23, 8 50, 9 25, 9 38, 10 09, 10 53 p. m.; 12 07, 12 41 night. SUNDAYS: 4 15, 8 43, 9 37, 10 28, 11 34 a. m.; 12 43, 1 13, 2 08, 3 13, 4 13, 5 13, 5 51, 5 58, 7 20, 8 13, 9 38, 10 13 p. m.

Leave **Centreville.** 4 18, 5 23, 5 51, 6 26, 6 51, 7 26, 7 48, 8 19, 8 43, 9 36, 10 00, 10 20, 11 01, 11 38, a. m.; 12 25, 1 16, 1 15, 2 51, 3 36, 4 45, 5 10, 5 40, 6 26, 6 53, 7 44, 8 52, 9 41, 10 11, 10 55, p. m.; 12 00, 12 18, night. SUNDAYS; 4 18, 8 45, 9 30, 10 30, a. m.; 12 45, 1 15, 2 11, 3 16, 4 16, 5 15, 6 01, 7 32, 8 16, 9 41, 10 16 p. m.

Leave **Bayonne,** 4 21, 5 26, 5 53, 6 28, 6 53, 7 16, 7 28, 7 51, 8 21, 8 50, 9 39, 10 02, 10 22, 11 03, 11 40 a. m.; 12 27, 1 18, 1 47, 2 07, 2 54, 3 39, 4 48, 5 12, 5 42, 6 29, 6 56, 7 15, 7 46, 8 58, 8 53, 9 43, 10 13, 10 57, p. m.; 12 12, 12 30 night. SUNDAYS, 4 21, 8 48, 9 41, 10 32, a. m.; 12 17, 1 18, 2 13, 3 18, 4 18, 5 18, 6 04, 7 35, 8 18, 9 45, 10 18 p. m.

Leave **Pamrapo,** 4 25, 5 28, 5 56, 6 31, 6 56, 7 19, 7 31, 7 53, 8 24, 8 53, 9 42, 10 05, 11 43 a. m.; 12 29, 1 21, 1 50, 2 10, 2 56, 3 42, 4 38, 1 51, 5 14, 5 15, 6 17, 6 32, 6 59, 7 17, 7 49, 8 31, 8 58, 9 46, 10 16, 11 00 p. m.; 12 14, 12 53, night. SUNDAYS, 4 25, 8 51, 9 44, 10 35, a. m.; 12 21, 1 21, 2 16, 3 21, 4 21, 5 21, 6 06, 7 38, 8 21, 9 46, 10 21 p. m.

Leave **Greenville.** 4 28, 5 30, 5 59, 6 34, 6 59, 7 22, 7 34, 7 17, 7 56, 8 27, 8 55, 9 45, 10 08, 10 28, 11 06, 11 46 a. m.; 12 32, 1 24, 1 52, 2 13, 2 59, 3 44, 4 41, 4 54, 5 16, 5 18, 6 05, 6 35, 7 02, 7 19, 7 52, 8 34, 9 01, 9 31, 9 48, 10 18, 11 02 p. m.; 12 17, 12 55 night. SUNDAYS, 4 28, 8 54, 9 46, 10 38 a. m.; 12 24, 1 24, 2 19, 3 24, 4 24, 5 24, 6 09, 7 42, 8 24, 9 49, 10 24 p. m.

Leave **Claremont,** 4 31, 5 38, 6 02, 6 37, 7 02, 7 37, 7 50, 8 30, 8 58, 9 48, 10 11, 11 11, 11 49 a. m.; 12 35, 1 27, 1 55, 3 01, 3 47, 4 57, 5 19, 5 51, 6 38, 7 05, 8 37, 9 01, 9 51, 10 21, 11 05 p. m.; 12 57 night. SUNDAYS, 4 31, 8 57, 9 50, 10 41 a. m.; 12 27, 2 22, 3 27, 4 27, 5 27, 6 12, 7 45, 8 47, 9 52, 10 27 p. m.

Leave **Communipaw,** 4 34, 5 35, 6 05, 6 39, 7 05, 7 39, 8 01, 8 32, 9 00, 9 50, 10 13, 11 13, 11 51 a. m.; 12 37, 1 29, 1 58, 3 09, 3 50, 4 59, 5 22, 5 53, 6 40, 7 07, 8 40, 9 06, 9 54, 10 24, 11 08 p. m.; 12 22, 12 59 night. SUNDAYS, 4 34, 8 59, 9 51, 10 43 a. m.; 12 29, 1 29, 2 24, 3 29, 4 29, 5 29, 6 14, 7 48, 8 29, 9 54, 10 29 p. m.

CENTRAL R. R. OF NEW JERSEY—Continued.

ALLENTOWN LINE.

Leave **foot of Liberty St.**, for **Reading and Harrisburg**, 7 00, 8 30 a. m., 1 00, 5 15 p. m. Sundays, 5 30 p. m. Due at Reading, 10 00 a. m., 1 25, 6 00, 10 23 p. m. Sundays, 10 23 p. m.; due at Harrisburg, 2 00, 3 10, 8 20 p. m.; 12 10 night. Sundays, 12 10 night.

For **Pottsville**, 7 00, 8 30 a. m., 1 00 p. m.; due at Pottsville, 11 35 a.m., 5 51, 7 15 p. m.

To New York.

Leave **Harrisburg**, 5 10 a. m., 1 25 p. m. Leave **Pottsville**, 5 50 a. m., 2 45 p. m. Leave **Reading**, 7 15 a. m., 3 30 p. m.; due in New York, 3 20, 9 50 p. m.

SOUTH BRANCH R. R.

Stations: Somerville, Ricefield, Flagtown, Neshanic, Woodfern, Three Bridges, Flemington.
Leave **foot of Liberty St.**, for **Flemington** and intermediate stations, 7 00, 8 30 a. m., 1 00, 4 30, 5 00 p. m. Sundays, 4 00 p. m.; due at Flemington 9 20, 11 10 a. m., 3 20, 6 20, 7 20 p. m. Sundays, 6 25 p. m.

To New York.

Leave **Flemington**, 6 55, 9 35 a. m., 1 10, 4 25, 6 50 p. m. Sundays, 8 00 p. m., due in New York, 8 52, 11 37 a. m., 3 20, 7 07, 9 50 p. m. Sundays, 10 45 p. m.

BOUND BROOK & SOMERVILLE TRAINS.

Leave **foot of Liberty St.**, for **Somerville**, stopping at Bound Brook, 4 00, 7 00, 8 30, 9 00, 10 15 a. m., 1 00, 2 30, *3 15, 4 30, 5 00, 5 45, 6 00, 6 30, 7 00, 8 30, 10 00, 11 30 p. m. SUNDAYS, 5 00, 9 00 a.m., 1 30, 4 00, 5 30, 9 30 p. m.
Arrive **Somerville**, 5 40, 8 34, 9 45, 10 40 a. m.; 12 07, 2 27, 4 20, 1 53, 5 40, 5 58, 6 38, 7 00, 7 25, 7 55, 8 38, 10 10, 11 40 p. m., 1 10 night. SUNDAYS, 6 40, 10 40 a. m., 3 10, 5 40, 7 04, 11 10 p, m. * Does not stop at Bound Brook.

To New York.

Leave **Somerville** (leave Bound Brook 8 minutes later), 6 00, 6 30, 7 30, 7 25, 7 35, 7 48, 8 26, 9 10, 10 15, 11 15 a. m., 12 55, 2 00, 3 25, 5 00, 5 40, 8 15, 8 40, 11 05 p. m. SUNDAYS, 8 30, 11 05 a. m.; 1 00, 4 50, 7 00, 8 50 p. m.
Arrive in **New York**, 7 40, 8 05, 8 20, 9 02, 8 52, 3 25, 9 30, 10 50, 11 37 a. m., 12 55, 2 32, 3 20, 5 00, 6 10, 7 07, 9 50, 10 10 p. m., 12 37 night. SUNDAYS, 10 05 a. m., 12 45, 2 10, 6 30, 8 45, 10 45 p. m.

HIGH BRIDGE BRANCH.

German Valley, Chester, Dover, Rockaway, Schooley's Mountain, Budd's Lake & Lake Hopatcong.

Stations: High Bridge, Califon, Vernoy, Middle Valley, German Valley, Chester Furnace, Chester, Naughrigh, Bartley, Flanders, Cary's, Drakesville, Kenvil, Hopatcong Junction, Morris Co. Junction, Minnisink, Lake Hopatcong, Hurd, Weldon, Ford, Ogden, Port Oram, Dover, Rockaway.
Leave **foot of Liberty St.**, at *4 00, 8 30 a. m., 4 30 p. m.; due at German Valley, 8 32, 10 42 a. m., 6 10 p. m.; due at Chester, 8 38, 11 00 a. m., 6 56 p. m.; due at Lake Hopatcong, 11 30 a. m., 7 35 p. m. (the *4 00 a. m. train from N. Y. connects for Lake Hopatcong on Mondays only); due at Rockaway, 9 25, 11 30 a. m., 7 24 p. m.

To New York.

Leave **Rockaway**, 6 35 a. m., 3 10, 5 37 p. m.; due in New York, 9 30 a. m., 9 50 p. m.
Leave **Lake Hopatcong**, 6 35 a. m., 5 10 p. m., Saturday, about 3 p. m.; due in New York, 9 30 a. m., 9 50 p. m., Saturday, 7 07 p.m.
Leave **Kenvil**, 6 35 a. m., 1 01, 6 00 p. m., Sunday, 5 10 p. m.; due in New York, 9 30 a. m., 7 07, 9 50 p. m., Sunday, 10 15 p. m.
Leave **Chester**, 7 05 a. m., 4 10, 6 15 p. m., Sunday, 6 15 p. m.; due in New York, 9 30 a. m., 7 07, 9 50 p. m., Sunday, 10 15 p. m.
Leave **German Valley**, 7 23 a. m., 4 29, 6 40 p. m., Sunday, 6 35 p. m.; due in New York, 9 30 a. m., 7 07, 9 50 p. m., Sunday, 10 15 p. m.

LEHIGH AND SUSQUEHANNA DIVISION.

For **" Fares to all Places,"** See Index.

Leave **Foot of Liberty St.**, for **Phillipsburg, Easton, Bethlehem, Allentown, Siegfried** and **Mauch Chunk**, stopping at intermediate stations, 7 00, 7 00, 8 30, a. m., 1 00, 3 15, 5 45, p. m.; due at Easton, 7 14, 10 10, 10 32 a. m., 3 45, 5 57, 8 17 p. m.; due at Bethlehem, 7 40, 10 44, 11 12 a. m., 4 12, 6 19, 8 39 p. m.; due at Allentown, 7 51, 11 00, 11 20 a. m., 4 30, 6 29, 8 48 p. m.; due at Mauch Chunk, 9 00 a. m., 12 05, 12 10, 5 40, 7 25, 9 50 p. m.
Leave **foot of Liberty St.**, for **White Haven, Wilkes Barre** and **Scranton**, 8 30 a. m., 3 45 p. m.; due at White Haven, 1 06, 8 10 p. m.; due at Wilkes Barre, 2 15, 9 50 p. m.; due at Scranton, 3 05, 10 10 p. m.

To New York.

Leave **Scranton**, 7 50 a. m., 3 00 p. m.; leave **Wilkes Barre**, 8 10 a. m., 3 35 p. m.; leave **White Haven**, 10 05 a. m., 4 31 p. m., stopping at intermediate stations; due in New York, 3 20, 9 50 p. m.
Leave **Mauch Chunk**, 5 45, 7 13, 11 02 a. m., 2 35, 5 20 p. m.; leave **Allentown**, 6 48, 8 14 a. m., 12 02, 3 11, 6 21 p. m.; leave **Bethlehem**, 6 58, 8 26 a. m., 12 11, 3 51, 6 31 p. m.; leave **Easton** (Phillipsburg 3 minutes later), 7 23, 8 57 a. m., 12 40, 4 15, 7 00 p. m.; due in New York, 9 30, 11 37 a. m., 3 20, 7 07, 9 50 p. m.

LEHIGH AND LACKAWANNA R. R.

Leave **foot of Liberty St.**, for **Chapman Quarries, Pen-Argyl** and **Bangor**, stopping at intermediate stations, 7 00 a. m., 3 45 p. m.; due at Chapman Quarries, 11 30 a. m., 7 13 p. m.; due at Pen-Argyl, 12 noon, 7 18 p. m.; due at Bangor, 12 10, 8 05 p. m.

To **New York.**—Leave **Bangor**, 6 50 a. m., 4 40 p. m. Leave **Pen-Argyl**, 7 01 a. m., 4 51 p. m., Leave **Chapman Quarries**, 7 34 a. m., 5 23 p. m.; due in New York, 11 37 a. m., 9 50 p. m. Also leave Pen-Argyl on Saturdays, 12 40 noon; due in New York, 7 07 p. m.

NESCOPEC BRANCH.

Leave **foot of Liberty St.**, for **Upper Lehigh** and intermediate stations, 8 30 a. m.; due at Upper Lehigh, 2 10 p. m.
Leave **Upper Lehigh**, 7 13 a. m., 3 45 p. m.; arrive in New York, 3 20, 9 50 p. m.

TAMAQUA BRANCH.

Leave **foot of Liberty St.**, for **Tamaqua, Pottsville, Mahanoy City, Shamokin**, 8 30 a. m., 3 45 p. m.; due at Tamaqua, 1 00, 8 20 p. m.; due at Pottsville, 2 25, 9 05 p. m.; due at Mahanoy City, 2 03, 9 51 p. m.; due at Shamokin, 3 20, 11 00 p. m.
For **Williamsport**, 8 30 a. m.; arrive at 5 57 p. m.

To New York.

Leave **Williamsport**, 9 00 a. m., 11 35 a. m.; arrive New York. 7 05, 9 50 p. m.
Leave **Shamokin**, 1 56, 6 40, 11 32 a. m., 2 10 p. m. Arrive New York, 11 35 a. m., 3 20, 7 05, 9 50 p. m.
Leave **Pottsville**, 5 45, 7 50 a. m., 12 40 p. m. Arrive New York, 11 37 a. m., 3 20, 7 07 p. m.
Leave **Tamaqua**, 6 28, 8 35 a. m., 1 45, 4 25 p. m. Arrive New York, 11 35 a. m., 3 20, 7 05, 9 50 p. m.

DRIFTON BRANCH.

Leave **foot of Liberty St.**, for **Drifton** and intermediate stations, 3 45 p. m.; due at Drifton, 9 05 p. m.
To **New York.**—Leave **Drifton**, 5 50 a. m.; due in New York, 11 37 a. m.

NANTICOKE BRANCH.

Leave **foot of Liberty St.**, for **Wanamie** and intermediate stations, 8 30 a. m.; on Saturdays, 3 45 p. m.; due at Wanamie, 4 20 p. m.; on Saturdays, 11 40 p. m.
To **New York.**—Leave **Wanamie**, 8 25, 11 05 a. m.; due in New York, 3 20, 9 50 p. m.

NEW JERSEY SOUTHERN DIVISION—C. R. R. of N. J.—Continued.

Distances, Stations and Fares—Single and Excursion.

M. Stations.	Fares Single.	Exc.	M. Stations.	Fares Single.	Exc.	M. Stations.	Fares Single.	Exc.	M. Stations.	Fares Single.	Exc.
	New York		30	Manchester	$1.70-$2.75		Egg Harbor	$3.16	$4.64	103	Woodruff's	$3.25-$5.25
18	Red Bank	$1.00	$1.50	45	Whitings	1.85-3.25		Atlantic City	3.25	4.75	104	Bridgeton Junc.	
16	Shrewsbury	1.00	1.50	50	Wheatland	1.95	3.55	78	Winslow	2.85	4.10	106	Bridgeton	3.25-5.25
15	Eatontown	1.00	1.50	53	Woodmansie	2.05	3.70	84	Cedar Lake	3.00-4.40	108	Bowentown	3.35-5.40
17	Pine Brook	1.05	1.60	58	Shamong	2.25-3.95	88	Landisville	3.15	1.65	111	Sheppard's	
21	Shark River	1.20	1.80	61	Harris	2.35	3.95	90	Wheat Road	3.20	4.75		Mills	3.45-5.55
24	Farmingdale	1.30	2.00	69	Atsion	2.60-4.00	92	Main Avenue	3.25-4.75	113	Greenwich	3.50-5.60
30	Squankum	1.35-2.05	71	Parkdale	2.70-4.00	94	Vineland	3.25	4.75	114	Bacon's Neck	3.55-5.70
32	Lakewood	1.45	2.35	76	Elm	2.75	4.00	97	Bradway	3.25-4.95	116	Bay Side	3.60	5.75
35	White's	1.65	2.55	78	Winslow Junc.	2.80-4.00	100	Rosenhayn	3.25-5.20			

LAKEWOOD, ATLANTIC CITY, VINELAND, BRIDGETON, BAYSIDE.

Leave foot of Liberty Street:

For **Red Bank, Lakewood** and **Manchester**, stopping at intermediate stations, 4 30, 8 15 a. m., 1 00, †2 30, 4 30 p. m. Arrive Manchester, 7 50, 10 58 a. m., 3 36, *4 35, 6 35 p. m. *Atlantic City Express.

For **Atlantic City** and intermediate stations, 4 30 a. m. 1 00, †2 30 p. m. Arrive Atlantic City, 10 15 a. m. 5 45, 16 15 p. m. †Atlantic City Express.

For **Vineland, Bridgeton, Bayside** and intermediate stations, 4 30 a. m., 1 00 p. m. Arrive Vineland, 9 17 a. m., 5 35 p. m.; arrive Bridgeton, 10 17 a. m., 6 10 p. m.; arrive Bayside, 10 48 a. m., 6 43 p. m.

Trains to New York.

Leave **Bayside**, stopping at intermediate stations, 7 15 a. m., 3 00 p. m.; leave **Bridgeton**, 7 50 a. m., 3 35 p. m.; leave **Vineland**, 8 24 a. m., 4 06 p. m.; leave **Winslow**, 8 58 a. m., 4 42 p. m. Arrive foot of Liberty Street, New York, 1 00, 8 40 p. m.

Leave **Atlantic City**, stopping at intermediate stations, 8 05, †9 10 a. m., 4 00 p. m.; leave **Atsion**, 9 28, †10 10 a. m., 5 20 p. m. Arrive New York, 1 00, *1 00, 8 40 p. m. *Atlantic City Express.

Leave **Manchester** (leave **Lakewood** 14 minutes later), 7 30, 10 28, *11 00 a. m., 3 36, 6 16 p. m. Arrive New York, 9 37 a. m., 1 00, *1 00, 6 15, 8 40 p. m. *Atlantic City Express.

Leave **Farmingdale**, 8 00, 10 58 a. m., 4 10, 6 45 p. m.; leave **Eatontown** (Shrewsbury 4 minutes later), 8 14, 11 18 a. m. 4 30, 7 04 p. m. Arrive New York, 9 37 a. m., 1 00, 6 15, 8 40 p. m.

Leave **Red Bank**, 8 22, 11 28, 11 45 a. m., 4 40, 7 13 p. m. Arrive New York, 9 37 a. m., 1 00, 1 00, 6 15, 8 40 p. m.

TRAINS TO TOMS RIVER, BARNEGAT, ETC.

Stations, Distances and Fares—Single and Excursion.

	Manchester		8 Toms River	$1.90-$3.00	16 Forked River	$2.20-$3.45	20 Waretown	$2.25-$3.65
5	Germania	$1.85	$3.00	12 Barnegat Park	2.00-3.25	17 Ostrom	2.20-3.50	23 Barnegat	2.35-3.80
7	Appollonio	1.90	3.00	11 Cedar Creek	2.10	3.35

Leave foot of Liberty Street, for **Toms River, Barnegat**, and intermediate stations, 4 30, 8 15 a. m., 1 00, 4 30 p. m. Arrive Toms River, 8 12, 11 20 a. m., 3 57, 6 55 p. m.; arrive Barnegat, 8 50, 11 58 a. m., 4 35, 7 33 p. m.

Trains to New York.

Leave **Barnegat**, stopping at intermediate stations, 6 30, 9 30 a. m., 2 40, 5 15 p. m.; leave **Toms River**, 7 10, 10 10 a. m., 3 18, 5 56 p. m. Arrive foot of Liberty St., New York, 9 37 a. m., 1 00, 6 15, 8 40 p. m.

ATLANTIC HIGHLANDS BRANCH.

Stations and Fare from New York—Single and Excursion.

| Red Bank | $1.00-$1.50 | Hopping | $1.00-$1.50 | Atlantic Highlands | $1.00-$1.50 | Port Monmouth | $1.00-$1.50 |
| Chapel Hill | 1.00-1.50 | Bay View | 1.00-1.50 |

Leave foot of Liberty St., via Red Bank, for **Atlantic Highlands, Port Monmouth** and intermediate stations, 8 15 a. m., 4 30 p. m. Arrive Atlantic Highlands, 10 15 a. m., 6 27 p. m.

Trains to New York.

Leave **Atlantic Highlands**, 7 45, 10 45 a. m., 4 00 p. m., stopping at intermediate stations. Arrive foot of Liberty St., New York, 9 37 a. m., 1 00, 6 15 p. m.

CUMBERLAND AND MAURICE RIVER BRANCH.

Stations, Distances and Fare from New York—Single and Excursion.

	Bridgeton Junction		6 Westcotts	$3.45-$3.60	11 Newport	$3.65-$5.95	19 Centreville	$3.90-$6.25
2	East Bridgeton	$3.35	$5.10	8 N. Cedarville	3.50-5.65	14 Dividing Creek	3.75-6.10	21 Port Norris	3.90-6.25
5	Fairton	3.40	5.50	9 Cedarville	3.60-5.85	17 Mauricetown	3.85-6.25	22 Long Reach	3.95-6.30

Leave foot of Liberty St, for **Cedarville, Mauricetown, Port Norris** and intermediate stations, 4 30 a. m. 1 00 p. m. Arrive Port Norris, 11 12 a. m., 7 05 p. m.

Trains to New York.

Leave **Long Reach**, 6 55 a. m., 2 35 p. m.; leave **Port Norris**, 7 00 a. m., 2 40 p. m.; leave **Mauricetown**, stopping at intermediate stations, 7 08 a. m., 2 48 p. m. Arrive foot of Liberty street, N. Y., 1 00, 8 40 p. m.

For "**Fares to all Places**" see Index.

M. Sandy Hook.	6 Seabright.	9 North Long Branch.	12 West End.
4 Highland Beach.	7 Low Moor.	10 Long Branch.	14 Branchport.
4 Navesink Beach	8 Galilee.	10 Chelsea Avenue.	13 Oceanport.
5 Normandie.	8 Monmouth Beach.	11 Avenue B.	15 Eatontown.
5 Rumson Beach.

Leave **Sandy Hook** for **Seabright, Long Branch, Branchport, Oceanport** and **Eatontown**, 5 35, 9 10 a. m., 1 55, 3 55 p. m. Arrive Seabright in 17 minutes; arrive Long Branch in 24 minutes; arrive Branchport in 10 minutes; arrive Oceanport in 45 minutes; arrive Eatontown in 50 minutes.

Leave **Highland Beach** for **Long Branch, Oceanport** and **Eatontown**, 6 03, 7 44, 9 20 a. m. (10 45 a. m. to Branchport), 2 03, 4 03, 5 11 p. m. Arrive Long Branch in 24 minutes; arrive Eatontown in 10 minutes.

To Highland Beach and Sandy Hook.

Leave **Eatontown** (leave Oceanport 4 minutes later), 8 15, 9 50, 11 18 a. m., 4 30, 5 40 p. m. (7 05 p. m. to Long Branch). Arrive Highland Beach in 38 minutes.

Leave **Branchport**, 6 45, 8 24, 10 02, 11 28 a. m., 12 47, 4 40, 5 55 p. m. (7 15 p. m. to Long Branch). Arrive Highland Beach in 23 minutes.

Leave **Long Branch** for **Highland Beach**, 6 49, 8 30, 10 07, 11 33 a. m., 12 50, 4 45, 6 00 p. m. Arrive in 19 minutes. Leave North Long Branch 2 minutes later; Monmouth Beach 4 minutes later; Galilee 6 minutes later; Low Moor 8 minutes later than time of leaving Long Branch.

Leave **Seabright**, 7 00, 8 41, 10 20, 11 46 a. m., 1 03, 4 56, 6 13 p. m. Leave Rumson Beach 2 minutes later; Normandie 4 minutes later; Navesink Beach 6 minutes later. Arrive Highland Beach in 8 minutes from Seabright.

Leave **Highland Beach** for **Sandy Hook**, 8 19, 11 54 a. m., 1 11, 6 21 p. m. Arrive Sandy Hook in 9 minutes.

PHILADELPHIA & READING R. R.
From C. R. R. of N. J. Depot, foot of Liberty St.

For "Fares to all Places," see Index.

Philadelphia,	Roseglen,	Port Kennedy,	Linfield,	Birdsboro,
Girard Avenue,	West Spring Mill,	Valley Forge,	Sanatoga,	Exeter,
Belmont,	West Conshohocken,	Perkiomen Junction,	Pottstown,	Neversink,
West Falls,	Swedeland,	Phœnixville,	Stowe,	Franklin Street,
Pencoyd,	Bridgeport,	Mingo,	Douglassville,	Reading.
West Manayunk.	Merion,	Royersford	Monocacy,	

Leave foot of **Liberty St.** for **Bridgeport** (Norristown), **Phœnixville, Pottstown** and **Reading**, stopping at intermediate stations, 4 00, 7 45, 11 00 a. m., 1 30, 3 15, 4 00, 5 30, 7 30 p. m., 12 night. Sundays, 9 00 a. m., 5 30 p. m.
Due at **Bridgeport,** 10 05, 10 37 a. m., 2 28, 4 40, 6 08, 6 38, 8 37 p. m., 12 10 night, 5 04 a. m. Sundays, 12 15 noon, 12 10 night.
Due at **Phœnixville,** 10 32, 10 55 a. m., 3 03, 5 00, 6 35, 6 58, 9 03 p. m., 12 30 night, 5 32 a. m. Sundays, 1 21 p. m., 12 30 night.
Due at **Pottstown,** 10 58, 11 17 a. m., 3 37, 5 26, 7 04, 7 21, 9 32 p. m., 12 55 night, 6 04 a. m. Sundays, 1 57 p. m., 12 55 night.
Due at **Reading,** 11 40, 11 50 a. m., 4 25, 6 00, 7 48, 7 55, 10 15 p. m., 1 30 night, 6 50 a. m. Sundays, 1 30 night.

To New York.
Leave **Reading,** *1 30, 5 00, 8 00, 10 15 a. m., 12 45, 3 30, 6 20 p. m.; due in New York, *9 30, 9 30 a. m., 12 10, 4 45, 6 10, 7 10 p. m., 12 37 night. *Daily.
Leave **Pottstown** (stopping at Phœnixville and Bridgeport), 5 00, 5 38, 6 55, 8 33, 10 50 a. m., 1 24, 4 03, 7 03 p. m. Sunday, 6 55 a. m. Due in New York, 9 30, 9 30, 10 50 a. m., 12 10, 3 15, 6 10, 7 10 p. m., 12 37 night. Sundays, 12 noon.

For Trains to other points on this Road, see Central R. R. of N. J.

LEHIGH VALLEY R. R.
Depots foot of Cortlandt and Desbrosses Sts.

Fare (Single and Excursion) to Flemington, $1.35, 2.20, Phillipsburg, 2.05, 3.25, Easton, 2.10, 3.30, Bethlehem, 2.45, 3.85, Allentown, 2.60, 4.10, Mauch Chunk, 3.45, 5.55, Wilkes Barre, 5.00, 7.50, Pittston, 5.00, 7.75, Waverly, 6.95, Buffalo, 9.25, Niagara Falls, 9.25.

Ticket Offices, 235 Broadway, foot of Cortlandt & Desbrosses Sts.; all Penn. R.R. Ticket Offices; Dodd's Transfer Co's Offices.

Flemington, Phillipsburg, Easton, Bethlehem, Allentown, Mauch Chunk, Wilkes Barre, Pittston, Sayre, Waverly, Buffalo, and Niagara Falls.

Leave **Cortlandt or Desbrosses Sts.,** for **Bethlehem, Allentown** and intermediate stations 6 50, †8 00, 11 00 a. m., 1 00, †3 40, 5 40, †7 00 p. m. Sundays: 8 00 a. m., 5 45, *7 00 p. m.; due in Allentown in 3 hours. Trains marked † are Express trains, stopping only at Flemington, Phillipsburg, Easton and Bethlehem.
For **Mauch Chunk** and intermediate stations, 8 00 a. m., 1 00, 3 40, 5 40, 7 00 p. m. Sundays: 8 00 a. m., 5 45, 7 00 p. m., due in Mauch Chunk in about 4 hours.
For **Wilkes Barre** and intermediate stations, 8 00 a. m., 1 00, 3 40, 7 00 p. m. Sundays: 7 00 p. m.; due at Wilkes Barre in 6 hours.
For **Sayre, Waverly** and **Elmira**, connecting, via Erie R. R., for **Buffalo** and **Niagara Falls,** 8 00 a. m., 7 00 p. m. Sundays: 7 00 p. m.; due Elmira 5 46 p. m., 4 34 a. m.; due at Niagara Falls, 12 11 night, 10 45 a. m.

Trains to New York.
Leave **Buffalo,** via Erie R. R., 9 15 a. m., *5 30 p. m.; due in New York 11 35 p. m., *7 50 a. m. *Daily.
Leave **Elmira,** stopping at Waverly, Sayre and intermediate stations, 8 05 a. m., 2 19, *10 27 p. m.; due in New York, 6 30, 12 15 p. m., *7 50 a. m. *Daily.
Leave **Wilkes Barre,** *2 10, 5 00, 8 35 a. m., 12 40, 3 00, 6 00 p. m.; due in New York, *7 50, 11 00 a. m., 3 30, 6 30, 9 50, 11 35 p. m. *Daily.
Leave **Mauch Chunk,** *4 05, 5 25, 7 10, †1 00 a. m., 3 00, 5 20, 7 55 p. m. Sundays: 4 05, 5 50 a. m., 3 55 p. m.; due in New York, *7 50, 9 50, 11 00 a. m., 3 30, 6 30, 9 50, 11 35 p. m. Sundays, 10 05 a. m.; 8 35 p. m. *Daily.
Leave **Easton (Phillipsburg,** 2 minutes later). *5 40, 7 20, 8 50 a. m., 12 55, 4 23, 7 05, 9 25. Sundays: 5 40, 7 35 a. m., 3 5. p. m.; due in New York, 7 50, 9 50, 11 00 a. m., 3 30, 6 30, 9 50, 11 35 p. m. Sundays: 7 50, 10 05 a. m., 8 35 p. m. *Daily.

BOSTON & ALBANY R. R.
Connecting Trains leave Grand Central Depot, 4th Ave. and 42d St.
For "through" trains between Springfield and Boston, see New York, New Haven & H. R. R. time table.

Distance, Station and Fare.

Albany,.........| 25	Chatham........67c.	48 Shaker Village $1 18	71 Middlefield...$1 72	101 West Springfield $2 40
2 Greenbush......05c.	31 East Chatham....80c.	51 Pittsfield.... 1 27	76 Chester...... 1 84	103 Springfield.... 2 44
8 Schodak,......33c.	35 Canaan........91c.	57 Dalton........ 1 39	83 Huntington... 1 97	
10 Van Hosen....37c.	40 State Line....$1 03	60 Hinsdale..... 1 48	87 Russell...... 2 06	
17 Kinderhook...50c.	42 Richmond Furnace 1 07	64 Washington... 1 57	90 Fairfield....	
20 Chatham Centre 55c.	43 Richmond.... 1 09	68 Becket....... 1 63	94 Westfield.... 2 24	

Leave **Albany** for **Chatham, Pittsfield, Springfield** and intermediate stations, *2 30, 7 00, 10 00 a.m., 2 30, *1 50, †5 00, 9 00 p. m. *Sundays also. †Does not run east of Pittsfield.
Due at **Chatham,** *3 20, 7 55, 10 48 a. m., 3 25, 5 33, 5 56, 9 55 p. m.
Due at **Pittsfield,** *4 20, 9 02, 11 40 a. m., 4 32, *6 22, 7 00, 10 57 p. m.
Due at **Springfield,** *6 05, 10 57 a. m., 1 25, 6 37, *7 55 p. m., 1 00 night.
Leave **Springfield** for **Albany** and intermediate stations, 3 30, 9 05, 11 30 a. m., 2 15, *6 05, *9 57 p. m.; due at Albany, 7 25 a. m., 1 00, 2 43, 6 10, *9 45 p. m., *1 30 night.
Leave **Pittsfield,** 5 34, 7 25, 11 11 a. m., 1 16, 4 19, *8 10, *11 53 p. m.; due at Albany, 7 25, 9 15 a. m., 1 00, 2 43, 6 10, *9 45 p.m., *1 30 night.
Leave **Chatham,** 6 33, 8 26 a. m., 12 10, 2 01, 5 18, *9 00 p. m., *12 42 night; due at Albany 7 25, 9 15 a. m., 1 00, 2 43, 6 10, *9 45 p. m., *1 30 night.

HUDSON & CHATHAM BRANCH.
Stations and Fare from Hudson—Hudson Upper, 15c.; Claverack, 19c.; Mellenville, 31c.; Pulvers, 35c.; Ghent, 44c.; Chatham, 49c.
Leave **Chatham** for **Hudson** and all stations, 8 30 a. m., 12 10, 2 10, 5 20, 6 10 p. m.; due at Hudson, 9 10 a. m., 1 00, 3 01, 6 05, 7 00 p. m.
Leave **Hudson** for **Chatham,** 7 05, 9 55, a. m., 12 25, 2 30, 4 30 p. m.; due at Chatham 7 50, 10 40 a. m., 1 25, 3 21, 5 15 p. m.

PITTSFIELD & NORTH ADAMS BRANCH.
Distance, Station and Fare.

North Adams	6 Maple Grove....24c.	12 Farnum.........42c.	— Junction,
4 Renfrew....19c.	8 Chesh. Harbor..26c.	14 Berkshire.....43c.	21 Pittsfield.........55c.
5 Adams .....22c.	10 Cheshire......34c.	17 Coltsville.....40c.	

Leave **Pittsfield** for **North Adams** and all stations, 7 30, 11 15 a. m., 1 40, 5 05, 8 15 p. m.; due at North Adams, 8 20 a. m., 12 05, 2 30, 5 55, 9 05 p. m.
Leave **North Adams** for **Pittsfield,** 6 20, 10 00 a. m., 12 15, 3 05, 6 20 p.m.; due at Pittsfield, 7 10, 10 50 a. m., 1 05, 3 55, 7 10 p. m.

ATHOL BRANCH.
Fare—Springfield to Boudsville, 53c.; to Athol, $1.18.
Leave **Springfield** for **Boudsville, Athol** and intermediate stations, 7 10 a. m., 6 10 p. m. Saturdays, †9 55 p. m.; due at Boudsville, 8 30 a.m., 7 30 p.m. Saturdays, 10 45 p.m.; due at Athol 9 55 a.m., 8 15 p.m. †Runs to Boudsville only.
Leave **Athol** for **Springfield,** 8 a. m., 5 38 p. m.; due at Springfield, 10 10 a. m., 5 38 p. m.
Leave **Boudsville,** 9 18 a.m., 1 19 p.m. Saturdays, 10 50 p.m.; due at Springfield 10 10 a.m., 5 38 p.m. Saturdays 11 42 p.m.

DELAWARE, LACKAWANNA AND WESTERN R. R.

Depot, foot of Barclay and Christopher Sts.

Ticket Offices, foot of Barclay & Christopher Sts., 429 Broadway, 26 Exchange Place.

MORRIS AND ESSEX DIVISION.

Stations, Distances and Fares—Single and Excursion.

M Hoboken		14 South Orange	40c- .65	28 Convent	.75-$1.15	55 Waterloo	$1.65-$2.25
7 Harrison	20c-30c	15 Maplewood	45c- .70	30 Morristown	.80- 1.25	60 Hackettstown	1.70- 2.45
8 Newark	20c-30c	16 Wyoming	50c- .75	32 Morris Plains	.90- 1.35	66 Port Murray	1.70- 2.75
9 Roseville	20c-30c	17 Milburn	50c- .80	36 Mount Tabor	$1.00- 1.40	70 Washington	1.70- 2.85
10 Grove St	25c-45c	18 Short Hills	55c- .85	37 Denville	1.05- 1.50	75 Broadway	1.85- 3.05
East Orange	26c-50c	19 Huntly	55c- .85	38 Rockaway	1.15- 1.60	79 Stewartsville	2.00- 3.20
11 Brick Church	28c-50c	20 Summit	55c- .85	42 Dover	1.25- 1.75	84 Phillipsburg	2.05- 3.25
Orange	30c-50c	22 N. Providence	60c- .95	47 Drakesville	1.40- 1.95	85 Easton	2.10- 3.30
12 Highland Av	35c-55c	23 Chatham	65c- $1.00	Hopatcong	1.45 2.05		
13 Mountain Station	38c-65c	26 Madison	70c- 1.10	51 Stanhope	1.55- 2.10		

** Leave Christopher St. same time as Barclay St. † Express train, makes no intermediate stops. ‡ Does not stop at Mount Tabor. § Does not stop at Drakesville or Waterloo.*

Leave foot of Barclay St. (leave foot of Christopher St. 5 minutes later).

For **Harrison,** 6 30, 7 30, 9 20 a. m., 1 30, 3 10, 6 10, *7 00, *8 30, *10 00, *10 45, 11 30 p. m., 12 night. Arrive Harrison in 31 minutes.

For **Newark,** 6 30, 7 00, 7 20, 7 30, 8 00, 8 10, 8 30, 9 10, 9 20, 9 30, 10 10, 10 30, 11 10, 11 30 a. m., 12 00 m., and 12 10, 12 30, 12 40, 1 30, 2 10, 2 30, 3 10, 3 30, 3 40, 4 00, 4 30, 4 40, 5 00, 5 10, 5 20, 5 30, 5 50, 6 00, 6 10, 6 20, *6 30, *7 00, *8 00, *8 30, *9 00, *10 00, *10 45, 11 30 and 12 00 p. m. Arrive Newark in 33 minutes.

For **Orange** (all stations), **Mountain Station** and **South Orange,** 6 30, 7 00 (7 20 to Orange Station and South Orange), 7 30, 8 00, 8 30 (9 10 to Orange Station), 9 20, 10 10, 11 10 a. m., 12 10, 12 40, 1 30, 2 30, 3 10, 3 30, 4 00, 4 30 (4 50 to Orange Station, Highland Ave., Mountain Station and South Orange), 5 00, 5 20 (5 40, except Grove St.), 5 50 (6 00 to Brick Church and Orange St'n), 6 10, *6 30, *7 00, *8 00, *8 30, *9 00, *10 00, *10 45, 11 30 p. m., 12 00 night. Arrive at Roseville Ave. in 38 minutes; Grove St., 40 minutes; East Orange, 42 minutes; Brick Church, 44 minutes; Orange Station, 47 minutes; Highland Avenue, 50 minutes; Mountain Station, 53 minutes; South Orange, 55 minutes.

For **Maplewood, Wyoming, Milburn and Short Hills,** (7 20, Milburn only), 7 30, 8 30, 10 10, 11 10 a. m., 1 30, 2 30, 4 00, 4 30, (5 20, Milburn & Short Hills), 5 40, (6 00, Milburn & Short H.), 6 10, *6 30, *8 00, *9 00, *10 00 p. m. Arrive Milburn in 1 hour, Short Hills 1 hour, 7 minutes.

For **Huntly,** 7 30, 10 10 a. m., 4 30, 5 40 p. m., arrive in 1 hour, 10 minutes.

For **Summit,** 7 20, 7 30, 8 30, 9 10, 10 10, 11 10 a. m., 12 m., (1 20 on Saturdays only), ‡1 30, 2 30, 3 30, 4 00, 4 30, 5 00, 5 20, 5 40, 6 00, 6 10, *6 30, *8 00, *9 00, *10 00 p. m., (12 night Wed. only). Arrive Summit in 1⅙ hours.

For **New Providence,** 7 30, 9 10, 10 10 a. m., 2 30, 4 30, 5 20, 6 00, *6 30, *8 00 p. m., (12 night Sat. only).

For **Chatham,** 7 20, 7 30, 9 10, 10 10, 11 10 a. m., 12 m., (1 20 Sat. only), 2 30, 3 30, 4 30, 5 20, 6 00, *6 30, *8 00, *10 00 p. m., (12 night Sat. only). Arrive Chatham in 1½ hours.

For **Madison,** 7 20, 9 10, 10 10, 11 10 a. m., 12 m., (1 20 Sat. only), 2 30, 3 30, 4 00, 4 30, 5 00, 5 20, 6 00, *6 30, *8 00, *10 00 p. m. (12 night Sat. only). Arrive Madison 1 hour, 20 minutes.

For **Convent** (Signal Station), 7 20, 9 10, 10 10, 11 10 a. m., 2 30, 4 30, 5 20, 6 00, *6 30, *8 00, *10 00 p. m., (12 night Sat. only). Arrive Convent in 1 hour 25 minutes.

For **Morristown,** 7 20, 9 10, 10 10, 11 10 a. m., 12 m., (1 20 Sat. only), 2 30, 3 30, 4 00, 4 30, 5 00, 5 20, 6 00, *6 30, *8 00, *10 00 p. m., (12 night Sat. only). Arrive Morristown in 1½ hours.

For **Dover,** stopping at Morris Plains, Mt. Tabor, Denville and Rockaway, †7 20, 7 20, †9 00, 9 10, 10 10 a. m., 12 00 m., †1 00, ‡3 30, †4 10, 4 30, ‡5 20, *†7 00, *8 00, †*9 00 p. m., Sundays †*9 00 p. m. Arrive at Dover †Express trains in 1⅝ hours; accommodation trains in 2 hours.

For **Hackettstown** and intermediate stations, 7 20, †9 00 a. m., 12 00 m., §1 00, 3 30, 4 10, 5 20, *†7 00, *†9 00 p. m. Sundays, *†9 00 p. m. Arrive in 2 hours.

For **Port Murray,** 7 20 a. m., 12 m., 3 30 p. m. Arrive in 2⅝ hours.

For **Washington,** 7 20, 9 00 a. m., 12 m., 1 00, 3 30, 4 10, *7 00, *9 00 p. m. Sundays, *9 00 p. m. Arrive in 2¾ to 3 hours.

For **Easton,** stopping at Broadway, Stewartville and Phillipsburg, 7 20 a. m., 1 00, 4 10 p. m. Arrive **Easton,** 10 52 a. m., 3 40, 7 05 p. m.

To New York.

Leave **Easton,** 7 15 a. m., 1 00, 7 08 p. m. Arrive New York, 10 25 a. m., 4 35, 10 50 p. m.

Leave **Washington,** 4 40, 5 10, 7 25, 7 44, 10 25 a. m., 12 42, 1 38, 3 50, 6 18, 7 30, 7 41 p. m. Sundays, 1 40, 5 10, 7 25 a. m., 7 30 p. m. Arrive **New York** in 2 to 3 hours.

Leave **Hackettstown,** 4 59, 5 29, 6 55, 7 43, 8 05, 10 42 a. m., 1 00, 1 58, 4 07, 7 05, 7 51, 8 03 p. m. Sundays, 4 59, 5 29, 7 43 a. m., 7 51 p. m. Arrive New York in 2 hours.

Leave **Dover,** 5 38, 6 06, 6 55, 7 31, 8 19, 8 45, 11 15, 11 20 a. m., 12 45, 1 36, 2 44, 4 41, 5 55, 7 38, 8 36, 8 55 p. m. Sundays, 5 38, 6 06, 8 19 a. m., 8 36 p. m. Arrive New York in 1¼ to 2 hours.

Leave **Morristown,** 6 30, 6 55, 7 21, 7 55, 8 02, 8 25, 9 12, 10 30, 11 48 a. m., 1 15 (2 55, Saturdays only), 3 15, 4 35, 6 25, 8 05, 9 30 p. m. Arrive New York in 1 to 1½ hours.

Leave **Madison,** 6 40, 7 05, 7 30, 8 02, 8 11, 8 32, 9 20, 10 40, 11 57 a. m., 1 25 (3 05, Saturdays only), 3 24, 4 15, 6 34, 8 15, 9 39 p. m. Arrive New York in 1¼ hours.

Leave **Chatham,** 6 15, 6 46, 7 10, 7 34, 8 16, 9 25, 9 35, 10 46 a. m., 12 02, 1 31 (3 10, Saturdays only), 3 30, 4 51, 6 39, 8 21, 9 44 p. m. Arrive New York in 1 to 1¼ hours.

Leave **Summit,** 6 25, 6 55, 7 05, 7 18, 7 42, 7 48, 8 11, 8 25, 8 45, 9 32, 9 44, 10 15, 10 55 a. m., 12 10, 1 39, 2 55 (3 17, Saturdays only), 3 38, 5 02, 6 48, 7 55, 8 29, 9 51, 10 42 p. m. Arrive New York in 1 hour.

Leave **Huntly,** 6 27, 7 07, 9 45 a. m., 1 40, 2 57 p. m. Arrive New York in 1 hour, 10 minutes.

Leave **Short Hills** 7 00, 7 24, 7 48, 7 53, 8 29, 8 50, 9 50, 10 20, 11 00 a. m., 12 15, 1 44, 3 00, 5 08, 6 52, 7 59, 8 31, 10 47 p. m. Arrive New York in 1 hour.

Leave **Milburn** 6 35, 7 01, 7 14, 7 28, 7 51, 7 56, 8 33, 8 51, 9 53, 10 25, 11 04 a. m., 12 18, 1 48, 3 05, 3 25, 3 46, 5 12, 6 57, 8 05, 8 38, 9 58, 10 51 p. m. Arrive New York in 1 hour.

Leave **Wyoming** (Signal Station), 6 37, 7 06, 7 16, 7 30, 7 58, 9 55, 10 27, 11 06 a. m., 1 50, 3 07, 5 14, 6 59, 8 07, 8 40, 10 53 p. m. Arrive New York in 50 minutes.

Leave **Maplewood** 6 40, 7 09, 7 32, 8 00, 8 58, 9 57, 10 20, 11 07 a. m., 12 22, 1 53, 3 09, 5 17, 7 01, 8 10, 8 43, 10 56 p. m. Arrive New York in 50 minutes.

Leave **South Orange** (Mountain Station 2 minutes later; Hi'land Avenue 4 minutes later), 5 48, 6 00, 6 44, 7 13, 7 24, 7 38, (8 00 S. Orange only), 8 08, 8 25, 9 02, 9 25, 10 02, 10 35, 11 13, 11 55 a. m., 12 26, 1 15, 1 57, 2 45, 3 15, (3 52 S. Orange only), 4 25, 4 43, 5 22, 6 03, 6 30, 7 05, 7 45, 8 15, 8 46, 9 30, (10 04 S. Orange only), 10 30, 11 00 p. m., 12 33 night.

Leave **Orange** 5 57, 6 08, 6 53, 7 22, 7 32, 7 47, 7 52, 8 06, 8 17, 8 33, 8 43, 9 10, 9 34, 9 50, 10 12, 10 41, 11 22 a. m., 12 01, 12 36, 1 24, 2 07, 2 54, 3 24, (3 40 Sat only), 3 58, 4 33, 4 53, 5 31, 6 13, 6 39, 7 15, 7 54, 8 23, 8 55, 9 39, 10 10, 10 40, 11 08 p. m., 12 42 a. m. Arrive New York in 40 minutes.

Leave **Brick Church** (Orange), 6 00, 6 11, 6 56, 7 25, 7 36, 7 55, 8 08, 8 36, 9 12, 9 37, 10 15, 10 47, 11 25 a. m., 12 07, 12 39, 1 27, 2 10, 2 57, 3 27, 4 36, 4 57, 5 34, 6 16, 6 42, 7 18, 7 57, 8 26, 8 58, 9 42, 10 43, 11 11 p. m., 12 45 a. m. Arrive New York in 38 minutes.

Leave **East Orange** 6 02, 6 13, 6 58, 7 27, 7 38, 7 57, 8 10, 8 38, 9 14, 9 39, 10 17, 10 49, 11 27 a. m., 12 09, 12 41, 1 29, 2 12, 2 53, 3 29, 4 34, 4 59, 5 37, 6 18, 6 44, 7 20, 7 59, 8 28, 9 00, 9 44, 10 45, 11 13 p. m., 12 47 night. Arrive New York in 36 minutes.

Leave **Grove Street** (Orange), 6 04, 6 15, 7 00, 7 29, 7 40, 7 59, 8 12, 8 40, 9 16, 9 41, 10 19, 10 51, 11 29 a. m., 12 11, 12 43, 1 31, 2 14, 3 01, 3 31, 4 40, 5 01, 5 40, 6 20, 6 46, 7 22, 8 01, 8 30, 9 02, 9 46, 10 47, 11 15 p. m., 12 49 a. m. Arrive New York in 34 minutes.

Continued on next page.

DELAWARE, LACKAWANNA AND WESTERN R. R.—Continued.

Morris & Essex Division—Trains to New York.

Leave **Roseville Avenue**, 6 06, 6 18, 7 03, 7 42, 7 52, 8 14, 8 43, 9 41, 10 22, 10 53, 11 32 a. m., 12 14, 12 46, 1 33, 2 17, 3 01, 3 34, 4 04, 4 35, 5 09, 5 43, 6 23, 6 48, 7 25, 8 04, 8 32, 9 05, 9 48, 10 50, 11 17 p. m., 12 51 night. Arrive New York in 31 minutes.

Leave **Newark** at 6 11, 6 23, 7 08, 7 20, 7 37, 7 47, 7 57, 8 07, 8 11, 8 19, 8 48, 8 51, 9 24, 9 30, 9 49, 10 00, 10 27, 10 47, 10 58, 11 37, 11 50 a. m., 12 19, 12 51, 12 58, 1 38, 1 58, 2 22, 3 09, 3 39, 3 47, 4 09, 4 48, 4 55, 5 08, 5 39, 5 48, 6 28, 6 53, 7 30, 8 08, 8 37, 9 10, 9 53, 10 23, 10 55, 11 22 p. m., 12 56 a. m. Arrive New York in 27 minutes.

Leave **Harrison**, 6 43, 6 25, 7 10, 7 30, 7 49, 9 51, 10 23, 11 00 a. m., 12 21, 3 11, 3 11, 4 50, 5 10, 6 30, 6 55, 8 10, 9 12, 9 55, 10 57, 11 24 p. m., 12 58 night. Arrive New York in 25 minutes.

NEWARK AND BLOOMFIELD BRANCH.

Leave Christopher St. same time as Barclay St.

Fare, Single and Excursion—Watsessing 28c., 45c., Bloomfield 30c., 50c., Glen Ridge, 33c., 55c., Montclair 35c., 60c.

Leave foot of Barclay St. (leave Christopher St. 5 minutes later) for **Watsessing, Bloomfield, Glen Ridge and Montclair**, 6 30, 7 20, 8 10, 9 30, 10 30, 11 30 a. m., 12 30 (1 20, Saturdays only), 2 10, 3 40, 4 20, 1 40, 5 10, 5 30, 6 20, *7 00, *8 30, *10 00, 11 30 p. m. Arrive Watsessing in 42 minutes; Bloomfield, 44 minutes; Glen Ridge, 46 minutes; Montclair, 48 minutes.

Leave **Montclair**, 6 03, 6 50, 7 15, 7 52, 8 28, 9 15, 10 30, 11 35 a. m., 12 10, 1 10 12 30. Saturdays only), 3 30, 4 10, 5 20, 5 45, 6 10, 6 38, 8 15, 9 35, 11 05 p. m., 12 40 night. Arrive New York in 45 minutes.

Leave Glen Ridge 3 minutes later; Bloomfield, 4 minutes later; Watsessing, 6 minutes later than time of leaving Montclair.

BOONTON BRANCH.

Leave Christopher St. same time as Barclay St.

Stations, Distances and Fares—Single and Excursion.

Hoboken		9 Delawanna...35c.-45c.	16 West Paterson...50c.-70c.	25 Whitehall...80c.-$1 05
4 Secaucus...15c.-25c.	11 Passaic...40c.-55c.	18 Little Falls...55c.-80c.	24 Montville...85c.-1 15
7 Kingsland...25c.-35c.	12 Clifton...45c.-65c.	21 Mountain View...70c.-90c.	30 Boonton...95c.-1 25
8 Lyndhurst...35c.-40c.	15 Paterson...50c.-70c.	23 Lincoln Park...75c.-95c.	34 Denville...$1 05-1 50

Leave foot of Barclay St. (leave Christopher St. 5 minutes later) for **Paterson, Boonton** and intermediate stations, 6 50, 10 30, 1 10, 5 30 p. m. (6 20 p. m. to Lyndhurst). Arrive at Paterson, 7 47, 11 25 a. m., 5 07, 6 27 p. m.; at Boonton, 8 23 a. m., 12 00 m., 5 48, 7 05 p. m.

For **Paterson** and **Boonton** only (Express trains), 7 20, 9 00 a. m., 1 00, 4 10, *7 00, *9 00 p. m., Sundays, *7 00, *9 00 p. m. Arrive Paterson in 42 minutes; Boonton in 1 hour, 5 minutes.

For **Denville**, 1 00, 4 10 p. m. Arrive, 2 55, 6 03 p. m.

To New York,

Leave **Denville**, 7 50 a. m., 3 05, 6 10 p. m. Arrive New York, 9 25 a. m., 4 45, 8 50 p. m.

Leave **Boonton**, 5 56, 6 24, 7 00, 8 04, 8 35, 11 30 a. m., 12 30, 1 53, 3 18, 4 57, 7 50, 8 54 p. m., Sundays, 5 56, 6 23, 8 35 a. m. Arrive New York in 1¼ hours.

Leave **Paterson**, 6 26, 6 49, 7 33, 8 38, 9 01, 11 55 a. m., 1 10, 2 19, 3 50, 5 23, 8 10, 9 26 p. m., Sundays, 6 24, 6 49, 9 01 a. m. Arrive New York in 39 minutes.

Leave **Lyndhurst**, 6 07, 6 37, 7 19, 8 54 a. m., 1 35, 4 45 p. m., Sundays, 6 37 a. m. Arrive New York in 27 minutes.

SUSSEX R. R.

Fare, Single and Excursion—Andover $1.85, $2.65, Newton $2.00, $2.95, Lafayette $2.15, $3 25, Branchville $2.35, $3.50, Franklin $2.45, $3.60.

Leave foot of Barclay St. (leave Christopher St. 5 minutes later) for **Waterloo, Andover, Newton, Lafayette and Branchville**, 7 20 a. m., 12 00 m., 4 10 p. m. Arrive Andover, 10 16 a. m., 2 55, 6 25 p. m.; Newton, 10 29 a. m., 3 15, 6 38 p. m.; Lafayette, 10 43 a. m., 3 30, 6 52 p. m.; Branchville, 11.00 a. m., 3 50, 7 08 p. m.

For **Waterloo, Andover** and **Newton** only, 5 30 p. m. Arrive Andover, 8 35 p. m.; Newton 8 50 p. m.

For **Sparta Station** and **Franklin**, 7 20 a. m., 12 00 m. Arrive Franklin, 11 10 a. m., 5 03 p.m.

To New York.

Leave **Franklin**, 12 45, 5 30 p. m. Arrive New York, 4 35, 10 35 p. m.

Leave **Branchville**, 6 45 a. m., 1 05, 6 10 p. m.; leave **Lafayette**, 7 00 a. m., 1 20, 6 35 p. m. Arrive New York, 10 25 a. m., 4 35, 10 35 p. m.

Leave **Newton** (leave Andover 13 minutes later), 6 30, 7 15 a. m., 1 35, 7 05 p. m. Arrive New York, 9 15, 10 25 a.m., 4 35, 10 35 p. m.

PASSAIC AND DELAWARE R. R.

Stations, Distances and Fares—Single and Excursion.

Hoboken	25 Murray Hill...70c.-$1 00	29 Stirling...90c.-$1 20	31 Basking Ridge.$1 05-$1 40
20 Summit	26 Berkeley Heights...70c.-1 00	30 Millington...95c.-1 25	35 Bernardsville...1 10-$1 45
22 West Summit...65c.-95c.	27 Gillette...1 15	32 Lyons...90c.-1 30	

Leave **foot of Barclay St.** (leave Christopher St. 5 minutes later) for **Bernardsville** and intermediate stations, 7 20, 9 10 a. m., 3 30, 4 30, 5 20 p. m. Arrive Bernardsville, 9 25, 10 40 a. m., 5 10, 6 10, 7 05 p. m.

Leave **Bernardsville**, stopping at all intermediate stations, 7 03, 7 52, 8 50 a. m., 3 00, 5 35 p. m. Arrive New York, 8 35, 9 15, 10 25 a. m., 4 35, 7 55 p. m.

BLOOMSBURG DIVISION.

Stations, Distances and Fares—Single and Excursion.

Scranton...$4 35-$6 75	16 Bennett...$4 90 $7 45	34 Shickshinny...$5 25-$8 05	56 Bloomsburg...$5 35-$8 05
1 Bellevue...4 40- 6 80	17 Kingston...4 95- 7 50	34 Hick's Ferry...5 30 8 15	58 Rupert...5 35- 8 75
3 Taylorville...4 45- 6 85	Wilkes-Barre...4 95- 7 50	37 Beach Haven...5 30 8 25	60 Catawissa...5 35 8 75
6 Lackawanna...4 55- 7 05	19 Plymouth June.	44 Berwick...5 30- 8 35	68 Danville...5 65- 9 00
9 Pittston...4 65- 7 15	20 Plymouth...5 00- 7 65	47 Brier Creek...5 30- 8 40	71 Chulasky...5 80- 9 05
10 West Pittston...4 70- 7 25	22 Avondale...5 10- 7 75	48 Willow Grove...8 20 8 45	73 Cameron...5 90- 9 10
12 Wyoming...4 75- 7 35	24 Nanticoke...5 15- 7 80	50 Lime Ridge...5 30- 8 50	80 Northumberland 6 05 9 25
14 Maltby...4 85- 7 40	27 Hunlock's...5 25- 7 95	51 Espy...5 30- 8 85	

Leave foot of Barclay and **Christopher Sts.**, via Scranton, for **Wilkes-Barre, Plymouth** and intermediate stations, 9 00 a. m., 1 00, 4 10, 7 00 p. m. Arrive at Wilkes-Barre, 3 00, 7 27, 10 40 p. m., 7 18 a. m.; at Plymouth, 2 55, 7 16, 10 30 p. m., 7 10 a. m.

For **Nanticoke**, 9 00 a. m., 1 00, 7 00 p. m. Arrive, 3 05, 7 25 p. m., 7 19 a. m.

For **Northumberland** and intermediate stations, 9 00 a. m., 1 00, 7 00 p. m. Arrive Northumberland, 5 15, 9 45 p. m., 9 24 a. m.

To New York.

Leave **Northumberland**, stopping at intermediate stations, 6 15, 10 00 a. m., 1 35, 5 40 p. m. Arrive New York, 2 55, 6 00, 8 50 p. m., 7 10 a. m.

Leave **Plymouth**, 7 10, 8 33 a. m., 12 15, 3 35, 7 59 p. m.; leave **Wilkes-Barre** (Branch), 7 00, 8 10 a. m., 12 05, 3 15, 7 45 p. m. Arrive New York, 12 25, 2 55, 6 00, 8 50 p. m., 7 10 a. m.

Continued on next page.

DELAWARE, LACKAWANNA & WESTERN R. R.—Continued.

MAIN LINE.
*Trains marked * run daily.*

Stations, Distances and Fares—Single and Excursion.

M.	New York		95 Spragueville....	$2 65–$1 20		155 Dalton........	$1 75– 7 35		329 RichfieldSpring:$5 65-10 75
	Junction		99 Henryville	2 75– 4 35		157 La Plume.....	1 80– 7 50		301 Utica .... 5 00 ......
	— Changewater.	$1 80–	101 Cresco.........	2 95– 4 60		159 Factoryville...	1 90– 7 60		285 Syracuse....... 6 00–10 00
66	Washington....	1 70– 2 85	110 Mount Pocono.	3 15– 4 90		165 Nicholson.....	5 00– 7 70		320 Oswego........ 6 50 10 00
51	Oxford Furnace	1 85– 3 15	113 Pocono Summit	3 25– 5 05		171 Foster.........	5 00– 7 70		228 Owego......... 5 50– 8 85
75	Bridgeville.....	1 95– 3 35	118 Tobyhanna....	3 40– 5 40		175 Kingsley's.....	5 00 7 70		
77	Manunka Chunk	2 05– 3 40	123 Gouldsboro.....	3 40 5 70		178 Montrose......	5 00– 7 75		364 Ithaca........... 6 50 10 50
79	Delaware.......	2 05– 3 15	131 Moscow.......	3 90 6 15		185 New Milford..	5 00– 7 75		215 Waverly...... 5 75– 9 60
82	Portland.......	2 15– 3 60	134 Dunning.......	4 00– 6 30		192 Great Bend.....	5 00– 7 75		263 Elmira......... 6 00 10 25
87	Water Gap.....	2 25– 3 80	145 Scranton......	4 35– 6 25		197 Conklin........	5 00– 7 85		250 Bath........... 6 00
91	Stroudsburg....	2 50– 4 00	151 Clark'sSummit	4 60 7 15		207 Binghamton...	$5 00–$8 00		410 Buffalo........ 8 50
			154 Glenburn.....	$4 70 $7 30					

Leave foot of Barclay and Christopher Sts. for **Manunka Chunk, Stroudsburg, Scranton** and intermediate stations, 7 30, 9 00 a. m., 1 00, 4 10, *7 00, *9 00 p.m. Arrive **Manunka Chunk**, 10 15, 11 31 a. m., 3 40, 7 00, *9 31, *11 45 p. m.; arrive **Stroudsburg**, 10 52 a. m., 12 00 m., 1 13, 7 35, *10 03 p. m., *12 49 night; arrive **Scranton**, 12 45, 1 35, 6 00, 9 25, *11 40 p. m., *2 10 a. m.

For **Binghamton, Owego** and intermediate stations, 7 30, 9 00 a. m., 1 00, *7 00, *9 00 p. m. Arrive **Binghamton**, 3 20, 3 35, 8 25 p. m., *1 40, *4 15 a. m.; arrive **Owego**, 4 15, 9 08 p. m., *2 17, *5 02 a. m.

For **Ithaca**, 9 00 a.m., *9 p. m. Arrive Ithaca, 5 45 p.m., *6 40 a. m.

For **Utica** and **Richfield Springs**, 9 00 a.m., *9 00 p. m. Arrive Utica, 7 30 p.m.. *7 55 a. m. Arrive Richfield Springs, 7 55 p. m. ,*8 05 a. m. except Sundays).

For **Syracuse and Oswego**, 9 00 a.m., *9 00 p. m. Arrive Syracuse, 6 40 p.m., *7 10 a.m. Arrive Oswego, 7 25 p.m., *8 30 a.m.

For **Waverly, Elmira, Bath** and **Buffalo**, 9 00 a. m. (to Waverly and Elmira only), *7 00, *9 00 p. m. Arrive **Waverly**, 1 47, 9 40 p.m., *2 16, *5 40 a. m. Arrive **Elmira**, 5 15, 10 10 p.m., *3 15, *6 15 a.m. Arrive **Bath**, 6 22 p. m., *4 18, 7 35 a. m. Arrive **Buffalo**, 9 50 p. m., *7 20, *11 45 a.m.

Trains to New York.
*Trains marked * run daily.*

Leave **Buffalo**, 9 00 a. m., *6 15, *9 35 p.m. Arrive New York, *7 30, *9 40 a. m.
Leave **Bath**, *12 30, 8 18 a. m., 12 28, *9 10 p.m. Arrive New York, 9 00 a.m., 4 00, 9 00 p. m., *7 30 a. m.
Leave **Elmira**, *1 39, 5 40, 9 40 a.m., 1 21, *10 46 p.m. Arrive New York, *9 10 a.m., 3 00, 6 00, 9 00 p. m., *7 30 a.m.
Leave **Waverly**, 6 13, 10 10, 1 17, *11 15 p.m. Arrive New York, 3 00, 6 00, 9 00 p. m., *7 30 a.m.
Leave **Ithaca**, 7 30 a. m., 12 30, *7 30 p.m. Arrive New York, 6 00, 9 00 p. m., *7 10 a. m.
Leave **Owego**, *2 11, 6 46, 10 13 a.m., 2 13, *11 49 p. m. Arrive New York, *9 10 a.m., 3 00, 6 00, 9 00 p. m., *7 30 a. m.
Leave **Oswego**, 7 15 a. m., *7 40 p.m. Arrive New York, 6 00 p. m., *7 10 a.m.
Leave **Syracuse**, 9 00 a. m., *9 00 p.m. Arrive New York, 6 00 p.m., *7 10 a. m.
Leave **Richfield Springs**, 9 15 a. m., 8 45 p.m. Arrive New York, 9 00 p. m., 7 10 a. m.
Leave **Utica**, 6 15, 11 15 a. m., *9 00 p.m. Arrive New York, 6 00, 9 00 p.m., 7 10 a. m.
Leave **Binghamton**, *12 25, *3 15, 7 30, 11 40 a.m., 2 48, *11 15 p.m. Arrive New York, *7 30, *9 10 a.m., 3 00, 6, 9 p.m., *7 10 a.m.
Leave **Scranton**, *1 59, *2 30, *5 00, 8 00, 9 50 a.m., 1 25, 4 31 p. m. Arrive New York, *7 10, *7 30, 9 10 a.m., 12 30, 3 00, 6, 9 00 p.m.
Leave **Stroudsburg**, *3 39, *4 13, *6 32, 9 38, 11 43 a.m., 3 00, 6 01 p. m. Arrive New York, *7 10, *7 30, 9 10 a.m., 12 30, 3 00, 6 00, 9 00 p.m.
Leave **Manunka Chunk**, *4 12, *4 11, *7 00, 10 04 a.m., 12 17, 3 30, 6 29, 6 45 p.m. Arrive New York, *7 10, *7 30, *9 40 a. m., 12 30, 3 00, 6 00, 9 00, 10 30 p. m.

LEHIGH & HUDSON RIVER R. R.

New York connections as follows: At Greycourt with Erie R. R.; at Franklin Junction with New York, Sus. & W. R. R., and Sussex R. R.; at Belvidere with Pennsylvania R. R.

Stations, Distances and Fares from Greycourt.

Greycourt.		10 Warwick........	33c.	21 Hamburg......	75c.	39 Andover.......	$1 20
4 Sugar Loaf.......	13c.	13 New Milford...	40c.	26 Franklin Junction..	80c.	51 Great Meadows..	1 55
6 Lake............	18c.	18 Vernon.........	51c.	30 Lake Grinnell..	93c.	58 Buttsville......	1 75
8 Stone Bridge.....	27c.	22 McAfee........	63c.	33 Sparta Junction...	$1 00	63 Belvidere......	1 90

Leave Greycourt for **Warwick** and intermediate stations. 8 00, 8 15, 11 01 a. m., 3 18, 6 30 p. m., Sundays, 10 57 a. m. Arrive in 30 to 40 minutes.

For **Belvidere** and intermediate stations, 8 45 a. m., 3 18 p.m., Sundays, 10 57 a.m. Arrive **Franklin Junction**, 10 18 a. m., 5 10 p. m., Sundays, 12 36 p. m. Arrive **Belvidere**, 12 15, 7 30 p. m., Sundays, 2 20 p. m.

Trains to Greycourt.

Leave **Belvidere**, stopping at intermediate stations, 8 05 a. m., 3 32 p. m., Sundays, 2 50 p. m.; leave **Franklin Junction**, 10 55 a. m., 5 10 p. m., Sundays, 1 25 p. m. Arrive Greycourt, 12 40, 7 15 p. m., Sundays, 6 25 p. m.
Leave **Warwick**, 7 05, 9 55 a. m., 12 05, 1 35, 6 18 p. m., Sundays, 5 36 p. m. Arrive Greycourt, 7 30, 10 20 a. m., 12 40, 5 15, 7 12 p. m., Sundays, 6 25 p. m.

MERIDEN, WATERBURY AND CONNECTICUT RIVER R. R.

Via New York, New Haven and H. R. R., Grand Central Depot. For "Fares to all Places," see Index.

Leave Grand Central Depot, 5 01, 8 00 a. m., 1 00 p.m., for **Waterbury**, East Farms, Summit, Prospect, West Cheshire, Southington Road. Arrive Southington Road, 9 44 a. m., 1 41, 5 17 p. m.
For **Meriden**, Highland, Smiths, Westfield, Cromwell, 5 01, 11 00 a. m., 3 00 p.m. Arrive Cromwell, 10 28 a.m., 2 25, 6 16 p. m.

To Meriden, Waterbury and New York.

Leave **Cromwell**, 6 30 a. m., 12 13, 4 05 p. m. Arrive Meriden, 7 02 a. m., 12 31, 4 10 p. m.
Leave **Meriden**, 7 02, 9 25 a. m., 12 51, 1 55 p.m. Arrive Waterbury, 7 18, 10 18 a. m., 1 35, 5 45 p. m. Arrive **New York**, 11 05 h. m., 2 15, 6 00, 9 00 p. m.

NEWBURG, DUTCHESS AND CONNECTICUT R. R.

Connect via New York Central and Hudson River R. R. Passengers from Newburgh will leave by Newburgh and Fishkill Ferry and Stage to Mattewan. Passengers for Newburgh will change at Mattewan, taking Stages of Newburgh Transfer Co.

Stations and Distances.

Newburg		8 Brinckerhoff		21 Moores		39 Stissing		54 Winchell's
Dutchess Junction		12 Hopewell		24 Verbank		41 Attlebury		58 Millerton
1 Wicopee		13 Clove Junction		27 Collins		44 Pine Plains		
2 Mattewan		16 Arthursburgh		29 Millbrook		46 Bethel		
4 Glenham		17 Lagrange		33 Shunpike		49 Shekomeko		
6 Fishkill Village		19 Billing's		36 Bangall		52 Husted		

Leave Grand Central Depot for **Stissing, Pine Plains** and intermediate stations, 8 00 a. m., 3 58 p. m. Arrive Pine Plains, 12 06, 8 04 p. m. For **Millerton** and intermediate stations, 8 00 a. m. Arrive, 12 50 p. m.

Trains to New York.

Leave **Millerton**, 6 05 a. m., 3 15 p. m., Sundays, 3 15 p. m. Arrive New York, 10 45 a. m., 9 25 p. m., Sundays, 9 25 p. m.
Leave **Pine Plains**, 7 00, 9 36 a. m., 4 34 p. m., Sundays, 4 34 p.m. Leave **Hopewell**, 8 18 a. m., 1 21, 6 37 p. m., Sundays, 6 37 p. m. Arrive New York, 10 45 a. m., 6 30, 9 25 p. m., Sundays, 9 25 p. m.

PROSPECT PARK AND CONEY ISLAND R. R.

Horse car routes to Depot, cor. 9th Avenue and 20th Street. From Fulton Ferry or Bridge Depots.—The 7th Avenue line, Vanderbilt Avenue line and Smith Street line. From Hamilton Ferry—via 9th or 15th Street Lines. Excursion Fare to West Brighton Beach, 30 cents.

§ *Trains will stop at the Grand Stand, Brooklyn Jockey Club Race Course, on Race Days only, and on those days will not stop at King's Highway Station between the hours of 11 30 a. m. and 6 30 p. m.*

Special Excursion Tickets to Brooklyn Jockey Club Race Course on Race Days, 25 Cents.

Leave cor. 9th Ave. and 20th St., Brooklyn for **Parkville, Gravesend, West Brighton Beach**, (Coney Island) and intermediate stations, *6 00, *7 00, 8 00, 9 00, 10 00, 11 00 a. m., 12 00 m., 1 00, 2 00, 3 00, 4 00, 5 00 6 00, 7 00, 8 00, 9 00 p. m. (On Saturdays 12 00 night.) **Do not run on Sunday.* Arrive Parkville in 6 minutes; King's Highway in 11 minutes; Gravesend in 13 minutes; West Brighton Beach in 18 minutes.

§For **Brooklyn Jockey Club** (Grand Stand), 12 m., 1 00, 2 00, 3 00, 4 00, 5 00, 6 00 p. m. Arrive Grand Stand in 12 minutes.

Trains to Brooklyn.

Leave **Grand Stand**, 12 36, 1 36, 2 36, 3 36, 4 36, 5 36, 6 36 p. m. Arrive cor. 9th Ave. and 20th St., Brooklyn in 12 minutes.

Leave **West Brighton Beach**, *6 30, *7 30, 8 30, 9 30, 10 30, 11 30 a. m., 12 30, 1 30, 2 30, 3 30, 4 30, 5 30, 6 30, 7 30, 8 30, 9 30 p. m. (Saturdays only, 12 25 night); leave Van Sicklen Station 1 minute later, Gravesend 5 minutes later, Kings' Highway 7 minutes later, Woodlawn Station 9 minutes later, Washington Cemetery 11 minutes later, Parkville 12 minutes later. Arrive cor. 9th Ave. and 20th St. Brooklyn, in 18 minutes from West Brighton Beach. **Do not run on Sundays.*

PROVIDENCE AND SPRINGFIELD R. R.

Connect from New York via N. Y., N. H. & H. R. R., Shore Line Division.

Leave **Providence** for **Enfield, Georgiaville, Oakland**, and **Pascoag**, stopping at all intermediate stations, 9 45 a. m., 1 15, 4 15, 6 20 p. m. (Saturdays only 11 15 p. m.) Arrive Pascoag, 10 56 a. m., 2 30, 5 30, 7 35 p. m. (Saturdays only, 12 30 night.)

Leave **Pascoag**, 5 35, 7 10 a. m., 12 30, 4 15 p. m. (Saturdays only, 5 40 p. m.); leave **Georgiaville**, 6 14, 7 49 a. m., 1 13, 4 54 p. m. (Saturdays only, 6 19 p. m.). Arrive Providence, 6 45, 8 20 a. m., 1 40, 5 20 p. m. (Saturdays only, 6 50 p. m.).

WEST SHORE R. R.

Depots foot of Jay and W. 42 Sts, and Weehawken. Ticket Offices: 1,271, 363, 785, 942 Broadway; 12 Park Place, 2 Centre St. 153½ Bowery, and foot of Jay and W. 42d Sts. Brooklyn, 333 Washington, Annex Office, foot of Fulton St., 730 Fulton St., 215 Atlantic Ave., 398 Bedford Ave., near Broadway.

Local Stations and Trains from New York.

M.	Stations.	Fare.	Exc.	M.	Stations.	Fare.	Exc.	M.	Stations.	Fare.	Exc.	M.	Stations.	Fare.	Exc.
	New York, Weehawken,			19	Tappan	55c.	$1.00	36	Tomkins' Cove	80c.	$1.35	52	Cornwall	$1.08	$2.00
1	New Durham	14c.	25c.	20	Orangeburgh	55c.	1.00	39	Jones' Point (Peekskill by Ferry)	80c.	1.40	56	Newburgh (Fishkill by Ferry)	1.16	2.25
5	Little Ferry	23c.	40c.	21	Blauveltville	60c.	1.00	41	Iona Island	85c.	1.50	60	Roseton	1.28	2.11
6	Ridgefield Park	25c.	40c.	22	Rockland Park	60c.	1.00	42	Fort Montgomery	90c.	1.60	63	Hampton	1.28	2.53
7	Hackensack	29c.	50c.	24	West Nyack	60c.	1.00	46	Cranston's (Hig'nd Falls)	98c.	1.75	64	Marlborough	1.28	2.56
9	Teaneck	30c.	50c.	26	Valley Cottage	65c.	1.10	47	West Point (Garrisons by Ferry)	98c.	1.75	68	Milton	1.38	2.73
10	West Englewood	35c.	60c.	28	Congers (Rockland Lake)	75c.	1 20					72	Highland (P'keepsie by Ferry)	1.19	2.90
12	Bergenfields	40c.	70c.	32	Haverstraw Village	80c.	1.20								
12	Schraalenburgh	40c.	75c.	33	W. Haverstraw	80c.	1.20								
16	Harrington	45c.	85c.	34	Stony Point	80c.	1.20								
17	West Norwood	50c.	90c.												

**Daily. †Express train, makes no stops between New Durham and Haverstraw.*

Leave foot of Jay St. (leave **foot W. 42d St.** 15 minutes later),

For **Teaneck, Bergenfields, West Nyack, West Haverstraw**, and intermediate stations, *3 00, *7 00, 8 10, *†9 40, *10 00, †11 15 a. m., 1 30, †3 15, 3 55, 5 00, *6 10, *†8 00, 8 30 p. m. Arrive Teaneck in 30 minutes; arrive Bergenfields in 1 hour; arrive West Nyack in 1½ hours; arrive West Haverstraw in 1¾ hours.

For **Stony Point**, *3 00, *7 00, *10 00 a. m., 3 45, 3 55, 5 00, 8 30 p. m. Arrive Stony Point in 1¾ hours.

For **Tomkin's Cove**, *3 00, *7 00, *10 00 a. m., 3 55, 5 00, 8 30 p. m. Arrive in 2 hours.

For **Jones Point**, *7 00, *10 00 a. m., 3 55, 5 00, 8 30 p. m. Arrive in 2 hours 5 minutes.

For **Iona Island** (signal station), *7 00, *10 00 a. m., 3 45, 3 55, 5 00, 8 30 p. m. Arrive in 2 hours 7 minutes.

For **Fort Montgomery**, *3 00, *7 00, *10 00 a. m., 3 55, 5 00, 8 30 p. m. Arrive in 2 hours 10 minutes.

For **Cranston, West Point, Cornwall, Newburg**, *3 00, *7 00, *9 40, *10 00, 11 15 a. m., 3 45, 3 55, 5 00 (*5 10 not West Point), *8 00, 8 30 p. m. Arrive Cranstons in 2 hours 5 minutes; arrive West Point in 2¼ hours; arrive Cornwall in 2 hours 25 minutes; arrive Newburg in 2½ hours.

For **Roseton**, *3 00, 7 00 a. m., 3 15 p. m. Arrive in 2 hours 40 minutes.

For **Hampton**, *7 00 a. m., 3 15 p. m. Arrive *9 47 a. m., 6 07 p. m.

For **Marlborough**, *3 00, *7 00, *9 40, 11 15 a. m., 3 45, *8 00 p. m. Arrive Marlborough, *5 49, *9 53 a. m., *12 04, 1 40, 6 12, *10 55 p. m.

For **Milton**, *3 00, *7 00, *9 40 a. m., 3 45 p. m. Arrive Milton, *5 58, *9 57 a. m., *12 11, 6 20 p. m.

For **Highland**, *3 00, *7 00, *9 40, 11 15 a. m., 3 45, *8 00 p. m. Arrive in 3 hours.

Local Trains to New York.

Leave **Highland**, 6 57, *7 40 a. m., 12 23, *4 34, 6 41, *8 11 p. m. Arrive New York, 3¼ hours.

Leave **Milton** (Signal Station), 7 05, 7 47 a. m., 12 30, *4 42, *6 53 p. m. Arrive New York in 3 hours 5 minutes.

Leave **Marlborough**, 7 13, *7 55 a. m., 12 38, *4 47, *7 01 p. m. Arrive New York in 3 hours.

Leave **Hampton**, 7 16 a. m., *7 04 p. m. Arrive New York, 9 15 a. m., *10 p. m.

Leave **Roseton**, 7 21 a. m., *4 51, 7 10 p. m. Arrive New York, 9 15 a. m., *7 00, *10 p. m.

Leave **Newburg**, *5 45, 6 00, 6 50, 7 30, *8 10 a. m., 12 52, *1 20, 4 10, *5 02, *7 19, *8 35 p. m.; leave **Cornwall**, *5 55, 6 10, 7 00, 7 39, *8 20 a. m., 1 02, *1 30, 4 20, *5 11, *7 30, *8 45 p. m. Arrive New York in 2¼ hours from Newburg and in 2 hours 5 minutes from Cornwall.

Leave **West Point** (leave Cranston 2 minutes later), 6 20, 7 10, 7 49, *8 31 a. m., 1 12, *1 41, 4 30, *5 21, 7 12, *8 56 p. m. Arrive New York in 1¾ hours.

Leave **Fort Montgomery**, 6 30, 7 20 a. m., *1 50, *4 40, *7 55 p. m. Arrive New York in 1 hour 40 minutes.

Leave **Iona Island** (Signal Station), 6 34, 7 24 a. m., *1 55, 4 44, *8 00 p. m. Arrive New York in 2 hours.

Leave **Jones Point**, 6 38, 7 28 a. m., *1 59, 4 48, *8 05 p. m. Arrive New York, 8 15, 9 15 a. m., *3 40, 6 25, *10 00 p. m.

Leave **Tomkins Cove**, 6 43, 7 33, *8 52 a. m., *2 05, 4 54, *8 13 p. m. Arrive in New York in 1½ hours.

Leave **Stony Point**, 6 47, 7 37, 8 10, *8 56 a. m., *2 10, 4 57, *8 18 p. m. Arrive New York in 1 hour 25 minutes.

Leave **West Haverstraw**, stopping at intermediate stations, 5 30, 6 54, *7 49, 8 14, 9 00, 10 45 a. m., *1 38, *2 14, 3 50, 5 00, *†5 48, *8 24 p. m. Arrive in New York—Express trains in 1 hour 5 minutes; accommodation trains 1 hour 20 minutes.

Leave **West Nyack**, 5 51, 7 03, *8 01, 11 03 a. m., *2 35, 4 08, 5 19, *6 05, *8 48 p. m.; leave **Tappan**, 6 04, 7 20, *8 14, 11 19 a. m., *2 46, 4 19, 5 31, *9 00 p. m.; leave **Bergenfields**, 6 21, 7 35, *8 31, 11 36 a. m., *3 02, 4 33, 5 47, *9 17 p. m. Arrive New York in 1 hour 10 minutes from West Nyack; in 1 hour from Tappan; in 45 minutes from Bergenfields.

For trains to and from the West see following pages.

WEST SHORE R. R.—Continued.
TRAINS GOING West.

Miles.	STATIONS.	Fare.	59 A.M.	61 A.M.	51 A.M.	57 P.M.	65 P.M.	53 P.M.	55 P.M.	
	L've New York, foot Jay St., N. R.		3 00	7 00	9 30	11 15	3 45	5 10	8 00	
	" New York, foot W. 42d St.		3 15	7 15	9 35	11 30	4 00	6 00	8 15	
	L've Brooklyn, by Annex.					10 30	3 00			
	" Jersey City, P. R. R. Station					11 20	3 10			
	" Hoboken, West Shore Station					11 30	3 30			
	L've Weehawken		3 30	7 30	10 10	11 45	4 15	6 15	8 30	
16.5	" Cranston's (Highland Falls)	$ 98	*5 06	9 12	11 28	1 03	5 34	7 25	10 10	
47.4	" West Point (Garrisons by ferry)	98	5 08	9 14	11 31	1 05	5 36		10 13	
52.3	Arr. Cornwall	1 08	5 19	9 24	11 41	1 15	5 46	7 34	10 25	
56.7	Arr. Newburgh (Fishkill by ferry)	1 16	5 31	9 35	11 50	1 24	5 56	7 43	10 35	
72.3	" Highland (Poughkeepsie by ferry)	1 49	6 08	10 04	12 19	1 54	6 28		11 10	
88.2	" Kingston	1 76	6 45	10 35	12 50	2 25	7 00	8 33	11 45	
88.2	L've Kingston		$7 00	10 45	1 00	2 35	7 10	8 40	11 55	
110.0	Arr. Catskill	2 18	7 42	11 27	1 40	3 11	7 50	9 15	12 42	71
128.2	" Coeyman's Junction	2 58	8 15	12 00	2 15	3 45	8 25	9 45	1 20	
141.3	" Albany	3 10	9 00	12 10	2 35	4 30	9 05	10 25	2 03	
	L've Albany, Coeyman's Junction			P.M.			P.M.		A.M.	
	" Albany, D. & H. C. Co's R. R.		8 35	$12 25	3 30			9 08		Daily ex. Sunday
152.6	Arr. South Schenectady	3 11	9 25		3 05	4 10				
159.6	" Rotterdam Junction	3 38	9 30		3 18	5 00		10 10	2 40	
168.1	" Amsterdam	3 76	9 50		3 37	5 16			3 07	
178.1	" Fultonville (Fonda)	3 98	10 15		3 55	5 36			3 27	
194.3	" Canajoharie (Palatine Bridge)	4 20	10 38		4 15	6 00		11 10	3 50	A.M.
193.8	" Fort Plain	4 28	10 45		4 20	6 07			3 58	7 08
205.5	" Little Falls	4 58	11 15		4 45	6 38			4 24	7 52
216.5	" Mohawk	4 72	11 28			6 51				
218.7	" Ilion	4 78	11 32			6 55			4 46	8 20
229.0	" Frankfort	4 82	11 38		5 05	7 00		12 25	5 03	8 04
231.8	" Utica	5 00	12 02		5 20	7 20		12 45	5 24	8 26
251.8	Arr. Oneida Castle (Oneida)	5 54	12 45		6 04	P.M.			6 10	9 10
257.4	" Canastota (E. C. & N. R. R.)	5 64	12 55		6 13				6 25	9 27
278.3	" Syracuse	6 06	1 45		6 50		A.M.	2 10	7 10	10 15
320.2	Arr. Newark	7 08	3 34		8 10	See foot note.	6 35	3 28	9 10	11 58
339.0	Arr. Rochester	7 68	4 35		9 30		7 55	4 25	10 10	1 00
429.0	Arr. Buffalo	8 50	7 00		11 40		10 10	6 25	12 30	P.M.
446.9	" Niagara Falls	8 50			12 33			7 25	1 30	
449.0	" Suspension Bridge	8 50			12 40			7 32	1 10	
				P.M.		A.M.	A.M.	A.M.	P.M.	

; Stop for, or to leave New York or New England passengers only.   Daily.   § Daily except Sunday.   *Stop on signal.
Trains No. 51, 53, 55 and 61 run daily. Train No. 59 will run daily between New York and Kingston, and daily, except Sunday, west of Kingston. All other trains daily, except Sundays. Train No. 57 runs to the New York Central station, Utica, and not to West Shore station. Trains 51 and 55 will stop at all stations west of Frankfort to let off passengers coming from New York or New England points.

ARRANGEMENT OF PARLOR AND SLEEPING CARS.

No. 51.—Sleeping Cars, New York to Chicago, via Port Huron, daily. **No. 57.**—Drawing Room Cars, Jersey City to Albany, daily, except Sunday. **No. 55.**—Sleeping Cars, New York to Toronto; New York to Chicago, via Port Huron, daily. **No. 53.**—Sleeping Cars, New York to Chicago, via Niagara Falls Short Line; New York to St. Louis, via Michigan Central R. R.; Buffalo to St. Louis, via Grand Trunk R. R., daily. **No. 65.**—Drawing Room Car, New York to Albany daily, except Sunday.

HIGH WATER AT SANDY HOOK, N. J.
In the a.m. columns hours designated by o mean midnight; in the p.m. columns 12 h. 0 m. means noon.

Date	APRIL		MAY		JUNE		JULY		AUGUST		SEPT.		OCT.		NOV.		DEC.	
	A.M.	P.M.	A.M.	P.M.	A.M.	P.M.	A.M.	P.M.	A.M.	P.M.	A.M.	P.M.	A.M.	P.M.	A.M.	P.M.	A.M.	P.M.
	Time h.m.	Time h.m.	Time h.m.	Time h.m.	Time h.m.	Time h.m.	Time h.m.	Time h.m.	Time h.m.	Time h.m.	Time h.m.	Time h.m.	Time h.m.	Time h.m.	Time h.m.	Time h.m.	Time h.m.	Time h.m.
1	8 27	8 45	8 08	8 51	9 36	9 43	9 27	9 28	10 22	10 36	11 51		0 08	12 21	1 32	2 03	2 38	2 57
2	9 11	9 25	8 48	9 27	9 58	10 03	10 06	11 31		12 09	1 26	1 51	1 28		2 50	3 13	3 43	4 05
3	9 52	10 02	10 10	9 30	10 34	10 31	10 42	10 51		12 49	2 05	2 38	2 26	4 00		3 50	4 42	5 06
4	10 32	10 40	10 31	10 32	11 22	11 17	11 32	11 42	0 45	1 13	2 30	2 53	3 16	3 29	4 58	5 22	5 33	5 59
5	11 12	11 16	11 11	11 11	11 56			12 31	1 10	3 17	3 25	3 54	4 16	4 32	5 52	6 17	6 19	6 46
6	11 53	11 57	11 52	11 54	0 06	12 51	0 45	1 36	2 49	3 20	4 25	5 12	5 31	6 40	7 07	6 59	7 29	
7		12 37		12 35	1 08	1 56	1 57	2 43	3 54	1 39	5 31	5 46	6 05	6 30	7 23	7 52	7 57	8 07
8	0 12	1 26	0 46	1 30	2 17	3 03	3 07	3 46	4 51	5 13	6 21	6 40	6 55	7 20	8 08	8 38	8 10	8 42
9	1 02	2 18	1 49	2 32	3 30	4 11	4 15	4 13	5 49	6 06	7 18	7 32	7 42	8 09	9 18	9 19	9 13	9 42
10	1 34	3 11	2 50	3 15	4 37	5 10	5 16	5 39	6 42	6 56	8 00	8 16	8 39	8 54	9 16	10 23	9 50	10 20
11	2 49	4 07	3 37	4 26	5 37	6 02	6 11	6 31	7 32	7 42	8 45	8 59	9 28	9 36	10 25	11 31	10 32	11 03
12	4 30	5 02	5 03	5 32	6 32	6 52	7 02	7 17	8 22	8 35	9 34	9 50	9 48	10 29	10 21	11 01	10 59	10 57
13	5 27	5 55	6 00	6 25	7 25	7 40	7 53	8 03	9 11	9 26	10 19	10 28	10 27	11 01	10 58	11 39	10 59	11 39
14	6 21	6 46	6 54	7 15	8 15	8 27	8 43	8 52	9 54	10 11	11 05	11 31	11 01	11 42	11 58		11 45	
15	7 12	7 35	7 46	8 02	9 04	9 13	9 33	9 41	10 48	11 09	11 50		11 11		0 22	12 25	0 32	12 25
16	8 04	8 24	8 31	8 45	9 45	10 01	10 24	10 32	11 40		0 23	12 37	0 25	12 26	1 11	1 20	1 19	1 17
17	8 54	9 10	9 26	9 30	10 47	10 51	11 14	11 27		0 03	12 31	1 14	1 18	1 16	2 00	2 24	2 44	2 59
18	9 44	9 59	10 15	10 30	11 31	11 47			12 10	1 00	1 29	2 01	2 00	2 08	3 03	3 30	3 37	3 57
19	10 35	10 56	11 08	1 14		12 38	0 20	1 31	1 58	2 27	3 04	2 55	3 12	1 35	4 33	4 54	5 00	
20	11 29	11 39		12 05	0 19	1 41	1 01	1 31	2 12	2 55	3 14	3 40	3 54	4 01	5 08	5 35	5 36	6 05
21			12 26	0 10	1 01	1 52	2 16	2 36	3 11	3 47	4 04	4 42	5 08	6 01	6 30	6 35	6 24	
22	0 35	1 27	1 10	2 05	3 06	3 17	3 37	4 04	1 05	4 45	5 07	5 47	5 25	6 00	6 51	7 21	7 11	7 45
23	1 35	2 29	2 18	3 10	1 10	4 11	1 31	4 50	5 03	5 47	6 07	6 35	6 52	7 37	8 10	8 01	8 37	
24	2 39	3 31	3 28	4 12	5 05	5 27	5 19	5 31	6 08	6 18	6 52	7 18	7 12	7 42	8 21	9 01	9 48	9 29
25	3 16	4 34	4 34	5 07	5 52	6 01	6 04	6 08	6 41	6 49	7 02	7 54	7 50	8 50	9 10	9 49	9 30	10 19
26	4 51	5 28	5 26	5 50	6 36	6 45	6 58	7 07	7 20	7 29	7 49	8 28	9 01	9 47	9 51	10 38	10 25	11 13
27	5 49	6 15	6 13	6 38	7 11	7 29	7 50	8 03	8 08	8 19	9 04	9 20	9 54	10 39	10 45	11 35	11 19	
28	6 30	7 01	7 03	7 16	7 54	8 13	8 39	8 49	8 53	9 07	9 50	10 24	10 58	11 38			0 07	12 21
29	7 25	7 42	7 45	7 50	8 22	8 49	9 11	10 06	10 32	11 07	11 47		0 30	12 38	1 10	1 20		
30	8 10	8 19	8 22	8 51	9 02	9 11	10 06	10 32	11 30			1 32	1 45	2 16	2 30	3 28		
31			8 51	8 59			9 36	9 50	10 52	11 28			0 51	12 58			3 20	3 42

WEST SHORE R. R.—Continued.
TRAINS COMING EAST.

STATIONS.	56	78	54	58	62	60	52	72	72
	P. M.	P. M.	P. M.			A. M.	A. M.		
L've Suspension Bridge	4 40		8 10			68 43	8 17		
" Niagara Falls	4 48		8 16			3 51	8 53		
L've Buffalo	6 20	3 15	9 25			$5 00	9 55		
L've Rochester	8 20	5 10	11 15			7 25	11 15		1 00
Arr. Newark	9 10	6 40	12 04			8 25	12 36	P. M.	5 01
L've Syracuse	10 35	P. M.	1 25			10 10	2 15	4 30	6 15
Arr. Canastota (E. C. & N. R. R.)	11 15					10 58		5 10	
" Oneida Castle, Oneida					A. M.	11 04		5 20	
L've Utica	12 08		2 17	6 50		11 46	3 20	6 06	
Arr. Frankfort	12 30		3 05	7 10		12 10	3 45	6 30	
" Ilion				7 15		12 19	3 54	6 36	
" Mohawk		66		7 19		12 23		6 40	
" Little Falls	12 50		38 27	7 51		12 57	1 09	6 56	
" Fort Plain	*1 27			8 03		1 13	1 33	7 20	
" Canajoharie (Palatine Bridge)	1 33		3 55	8 09		1 15	4 38	7 35	
" Fultonville (Fonda)		Daily except Sunday.		8 33		1 40	1 57	P. M.	
" Amsterdam	2 10			8 53		2 02	5 13		
" Rotterdam Junction	2 25		4 41	9 10		2 30	5 26		
" South Schenectady				9 24		2 45			
Arr. Albany, D. & H. C. Co's R. R.				$6 55	10 10		5 05	$7 15	
" Albany, Coeyman's Junction	4 15	A. M.			P. M.		P. M.	P. M.	
L've Albany	2 50	4 20	4 55	9 50	2 00	4 00	5 30		
" Coeyman's Junction	3 35	5 00	5 40	10 30	2 45	4 15	6 25		
Arr. Catskill	4 05	5 34	6 15	11 03	3 17	5 19	6 58		
" Kingston	4 45	6 15	6 55	11 45	3 55	6 00	7 35		
L've Kingston	4 50	6 25	7 00	11 55		6 10	7 45		
Arr. Highland (Po'keepsie by ferry)		6 57	7 40	12 23		6 44	8 11		
" Newburgh (Fishkill by ferry)	5 45	7 30	8 10	12 52	5 02	7 19	8 36		
L've Cornwall	5 55	7 39	8 20	1 02	5 11	7 30	8 46		
Arr. West Point (Garrison's by ferry)		7 49	8 31	1 12	5 21	7 42	8 56		
" Cranston's (Highland Falls)		7 51	8 33	1 14	5 23	7 45	8 59		
" Weehawken	7 30	9 05	10 10	2 40	6 50	9 50	10 20		
Arr. New York, foot W. 42d St	7 40	9 15	10 10	2 50	7 00	10 05	10 30		
" New York, foot Jay St., N. R.	7 55	9 30	10 25	3 05	7 15	10 15	10 45		
	A. M.	A. M.	A. M.				P. M.	P. M.	
Arr. Hoboken, West Shore Station				3 00	7 10				
" Jersey City, P. R. R. Station				3 10	7 20				
" Brooklyn, Brooklyn Annex				3 50	7 50				
				A. M.	P. M.				

‡ Stop for, or to leave, New York or New England passengers only.
* Stop on Signal. Daily. § Daily, except Sunday. c Daily, except Monday.

Trains Nos. 52, 54, 56 and 62 run daily. Train No. 60 will run daily between Kingston and New York, and daily, except Sunday, west of Kingston. All other trains daily, except Sunday. Train No. 54 will stop at stations between Suspension Bridge and Coeyman's Junction; and Trains Nos. 52 and 56 will stop at any station to let off passengers holding foreign tickets to local stations, sold at points west of Buffalo or Clifton. On Sunday Train No. 52 will stop at West Haverstraw at 9 26 p. m., and No. 56 will stop at Cranston's at 6 06 a. m. Train No. 58 leaves from the New York Central station at Utica, and not from the West Shore station.

STATEN ISLAND RAPID TRANSIT R. R.
PERTH AMBOY DIVISION.
Fare from New York to all stations, 10 cents; from station to station, 5 cents.

Leave foot of Whitehall St., for St. George, Gra-mere, Garretson, Grant City, New Dorp, Court House, Giffords, Eltingville, Annadale, Huguenot, Princess Bay, Pleasant Plains, Richmond Valley, Tottenville and Perth Amboy, daily except Sunday, 6 30, 7 20, 9 30 and 11 30 a. m.; 1 30, 3 30, 4 30, 5 10, 5 50, 6 30, 7 40 and *10 00 p. m. and †12 15 night. *Sundays*, 8 00, 9 00, 10 00 and 11 00 a. m.; 1 00, 2 00, 4 00, 5 00, 6 00, 7 00 and 8 00 p. m.

Leave Perth Amboy, stopping at Tottenville 10 minutes later, and all intermediate stations, 6 25, 7 05, 7 35, 8 05, 9 25 and 11 25 a.m.; 1 55, 3 35, 5 15 and 6 30 p.m., *Sundays*, 7 10, 8 10, 9 10, 10 10 a.m., and 12 10, 1 10, 3 10, 4 10, 5 10, 6 10 and 7 10 p.m.

Leave Tottenville for New York and intermediate stations. Additional trains at 5 35 a. m. and *9 40 p. m.

RAPID TRANSIT DIVISION.
From foot of Whitehall St.

Leave New York for St. George, Tompkinsville, Stapleton, Clifton, Rosebank, Fort Wadsworth, Arrochar, New Brighton, Snug Harbor, Livingston, West Brighton, Port Richmond, Tower Hill, Elm Park and Erastina, daily, except Sunday, 5 30, 6 00, 6 30, 7 20, 7 50, 8 10, 8 30, 9 00, 9 30, 10 00, 10 30, 11 00 and 11 30 a. m.; 12 00 m.; 12 30, 1 00, 2 00, 2 30, 3 00, 3 30, 4 00, 4 30, 4 50, 5 10, 5 30, 5 50, 6 10, 6 30, 7 00, 7 40, 8 20, 9 00, 10 00, 11 00 and 11 30 p. m. and 12 15 night. *Sundays*, 6 00, 7 00, 8 00, 9 00, 10 00, 10 30, 11 00 and 11 30 a. m.; 12 00 m.; 12 30, 1 00, 1 30, 2 00, 2 30, 3 00, 3 30, 4 00, 4 30, 5 30, 6 00, 6 30, 7 00, 7 30, 8 00, 8 30, 9 00, 9 40, 10 20, 11 00 and 11 30 p. m.

Leave Erastina for Arrochar, New York and intermediate stations, daily, except Sundays, 5 00, 5 30, 5 55, 6 30, 7 00, 7 20, 7 40, 8 00, 8 20, 8 40, 9 00, 9 30, 10 00, 10 30, 11 00 and 11 30 a. m.; 12 00 m.; 12 30, 1 00, 1 30, 2 00, 2 30, 3 00, 3 30, 4 05, 4 30, 4 50, 5 10, 5 30, 5 55, 6 10, 6 30, 7 05, 7 45, 8 25, 9 05, 10 05, and 11 05 p. m. *Sundays*, 6 00, 7 00, 8 00, 8 30, 9 00, 9 25, 9 55, 10 25, 10 55, 11 25 and 11 55 a. m.; 12 25, 12 55, 1 25, 1 55, 2 25, 2 55, 3 25, 3 55, 4 25, 4 55, 5 25, 5 55, 6 25, 6 55, 7 25, 7 55, 8 40, 9 20, 10 00 and 10 40 p. m.

Leave Erastina for Arrochar and intermediate stations, daily. Additional trains at 11 30 p. m. *Sundays*, 11 10 p. m.

Leave Arrochar for Erastina, New York and intermediate stations, daily, except Sundays, 5 38, 6 33, 7 03, 7 23, 7 43, 8 03, 8 23, 8 43, 9 08, 9 33, 10 03, 10 33, 11 03 and 11 33 a. m.; 12 03, 12 33, 1 03, 1 33, 2 03, 2 33, 3 03, 3 33, 4 08, 4 33, 4 58, 5 18, 5 33, 5 53, 6 13, 6 38, 7 08, 7 38, 8 28, 9 08, 10 08 and 11 08 p. m. *Sundays*, 7 00, 8 00, 8 30, 9 00, 9 25, 9 55, 10 25, 10 55, 11 25 and 11 55 a. m.; 12 25, 12 55, 1 25, 1 55, 2 25, 2 55, 3 25, 3 55, 4 25, 4 55, 5 25, 5 55, 6 25, 6 55, 7 25, 7 55, 8 40, 9 00, 9 20, 10 00 and 10 40 p. m.

Leave Arrochar for Erastina and intermediate stations, Sundays, 11 10 p. m. also.
Leave Clifton for New York and intermediate stations, daily, except Sunday, 5 10, 5 40 a. m. Sundays, 6 10 a. m. also.
Leave St. George for Whitehall St., daily, except Sunday, 5 20, 5 50, 6 15, 6 50, 7 20, 7 40, 8 00, 8 20, 8 40, 9 00, 9 20, 9 50, 10 20, 10 50, 11 20 and 11 50 a. m.; 12 20, 12 50, 1 20, 1 50, 2 20, 2 50, 3 20, 3 50, 4 20, 4 50, 5 10, 5 30, 5 50, 6 20, 6 50, 7 30, 8 10, 8 50, 10 30 and 11 30 p. m. *Sundays*, 7 20, 7 40, 8 00, 8 20, 8 50, 9 15, 9 45, 10 15, 10 45, 11 15 and 11 45 a. m.; 12 15, 12 45, 1 15, 1 45, 2 15, 2 45, 3 15, 3 45, 4 15, 4 45, 5 15, 5 45, 6 15, 6 45, 7 15, 7 45, 8 15, 9 00, 9 40, 10 20 and 11 p. m.

* Will not run Saturdays or Sundays. † Saturday nights only. Fare, New York to Perth Amboy, 40 cents.

NEW YORK & LONG BRANCH R. R.

Notice.—No trains stop at Asbury Park, Ocean Grove, or Key East on Sundays.

Depots :—Central R. R. of N. J., foot of Liberty St., N. R.; Pennsylvania R. R., foot of Cortlandt and Desbrosses Sts., N. R.

STATIONS, DISTANCES AND FARES FROM NEW YORK.

M.	Fare. Single, Exc.	M.	Fare. Single, Exc.	M.	Fare. Single, Exc.	M.	Fare. Single, Exc.
26 Perth Amboy		43 Red Bank	$1.00-$1.50	51½ N. Asbury Pk	$1.20-$1.85	61 Sea Girt	$1.35-$2.15
27 South Amboy	.70c- $1.10	45½ Little Silver	1.00- 1.50	55 Asbury Park	1.20- 1.85	61½ Manasquan	1.40- 2.25
28 Morgan	.70c- 1.15	46 Branchport	1.00- 1.50	55 Ocean Grove	1.20- 1.85	62 Brielle	1.40- 2.25
30 Cliffwood	.70c- 1.25	49 Long Branch	1.00- 1.50	57 Key East	1.25- 2.00	63½ Point Pleasant	1.45- 2.35
31 Matawan	.70c- 1.25	50 West End	1.00- 1.50	57½ Ocean Beach	1.25- 2.00		
35 Hazlet	.75c- 1.25	51 Elberon	1.00- 1.60	58½ Como	1.30- 2.05		
37 Middletown	.80c- 1.50	53 Deal Beach	1.00- 1.75	59½ Spring Lake	1.30- 2.10		

Via CENTRAL R. R. of N. J., Leave foot of Liberty St. for **Long Branch, Ocean Grove, Asbury Park** and **Point Pleasant**, stopping at **Red Bank** and intermediate stations, 1.30, 8.15, 11.15 a. m., 1.00, 4.00, 1.30, 6.10 p. m. Sundays, 1.00, 9.00 a. m.
Due at **Long Branch**, 6.15, 10.05 a. m., 12.50, 2.13, 5.10, 5.36, 7.55 p. m. Sundays, 5.50, 10.40 a. m.
Due at **Ocean Grove**, 7.00, 10.30 a. m., 1.05, 2.58, 5.55, 6.11, 8.10 p. m. None on Sundays.
Due at **Point Pleasant**, 7.25, 10.45 a. m., 1.30, 3.20, 6.20, 6.30, 8.35 p. m. Sundays, 6.25, 11.15 a. m.

Via PENNSYLVANIA R. R.—Leave foot of Cortlandt and Desbrosses Sts. for **Long Branch, Ocean Grove, Asbury Park** and **Point Pleasant**, stopping at **Red Bank** and intermediate stations, 9.10 a. m., 12 noon, 1.30, 5.00 p. m. Sundays, 9.45 a. m., 5 p. m.
Due at **Long Branch**, 10.50 a. m., 1.15, 5.51, 6.45 p. m. Sundays, 11.10 a. m., 6.45 p. m.
Due at **Ocean Grove**, 11.05 a. m., 2.00, 6.06, 7.00 p. m. None on Sundays.
Due at **Point Pleasant**, 11.30 a. m., 2.25, 6.25, 7.25 p. m. Sundays, 12.15, 7.20 p. m.

Trains to New York

From the following places, stopping at intermediate stations:
Via CENTRAL R. R. OF N. J.—Leave **Point Pleasant**, 5.50, 6.35, 7.30, 10.35 a. m., 3.50, 6.20 p. m. Sundays, 7.15 a. m., 3.50 p. m.
Leave **Ocean Grove** (Asbury Park), 6.15, 6.56, 7.55, 11 a. m., 1.15, 6.45 p. m. None on Sundays.
Leave **Long Branch**, 6.30, 7.12, 8.10, 11.15 a. m., 1.30, 7.00 p. m. Sundays, 7.55 a. m., 4.30 p. m.
Leave **Red Bank**, 6.43, 7.25, 8.25, 11.35 a. m., 1.45, 7.15 p. m. Sundays, 8.08, 4.15 p. m.
Leave **Matawan**, 7.00, 7.44, 8.39, 11.52 a. m., 2.15, 5.03, 7.32 p. m. Sundays, 8.26 a. m., 5.03 p. m.
Foregoing trains **arrive in New York**, foot of Liberty St., at 8.10, 8.55, 9.37 a. m., 1.00, 3.30, 6.15, 8.40 p. m. Sundays, 9.35 a. m., 6.15 p. m.
Additional trains leave South Amboy, 8.18, 8.53 a. m., and arrive in New York, 9.17, 9.52 a. m.

Via PENNSYLVANIA R. R. Leave **Point Pleasant**, 6.25, 8.50 a.m., 12.50, 5.10 p.m. Sundays, 8.55 a.m., 5.10 p.m.
Leave **Ocean Grove** (Asbury Park), 6.50, 9.15 a. m., 1.15, 5.35 p. m. None on Sundays.
Leave **Long Branch**, 7.00, 9.30 a. m., 1.30, 5.50 p. m. Sundays, 9.30 a. m., 5.50 p. m.
Leave **Red Bank**, 7.19, 9.44 a. m., 1.43, 6.00 p. m. Sundays, 9.43 a. m., 6.06 p. m.
Leave **Matawan**, 7.36, 10 a. m., 2.01, 6.26 p. m. Sundays, 10 a. m., 6.26 p. m.
Foregoing trains **arrive in New York**, foot of Cortlandt and Desbrosses Sts., 8.10, 11.10 a. m., 3.10, 7.10 p. m. Sundays, 11.05 a. m., 7.50 p. m.

CAMDEN AND ATLANTIC R. R.

Via Pennsylvania R. R. foot of Cortlandt and Desbrosses Streets.

Stations, Distances and Fares from Phila'elphia.

M.							
Philadelphia		9 Ashland	27c.	24 Ancora	65c.	44 Germania	$1.00
Shackamaxon St.		11 Kirkwood	31c.	27 Winslow Junction	70c.	46 Pomona	1.00
Market Street.		15 Berlin	40c.	30 Hammonton	81c.	49 Doughty's	1.00
1 Camden.		19 Atco	50c.	34 Da Costa	81c.	52 Absecon	1.00
1 Collingswood	14c.	22 Chesilhurst	58c.	36 Elwood	91c.	57 Drawbridge	1.00
6 Haddonfield	20c.	22 Waterford	60c.	41 Egg Harbor	$1.00	58 Atlantic City	1.00

Leave foot of Cortlandt or Desbrosses Sts., via Philadelphia and Camden, for **Hammonton, Absecon** and **Atlantic City**, stopping at intermediate stations, *11.10 a. m., 1.00, *2.60 p. m., Sundays 10.00 a. m. Arrive Hammonton 3.51, 5.15, 5.56 p. m.; Sundays, 5.29 p. m. Arrive Atlantic City, 4.30, 6.47, 6.37 p. m. Sundays, 6.22 p. m. An additional accommodation train leaves Philadelphia and Camden daily, at 8.00 a. m. Arrive at Atlantic City, 10.10 a. m. daily. *Express trains making no intermediate stops after leaving Philadelphia.

Trains to New York.

Leave **Atlantic City** for Philadelphia, stopping at intermediate stations, 7.00, *10.15 a. m., 3.20, †4.40 p. m., Sundays, 7.50 a. m., 4.00 p. m.; leave **Hammonton**, 7.54, *11.00 a. m., 4.16, 15.21 p. m., Sundays, 8.43 a. m., 5.04 p. m. Arrive Philadelphia 9.05, *11.50 a. m., 5.35, *6.10 p. m., Sundays, 10.05 a. m., 6.20 p. m. **Arrive New York**, 12.15, 13.45, 9.45, 19.45 p. m., Sundays, 3.45, 9.15 p. m. †*Express trains.*

Local trains leave **Philadelphia** for **Hammonton** and intermediate stations, 10.45 a. m., 6.00 p. m. (11.30 p. m. to Atco). Arrive Hammonton, 12.18, 7.28 p. m.
Leave **Hammonton**, 6.05 a. m., 12.20 p. m. Arrive Philadelphia, 7.35 a. m., 1.50 p. m.
Leave **Waterford**, 5.24, 6.24 a. m., 12.17, 7.40 p. m. Arrive Philadelphia, 6.35, 7.35 a. m., 1.50, 8.50 p. m.
Longport trains leave **Atlantic City**, stopping at intermediate stations, 9.30 a. m., 1.17 p. m. (10.14 a. m., Wednesday and Saturday only.) Returning leave **Longport**, 6.55 a. m., 5.25 p. m. (2.40 p. m. Wednesday and Saturday only.)

Stations and Distances.

M Philadelphia	6 Haddonfield.	11 Locust Grove.	17 Melrose.
Market Street.	8 Freeman.	12 Cropwell.	18 Medford.
1 Camden.	9 Lodi.	13 Marlton.	22 Lumberton.
1 Collingswood.	10 Springdale.	15 Elmwood Road.	25 Mt. Holly.

Leave **Philadelphia** (Vine Street) for **Collingswood** and **Haddonfield**, 6.30, 7.30, 8.00, 10.00, 10.45 a. m., 12 m., 2.00, *3.10, 4.30, *5.00, 5.30, 6.01, 6.30, *7.30, 10.30, 11.30 p. m. Sundays, 8.00, *9.15 a. m., 1.00, 4.00, *5.30, *9.30 p. m. Arrive Haddonfield in 30 minutes. *Trains marked † leave Market Street Station.*
For **Medford** and **Mt. Holly**, stopping at intermediate stations; from Vine St. Station, 7.30, 10.00 a. m.; from Market St. Station, 3.10, 5.00 p. m.; Sundays, 9.15 a. m. (to Medford only), 5.30 p. m. Arrive Medford 8.32, 11.40 a. m.; 4.15, 6.07 p. m. Sundays, 10.30 a. m., 6.32 p. m.; arrive at Mt. Holly, 8.52 a. m., 12 m., 4.35, 6.28 p. m., Sundays, 6.52 p. m.

Trains to Philadelphia.

Leave **Mount Holly**, 6.17, 9.32 a. m., 12.25, 5.00 p. m., Sundays, 7.15 a. m.; leave **Medford**, 7.08, 9.50 a. m., 12.55, 5.37 p. m., Sundays, 7.44 a. m., 3.50 p. m. Arrive Philadelphia, 8.40, 10.50 a. m., 2.05, 6.35 p. m., Sundays 8.50 a. m., 4.50 p. m.
Leave **Haddonfield** (Collingswood 5 minutes later), 6.05, 7.05, 7.35, 7.47, 8.11, 10.20 a. m., 12.50, 1.07, 1.40, 3.35, 5.08, 6.10, 7.05, 8.25, 9.50, 11.07 p. m., Sundays, 8.25, 9.36 a. m., 2.30, 4.23, 5.55, 10.20 p. m. Arrive Philadelphia in 30 minutes.

HOURS OF CLOSING DOMESTIC AND CANADA MAILS.

The time here given is official, but mails made up at the Post Office between 12 night and 7 a. m. we have purposely omitted (excepting where such hours represent the only *Sunday* dispatch), believing a report of those mails unnecessary to ordinary correspondents. Mails with s prefixed close on Sunday also.

STATES.	HOURS OF CLOSING.
Alabama,	1, 2.30, s3.30, s8, 11 p. m.
Alaska Ter.,	s7.30 p. m.
Arizona,	s8 a. m., s7.30 p. m.
Arkansas,	s8 a. m., s7.30 p. m.
California,	s8 a. m., s7.30 p. m.
Colorado,	s8 a. m., s7.30 p. m.
Connecticut,	7.30, 9.30, 11.30 a. m., s2.30, s9.30, s10 p. m.
Dakota,	8.30 a. m., s7.30 p. m.
Delaware,	7.30, 10 a. m., 1, s8 p. m.
Dist. Columbia,	7.30, 9 a. m., 1, s2.30, 3.30, s8, s11 p. m.
Florida,	s3.30 a. m., s8 p. m.
Georgia,	7.30 a. m., 1, s3.30, s8, 11 p. m.
Idaho,	s8 a. m., s9.30 p. m.
Illinois,	s8 a. m., s7.30 p. m.
Indiana,	s8 a. m., 5.30, 7 p. m.
Indian Ter.,	s8 a. m., s7.30 p. m.
Iowa,	8.30 a. m., s7.30 p. m.
Kansas,	s8 a. m., s7.30 p. m.
Kentucky,	s8 a. m., 7 p. m.
Louisiana,	s8 a. m., 2.30, s3.30, 7, s8, 11 p. m.
Maine,	7.30, 9.30 a. m., s2.30, s9.30 p. m.
Maryland,	7.30, 9 a. m., 12 m., s2.30, 3.30, 7, s8, s11 p. m.
Massachusetts,	7.30, 9.30, 11.30 a.m., 1.30, s2.30, 3.30, s9.30 p. m.
Michigan,	8.30 a. m., s1.30, s7.30 p. m.
Minnesota,	8 a. m., s1.30, s7.30 p. m.
Mississippi,	s8 a. m., 7 p. m.
Missouri,	s8 a. m., s7.30 p. m.
Montana,	8.30 a. m., s7.30 p. m.
Nebraska,	8.30 a. m., s7.30 p. m.
Nevada,	s8 a. m., s7.30 p. m.
New Hampshire,	7.30 a. m., s2.30, s9.30 p. m.
New Jersey:	
Asbury Park and Long Branch,	7 a. m., 12 m., 3 p. m.
Jersey City,	s8, 10 a. m., 12 m., 2.30, 5.30, 7, 8, s11 p. m.
Newark,	7.30, 9.30, 11 a. m., 1, 2.30, 3.30, 5.30, s8 p. m.
New Brunswick,	7.30, 10 a. m., 12 m., 3.30 p. m.
Orange,	11 a. m., 2.30, 7 p. m.
Paterson,	3, 11 a. m., 2.30, 3.30 p. m.
Trenton,	7.30, 10 a. m., 12 m., 3.30, s8 p. m.
New Mexico,	s8 a. m., s7.30 p. m.
New York:	
Albany,	9, 10 a. m., 2.30, 5, 7.30, s10 p. m.
Auburn,	s8 a. m., 5, s7.30 p. m.
Binghamton,	8 a. m., s8 p. m.
Brooklyn,	every half hour from 7 a. m. to 4 p. m., then hourly to s9 p. m., then occasionally to 7 a. m.
Buffalo,	9 a. m., s4.30, s7.30, s10 p. m.
Catskill,	s3, 10 a. m., 2, s7.30 p. m.
Elmira,	8 a. m., s8 p. m.
Flushing,	6 a. m., 1, 3.30 p. m.
Greenport,	2, s10 p. m.
Newburgh,	10 a. m., 1, 2.30, s5, 10.30 p. m.
Oswego,	4, s8 p. m.
Poughkeepsie,	s3, 9 a. m., 1, 2.30 p. m.
Rochester,	9 a. m., s4.30, s7.30, 10 p. m.
Rome,	s3 a. m., s7.30 p. m.
Saratoga Springs,	s3, 9 a. m., 5, 10.30 p. m.
Staten Island,	about 6 times a day.
Syracuse,	s3 a. m., s7.30, s9.30 p. m.
Troy,	s3, 9, 10 a. m., 2.30, s5, 7.30, 10.30 p. m.
Utica,	s3 a. m., 5, s7.30, 10 p. m.
West Point,	3 a. m., 2.30 p. m.
Yonkers,	s3, 9 a. m., 12.30, 2.30, 4.30 p. m.
North Carolina,	7.30 a. m., 1, s3.30, s8, 11 p. m.
Ohio,	s3.30, s8 a. m., 7 p. m.
Cleveland and Toledo,	s3.30, 8.30 a. m., s4.30, s7.30 p. m.
Oregon,	s8.30 a. m., s7.30 p. m.
Pennsylvania,	s3.30 a. m., 8 a. m., 1, 5.30, 7 p. m.
Philadelphia,	7.30, 9, 10, 11.30 a. m., 12 m., 1, 3.30, s5.30, s7, s8, s11 p. m.
Rhode Island,	7.30, 11.30 a. m., 3.30, s10 p. m.
South Carolina,	7.30 a. m., s3.30, s8, 11 p. m.
Tennessee,	s3.30, s8 a. m., 7 p. m.
Texas,	s3.30 a. m., 2.30, s3.30 p. m.
Utah,	s8 a. m., s7.30 p. m.
Vermont,	s5, 10.30 p. m.
Virginia,	7.30 a. m., s8 p. m.
Washington, D. C.,	7.30, 9 a. m., 1, s2.30, 3.30, s8, s11 p.m.
Washington Ter.,	s3.30 a. m., s7.30 p. m.
West Virginia,	7.30 a. m., s8 p. m.
Wisconsin,	8.30 a. m., s4.30, s7.30 p. m.
Wyoming,	s8 a. m., s7.30 p. m.
CANADA.	
British Columbia and Manitoba,	8.30 a. m., s7.30 p. m.
New Brunswick, Nova Scotia and P. E. Island,	9.30 a. m., s9.30 p. m.
Ontario,	9 a. m., 4, s7.30 p. m.
Quebec,	3 a. m., s5 p. m.

FOR THE RECEPTION OF LETTERS TOO LATE FOR MAILS AT THE POST OFFICE.

Red Boxes have been placed at the Grand Central Station, in the Pennsylvania R. R. Station at Jersey City, and in N. Y., L. E. & W. R. R. Station, Jersey City. They are to be used as follows :

Grand Central Station.—The one in Vanderbilt Avenue, near Baggage Entrance of New York Central & Hudson River R. R., is exclusively for letters going to places on the route of the N. Y. C. & H. R. R. R. and beyond, by s4.35 and 8 a. m., and 3.58 and s9 p. m. trains. Collections will be made 10 minutes previous to starting of trains. For 9 p. m. train no letters should be posted for places south of Rhinecliff, N. Y.

The Box near the Passenger Exit in 42d Street is exclusively for letters going to places on the routes of N. Y., N. H. & H. R. R., and beyond, by 5.02 and 9.01 a. m., and s4.01, s4.05, s11.01 and s11.31 p. m. trains. Collections will be made 10 minutes previous to starting of trains. No letters for Western Vermont should be placed in this box, and no letters for points West of South Norwalk should be deposited for the 11.01 and 11.31 p. m. trains.

The Box for the Harlem R. R. is near the Baggage Entrance of that road in Vanderbilt Avenue. Mails will be taken from this box at 8.15 a. m. and 3.40 p. m., for the 8.20 a. m. and 3.75 p. m. trains.

Put no letters for NEW YORK CITY, or for the Southern States, in the *Red Boxes* at Grand Central Station.

Pennsylvania R. R. Station, Jersey City.—A Red Box is placed in the Passengers' Waiting Room exclusively for mail destined to points local to the N. Y. Division Pennsylvania R. R., and South and West of Philadelphia, Pa., by s4.45, 8.15, 8.23 and 8.43 a. m. and 4.52, s6.45, 8 and s9.15 p. m. trains. Collections will be made 10 minutes previous to starting of trains. No mail for Northern New Jersey, New York, or New England should be posted in this box. For the 8.15 a. m. train only letters for points on the Lehigh Valley R. R. should be placed in this box, and for the 8.23 a. m. train only letters for points on the N. Y., Susquehanna & Western R. R.

N. Y., L. E. & W. R. R. Station, Jersey City.—A Red Box is placed in the Passengers' Waiting Room for the reception of letters to be forwarded by trains as follows : N. Y., L. E. & W. R. R., 5.00, 8.05 a. m., 4.44 and 8.50 p. m. Northern R. R. of N. J., 8.33 a. m. and 4.15 p. m. N. J. & N. Y. R. R., 8.08 a. m. N. Y. & Greenwood Lake R. R., 8.37 a. m. Collections will be made 10 minutes previous to starting of trains.

MISCELLANEOUS.

Arrears & Assessments Collection Bureau, Office, 35 Stewart Building, 276 Broadway.
Board of Assessors, Office, 11½ City Hall.
Building Inspection Bureau, Office, 157 E. 67th.
Commissioner of Jurors, Office, 127 Stewart Building, 276 Broadway.
Custom House, cor. of Wall and William Sts. Open every day except Sundays and Holidays, from 9 a. m. to 4 p. m.; on holidays, usually open from 9 to 10 a. m. for Entrance and Clearance of Vessels.
   Collector's Office, in Custom House.
   Auditor's Office, in Custom House.
   Barge Office, Battery Park.
   Cashier's Office, in Custom House.
   Deputy Surveyor's Office, in Barge Office.
   Naval Officer's Office, 22 Exchange Place.
   Sample Offices, 254 West.
   Surveyor's Office, in Custom House.
   Public Stores, Washington and Laight Sts.
Excise Department, Office, 54 Bond.
Fire Department, Office, 157 E. 67th.
Health Department, Office, 301 Mott.

Inspectors & Sealers of Weights & Measures.
First District, H. H. Masterson, Inspector, 46 W. 62d ; S. R. Porter, Jr., Sealer, 196 Chrystie.
Second District.—Wm. Martin, Inspector, 231 Mulberry ; Michael Hahn, Sealer, 212 E. 96th.

National Guard, Location of Armories.
Arsenal, Seventh Ave. and W. 35th.
1st Brigade, Headquarters, 6 Pine.
1st Battery, 14th, near Ninth Ave.
2d Battery, Seventh Ave., near 52d.
7th Regiment, Park Ave. and 67th St.
8th Regiment, Broadway and 35th.
9th Regiment, 224 W. 26th.

11th Regiment, Disbanded.
12th Regiment, cor. Ninth Ave. and 61st.
23d Regiment, 14th St., near 6th Ave.
69th Regiment, cor. Third Ave. and 7th St.
71st Regiment, Broadway and 45th.
U. S. Army (War Dept.) Building, cor. Whitehall & Pearl Sts.

Public Charities & Correction Department, Office, cor. 11th St. & 3d Ave., has in charge the following hospitals, etc.; for ferries to Blackwell Island &c. see below:
Almshouse, Blackwell's Island.
Bellevue Hospital, foot E. 26th St.
Charity Hospital, Blackwell's Island.
City Prison, Franklin & Centre Sts.
Colored Home, 65th St. and 1st Ave.
Colored Orphan Asylum, 10th Ave and 143d St.
District Prisons.
Emergency for Women, 223 E. 26th.
Epileptic & Incurable Hospitals, Blackwell's Island.
Gouverneur Hospital, cor. Gouverneur Slip & Front.
Harlem Hospital, foot E. 120th.
Homœopathic Hospital, Ward's Island.
Idiot Hospital, Randall's Island.
Infants' Hospital, Randall's Island.
Insane Asylum, Ward's Island.
Lunatic Asylum, Blackwell's Island.
Medical & Surgical Relief for Out-door Poor, foot E. 26th.
Nursery Hospital, Randall's Island.
Out-door Poor Department, Supt's. Office, cor. 11th St. & 3d Av
Penitentiary, Blackwell's Island.
Workhouse, Blackwell's Island.
   { Blackwell's Island Ferry, foot of E. 26th, 52d, 76th St.
Ferries { Randall's Island Ferry, foot E. 26th and 120th Sts.
   { Ward's Island Ferry, " "
Street Cleaning Department, Office, 51 Chambers.
Tax Collection Bureau, Receiver's Office, 57 Chambers.

STORAGE WAREHOUSES.

Acker & Co., Office, 74 South.
American Docks, Staten Island ; Office, 50 Cotton Exch., N.Y.
Appraiser's Office, 102 Washington.
Atlantic Dock, at Hamilton Ferry, Bkln.; Office, 361 Produce Ex.
Baker & Williams ; Office, 271 Water, 510 Washing'n, 72 Beaver.
Baltic, foot of Baltic St., Bkln.; Office, 5 Hanover St.
Bartlett, near Wall St. Ferry, Bkln.; Office, 5 Hanover St.
Bellows ; Office, 127 Front.
Bluxome & Co.; Office, 54 Washington.
Brooklyn Grain Warehousing Co., 103 Produce Exchange.
Brooklyn Tobacco Inspection, Water & Dock Sts., Dows & Co., Room M, Produce Exchange.
Casey's, 151 Leroy.
Clinton, Atlantic Dock, Bkln.; Office, 361 Produce Exchange.
Columbia, foot of Pacific St., Bkln.; Office, 103 Produce Ex.
Coe-Lawrence, Son & Gerrish: Offices, 103 Front, 755 Water & 221 South.
Commercial, Atlantic Dock, Bkln.: Office, 5 Hanover St.
Congress, foot of Congress St., Bkln.; Office, 5 Hanover St.
Doane ; Office, 302 Greenwich.
Dows, foot of Pacific St., Bkln.; Office, 103 Produce Exchange.
Driggs, E. F. & Co.; Office, 271 South & 113 Water.
Driggs, M. S. & Co.; Office, 280 South & 72 Beaver.
Empire, Water St., n. Fulton Ferry, Bkln.; Office, 5 Hanover.
Empire Warehousing Co.; Office, 5 Hanover.
Excelsior, 384 W. 11th.
Excelsior, Atlantic Dock, Bkln.; Office, 207 Produce Exchange.
Export Lumber Co., Long Island City ; Office, 88 Wall.
Finke Tobacco Inspection, 149 Water.
Finlay, Atlantic Dock, Bkln.; Office, 5 Hanover St.
Franklin, Atlantic Dock, Bkln.; Office, 5 Hanover St.
Fulton—cor. Water & Dock Sts., Bkln.; Office, Room M, Produce Exchange.
Gentle's ; Office, 227 Pearl.
German American, ft. of Partition St., Bkln.; Office, 19 Old St.
Grain Warehousing Co., Atlantic Dock, Bkln.; Office, 207 Produce Exchange.
Hamburg, foot of 1st St., Hoboken.
Harbeck, near Wall St. Ferry, Bkln.; Office, 5 Hanover St.
Hobby's, 286 South.
Hobby's, 110 Washington.
Hoboken, foot of 4th St.

Hoboken (Bonded), foot of 3d St.
Jarvis & Co., Clinton & South Sts., and 13th & Provost Sts., Jersey City ; Office, 60 Broad.
Jersey City, foot of Grand St.
Kelsey, foot of Irving St., Bkln.; Office, 5 Hanover St.
Kimberly & Co., 6 Bridge.
Knickerbocker ; Office, 5 E. 14th & 125 E. 24th.
Laimbeers, Atlantic Dock, Bkln.; Office, 207 Produce Ex.
Lawrence, Son & Gerrish: Office 221 South, 103 Front, 755 Water
Laytons, 62 South.
Linde, F. C. & Co.; Office, cor Varick & Laight Sts.
Linde Tobacco Inspection ; Office, 142 Water.
Lockwood, C. B. & Co., 361 Produce Exchange.
Manhattan, Lexington Ave. & 41st.
Martins, near Wall St. Ferry, Bkln.; Office, 109 Water.
Mediterranean, at Wall St. Ferry, Bkln: Office, 5 Hanover St.
Merchants, 32 Jay ; Office, 65 Beaver.
Merchants, foot of Van Dyck St., Bkln.; Office, 5 Hanover St.
Miller's ; Office, 88 Pearl.
Morewood's ; Office, 237 South & 87 Front.
National—Communipaw, N. J.; Office, 55 Broadway.
N.Y. Warehousing Co., foot Van Brant St., Bkln; Office, 52 B'way
Nichols ; Office, 138 W. 12th & 28 So. William.
Phillips Tobacco Co.; Office, 188 Pearl.
Pierrepont, near Wall St. Ferry, Bkln.; Office, 5 Hanover St.
Pintos, Atlantic Dock, Bkln.; Office, 159 Produce Exchange.
Prentice, near Wall St. Ferry, Bkln.; Office, 5 Hanover St.
Public Stores, cor. Laight & Washington Sts.
Roberts, near Wall St. Ferry, Bkln.; Office, 5 Hanover St.
Robinson, foot of Congress St., Bkln.; Office, 5 Hanover St.
Robinson, 52 Greenwich.
Shaw's ; Office, 65 Water.
Stranahan Storage & Tobacco Inspection, foot of King St., Bkln.; Office, 361 Produce Exchange.
Tower's, 281 West.
Union, foot of Sedgwick St., Bkln.; Office, 5 Hanover St.
United States, foot of Degraw St., Bkln.
Watson, near Wall St. Ferry, Bkln.; Office, 5 Hanover St.
Waverly, foot of 26th St., Bkln.; Office, 5 Hanover St.
Woodruff, foot of Joralemon St., Bkln.; Office, 5 Hanover St.
Wood's, 311 West.

STORAGE FOR FURNITURE, ETC.

Baker's ; Office, 164 E. 125th.
Brigg's, 207 E. 59th.
Brown's, 292 E. 23d.
Carrington, 384 3d Ave.
Clinton, 245 E. 35th.
Curtis, 1601 Broadway.
De Boes, B. H. & Co., 1342 3d Ave.
Deweys, 164 E. 126th.
Empire, 88 Wooster.
Empire, 388 Hudson.
Globe, 305 E. 61st.

Haeger's, 300 W. 34th.
Harlem, 125 E. 129th.
Hayes & Co., 311 W. 48th.
Hetherington, 102 E. 63d.
Knickerbocker, 121 E. 24th.
Manhattan, Lexington Ave. & 41st.
Martin, A. & Son, 165 W. 32d.
Metropolitan, 202 Mercer.
Meyers, H. M., 300 W. 11th.
Morgan's, 232 W. 47th.
Muxlow's, 1283 3d Ave.

N. Y. Storage, 109 E. 44th.
Standard, Broadway. cor. 53d.
Star, 103 W. 33d.
Sylvan, 2191 3d Ave.
Timmins, cor. 6th Ave. & 125th.
Union, 285 Hudson.
Union, 121 E. 23d.
Union Square, 80 University Pl.
United States, 10th St. & 3d. Ave.
Yorkville, 169 E. 85th.

NATIONAL AND STATE BANKS.

For Savings Banks, see below.

Bank Clearing House, 14 Pine St. Sub-Treasury, cor. Wall, Nassau and Pine Sts. Banks are open every day, except Sundays and legal holidays, from 10 a. m. to 3 p. m., and on Saturdays only from 10 a. m. to 12 m. Commercial paper, except sight or demand bills, falling due on Saturday, is payable on the following business day.

Note.—In the following arrangement of names, the only bank title given is the one commonly used. The prefix "Bank of" and "National Bank of," etc., being confusing to many who have occasion to look for the location of a bank. Bank of America will be found under A. Bank of New York, under N. National Bank of Commerce, under C.

American, 46 Wall.
American Exchange National, 128 B'way.
Assets State Bank, 42 New.
Bowery, 62 Bowery.
Broadway, 237 Broadway.
Butcher's and Drover's, 124 Bowery.
Central National, 320 Broadway.
Chase, 15 Nassau.
Chatham, 192 Broadway.
Chemical, 270 Broadway.
Citizen's, 401 Broadway.
City, 52 Wall.
Clinton, 112 Hudson.
Columbia, 501 Fifth Av.
Commerce, 29 Nassau.
Commercial, 78 Wall.
Continental, 7 Nassau.
Corn Exchange, 14 William.
Deposit, 55 Liberty.
East River, 682 Broadway.
East Side, 459 Grand.
Eleventh Ward, 147 Av. D.
Empire, 640 Broadway.
Fifth Av., 531 Fifth Av.
Fifth National, 300 Third Av.
First National, 2 Wall.
Fourteenth St., 3 East 14th.
Fourth National, 14 Nassau.
Gallatin, 36 Wall.
Gansevoort, cor. 9th Av. & 14th St.
Garfield, 79 West 23d.
German American, 50 Wall.
German Exchange, 380 Bowery.
Germania, 215 Bowery.
Greenwich, 402 Hudson.
Hamilton, 278 West 125th.
Hanover, 11 Nassau.
Harlem, 211 West 125th.
Home, 383 West 12d.
Hudson River, c. Ninth Av. and 72d.
Importer's & Trader's, 217 Broadway.
Irving, 287 Greenwich.
Leather Manufacturer's, 29 Wall.
Lenox Hill, 1248 Third Av.
Lincoln, 32 East 42d.
Madison Square, 202 Fifth Av.
Manhattan Company, 40 Wall.
Marine, Receiver's Office, 80 Wall.
Market and Fulton, c. Fulton and Gold.
Mechanic's, 33 Wall.
Mechanic's & Trader's, B'way & Broome.
Mercantile, 191 Broadway.
Merchant's, 42 Wall.
Merchant's Exchange, 257 Broadway.
Metropolitan, In liquidation, 2 Wall.
Metropolis, 29 Union Square.
Mount Morris, 85 East 125th.
Murray Hill, 760 Third Av.
Nassau, 9 Beekman.
New Amsterdam, 1.134 Broadway.
New York, N. B. A., 48 Wall.
New York County, 79 Eighth Av.
New York, State of, 33 William.
New York Nat. Exchange, 136 Chambers.
New York Produce Exchange, Produce Exchange Building.
Ninth National, 409 Broadway.
Ninth Av., 2 Ninth Av.
Nineteenth Ward, 953 Third Av.
North America, cor. Nassau & Cedar Sts.
North River, 187 Greenwich.
Oriental, 122 Bowery.
Pacific, 470 Broadway.
Park, 214 Broadway.
People's, 365 Canal.
Phenix, 99 Wall.
Produce Exchange, Produce Exc. B'l'g.
Republic, 2 Wall.
Riverside, c. Eighth Av. and 57th.
Seaboard, 18 Broadway.
Second National, 190 Fifth Av.
Seventh National, 184 Broadway.
Shoe and Leather, 271 Broadway.
Sixth National, 1,292 Broadway.
St. Nicholas, 120 Broadway.
State of New York, 33 William.
Stuyvesant, cor. 5th Av. & 125th St.
Third National, 20 Nassau.
Tradesmen's, 291 Broadway.
Twelfth Ward, 153 East 125th.
Twenty-third Ward, Third Av. & 116th.
Union, 747 Fifth Av.
Union Nat'l, in liquidation, 39 William.
Union Square, 8 Union Square.
United States, 1 Broadway.
Western, 120 Broadway.
West Side, 481 Eighth Av.

Bank Agencies, &c.

Bank of British North America, 52 Wall.
Bank of California, 16 Wall.
Bank of Montreal, 59 Wall.
Canadian Bank of Commerce, 16 Exchange place.
Cheque Bank of London, 2 Wall.
Merchant's Bank of Canada, 61 Wall.
Nevada Bank of San Francisco, 62 Wall.

SAVINGS BANKS AND THEIR BUSINESS HOURS.

American, 501 Fifth Av.; 9 a. m. to 4 p. m., and on Monday, 6 to 8 p. m. also.
Bank for Savings, 67 Bleecker; 10 a. m. to 2 p. m., and on Wed. and Fri., 4 to 6 p. m. also.
Bowery, 130 Bowery; 10 a. m. to 3 p. m., and on Monday, 10 a. m. to 7 p. m.
Broadway, 4 Park Place; 10 a. m. to 3 p. m.
Citizen's, 58 Bowery; 10 a. m. to 3 p. m.
Dry Dock, 343 Bowery; 10 a. m. to 3 p. m., and on Monday, 5 to 7 p. m. also.
East River, 3 Chambers; 10 a. m. to 3 p. m.
Emigrant Industrial, 51 Chambers; 10 a. m. to 4 p. m.
Excelsior, 118 West 23d; 10 a. m. to 3. p. m., and on Saturday 6 to 8 p. m. also, except July and August.
Franklin, 658 Eighth Av.; 10 a. m. to 3 p. m., and on Monday 6 to 8 p. m. also.
German, c. Fourth Av. and 14th; 10 a. m. to 3 p. m., and on Monday, 10 a. m. to 8 p. m.
Greenwich, 73 Sixth Av.; 10 a. m. to 3 p. m.
Harlem, 2,381 Third Av.: 10 a. m. to 3 p. m., and on Monday, 6 to 8 p. m. also.
Institution for the Savings of Merchants' Clerks, 20 Union Square; 10 a. m. to 3 p. m., and on Thursday, 5 to 7 p. m. also.
Irving, 96 Warren; 10 a. m. to 3 p. m.
Manhattan, 644 Broadway; 10 a. m. to 4 p. m., and on Saturday, 10 a. m. to 12 m.
Metropolitan, 1 Third Av.; 10 a. m. to 3 p. m., and on Monday, 5 to 7 p. m. also.
New York, 81 Eighth Av.; 10 a. m. to 3 p. m., and on Monday, 6 to 8 p. m. also.
North River, 474 Eighth Av.; 10 a. m. to 3 p. m., and on Monday and Saturday, 6 to 8 p. m. also, except Saturday nights in July and August.
Seamen's, 74 Wall; 10 a. m. to 3 p. m.
Union Dime, 54 West 32d; 10 a. m. to 3 p. m., and on Monday, 10 a. m. to 7 p. m.
West Side, 56 Sixth Av.; 9 a. m. to 3 p. m., and on Monday and Saturday, 6 to 8 p. m. also.

SAFE DEPOSIT COMPANIES.

American, 2 E. 42d.
Bankers', 4 Wall.
Bank of New York, 48 Wall.
Central, 3 E. 14th.
Garfield, 6th Av. & 23d.
Lincoln, 32 E. 42d.
Manhattan, [and storage], 346 Broadway.
Manhattan Warehouse, 42d St. & Lexington Av.
Mercantile, 122 Broadway.
Mount Morris, Park Av. c. 125th.
Nassau, Beekman cor. Nassau.
New York County, 79 8th Av.
North River, 197 Greenwich.
Park Bank, 214 Broadway.
Produce Exchange, Broadway & Beaver St.
Safe Deposit Co. of New York, 140 Broadway.
State, 35 William.
Stock Exchange, 10 Broad.
Stuyvesant, 1 3d Av.
Tiffany & Co., 15 Union Sq.

TRUST, INVESTMENT AND MORTGAGE COMPANIES.

American Dock & Trust Co., Cotton Exchange Building.
American Investment Co., 150 Nassau.
American Land Mortgage Guar. & Debenture Co., 39 Broad.
American Loan & Trust Co., 113 Broadway.
Atlantic Trust Co., 39 William.
Central Trust Co., 54 Wall.
Des Moines Loan & Trust Co., 38 Park Row.
Eastern Car Trust Co., 11 Wall.
Equitable Trust Co., 42 Pine.
Equitable Mortgage Co., 208 Broadway.
Farmers' Loan & Trust Co., 20 William.
Fidelity Indorsing & Guarantee Co., 107 Broadway.
Fidelity Loan & Trust Co., 37 Wall.
Guaranty & Indemnity Co., 52 Broadway.
Guaranty Investment Co., 191 Broadway.
Hamilton Loan & Trust Co., 150 Broadway.
Holland Trust Co., 7 Wall.
Interstate Loan & Trust Co., 170 Broadway.
Jarvis-Conklin Mortgage Co., 239 Broadway.
Knickerbocker Trust Co., 234 5th Av.
Lombard Investment Co., 150 Broadway.
Manhattan Trust Co., 10 Wall.
Mercantile Trust Co., 120 Broadway.
Merchants' Loan & Trust Co., 58 New.
Metropolitan Trust Co., 37 Wall.
Mutual Trust Co., 31 Broadway.
New England Loan & Trust Co., 100 Broadway.
N. Y. Guaranty & Indemnity Co., 52 Broadway.
N. Y. Life Ins. & Trust Co., 52 Wall.
Real Estate Loan & Trust Co., 58 New.
Title Guarantee & Trust Co., 55 Liberty.
Union Trust Co., 73 Broadway.
U. S. Mortgage Co., 32 Nassau.
United States Trust Co., 49 Wall.
Western Loan & Trust Co., 2 Wall.

NEW YORK AND HARLEM R. R.

M.	Stations.	Fare. Single, Ex.	M.	Stations.	Fare. Single, Ex.	M.	Stations.	Fare. Single, Ex.	M.	Stations.	Fare. Single, Ex.
	Grand Central St'n		13	Mount Vernon..	.28- .45	44	Golden's Bridge	$1.05-$1.85	84	Amenia	$2.05-$3.45
	86th Street...	5c.	15	Bronxville......	.35- .55	47	Somer's Centre.	1.10- 2.00	87	Sharon Station.	2.13- 3.55
	110th Street.	5c.	16	Tuckahoe..... ..	.38- .60	51	Lake Mahopac..	1.10- 2.00	88	Coleman's	
4	Harlem (125th St.).	6c.-10c.	18	Scarsdale.......	.45- .75	46	Purdy's.........	1.13- 1.90	92	Millerton	2.28- 3.75
4	Mott Haven (138th)	6c.-10c.	20	Hartsdale	.48- .80	48	Croton Falls....	1.15- 2.00	95	Mount Riga	
5	Melrose...........	10c.-20c.	22	White Plains...	.50- .90	52	Brewsters..... ..	1.25- 2.15	99	Boston Corners	2.45- 4.00
6	Morrisania.......	10c.-20c.	25	Kensico..........	.58-$1.05	55	Dykeman's.....	1.33- 2.30	104	CopakeI'nW'ks	2.58- 4.20
7	Central Morrisania	12c.-24c.	28	Unionville......	.68- 1.20	58	Towner's.	1.40- 2.45	108	Hillsdale.......	2.68 4.40
7	Tremont....... ..	12c.-24c.	30	Pleasantville ...	.73- 1.25	60	Patterson	1.48- 2.55	111	Craryville......	2.73- 4.50
8	Fordham..........	15c.-30c.	33	Chappaqua.....	.78- 1.40	63	Pawling	1.55 2.65	115	Martindale.. .	2.83- 4.50
9	Bedford Park St'n.	20c.-35c.	37	Mount Kisco...	.88- 1.55	69	South Dover....	1.70- 2.85	118	Philmont......	2.90- 4.50
10	Williams Bridge..	22c.-35c.	39	Bedford...... ..	.95- 1.65	76	Dover Plains...	1.85- 3.10	124	Ghent.........	2.96- 4.50
11	Woodlawn........	25c.-35c.	42	Katonah........	$1.00- 1.75	84	Wassaic...	1.98 3.25	127	Chatham	3.00- 4.50

Stage Connections and Miles – Mount Vernon for Yonkers 3. White Plains for Tarrytown 6, Kensico for Armonk 6, Pleasantville for Sing Sing 5. Sharon Station for Sharon, Conn., 2½ miles.

☞ Jerome Park Race Track at Fordham. Fleetwood Race Track at Melrose. Y.M.C.A.—Athletic Department at Mott Haven.

* *Express trains.* + *Stops only at Mt. Kisco, Katonah and Brewsters.*

Leave Grand Central Depot for **Williams Bridge, Woodlawn, Mt. Vernon. Tuckahoe** and intermediate stations, 6 00, *6 20, 7 00, 7 40, 8 35, 9 05, 9 35 (10 35, Woodlawn and Mt. Vernon), 10 37, 11 20 a. m., 12 35, 1 05, 1 35, *2 05, 2 35, 3 27, 4 12, *4 15, 4 35, *5 13, 5 15, 5 20, 5 50, 6 06, 6 18, 6 38, 6 42, 7 40, 8 40, 10 05, 11 45 p. m., Sundays, 9 05, 10 45 a. m., 1 35 (2 20 except Wms. Bridge), 2 35, *4 15, *5 03, 5 15, 7 00, 10 05 p. m. Arrive at Williams Bridge in 25 minutes; at Woodlawn in 30 minutes; at Tuckahoe in 35 minutes.

For **White Plains** and intermediate stations. *6 20, 7 40, 9 05, *10 35, 11 20 a. m., 1 05, 2 05, 2 35, 4 15, 4 35, 5 13, 5 15, 5 50, 6 06, 6 38, 6 42, 7 40, 8 40, 10 05, 11 45 p.m., Sundays, *6 15, 9 05, *9 45, 10 45 a.m., 2 35, 5 03, 7 00, 10 05 p.m. Arrive White Plains in 1 hour.

For **Bedford, Katonah, Croton Falls** and intermediate stations, 6 20, 10 35 a. m., 2 05, 4 15, 5 13, 6 38 p. m., Sundays, 6 15, 9 45 a. m., 5 03 p. m. Arrive at Bedford in 1½ hours; at Croton Falls in 1¾ hours.

For **Lake Mahopac,** 10 35 a. m., 4 15, 5 13 p. m., Sundays, 9 45 a. m. Arrive Lake Mahopac in 1 hour, 55 minutes.

For **Pawling** and intermediate stations, 6 20, 10 35 a. m., 2 05, +3 25, 4 15, 5 13 p. m., Sundays, 9 45 a. m., 5 03 p. m. Arrive Pawling in 2¼ hours.

For **Dover Plains, Amenia, Millerton** and intermediate stations, 6 20, 10 35 a. m., 3 25, 4 15 p. m., Sundays, 9 45, a. m. Arrive Millerton, 0 33 a. m., 1 55, 6 11, 7 25 p. m., Sundays, 1 15 p. m.

For **Hillsdale, Chatham** and intermediate stations, 6 20, 10 35 a. m., 3 25 p. m., Sundays, 9 45 a. m. Arrive Chatham, 10 43 a. m., 3 05, 7 24 p. m., Sundays, 2 30 p. m. **For Pittsfield and North Adams,** take the 3 25 p. m. train from Grand Central Depot.

Trains to New York.

Trains stop at intermediate stations.

Leave **Chatham,** 8 30 a. m., 12 25, 1 45 p. m., Sundays, 3 00 p. m. Arrive New York, 12 20, 5 20, 8 55 p. m., Sundays, 7 40 p. m.

Leave **Millerton,** 7 00, 9 33 a. m., 1 36, 5 51 p. m., Sundays, 7 00 a. m., 4 15, 5 10 p. m. Arrive New York in 3 hours.

Leave **Pawling,** 6 20, 7 55, +10 35, 10 50 a. m., 2 40, 6 55, 7 45 p. m., Sundays, 7 55 a. m., 5 20, 7 45 p. m. Arrive New York in 2 hours, 10 minutes.

Leave **Croton Falls,** 5 40, 6 49, 8 26, 11 24 a. m., 3 28, 7 25, 8 57 p. m. Sundays, 8 26 a. m., 5 53, 8 57 p. m. Arrive New York in 1¾ hours.

Leave **Lake Mahopac,** 8 15, 11 08 a. m., 3 23 p. m., Sundays, 5 35 p. m. Arrive New York in 2 hours.

Leave **Katonah,** 5 55, 7 04, 8 10, 11 12, 11 38 a. m., 3 48, 7 38 p. m., Sundays, 8 40 a. m., 6 08, 9 32 p. m. Arrive New York in 1 hour 20 minutes.

Leave **Bedford,** 6 00, 7 09, 8 45, 11 41 a. m., 3 51, 7 41, 9 47 p. m., Sundays, 8 45 a. m., 6 11, 9 17 p. m. Arrive New York in 1¼ hours.

Leave **White Plains,** 5 25, 6 18, 6 38, 7 13, 7 30, *7 47, 8 29, *9 20, 9 31, 10 10, *11 43 a. m., 12 21, 1 27, 2 50, 3 45, 4 33, 5 15, 6 20, *8 16, 8 21, 10 20, *11 07 p. m., Sundays, 7 13, 8 50, 9 20, 10 40 a. m., 1 00, 5 55, 6 55, 7 00, *11 07 p. m. Arrive New York in 1 hour.

Leave **Tuckahoe** (Mt. Vernon 8 minutes later, Woodlawn 10 minutes later), 5 30, 5 40, 6 32, 6 51, 7 03, 7 26, 7 43, 8 03, 8 42, 9 06, 9 47, 10 12, 10 54, 11 17 a. m., 12 35, 12 43, 1 42, 2 00, 3 03, 3 30, 3 59, 4 25, 4 47, 5 08, 5 28, 6 55, 8 33, 10 33 p. m., Sundays, 7 26, 9 02, 10 54 a. m., 1 17, 4 52, 5 43, 7 16 p. m. Arrive New York in 50 minutes.

Leave **Williams Bridge,** 5 46, 5 58, 6 47, 7 04, 7 18, 7 41, 7 55, 8 17, 8 57, 9 21, 10 02, 10 28, 11 11, 11 32 a. m., *12 49, 12 59, 1 58, 2 17, 3 18, 3 45, 4 14, 4 30, *4 58, 5 13, 6 52, 7 11, 8 48, 10 49 p. m., Sundays, 7 41, 9 17, 11 11 a. m., 1 33, 3 45, 5 10, 5 58, 7 31 p. m. Arrive Grand Central Depot in 25 minutes.

Leave **Mott Haven,** 6 05, 6 19, 7 06, 7 14, 7 38, 8 19, 8 36, 9 16, 9 50, 10 19, 10 46, 11 28, 11 50 a. m., 12 59, 1 17, 2 16, 2 36 3 37, 4 05, 4 32, 4 57, 5 09, 6 00, 7 09, 7 28, 8 46, 9 08, 11 07 p. m., Sundays, 9 36, 11 28 a. m., 1 51, 4 05, 5 29 6 15, 7 56 p.m. Arrive Grand Central Depot in 11 minutes.

BROOKLYN BANKS.

Bedford, cor. Bedford Av. & Halsey St.
Broadway, c. Broadway & Flushing Av.
Brooklyn, cor. Fulton and Front Sts.
City (National), 357 Fulton.
Commercial, 363 Fulton.
First National, cor. Kent Av. & B'dway.
Fulton, 361 Fulton.
Kings County, 12 Court St.
Long Island, 186 Remsen.
Manufacturers, 61 Broadway.
Mechanics, cor. Court & Montague Sts.
Mechanics and Traders, cor. Greenpoint Av. and Franklin St.
Nassau, cor. Court and Remsen Sts.
Sprague, cor. 4th and Atlantic Avs.
Twenty-Sixth Ward, Atlantic Av. near Manhattan Crossing.
Wallabout, cor. Myrtle and Clinton Avs.

Savings Banks and their Business Hours.

Brooklyn, 223 Fulton St. Open daily, 10 a. m. to 3 p. m., and on Monday from 5 to 7 p. m. also.

Bushwick, 466 Grand St. Open, 10 a. m. to 2 p. m.; on Saturdays, 10 a. m. to 12 noon; on Mondays, 10 a. m. to 2 p. m. and 5 to 8 p. m.

City, cor. 4th and Flatbush Avs. Open, 9 a. m. to 3 p. m.; Saturday, 9 a. m. to 12 noon; on Monday, 9 a. m. to 3 p. m. and 6 to 8 p. m.

Dime of Brooklyn, cor. Court and Remsen Sts. Open daily. 9 a. m. to 3 p. m.; on Mondays, 9 a. m. to 3 p. m. and 5 to 7 p. m.

Dime of Williamsburg, 52 Broadway. Open, 10 a. m. to 3 p. m.; on Saturdays, 10 a. m. to 12 noon; on Mondays, 10 a. m. to 3 p. m. and 5 to 7 p. m.

East Brooklyn, 643 Myrtle Av. Open daily from 9 a. m. to 3 p. m., and on Mondays from 7 to 9 p. m. also.

East New York, cor. Atlantic and Van Siclen Avs.

German, cor. Broadway and Boerum. Open, 10 a. m. to 2 p. m.; on Saturdays, 10 a. m. to 12 noon; on Mondays, 10 a. m. to 2 p. m. and 5 to 8 p. m.

Germania, 375 Fulton. Open, 9 a. m. to 3 p. m.; on Saturdays, 9 a. m. to 12 noon; on Mondays, 9 a. m. to 3 p. m. and 5 to 7 p. m.

Greenpoint, cor. Manhattan Av. and Noble St. Open, 10 a. m. to 2 p. m., and on Monday from 6 to 8 p. m. also.

Kings County Savings Institution, cor. Broadway and Bedford Av. Open, 9 a. m. to 3 p. M.; on Saturday, 9 a. m. to 12 noon; on Mondays, 9 a. m. to 3 p. m. and 4 to 7 p. m.

South Brooklyn Savings Institution, 160 Atlantic Av. Open, 9 a. m. to 3 p. m.; on Saturdays, 9 a. m. to 12 noon; on Mondays, 9 a. m to 3 p. m. and 6 to 8 p. m.

Williamsburg, cor. Broadway and Driggs St. Open, 10 a. m. to 3 p. m.; on Saturdays, 10 a. m. to 12 noon; on Mondays, 10 a. m. to 3 p. m. and 4 to 7 p. m.

SAFE DEPOSIT AND TRUST COMPANIES.

Brooklyn City Safe Deposit Co., cor. Montague & Clinton Sts.
Brooklyn Trust Co., 177 Montague.
Franklin Trust Co., 186 Remsen.
Long Island Loan and Trust Co., 203 Montague.
Long Island Safe Deposit Co., cor. Fulton and Front Sts.
Nassau Loan and Trust Co., 101 Broadway.

PENNSYLVANIA R. R.

DEPOTS FOOT OF CORTLANDT AND DESBROSSES STREETS.

☞ *For Local Trains between New York and all Stations see 3d page following this.*

Eastern Standard Time is given at all stations east of Pittsburg, and Central Standard Time at all points west thereof.

Tickets, Baggage Checks, etc., can be obtained at the offices of the Company, as follows: 1, 435, 849, 944 Broadway, 1 Astor House, and foot of Cortlandt and Desbrosses streets; also in Jersey City at the Depot.

Trains for Philadelphia.

Fare $2.50; Excursion Fare $4.40, good for 5 days.

Leave New York.	Leave Brooklyn.	Arrive Philadelphia.	
6.30 a.m.		8.48 a.m.	3 FAST EXPRESS TRAINS are now run from New York to Camden, via Trenton, leaving New York at 8 a.m., 12.20, 4 p.m.; Brooklyn 7.30 a.m., 12 m., 3.30 p.m.; arriving at Philadelphia at 10.50 a.m. 3.10 and 6.40 p.m.
7.30 "	7.00 a.m.	9.55 "	
8.00 "	7.30 "	10.10 "	
8.30 "	8.00 "	11.08 "	
*9.00 "	8.30 "	11.13 "	
†9.00 "	8.30 "	11.30 "	SUNDAY TRAINS leave Brooklyn 8.30 (Limited Express 8.30 a.m.), 9.30 a.m., 3.30, 4.00, 4.30, 5.30, 6.00, 6.30, 7.30, 8.30 and 11 p.m. Leave New York 6.15, 9.00 (Limited Express 9.00 a.m.), 10.00 a.m., 4.00, 4.30, 5.00, 6.00, 6.30, 7.00, 8.00 and 9.00 p.m., and 12.15 night.
†10.00 "	9.30 "	12.25 p.m.	
11.00 "	10.30 "	1.30 "	
11.10 "	10.30 "	2.30 "	
12.20 p.m.	12.00 noon	2.47 "	
1.00 "	12.30 "	3.50 "	
2.00 "	1.30 p.m.	4.20 "	
3.00 "	2.30 "	5.12 "	
*3.30 "	3.00 "	5.43 "	
4.00 "	3.30 "	6.05 "	
4.30 "	4.00 "	6.47 "	All Sunday trains except the 6.15 a.m., 5.00, 6.00 and 7.00 p.m., have Parlor or Sleeping cars attached.
4.40 "	4.00 "	7.33 "	
5.00 "	4.30 "	7.50 "	
6.00 "	5.30 "	8.30 "	
6.30 "	6.00 "	9.00 "	THE LIMITED EXPRESS TRAINS leaving New York at 9.00 and 10.00 a.m, are composed entirely of Pullman Parlor Cars, on which an extra rate of fare is charged.
7.00 "	6.30 "	10.35 "	
8.00 "	7.30 "	10.50 "	
9.00 "	8.30 "	11.47 "	
12.15 n't	11.00	3.25 a.m.	

All trains except those marked † stop at Germantown Junction.

PULLMAN SLEEPING CAR for train leaving New York 12.15 midnight, daily, will be placed in Station at Jersey City, open to receive passengers at 10.00 p.m.

Trains for New York.

Leave Philadelphia.	Arrive New York.	Arrive Brooklyn.	
12.01 n't	3.50 a.m.		3 FAST EXPRESS TRAINS are now running from Camden to New York, via Trenton, leaving Station, foot of Market St. at 9, 11.40 a.m. and 4.30 p.m., arriving at New York 11.40 a.m.,2.10,7.20 p.m., and Brooklyn 11.45 a.m., 2.45, 7.45 p.m.
*3.20 a.m.	6.20 "	6.15 a.m.	
4.05 "	6.50 "	7.15 "	
†1.40 "	7.10 "	7.15 "	
*5.35 "	8.00 "	8.15 "	
6.50 "	9.30 "	9.45 "	
7.30 "	9.30 "	9.45 "	
8.20 "	10.40 "	10.45 "	SUNDAY TRAINS leave Philadelphia (Broad St. Station) 12.01 night, 3.20, 4.05, 4.40, 5.35, 8.30 and 9.40 a.m., 12.49, 1.40, 3.20 (Limited Express 4.50), 5.28, 6.95, 7.12 and 8.12 p.m.
8.30 "	11.30 "	11.45 "	
9.10 "	11.30 "	12.15 p.m.	
11.00 "	1.20 p.m.	1.15 "	
11.15 "	2.00 "	2.15 "	
12.00 n'n	2.10 "	2.45 "	
12.10 p.m.	3.20 "	3.45 "	
†1.14 "	3.30 "	3.45 "	All Sunday trains except the 8.30 a.m. have Parlor or Sleeping Cars attached.
†1.40 "	4.00 "	4.15 "	
2.30 "	1.50 "	5.15 "	
3.30 "	5.50 "	6.15 "	
4.30 "	6.20 "	6.45 "	THE LIMITED EXPRESS TRAINS leaving at 1.11 and 1.50 p.m. are composed entirely of Pullman Parlor Cars, on which an extra rate is charged.
4.50 "	7.00 "	7.15 "	
5.00 "	7.20 "	7.45 "	
6.00 "	8.50 "	9.15 "	
6.35 "	9.20 "	9.45 "	
*7.12 "	9.35 "	9.45 "	
8.12 "	10.15 "	10.45 "	
9.50 "	12.20 a.m.		

All trains except those marked † leave Germantown Junction 9 minutes after leaving Philadelphia.

PULLMAN SLEEPING CARS open to receive passengers at 10.40 p.m., are run every night on train leaving at 12.01 night, arriving in New York at 3.50 a.m. Passengers may rest undisturbed until 7.00 a.m.

NEW YORK AND CHICAGO.

Distance from New York.		Fare.	N. Y. & CHICAGO LIMITED. (Extra Fare.) Leaves every day and runs through.	FAST LINE. Leaves every day. Train leav'g New York on Saturday does not run beyond Pittsburg on the P., F. W. & C. Ry.; connects for Chicago via C., St. L. & P. R. R. daily.	WESTERN EXP. Leaves every day and runs through.	PACIFIC EXPRESS. Leaves every day and runs through via P., Ft. W. & C. Ry. Train leaving N. Y. on Saturday does not connect via C., St. L. & P. R. R.
	Leave New York		9.00 a.m.	9.00 a.m.	6.30 p.m.	8.00 p.m.
9	" Newark	$ 15		9.30 "	6.50 "	8.32 "
57	" Trenton	1 70		10.33 "	8.05 "	9.30 "
91	" Philadelphia	2 50	11.20 "	11.30 "	9.20 "	11.25 "
196	" Harrisburg	5 50	2.00 p.m.	3.40 p.m.	12.25 a.m.	3.10 a.m.
444	Arrive Pittsburg, Eastern Time	10 50	8.30 "	11.55 "	7.45 "	12.45 p.m.
	" Pittsburg, Central Time		7.30 "	10.55 "	6.45 "	11.45 a.m.
	Leave Pittsburg, Central Time		7.45 "	11.20 "	7.25 "	1.00 p.m.
619	Arrive Mansfield	15 25		6.20 a.m.	1.09 p.m.	8 10 "
689	" Crestline	15 25	1.35 a.m.	6.55 "	1.35 "	8.45 "
764	" Fort Wayne	16 75	4.54 "	12.20 p.m.	5.10 "	1.35 a.m.
912	" Chicago (via P., F. W. & C. Ry.)	20 00	9.00 "	6.05 "	9.30 "	7.00 "
	Leave Pittsburg, Central Time (via Pan Handle Route)			11.15 "		12.05 noon.
834	Arrive Logansport	19 00		12.45 noon.		2.40 a.m.
	" (via C., St. L. & P. R. R.)					
953	" Chicago (via C., St. L. & P. R. R.)	20 00		6.30 p.m.		7.20 "

NEW YORK, INDIANAPOLIS AND ST. LOUIS.

Dist. from New York.	For hours at Stations between New York and Pittsburg, see New York and Chicago Time Table.		Fare.	FAST LINE. Leaves every day and runs through.	WESTERN EXP. Leaves every day and runs through.
	Leave New York			9.00 a.m.	6.30 p.m.
91	" Philadelphia	For		11.50 "	9.20 "
444	Arrive Pittsburg, Eastern Time	Arrangement	$10 50	11.55 p.m.	7.15 a.m.
	" Pittsburg, Central Time	of		10.55 "	6.45 "
	Leave Pittsburg, Central Time			11.15 "	7.50 "
487	Arrive Steubenville	Through Cars,	12 00	12.45 a.m.	9.00 "
604	" Newark		15 25	4.25 "	1.25 p.m.
637	" Columbus	see	16 25	5.30 "	2.50 "
825	" Indianapolis		19 00	11.46 "	10.30 "
888	" Terra Haute	Next Page.	21 25	2.00 p.m.	1.30 a.m.
965	" Effingham		23 00	4.20 "	3.45 "
996	" Vandalia		24 00	5.15 "	4.48 "
1065	" St. Louis		24 25	7.30 "	7.00 "

PENNSYLVANIA R. R.—Continued.

NEW YORK, COLUMBUS, CINCINNATI AND THE SOUTH.

Distance from New York.	For hours at Stations between New York and Pittsburg, see New York and Chicago Time Table.	Fare.	N. Y. & CHICAGO LIMITED. Leaves every day and runs through.	FAST LINE. Leaves New York daily and runs through to Cincinnati, Connects for Louisville week days.	WESTERN EXP. Leaves every day and runs through.	PACIFIC EXP. Leaves every day. Train leav'g New York on Saturday does not run west of Pittsburg.
	Leave New York...........		9.00 a.m.	9.00 a.m.	6.30 p.m.	8.00 p.m.
91	" Philadelphia.........	$2 50	11.20 "	11.50 "	9.20 "	11.25 "
444	Arrive Pittsburg, Eastern Time...	10 50	8.30 p.m.	11.55 p.m.	7.45 a.m.	12.15 noon.
	" Pittsburg, Central Time....		7.30 "	10.55 "	6.45 "	11.45 a.m.
	Leave Pittsburg, Central Time.....		8.00 "	11.15 "	7.30 "	12.05 p.m.
637	Arrive Columbus..............	16 25	2.25 a.m.	5.30 a.m.	2.30 p.m.	7.25 "
757	" Cincinnati.............	18 00	7.10 "	10.00 "	6.40 "	....
807	" Louisville..............	21 50	11.30 "	7.20 p.m.	11.45 "	....

Connecting via Louisville and Nashville R. R. for

	Arrive Nashville...........	$25 65	7.40 p.m.		6.50 a.m.	
	" Memphis...........	29 40	5.15 a.m.		2.40 p.m.	
	" New Orleans........	34 00	7.20 p.m.		7.00 a.m.	
	" Galveston..........	46 30	12.01 noon.		8.25 "	

NEW YORK, CLEVELAND AND TOLEDO.

Dist. from New York.	For hours at Stations between New York and Pittsburg, see New York and Chicago Time Table.	Fare.	FAST LINE. Leaves every day and connects through to Cleveland. Train leaving New York on Saturday does not for Toledo.	WESTERN EXP. Leaves every day. Train leav'g New York on Saturday does not connect on Saturday does not for Cleveland.	PACIFIC EXPRESS. Leaves every day leaving New York or not connect for Toledo, Toledo.		
	Leave New York...............		9.00 a.m.	6.30 p.m.	8.00 p.m.
91	" Philadelphia..........	$2 50	11.50 "	9.20 "	11.25 "
444	Arrive Pittsburg, Eastern Time.........	10 50	11.55 p.m.	7.45 a.m.	12.45 noon.
	" Pittsburg, Central Time.............		10.55 "	6.45 "	11.45 a.m.
	Leave Pittsburg, Central Time...........		11.05 "	7.25 "	12.50 p.m.
527	Arrive Alliance..........................	12 00		10.15 "	....
593	" Cleveland..........................	13 00	5.25 a.m.	12.50 p.m.	6.55 "
619	" Mansfield..........................	15 25	5.55 "	1.09 "	8.10 "
705	" Toledo............................	16 25	9.15 "	4.15 "	11.25 "

ARRANGEMENT OF THROUGH CARS.

Fast Line. Vestibule Sleeping Car New York to St. Louis. Sleeping Car Pittsburg to Cincinnati. Sleeping Car Altoona to Chicago. Vestibule Parlor Car New York to Pittsburg. Sleeping Car Pittsburg to Cleveland. Sleeping Car Pittsburg to Toledo ; car open at 10.00 p. m. Dining Car Philadelphia to Altoona. Passenger Coach New York to Pittsburg. Passenger Coach Philadelphia to Pittsburg.

(NOTE.—Tickets will be sold at New York, Jersey City and Philadelphia, good for a seat in Parlor Car to Pittsburg, and a berth in sleeper from Pittsburg to Cincinnati.)

New York and Chicago Limited.—Vestibule Sleeping Cars New York to Chicago. Vestibule Sleeping Car New York to Cincinnati. Vestibule Sleeping Car Pittsburg to Cincinnati. Vestibule Dining Car New York to Pittsburg, and Fort Wayne to Chicago. Vestibule Smoking Car New York to Chicago. Sleeping Car Pittsburg to Indianapolis.

Western Express.—Vestibule Sleeping Car New York to St. Louis. Vestibule Buffet Sleeping Car New York to Memphis. Vestibule Sleeping Car New York to Chicago. Sleeping Cars Philadelphia to Pittsburg. Vestibule Sleeping Car New York to Cincinnati. Vestibule Buffet Sleeping Car New York to New Orleans. Passenger Coach New York to Pittsburg. Dining Car New York to Philadelphia.

Pacific Express.—Vestibule Buffet Sleeping Car New York to Chicago. Sleeping Car Philadelphia to Pittsburg, open at 10.00 p. m. Sleeping Car Philadelphia to Altoona. Passenger Coach New York to Pittsburg. Buffet Sleeping Car New York to Memphis (via Shenandoah Valley R. R.) Sleeping Car New York to Chicago via C., St. L. & P. R. R. Passenger Coach Philadelphia to Pittsburg.

PIEDMONT AIR LINE AND ATLANTIC COAST LINE.

Leave New York by Pennsylvania Railroad, foot of Cortlandt and Desbrosses streets. For arrangement of Through Cars, see "Pennsylvania Route to Washington and the South."

Piedmont Air Line.

*RUN ON SUNDAYS ALSO.	Fare.	Fast Mail.	Southern Express.
Lv. New York.............		*12.15 n't	*4.30 p.m.
" Philadelphia............		7.20 a.m.	6.57 "
" Baltimore...............		9.00 "	9.30 "
" Washington.............		11.24 "	11.00 "
Ar. Danville, Va............	$13 65	8.30 p.m.	8.05 a.m.
" Charlotte, N. C..........	18 00	1.55 a.m.	12.40 n'n
" Atlanta, Ga..............	24 00	11.00 "	9.40 p.m.
" Macon, Ga...............	25 00	8.15 p.m.	3.58 a.m.
" Montgomery, Ala.........	28 50	7.00 "	7.25 "
" Birmingham.............	26 80	8.20 p.m.	6.30 a.m.
" Mobile..................	32 00	2.10 a.m.	1.55 p.m.
" New Orleans............	34 00	7.00 a.m.	7.20 p.m.
" Galveston...............	46 30	9.20 a.m.	12.05 n'n
" San Francisco, 4th day } from New Orleans......}	91 75	8.15 p.m.	....
Ar. City of Mexico, 5th day } from New Orleans......}	85 20	7.15 a.m.	....

Atlantic Coast Line.

	Fare.	Runs every day.	Daily except Sunday.
Lv. New York.................		12.15 a.m.	8.30 a.m.
" Philadelphia.............		7.20 "	11.28 "
" Baltimore................		9.00 "	2.00 p.m.
" Washington..............		10.57 "	3.10 "
Ar. Richmond................		2.38 p.m.	7.45 "
" Wilmington, N. C.........	$16 95	9.55 "	3.55 a.m.
" Charleston, S. C..........	23 00	4.00 a.m.	10.55 "
" Savannah, Ga............	21 00	6.41 "	2.15 p.m.
Ar. Brunswick, Ga............	27 00	12.50 p.m.	....
" Thomasville..............	20 50	1.40 p.m.	....
Ar. Jacksonville, Fla.........	27 75	12.00 n'n	8.30 p.m.
" St. Augustine.............	32 50	3.15 p.m.	....
" Tampa, Fla...............	35 70	10.00 p.m.	....

For arrangement of Through Cars, see next page.

PENNSYLVANIA R. R.—Continued.

PENNSYLVANIA ROUTE—WASHINGTON AND THE SOUTH.

Connect from Brooklyn, via Annex, foot of Fulton St.	Fare.	Fast Mail.	Washington Mail.	Washington Fast Exp.	Southern Day Exp.	§Washington Limited.	Washington Day Exp.	Washington Exp.	§Congress. Limited.	Fast Southern Exp.	Southern Night Exp.	Washington Exp.
Lv. New York		¶6.20am	8.00am	8.30am	10.00am	1.00pm	2.00pm	*3.40pm	*4.30pm	*9.00pm	*12.15am
" Jersey City		*4.15am	6.34 "	8.13 "	8.43 "	10.15 "	1.15 "	2.13 "	3.51 "	4.43 "	9.15 "	12.30 "
Ar. Philadelphia	$2.50	6.50 "	8.48 "	10.10 "	11.08 "	12.25pm	3.50 "	4.20 "	......	6.47 "	11.47 "	3.35 "
Lv. "		7.20 "	9.10 "	10.20 "	*11.18 "	12.35 "	4.05 "	4.30 "	5.14 "	6.57 "	11.57 "	3.50 "
Ar. Chester	2 90	......	9.42 "	......	11.45 "	......	4.26 "	......	......	7.19 "	12.25am	4.21 "
" Wilmington	3 25	8.04 "	10.12 "	11.00 "	12.06pm	1.17 "	4.46 "	5.13 "	6.33 "	7.40 "	12.49 "	4.46 "
" Baltimore	5 30	9.40 "	12.25pm	12.35pm	2.00 "	2.55 "	6.50 "	6.59 "	8.06 "	9.25 "	2.40 "	6.45 "
" Annapolis	6 45	......	......	1.48pm	6.30pm	6.30pm	......	......	......	......	......	*9 05am
Ar. Washington	6 50	*10.45am	*2.15pm	1.42pm	*3.10pm	4.00pm	*8.30pm	8.10pm	*9.12pm	*10.35pm	*1.10am	*8.00am
" Alexandria	6 95	11.14 "	*4.00 "	2.25 "	*4.00 "	4.45 "	......	......	10.25 "	*11.57 "	4.49 "	*9.00 "
" Fredericksburg	8 85	12.45pm	......	......	*5.36 "	......	......	......	......	......	6.36 "	......
" Richmond	10 35	2.38 "	......	......	*7 45 "	......	......	......	......	......	8.50 "	......

¶On Sundays this train leaves New York at 6.15 a. m. *Every day. †Daily, except Sunday. §Train is composed entirely of Parlor Cars, on which an extra rate of fare is charged.

Trains to New York.

STATIONS.	Fast Express.	New York Express.	§Limited Express.	New York Express.	New York Express.	Boston Express.	§Congressional Limited.	New York Express.	Night Express.	Night Express.
Richmond [Leave	......	......	......	......	*7.32 a.m	......	†11.07 a.m	†11.07 a.m	......	*6.25p.m
Fredericksburg	......	......	......	......	9.27 "	......	1.30 p.m	1.30 p.m	......	8.47 "
Alexandria	6.05 a.m	*8.00 a.m	*9.10 a.m	10.15 a.m	11.07 "	†1.20 p.m	3.21 "	3.21 "	*9.32 p.m	10.42 "
Washington	7.20 "	*9.00 "	*9.40 "	11.00 "	*11.40 "	*2.10 "	*3.45 "	*4.10 "	*10.00 "	*11.20 "
Annapolis [Leave	6.40 a.m	*8.37 a.m	......	......	......	†2.05 p.m	†2.05 p.m	*4.10 p.m	......	......
Baltimore [Leave	8.25 a.m	*10.08 a.m	10.15 a.m	12.05 p.m	*12.45 p.m	*3.20 p.m	*4.40 p.m	*5.17 p.m	*11.35 p.m	*12.40 a.m
Wilmington	10.07 "	11.51 "	12.28 p.m	1.39 "	2.27 "	5.24 "	6.26 "	7.06 "	2.00 a.m	2.52 "
Chester	......	12.10 p.m	......	......	......	5.44 "	......	7.26 "	2.28 "	3.16 "
Philadelphia { Ar	10.47 "	12.35 "	1.05 "	2.30 "	3.10 "	6.06 "	7.17 "	7.49 "	3.00 "	3.45 "
{ Lv	11.00 "	12.46 "	1.14 "	2.30 "	3.20 "	6.35 "	......	8.12 "	3.20 "	4.05 "
Jersey City [Arrive	1.12 p.m	3.15 "	3.20 "	4.42 "	5.42 "	9.10 "	9.13 "	10.28 "	6.10 "	6.42 "
New York [Arrive	1.20 "	3.20 "	3.30 "	4.50 "	5.50 "	*9.20 "	*9.20 "	*10.35 "	*6.20 "	*6.30 "

ARRANGEMENT OF THROUGH CARS.—Southward.

Fast Mail.—Passenger Coaches Philadelphia to Washington. Buffet Sleeping Car Washington to Jacksonville (via Atlantic Coast Line). Buffet Sleeping Car Washington to Charleston (via Atlantic Coast Line). Passenger Coach Washington to Wilmington, N. C.

Washington Mail.—Passenger Coach New York to Washington.

Washington Fast Express.—Parlor Car New York to Washington. Passenger Coach New York to Washington.

Southern Day Express.—Buffet Parlor Car New York to Washington. Buffet Sleeping Car Washington to Jacksonville (via Atlantic Coast Line). Parlor Car Washington to Richmond. Passenger Coaches New York to Richmond.

Washington Limited.—Buffet Parlor Cars New York to Washington.

Washington Day Express.—Passenger Coaches New York to Washington.

Washington Express.—Buffet Parlor Car New York to Washington. Passenger Coaches New York to Washington.

Congressional Limited.—Buffet Parlor Cars New York to Washington. Dining Car New York to Washington.

Fast Southern Express.—Parlor Cars New York to Washington. Buffet Sleeping Car Washington to New Orleans (via Piedmont Air Line). Passenger Coaches New York to Washington.

Southern Night Express.—Sleeping Car New York to Washington. Buffet Sleeping Car New York to Tampa (via Atlantic Coast Line). Buffet Sleeping Car New York to Thomasville (via Atlantic Coast Line). Sleeping Car Philadelphia to Washington, open to receive passengers at 10.00 p. m. Passenger Coaches New York to Washington. Passenger Coach Washington to Wilmington, N. C.

Washington Express.—Sleeping Car New York to Washington. Buffet Sleeping Car New York to Atlanta (via Piedmont Air Line). Buffet Sleeping Car Washington to New Orleans (via Kennesaw Route). Passenger Coach New York to Washington.

Cape Charles Route,
via Pennsylvania R. R.

Southward.	Trains run every day.	Northward.
8.00 p. m. Leave	....New York.... Arrive	8.00 a. m.
11.20 " "	....Philadelphia.... "	5.10 "
12.05 a. m. "	....Wilmington.... "	4.15 "
3.15 " "	....Delmar.... "	1.00 "
7.20 " "	....Cape Charles.... "	9.00 p. m.
9.20 " Arrive	..Old Point Comfort. Leave	6.45 "
10.20 " "	....Norfolk.... "	5.45 "
10.40 " Arrive	....Portsmouth.... Leave	5.15 "

Bay Line,
via Pennsylvania R. R.

Southward.	Trains run daily except Sunday.	Northward.
2.00 p. m. Leave	....New York.... Arrive	1.20 p. m.
4.30 " "	....Philadelphia.... "	10.47 a. m.
7.00 " "	{ Baltimore, via Bay Line / Steamers from... / ...Canton Wharf.... }	8.00 "
7.00 a. m. Arrive	..Old Point Comfort.. Leave	8.15 p. m.
8.00 " "	....Norfolk.... "	7.25 "
8.30 " "	....Portsmouth.... "	7.10 "

VIA CAMDEN AND ATLANTIC R. R.

From Pennsylvania R. R. Depot, foot of Cortlandt and Desbrosses Sts.

Leave foot of **Cortlandt** or **Desbrosses Sts.**, for **Camden** and **Atlantic City**, 12 20, 2 00 p.m., arrive at Atlantic City, 4 30, 6 37 p. m.

Leave **Atlantic City** for **New York**, 10 15 a. m., 4 40 p. m., arrive at New York, 2 10, 9 35 p. m.

VIA WEST JERSEY R. R.

From Pennsylvania R. R. Depot, foot of Cortlandt and Desbrosses Sts.

Leave foot of **Cortlandt** or **Desbrosses Sts.**, via Camden, for **Atlantic City**, 1 00 p. m., arrive Atlantic City, 5 40 p. m.

Leave **Atlantic City** for **New York**, 7 30 a. m., 3 00 p. m. Sundays, 4 10 p. m., arrive New York, 11 40 a. m., 7 20 p. m. Sundays, 9 20 p. m.

Leave foot of **Cortlandt** or **Desbrosses Sts.**, for **Cape May**, via Camden, 1 00 p. m., arrive at Cape May at 6 00 p. m.

Leave **Cape May** for **New York**, 7 20 a. m., 3 25 p. m. Sundays, 3 20 p. m., arrive New York, 2 00, 9 20 p. m. Sundays, 9 35 p. m.

PENNSYLVANIA R. R.—Continued.

LOCAL TRAINS NEW YORK DIVISION.

M.	Stations.	Fare.	Exc.
	New York		
1	Jersey City		
3	Marion	10c.	20c.
4	Meadows	14c.	25c.
8	Harrison	15c.	25c.
9	Centre St., Newark	15c.	25c.
9	Market St	15c.	25c.
9	Chestnut St	15c.	25c.
10	Emmet St	15c.	25c.
11	Waverly	25c.	40c.
13	North Elizabeth		
14	Elizabeth	25c.	40c.
15	South Elizabeth		
17	Linden	35c.	60c.
19	Scott Avenue		
19	Rahway	40c.	65c.
20	Perth Amboy Junction	45c.	70c.
21	Avenel	50c.	75c.
22	Edgar's	53c.	75c.
23	Woodbridge	55c.	85c.
24	Spa Spring	57c.	$1.00

M.	Stations.	Fare.	Exc.
26	Perth Amboy	60-	$1.00
21	Houtenville	50-	.85
22	Iselin	60-	.90
24	Menlo Park	65-	.95
25	Robinvale	.70-	1.00
26	Metuchen	.75-	1.05
29	Stelton	.80-	1.20
31	New Brunswick	.90	1.30
32	New Brunswick (Suydam St.)		
33	Millstone Junc.	$1.00	1.40
34	Voorhees	1.04	1.47
35	Clyde	1.10	1.54
36	Middlebush	1.14	1.62
39	East Millstone	1.26-	1.79
35	Franklin Park	1.07-	1.56
38	Dean's	1.16	1.74
41	Monmouth Junction	1.24-	1.95
45	Kingston	1.42	2.29
47	Rocky Hill	1.50	2.31
44	Schalk's	1.34	2.10
45	Plainsboro	1.37-	2.20

M.	Stations.	Fare	Exc.
47	Princeton Junc.	$1.42-	$2.30
50	Princeton	1.51-	2.40
51	Lawrence	1.54-	2.50
56	Trenton	1.70-	2.75
57	South Trenton		
58	Morrisville	1.71	2.90
60	Penn Valley	1.82	2.94
61	Wheat Sheaf	1.85-	3.00
63	Tullytown	1.90-	3.08
64	Cold Spring	1.94	3.15
67	Bristol	2.02-	3.27
70	Schenck's	2.10-	3.41
71	Eddington	2.14-	3.48
72	Cornwell's	2.18	3.51
73	Andalusia	2.19-	3.56
73	Borie's	2.21-	3.60
74	Torresdale	2.24	3.65
75	Pierson's	2.27	3.69
76	Pennypack	2.30-	3.71
77	Holmsburg Junction	2.32	3.78

M.	Stations.	Fare.	Exc.
78	Tacony	$2.35-	$3.83
79	Wissinoming	2.39	3.89
79	Fitler's	2.40-	3.91
80	Bridesburg	2.41-	3.93
81	Frankford	2.43-	3.97
81	Frankford Junction	2.46-	4.00
84	Kensington	2.50-	4.00
82	Harrowgate	2.47-	4.00
84	North Penn Junction	2.50-	4.00
84	Eleventh St	2.50	4.00
85	Germantown Junction	2.50-	4.00
86	Twenty-second Street	2.50-	4.00
86	Ridge Ave.	2.50-	4.00
87	Engelside	2.50-	4.00
88	Zoological Garden	2.50-	4.00
90	Philadelphia	2.50-	4.10

Leave foot of Cortlandt and Desbrosses Sts.:

For **Marion,** 5 00, 6 00, 6 30, 6 40, 7 00, 7 40, 8 10, 8 30, 9 20, 10 10, 10 40 a. m., 12 m., 12 30, 1 40, 2 30, 3 20, 4 30, 5 10, 5 30, 6 10, 6 20, 7 00, 7 30, 8 30, 9 15, 10 15, 11 15 p. m. *Sundays,* 8 00, 9 00, 10 30, 11 00 a. m., 12 m., 1 00, 2 00, 3 00, 4 00, 4 30, 5 45, 6 20, 6 45, 7 00, 8 00, 8 30, 9 00, 9 30, 10 15, 11 p. m. Arrive Marion in 20 minutes.

For **Meadows,** 6 00, 8 10, 9 20, 10 10 a. m., 2 00 p. m. Arrive in 21 minutes.

For **Harrison,** 6 00, 7 00, 8 10 a. m., 12 30, 2 30, 4 40, 5 30, 6 10, 7 30, 8 30, 10 15, p. m. *Sundays,* 11 00 a. m., 12 m., 1 00, 2 00, 4 00, 4 30, 5 45, 6 45, 11 00 p. m. Arrive in 30 minutes.

For **Newark** (Centre Street), 5 00, 6 00, 7 00, 7 30, 8 10, 9 20, 10 10, 10 40, 11 10 a. m., 12 00 m., 12 30, 1 40, 2 30, 4 10, 4 40, 5 10, 5 30, 6 20, 6 40, 7 00, 7 30, 8 30, 10 15, 11 45 p. m. Arrive in 31 minutes.

For **Newark** (Market St.), 5 00, 6 00, 6 30, 6 40, 7 00, 7 30, 7 40, 8 10, 8 30, 9 10, 9 20, 10 10, 10 40, 11 00, 11 10 a. m., 12 m., 12 30, 1 00, 1 40, 2 00, 2 30, 3 00, 3 20, 3 50, 4 00, 4 10, 4 30, 4 40, 4 50, 5 00, 5 10, 5 20, 5 30, 5 40, 5 50, 6 00, 6 10, 6 20, 6 30, 6 40, 7 00, 7 30, 8 30, 9 15, 10 15, 11 45 p. m., 12 15 night. *Sundays,* 6 15, 8 00, 9 00, 9 45, 10 00, 10 30, 11 00 a. m., 12 m., 1 00, 2 00, 3 00, 4 00, 4 30, 5 00, 5 45, 6 30, 6 45, 7 00, 7 30, 8 00, 8 30, 9 00, 9 30, 10 15, 11 00 p. m., 12 15 night. Arrive in 30 minutes.

For **Newark** (Chestnut Street), 5 00, 6 00, 6 30, 6 40, 7 00, 7 30, 7 40, 8 10, 8 30, 9 10, 9 20, 10 10, 10 40, 11 20 a. m., 12 m., 12 30, 1 00, 1 40, 2 00, 2 30, 3 00, 3 20, 3 50, 4 10, 4 40, 5 10, 5 20, 5 30, 5 50, 6 00, 6 10, 6 30, 6 40, 7 00, 7 30, 8 30, 9 15, 10 15, 11 45 p. m. 12 15 night. *Sundays,* 8 00, 9 00, 10 30, 11 00 a. m., 12 m., 1 00, 2 00, 3 00, 4 00, 4 30, 5 45, 6 30, 6 45, 7 00, 7 30, 8 00, 8 30, 9 00, 9 30, 10 15, 10 40 p. m., 12 15 night. Arrive in 35 minutes.

For **Newark** (Emmett Street), 5 00, 6 00, 6 40, 7 00, 7 30, 7 40, 8 10, 8 30, 9 20, 10 10, 10 40 a. m.: 12. m., 12 30, 1 40, 2 30, 3 50, 4 30, 5 10, 5 30, 6 00, 6 10, 6 20, 6 40, 7 30, 8 30, 10 15, 11 45 p. m. *Sundays,* 9 00, 10 30, 11 00 a. m., 12 00 m., 1 00, 2 00, 3 00, 4 00, 4 30, 5 45, 6 45, 7 30, 8 00, 8 30, 9 00, 9 30, 10 15 p. m. Arrive in 37 minutes.

For **Waverly,** 5 00, 6 00, 6 40, 7 30, 7 40, 8 10, 8 30, 10 10, 10 40 a. m., 12 00 m., 12 30, 1 40, 2 30, 3 50, 4 40, 6 30, 7 30, 8 30, 10 15, 11 45 p. m., *Sundays,* 9 00, 10 30, 11 00 a. m., 12 00 m., 1 00, 2 00, 3 00, 4 00, 5 45, 6 30, 6 45, 8 30, 9 00, 9 30, 10 15 p. m. **Arrive Waverly** in 37 minutes.

For **Elizabeth** and **Rahway,** 6 30, 7 00, 7 20, 7 40, 8 00, 9 10, 9 20, 10 10, 11 00, 11 10 a. m., 12 00 m., 12 30, 1 00, 2 00, 2 30, 3 00, 3 20, 4 00, 4 10, 4 30, 4 50, 5 00, 5 10, 5 20, 5 30, 5 40, 5 50, 6 00, 6 10, 6 20, 6 40, 7 00, 7 30, 8 30, 9 15, 10 15, 11 45 p. m., 12 15 night, *Sundays,* 6 15, 8 00, 9 00, 9 45, 10 00, 11 00 a. m., 12 m., 1 00, 2 00, 3 00, 4 00, 4 30, 5 00, 5 45, 6 30, 7 00, 7 30, 8 00, 8 30, 9 00, 9 30, 10 15, 11 00 p. m., 12 15 night. Arrive Elizabeth in 45 minutes; arrive Rahway in 55 minutes.

For **Woodbridge,** 6 00, 9 10, 10 10 a. m., 12 m., 2 30, 4 10, 5 00, 5 50, 6 40, 11 45 p. m., Sundays, 9 45 a. m., 5 00, 9 30 p. m. Arrive Woodbridge in 1 hour.

For **Perth Amboy,** 6 00, 10 10 a. m., 2 30, 4 10, 5 30, 6 40, 11 45 p. m., Sundays, 9 30 p. m. Arrive Perth Amboy in 1 hour 10 minutes.

For **Metuchen** and intermediate stations, 6 30, *6 50, *8 00, 9 20, *11 00, 11 10 a. m., 1 00, 2 00, 3 00, *3 40, *4 00, 4 50, *5 00, 5 40, 6 00, 7 00, *9 00, 10 15 p. m., *12 15 night. Sundays, *8 00, 9 00 a. m., 12 m., 1 00, 4 30, *5 00, 5 45, 7 00, 8 30 p. m., *12 15 night. Arrive Metuchen in 1 hour. **Express trains.*

For **New Brunswick,** *6 20, 6 30, *7 20, *8 30, 9 20, 11 10 a. m., *12 20, *1 00, 2 00, 3 00, *4 00, *4 40, 4 50, 5 00, 6 00, 7 00, *9 00, 10 15 p. m., *12 15 night, Sundays *6 45, 9 00, *10 a. m., 12 m., 1 00, 4 30, *5 00, 7 00, *8 00, 8 30, *9 00 p. m., *12 15 night. Arrive New Brunswick in 1 to 1¼ hours. **Express trains.*

For **East Millstone** and intermediate stations, 6 30 a. m., 12 20, 3 00, 4 50 p. m. Arrive East Millstone in 1¾ hours.

For **Monmouth Junction** and intermediate stations, 6 30, *7 20, 11 10 a. m., 2 00, 4 00, 4 40, 5 00, 7 00 p. m., *12 15 night, Sundays, *6 45, *10 00 a. m., *5 00, 7 00 p. m., *12 15 night. Arrive Monmouth Junction in 1½ hours. **Express trains.*

For **Kingston, Rocky Hill,** 7 20 a. m., 4 00 p. m. Arrive Rocky Hill in 2 hours.

For **Princeton,** 6 30, 8 30, 11 10 a. m., 1 00, 2 00, 4 40, 7 00 p. m. Arrive Princeton in 1¾ hours.

For **Trenton** and intermediate stations, *6 20, 6 30, *7 20, *8 00, *8 30, *9 00, (*10 00 a. m., extra fare), *11 00, 11 10 a. m., *12 20, 1 00, 2 00, 3 00, *4 00, 4 40, *5 00, *6 00, *6 30, 7 00, *8 00, *9 00 p. m., 12 15 night, Sundays, *6 45, *9 00, *10 00 a. m., *4 00, 5 00, *6 00, *6 30, 7 00, *8 00, *9 00 p. m., 12 15 night. Arrive Trenton—Express trains in 1½ hours. Accommodation trains in 2 hours. **Express trains.*

For **Bristol, Frankford,** and intermediate stations, *6 20, *7 20, 8 00, *8 30, 10 00, 11 10 a. m., 1 00, 2 00, 4 00, 4 40, *5 00, 6 30, 7 00 p. m., 12 15 night, Sundays, 6 45, 10 00 a. m., *5 00, 7 00 p. m. (*9 00 to Bristol), 12 15 night. Arrive Bristol 2 hours 6 minutes; arrive Frankford in 2½ hours. **Express Trains.*

For **Kensington,** 6 20, 7 20, 8 00, 8 30, 10 00, 11 10 a. m., 1 00, 4 00, 4 40, 6 30, 7 00 p. m. Arrive in 2 to 3 hours.

☞ For trains to and from Germantown Junction and Philadelphia, see page 97.

Trains to New York.

** Express trains. Trains stop at intermediate stations unless marked *.*

Leave **Kensington,** 6 50, 7 40, 8 35, 10 10, 11 15 a. m., 12 05, 1 58, 2 52, 5 35, 6 10, 7 34, 11 25 p. m., *Sundays,* 8 25 a. m. Arrive New York in 2 to 3 hours.

Leave **Frankford,** 12 30, 7 08, 7 57, 8 53, 10 28, *11 36 a. m., 12 21, 2 15, 3 00, 5 51, 6 19, 6 25, 7 50, 9 40, 10 07 p. m., Sundays, 12 30, 8 51, 9 13 a. m., 2 31, *5 45 p. m. Arrive New York in 2¼ hours.

Leave **Bristol,** 1 05, *7 29, 8 30, 9 16, 11 02, *11 56 a. m., 12 51, 2 51, 3 41, *5 34, 6 42, *7 14, 8 21, 10 23 p. m., Sundays, 1 05, 9 16 a. m., 3 05, *6 05, *7 14, *8 16 p. m. Arrive New York in 2 hours.

Leave **Trenton,** 1 35, *4 20, *5 00, *5 30, *6 21, 7 10, *7 45, *9 10, 9 37, *10 08, *11 50 a. m., 12 15, *12 47, *1 40, (*2 03 extra fare), *2 28, *3 20, *4 10, *4 50, 5 05, *5 50, *7 00, *7 32, *8 02, *9 02, *10 38 p. m., Sundays, *1 35, *5 00, *5 30, *9 37 a. m., *1 40, *4 10, 6 20, *7 32, *9 02 p. m. Arrive New York—Express trains in 1½ hours; Accommodation trains in 1 hour 50 minutes.

PENNSYLVANIA R. R.—Continued.

Trains to New York—Continued.

**Express trains.—Trains stop at intermediate stations unless marked *.*

Leave **Princeton,** 7 10, 8 55, 9 38 a. m., 12 13, 1 40, 5 00, 5 50, 7 30 p. m. Arrive New York in 1½ hours.
Leave **Rocky Hill,** 7 00, 11 50 a. m.; leave **Kingston,** 7 13 a. m., 12 03 p. m. Arrive New York in 2 hours.
Leave **Monmouth Junction,** 2 04, *5 30, 7 35, *8 08, *9 20, 10 01, *10 28 a. m., 12 39, 1 20, *2 01, 5 31, *6 12, 7 22, *10 56 p. m., Sundays, 2 01, *5 50, *10 01 a. m., *2 04, 6 41, *7 56 p. m. Arrive New York in 1½ hours
Leave **East Millstone,** 6 55, 8 40 a. m., 2 15, 5 00 p. m. Arrive New York in 2 hours
Leave **New Brunswick,** *2 25, *5 02, *5 40, 6 30, 7 20, *8 00, *8 22, 9 05, *10 19, *10 43, 11 10 a. m., *12 55, 1 40, *2 20, 3 10, *3 53, *5 22, 5 49, *6 25, *7 41, *8 13, *9 36, 11 00 p. m., Sundays, 2 25, *5 40, *6 03, 8 05, 10 19 a. m., 12 05, 1 55, *2 20, 4 05, *4 46, 6 30, 6 55, *8 13, *9 36 p. m. Arrive New York in 1 hour.
Leave **Metuchen,** 2 37, *5 12, 6 10, *6 57, 7 30, *8 08, *8 58, 9 15, *10 05, 11 20 a.m., *1 04, 1 51, *2 35, 3 20, *5 40, 5 50, *7 51, *8 52, *10 40, 11 19 p. m., Sundays, *2 37, *6 57, 8 15, 9 13, *10 28 a. m., 12 15, 2 05, 4 15, 6 40, 7 06, *7 40 p. m.
Leave **Perth Amboy** (leave Woodbridge 6 minutes later), 6 16, 6 50, 7 06, 7 40 a. m., 12 28, 5 10, 5 42 p. m., Sundays, 9 16 a. m. Extra trains leave Woodbridge 10 23 a. m., 2 24, 6 53 p. m., Sundays, 10 23 a.m., 6 51 p. m. Arrive New York in 1 hour.
Leave **Rahway,** 2 49, 5 35, 6 05, 6 34, 6 54, 7 08, 7 25, *7 39, 7 46, 7 57, *8 18, 8 23, *8 38, *9 08, 9 33, 10 07, *10 30, *10 40, 11 35 a. m., 12 45, *1 13, 1 42, 2 05, *2 32, 3 35, 4 32, 5 26, 5 57, *6 13, 6 47, *6 59, 7 18, 7 43, *8 03, 8 18, 8 59, 9 40, 10 25, 11 31 p. m., Sundays, 2 19, *5 59, *7 05, 7 42, 8 30, *9 23, 9 33, 9 58, *10 30, *10 10 a.m., 12 30, 1 32, 2 20, *2 36, 3 32, 4 32, 5 22, 6 52, *7 02, *7 18, *8 32, 9 03, 10 03, 11 33 p. m. Arrive New York in 45 minutes.
Leave **Elizabeth,** 3 02, 5 34, 5 46, 6 10, 6 17, 6 47, 7 01, 7 15, 7 20, 7 38, 7 50, 7 57, 8 08, 8 28, 8 33, 8 48, 9 17, 9 46, 10 19, 10 23, 10 38, 10 49, 11 07, 11 47 a. m., 12 57, 1 23, 1 54, 2 18, 2 40, 2 45, 2 52, 3 17, 4 45, 5 38, 6 09, 6 23, 6 57, 7 09, 7 30, 7 55, 8 13, 8 28, 9 11, 9 50, 10 37, 11 42 p. m., Sundays, 3 02, 6 10, 7 54, 8 45, 9 32, 9 47, 10 12, 10 38, 10 49 a. m., 12 43, 1 44, 2 33, 2 45, 3 45, 4 45, 5 31, 7 05, 7 12, 7 28, 7 58, 8 42, 9 15, 10 16, 11 46 p. m. Arrive New York in 40 minutes.
Leave **Waverly,** 6 05, 7 37, 8 22, 9 10, 9 26, 10 23 a. m., 12 20, 1 01, 2 00, 2 23, 3 22, 4 10, 4 49, 5 24, 5 42, 6 13, 6 37, 7 15, 7 35, 7 59, 9 55, 10 41 p. m., Sundays, 8 00, 8 50, 10 17, 11 30 a. m., 12 40, 1 50, 2 40, 3 51, 4 51, 6 50, 7 10, 8 37, 9 20, 9 50, 10 21, 11 51 p. m.
Leave **Newark** (Emmett St.) 5 51, 6 08, 6 24, 6 54, 7 40, 7 45, 8 05, 8 25, 8 39, 9 13, 9 30, 9 54, 10 55, 11 51 a. m., 12 24, 1 01, 2 04, 2 26, 3 25, 3 51, 4 12, 4 51, 5 27, 6 16, 6 39, 7 18, 7 38, 8 02, 8 35, 9 58, 10 44, 11 51 p. m., *Sundays*, 8 03, 8 53, 9 56, 10 21, 11 53 a. m., 12 52, 1 54, 2 44, 3 54, 4 51, 5 11, 6 54, 7 13, 8 40, 9 23, 9 53, 11 54 p. m. Arrive New York in 36 minutes.
Leave **Newark** (Chestnut St.), 3 12, 5 56, 6 10, 6 26, 6 56, 7 12, 7 42, 7 47, 8 07, 8 27, 8 41, 9 15, 9 32, 9 56, 10 27, 10 57, 11 56 a. m., 12 25, 1 06, 2 06, 2 28, 3 27, 3 56, 4 16, 4 54, 5 20, 5 47, 6 18, 6 30, 6 41, 7 04, 7 21, 7 41, 8 05, 8 38, 9 19, 10 00, 10 46, 11 53 p. m., *Sundays*, 8 05, 8 56, 9 59, 10 25, 10 57, 11 56 a. m., 12 55, 1 56, 2 46, 3 56, 4 56, 5 43, 6 56, 7 16, 7 22, 8 43, 9 26, 9 56, 10 25, 11 56 p. m. Arrive New York in 34 minutes.
Leave **Newark** (Market Street), 3 16, 5 47, 6 00, 6 12, 6 30, 7 00, 7 15, 7 30, 7 45, 7 52, 7 57, 8 10, 8 19, 8 30, 8 38, 8 43, 8 57, 9 18, 9 31, 10 00, 10 30, 10 48, 11 00, 11 17 a. m., 12 m., 12 30, 1 10, 1 35, 2 10, 2 32, 2 48, 2 57, 3 02, 3 30, 4 00, 4 20, 5 01, 5 31, 5 50, 6 06, 6 21, 6 33, 6 45, 6 58, 7 06, 7 19, 7 23, 7 45, 8 00, 8 24, 8 40, 9 22, 10 04, 10 50, 11 56 p. m., Sundays, 3 16, 8 00, 9 00, 10 02, 10 30, 10 48, 11 00 a. m., 12 00 m., 1 00, 2 00, 2 50, 2 57, 4 00, 5 00, 5 46, 7 00, 7 20, 7 25, 7 39, 8 10, 8 47, 9 30, 10 00, 10 30 p. m., 12 00 night. Arrive New York in 33 minutes.
Leave **Newark** (Centre Street), 6 03, 6 15, 6 33, 7 03, 7 17, 7 48, 7 54, 8 34, 8 46, 9 37, 10 03, 10 33, 11 03 a. m., 12 03, 12 33, 1 13, 2 13, 2 35, 3 32, 4 03, 4 23, 5 04, 5 31, 5 53, 6 24, 6 48, 7 26, 7 48, 8 12, 9 21, 10 07, 10 53 p. m. Arrive New York in 30 minutes.
Leave **Harrison,** 6 05, 6 17, 6 35, 7 05, 7 36, 8 35, 9 40, 10 35 a. m., 12 35, 1 15, 2 15, 4 05, 4 25, 5 37, 6 26, 7 29, 8 14, 10 55 p. m., *Sundays*, 8 11, 9 03, 10 33 a. m., 12 02, 1 03, 2 05, 2 53, 4 05, 5 01, 7 03, 9 33 p. m. Arrive New York in 25 minutes.
Leave **Meadows,** 12 08, 5 00, 6 20 p. m. Arrive New York in 22 minutes.
Leave **Marion,** 6 12, 6 25, 6 42, 7 14, 7 56, 8 04, 8 44, 8 56, 9 47, 10 13 a. m., 12 14, 12 43, 1 21, 2 23, 2 43, 3 43, 4 13, 4 33, 5 14, 5 44, 6 01, 6 37, 6 57, 7 17, 7 36, 8 00, 8 22, 8 50, 9 33, 10 17, 11 03 p. m., 12 05 night., *Sundays*, 8 19, 9 15, 10 16, 10 45 a. m., 12 15, 1 15, 2 13, 3 00, 4 13, 5 57, 7 15, 7 32, 8 56, 9 41, 10 13, 10 43 p. m., 12 14 night. Arrive New York in 16 minutes.

BRYN MAWR AND PAOLI TRAINS.

Leave Cortlandt and **Desbrosses Sts.,** via Philadelphia, for **Bryn Mawr** and **Paoli,** 6 20, 8 00, 9 00, 10 00, 11 10 a. m., 12 20, 1 00, 2 00, 3 20, 4 00 (4 30 to Bryn Mawr), 5 00, 6 30, 8 00 p. m., Sundays, 6 15, 9 00, 10 00 a. m., 4 00, 5 00, 6 30 p. m. (8 00 p. m. to Bryn Mawr). Arrive Bryn Mawr in 3¼ hours; arrive Paoli in 3⅓ hours.
Leave **Paoli** (leave Bryn Mawr 23 minutes later), 5 55, 6 25, 7 17, 8 25, 9 25, 10 25, 11 55 a. m., 12 25, 1 25, 1 55, 2 55, 3 25 (4 18 from Bryn Mawr), 5 25, 5 55, 6 55, 8 55, 10 55 p. m., Sundays, 7 25, 8 13 a. m. (11 48 a. m., from Bryn Mawr), 12 40, 2 18, 4 18, 4 57, 5 48 (6 18 from Bryn Mawr), 10 25 p. m. Arrive New York in 4 hours.

Manayunk, Norristown, Phoenixville, Pottstown, Birdsboro, Reading, Hamburg, Pottsville.

Leave foot of Cortlandt or **Desbrosses Sts.** for **Manayunk** and **Norristown,** 12 15, 6 20, 8 00, 9 00, 11 00 a. m., 12 20, 1 00, 2 00, 3 30, 4 00, 5 00, 6 30, 8 00 p. m., Sundays, 12 15, 6 15, 10 a. m., 4 00, 5 00, 6 30 p. m. Arrive Manayunk in 2¾ hours; arrive Norristown in 3¼ hours.
For **Phoenixville, Pottstown, Birdsboro** and **Reading,** 12 15, 11 00 a. m., 1 00, 4 00 p. m., Sundays, 6 15, 10 00 a. m. Arrive Phoenixville, 7 28 a. m., 3 34, 5 03, 7 39 p. m., Sundays, 10 37 a. m., 2 28 p. m.; arrive Pottstown, 7 55 a. m., 4 01, 5 27, 8 07 p. m., Sundays, 11 03 a. m. 2 56 p. m.; arrive Reading, 8 40 a. m., 5 00, 6 00, 8 45 p. m., Sundays, 11 50 a. m., 3 45 p. m.
For **Hamburg** and **Pottsville,** 12 15, 11 00 a m., 1 00 p. m., Sundays, 6 15, 10 00 a. m. Arrive **Pottsville,** 10 04 a. m., 6 20, 7 07 p. m., Sundays, 1 11, 5 06 p. m.

GERMANTOWN AND CHESTNUT HILL BRANCH.

Fare to Chestnut Hill $1.60 Excursion $4.20.

Leave foot of Cortlandt or **Desbrosses Sts.,** via Germantown Junction, for **Chestnut Hill** and intermediate stations, 6 20, 7 20, 8 30, 11 00 a. m. 12 20, 1 00, 2 00, 3 00, 4 00, 4 30, 5 00, 6 00, 6 30, 8 00, 9 00 p. m., Sundays, 6 15, 9 00, 10 00 a. m., 4 30, 5 00, 6 30, 8 00 p. m. Arrive Chestnut Hill in about 3 hours.
Leave **Chestnut Hill,** 6 30, 7 15, 8 07, 8 20, 9 15, 10 46 a. m., 12 26, 2 10, 2 45, 3 10, 4 46, 5 45, 6 20, 7 45, 9 05, 11 59 p. m., Sundays, 7 15, 9 28 a. m., 12 30, 2 34, 4 34, 6 24, 7 29, 10 20 p. m. Arrive New York in about 2⅓ hours.

BELVIDERE DIVISION.

M.	Stations.	Fare.	Exc.	M.	Stations.	Fare.	Exc.	M.	Stations.	Fare.	Exc.	M.	Stations.	Fare.	Exc.
	Trenton……	$1.70-	$1.75	16	Lambertville…	$2.19	$3.56	22	Bull's Island…	$2.30-	$3.89	50	Phillipsburg…	$3.23	$5.29
1	Warren Street			18	Flemington Br.: Alexauken	2.25-	3.66	24	Byram……	2.41-	3.98		Easton		
4	Asylum……	1.82-	2.95	19	Mt. Airy…	2.30-	3.71	26	Tumble……	2.50	4.08	51	Lopatcong ….	3.25	5.33
5	Wilburtha……	1.85-	3.00	20	Bowne….	2.32	3.78	28	Kingwood ….	2.55-	4.17	53	Harmony……	3.37-	5.53
6	Scudder's Falls	1.91-	3.10	22	Boss Road.	2.37-	3.87	31	Frenchtown….	2.66-	4.31	57	Martin's Creek.	3.44	5.64
7	Somerset……	1.94-	3.11	23	Ringoes….	2.40	3.91	35	Milford ……	2.76-	4.51	59	Hutchinson's…	3.49	5.73
9	Washington			24	Muirhead's.	2.43	3.97	38	Holland……	2.86-	4.67	60	Roxburg ……	3.58	5.80
	Crossing….	1.98-	3.22	26	Copper Hill	2.48-	4.05	41	Riegelsville….	2.96	4.85	64	Belvidere……	3.65	5.99
10	Titusville……	2.02	3.28	28	Flemington	2.55-	4.16	45	Carpenterville..	3.07-	5.03	67	Manunka		
12	Moore's ……	2.09-	3.39	19	Stockton……	2.20-	3.73	50	Lehigh Junc ..	3.22	5.29		Chunk …	3.71-	6.15

Trenton, Lambertville, Flemington, Lehigh Junction, Easton and Manunka Chunk.

Leave foot of Cortlandt and **Desbrosses Sts.** for **Lambertville** and intermediate stations, 7 20, 11 00 a. m., 2 00, 3 00, 5 00 p. m. Arrive Lambertville, 9 42 a. m., 1 35, 4 25, 5 21, 7 40 p. m.
For **Flemington** and intermediate stations, 7 20, 11 00 a. m., 3 00 p. m. Arrive Flemington, 10 12 a. m., 2 55, 6 02 p. m.
For **Lehigh Junction, Easton, Manunka Chunk** and intermediate stations, 7 20, 11 00 a. m., 3 00, 5 00 p. m. Arrive Lehigh Junction, 10 38 a. m., 2 44, 6 21, 8 49 p. m.; arrive Easton, 10 43 a. m., 2 50, 6 25, 8 53 p. m.; arrive Manunka Chunk, 11 20 a. m., 3 30, 7 00, 9 30 p. m.

Trains to New York.

Leave **Manunka Chunk,** 7 00, 10 15 a. m., 12 20, 3 45, 6 30 p. m.; leave **Easton,** 7 26, 10 46 a. m., 1 00, 4 20, 7 02 p. m.; leave **Lehigh Junction,** 7 27, 10 47 a. m., 1 01, 4 21, 7 03 p. m.; leave **Lambertville,** 8 30, 11 52 a. m., 2 08, 5 30, 8 00 p. m. Arrive New York, 10 40 a. m., 2 10, 4 50, 8 50, 10 35 p. m.
Leave **Flemington,** 7 50 a. m., 12 40, 4 45 p. m. Arrive New York, 10 40 a. m., 4 50, 8 50 p. m.

PENNSYLVANIA R. R.—Continued.
AMBOY DIVISION.
The fares here given are via Rahway.

M.	Stations.	Fare.	Exc.	M.	Stations.	Fare.	Exc.	M.	Stations.	Fare.	Exc.	M.	Stations.	Fare.	Exc.
	South Amboy	.70c.	$1.10	24	Windsor	$1.30	$2.30	42	Mt. Holly Junc.			53	Palmyra	$2.03	$3.77
2	Kriston	80c.	1.30	27	Newtown	1.38	2.45	43	Burlington	$1.78	$3.26	53	West Palmyra	2.05	3.79
7	Old Bridge	86c.	1.46	30	Yardville	1.47	2.63	45	Edgewater Park	1.84	3.38	54	Morris	2.08	3.85
8	Bloomfield	90c.	1.54	33	Bordentown	1.54	2.79	46	Beverly	1.86	3.42	56	Delair	2.10	3.91
9	Spotswood	91c.	1.57	34	White Hill	1.57	2.85	47	Perkins	1.88	3.46	56	Fish House	2.12	3.94
11	Helmetta	96c.	1.67	36	Kinkora	1.62	2.91	48	Delanco	1.92	3.53	57	Beideman's	2.15	4.00
13	Jamesburg	$1.00	1.75	37	Knickerbocker			49	Riverside	1.93	3.56	58	Pavonia	2.16	4.00
15	Prospect Plains	1.10	1.90		Row	1.64	2.99	50	Cambridge	1.95	3.60	60	Haddon Avenue	2.22	4.00
17	Cranbury	1.14	1.98	38	Florence	1.67	3.03	50	Taylor	1.97	3.64	60	Camden	2.22	4.00
20	Hightstown	1.21	2.13	41	Stevens	1.73	3.16	52	Riverton	2.02	3.73	61	Philadelphia	2.25	4.00

Leave foot of Cortlandt or Desbrosses Sts., for **Jamesburg, Hightstown, Bordentown** and intermediate stations, 9.10 a. m., 5.00 p. m. Arrive Jamesburg, 10.42 a. m., 6.36 p. m.; arrive Bordentown, 11.31 a. m., 7.28 p. m.
For **Burlington, Camden, Philadelphia** and intermediate stations, 9.00, 11.10 a. m., 12.20, 1.00, 2.00, 4.00, 5.00, 8.00 p. m., Sundays, 10.00 a. m., 6.00 p. m. Arrive Burlington in 2½ hours; arrive Camden and Philadelphia in 3 hours.

Trains to New York.
Leave **Philadelphia** (leave Camden 10 minutes later), 6.20, 7.20, 9.00, 10.30, 11.40 a. m., 12.00 m., 2.30, 3.30, 4.00, 4.30, 5.30, 7.30 p. m., Sundays, 9.15 a. m., 5.15 p. m. Arrive New York in 3 hours.
Leave **Burlington**, 7.10, 8.03, 9.37, 11.21 a. m., 12.46, 1.00, 3.21, 4.29, 4.44, 5.17, 6.19, 8.23 p. m., Sundays, 10.19 a. m., 6.42 p. m. Arrive New York in 2½ hours.
Leave **Bordentown**, 6.30, 7.20, 8.37, 9.55, 11.47 a. m., 12.31, 1.25, 3.45, 4.52, 5.00, 5.36, 6.41, 8.45 p. m., Sundays, 6.30, 10.43 a. m., 7.08 p. m. Arrive New York in 2 hours.
Leave **Hightstown**, 7.25, 8.30, 9.02 a. m., 5.21 p. m.; leave **Jamesburg**, 7.50, 9.10, 9.35 a. m., 5.41 p. m. Arrive New York, 9.20, 11.30, 11.40 a. m., 7.30 p. m.

Burlington Branch—Leave **Burlington** for **Mount Holly**, 8.20, 10.05, 11.58 a. m., 3.32, 5.18, 7.33 p. m. Arrive Mount Holly in 25 minutes.
Leave **Mount Holly** for **Burlington**, 6.42, 9.02, 10.50 a. m., 2.50, 4.38, 6.00 p. m. Arrive Burlington in 25 minutes.
Medford Branch—Leave **Mount Holly** for **Medford**, 6.47, 9.32 a. m., 12.25, 5.00 p. m., Sundays, 7.15 a. m. Arrive Medford in 27 minutes.
Kinkora Branch Leave **Kinkora** for **Lewistown**, 8.25, 9.50 a. m., 3.37, 5.42 p. m., Sundays, 7.21 a. m. Arrive Lewistown in 22 minutes.
Leave **Lewistown**, 7.30, 9.16 a. m., 2.32, 5.05 p. m., Sundays, 6.29 p. m. Arrive Kinkora in 22 minutes.
Vincentown Branch Leave **Ewansville**, 9.28 a. m., 12.42, 2.37, 3.10, 6.27 p. m. Arrive Vincentown in 12 minutes.
Leave **Vincentown**, 7.00 a. m., 12.30, 1.55, 3.10, 4.05 p. m. Arrive Ewansville in 22 minutes.
Pemberton and Hightstown R. R. Leave **Hightstown** for **North Pemberton** and **Birmingham**, 7.30, 10.00 a. m., 7.23 p. m. Arrive Birmingham, 8.52 a. m., 12.38, 8.29 p. m.
Leave **Birmingham** (North Pemberton 6 minutes later), 8.04 a. m., 1.45, 5.08 p. m. Arrive **Hightstown**, 9.00 a. m., 5.20, 6.25 p. m.

POINT PLEASANT, TOM'S RIVER, WHITINGS, MOUNT HOLLY AND PHILADELPHIA.
Leave **Point Pleasant** for Berkeley, Seaside Park, Island Heights and Tom's River, 11.30 a. m., and on Mondays and Saturdays only, 3.05 p. m. Arrive Tom's River, 1.12 p. m., and on Mondays and Saturdays at 4.05 p. m.
Leave **Island Heights** for **Whitings, Mount Holly and Philadelphia**, 7.50 a. m., 3.55 p. m. Arrive Mount Holly, 9.10 a. m., 5.10 p. m.; arrive Philadelphia, 10.01 a. m., 6.00 p. m.
Leave **North Pemberton** for **Merchantville and Philadelphia**, 6.30, 7.35 a. m., 12.32, 2.30, 4.10, 8.45 p. m., Sundays, 8.12 a. m. Arrive Merchantville in 1 hour; arrive Philadelphia in 1¼ hours.
Leave **Mount Holly** for **Merchantville, Camden and Philadelphia**, 5.30, 6.00, 6.52, 7.22, 8.00, 9.10, 11.20 a. m., 12.51, 2.15, 4.28, 5.10, 6.15, 8.11, 10.50 p. m., Sundays, 8.13 a. m., 12.05, 5.30, 7.50 p. m. Arrive Merchantville in 36 minutes; arrive Camden and Philadelphia in 1 hour.

FREEHOLD AND JAMESBURG R. R.
The fares here given are via Monmouth Junction and are higher than rates via Rahway and South Amboy. New York connections for this road are mostly made via Monmouth Junction.

M.	Stations.	Fare.	Exc.	M.	Stations.	Fare.	Exc.	M.	Stations.	Fare.	Exc.	M.	Stations.	Fare.	Exc.
	Monmouth Jun.	$1.24	$1.95	11	Tracy's	$1.50	$2.00	20	Howell	$1.60	$2.10	28	Allaire	$1.75	$2.25
2	Dayton		1.30	2.00	14	Englishtown	1.50	2.00	21	Fairfield	1.62	2.10	30	Allenwood	1.75	2.35
6	Jamesburg	1.41	2.00	14	Tennent	1.50	2.00	23	Yellowbrook			32	Manasquan	1.75	2.35
7	Low Jamesburg	1.43	2.00	17	Freehold	1.50	2.00	25	Farmingdale	1.70	2.10	33	Sea Girt	1.75	2.35
9	Hoffman's	1.45	2.00												

Leave foot of Cortlandt or Desbrosses Sts. for **Jamesburg, Freehold, Farmingdale, Manasquan and Sea Girt,** 7.20, 11.10 a. m., 1.00, 5.00 p. m. Arrive Jamesburg, 9.35 a. m., 1.10, 5.10, 6.45 p. m.; arrive Freehold, 10.01 a. m., 1.40, 6.00, 7.12 p. m.; arrive Farmingdale, 10.16 a. m., 1.57, 6.14, 7.28 p. m.; arrive Sea Girt, 10.33 a. m., 2.16, 6.33, 7.46 p. m.

Trains to New York.
Leave **Sea Girt** (Manasquan 2 minutes later), 6.15, 8.11 a. m., 12.43, 4.35 p. m.; leave **Farmingdale**, 6.32, 8.43 a. m., 1.02, 4.51 p. m.; leave **Freehold**, 6.48, 8.50 a. m., 1.19, 5.10 p. m.; leave **Jamesburg**, 7.15, 9.19 a. m., 1.45, 5.37 p. m. Arrive New York, 9.00, 11.30 a. m., 3.40, 7.20 p. m.

DOCK MASTERS.
Office of Department of Docks, Pier A N. R. (Battery).

EAST RIVER.
District No. 1. Charles H. Thompson, dockmaster. Office, 83 Coenties Slip. From Castle Garden to and including west side of Pier 16, foot of Wall St.
District No. 3.—Edward Abeel, dockmaster. Office, 262 South St. From east side of Pier 16, foot of Wall St., to Pier 45, between Rutger's Slip and Jefferson St.
District No. 5. Charles H. Pendergast, dockmaster. Office, 271 South St. From Pier 45, between Rutger's Slip and Jefferson St., to Pier (old) 69, foot of 10th St.
District No. 7.—Charles Hutchinson, dockmaster. Office, foot E. 17th St. From Pier (old) 69, foot 10th, to 54th St.
District No. 9.—Geo. A. Bourhon, dockmaster. Office, 559 E. 86th St. From 54th to 164th St.
District No. 11. David W. Bogert, acting dockmaster. Office, 109th St. Har. River. From 93d St. to Kingsbridge, also Bronx River.

NORTH RIVER.
District No. 2. David W. Bogert, dockmaster. Office, foot Duane St. From Pier A to Pier (new) 27, foot of Hubert St.
District No. 4. Patrick Carley, dockmaster. Office, foot Barrow St. From Pier (new) 27, foot Hubert St., to W. 11th St.
District No. 6.—Chas. B. Husted, dockmaster. Office, foot W. 18th St. From W. 11th St. to W. 23d St.
District No. 8. Patrick J. Brady, dockmaster. Office, foot W. 30th St. From W. 23d St. to W. 42d St.
District No. 10. Joseph B. Erwin, dockmaster. Office, foot W. 57th St. From W. 42d St. to W. 60th St.
District No. 12. John J. Ryan, dockmaster. Office, foot W. 79th St. From W. 60th St. to Yonkers, Spuyten Duyvil and Kingsbridge.

WEST JERSEY R. R.

Via Pennsylvania R. R. foot of Cortlandt and Desbrosses Streets.

Leave Philadelphia for **Newfield** and **Atlantic City**, stopping at intermediate stations, 8.20, 8.50 a. m., 3.10, †4.00 p. m., Sundays, 8.00, †8.45 a. m., 4.45 p. m. Arrive Atlantic City, 10.37, †10.30 a. m., 5.30, †5.40 p. m., Sundays, 10.48, †10.25 a. m., 7.02 p. m.

† *Express trains, make no stops between Camden and Pleasantville.*

Trains to Philadelphia.

Leave **Atlantic City**, 7.15, †7.30 a. m., †3.00, 3.05 p. m., Sundays, 7.30 a. m., 3.55, †4.10 p. m. Arrive Philadelphia, 9.50, †9.40 a. m., 1.40, 5.20 p. m., Sundays, 9.35 a. m., 6.20 p. m., †5.50 p. m.

Leave **Newfield**, 8.00 a. m., 3.58 p. m., Sundays, 8.19 a. m., 4.44 p. m. Arrive Philadelphia, 9.50 a. m., 5.20 p. m., Sundays, 9.35 a. m., 6.20 p. m.

Somers Point Branch.—Leave **Philadelphia** for **Somers Point**, 8.50 a. m., 4.00 p. m., Sundays, 8.45 a. m. Arrive in 2 hours.

Leave **Somers Point**, 7.05 a. m., 2.15 p. m., Sundays, 3.15 p. m. Arrive Philadelphia in 2 hours.

Woodbury, Pennsgrove, Wenonah, Glassboro, Clayton, Bridgeton.

Leave Philadelphia for **Woodbury** and intermediate stations, 6.10, 8.00, 8.20, 9.30, 10.30 a. m., 12.00 m., 1.30, 3.10, 1.40, 4.30, 5.00, 5.20, 5.40, 6.00, 6.30, 7.30, 10.45, 11.30 p. m., Sundays, 8.00, 8.15 a. m., 12.30, 4.45, 5.15, 9.30 p. m. Arrive Woodbury in 30 minutes.

For **Pennsgrove** and intermediate stations, 8.00, 10.30 a. m., 3.10, 5.40 p. m., Sundays, 8.15 a. m., 5.15 p. m. Arrive Pennsgrove in 2 hours.

For **Glassboro**, 6.10, 8.00, 8.20, 9.30, 10.30 a. m., 12.00 m., 3.10, 3.30, 4.30, 5.00, 5.20, 6.30, 11.30 p. m., Sundays, 8.00 a. m., 4.45 p. m. Arrive Glassboro in 50 minutes.

For **Clayton**, 8.20 a. m., 12.00 m., 3.10, 5.20 p. m., Sundays, 8.00 a. m., 4.45 p. m. Arrive in 1 hour.

For **Elmer** and **Bridgeton**, 8.00 a. m., 12.00 m., 3.30, 5.00, 6.30 p. m., Sundays, 8.00 a. m., 4.45 p. m. Arrive Bridgeton in 1¾ hours.

Trains to Philadelphia.

Leave **Bridgeton**, stopping at intermediate stations, 7.00, 8.05 a. m., 12.15, 3.00, 5.10 p. m., Sundays, 8.00 a. m., 4.50 p. m. Arrive Philadelphia in 1¾ hours.

Leave **Glassboro**, 5.50, 6.20, 7.07, 7.34, 7.40, 8.12, 8.50, 11.00 a. m., 12.00 m., 1.05, 3.46, 4.30, 5.21, 5.51, 7.40 p. m., Sundays, 8.46 a. m., 5.32 p. m. Arrive Philadelphia in 1 hour 50 minutes.

Leave **Pennsgrove**, 6.55, 8.15 a. m., 12.20, 4.55 p. m., Sundays, 7.30 a. m., 4.30 p. m. Arrive Philadelphia in 1¾ hours.

Leave **Woodbury**, 6.07, 6.38, 7.28, 7.17, 8.00, 8.35, 9.21, 11.20 a. m., 12.20, 1.26, 3.00, 4.05, 4.49, 5.08, 5.35, 6.10, 7.02, 8.03, 8.50, 11.07 p. m., Sundays, 8.32, 9.04 a. m., 3.00, 5.42, 5.52, 10.21 p. m. Arrive Philadelphia in 30 minutes.

VINELAND, MILLVILLE, PORT NORRIS AND CAPE MAY.

Leave Philadelphia for **Vineland**, **Millville**, **Manumuskin** and intermediate stations, 8.20, 9.00 a. m., 12.00 m., 3.10 (3.50 to Millville) 5.20 p. m., Sundays, 8.00 a. m., 4.45 p. m. Arrive Vineland in 1¼ hours; arrive Manumuskin in 1¾ hours.

For **Mauricetown, Port Norris** and intermediate stations, 8.20 a. m., 12.00 m., 5.20 p. m., Sundays, 4.45 p.m. Arrive Mauricetown, 10.48 a. m., 2.17, 7.08 p. m., Sundays, 6.48 p. m.; arrive Port Norris, 10.51 a. m., 2.55, 7.41 p. m., Sundays, 7.16 p. m.

For **Cape May City** and intermediate stations, 9.00 a. m., 3.10, 3.50 p. m., Sundays, 8.00 a. m. Arrive Cape May City, 11.35 a. m., 6.18, 6.00 p. m., Sundays, 11.03 a. m.

Trains to Philadelphia.

Leave **Cape May City**, 6.50, 7.20 a. m., 3.25, p. m., Sundays, 3.20 p. m.; leave Cape May C. H. 17 minutes later. Arrive Philadelphia, 9.50, 9.30 a. m., 6.00 p. m., Sundays, 6.20 p. m.

Leave **Port Norris**, 5.55, 11.20 a. m., 2.35 p. m., Sundays, 7.03 a. m. Arrive Philadelphia in 3½ hours.

Leave **Manumuskin** (leave Millville 12 minutes later), 6.36, 7.51 a. m., 8.21 a. m. from Millville, 12.03, 3.20, 4.26 p. m., Sundays 7.16 a. m., 4.20 p. m.; leave **Vineland**, 7.01, 8.19, 8.30 a. m., 12.27, 3.56, 4.51 p. m., Sundays, 8.11 a. m., 4.56 p. m. Arrive Philadelphia in 2 hours from Manumuskin; in 1¾ hours from Vineland.

PHILADELPHIA AND SALEM TRAINS.

Leave **Philadelphia** (via Glassboro), 8.00 a. m., 3.30 p. m. Arrive Salem, 10.30 a. m., 5.17 p. m.

Leave **Salem**, 7.30 a. m., 2.17 p. m. Arrive Philadelphia, 9.30 a. m., 4.40 p. m.

Leave **Philadelphia** (via Swedesboro), 8.20 a. m., 1.30, 4.40, 5.40 p. m., Sundays, 8.15 a. m., 5.15 p. m. Arrive Swedesboro in 1 hour; arrive Salem in 1¾ hours.

Leave **Salem**, 6.45, 7.40 a. m. 12.20, 4.00 p. m., Sundays, 7.20 a. m., 4.30 p. m.; leave **Swedesboro**, 7.24, 8.40 a. m., 12.58, 4.40 p. m., 7.58 a. m., 5.11 p. m. Arrive Philadelphia 8.30, 9.00 a. m., 2.00, 5.40 p. m. Sundays, 9.05 a. m., 6.20 p. m.

Sea Isle and Ocean City Branch Leave **Philadelphia**, for Sea Isle City and Ocean City, 9.00 a.m., 3.50 p.m., Sundays, 8.00 a. m. Arrive at Ocean City, 11.38 a. m., 6.30 p. m., Sundays, 11.09 a. m.

Leave **Ocean City**, 6.30 a. m., 3.20 p. m., Sundays, 3.17 p. m. Arrive Philadelphia, 9.30 a. m., 6.00 p. m., Sundays, 6.20 p. m.

Five-Mile Beach Branch. Leave **Philadelphia** for **Anglesea** and **Holly Beach**, 9.00 a. m., 3.50 p. m., Sundays 8.00 a. m. Arrive Holly Beach, 12.01, 6.35 p. m., Sundays, 11.20 a. m.

Leave **Holly Beach**, 6.21 a. m., 3.00 p. m., Sundays, 2.55 p. m. Arrive Philadelphia, 9.30 a. m., 6.00 p. m., Sundays, 6.20 p. m.

BOARD OF PORT WARDENS.

Office of Wardens of Port, 17 South St., New York,—William H. Leaycraft, President; F. G. Comstock, Vice-Pres.; William Conselyea, Secretary; C. W. Meade, Treas., and in charge of Auctions; A. W. Dodge, Collector.
C. W. Meade, from Pier 1 N. R. to Pier 21 N. R.
Isaac W. Edsall, Pier 22 N. R. to Pier 36 N. R.
F. G. Comstock, Pier 37 N. R. upwards.
W. G. Watt, Pier 1 E. R. to Pier 40 E. R.

William H. Leaycraft, Pier 41 E. R. to Coe's Stores.
H. A. Barnum, from Coe's Stores, Williamsburgh, Greenpoint and Hunters Point.
J. S. Kidder, from Navy Yard to South Ferry, Brooklyn.
Hiram Calkins, from South Ferry to and including Atlantic Dock, Brooklyn.
Edward Toothill, from Atlantic Basin to Gowanus Bay, Brooklyn.

FOREIGN EXPRESSES.

American Express Company.—Principal office. 65 Broadway.
American Foreign and European Express.— Davis, Turner & Co., 31 Broadway.
Baldwin's European Express.—Baldwin, Bros. & Co., 53 Broadway.
Contanseau Foreign Express Co. L. Contanseau, V. Pres., 69 and 1,420 Broadway.
Downing's Foreign Express.—R. F. Downing & Co., 20 Exchange Place., 63 Beaver St.
E. Losee's European Express.— 111 Broadway.
Hensel, Bruckman & Lorbacher, Parcel Agency Imperial German Mail. 25 William St.

Merchants' Lightning Foreign Express.—R. F. Laug. 40 Exchange Place.
Morris' European and American Express.—L. W. Morris & Son, 18 and 20 Broadway.
Pitt & Scott's Foreign Express.—35 Broadway.
Stoglich & Baese European Package Express.— 76 Williams St.
The Foreign Express Co. 207 Broadway.
The Transatlantic Express. J. Ter Kuile, Prop., 31 Broadway.
Wells, Fargo & Co. European Express.—61 Broadway.
Wolff's European Express. 45 Broadway.

SAILING VESSEL LINES
FOR FOREIGN PORTS.

We have inserted the frequency of sailings of the different lines where any regular interval is adhered to by the lines.

Adelaide, South Australia. "Kangaroo Line." Every 3 to 6 weeks. Mailler & Quereau. 51 Stone St.
Alicante, Spain.—R. De Florez & Co., 24 Stone St.
" " Miller & Houghton, 32 South St.
Almeria, Spain.—R. De Florez & Co., 24 Stone St.
Antofogasta, Chili.—"Merchant's Line." W. R. Grace & Co., Hanover Square.
Antigua, West Indies, G. A. Brett, Son & Co., 41 South St.
" " Miller, Bull & Co., 18 South St.
" " G. F. Lough & Co., Produce Exchange.
Arica, Peru.—Every 3 or 4 months. W. R. Grace & Co., Hanover Square.
Arroyo, Porto Rico.—Miller, Bull & Co., 18 South St.
" " G. A. Brett, Son & Co., 41 South St.
Aspinwall, U. S. of Col.—Miller, Bull & Co., 18 South St.
" " G. A. Brett, Son & Co., 41 South St.
" " Miller & Houghton, 32 South St.
Auckland, New Zealand. "Pioneer Line," once a month, R. W. Cameron & Co., 24 So. William St.
" " "Kangaroo Line." Every 3 to 6 weeks, Mailler & Quereau, 51 Stone St.
Aux Cayes, Hayti.—F. C. Elliot, 26 South St.
Azua, St. Domingo,—J. B. Vicini & Co., 91 Wall St.
Baracoa, Cuba,—Miller, Bull & Co., 18 South St.
Barbadoes, West Indies, G. F. Lough & Co., Produce Exchange.
Barcelona, Spain,—R. De Florez & Co., 24 Stone St.
Barcelona, Venezuela, Every 2 months, S. Dominici's Sons, 81 New St.
Bassa, Africa, Yates & Porterfield, 57 South St.
Bermuda.—G. F. Lough & Co., Produce Exchange.
" Scammell Brothers, 29 Beaver St.
Bilboa, Spain, R. De Florez & Co., 24 Stone St.
Brisbane, Queensland. "Pioneer Line." Once a month, R. W. Cameron & Co., 24 So. William St.
" " "Australasian Line." R. W. Forbes & Son, 14 South William St.
" " "Merchants' Line." Arkell & Douglass, 25 Whitehall St.
" " "Kangaroo Line." Every 3 to 6 weeks. Mailler & Quereau, 51 Stone St.
Buenos Ayres, Argentine Republic,—"Old Regular Line." John Norton & Sons, 90 Wall St.
" " Paul F. Gerhard & Co., 8 Broad St.
" " J. E. Ward & Co., 113 Wall St.
" " Miller & Houghton, 32 South St.
Cadiz, Spain,—"Regular Line," R. De Florez & Co., 24 Stone St.
Caibarien, Cuba, "Independent Line." E. Sanchez y Dolz, 117 Pearl St.
" " Regular Line, Waydell & Co., 21 Old Slip.
Callao, Peru,—"Merchants' Line." Every 3 months. W. R. Grace & Co., Hanover Square.
Campeachy, Mexico, B. F. Metcalf & Co., 120 Front St.
Cape Town, C. G. H.—"Dispatch Line." John Norton & Sons, 90 Wall St.
" " Corner Bros. & Co., 128 Pearl St.
Cardenas, Cuba. "Independent Line." E. Sanchez y Dolz, 117 Pearl St.
" " Miller & Houghton, 32 South St.
" " G. A. Brett, Son & Co., 41 South St.
Carupano.—G. A. Brett, Son & Co., 41 South St.
" " Every two months, S. Dominici's Sons, 81 New St.
Cayenne, F. G. G. A. Brett, Son & Co., 41 South St.
Cette, France, R. De Florez & Co., 24 Stone St.
Cienfuegos, Cuba, "Independent Line." E. Sanchez y Dolz, 117 Pearl St.
" " J. & G. Fowler, 131 Pearl St.
Coquimbo, Chili.—W. R. Grace & Co., Hanover Square.
Cumana, Venezuela,—Every two months. S. Dominici's Sons, 81 New St.
Delagoa Bay, South Africa, "Merchants' Line." Arkell & Douglass, 25 Whitehall St.
Demerara.—Howland & Aspinwall, 54 South St.
" G. F. Lough & Co., Produce Exchange.
" Miller, Bull & Co., 18 South St.
Dominica, West Indies, Howland & Aspinwall, 54 South St.
Dunedin, New Zealand. "Pioneer Line." Once a month. R. W. Cameron & Co., 24 South William St.
" " "Kangaroo Line," every 3 to 6 weeks. Mailler & Quereau, 51 Stone St.
East London, South Africa.—"Merchants' Line." Arkell & Douglass, 25 Whitehall St.
" " "Dispatch Line." John Norton & Son, 90 Wall St.
" " Corner Bros. & Co., 128 Pearl St.
Eten, Peru.—W. R. Grace & Co., Hanover Square.
Freemantle, Australia. "Pioneer Line." Once a month. R. W. Cameron & Co., 24 So. William St.
Frontera, Mexico.—Theland Brothers, 87 Broad St.
" " B. F. Metcalf & Co., 120 Front Street.
Genoa, Italy.—R. De Florez & Co., 24 Stone St.
" " Miller & Houghton, 32 South St.
Gibara, Cuba.—Every month. Mosle Brothers, 52 Exchange Place.
Gibraltar.—Miller & Houghton, 32 South St.
" "Regular Line." R. De Florez & Co., 24 Stone St.
Gonaives, Hayti.—G. A. Brett, Son & Co., 41 South St.
" " F. C. Elliot, 26 South St.
Guantanamo, Cuba.—Miller & Houghton, 32 South St. Waydell & Co., 21 Old Slip.
" " Waydell & Co., 21 Old Slip.
Guadaloupe, West Indies.—Howland & Aspinwall, 54 South St.
" " Miller, Bull & Co., 48 South St.
" " G. F. Lough & Co., Produce Exchange.
Guayaquil, Ecuador.—W. R. Grace & Co., Hanover Square.
Havana, Cuba. "Independent Line." E. Sanchez y Dolz, 117 Pearl St.
Hayti, West Indies.—"People's' Line." Every two weeks. F. C. Elliot, 26 South St.
" " G. A. Brett, Son & Co., 41 South St.
" " Miller & Houghton, 32 South St.
Hobart, Tasmania.—"Australasian Line." R. W. Forbes & Son, 14 So. William St.
" " "Pioneer Line." Once a month. R. W. Cameron & Co., 24 So. William St.
Iquique, Peru.—"Merchants' Line." Once in three months. W. R. Grace & Co., Hanover Square.
Kingston, Jamaica. Miller, Bull & Co., 18 South St.
Laguna, Mexico,—B. F. Metcalf & Co., 120 Front St.
Leghorn.—Miller & Houghton, 32 South St.
Liberia, Africa.—Yates & Porterfield, 57 South St.

The only Guide published giving the Rate of every Hotel in N. Y. City, Baltimore, Boston, Philadelphia and Washington.

SAILING VESSEL LINES.—Continued.

Lisbon, Portugal.—Hagemeyer & Brunn, 47 Pearl St.
Lyttleton, New Zealand.—"Pioneer Line" once a month. R. W. Cameron & Co., 23 So. William St.
" " "Kangaroo Line" every 3 to 6 weeks. Mailler & Quereau, 51 Stone St.
Macoris, St. Domingo.—G. A. Brett, Son & Co., 41 South St.
" " J. B. Vicini & Co., 91 Wall St.
" " "Porvenir Line." Hugh Kelly, 71 Wall St.
Madeira, Hagemeyer & Brunn, 47 Pearl St.
Malaga.—R. De Florez & Co., 24 Stone St.
Manzanilla, Cuba.—"Independent Line." E. Sanchez y Dolz, 117 Pearl.
" " Thomas J. Owen & Co., 68 South St.
" " "Porvenir Line." Hugh Kelly, 71 Wall St.
Marseilles, France.—R. De Florez & Co., 24 Stone St.
" " Miller & Houghton, 32 South St.
Martinique, West Indies.—Miller, Bull & Co., 48 South St.
" " Howland & Aspinwall, 54 South St.
" " G. F. Lough & Co., Produce Exchange.
Matanzas, Cuba.—"Independent Line." E. Sanchez y Dolz, 117 Pearl St.
" " Miller & Houghton, 32 South St.
" " G. A. Brett, Son & Co., 41 South St.
Melbourne, Australia.—"Merchants' Line." Arkell & Douglass, 25 Whitehall St.
" " "Pioneer Line" once a month. R. W. Cameron & Co., 23 So. William St.
" " "Kangaroo Line" every 3 to 6 weeks. Mailler & Quereau, 51 Stone St.
" " Arnold, Cheney & Co., 158 Water St.
Mollendo, Peru.—W. R. Grace & Co., Hanover Square.
Monte Christi, San Domingo.—Miller, Bull & Co., 48 South St.
Montevideo, Uruguay.—"Old Regular Line." John Norton & Sons, 90 Wall St.
" " J. E. Ward & Co., 113 Wall St.
Monrovia, Africa.—Yates & Porterfield, 57 South St.
Nelson, New Zealand.—"Pioneer Line" once a month. R. W. Cameron & Co., 23 So. William St.
" " "Australasian Line." R. W. Forbes & Son, 11 So. William St.
Nuevitas, Cuba. "Independent Line." E. Sanchez y Dolz, 117 Pearl St.
" " Every month. Mosle Brothers, 52 Exchange Place.
" " G. A. Brett, Son & Co., 41 South St.
Oporto, Portugal. Hagemeyer & Brunn, 47 Pearl St.
Pasages, Spain. R. De Florez & Co., 24 Stone St.
Pelotas, Brazil, Paul F. Gerhard & Co., 84 Broad St.
" " Every 3 months. Thomas Norton, 104 Wall St.
Pimental, Peru.—W. R. Grace & Co., Hanover Square.
Pisco, Peru, W. R. Grace & Co., Hanover Square.
Port-au-Prince. "People's Line" every two weeks. F. C. Elliott, 26 South St.
" " "Brett's Line." G. A. Brett, Son & Co., 41 South St.
Port Chalmers, New Zealand. "Pioneer Line" once a month. R. W. Cameron & Co., 23 So. William St.
Port Elizabeth, Algoa Bay. "Dispatch Line." John Norton & Sons, 90 Wall St.
" " Corner, Bros. & Co., 128 Pearl St.
Port Natal, South Africa.—Corner Bros. & Co., 128 Pearl St.
" " "Merchants' Line." Arkell & Douglass, 25 Whitehall St.
Porto Alegre, Brazil, Paul F. Gerhard & Co., 84 Broad St.
Porto Plata, Hayti.—G. A. Brett, Son & Co., 41 South St.
" " Miller & Houghton, 32 South St.
" " "Porvenir Line." Hugh Kelly, 71 Wall St.
Porto Rico, West Indies.—Miller & Houghton, 32 South St.
" " G. A. Brett, Son & Co., 41 South St.
Progreso, Mexico. B. F. Metcalf & Co., 120 Front St.
Rio de Janeiro, Brazil. Every 6 weeks. Thomas Norton, 104 Wall St.
Rio Grande do Sul, Brazil. Paul F. Gerhard & Co., 84 Broad St.
" " Every 3 months. Thomas Norton, 104 Wall St.
Rosario, Argentine Republic.—"Old Regular Line." John Norton & Sons, 90 Wall St.
" " Paul F. Gerhard & Co., 84 Broad St.
" " J. E. Ward & Co., 113 Wall St.
Samana.—"Porvenir Line." Hugh Kelly, 71 Wall St.
Santo Domingo, St. Domingo.—G. A. Brett, Son & Co., 41 South St.
" " J. B. Vicini & Co., 91 Wall St.
" " "Porvenir Line." Hugh Kelly, 71 Wall St.
San Fernando, Venezuela.—Miller & Houghton, 32 South St.
Santos, Brazil. Every month. Thomas Norton, 104 Wall St.
Sierra Leone, Africa. Yates & Porterfield, 57 South St.
St. Croix, West Indies. Miller & Houghton, 32 South St.
St. Jago de Cuba, Cuba.—G. A. Brett, Son & Co., 41 South St.
" " Miller & Houghton, 32 South St.
" " Waydell & Co., 21 Old Slip.
St. Kitts, West Indies.—Howland & Aspinwall, 54 South St.
" " G. F. Lough & Co., Produce Exchange.
St. Martin, " G. F. Lough & Co., Produce Exchange.
St. Thomas, " Every month. Miller, Bull & Co., 48 South St.
" " G. F. Lough & Co., Produce Exchange.
" " Miller & Houghton, 32 South St.
Sydney, N. S. W.—"Pioneer Line," once a month. R. W. Cameron & Co., 23 South William St.
" " "Kangaroo Line" every 3 to 6 weeks. Mailler & Quereau, 51 Stone St.
" " "Merchant's Line." Arkell & Douglass, 25 Whitehall St.
" " Arnold, Cheney & Co., 158 Water St.
Talcahuano, Chili. Once in three months. W. R. Grace & Co., Hanover Square.
Tampico, Mexico. Theband Brothers, 87 Broad St.
" " B. F. Metcalf & Co., 120 Front St.
Tarragona, Spain, R. De Florez & Co., 24 Stone St.
Tasmania.—"Australasian Line." R. W. Forbes & Son, 11 So. William St.
" " "Pioneer Line." Once a month. R. W. Cameron & Co., 23 So. William St.
Trinidad.—Miller & Houghton, 32 South St.
" " Howland & Aspinwall, 54 South St.
" " Miller, Bull & Co., 48 South St.
" " G. F. Lough & Co., Produce Exchange.
Tunas de Zaza, Cuba. Three or four times a year. J. A. Del Valle, 55 Broadway.
" " "Independent Line." E. Sanchez y Dolz, 117 Pearl St.
Tuxpan, Mexico.—Theband Brothers, 87 Broad St.
" " B. F. Metcalf & Co., 120 Front St.
Valparaiso, Chili. "Merchants' Line" once a month. W. R. Grace & Co., Hanover Square.
Vera Cruz, Mexico.—Theband Brothers, 87 Broad St.
" " B. F. Metcalf & Co., 120 Front St.
" " G. A. Brett, Son & Co., 41 South St.
" " Tupper & Beattie, 116 Wall St.
Vigo, Spain. R. De Florez & Co., 24 Stone St.
Wellington, New Zealand. "Pioneer Line." Once a month. R. W. Cameron & Co., 23 So. William St.
" " "Kangaroo Line" every 3 to 6 weeks. Mailler & Quereau, 51 Stone St.
" " "Australasian Line." R. W. Forbes & Son, 11 So. William St.

SAILING VESSEL LINES.—Continued.
DOMESTIC PORTS.

Alexandria, Va.,—J. A. Van Brunt, 75 South.
" Slaght & Bailey, 41 South.
Augusta, Maine.—Rackett & Bro., 52 South.
Baltimore, Md.,—Slaght & Bailey, 41 South.
" Regular Line, J.A. Van Brunt, 75 South.
Bangor, Maine.—Rackett & Bro., 52 South.
Bath, Maine.—Rackett & Bro., 52 South.
Beaufort, N. C.—J. A. Van Brunt, 75 South.
Brunswick, Ga.—Every 3 weeks. Warren Ray, 62 South.
" J. A. Van Brunt, 75 South.
" Slaght & Bailey, 41 South.
Boston, Mass.,—Jed Frye & Co., 47 Water.
" J. A. Van Brunt, 75 South.
Bucksville, S. C.—Every 10 days. F.V.L.Jones, 83 South.
Calais, Maine.—Jed Frye & Co., 47 Water.
Cedar Keys,—Once a month, N.A.Benner & Co.,19 Old Sl.
Charleston, S.C.—Regular Line, J.A.Van Brunt, 75 South.
" Slaght & Bailey, 41 South.
City Point, Va.—J. A. Van Brunt, 75 South.
" Slaght & Bailey, 41 South.
Conway, S. C.—Every 10 days, F. V. L. Jones, 83 South.
Eastport, Maine,—Jed Frye & Co., 47 Water.
Fall River, Mass.—Rackett & Bro., 52 South.
Fernandina, Fla.,—J. A. Van Brunt, 75 South.
" Slaght & Bailey, 41 South St.
Galveston, "Atlantic Line." Tupper & Beattie,116 Wall.
" Every 2 weeks. N.A Benner & Co.,19 Old Slip.
Georgetown, D. C.—J. A. Van Brunt, 75 South.
Georgetown, S,C.—Every 10 days. F.V.L.Jones,83 South.
Green Cove Springs, Every 2 months. W. Ray,62 South.
Jacksonville, Fla., Slaght & Bailey, 41 South.
" Regularly. Warren Ray, 62 South.
" J. A. Van Brunt, 75 South.
Key West,—Every 2 weeks. N.A.Benner & Co.,19 Old Slip.
Lubec, Maine,—Jed Frye & Co., 47 Water.
Mobile, Every 2 weeks. N. A. Benner & Co., 19 Old Slip.
" J. A. Van Brunt, 75 South St.
New Bedford, Mass., Rackett & Bro., 52 South.
Newbern, N. C. Slaght & Bailey, 14 South.
Newburyport, Mass. Rackett & Bro., 52 South.
" Jed Frye & Co., 47 Water.
New Haven, Conn. Rackett & Bro., 52 South.
New London, Conn.—Rackett & Bro., 52 South.

New Orleans, "Despatch Line." N.H.Brigham,96 Wall.
" "Atlantic Line." Tupper & Beattie,116 Wall.
Newport, R. I. Rackett & Bro., 52 South.
Newport News, Va. J. A. Van Brunt, 75 South.
Norfolk, Va. Regular Line. J. A. Van Brunt, 75 South.
" Slaght & Bailey, 41 South.
Palatka, Fla. Every 3 weeks. Warren Ray, 62 South.
Peach Tree, N.C. Every 10 days. F.V.L.Jones, 83 South.
Pensacola,—Once a month. N.A.Benner & Co.,19 Old Sl.
Petersburgh, Va. J. A. Van Brunt, 75 South.
Philadelphia, Pa, J. A. Van Brunt, 75 South.
" Slaght & Bailey, 41 South.
Plymouth, Mass.—Jed Frye & Co., 47 Water.
Port Harrelson, N. C. Every 10 days. F. V. L. Jones.
" 83 South.
Portland, Maine.—Jed Frye & Co., 47 Water.
Portland, Ore. "Despatch Line." Sutton & Co.,82 South.
Port Royal, N. C. J. A. Van Brunt, 75 South.
" Slaght & Bailey, 41 South.
Portsmouth, N. H. Jed Frye & Co., 47 Water.
Portsmouth. Va. Slaght & Bailey, 41 South.
" J. A. Van Brunt, 75 South St.
Pot Bluff, S. C. Every 10 days. F.V.L. Jones, 83 South.
Providence, R. I. Jed Frye & Co., 47 Water.
" Rackett & Bro., 52 South.
Richmond, Va. Regular Line. J.A.Van Brunt. 75 South.
" Slaght & Bailey, 41 South.
Saco, Maine. Jed Frye & Co., 47 Water.
San Francisco, Cal. "Despatch Line." Every two
" weeks. Sutton & Co., 82 South.
" Every 3 to 4 weeks. Dearborn & Co., 104 Wall.
Savannah, Ga. Slaght & Bailey, 41 South.
" Regular Line, J.A.Van Brunt, 75 South.
St. Augustine, Fla. Regularly. Warren Ray, 62 South.
" J. A. Van Brunt, 75 South.
Tampa, Fla. Once a month, N.A.Benner & Co.,19 Old Slip
Washington, D. C. Slaght & Bailey, 41 South.
" J. A. Van Brunt, 75 South.
Washington, N. C. J. A. Van Brunt, 75 South.
West Point, Va. J. A. Van Brunt, 75 South.
Wilmington, Del. Rackett & Bro., 52 South.
Wilmington, N. C. Slaght & Bailey, 41 South.
" J. A. Van Brunt, 75 South.

ULSTER AND DELAWARE R. R.

via West Shore R. R. to Kingston, or via N. Y. C. & H. R. R. R. to Rhinebeck, and ferry to Rondout
Stations. Distances and Fare from Rondout.

M.	Stations.	Fare.	M.	Stations.	Fare.	M.	Stations.	Fare.	M.	Stations.	Fare.
	Rondout		17	Broadhead's Bridge	.54c.	36	Big Indian	$1.08	53	Halcottville	$1.50
2	Kingston	.5c.	18	Shokan	.54c.	39	Pine Hill	1.20	59	Roxbury	1.77
4	Higginsville		21	Boiceville	.63c.	41	Grand Hotel Station	1.23	65	Grand Gorge	1.95
8	Stony Hollow	.27c.	24	Mt. Pleasant	.72c.	44	Griffin's Corners	1.32		South Gilboa	2.13
9	West Hurley	.31c.	27	Phoenicia	.81c.	48	Arkville	1.44	70	Stamford	2.22
12	Olive Branch	.36c.	32	Allaben	.96c.	51	Kelly's Corners	1.53	78	Hobart	2.34
15	Brown's Station	.45c.	33	Shandaken	.99c.						

VIA WEST SHORE R. R.

Leave foot of Jay St, (leave foot W. 42d St. 15 minutes later):
For Kingston, Phoenicia, Arkville, and intermediate stations, 3.00, 7.00, 11.15 a. m., Sundays. 8.00 a. m. Leave Rondout, 7.40,11.30 a. m., 2.10 p. m., Sundays, 7.10 a. m. Arrive Phoenicia, 9.01 a. m., 2.05, 4.10 p. m., Sundays, 9.02 a. m. Arrive Arkville, 10.26 a. m., 4.50, 5.24 p. m., Sundays, 10.26 a. m.
For Roxbury, Stamford, Hobart and intermediate stations, 3.00, 11.15 a. m., Sundays, 3.00 a. m. Arrive Roxbury, 10.51 a. m., 5.58 p. m., Sundays, 10.54 a. m.; arrive Hobart, 11.40 a. m., 6.45 p. m., Sundays, 11.40 a. m.

VIA NEW YORK CENTRAL AND HUDSON RIVER R. R.

Leave Grand Central Depot (42d St. and 4th Av.):
For Rondout (Ferry from Rhinebeck), Phoenicia, Arkville, and intermediate stations, 8.00, 10.30 a. m. Arrive Phoenicia, 2.40, 4.10 p. m.; arrive Arkville, 4.50, 5.28 p. m.
For Roxbury, Stamford, Hobart, and intermediate stations, 10.30 a. m. Arrive Hobart, 6.45 p. m.

Trains to New York.

Leave Hobart, 7.10 a. m., 1.40 p. m., Sundays, 1.40 p. m.; leave Stamford. 7.30 a. m., 1.50 p. m., Sundays, 1.50 p. m.; leave Grand Gorge, 8.10 a. m., 2.10 p. m., Sundays, 2.10 p. m.; leave Roxbury, 8.25 a. m., 2.25 p. m., Sundays, 2.25 p. m.; leave Halcottville, 8.58 a. m., 2.38 p. m., Sundays, 2.38 p. m. Arrive Kingston, 11.16 a. m., 5.20 p. m., Sundays, 5.20 p. m.; arrive Rondout, 10.20, 11.25 a. m., 5.30 p. m., Sundays, 5.30 p. m., arrive New York via West Shore R. R., 2.50, 10.00 p. m., Sundays, 10.00 p. m.; via N. Y. C. & H. R. R., 3.25, 8.50 p. m., Sundays, 8.50 p. m.
Leave Arkville (stopping at intermediate stations), 5.15, 8.54 a. m., 2.55 p. m., Sundays, 2.55 p. m., leave Phoenicia, 7.30, 10.07 a. m., 4.10 p. m., Sundays, 4.10 p. m.; leave Shokan, 8.10, 10.40 a. m., 4.32 p. m., Sundays, 4.32 p. m.; leave West Hurley, 8.20, 10.51 a. m., 4.58 p. m., Sundays, 4.58 p. m. Arrive Kingston, 10.10, 11.16 a. m., 5.20 p. m., Sundays, 5.20 p. m.; arrive Rondout, 10.20, 11.25 a. m., 5.30 p. m., Sundays, 5.30 p. m.; arrive New York via West Shore R. R., 2.50, 10.00 p. m., Sundays, 10.00 p. m.; via N. Y. C. & H. R. R., 2.12, 3.25, 8.50 p. m., Sundays, 8.50 p. m.

STONY CLOVE AND CATSKILL MOUNTAIN R. R.

Stations and fare from Phoenicia—Chichesters, 10c.; Lanesville, 40c.; Edgewood, 60c.; Stony Clove, 96c.; Kaaterskill Junction, 8c. $1.10c.; Hunter, $1.10.
Leave Phoenicia for Hunter and intermediate stations, 9.05 a. m., 4.10 p. m. Arrive Hunter, 10.10 a. m., 5.05 p. m.
Leave Hunter, stopping at intermediate stations, 8.00 a. m., 3.10 p. m. Arrive Phoenicia, 8.55 a. m., 4.00 p. m.
Kaaterskill R. R. trains will begin running about June 20th.

ACCIDENT INSURANCE COMPANIES.

American Accident Indemnity Association, 5 Beekman.
Coöperative Life & Accident, 171 B'way.
Employers' Liability Assurance Corporation of London, 54 Pine.
Fidelity & Casualty Co., 214 Broadway.
Guaranty Mutual, 35 Park Row.
Mercantile Mutual, 137 Broadway.
Merchants' Casualty, 21 Park Row.
National, 280 Broadway.
Provident Fund Society, 280 Broadway.
Traders' & Travelers', 287 Broadway.
Travelers', 110 Broadway.
United States Mutual, 320 Broadway.
Women's Mutual Ins. & Accident Co., 128 Broadway.

LIFE INSURANCE COMPANIES.

Ætna of Hartford, 167 Broadway.
Bankers' & Merchants' Alliance, 32 Thomas.
Berkshire of Massachusetts, 271 B'way.
Brooklyn, 51 Liberty.
Citizens' Mutual, 115 Broadway.
Connecticut Mutual of Hartford, 1 Wall.
Coöperative Life & Accident of U. S., 171 Broadway.
Equitable, 120 Broadway.
Equitable Reserve Fund, 169 Broadway.
Family Fund Society, 280 Broadway.
Fidelity Mutual of Philadelphia, 13 Park Row.
Germania, 20 Nassau.
Globe Mutual Benefit, 73 Park Row.
Hancock, John, Mutual of Boston, 28 Union Square.
Hartford Life & Annuity, 189 Broadway.
Home Benefit Society, 161 Broadway.
Home Benefit Association, 137 B'way.
Home, 254 Broadway.
Home Provident Safety Fund, 891 Liberty.
Homœopathic Mutual (in liquidation), 117 W. 42d.
Income & Life, 265 Broadway.
Life & Accident Ins. Corp., 132 Nassau.
Life Union, 234 Broadway.
Manhattan, 156 Broadway.
Massachusetts Mutual of Springfield, 243 Broadway.
Mercantile Benefit, 319 Broadway.
Metropolitan, 32 Park Place.
Mutual, 32 Nassau.
Mutual Benefit of America, 280 B'way.
Mutual Reserve Fund, 38 Park Row.
National Alliance, 5 Beekman.
New England Mutual, 320 Broadway.
New York, 346 Broadway.
New York Life and Trust, 52 Wall.
New York Life Ins. Credit Co., 13 Park Row.
New York Safety Reserve Fund, 197 Greenwich.
Northern Assurance Co., of London, 25 Pine.
Northwestern Mutual, 13 Park Row.
Protective, 44 Broadway.
Provident Savings, 120 Broadway.
Prudential, 224 Centre.
St. Lawrence, 7 Beekman.
Security Mutual Benefit, 233 Broadway.
State Mutual, of Worcester, 189 B'way.
Travelers', 110 Broadway.
Union Mutual, of Portland, 96 B'way.
United Life and Accident, 14 Broadway.
United States, 261 Broadway.
Washington, 21 Cortlandt.
Women's Mutual Ins. and Accident Co., 128 Broadway.

MARINE INSURANCE COMPANIES.

See also under "Fire Insurance Companies."

Atlantic Mutual, 51 Wall.
Board (National) Marine Underwriters, 25 William.
Boston, 43 Wall.
British and Foreign, of Liverpool, Cotton Exchange Building.
China Mutual, 16 Exchange Place.
Commercial Mutual, 42 Wall.
Delaware Mutual, of Phila., 75 Beaver.
Dresden, 18 Exchange Place.
India Mutual, of Boston, 16 Exchange pl.
London, 77 Beaver.
Mercantile, of Boston, 141 Broadway.
National Board of Marine Underwriters, 25 William.
New York Mutual, 61 William.
North America, 16 Exchange Place.
Saint Louis, 120 Broadway.
Sea, of Liverpool, 77 Beaver.
South and North American Lloyds, 33 Liberty.
Switzerland, of Zurich, 18 Exchange pl.
Thames & Mersey, of Liverpool, 69 Wall.
Union, of Liverpool, 51 Wall.
Union of Philadelphia, 16 Exchange pl.
United States Lloyds, 50 Wall.
Universal, of London, 1 Hanover.

MISCELLANEOUS INSURANCE COMPANIES.

American Steam Boiler, 120 Broadway.
American Surety Company, 160 B'way.
German Am. Real Estate Title Guarantee Co., 34 Nassau.
Fidelity & Casualty, 214 Broadway.
Guarantee Company of North America, 111 Broadway.
Hartford Steam Boiler, 285 Broadway.
Lawyers' Title [Real Estate], 120 B'way
Lloyds [Plate Glass], 68 William.
Metropolitan [Plate Glass], 66 Liberty.
Protective Live Stock Mutual, 116 W. 23d.

MERCANTILE AND TRADE ASSOCIATIONS, EXCHANGES, ETC.

Ale Brewers' Ass'n. of N. Y. & N. J., 24 Park Pl.
American Horse Exchange, 1634 Broadway.
Associated Press, 195 Broadway.
Bankers' Association, 78 William.
Board of Trade & Transportation, 55 Liberty.
Brewers' Exchange, 2 Irving Pl.
Brewers' Exchange, cor. Worth St. and Park Row.
Building Material Exchange, 63 Liberty.
Carpet Trade Association, 115 Worth.
Cattle Exchange, 1634 Broadway.
Chamber of Commerce, 36 Nassau.
China & Glass Importers & Jobbers' Ass'n., 61 Park Pl.
Clothing Manufacturers' Ass'n, 96 Spring.
Coal Exchange, 1 Broadway.
Coal & Iron Exchange, cor. Cortlandt & New Church.
Coffee Exchange, 141 Pearl.
Consolidated Stock & Petroleum Exchange, 60 Broadway.
Confectioners' Association, 23 Jay.
Cotton Exchange, Beaver & William.
Electrotypers & Stereotypers' Ass'n., 19 Park Pl.
Exchange for Woman's Work, 329 5th Ave.
Foreign Fruit Exchange, 21 State.
Furniture Board of Trade, 62 Bowery.
Hardware Board of Trade, 6 Warren.
Horse Exchange, 1634 Broadway.
Ice Exchange, 389 8th Ave.
Importers' & Grocers' Exchange, 107 Water.
Iron & Steel Wire Association, 116 Broadway.
Italian Chamber of Commerce, 22 State.
Jewelers' Association, 146 Broadway.
Jewelers' Board of Trade, 41 Maiden Lane.
Jewelers' League, 170 Broadway.
Lager Beer Brewers' Board of Trade, 2 Irving Pl.
Leaf Tobacco Board of Trade, 178 Pearl.
Madison Avenue Depository & Exchange for Women's Work, 640 Madison Ave.
Manhattan Stock Exchange, 69 New.
Maritime Exchange, Produce Exchange Building, Broadway & Beaver St.
Master Car Builders' Association, 45 Broadway.
Mechanics' & Traders' Exchange, 14 Vesey.
Mercantile Exchange, 6 Harrison.
Mercantile Jobbers' Association, 530 Broadway.
Merchants' Association, 6 Harrison.
Metal Exchange, 234 Pearl.
Milk Exchange, 6 Harrison.
Musical Exchange, 32 E. 4th.
Naval Stores & Tobacco Exchange, 113 Pearl.
N. Y. Petroleum Ex. & Stock Board, 62 Broadway.
North American Exchange Co., 57 Broadway.
Pattern Makers' Association, 73 Ludlow.
Produce Exchange, Broadway & Beaver.
Public Grain & Stock Exchange, 18 Broadway.
Real Estate Exchange & Auction Rooms, 59 Liberty.
Spanish Chamber of Commerce, 19 Whitehall.
Shipmasters' Association, 37 William.
Silk Association of America, 446 Broome.
Stationers' Board of Trade, 99 Nassau.
Stock Exchange, 10 Broad and 13 Wall.
Undertakers' Association, 301 W. 2d.
U. S. Brewers' Association, 2 Irving Pl.
Vessel Owners and Captains' National Ass'n., 1 Broadway.

BROOKLYN, BATH AND WEST END R. R.

Trains stop on signal at Blythebourne, Weirs' Hill, Bensonhurst and Club House.

Except Sunday. † Wednesday and Saturday only.

Fares from New York Single and Excursion. West Brooklyn, 10c., 20c.; Blythebourne, 15c., 25c.; Bath Beach Junction, 20c., 30c.; New Utrecht, 20c., 35c.; Bath Beach, 20c., 35c.; Bensonhurst, 20c., 35c.; Unionville, 25c., 35c.; Club House, 25c., 35c.; Coney Island, 25c., 40c.

Leave **5th Av. and 27th St., Brooklyn**, for **West Brooklyn, Bath Beach, Unionville** and **Coney Island**, (Daily) *6.30, 8.00, 8.30, 9.30, 10.30, 11.30 a. m., 12.30, 1.30, 3.35, 4.30, 5.00, 6.00, 6.30, 7.30, 10.15 p. m., †12.15 night. Arrive West Brooklyn in 8 minutes; arrive Bath Beach in 19 minutes; arrive Unionville in 22 minutes; arrive Coney Island in 30 minutes.

Leave **Ferry Depot, 2d Av. and 39th St**, (Ferry from Whitehall St. N. Y.) Daily, *8.00, 8.30 a. m., 5.00, 6.00, 6.30, 7.00 p. m. Arrive Bath Beach in 19 minutes; arrive Coney Island in 30 minutes.

Trains to Brooklyn.

Leave **Coney Island** (Daily), 7.20, 7.50, 8.50, 9.50, 10.50, 11.50 a. m., 12.50, 1.50, 2.50, 3.50, 4.20, 5.20, 5.50, 6.45, 8.10, †11.00 p. m. Arrive 5th Av. and 27th St. in 30 minutes.

Leave **Unionville** (Daily), *5.45, 7.26, 7.56, 8.56, 9.56, 10.56, 11.56, a. m., 12.56, 1.56, 2.56, 3.56, 4.26, 5.26, 5.56, 6.51, 8.16, †11.06 p. m. Arrive 5th Av. and 27th St. in 25 minutes.

Leave **Bath Beach** (Daily), *5.50, 7.31, 8.01, 9.01, 10.01, 11.01 a. m., 12.01, 1.01, 2.01, 3.01, 4.01, 4.31, 5.31, 6.01, 6.56, 8.51, †11.11 p. m. Arrive 5th Av. and 27th St., in 19 minutes.

Leave **West Brooklyn** (Daily), *6.02, 7.42, 8.12, 9.12, 10.12, 11.12 a. m., 12.12, 1.12, 2.12, 3.12, 4.12, 4.42, 5.42, 6.12, 7.07, 9.02, †11.22 p. m. Arrive 5th Av. and 27th St. in 8 minutes.

Trains for **3d Av. and 39th St. Ferry** (to Whitehall St. New York), leave **Coney Island**, *7.20, 7.50 a. m., 1.20, 5.20, 5.50 p. m.; leave Unionville, 6.55 a. m., and every 6 minutes after leaving Coney Island; leave Bath Beach 7.00 a. m. and every 11 minutes after leaving Coney Island.

NEW YORK AND SEA BEACH RY.

Stations: Bay Ridge, Bath Beach Junction, Mapleton, Woodlawn Park, King's Highway, Gravesend, Coney Island.
Fare, New York to Coney Island 25 cents; excursion, 40 cents.

Leave **foot of Whitehall St**, via Bay Ridge, for **Coney Island** and way stations (daily, except Sundays), 8.00 a. m., 3.45, 4.50, 5.55 p. m. Arrive Coney Island in 60 minutes.

Leave **3d Av. and 65th St. Brooklyn** for **Coney Island**, 7.37, 8.42 a. m., 4.42, 5.47, 6.22 p. m.

Leave **Coney Island** for New York (foot Whitehall St.), Brooklyn and way stations (daily, except Sundays), 8.20, 9.20 a. m., 4.55 p. m.; for Brooklyn only, 5.55, 6.15 p. m.

BROOKLYN AND BRIGHTON BEACH R. R.

For Bedford Station take Kings County and Brooklyn Elevated Railways to Franklin Ave. Station.
For Prospect Park Station, take Flatbush, Franklin and Nostrand Avenue Horse Cars.
Fare from Bedford Station to Brighton Beach, 25 cents; excursion 35 cents.

Leave **Bedford Station** for **Sheepshead Bay** and **Brighton Beach**, daily at *6.30, 8.30, 11.00 a. m., 1.30, 2.30, 3.30, 5.30, 7.00 p. m., †on Saturdays only, 11.45 p. m., *Not on Sundays. Arrive Sheepshead Bay in 20 minutes; arrive Brighton Beach in 25 minutes.

Leave **Brighton Beach** leave Sheepshead Bay 5 minutes later) for **Bedford Station** daily at *7.50, 9.00 a. m., 12.30, 2.00, 3.00, 5.00, 6.00, 7.30 p. m., (on Sunday mornings only, 12.15 a. m.) *Not on Sundays. Arrive Bedford Station in 25 minutes.

Trains leave Bergen, Butler and Prospect Park stations a few minutes later than Bedford Station time.
All trains stop on signal at Parkville, Greenfield, King's Highway and Neck Road.

CONEY ISLAND AND BROOKLYN R. R.

Fare to Coney Island, 10 cents—Time to Coney Island, 1 hour.

Horse Cars leave cor. **15th St. and 9th Av, Brooklyn** for **Parkville, Gravesend** and **Coney Island** every two hours from 8.00 a. m. to 8.00 p. m. daily.

Leave **Coney Island** for **Brooklyn** every two hours from 7.00 a. m. to 7.00 p. m. daily.

CATSKILL MOUNTAIN AND CAIRO RYS.

Trains on this road will begin running to Cairo about May 1st to 10th, and to Palenville about June 15th.

ELMIRA, CORTLAND AND NORTHERN R. R.,

via Erie, N. Y. Central, or D. L. & W. R. Rs.

Stations, Distances and Fares from Elmira.

M	Elmira		45	Brookton	$1 32	73	Loring's	$2 12	108	Chittenango Falls	$2 90
6	Horseheads	12c	49	Besemer	1 37	75	East River	2 17	111	Perryville	2 65
10	Breesport	32c	51	Ithaca	1 42	77	East Homer	2 22	115	Cottons	
14	Erin	42c	53	Varna		82	Truxton	2 30	116	Clockville	
17	Park Station	52c	54	Snyder's	1 57	83	Cran's Mills	2 35	119	Canastota	2 65
21	Swartwood	67c	57	Etna	1 67	87	Cayler	2 40	125	Lakeside	2 90
25	Van Etten	77c	60	Freeville	1 72	90	De Ruyter	2 45	126	Oneida Creek	2 85
28	Spencer	85c	62	Malloryville	1 82	95	Shed's Corners	2 50	126	Verona Beach	2 85
32	West Candor	97c	63	McLean	1 82	98	Woolstock	2 50	127	Sylvan Beach	2 90
34	North Candor	$1 02	69	Chicago	1 92	103	Delphi	2 55	128	Sylvan	2 95
38	Wilseyville	1 12	67	South Cortland		103	Rippleton	2 60	131	Vienna	2 95
42	White Church	1 27	70	Cortland	2 00	104	Cazenovia	2 60	131	McConnellville	3 10
44	Caroline Junction		71	Cortland Junction	2 00	107	Bingley		140	Camden	3 25

Leave **Elmira** for **Cortland, Canastota** and intermediate stations, 7.00 a. m., 1.30 p. m., Sundays, 8.00 a. m. Arrive Cortland, 9.15 a. m., 7.07 p. m., Sundays, 10.31 a. m.; arrive Canastota, 11.45 a. m., 9.15 p. m., Sundays, 12.23 p. m.

Leave **Canastota** for **Camden**, 8.20 a. m., 4.30, 6.00 p. m. Arrive Camden, 9.25 a. m., 5.10, 6.50 p. m.

Trains to Elmira.

Leave **Camden** for **Canastota**, 7.00, 10.30 a. m., 4.30 p. m. Arrive Canastota, 7.50 a. m., 12.00 m., 5.30 p. m.

Leave **Canastota** for **Cortland** and **Elmira**, 7.05 a. m., 12.55 p. m., Sundays, 3.25 p. m.; leave **De Ruyter**, 8.05 a. m., 2.01 p. m., Sundays, 4.42 p. m.; leave **Cortland**, 8.52 a. m., 2.45 p. m., Sundays, 5.30 p. m.; leave **Spencer**, 10.32 a. m., 4.42 p. m., Sundays, 6.52 p. m.; **Arrive Elmira**, 11.45 a. m., 5.20 p. m., Sundays, 8.05 p. m.

EXPRESS COMPANIES.

The Companies here mentioned do a "through" business, taking goods for different sections of the country.

Adams: Main office, 59 Broadway. Branch offices, 684 Broadway, 12 W. 23d, 10 E. 42d, 309 Canal, 122 W. Broadway, 2 Exchange Pl., Jersey City.

American: Main office, 65 Broadway. Branch offices, 3 Park Pl., 40 Hudson, 502, 314, 490 Canal, 696, 785, 940, 942 Broadway, 15, 27 E. 14th, 30th St. & 10th Ave., 15th St. cor. Vanderbilt Ave., Grand Central Depot, 18th St. cor. Madison Ave., 536 St. cor. 8th Ave., 126 E. 125th St., and 3 Hudson St., J. C.

Baltimore & Ohio, now United States Express.

Dodd's, see at N. Y. Transfer Co.

Earle & Prew, see New York & Boston Despatch.

Erie, now Wells, Fargo & Co.

International: Main office, 280 Canal. Branch offices, 49, 207, 683, 1313 Broadway, 101 Mercer, 72 W. 125th, 142 West, 11 E. 14th.

Long Island: Main office, foot of New Chambers St., E. R., and foot of E. 34th St. Branch offices, 683, 912, 1313 Broadway, 11 E. 14th, 206 Canal, 142 West, 62 W. 125th. In Brooklyn, L. I. R. R. Depot, cor. Flatbush and Atlantic Aves., 333 Fulton St., and 107 Broadway, E.D., and Long Island City.

National: Main office, 145 Broadway. Branch offices, 300 Canal, 785, 940 Broadway, 12 Park Pl., cor. 47th St. and Madison Ave., foot of Jay St., 111 Hudson St., Jersey City, and West Shore Depot, Weehawken.

New England Despatch, see International Express.

New York & Boston Despatch: Main office, 394 Canal St. Branch offices, 910 Broadway, 45 Church St.

New York Transfer Co.: 1323 Broadway. Branch offices, 296, 849, 944 Broadway, 1 Astor House, 737 6th Ave., 131 E. 125th St., 214 W. 125th St., 18 Exchange Pl., Jersey City. 4 Court, 52 Nassau, 860 Fulton, 98 Broadway, Brooklyn.

Philadelphia & Reading, now Adams Express.

Southern, see at Adams Express.

United States: Main office, 49 Broadway. Branch offices, 683, 946, 1313, 1140 Broadway, 142 West, 296 Canal, 11 E. 11th, foot Christopher and Whitehall Sts. In Jersey City, 66 Montgomery St., and D., L. & W. Depot, Hoboken.

Wells, Fargo & Co.: Main office, 63 Broadway. Branch offices, 317, 711, 957 Broadway, 81 Liberty, 322 Canal, 153 Bowery, 254 8th Ave., foot Chambers and W. 23d St. In Brooklyn, 331 Fulton St., and 107 Broadway, E.D. In Jersey City, 64 Pavonia Ave. & 62 Montgomery St. and Erie Depot.

Westcott: Main office, 12 Park Place. Branch offices, 785, 942 Broadway, 311 Canal, Grand Central Depot, foot of Barclay, Christopher, Jay and W. 42d Sts. In Brooklyn, 333 Washington, 19 Bergen St., 398 Bedford Ave., E. D.

LOCAL EXPRESSES.

American Union, 312 Canal.
Ames, 101 Mercer, 1 Hudson, 12 Fulton.
Benjamin, 117 John, 3 Hudson, 97 Mercer.
Biglin, Castle Garden and 308 Washington.
Bowron, 12 Fulton, 1 Hudson, 785 Broadway.
Brisk, 1 Hudson, 84 Cortlandt, 101 Mercer.
Brooklyn, Bath & West End, 39th St. Ferry Depot, foot Whitehall St., 313 Canal, 31 Hudson.
Consolidated, 312 Canal, 4 Old Slip, 76 Cortlandt.
Coop, 117 John, 97 Mercer, 153 West Broadway.
Dodd & Child, 296 Canal, 683, 844 Broadway, 11 E. 14th, Cortlandt and Desbrosses Sts. Ferry.
Dunlap's, 311 W. 24th, 153 W. Broadway, 97 Mercer.
Fuller Ex. Co., 135th St. & 4th Ave. and 216 Duane.
Fuller Paterson Ex., 153 W. B'way, 117 John, 97 Mercer.
Furniture Van Co., 2348 8th Ave.
Hackensack Despatch, 94 Barclay, 109 Murray.
Hudson County, 1 Hudson, 206 Greenwich.
Independent, 320 Pearl, 155 E. 32d, cor. 145th & 3d Ave.
Inman Hall, 84 Cortlandt, 3 Hudson, 36 Church.
Kelly, 3 Hudson, 64 Beekman, 167 Washington.
Knickerbocker, 117 John, 101 Mercer, 1 Lispenard.
Lary's, 192 Chambers.
Manhattan, cor. 42d St. and 4th Ave.
Merchants, 3 Hudson, 153 W. B'way, 101 Mercer.
Metropolitan Express & Van Co., 201 Mercer, 312 Canal, 45 Church.
Moore's, 3 Hudson, 11 E. 11th, 12 Fulton, 296 Canal.
Morris Ex. Co., 117 John, 76 Cortlandt, 296 Canal.
N. Y. & Harlem Despatch, 1 Hudson, 78 E. 125th.
Ogden Ex. Co., 153 W. B'way, 1 Hudson, 4 Old Slip.
Patterson's, 117 John, 153 W. B'way, Barclay St. Ferry.
People's, 1 Hudson, 101 Mercer.
Piercy's, 23 Astor Pl., cor. B'way & Howard, 46 W. 131st.
Remsen, 117 John.
Smith's, 117 John, 12 Fulton, 28 Church.
Stanton, 312 Canal, 12 Fulton, 153 West Broadway.
Turnir, 76 Cortlandt, 1 Hudson, 153 W. Broadway.
Union Transfer, 467 4th Ave., 123 E. 22d.
Van Nostrand's, 97 Mercer, 117 John, 153 W. B'dway.
Washington Ex. & Van Co., cor. 8th Ave. & 124th St.
Weed & Paul, 153 W. B'way, 117 John, 97 Mercer.

CANAL LINES.

Baltimore, Md., New York and Baltimore Transportation Line.—Steamers leave Pier 7 N. R. (foot of Rector St.) daily except Sunday 5.00 p. m. Freight received to 3.00 p. m. Time of trip 56 hours. H. C. Foster, agent, on Pier 7 N. R.

Clyde's Line. See at "Philadelphia."

Erie Canal Line. Forwarders of merchandise, coal, iron, etc., to all points West via Erie Canal and South via Delaware and Raritan Canal and to Montreal and Ottawa, Canada. Sherman Peirie, 112 Broad St.

Inland Transportation Company, Canal, Rail and Lake line to points in the West, Northwest, Southwest, Buffalo and Canada. Mark goods for canal shipment "I. T. Line" and ship at Pier 3 E. R. Geo. W. Stillwell, Jr., Manager, 111 Broad St.

International Canal Line.—Forwarders of all kinds of freight between New York, Montreal, Quebec and Ottawa and all intermediate points, ship Pier 6 E. R. G. W. Hunt, agent, 149 Broad St.

Ithaca Line.—Freight received daily Pier 3 E. R. Apply to W. B. Walsh, agent, 111 Broad St.

Merchants' Northern and Western Line, via Erie and Champlain Canals and Lake Champlain; cargo lots only. Ira W. Mole, agent, 9 South St.

Merchants' and Tanners' Line. From Bulkhead, between Franklin and Harrison Sts., N. R., Wednesday and Saturday 3.30 p. m. Freight received daily 5 p. m. for Eddyville, Creek Locks, Rosendale, High Falls, Alligerville, Accord, Port Jackson, Middleport, Port Ben, Napanoch, Ellenville, Homowack, Phillipsport, Summitville, Wurtsboro, Westbrookville, Cuddebackville, Huguenot, Port Jervis, Barryville. Johnson Decker, agent, on Pier.

Merchants' Transportation Company.—(Bonded Line) via Erie Canal to Buffalo, thence by rail and lakes to all points West and Southwest and via Oswego and Rouse's Point to Canada. H. N. Holt, agent, rooms 83 and 84, 1 Broadway.

Merchants' Western Line, and Buffalo Creek Transfer Railroad Co.'s bonded line via Erie - canal and lakes or rail, for shipment of freight from New York to Western points. Frank Williams & Co., 110 Broad St.

New York and Canada Line.—For full cargoes only to points on Erie Canal, Lake Champlain, Champlain Canal, Montreal, St. John and Quebec. N. R. Moe, agent, 9 South St.

New York and Montreal Transportation Co.—Forwarders of freight of all kinds to all points North and West via canal, lake or rail. N. R. Moe & Co., agents, 9 South St.

Philadelphia, Pa., Clyde's New York and Philadelphia Line, via Canal, leaves Pier 39½ E. R. daily except Sunday 5 p. m., freight received to 4.30 p. m. W. P. Clyde & Co., agents, on Pier.

Syracuse and Oswego Line.—Freight received for Rome, Syracuse, Rochester and all intermediate points on Erie Canal. Mark Goods "S. & O. Line" and ship at Pier 3 E. R. W. B. Walsh, agent, 111 Broad St.

Utica Line.—Freight received for Utica, Lowville, Carthage, Watertown and points on R. W. & O. R. R. via Utica, also on D. L. & W. R. R. and D. & H. Canal Co. R. R. via Utica, ship at Pier 3 E. R. W. B. Walsh, agent, 111 Broad St.

Western Transit Company (all water freight line). Merchandise forwarded via Hudson River, Erie Canal and steamers on the lakes to Chicago, Milwaukee, Cleveland and Detroit and via, connecting railroads to all points in the West, Northwest and Southwest. Mark "W. T. Co.", ship at Pier 7 E. R. Gibson L. Douglass, agent, 94 Wall St.

DIRECTIONS FOR REACHING VARIOUS PLACES.

For Time Tables see Index on front pages.

Route No.	Railroad (or Route on which the place is located).	Location of Depot (or Ferry to Depot).
1	Adirondack R. R.	Via Hudson River and West Shore R. Rs.
3	Baltimore & Ohio	Via Central R. R. of N. J. (to Philadelphia), foot Liberty St.
4	Bennington & Rutland	Via Hudson River R. R., Grand Central Depot.
5	Boston & Albany	Grand Central Depot, 42d St. and Fourth Ave.
6	Brooklyn, Bath & West End	Foot of Whitehall St.; also Fifth Ave. and 25th St., Brooklyn.
7	Brooklyn & Brighton Beach	Flatbush Ave. n. City Line, and Franklin Ave., Brooklyn.
8	Brooklyn & Rockaway Beach	Opposite Howard House, East New York.
9	Buffalo, Rochester & Pittsburgh	Via New York Central or Erie R. R.
10	Camden & Atlantic	Via Penn R. R. foot of Cortlandt and Desbrosses Sts.
11	Cars from Fulton Ferry or Bridge Depots, Brooklyn.	
12	Catskill Mountain & Cairo	Grand Central Depot, and foot of Jay and West 42d Sts.
13	Central of New Jersey	Foot of Liberty St.
13a	Bound Brook Route(Phila.New Line)	" " "
13c	Lehigh & Susquehanna Division	" " "
13e	Newark & New York R. R	" " "
13g	New Jersey Southern Division	Foot of Rector and Liberty Sts.
14	Central Vermont	Grand Central Depot, Fourth Ave. and 42d St.
15	Chateaugay	Grand Central Depot, and foot of Jay and West 42d Sts.
16	Coney Island & Brooklyn (horse cars), 15th St. and City Line, Brooklyn.	
17	Connecticut River	Via New Haven R. R., Grand Central Depot.
20	Delaware & Hudson Canal	Grand Central Depot, and foot of Jay and West 42d Sts.
20a	Pennsylvania Division	Via Cen. R. R. of N. J., Lehigh Valley or D. L. & W. R. Rs.
20b	Susquehanna Division	Via New York Central, West Shore or Erie R. R.
21	Delaware, Lackawanna & Western	Foot of Barclay and Christopher Streets.
21a	Bloomsburgh Division	" " " " "
21c	Morris & Essex Division	" " " " "
21e	Passaic & Delaware R. R	" " " " "
21f	Sussex R. R	" " " " "
23	Elmira, Cortland & Northern	Via Erie, New York Central, or D. L. & W. R. R. Erie, see "New York, Lake Erie & Western."
28	Ferry from New York, see Index for "Ferries."	
29	Fitchburg	Via Hudson River R. R., Grand Central Depot.
30	Fonda, Johnstown & Gloversville	Via New York Central R. R.. Grand Central Depot.
31	Freehold & New York	Foot of Liberty, Cortlandt and Desbrosses Sts.
35	Hartford & Conn. Western	Via New Haven R. R., Grand Central Depot.
36	Housatonic	Via New Haven R. R., Grand Central Depot.
36a	Danbury & Norwalk R. R	" " " " "
38	Lebanon Springs	Via Hudson River R. R., Grand Central Depot.
39	Lehigh & Hudson River	Via Erie R. R., foot of Chambers and West 23d Sts.
40	Lehigh Valley	Via Penn R. R., foot of Cortlandt and Desbrosses Sts.
40a	Southern Central Division	
40b	Geneva, Ithaca & Sayre	" " " " "
41	Long Island	Foot of James' Slip and E. 34th Sts., also Flatbush Ave., Bklyn.
41a	Atlantic Ave. Branch	Flatbush & Atlantic Ave., Brooklyn.
41b	Long Beach Branch	Foot of James' Slip and E. 34th Sts., also Flatbush Ave., Bklyn.
41c	Manhattan Beach Division	" " " " "
43	Meriden, Waterbury & Conn. River	Via New Haven R. R., Grand Central Depot.
45	Newburgh, Dutchess & Connecticut	Via Hudson River R. R., Grand Central Depot.
46	New Haven & Derby	Via New Haven R. R., Grand Central Depot.
47	New Jersey & New York	Foot of Chambers and West 23d St.
48	New London Northern	Via New Haven R. R., Grand Central Depot.
49	New York & Greenwood Lake	Foot of Chambers and West 23d Sts.
50	New York & Long Branch	Foot of Liberty, Cortlandt and Desbrosses Sts.
51	New York & Massachusetts	Via Hudson River R. R., Grand Central Depot.
52	New York & New England	Grand Central Depot, Fourth Ave. and 42d St.
53	New York & Northern	155th St. and Eighth Ave.

DIRECTIONS FOR REACHING VARIOUS PLACES.—*Continued.*

Route No.	Railroad (or Route on which the place is located).	Location of Depot (or Ferry to Depot).
54	New York & Rockaway Beach	Foot of James' Slip and E. 34th St., also Flatbush Ave., Bklyn.
55	New York & Sea Beach	Foot of Whitehall St., N. Y., and 65th St., Bay Ridge.
56	New York Central & Hudson River	Grand Central Depot, 42d St. and 4th Ave., and Fourth Ave. & 125th & 138th Sts., also Tenth Ave. and 30th St.
56a	New York and Harlem Division	Fourth Ave. and 42d, 86th, 110th, 125th & 138th Sts.
57	New York, Lake Erie & Western	Foot of Chambers and West 23d Sts.
58	New York, New Haven & Hartford	Grand Central Depot, Fourth Ave. and 42d St.
58a	Naugatuck Division	" " " " "
58c	Northampton Division	" " " " "
58d	Valley Division	" " " " "
59	New York, Ontario & Western	Foot of Jay and West 42d Sts.
62	New York, Providence & Boston	Via New Haven R. R., Grand Central Depot.
62a	Narragansett Pier R. R.	" " " " "
62b	Newport & Wickford R. R.	" " " " "
63	New York, Susquehanna & Western	Foot of Cortlandt and Desbrosses Sts.
64	Northern Adirondack	Via Hudson River and West Shore R. Rs.
65	Northern of New Jersey	Foot of Chambers and West 23d Sts.
66	Old Colony	Via Fall River Line, foot Murray St.
67	Pennsylvania	Foot of Cortlandt and Desbrosses Sts.
67a	Amboy Division	" " " " "
67b	Belvidere Division	" " " " "
67c	Freehold & Jamesburg R. R.	" " " " "
68	Philadelphia & Reading	Foot of Liberty St.
69	Philadelphia, Wilmington & Baltimore	Via Penn R. R. foot of Cortlandt and Desbrosses Sts.
71	Port Jervis, Monticello & New York	Via Erie, or N. Y., Ontario & Western R. Rs.
72	Prospect Park & Coney Island	Cor. Ninth Ave. and 20th St., Brooklyn.
73	Providence & Springfield	Via New Haven R. R., Grand Central Depot.
74	Providence & Worcester	Via New Haven R. R., Grand Central Depot.
75	Rome, Watertown & Ogdensburg	Via New York Central R. R., Grand Central Depot.
78	Shepaug, Litchfield & Northern	Via New Haven R. R., Grand Central Depot.
80	Staten Island	Foot of Whitehall St.
82	Steamboats for Hudson River towns	See Index for time table, etc.
83	Steamboats for other than Hudson River towns	See Index for time table, etc.
84	Steamships, places reached by	For piers, etc., see Index for "Steamship Lines."
85	Syracuse, Geneva & Corning	Via New York Central and Erie R. Rs.
86	Tuckerton	Via Central of N. J. and Penn. R. Rs.
87	Ulster & Delaware	Via Hudson River R. R. and West Shore R. R.
87a	Kaaterskill R. R.	" " " " "
87b	Stony Clove & Catskill Mountain	" " " " "
88	Union Transportation Company	Via Penn. R. R., foot of Cortlandt and Desbrosses Sts.
90	Wallkill Valley	Via West Shore R. R., foot of Jay and West 42d Sts.
94	West Jersey	Via Penn R. R., foot of Cortlandt and Desbrosses Sts.
95	West Shore R. R.	Foot of Jay and West 42d Sts.

BROOKLYN, CANARSIE & ROCKAWAY BEACH R. R.

Connections made by

Atlantic Ave. "Rapid Transit" and Brooklyn Elevated R. R. to (Howard House) East New York, from Flatbush Ave., Fulton Ferry, Brooklyn Bridge or Broadway Ferry.

Trains leave **Howard House, East New York,** for Canarsie Shore, 6 30, 7 30, 9 00, 10 15, 11 30 a. m., 1 00, 2 30 3 45, 4 50, 6 00, 7 15 p. m., *Saturdays,* 8 15, p. m., *Sundays only* every hour from 8 30 a. m. to 7 30 p. m.

Trains leave **Canarsie Shore** at 5 45, 7 00, 8 30, 9 30, 11 00 a. m., 12 30, 2 00, 3 15, 4 15, 5 30, 6 30 p. m., *Saturdays,* 7 15. p. m., *Sundays only* every hour from 8 00 a. m. to 7 00 p. m.

No Steamboats running to Rockaway Beach.

The Coupon Information contained in this Guide is furnished by the Banks and Bankers, who have signified their willingness to co-operate with us in giving the public correct information.

DIRECTIONS AND EXPRESS TO VARIOUS PLACES

Selected from time tables of Railroads in New York, New Jersey, Pennsylvania, Connecticut, and adjacent States.

For Name of Railroad or Route on which the place is located, see at corresponding numbers on preceding pages.

For Offices of all Express Companies, see page 100.

Express Company Names Abbreviated as follows:

Ad.—Adams.	L. I.—Long Island.	U. S.—United States.
Am.—American.	Nat.—National.	W. F. & Co.—Wells, Fargo & Co.
Int'l.—International.	N. Y. & B.—New York & Boston Dispatch.	

Route.	Place and Express.	Route	Place and Express.	Route	Place and Express.
57	Abbott's Road, N.Y.—W.F.&Co.	62	Arkwright, R. I.—Ad.	13g	Barnegat Park, N. J.—Ad.
3, 69	Aberdeen, Md.—U. S.; Ad.	19	Arlington, N. J.—W. F. & Co.	67a	Barnegat Pier, N. J.—Ad.
52	Abington, Conn.—Ad.	4	Arlington, Vt.—Nat.	13c	Barnesville, Pa.—Ad.; U. S.
66	Abington, Mass.—Nat.; Ad.	67	Arnold, Clearfield Co., Pa.—Ad.	71	Barnum's, N. Y.—W. F. & Co.
10	Abecon, N. J.—Ad.	58	Arnolds, Conn.—Ad.	41b	Barnum's Island, L. I.—L. I.
66	Acton, Mass.—Nat.; Ad.	52	Arnold's Mills, R. I.—Ad.	4	Barnumville, Vt.—Nat.
91	Acton, N. J.—Ad.	57	Arnot, Pa.—W. F. & Co.	11	Barre, Vt.—Nat.; Ad.
66	Acushnet, Mass.—N. Y. & B.	80	Arrochar, S. I.—U. S.	10	Barre's Corners, L. I.—Local.
5	Adams, Mass.—Am.; Ad.	45	A Thornburg, N. Y.—Am.	5	Barre Plains, Mass.—Ad.
75	Adams, N. Y.—Am.	54	Arverne, L. I.—L. I.	56, 82	Barrytown, N. Y.—Am.
56	Adams Basin, N. Y.—Am.	13	Asbury, N. J.—U. S.; Ad.	59	Bartlett, N. Y.—Nat.
75	Adams Centre, N. Y.—Am.	79	Asbury, N. Y.—U. S.	13	Bartley, N. J.—U. S.; Ad.
52	Adamsdale, Mass.—Ad.	50	Asbury Park, N. J.—U. S.; Ad.	68	Barto, Pa.—Ad.
57	Addison, N. Y.—W. F. & Co.; U. S.	68	Ashcroft, Mass.—Ad.	57	Barton, N. Y.—W. F. & Co.
57	Adrian, N. Y.—W. F. & Co.	52	Ashcroft, Mass.—Ad.	14	Bartonsville, Vt.—Nat.; Ad.
20	Afton, N. Y.—Nat.	9	Ashford, Cattaraugua, N. Y.—Am.	58	Barrow, N. Y.—Ad.
56, 95	Akron, N. Y.—Nat.; Am.	53	Ashford, Westchester, N. Y.—Am.	21c	Basking Ridge, N. J.—U. S.
via 57	Akron, O.—Ad.; Am.; W.F.&Co.	5	Ashland, Mass.—Ad.	56, 57	Batavia, N. Y.—W.F.&Co.; U.S.
95	Alabama, N. Y.; Nat.	19	Ashland, N. J.—Ad.	via 58	Bath, Me.—Nat.; Ad.; N.Y & B.
67	Alba, Pa.—Ad.	10, 13c	Ashland, Pa.—Ad.	21, 57	Bath, N. Y.—W. F. & Co.
50,95,82	Albany, N. Y.—Nat.; Am.	13c	Ashley, Pa.—U. S.; Ad.	13c	Bath, Pa.—U. S.; Ad.
41	Albertsons, L. I.—L. I.	36	Ashley Falls, Mass.—Ad.	6, 55	Bath Beach, L. I.—B. B. & W. E.
56	Albion, Orleans Co., N. Y.—Am.	71	Ashton, R. I.—N. Y. & B.	58	Bay Chester, N. Y.—Ad.
41	Albion, R. I.—N. Y. & B.	17	Ashuelot, N. H.—Ad.	67a	Bay Head, N. J.—Ad.
14	Alburgh, Vt.—Am.	66	Assonet, Mass.—N. Y. & B.	84	Bayonne, N. J.—U. S.
14	Alburgh Springs, Vt.—Am.	28, 84	Astoria, L. I.—Bowing.	41	Bayport, L. I.—L. I.
68	Albutus, Pa.—Ad.	67b	Asylum Station, N. J.—Ad.	83	Bay Ridge, L. I.—Kelly.
21, 57	Alden, N. Y.—W. F. & Co.; U. S.	10	Atco, N. J.—Ad.	11	Bayshore, L. I.—L. I.
13c	Alden, Pa.—U. S.	67	Atglen, Pa.—Ad.	13g	Bayside, N. J.—Ad.; U. S.
75	Alder Creek, N. Y.—Am.	57	Athenia, N. J.—W. F. & Co.	62	Bay Side, R. I.—Ad.
21, 57	Alexander, N. Y.—W. F. & Co.; Am.; U. S.	82	Athens, N. Y.—Nat.	11	Bay Side, L. I.—L. I.
75	Alexandria Bay, N. Y.—Am.	10	Athens, Pa.—Ad.	3, 60	Bayview, Md.—Ad.; U. S.
67b	Alexauken, N. J.—Ad.	5, 29	Athol, Mass.—Nat.; Ad.	13g	Bayview, N. J.—Ad.; U. S.
57	Alfred, N. Y.—W. F. & Co.	via13,67	Atlantic City, N. J.—Ad.	13	Bay Way, N. J.—Ad.; U. S.
87	Allaben, N. Y.—Am.	13g, 84	Atlantic Highlands, N. J.—U. S.	86	Beach Haven, N. J.—Ad.
97c	Allaire, N. J.—Ad.	13g	Atsion, N. J.—U. S.; Ad.	21a	Beach Haven, Pa.—U. S.
39	Allamuchy, N. J.—W. F. & Co.	57	Attlebury, N. Y.—W. F.; Am.; U. S.	86	Beach View, N. J.—Ad.
57	Allegany, N.Y.—W.F.&Co.; Am.	45	Attlebury, N. Y.—Am.	58a	Beacon Falls, Conn.—Ad.
via 67	Alleghany, Pa.—Ad.; Am.	52	Atwaters, N. Y.—U. S.; Ad.	68	Beaver, Pa.—Ad.; Am.
57	Alleudale, N. J.—W. F. & Co.	52	Auburn, Mass.—Ad.	57	Beaver Dam, N. Y.—W. F. & Co.
74	Allendale, R. I.—N. Y. & B.	68	Auburn, Pa.—Ad.	40	Beaver Meadow, Pa.—Ad.
13c, 40	Allentown, Pa.—U. S.; Ad.	62	Auburn, R. I.—Ad.	68	Bechtelsville, Pa.—Ad.
67c	Allenwood, N. J.—Ad.	5	Auburndale, Mass.—Ad.	5	Becket, Mass.—Nat.; Ad.
13c	Allenwood, Pa.—Ad.	10	Audenreid, Pa.—Ad.	58	Beckley's, Conn.—Ad.
via 57	Alliance, Ohio.—Ad.	via 58	Augusta, Me.—Nat; NY & B; Ad	56a	Bedford, N. Y.—Am.
91	Alloway, N. J.—Ad.	56	Aurelius, N. Y.—Am.	28	Bedford Park, N. Y.—Am.
54	Almond, N. Y.—W. F. & Co.	95	Aurieville, N. Y.—Nat.	23	Bedloe's Island, N. Y.—By Boat.
20	Altamont, N. Y.—Nat.	21	Aurora, N. Y.—U. S.; Ad.	45	Beekman, N. Y.—Ad.
57	Alton, Pa.—W. F. & Co.	20	Ausable, N. Y.—Ad.	29	Beekmantown, N. Y.—Nat.
44	Altoona, Pa.—Ad.	via 20	Ausable Chasm, N. Y.—Nat.	via58,57,81	Belfast, Me.—Nat.; Ad.; Int.
58	Amawalk, N. Y.—Am.	67	Avenel, N. J.—Ad.	62	Bellefonte, R. I.—Ad.
56, 95	Amboy, N. Y.—Nat.	13	Avenue A, N. J.—Ad.; U. S.	14a	Belle Mead, N. J.—Ad.
56a	Amenia, N. Y.—Am.	13g	Avenue H, N. J.—Ad.; U. S.	94	Belle Plain, N. J.—Ad.
18	Amherst, Mass.—Nat.; Ad.	21, 57	Avoca, N. Y.—W. F. & Co.; U. S.	57	Belleville, N. J.—W. F. & Co.
41	Amityville, L. I.—L. I.	58c	Avon, Conn.—Ad.	62b	Belleville, R. I.—Ad.
56, 95	Amsterdam, N. Y.—Nat.; Am.	66	Avon, Mass.—Ad.	60	Bellevue, Del.—Ad.
91	Ancora, N. J.—Ad.	21	Avon, N. Y.—W. F. & Co.	21a	Bellevue, Pa.—Ad.
35	Ancram, N. Y.—Am.	68	Avon, Pa.—Ad.	41	Bellmore, L. I.—L. I.
51	Ancram Lead Mines, N. Y.—Am.	57	Avondale, N. J.—W. F. & Co.	17	Bellows Falls, Vt.—Ad.; Nat.
67	Andalusia, Pa.—Ad.	21a	Avondale, Pa.—Ad.	11	Bell Port, L. I.—L. I.
52	Andover, Conn.—Ad.	20	Ayer, Mass.—Nat.	67	Bellwood, Pa.—Ad.
21f	Andover, N. J.—W.F.&Co.; U. S.	41	Babylon, L. I.—L. I.	57	Belmont, N. Y.—W. F. & Co.
57	Andover, N. Y.—W. F. & Co.	13g	Bacon's Neck, N. J.—Ad.; U. S.	68	Belmont, Pa.—Ad.
9	Annadale, S. I.—U. S.	3	Bailey's, Md.—Ad.	67b	Belvidere, N. J.—W.F.&Co.; Ad.
19	Annandale, N. J.—U. S.	35	Bainbridge, N. Y.—Nat.	57	Belvidere, N. Y.—W. F. & Co.
via 67	Annapolis, Md.—Ad.; U. S.	44	Baiting Hollow, L. I.—L. I.	13a	Benezet, Pa.—Ad.; U. S.
via56,57	Ann Arbor, Mich.—Am.	67	Bala, Pa.—Ad.	94	Bennett, N. J.—Ad.
68	Annville, Pa.—Ad.	20	Baldwin, N. Y.—Am.	67	Bennett, Pa.—Ad.
68	Anselma, Pa.—Ad.	53	Baldwin Place, N. Y.—Am.	4, 38	Bennington, Vt.—Nat.
58a, 46	Ansonia, Conn.—Ad.; U. S.; Int'l.	11	Baldwins, L. I.—L. I.	6	Bensonhurst, L.I.—B. B. & W. E.
52	Anthony, R. I.—Ad.	21	Baldwinsville, N. Y.—Nat.; U. S.	56, 95	Bergen, N. Y.—Nat.
45	Antrim, Pa.—Am.	5	Baldwinsville, Mass.—Nat.; Ad.	95	Bergenfields, N. J.—Ad.; Nat.
75	Antwerp, N. Y.—Am.	20	Balstoa, N. Y.—Nat.	13, 84	Bergen Point, N. J.—U. S.
21	Apalachin, N. Y.—U. S.	52	Baltic, Conn.—Ad.	67a	Berkeley, N. J.—Ad.
13g	Apollonia, N. J.—U. S.	3, 69, 84	Baltimore, Md.—Ad.; U. S.	74	Berkeley, R. I.—Ad.
62	Appoquag, R. I.—U. S.; Ad.	86	Bamber, N. J.—Ad.	21c	Berkeley Heights, N. J.—U. S.
21	Apulia, N. Y.—U. S.	45	Bangall, N. Y.—Am.	5	Berkshire, Mass.—Ad.; Nat.
54	Aqueduct, L. I.—L. I.	via58,81	Bangor, Me.—Ad.; Nat.; Int'l.	40a	Berkshire, N. Y.—Ad.
57	Ararat Summit, Pa.—W.F. & Co.	13c	Bangor, Pa.—U. S.; Ad.	58	Berlin, Conn.—Ad.
39	Archbald, Pa.—Nat.	78	Bantam, Conn.—Ad.	69	Berlin, Md.—Ad.; U. S.
62	Arctic, R. I.—Ad.	61	Bardons, N. Y.—Ad.	58	Berlin, N. Y.—Ad.
57	Arden, N. Y.—W. F. & Co.	via 58	Bar Harbor, Me.—Ad.;Nat.;Int'l.	38	Berlin, N. Y.—Nat.
53	Ardsley, N. Y.—Am.	3	Barksdale, Md.—U. S.	68	Bern, Pa.—Ad.
57	Arkport, N. Y.—W. F. & Co.	13g	Barnegat, N. J.—U. S.; Ad.	21c	Bernardsville, N. J.—U. S.
57	Arkville, N. Y.—Nat.; Am.	86	Barnegat City, N. J.—Ad.	59	Bernhards Bay, N. Y.—Nat.

DIRECTIONS AND EXPRESS TO VARIOUS PLACES—Continued.

For Explanation of Abbreviations used, see page 112.

21a	Berwick, Pa.—U S	68	Bridgeport, Pa.—Ad	3, 69.	Canton, Md.—Ad
23	Besemer, N. Y.—Natl Am	13g, 91	Bridgeton, N. J.—Ad	75	Canton, N. Y.—Am
13a	Bethayres, Pa.—Ad	69	Bridgeville, Del.—Ad	69	Cape Charles, Va.—Ad
36a	Bethel, Conn. Ad	21	Bridgeville, N. J.—U S	94	Cape May, N. J.—Ad
45	Bethel, N. Y.—Am	96	Bridgewater, Mass. Ad	94	Cape May C. H., N. J.—Ad
14	Bethel, Vt. Natl	21	Bridgewater, N. Y.—U S	75	Cape Vincent, N. Y.—Am
13c, 40	Bethlehem, Pa.—Ad	50	Brielle, N. J. Ad	20a, 57	Carbondale, Pa.—U S; Natl
67a	Beverly, N. J. Ad	75	Brier Hill, N. Y.—Am	47	Carlstadt, N. J. U S
57, 21	Big Flats, N. Y.—U S; W F & Co	5	Brighton, Mass.—Ad	75	Carlton, N. Y. Am
87	Big Indian, N. Y.—Am; Natl	56	Brighton, N. Y. Am	75	Carlyon, N. Y.—Am
57	Big Island, N. Y.—W F & Co	7	Brights Beach, L. I.—Remsen	via 56	Carmansville, N. Y.—Am
57	Big Shanty, Pa. W F & Co	17	Brightwood, Mass.—Ad	53	Carmel, N. Y.—Am
45	Billings, N. Y.—Am	45, 52	Brinckerhoff, N. Y.—Am	62	Caro Inn, R. I.—Ad
21, 57	Binghamton, N. Y.—Natl; U S	67	Brintons, Pa.—Ad	21	Caroline, N. Y.—U S
90	Binnewater, N. Y. U S	21	Brisbin, N. Y.—U S	67b	Carpenterville, N. J.—Ad
87,	Bird-in-Hand, Pa—Ad	52	Bristol, Conn.—Ad	57	Carrollton, N. Y. W F & Co
68	Birdsboro, Pa—Ad	67	Bristol, Pa.—Ad	13	Carteret, N. J.—Ad
46	Birmingham, Conn.—Ad Int'l	66	Bristol, R. I.—Int'l	75	Carthage, N. Y.—Am
67a	Birmingham, N. J.—Ad	66	Bristol Ferry, R. I.—Int'l	13	Cary's, N. J.—Ad
58	Black Hall, Conn.—Ad	52	Broad Brook, Conn.—Ad	58	Casanova, N. Y.—Ad
29	Blackinton, Mass.—Natl	54	Broad Channel, L. I. L I	40a	Cascade, N. Y.—U S
58	Black Point, Conn.—Ad	21c	Broadway, N. J.—U S; Natl	85	Cascade Mills, N. Y.—Am
40	Black Ridge, Pa.—Ad	86	Brockport, N. Y.—Am	57	Castile, N. Y.—W F & Co
75	Black River, N. Y.—Am	83	Brockways, Conn.—Ad	56	Castleton, N. Y.—Am
56	Black Rock, N. Y. Am; U S	66	Brockton, Mass.—Ad	20	Castleton, Vt. Natl
52	Blackstone, Mass.—Ad	13c	Brodhead, Pa.—Ad	75	Castor Land, N. Y.—Am
83	Blackwells Island, N. Y.—Local	87	Brodhead's Bridge, N. Y.—Am	13c, 40	Catasauqua, Pa.—Ad;
61	Blairstown, N. J.—Natl	56a	Bronxville, N. Y.—Am	21a	Catawissa, Pa.—Ad; U S
67	Blairsville Int'sec , Pa.—Ad	9	Bronxdale, N. Y. Am	40a	Cato, N. Y.—Ad; U S
68	Blandon, Pa.—Ad	36	Brookfield, Conn Ad	95, 82	Catskill, N. Y.—Am; Natl
65, 95	Blauveltville, N. Y.—W F & Co	88	Brookfield, Mass. Ad; Natl	56	Catskill Station, N. Y.—Am
9	Bliss, N. Y.—Am	11	Brookhaven, L. I. L I	57	Cattaraugus, N. Y.—W F & Co
11	Blissville, L. I.—Bowron	74, 55	Brooklyn Jockey Club, L. I.	21	Cattatunk, N. Y.—U S
96	Block Island, R. I.—Ad; N Y & B	68	Brookside, Pa.—Ad	56	Caughdenoy, N. Y.—Natl
21	Blodgetts Mills, N. Y.—U S	14	Brooksville, Vt. Natl	14	Cavendish, Vt.—Natl
21, 57	Bloods, N. Y.—U S; W F & Co	23	Brookton, N. Y.—Am; Natl; U S	40b, 56	Cayuga, N. Y. Ad; Am; U S
35	Bloomfield, Conn.—Ad	83	Brown's Dock, N. J.—Ad	23	Cazenovia, N. Y.—Am; Natl
40, 21a	Bloomfield, Essex Co., N. J.—U S	67a	Brown's Mills, N. J.—Ad	13g	Cedar Creek, N. J.—Ad
67a	Bloomfield, N. J.—W F & Co	87	Brown's Station, N. Y.—Natl	40	Cedar Grove, N. Y.—W F & Co
29	Bloomingburgh, N. Y.—Natl	75	Brownville, N. Y.—Am	13g	Cedar Lake, N. J.—Ad
63	Bloomingdale, N. J.—Natl	40	Brownsville, Pa.—Ad	14	Cedar River, N. Y. Natl
15	Bloomingdale, N. Y.—Natl	via 58	Brunswick, Me.—Ad; N Y & B	13g	Cedarville, N. J.—Ad
15	Bloomingdale, N. Y.—Natl	67	Bryn Mawr, Pa. Ad	21	Cedarville, N. J.—U S
57	Blooming Grove, N. Y.—W F & Co	67a	Buckingham, N. J.—Ad	52	Centerville, R. I. Ad
21a	Bloomsburg, Pa.—Ad; U S	52	Buckland, Conn. Ad	20b	Central Bridge, N. Y.—Natl
13, 40	Bloomsbury, N. J.—Ad	40	Buck Mountain, Pa.—Ad	40	Centralia, Pa. Ad
57	Blossburg, Pa.—W F & Co	57, 84	Bucksport, Me.—Int'l	41	Central Islip, L. I.—L I
1	Blue Mountain Lake, N. Y. Nat	21c, 13	Budd's Lake, N. J.—U S	56a	Central Morrisania, N. Y.—Am
via 41	Blue Point, L. I.—L I	94	Buena Vista, N. J.—Ad	41	Central Park, L. I. L I
6	Blythebourne, L. I.—Local	57, 56, 94, 40	Buffalo, N. Y.—Am; Natl	59, 73	Central Square, N. Y. Am; Natl
63	Bogota, N. J.—Natl	5	Bulls Head, N. Y.—U S	57	Central Valley, N. Y.—W F & Co
87,	Boiceville, N. Y.—Am	67b	Bull's Island Station, N. J.—Ad	52	Central Village, Conn.—Ad
52	Bolton, Conn.—Ad	57	Ballville, N. Y.—W F & Co	38	Centre Berlin, N. Y. Natl
20	Bolton, N. Y.—Ad	59	Bandys, N. Y.—Natl	73	Centredale, R. I.—N Y & B
14	Bolton, Vt.—Natl	58c	Burlington, Conn.—Ad	38	Centre Lebanon, N. Y.—Natl
5	Bondsville, Mass.—Ad; Natl	67a	Burlington, N. J.—Ad	14	Centre Rutland, Vt.—Natl
69	Bonnaffon, Pa.—Ad	14	Burlington, Vt.—Natl	20a	Centre Village, N. Y.—Natl
21c	Boonton, N. J.—U S	via 58	Burham, Me.—Natl	58c	Centreville, Conn.—Ad
75	Boonville, N. Y.—Am	52	Burnhams, Conn.—Ad	69	Centreville, Md.—Ad
67a	Bordentown, N. J.—Ad	57	Burns, N. Y.—W F & Co	13	Centreville, N. J. U S
67	Borie's, Pa.—Ad	52	Burnside, Conn.—Ad	13	Centreville, Cumb'l'd Co., N. J.—Ad
58, 83	Boston, Mass.—Ad; Int'l	50	Burnside, N. Y.—Natl	59	Centreville, N. Y.—Natl
56a	Boston Corners, N. Y.—Am	58a	Burrville, Conn.—Ad	68	Centreville, Pa.—Ad
36	Botsford, Conn.—Ad	41	Bushwick, L. I. Weed & P.	67a	Chadwick, N. J.—Ad
39	Bouckville, N. Y.—Natl	67	Bustleton, Pa.—Ad	21	Chadwicks, N. Y.—U S
13, 40	Bound Brook, N. J.—Ad	63	Butler, N. J.—Natl	21	Changewater, N. J.—U S
66	Bourne, Mass.—N Y & B	62	Buttonwoods, R. I.—Ad	13g	Chapel Hill, N. J.—Ad
13g	Bowentown, N. J.—Ad	87	Buttsville, N. J.—W F & Co	35	Chapinville, Conn.—Ad
66	Bowenville, Mass—N Y & B	67	Buttsville, N. J.—Am	56	Chapinville, N. J.—Am
54	Bower's, Pa.—Ad	66	Buzzard's Bay, Mass.—N Y & B	52	Chaplin, Conn.—Ad
83	Bowery Bay Beach, L. I.—Dowron	68	Byers, Pa.—Ad	13c	Chapman Quarries, Pa.—Ad
13c	Bowmans, Pa.—Ad; U S	67b	Byram, N. J.—U S	56a	Chappaqua, N. Y.—Am
95	Bowmansville, N. Y.—Natl	95	Byron Centre, N. Y.—Natl	69	Charlestown, Md.—Ad
67b	Bowne, N. J.—Ad	15	Cadyville, N. Y.—Natl	17	Charlestown, N. H.—Natl
68	Boyertown, Pa.—Ad	12	Cairo, N. Y.—Am; Natl	75	Charlotte, N. Y.—Am
31	Bradevelt, N. J.—Natl	21	Caldwell, N. J.—Ad	1	Charlotte, N. Y.—Natl
57	Bradford, Pa. Am; U S; Natl	56, 57	Caledonia, N. Y.—W F & Co	63	Charlotteburgh, N. J.—Natl
13	Bradshaw, Md.—U S	13	Califon, N. J.—Ad	58a	Chariton, Mass.—Natl
13g	Bradway, N. J.—Ad	57	Calicoon, N. Y.—W F & Co	58	Charter Oak, Conn.—Ad
38	Brainards, N. Y.—Natl	69	Cambridge, Md.—Ad	69	Chases, Md. Ad
13g, 50, 83	Branchport, N. J.—Ad	20	Cambridge, N. Y.—Natl	66	Chatham, Mass.—N Y & B
36a	Branchville, Conn.—Ad	3	Cambridge, Ohio.—Am	21c	Chatham, N. J.—U S
21f	Branchville, N. J.—U S	67a	Camden, N. J. Ad	5, 56a	Chatham, N. Y.—Am; Natl
14	Brandon, Vt.—Natl	23, 75	Camden, N. Y.—Am; Natl	5	Chatham Centre, N. Y. Am
57	Brandis, Pa.—W F & Co	56	Camelot, N. Y.—Am	75	Chaumont, N. Y.—Am
58	Branford, Conn.—Ad	57	Cameron, N. Y. W F & Co	20	Chazy, N. Y.—Natl
17	Brattleboro, Vt.—Ad	21c	Cameron, Pa.—Ad	16	Chazy Lake, N. Y.—Natl
23	Breesport, N. Y.—Am; Natl	57	Cameron Mills, N. Y.—W F & Co	58c	Chepsside, Mass. Ad
41	Brentwood, L. I.—L I	56	Camillus, N. Y.—Am	57	Cheektowaga, N. Y.—W F & Co
41	Breslau, L. I.—L I	21, 57	Campbell, N. Y. U S; W F & Co	66	Chelsea, S. I.—U S
75	Brewerton, N. Y.—Am	57, 59	Campbell Hall, N. Y. Natl; U S	57	Chemung, N. Y.—W F & Co
66	Brewster, Mass.—N Y & B	66	Campello, Mass.—Ad	21	Chenango Bridge, N. Y.—U S
59, 56a	Brewsters, N. Y. Am	via 58	Canaan, Conn.—Ad	21	Chenango Forks, N. Y.—U S
21a	Briar Creek, Pa.—U S	via 56	Canandaigua, N. Y.—Am; Ad	35	Cherry Brook, Conn.—Ad
21c	Brick Church, N. J.—U S	57	Canisteo, N. Y.—W F & Co	47	Cherry Hill, N. J.—U S
40a	Brick Church, N. Y.—U S	36a	Cannon, Conn.—Ad	20b	Cherry Valley, N. Y. Natl
67	Bridesburg, Pa.—Ad	56	Canoe Camp, Pa.—W F & Co	58c	Cheshire, Conn.—Ad
11	Bridge Hampton, L. I.—L I	52	Canterbury, Conn.—Ad	5	Cheshire, Mass.—Ad; Am
58, 89	Bridgeport, Conn.—Ad; Intl	35	Canton, Conn.—Ad	5	Cheshire Harbor, Mass.—Ad

DIRECTIONS AND EXPRESS TO VARIOUS PLACES—Continued.

For Explanation of Abbreviations used, see page 112.

10	Chesilhurst, N. J.—Ad	80	Concord, S. I.—U S	21	Dalton, Pa.—U S
58d	Chester, Conn.—Ad	57	Conesus, N. Y.—W F & Co	via 58	Damariscotta, Me.—Natl; Ad
5	Chester, Mass.—Ad; Natl	7, 16, 41, 55, 72, 83	Coney Island, L. I.	3ia 52	Danbury, Conn.—Ad; Int'l.
13, 21c	Chester, N. J.—U S; W F & Co	58c	Congamond, Conn.—Ad	1	Danby, Vt.—Natl
57	Chester, Pa.—Ad; U S	95	Congers, N. Y.—Natl	52	Danielsonville, Conn.—Ad
69	Chester, Pa.—Ad; U S	62	Connineut, R. I.—Ad	15	Dannemora, N. Y.—Natl
11	Chester, Vt.—Natl	21	Conklin, N. Y.—U S	21, 57	Dansville, N. Y.—U S; W F
13	Chester Furnace, N. J.—Ad	21	Conklin Centre, N. Y.—U S	via 56	Danville, Ill.—Ad; Am; U S
68	Chester Springs, Pa.—Ad	1	Conklingville, N. Y.—Natl	21a	Danville, Pa.—Ad; U S
58	Chestnut Hill, Conn.—Ad	13a	Conshocken, Pa.—Ad	3, 69	Darby, Pa.—Ad; U S
49	Chestnut Hill, N. J.—W F & Co	88	Constable Hook, N. J.—Local	58	Darien, Conn.—Ad
13a	Chestnut Hill, Pa.—Ad	59	Constantia, N. Y.—Natl	21, 57	Darien, N. Y.—U S; W F & Co
via 56, 57, 67, 3	Chicago, Ill.—Ad; Am; U S	21c	Convent, N. J.—U S	68	Dauphin, Pa.—Ad
87b	Chichesters, N. Y.—Am	50	Cook's Falls, N. Y.—Natl	67a	Davenport, N. J.—Ad
17	Chicopee Centre, Mass.—Ad; Natl	67a	Cookstown, N. J.—Ad	83	Davids Island, N. Y.—Ad
17	Chicopee Falls, Mass.—Ad; Nat	20b	Coons, N. Y.—Natl	67a	Davis, N. J.—Ad
69	Childs, Md.—Ad	49	Cooper, N. J.—W F & Co	62	Davisville, R. I.—Ad
56, 95	Chili, N. Y.—Am	21, 57	Coopers, N. Y.—W F & Co	67c	Dayton, N. J.—Ad
3	Chillicothe, Ohio.—Ad; U S	20b	Cooperstown, N. Y.—Natl	57	Dayton, N. Y.—W F & Co
56, 95	Chittenango, N. Y.—Am; Natl	20	Cooperville, N. Y.—Am	via 56, 57, 67	Dayton, Ohio.—Ad; Am; U S
23	Chittenango Falls, N. Y.—Natl	35	Copake, N. Y.—Am	52	Dayville, Conn.—Ad
20	Chubbs Dock, N. Y.—Natl	56a	Copake Iron Works, N. Y.—Am	67a	Deacon's, N. J.—Ad
21a	Chulasky, Pa.—U S	40	Coplay, N. Y.—	50	Deal Beach, N. J.—Ad
7	Church Lane, L. I.—Smith's	5	Cordaville, Mass.—Ad	67	Deans, N. J.—Ad
86, 95	Churchville, N. Y.—Am; Natl	56	Corfu, N. Y.—Am	30	Dennsville, N. Y.—Natl
via 56, 57, 67, 3	Cincinnati, Ohio.—Ad; Am	1	Corinth, N. Y.—Natl	via 56	Decatur, Ill.—Am
57	Circleville, N. Y.—W F & Co	21, 57	Corning, N. Y.—Am; W F & Co	68	Deckertown, N. J.—Ad
83	City Island, N. Y.—Ad	57, 82, 95	Cornwall, N. Y.—Natl	58d, 83	Deep River, Conn.—Ad
52	City Mills, Mass.—Ad	36	Cornwall Bridge, Conn.—Ad	58c, 17	Deerfield, Mass.—Ad; Natl
13	Claremont, N. J.—Dodd & C.	67	Cornwall's, Pa.—Ad	via 58	Deer Isle, Me.—Ad
95	Clarence, N. Y.—Natl	17	Corona, N. Y.—Ad	41	Deer Park, L. I.—L I
56	Clarence Centre, N. Y.—Am	11	Corona, L. I.—I	75	Deer River, N. Y.—Am
41	Clarenceville, L. I.—Local	via 57	Corry, Pa.—Ad; Am; Natl; W F	3	Defiance, Ohio.—U S
4	Clarendon, N. Y.—Natl	21, 23	Cortland, N. Y.—Am; Natl	57	De Golias, Pa.—W F & Co
95	Clark's Mills, N. Y.—Natl	58	Cos Cob, Conn.—Ad	30	De Kays, N. J.—W F & Co
5	Claverack, N. Y.—Am	66, 83	Cottage City, Mass.—N Y & B	50	De Laucy, N. Y.—Natl
75	Clay, N. Y.—Am	35	Cottage Grove, Conn.—Ad	67a	Delanco, N. J.—Ad
69	Claymont, Del.—Ad	23	Cottons, N. Y.—Natl	40	Delano, Pa.—Ad
52	Clayton, Conn.—Ad	13c	Council Ridge, Pa.—Ad	21c	Delawanna, N. J.—U S
66	Clayton, Del.—Ad	80	Court House, S. I.—U S	21	Delaware, N. J.—U S Natl
94	Clayton, N. J.—Ad	40b	Coventry, N. Y.—U S	via 56	Delaware, Ohio.—Am
75	Clayton, N. Y.—Am	21	Coventry, R. I.—Ad	21, 63	Delaware Water Gap, Pa.—Natl
21	Clayville, N. Y.—U S	52	Covert, N. Y.—Ad; U S	59	Delhi, N. Y.—Natl
59	Cleveland, N. Y.—Natl	57	Covington, Pa.—W F & Co	69	Delmar, Del.—Ad
via 56, 57, 67	Cleveland, Ohio.—Ad; Am	85	Cowenesque, Pa.—Am	20b	Delmar, N. Y.—Natl
50	Cliffwood, N. J.—Ad	41	Cowenhovens, L. I.—Remsen	23	Delphi, N. Y.—Am; Natl
via 58	Clifton, Mass.—Ad; Natl	62	Cowessett, R. I.—Ad	05	Demarest, N. J.—W F & Co
21, 57	Clifton, N. J.—W F & Co	82, 95	Coxsackie, N. Y.—Am; Natl	59	Dennistons, N. Y.—Natl
80	Clifton, S. I.—U S	56	Coxsackie Station, N. Y.—Am	21c	Denville, N. J.—U S
56	Clifton Springs, N. Y.—Am	86	Cox Station, N. J.—Ad	57	Deposit, N. Y.—W F & Co
58	Clinton, Conn.—Ad	40	Coxton, Pa.—Ad	46, 58a, 83	Derby, Conn.—Ad
40	Clinton, N. J.—Ad	53	Crafts, N. Y.—Am	67	Derry, Pa.—Ad
59	Clinton, N. Y.—Natl	21	Craigs, N. Y.—U S	23	De Ruyter, N. Y.—Am; Natl
51	Clinton Corners, N. Y.—Am	57	Craigville, N. Y.—W F & Co	via 56	Detroit, Mich.—Am; U S
20b	Clintons, N. Y.—Natl	23	Crains Mills, N. Y.—Natl	via 58	Devereux, Mass.—Ad
23	Clockville, N. Y.—Natl	67a	Cranbury Station, N. J.—Ad	9	Devereux, N. Y.—Am
95	Closter, N. J.—W F & Co	50	Crane's Village, N. J.—Am.	50	Dewey, Mass.—Ad
45	Clove Valley, N. Y.—Am	13	Cranford, N. J.—Ad	56, 95	Dewitt, N. Y.—Natl
67	Club House, N. Y.—W F & Co	52	Cranston, R. I.—Ad	via 58	Dexter, Me.—Am
50	Clyde, N. J.—Ad	82, 95	Cranstons, N. Y.—Natl.	52	Diamond Hill, R. I.—Ad
56, 95	Clyde, N. Y.—Am; Natl	56a	Craryville, N. Y.—Am	64	Dickinson Centre, N. Y.—Am
13c	Clyde, Pa.—Ad	67a	Cream Ridge, N. J.—Ad	20d	Dickson, Pa.—U S
13c	Coaldale, Pa.—L—L	via 41	Creedmoor, L. I.—L I.	66	Dighton, Mass.—N Y & B
67b	Coal Port, N. S.—Ad	1	Creek Centre, N. Y.—Natl	67	Dilleville, Pa.—Ad
67	Coatesville, Pa.—Ad	58	Crescent Beach, Conn.—Ad	13g	Dividing Creek, N. J.—Ad
50	Cobalt, Conn.—Ad	21	Cresco, Pa.—L S	3	Dix, N. Y.—Natl
20b	Cobbskill, N. Y.—Natl	65	Creskill, N. J.—W F & Co	56, 82	Dobbs Ferry, N. Y.—Am
57	Cochecton, N. Y.—W F & Co	80	Creskill, S. I.—U S	via 21	Doddtown, N. J.—U S
82	Coeyman's, N. Y.—Natl	67	Cresson, Pa.—Ad.	52	Dorchester, Mass.—Ad; Natl
95	Coeyman's Junc., N. Y.—Natl	57	Cressona, Pa.—Ad.	10	Doughtys, N. J.—Ad
45	Coffin's, N. Y.—Am	via 57, 67	Crestline, Ohio.—Ad; Am	52	Douglas, Mass.—Ad
21	Cohasset, Mass.—Ad; Natl	69	Crisfield, Md.—Ad	68	Douglasville, Pa.—Ad
21, 57	Cohocton, N. Y.—W F & Co	50	Crittenden, N. Y.—Am	41	Douglaston, L. I.—L I
20	Cohoes, N. Y.—Natl	56	Crofts, N. Y.—Am	58	Dover, Del.—Ad
58	Colchester, Conn.—Ad	58d, 83	Cromwell, Conn.—Ad	via 58	Dover, Me.—Natl
59	Colchester, N. Y.—Natl	10	Cropwell, N. J.—Ad	via 58	Dover, N. H.—Natl
11	Colchester, Vt.—Natl	5, 82	Croton, N. Y.—Am	13, 21c	Dover, N. J.—U S
11, 83	Cold Spring, L. I.—L I	56a	Croton Falls, N. Y.—Am	56a	Dover Furnace, N. Y.—Am
56, 82	Cold Spring, N. Y.—Am	53	Croton Lake, N. Y.—Am	56a	Dover Plains, N. Y.—Am
59	Cold Water, N. Y.—Am	56	Croton Landing, N. Y.—Am	95	Downing, N. Y.—Natl
35	Colebrook, Conn.—Ad	9	Crown Point, N. Y.—Natl	67	Downingtown, Pa.—Ad
68	Colebrookdale, Pa.—Ad	56	Crugers, N. Y.—Am	13c	Drakes Point, Pa.—Ad
56a	Coleman's, N. Y.—Am	69	Crum Lynne, Pa.—Ad	21c, 13	Drakesville, N. J.—U S
62	Cole's, R. I.—Ad	63	Crystal Lake, N. J.—Natl	20	Dresden, N. Y.—Natl
11, 83	College Point, L. I.—L I	59	Crystal Run, N. Y.—Natl	85	Dresden, Yates Co., N. Y.—Am
20b	Colliers, N. Y.—W F & Co	57	Cuba, N. Y.—W F & Co	13c, 10	Drifton, Pa.—Ad
10	Collingswood, N. J.—Ad	3	Cumberland, Md.—Ad; U S	40a	Dryden, N. Y.—Ad; U S
5	Collins, Mass.—Ad	52	Cumberland Mills, R. I.—Ad	13c	Dryland, Pa.—Ad
58c	Collinsville, Conn.—Ad	21, 57	Curtis, N. Y.—U S; W F & Co	20b	Duaneburgh, N. Y.—Natl
5	Coltsville, Mass.—Ad; Am	57	Curwensville, Pa.—W F & Co	20	Du Bois, Pa.—Ad; Am; Natl
63	Columbia, N. J.—Ad	41	Cutchogue, L. I.—L I	67a	Dudley, N. J.—Ad
67, 68	Columbia, Pa.—Ad	14	Cuttingsville, Vt.—Natl	17	Dummerston, Vt.—Natl
67a	Columbus, N. J.—Natl	23	Cuyler, N. Y.—Am; Natl	07	Duncannon, Pa.—Ad
via 56, 57, 67, 3	Columbus, Ohio.—Ad; Am	57	Cuylerville, N. Y.—Am; W F	57	Dundee, N. J.—W F & Co
13, 28	Communipaw, N. J.—Dodd & Co	41a	Cypress Hills, L. I.—Local	85	Dundee, N. Y.—Am
59	Community, N. J.—Natl	57	Dale, N. Y.—W F & Co	63	Dundee Lake, N. J.—Natl
50	Como, N. J.—Ad	40	Dallas, Pa.—Ad	13	Dunellen, N. J.—Ad
20	Comstock, N. Y.—Natl	5	Dalton, Mass.—Ad; Natl	57	Dunkirk, N. Y.—Am; Natl
via 58	Concord, N. H.—N Y & B	57	Dalton, N. Y.—W F & Co	63	Dunnfield, N. J.—Natl

DIRECTIONS AND EXPRESS TO VARIOUS PLACES—Continued.

For Explanation of Abbreviations used, see page 112.

21 Durnings, Pa.—U S; W F & Co	35 Ellerslie, N. Y.—Am	45, 52 Fishkill Village, N. Y. Ad; Am
58 Dunwoodie, N. Y.—Am	9 Ellicottville, N. Y.—Am	59 Fish's Eddy, N. Y. Natl
59 Durhamville, N. Y.—Natl	52 Ellington, Conn. Ad	Fitchburg, Mass. N Y & B
21a Duryea, Pa. U S	23 Elliotts, Conn.—Ad	67 Fitlers, Pa. Ad
56 Dutchess, N. Y.—Am	80 Elliottville, S. I. U S	58 Five Mile River, Conn. Ad
41 Dutch Kills, L. I. Bowron	52 Ellis, Mass.—Ad	13, 40 Flagtown, N. J. Ad
66 Duxbury, Mass.—Ad; Natl	55 Ellithorpe, Conn. Ad	13 Flanders, N. J. Ad
48 Dwights, Mass. Ad	via 58 Ellsworth, Me.—Natl	11 Flatbush, L. I. Smith's
73 Dyerville, R. I. N Y & B	13g Elm, N. J. Ad	41c Flatlands, L. I. Smith's
56a Dykemans, N. Y. Ad; Am	91 Elmer, N. J. Ad	68 Fleetwood, Pa. Ad
29 Eagle Bridge, N. Y.—Natl	85 Elmer, Pa.—Am	56a Fleetwood Park, N. Y.—Turnir
56 Eagle Harbor, N. Y.—Am	37, 21, 40 Elmira, N. Y. Ad; Am; U S	13, 40, 67b Flemington, N. J.—Ad
48 Eagleville, Conn.—Ad	13 El Mora, N. J.—Ad	40a Flemingville, N. Y. U S
85 Earle's, N. Y. Am	80 Elm Park, S. I.—U S	58c Florence, Mass. Ad; Natl
21, 50 Earlville, N. Y.—U S; Natl	58 Elmsford, N. Y. Am	67a Florence, N. J.—Ad
15 East Albany, N. Y.—Am	52 Elmwood, Conn. Ad	57 Florida, N. Y.—W F & Co
58 East Berlin, Conn.—Ad	62 Elmwood, R. I.—Ad	41, 83 Flushing, L. I. L I
21 East Bethany, N. Y.—U S	10 Elmwood Road, N. J. Ad	3 Folsom, Pa.—U S
56 East Bloomfield, N. Y.—Am	80 Eltingville, S. I.—U S	56 Fonda, N. Y.—Am; Natl
59 East Branch, N. Y.—Natl	9 Elton, N. Y.—Am	13 Ford, N. J. Ad
66 East Brewster, Mass.—N Y & B	11 Elwood, N. J. Ad	56a Fordham, N. Y. Am
13g East Bridgeton, N. J. Ad	68 Emaus, Pa.—Ad	53 Fordham Heights, N. Y.—Am
5 East Brookfield, Mass.—Ad	52 Endicott, Mass.—Ad	40 Fords, N. J.—Ad
67 East Brunswick, N. J. Ad	5 Enfield, Mass.—Ad; Natl	41c Ford's Corners, L. I.—Smiths
21, 56, 57 East Buffalo, N. Y. U S	73 Enfield, R. I.—Ad	via 67 Forest, Ohio—Ad
35 East Canaan, Conn.—Ad	58 Enfield Bridge, Conn.—Ad	57 Forest City, Pa.—W F & Co
5 East Chatham, N. Y. Am	67 Engleside, N. J.—Ad	90 Forest Glen, N. Y.—U S
39 East Chester, N. Y.—W F & Co	65 Englewood, N. J.—W F & Co	94 Forest Grove, N. J.—Ad
56 East Clarence, N. J.—Am	94 English Creek, N. J.—Ad	52 Forestville, Conn.—Ad
56 East Creek, N. Y.—Am	67c Englishtown, N. J.—Ad	57 Forestville, N. Y.—W F & Co
4 East Dorset, Vt. Natl	40a Ensenore, N. Y. Ad; U S	57 Forge, L. I. L I
52 East Douglas, Mass.—Ad	68 Ephratah, Pa.—Ad	13g Forked River, N. J. Ad
43 East Farms, Conn.—Ad	80 Erastina, S. I. U S	56 Forks, N. Y.—Am
66 East Freetown, Mass.	via 58 Erie, Pa.—Ad; Am; Natl	20 Fort Ann, N. Y.—Natl
14 East Granville, Vt.—Natl	23 Erin, N. Y.—Am; Natl	80 Fort Columbus, S. I.—U S
83 East Haddam, Conn. Ad	67c Erneston, N. J. Ad	20 Fort Edward, N. Y.—Natl
66 Eastham, Mass. N Y & B	49 Erskine, N. J.—W F & Co	11 Fort Hamilton, L. I. Kelly
75 East Hamlin, N. Y.—Am	57 Erwins, N. Y.—W F & Co	95 Fort Hunter, N. Y.—Natl
58 East Hampton, Conn.—Ad	95, 82 Esopus, N. Y.—Natl	82 Fort Lee, N. J.—By Ferry
58c Easthampton, Mass.—Ad; Natl	20b Esperance, N. Y.—Natl	95 Fort Montgomery, N. Y.—Natl
52 East Hartford, Conn.—Ad	21a Espy, Pa.—U S	56, 95 Fort Plain, N. Y.—Am; Natl
58 East Haven, Conn.—Ad	58d, 13 Essex, Conn.—Ad	83 Fort Schuyler, N. Y.—Local
41 East Hinsdale, L. I.—L I	57 Essex, N. J.—W F & Co	20 Fort Ticonderoga, N. Y.—Natl
23 East Homer, N. Y.—Am; Natl	20 Essex, N. Y. Natl	80 Fort Wadsworth, S. I.—U S
75 East Kendall, N. Y. Am	14 Essex Junction, Vt.—Natl	56 Fort Washington, N. Y.—Am
67 East Liberty, Pa.—Ad	47 Etna, N. J.—U S	via 67, 56, 57 Fort Wayne, Ind.—Ad; U S
58 East Lyme, Conn. Ad	23 Etna, N. Y.—Am; Natl	21 Foster, Pa.—Ad; U S
67 East Millstone, N. J.—Ad	75 Evans Mills, N. Y.—Am	40 Foundryville, Pa.—Ad
67a East Moorestown, N. J.—Ad	via 67 Evansville, Ind.—Ad	80 Four Corners, S. I.—U S
11, 41a, 41c East New York, L. I.—Peoples	13 Evona, N. J.—Ad	68 Frackville, Pa. Ad
58 East Norwalk, Conn.—Ad	67a Evansville, N. J.—Ad	67 Frankford, Pa. Ad
66 Easton, Mass.—Natl	13a Ewing, N. J.—Ad	56, 95 Frankfort, N. Y.—Am; Natl
13, 21c, 40 Easton, Pa.—Ad; U S	via 58 Exeter, N. H.—Natl	48 Franklin, Conn. Ad
21c East Orange, N. J.—U S	21 Factoryville, Pa.—U S	52 Franklin, Mass.—Ad
56 East Pembroke, N. Y.—Am	80 Factoryville, S. I. U S	63, 21f Franklin, N. J.—U S; W F & Co
via 58 Eastport, Me.—Intl	58 Fairfield, Conn.—Ad	80 Franklin, N. Y.—Natl
41 Eastport, L. I.—L I	67c Fairfield, N. J.—Ad	59 Franklin Iron Works, N. Y.—Nat
17 East Putney, Vt.—Natl	58 Fair Haven, Conn.—Ad	67 Franklin Park, N. J.—Ad
13 East Rahway, N. J.—Ad	66 Fairhaven, Mass.—N Y & B	94 Franklinville, N. J.—Ad
58 East River, Conn.—Ad	83 Fair Haven, N. J. Ad	via 13, 67 Fredericksburg, Va.—Ad
23 East River, N. Y.—Natl	40a Fair Haven, N. Y.—Ad; U S	9 Freedom, N. Y.—Am
41b East Rockaway, L. I.—L I	20 Fairhaven, Vt.—Natl	31, 67c Freehold, N. J.—Ad
66 East Sandwich, Mass.—N Y & B	57 Fair Lawn, N. J.—W F & Co	48 Freeland, Pa. Ad
29 East Schaghticoke, N. Y.—Natl	47 Fairmount, N. J.—U S	10 Freeman, N. J.—Ad
75 East Steuben, N. Y.—Am	51 Fairmount, N. Y.—Am	57 Freeman, Pa.—W F & Co
66 East Taunton, Mass.—N Y & B	59 Fair Oaks, N. Y.—Natl	13c, 40 Freemansburg, Pa.—Ad
52 East Thompson, Conn.—Ad	56, 95 Fairport, N. Y.—Am; Natl	via 58 Freeport, Me.—Natl
58 East View, N. Y.—Am	13g Fulton, N. J. Ad	41 Freeport, L. I.—L I
58 East Wallingford, Conn.—Ad	65 Fair View, N. J.—W F & Co	23, 40a Freeville, N. Y. Ad; Am; U S
14 East Wallingford, Vt.—Natl	20a, 40 Fairview, Pa.—Am; Ad; Am; Natl	68 French Creek, Pa.—Ad
66 East Wareham, Mass.—N Y & B	56 Falkirk, N. Y. Am	20 French Mountain, N. Y.—Natl
40b East Waverly, N. Y.—U S	85 Fall Brook, Pa. W F & Co	67b Frenchtown, N. J.—Ad
52 East Webster, Mass.—Ad	66, 83 Fall River, Mass.—Int'l; N Y & B	41 Fresh Pond, L. I.—L I
41 East Williston, L. I.—L I	40b Falls, N. Y. U S	57 Friendship, N. Y.—U S; W F
20a East Windsor, N. Y.—Natl	58 Falls, Pa.—Ad	95 Fullers, N. Y.—Natl
52 East Windsor Hill, Conn.—Ad	59 Fallsburgh, N. Y.—Natl	21, 59, 75 Fulton, N. Y.—Am; U S; Natl
21 East Winfield, N. Y.—U S	56 Falls Village, Conn.—Ad	68 Fulton, Pa.—Ad
20b East Worcester, N. Y.—Natl	66 Falmouth, Mass.—N Y & B	95 Fultonville, N. Y.—Natl
59 Eaton, N. Y.—Natl	13 Fanwood, N. J. Ad	9 Gainesville, N. Y.—Am
13g Eatontown, N. J.—Ad	40b Farmer, N. Y.—Ad; U S	13g Galilee, N. J.—Ad
40 Ebervale, Pa.—Ad	9 Farmersville, N. Y.—Am	via 56, 57 Galion, Ohio—Am
40, 13c Eckley, Pa. Ad	13g, 67c Farmingdale, N. J. Ad	35 Gallatinville, N. Y.—Am
67 Eddington, Pa.—Ad	41 Farmingdale, L. I.—L I	67 Gallitzin, Pa.—Ad
67 Edgars, N. J. Ad	58c Farmington, Conn. Ad	20 Gansevoort, N. Y.—Natl
82 Edgewater, N. J.—See "Fort Lee"	69 Farmington, Del.—Ad	67 Gap, Pa.—Ad
82 Edgewater, S. I.—Brisk; U S	via 58 Farmington, Me.—Natl	9 Garbuttsville, N. Y. Am
67a Edgewater Park, N. J.—Ad	56 Farmington, N. Y.—Am	41 Garden City, L. I.—L I
69 Edgewood, Md. Ad	41 Far Rockaway, L. I.—L I	via 58 Gardiner, Me.—Natl
87b Edgewood, N. Y.—Am	75 Felt Mills, N. Y.—Am	90 Gardiner, N. Y.—U S
10 Egg Harbor City, N. J.—Ad	58d Fenwick, Conn.—Ad	29 Gardner, Mass.—Ad; Natl
95 Elba, N. Y.—Natl	65 Ferenbaugh's N. Y.—Am	63, 57 Garfield, N. J. W F; Natl
50 Elberon, N. J.—Ad	14 Ferrisburgh, N. Y.—Natl	80 Garretsons, S. I.—U S
67, 13 Elizabeth, N. J. Ad	20 Ferrona, N. Y. Natl	56, 82 Garrisons, N. Y.—Am
13, 83 Elizabethport, N. J. Ad	67a Ferns Bush, N. Y.—Natl	56 Garwoods, N. Y.—W F & Co
67 Elizabethtown, Pa.—Ad	13 Finderne, N. J. Ad	56 Gasports, N. Y.—Am
via 57, 56, Elkhart, Ind.—U S	41 Fire Island, L. I.—L I	14 Gassetts, Vt.—Natl
85 Elkland, Pa.—Am; U S; Natl	56 Fishers, N. Y.—Am	57 Geneseo, N. Y.—U S; W F & Co
69 Elkton, Md. Ad	67a Fish House, N. J.—Ad	56, 40b Geneva, N. Y.—Ad; Am; U S
59 Ellenville, N. Y.—Natl	56, 82 Fishkill, N. Y.—Am	40a Genoa, N. Y.—Ad; U S

DIRECTIONS AND EXPRESS TO VARIOUS PLACES—Continued.

For Explanation of Abbreviations used, see page 112.

59	Genung, N. Y.—Natl	58, 83	Greenwich, Conn.—Ad	13c	Hauto, Pa.—Ad; U S
11	Georgia, Vt.—Natl	5	Greenwich, Mass.—Ad	via 58	Haverhill, Mass.—Ad; Natl
73	Georgiaville, R. I.—N Y & B	13g	Greenwich, N. J.—Ad; U S	17, 82	Haverstraw, N. Y.—U S; Natl
30a	Georgetown, Conn.—Ad	02	Greenwich, R. I.—Ad	95	Haverstraw Village, N. Y.—Natl
68	Georgetown, Del.—Ad	60	Greenwood, Del.—Ad	69, 3	Havre-de-Grace, Md.—Ad
10	Germania, N. J.—Ad	62	Greenwood, R. I.—Ad	50	Hawley, N. Y.—Natl
13g	Germania, Ocean Co., N. J.—Ad	19	Greenwood Lake—W. F. & Co	37	Hawley, Pa.—W F & Co
56, 82	Germantown, N. Y.—Am	21	Greigsville, N. Y.—U S	36, 36a	52 Hawleyville, Conn.—Ad
13a	Germantown, Pa.—Ad	57	Greycourt, N. Y.—W F & Co	95	Haworth, N. J.—Natl
67	Germantown June., Pa.—Ad	29	Greylock, Mass.—Natl	57	Hawthorne, N. J.—W F & Co
13	German Valley, N. J.—Ad	52	Greystone, Conn.—Ad	58	Haydens, Conn.—Ad
47	Germonds, N. Y.—U S	87	Griffin's Corners, N. Y.—Am	58c	Haydenville, Mass.—Ad; Natl
56	Getzville, N. Y.—Am	83	Griggstown, N. J.—Ad	75	Haywards, N. Y.—Am
56a	Ghent, N. Y.—Am	56	Grimesville, N. Y.—Am	13c	Hazard, Pa.—Ad; U S
80	Giffords, N. Y.—U S	57	Griswold, N. Y.—W F & Co	58	Hazardville, Conn.—U S
5	Gilbertville, Mass.—Ad	52	Grosvenordale, Conn.—Ad	36	Hazlet, N. J.—Ad
83	Gildersleeve's Conn.—Ad	62	Groton, Conn.—Ad	40	Hazleton, Pa.—Ad
21c	Gilette, N. J.—U S	40a	Groton, N. Y.—Ad; U S	40	Hazleton Shops, Pa.—Ad
71	Gilman's, N. Y.—W F & Co	58	Grove Beach, Conn.—Ad	95	Hecla, N. Y.—Natl
40	Girardville, Pa—Ad	21	Groveland, N. Y.—U S	67a	Helmetta, N. J.—Ad
68	Glasgow, Pa.—Ad	20b	Guilderland, N. Y.—Natl	41	Hempstead, L. I.—L I
91	Glassboro, N. J.—Ad	65	Guilderland Centre, N. Y.—Natl	57, 95	Henrietta, N. Y.—Am; W F & Co
83	Glastonbury, Conn.—Ad	58	Guilford, Conn.—Ad	21	Henryville, Pa.—U S
58	Glenbrook, Conn.—Ad	59	Guilford, N. J.—Ad	36	Herkimer, N. Y.—Am; Natl
21	Glenburn, Pa—U S	59	Guilford Centre, N. Y.—Natl	68	Herndon, Pa.—Ad
68	Glen Carbon, Pa.—Ad	95	Granville, N. Y.—Natl	57	Herrick Centre, Pa.—W F & Co
11, 83	Glen Cove, L. I.—L I	6	Gunthersville, L. I.—Remsen	75	Hess Road, N. Y.—Am
36	Glendale, Mass.—Ad	28	Guttenburg, N. J.—Hudson Co	75	Heuvelton, N. Y.—Am
75	Glendale, N. J.—Am	57	Guymard, N. Y.—W F & Co	49	Hewitt, N. J.—W F & Co
11	Glendale, L. I.—L I	47, 63, 95	Hackensack, N. J.—U S; Natl	41	Hewletts, L. I.—L I
10, 13g	Glendon, Pa.—Ad	21c	Hackettstown, N. J.—U S	10	Hickory Run, Pa.—Ad
13	Glen Gardner, N. J.—Ad; U S	58d	Haddam, Conn.—Ad	21a	Hicks Ferry, Pa.—U S
52, 15	Glenham, N. Y.—Am	10	Hahnville, N. J.—Ad	41	Hicksville, L. I.—L I
41	Glen Head, L. I.—L I	1	Hadley, N. Y.—Natl	58d	Higganum, Conn.—Ad
83	Glen Island, N. Y.—Ad	58d, 83	Hadlyme, Conn.—Ad	87	Higginsville, N. Y.—Natl
67	Glen Loch, Pa.—Ad	62	Hainesburg, N. J.—Ad	13	High Bridge, N. J.—Ad; U S
60	Glenloden, Pa.—Ad	87a	Haines Corners, N. Y.—Am	58, 53	High Bridge, N. Y.—Am; Turnr
10	Glen Onoko, Pa.—Ad	67a	Hainesport, N. J.—Ad	14	Highgate Springs, Vt.—Natl
21c	Glen Ridge, N. J.—U S	87	Halcottville, N. Y.—Am; Natl	95	Highland, N. Y.—Natl
50	Glen Falls, N. Y.—Natl	57	Hales Eddy, N. Y.—W F & Co	13g	Highland Beach, N. J.—Ad; U S
20a	Glenside, Pa.—Ad	10a	Half Acre, N. Y.—U S	52	Highland Lake, Mass.—Ad
40	Glen Summit, Pa.—Ad	57	Halfmoon, N. Y.—Ad	58	Highland Mills, N. Y.—W F & Co
83	Glen Wood, L. I.—L I	66	Halifax, Mass.—Ad; Natl	83	Highlands, N. J.—Ad
56	Glenwood, N. Y.—Am	via 58	Halifax, N. S.—Adams	56	Highlands, N. Y.—Am
via 58	Gloucester, Mass.—Ad; Natl	via 58	Hallowell, Me.—Natl	67a	Hightstown, N. J.—Ad
91	Gloucester, N. J.—Ad	13c	Halls, Pa.—Ad	65	Highwood, N. J.—W F & Co
30	Gloversville, N. Y.—Am	56	Hall's Station, N. Y.—Am	57	Hillburn, N. Y.—W F & Co
56a	Golden's Bridge, N. Y.—Am	51	Halstead's, N. Y.—Am	47	Hillsdale, N. J.—U S
41	Good Ground, L. I.—L I	68	Hamburg, Pa.—Ad	56a	Hillsdale, N. Y.—Am
58a, 83	Goodspeeds, Conn.—Ad	63, 39	Hamburg, N. J.—Natl	62	Hills Grove, R. I.—Ad
57	Goshen, N. Y.—W F & Co	85	Hamden, N. Y.—Am	56	Himrod's, N. Y.—Ad; Am
21	Gouldsboro, Pa.—U S	13a	Hamilton, N. J.—Ad; U S	66	Hingham, Mass.—Ad
75	Gouverneur, N. Y.—Am	59	Hamilton, N. Y.—Natl; W F & Co	5	Hinsdale, Mass.—Ad
83	Governor's Isl., N. Y.—By Boat	75	Hamlin, N. Y.—Am	57	Hinsdale, N. Y.—Am; W F & Co
40	Gowen, Pa.—Ad	51	Hammels, L. I.—L I	58c	Hitchcock's, Conn.—Ad
3	Grafton, W. Va.—U S	68	Hammon, Pa.—Ad	87	Hobart, N. Y.—Am; Natl
58c	Granby, Conn.—Ad	75	Hammond, N. Y.—Am	28	Hoboken, N. J.—Dodd & C.
87	Grand Gorge, N. Y.—Am; Natl	10	Hammonton, N. J.—Ad	57	Hodgeville, N. Y.—W F & Co
87	Grand Hotel Station, N. Y.—Am	52	Hampton, Conn.—Ad	57	Hoffman, N. Y.—W F & Co
via 57, 56	Grand Rapids, Mich.—Ad; Am	via 58	Hampton, Mass.—Ad; Am	67c	Hoffman's, N. J.—Ad
65	Grandview, N. Y.—W F & Co	57	Hampton, N. Y.—W F & Co	56	Hoffman's, N. Y.—Am
80	Graniteville, S. I.—U S	57	Hancock, Conn.—Ad	57	Hohokus, N. J.—W F & Co
69	Grant City, S. I.—U S	57, 59	Hancock, N. Y.—Natl; W F & Co	40	Hokendauqua, Pa.—Ad
65	Granton, N. J.—W F & Co	57	Hankins, N. Y.—W F & Co	66	Holbrook, Mass.—Ad
35	Grant's, Conn.—Ad	75	Hannibal, N. Y.—Am	41	Holbrook, L. I.—L I
20	Granville, N. Y.—Natl	67a	Hanover, N. J.—Ad	75	Holland Patent, N. Y.—Am
80	Grasmere, S. I.—U S	13c	Hanover, Pa.—Ad	51	Hollands, L. I.—L I
59	Gratwick, N. Y.—Am	75	Harbor, N. Y.—Natl	67b	Holland Station, N. J.—Ad
72, 55, 6	Gravesend, L. I.—Remsen	10a	Harford, N. Y.—Ad	56	Holley, N. Y.—Am
60	Gray's Ferry, Pa.—Ad	10a	Harford Mills, N. Y.—Ad	11	Hollis, L. I.—L I
36	Great Barrington, Mass.—Ad	30	Harkness, N. Y.—Natl	67	Holmesburg, Pa.—Ad
75	Great Bend, N. Y.—Am	13a	Harlingen, N. J.—Ad; U S	67	Holmesburg June., Pa.—Ad
21, 57	Great Bend, Pa.—U S	67b	Harmony, N. J.—Ad	78c	Holyoke, Mass.—Ad; Natl
80	Great Kills, S. I.—U S	3	Harper's Ferry, W. Va.—U S	21	Homer, N. Y.—U S
30	Great Meadows, N. J.—W F & Co	20b	Harpersville, N. Y.—Natl	65	Homestead, N. J.—W F & Co
11, 83	Great Neck, L. I.—L I	95	Harrington, Del.—Ad	40	Homesville, Pa.—Ad
57	Great Notch, N. J.—W F & Co	95	Harrington, N. J.—Natl	10	Home's Ferry, Pa.—Ad
57	Great Valley, N. Y.—W F & Co	13g	Harris, N. J.—Ad; U S	30	Homowack, N. Y.—Natl
75	Greece, N. Y.—U S; Am	1	Harrisburg, N. Y.—Natl	59	Honeoye Falls, N. Y.—Am
50, 5	Greenbush, N. Y.—Am	67, 68	Harrisburg, Pa.—Ad	57	Honesdale, Pa.—Natl; W F & Co
21	Greene, N. Y.—U S	57, 67, 21c	Harrison, N. J.—Ad; U S	57	Hooper, N. Y.—W F & Co
52	Greene, R. I.—Ad	78	Harrison, N. Y.—Ad	29	Hoosick, N. Y.—Natl
52	Greeneville, Conn.—Ad	85	Harrison Valley, Pa.—Ad	29	Hoosick Falls, N. Y.—Natl
17	Greenfield, Mass.—Ad; Nat	78	Hardville, R. I.—Am	29	Hoosick June., N. Y.—Natl
7	Greenfield, L. I.—Remsen	67a	Hurrowgate, N. J.—Ad	21c	Horoseheads, N. Y.—U S
1	Greenfield, N. Y.—Natl	28	Harsimus Cove, N. J.—Dodd&C.	13c	Horse, Pa.—Ad; U S
52	Green Haven, N. Y.—Ad	58, 52, 83	Hartford, Conn.—Ad; Int'l	62	Hope, R. I.—Ad
30	Green Island, N. Y.—Am; Natl	67a	Hartford, N. J.—Ad	83	Hope, N. J.—Ad
11	Greenlawn, L. I.—L I	11	Hartford, Vt.—Natl	13a	Hopewell, N. J.—Ad
28	Greenpoint, N. Y.—Bowron	14	Hartland, Vt.—Natl	18, 52	Hopewell June., N. Y.—Ad; Am
11, 83	Greenport, L. I.—L I	56a	Hartsdale, N. Y.—Am	13g	Hopping, N. J.—Ad; U S
80	Green Ridge, S. I.—U S	28	Harts Island, N. Y.—Ad	52	Hop River, Conn.—Ad
59	Green Ridge, Pa.—U S; Natl	20b	Hartwick, N. Y.—Natl	59	Hornellsville, N. Y.—U S
67	Greensburg, Pa.—Ad	71	Hartwood, N. Y.—W F & Co	57	Hornerstown, N. J.—Ad
56	Green's Corners, N. Y.—Am	86	Harvey Centre, N. J.—Ad	13c	Horn's Springs, Pa.—Ad; U S
58	Green's Farms, Conn.—Ad	40	Harveys Lake, Pa.—Ad	23	Horseheads, N. Y.—U S
62	Greenville, L. I.—L I	66	Harwich, Mass.—Ad	21c	Horton, N. J.—U S
via 58	Greenville, Me.—Ad; Natl	56, 82	Hastings, Westc. Co., N. Y.—Am	25	Hoskins, Conn.—Ad
13	Greenville, N. J.—Ad	17	Hatfield, Mass.—Ad	57	Houghton Farm, N. Y.—W F

DIRECTIONS AND EXPRESS TO VARIOUS PLACES—Continued.

For Explanation of Abbreviations used, see page 112.

via 58 Houlton, Me.—Natl	75 Keene's, N. Y.—Am	87a Laurel House Station, N. Y.—Am
36 Housatonic, Mass.—Ad	20b Kelley's, N. Y.—Natl	13c Laurel Run, Pa.—Ad; U S
67 Hontenville, N. J.—Ad	87 Kelly's Corners, N. Y.—Am	40 Laury's, Pa.—Ad
66 Howard, R. I.—Ad	75 Kendall, N. J.—Ad	73 Lavallette, N. J.—Ad
67c Howell's, N. J.—Ad	29 Kendall, Pa.—Am; Natl	via 58 Lawrence, Mass.—N Y & B
57 Howell's, N. Y.—W F & Co	via 58 Kennebunk, Me.—N Y & B	67 Lawrence, N. J.—Ad
20b Howe's Cave, N. Y.—Natl	40 Kennedy, N. J.—Ad	41 Lawrence, L. I.—L I
57 Hoytville, Pa.—W F & Co	56a Kensico, N. J.—Am	12 Lawrenceville, N. Y.—Am
21 Hubbardsville, N. Y.—U S	57 Kensington, N. Y.—W F & Co	57 Lawrenceville, Pa.—Ad; Am
56, 82 Hudson, N. Y.—Am	67 Kensington, Pa.—Ad	67 Leaman Place, Pa.—Ad
28 Hudson City, N. J.—Dodd & C	36 Kent, Conn.—Ad	via 57 Leavittsburg, Ohio.—W F & Co
5 Hudson, Upper, N. Y.—Am	via 57 Kent, Ohio—Am	48 Lebanon, Conn.—Ad
71 Huguenot, N. Y.—W F & Co	13 Kenvil, N. J.—Ad	13 Lebanon, N. J.—Ad
80 Huguenot, S. I.—U S	85 Keuka Mills, N. Y.—Am	68 Lebanon, Pa.—Ad
75 Humaston, N. Y.—Am	50 Key East, N. J.—Ad	38 Lebanon Springs, N. Y.—Natl
68 Hummelstown, Pa.—Ad	31, 83 Keyport, N. J.—Ad	36 Lee, Mass.—Ad
87b Hunter, N. Y.—Am; Natl	21 Killawog, N. Y.—U S	58c Leeds, Mass.—Ad; Natl
28 Hunter's Point, L. I.—Bowron	9 Killbuck, N. Y.—Am	12 Leeds, N. Y.—Am
67 Huntingdon, Pa.—Ad	68 Kimberton, Pa.—Ad	13c Leemine, Pa.—Ad
5 Huntington, Mass.—Ad ; Natl	57 Kimbles, Pa.—W F & Co	67 Leesport, Pa.—Ad
41, 83 Huntington, L. I.—L I	5 Kinderhook, N. Y.—Am	58 Leetes Island, Conn.—Ad
21c Huntly, N. J.—U S	1 Kings, N. Y.—Natl	21 Lehigh, Pa.—U S
57 Hunts, N. Y.—W F & Co	30 Kingsboro, N. Y.—Am	40, 13c Lehigh Gap, Pa.—Ad
58 Hunts Point, N. Y.—Ad	53, 56 Kings Bridge, N. Y.—Am	40, 13c Lehighton, Pa.—Ad
13 Hurd, N. J.—Ad ; U S	40b Kings Ferry, N. Y.—Ad; U S	21 Leicester, N. Y.—U S
59 Hurleyville, N. Y.—Natl	7, 72,40c, 55 Kings Highway, L. I.—Local	14 Leicester Junction, Vt.—Natl
15 Husted, N. Y.—Am	21c Kingsland, N. J.—U S	36 Lenox, Mass.—Ad
67b Hutchinson's, N. J.—Ad	21 Kingsley, Pa.—U S	36 Lenox Furnace, Mass.—Ad
66 Hyannis, Mass.—N Y & B	68 Kingston, N. J.—Ad	58 Leonard's Bridge, Conn.—Ad
52 Hyde Park, Mass.—Ad	67 Kingston, N. J.—Ad	65 Leonia, N. J.—W F & Co
56, 82 Hyde Park, N. Y.—Am; Natl	95, 82 Kingston, N. Y.—Am; Natl	57, 56 Le Roy, N. Y.—Am; U S
41 Hyde Park, L. I.—L I	21 Kingston, Pa.—Ad; U S	40b Levanna, N. Y.—Ad; U S
20b Hyndsville, N. Y.—Natl	62 Kingston, R. I.—Ad	48 Leverett, Mass.—Ad
56, 95 Ilion, N. Y.—Am ; Natl	67a Kinkora, N. J.—Ad	40 Leviston, Pa.—Ad
67a Imlaystown, N. J.—Ad	40a Kinslers, N. Y.—U S	49 Lewes, Del.—Ad
via 67, 56, 57, 3 Indianapolis, Ind.—Ad; Am ; U S	67 Kinzers, Pa.—Ad	13c Lewisburg, Pa.—Ad
95 Indian Castle, N. Y.—Natl	57 Kinzua, Pa.—W F & Co	57 Lewis Run, Pa.—W F & Co
5 Indian Orchard, Mass.—Ad	57 Kipps, N. Y.—W F & Co	via 58 Lewiston, Me.—Natl
1 Indian River, N. Y.—Natl	59 Kirkland, N. Y.—Natl	56, 75 Lewiston, N. Y.—Am
58c Ingleside, Mass.—Ad	95, 56 Kirkville, N. Y.—Am; Natl	67b Lewtown, N. J.—Ad
41 Inwood, L. I.—L I	10 Kirkwood, N. J.—Ad	75 Leyden, N. Y.—Am
56 Inwood, N. Y.—Am ; Morris	57 Kirkwood, N. Y.—W F & Co	59 Liberty, N. Y.—Natl
94 Iona, N. J.—Ad	59 Kitchawan, N. Y.—Am	via 21c Liberty Corner, N. J.—Ad
94, 82 Iona Island, N. Y.—Natl	67 Kittanning Point, Pa.—Ad	59 Liberty Falls, N. Y.—Natl
via 58 Ipswich, Mass.—Ad ; Natl	56 Knoxville, N. Y.—Am	67 Lilly, Pa.—Ad
40a Ira, N. Y.—Ad ; U S	85 Knoxville, Pa.—Am; U S; Natl	via 67, 57 Lima, Ohio.—Ad
21c Ironia, N. J.—U S	41c Kowenhovens, L. I.—Smith's	75 Limerick, N. Y.—Am
9 Irvine Mills, N. Y.—Am	80 Kreischerville, S. I.—U S	21a Lime Ridge, Pa.—U S
57 Irving, N. Y.—Am	68 Kutztown, Pa.—Ad	36 Lime Rock, Conn.—Ad
56, 82 Irvington, N. Y.—Am	40 Laceyville, Pa.—Ad	9 Lime Rock, N. Y.—Am
67 Irwin, Pa.—Ad	21a Lackawanna, Pa.—U S	57 Limestone, N. Y.—Am; W F & Co
67 Iselin, N. J.—Ad	57 Lackawaxen, Pa.—W F & Co	21c Lincoln Park, N. J.—U S
41 Islip, L. I.—L I	86 Lacy, N. J.—Ad	9 Lincoln P'rk, N. Y.—Am
21, 23, 40b Ithaca, N. Y.—Ad ; Am; U S	75 Lafargeville, N. Y.—Am	67 Linden, N. J.—Ad
via 57, 56 Jackson, Mich.—Am ; U S	13c Lafayette, N. J.—Dodd & C.	57 Linden, N. Y.—W F & Co
62 Jackson, R. I.—Ad	20a Laflin, Pa.—U S	9 Lindley, N. Y.—Am
95 Jacksonburgh, N. Y.—Natl	45 Lagrange, N. Y.—Am	68 Linfield, Pa.—Ad
35 Jackson Corners, N. Y.—Am	40 La Grange, Pa.—Ad	83 Lindenmuville, N. Y.—U S
40c Jacksons, N. Y.—Am	78 Lake, Conn.—Ad	69 Linwood, Pa.—Ad
41, 4a Jamaica, L. I.—L I	39 Lake George, N. Y.—Natl	68 Lionville, Pa.—Ad
67a 67c Jamesburg, N. J.—Ad	12-21c Lake Hopatcong, N. J.—Ad; U S	78, 58a Lisle, N. Y.—U S
41 Jamesport, L. I.—L I	1 Lake Katrine, N. Y.—Natl	21 Litchfield, Conn.—Ad
via 57 Jamestown, N. Y.—Am.; Natl	1 Lake Luzerne, N. Y.—Natl	21 Litchfield, N. Y.—U S
5 Jamesville, Mass.—Ad	53, 56a Lake Mahopac, N. Y.—Am	59 Lititz, Pa.—Ad
21 Jamesville, N. Y.—U S	90 Lake Minnewaska, N. Y.—U S	49, 21c Little Falls, N. J.—W F & Co
40 Jenusville, Pa.—Ad	90 Lake Mohonk, N. Y.—U S	56, 95 Little Falls, N. Y.—Am; Natl
40, 13c Jeddo, Pa.—Ad	15, 64 Lake Placid, N. Y.—Natl	63, 95 Little Ferry, N. J.—Natl
18a Jenkintown, Pa.—Ad	40b Lake Ridge, N. Y.—U S	41 Little Neck, L. I.—L I
20a Jermyn, Pa.—U S; Natl	10 Lakeside, N. J.—Ad	59 Little Silver, N. J.—Ad
56a Jerome Park, N. Y.—Ames	23 Lakeside, Mad'n Co., N. Y.—Natl	57 Little Valley, N. Y.—W F & Co
28 Jersey City, N. J.—Dodd & Co	75 Lake Side, N. Y.—Am	21 Little York, N. Y.—U S
1 Jessup's Landing, N. Y.—Natl	57 Lake View, N. J.—W F & Co	75 Liverpool, N. Y.—Am
52 Jewett City, Conn.—Ad	35 Lakeville, Conn.—Ad	56 Livingston, N. Y.—Am
67a Jobstown, N. J.—Ad	78 Lake Waramaug, Conn.—Ad	80 Livingston, S. I.—U S
1 Johnsburg, N. Y.—U S, Natl	13g Lakewood, N. J.—Ad; U S	59 Livingston Manor, N. Y.—Natl
57 Johnsenburg, Pa.—Ad; W F & Co	67b Lambertville, N. J.—Ad	57 Livonia, N. Y.—W F & Co
20b Johnson's, N. Y.—Natl	29 Lamokin, Pa.—Ad	21 Llanwellwyn, Pa.—U S
29 Johnsonville, N. Y.—Natl	21 Lancaster, N. Y.—U S	83 Llewellyn, N. J.—Ad
30 Johnstown, N. Y.—Am	21, 57 Lancaster, Pa.—U S; W F & Co	83 Lloyd's Dock, N. Y.—U S
67 Johnstown, Pa.—Ad	67 Lancaster, Pa.—Ad	59 Lochiel, Pa.—Ad
95 Jones' Point, N. Y.—Natl	68 Landingville, Pa.—Ad	40a Locke, N. Y.—Ad; U S
68 Jonestown, Pa.—Ad	13g Landisville, Pa.—Ad	56, 57 Lockport, N. Y.—Am; W F & Co
20b Jonesville, N. Y.—Natl	67 Landisville, Pa.—Ad	13c Lockport, Pa.—Ad
5 Jonesville, N. Y.—Natl	57 Landrus, Pa.—W F & Co	40b Lockwood, N. Y.—Ad; U S
56, 95 Jordan, N. Y.—Am; Natl	40 Lansdown, N. J.—Ad	41 Locust Grove, L. I.—Reusen
78 Judd's Bridge, Conn.—Ad	58c Lanesborough, Pa.—U S; Natl	10 Locust Grove, N. J.—Ad
67a Juliustown, N. J.—Ad	30 Lanesville, Conn.—Ad	83 Locust Point, N. J.—Ad
40 Juniard, N. J.—Ad	87b Lanesville, N. Y.—Am	41 Locust Valley, L. I.—L I
87a Kaaterskill, N. Y.—Am; Natl	12a Langhorne, Pa.—Ad	47 Lodi, N. J.—U S
via 56, 57 Kalamazoo, Mich.—Am; U S	13c Lansford, Pa.—Ad; U S	10 Lodi, N. J.—Ad
63 Kalarama, N. J.—Ad	20 Lausingburgh, N. Y.—Natl	41b Long Beach, L. I.—L I
57, 21 Kanona, N. Y.—U S; W F & Co	20 Lapham's Mills, N. Y.—Natl	50, 13g, 83 Long Branch, N. J.—Ad; U S
56 Karner, N. Y.—Am	21 La Plume, Pa.—U S	30 Long Bridge, N. J.—W F & Co
75 Kasong, N. Y.—Am	58 Larchmont, N. Y.—Am	57 Long Eddy, N. Y.—W F & Co
13c Katellen, N. J.—Am; U S	57, 56 La Salle, N. Y.—Am; W F & Co	36 Long Hill, Conn.—Ad
56a Katonah, N. Y.—Am	50 Larson's Corners, N. Y.—Natl	28 Long Island City, L. I.—Bowron
49 Kearney, N. J.—W F & Co	67 Latrobe, Pa.—Ad	1 Long Lake, N. Y.—Natl
17 Keene, N. H.—Natl	41 Laurel Hill, L. I.—Weed & P	85 Long Point, N. Y.—Am

DIRECTIONS AND EXPRESS TO VARIOUS PLACES—Continued.

For Explanation of Abbreviations used, see page 112.

10	Long Port, N. J.—Ad	67b	Martin's Creek, N. J.—Ad	13c	Milton, Pa. Ad
13g	Long Beach, N. J.—Ad	57	Martinsville, N. Y.—W F & Co	11	Milton, Vt. Natl
74	Lonsdale, R. I.—Ad.	40a	Martville, N. Y.—Ad ; U S	95	Mindonville, N. Y.—Natl
56	Loonyville, N. Y.—Am	20b	Maryland, N. Y. Natl	41	Mineola, L. I. L I
15	Loon Lake, N. Y. Natl	67	Maryville, Pa.—Ad	67	Mineral Point, Pa.—Ad
57	Lordville, N. Y.—W F & Co	67a	Masonville, N. J. Ad	68	Minersville, Pa.—Ad
28	Losings, N. Y. Natl	11	Maspeth, L. I. L I	1	Minerva, N. Y. Natl
40	Lost Creek, Pa—Ad	48	Massapequa, Conn. Ad	13	Minisink, N. J.—Ad
via 67, 56, 57, 3	Louisville, Ky.—Ad	75	Messena Springs, N. Y. Am	20a	Minooka, Pa.—U S
21	Lounsberry, N. Y. U S	69	Masseys, Md.—Ad	95	Mohawk, N. Y.—Am
via 58	Lowell, Mass.—N Y & B	57	Mast Hope, Pa. W F & Co	20b	Mohawk, N. Y. Natl
67a	Lower Bordentown, N. J. Ad	50, 83	Matawan, N. J. Ad	48	Mohegan, Conn. Ad
13c	Lower Catasauqua, Pa. Ad	52	Mattapan, Mass. Ad ; Natl	68	Mohrsville, Pa. Ad
67c	Lower Jamesburg, N. J. Ad	66	Mattapoisette, Mass.—N Y & B	64	Moira, N. Y.—Am
53	Lowerre, N. Y. Am	52, 45	Matteawan, N. Y. Am	13g	Monmouth Beach, N. J.—Ad
21	Lowmanville, N. Y. U S	41	Mattituck, L. I. L I	67	Monmouth Junc., N. J. Ad
13g	Low Moor, N. J. Ad	40, 13c	Mauch Chunk, Pa.—Ad	68	Monocacy, Pa.—Ad
56	Low Point, N. Y.—Am	13	Maurers, N. J. Ad	39	Monroe, N. J.—U S
75	Lowville, N. Y. Am	94	Maurice River, N. J. Ad	57	Montow, N. Y. W F & Co
5	Ludlow, Mass.—Ad	13g	Mauricetown, N. J. Ad ; U S	65	Monsey, N. Y. W F & Co
76	Ludlow, N. Y.—Am	86	Mayeta, N. J.—Ad	48	Monson, Mass.—Ad
11	Ludlow, Vt.—Natl	30	Mayfield, N. Y. Am	18	Montague, Mass. Ad ; Natl
10b	Ludlowville, N. Y. Ad ; U S	94	May's Landing, N. J. Ad	21c, 19	Montclair, N. J.—U S; W F
67c	Lumberton, N. J. Ad	63	Maywood, N. J. Natl	19	Montclair Heights, N. J. W F
1	Luxerne, N. J. Natl	39	McAfee, N. J. W F & Co	95	Montezuma, N. Y. Natl
40	Luzerne, Pa. U S	75, 23	McConnellsville, N. Y. Am	57	Montgomery, N. Y. U S
58, 83	Lyme, Conn. Ad	23	McLean, N. Y. Am	13c	Montgomery, Pa. Ad
21c	Lyndhurst, N. J. U S	57	McNair, N. Y. W F & Co	57	Monticello, N. Y. W F & Co
75	Lyndonville, N. Y. Am	67	McVeytown, Pa. Ad	13c	Mortonsville, Pa. Ad
via 58	Lynn, Mass. Ad ; Natl; N Y & B	59	Meadow Brook, N. Y. Natl	58	Montowese, Conn. Ad
15	Lyon Mountain, N. Y. Natl	67	Meadows, N. J. Ad	14	Montpelier, Vt. Natl
21c	Lyons, N. J. U S	via 57	Meadville, Pa. Ad ; W F & Co	20, 14	Montoud, Que. Natl
56, 95	Lyons, N. Y. Am; Natl	59	Mechanicstown, N. Y. Natl	56	Montrose, N. Y.—Am
68	Lyons, Pa. Ad	52	Mechanicsville, Conn. Ad	21	Montrose, Pa. Ad; U S
56, 95	Macedon, N. Y. Am; Natl	20	Mechanicville, N. Y. Natl	47	Montvale, N. J.—U S
9	Machias, N. Y. Am	67a	Medford, N. J. Ad	48	Montville, Conn. Ad
8	Macombs Dam, N. Y. Am	41	Medford, L. I. L I	20	Moores Junc., N. Y. Natl
68	Macungie, Pa. Ad	69	Media, Pa. Ad	13c	Moores, N. J. Ad
58	Madison, Conn. Ad	56	Medina, N. Y. Am	67b	Moore's, N. J. Ad
21c	Madison, N. J. U S	40	Mehoopany, Pa. Ad	20a	Moosic, Pa. U S
69	Magnolia, Md. Ad	5	Mellenville, N. Y. Am	52	Moosup, Conn. Ad
40, 13c	Mahanoy City, Pa. Ad	52	Melrose, Conn. Ad	10a	Moravia, N. Y. U S
13c	Mahanoy Plain, Pa. Ad	10	Melrose, N. J. Ad	85	Moreland, N. Y. Am
53	Mahopac Falls, N. Y. Am	56a	Melrose, N. Y. Natl	41	Moriches, L. I. L I
57	Mahwah, N. J. W F & Co	57	Melrose, N. Y. Am	36a	Morrisania, N. Y. Am
94	Malaga, N. J. Ad	20a	Melrose, Pa. W F & Co	58, 56	Morris Dock, N. Y. Am
95, 82	Malden, N. Y. Natl	95, 56	Memphis, N. Y. Am; Natl	15	Morrisonville, N. Y. Natl
75	Mallory, N. Y. Am	67	Menlo Park, L. I. L I	11a	Morris Park, L. I. L I
21a	Maltby, Pa.—U S	67a	Merchantville, N. J. Ad	21c	Morris Plains, N. J. U S
67	Malvern, Pa Ad	58	Meriden, Conn. Ad ; Int'l	57	Morris Run, Pa. W F & Co
58, 83	Mamaroneck, N. Y. Ad	68, 67	Merion, Pa. Ad	21c	Morristown, N. J. U S
86	Manahawken, N. J. Ad	41	Merrick, L. I. L I	75	Morrisville, N. Y. Am
50, 67c	Manasquan, N. J. Ad	40a	Merrifield, N. Y. Ad ; U S	59	Morrisville, N. Y. Natl
68	Manatawny, Pa. Ad	48	Merwinsville, Conn. Ad	67	Morrisville, Pa. Ad
13a	Manayunk, Pa. Ad	53	Mertins, N. Y. Am	21	Moscow, Pa. U S
52	Manchester, Conn. Ad	68	Mertztown, Pa. Ad	53	Mosholu, N. Y. Am
via 58	Manchester, Mass. Ad	36	Merwinsville, Conn. Ad	56a, 58	Mott Haven, N. Y. Am
via 58	Manchester, N. H. N Y & B	10	Meshoppen, Pa. Ad	59	Mountain Dale, N. Y. Natl
13g	Manchester, N. J. Ad; U S	67	Metuchen, N. J. Ad	12	Moun'n House Sta, N. Y. Am
1	Manchester, Vt. Natl	75	Mexico, N. Y. Am	21c	Mountain Station, N. J. U S
41c	Manhattan Beach, L. I. L I	67	Mexico, Pa. Ad	21c, 49	Mountain View, N.J. W F & Co
via 56	Manhattanville, N. Y. Am	66	Middleboro, Mass.—Ad	57	Mountainville, N. Y. W F & Co
56	Manlius, N. Y. Am; Natl	11	Middlebury, Vt. Natl	67b	Mount Airy, N. J. Ad
85	Manlius Centre, N. Y. Natl	67	Middlefield, N. J. Ad	52	Mount Bowdoin, Mass. Ad
75	Mannsville, N. Y. Am	58	Middlefield, Conn. Ad	68	Mount Carbon, Pa. Ad
41	Manor, L. I. L I	5	Middlefield, Mass. Ad	58c	Mount Carmel, Conn. Ad
48	Mansfield, Conn.—Ad	20	Middle Granville, N. Y.—Natl	40, 13c	Mount Carmel, Pa.—Ad
via 57, 67, 3	Mansfield, Ohio Ad	83	Middle Haddam, Conn. Ad	67a	Mount Holly, N. J. Ad
57	Mansfield, Pa. Ad; W F & Co	56	Middleport, N. Y. Am	14	Mount Holly, Vt. Natl
67a	Mantoloking, N. J.—Ad	14	Middlesex, Vt. Natl	58	Mount Hope, N. Y. Am
74	Manton, R. I.—Ad	58, 58d, 83	Middletown, Conn. Ad	57	Mount Jewett, Pa. W F & Co
94	Manunusink, N. J. Ad	69	Middletown, Del. Ad	67	Mount Joy, Pa. Ad
21, 67b	Manunka Chunk, N. J. U S	67a	Middletown, N. J. Ad	56a	Mount Kisco, N. Y. Am
74	Manville, R. I.—Ad	57, 59, 63	Middletown, N. Y. Natl	95	Mount Marion, N. Y. Natl
5	Maple Grove, Mass.—Ad	67	Middletown, Pa. Ad	21, 57	Mount Morris, N. Y. Am; U S
11	Maple Grove, L. I. L I	13	Middle Valley, N. J. Ad	31	Mount Pleasant, N. J. Ad
67a	Maple Shade, N. J. Ad	69	Midland Park, N. J. Ad	94	Mount Pleasant, N. J. Ad
40a	Mapleton, N. Y. Ad; U S	57	Midmond, Pa. W F & Co	87	Mount Pleasant, N. Y. Am
41c	Mapleton, L. I. Remsen	19	Midvale, N. J. U S ; W F & Co	21	Mount Pocono, Pa. U S
21c	Maplewood, N. J.—U S	67	Mifflin, Pa.—Ad	56a	Mount Vigo, N. Y. Am
95	Maplewood, N. Y. Am; Natl	40	Milan, Pa. Ad	35	Mount Ross, N. Y. Am
21	Marathon, N. Y. U S	21c	Milburn, N. J. U S	56	Mount St. Vincent, N. Y.—Am
via 58	Marblehead, Mass. Ad; Natl	58	Milford, Conn. Ad	21c	Mount Tabor, N. J. U S
56	Marcellus, N. Y. Am	30b	Milford, N. Y. Natl	48	Mount Tobey, Mass. Ad
75	Marcy, N. Y.—Am	67b	Milford Station, N. J. Ad	17	Mount Tom, Mass.—Ad
83	Mariner's Harbor, S. I. U S	13	Millbrook, N. Y.—Am; Natl	67	Mount Union, Pa.—Ad
66	Marion, Mass.—N Y & B	74, 5	Millbury, Mass.—Ad	59	Mount Upton, N. Y. Natl
67	Marion, N. Y. Natl	20a	Mill Creek, Pa. U S	56a, 58	Mount Vernon, N. Y.—Ad; Am
83	Marlborough, N. J. Natl	40	Millers, Pa. W F & Co	67b	Mulrhead, N. J.—Ad
95, 82	Marlborough, N. Y. Natl	56	Millers Corners, N. Y.—Am	9	Mumford, N. Y. Natl
10	Marlton, N. J. Ad	48	Millers Falls, Mass. Ad; Natl	13c	Muncy, Pa. Ad
58d	Maromas, Conn. Ad	56a	Millerton, N. Y. Am	59	Munnsville, N. Y.—Natl
21	Marshall, N. Y. U S	57	Millerton, Pa. W F & Co	56	Murray, N. Y. Am
66	Marshfield, Mass. Ad	21c	Millington, N. J. U S	21c	Murray Hill, N. J.—U S
48	Marshland, S. I. U S	40	Mill Plain, Conn. Ad	68	Myerstown, Pa. Ad
66, 83	Martha's Vineyard. N Y & B	40a	Milltone Junc., N. J. Ad	82	Mystic Conn.—Ad
56a	Martindale, N. Y. Am	52, 74	Millville, Mass. Ad	21a, 13c	Nanticoke, Pa. Ad; U S
75	Martinsburg, N. Y.—Am	94	Millville, N. J. Ad	66	Nantucket, Mass. N Y & B
3	Martinsburg, W. Va. U S	95, 82	Milton, N. Y. Natl	47-65	Nannet, N. Y.—U S; W F & Co

DIRECTIONS AND EXPRESS TO VARIOUS PLACES—Continued.

For Explanation of Abbreviations used, see page 112.

62a Narragansett Pier, R. I.—Ad	4 North Bennington, Vt.—Natl	56 Oriskany, N. Y. Am
57 Narrowsburg, N. Y. W F & Co	35 North Bloomfield, Conn. Ad	59 Oriskany Falls, N. Y.—Natl
84 Nashua, N. H.— N Y & B	13 North Branch, N. J. Ad	75 Orleans Corners, N. Y.—Am
5 Natick, Mass. Ad.	74 Northbridge, Mass. Ad	50 Orrs Mills, N. Y. Natl
62, 52 Natick, R. I.—Ad	5 North Brookfield, Mass.—Ad	via 67 Orrville, Ohio. Ad
58a Naugatuck, Conn.—Ad	21 North Brookfield, N. Y. U S	67a Ortley, N. J. Ad
49 Naughright, N. J. Ad	13g North Cedarville, N. J. Ad	52 Osborn, Conn. Ad
13g Navesink, N. J. Ad	14 North Clarendon, Vt. Natl	20b Osborn Hollow, N. Y. Natl
5* Neely Town, N. Y. W F & Co	1 North Creek, N. Y. Natl	56 Oscawanna, N. Y.—Am
85 Nelson, Pa.—Am.	58d North Cromwell, Conn. Ad	85 Osceola, Pa. Am; U S; Natl
53 Nepperhan, N. Y. Am	5 North Dana, Mass. Ad	12 Ostrom, N. J. Ad
13a Neshanning Falls, Pa. Ad	69 North-East, Md.—Ad	13g
13, 40 Neshanic, N. J.—Ad	67 North Elizabeth, N. J. Ad	59, 21, 75 Oswego, N. Y. Am; U S; Natl
13c Nesquehoning, Pa. Ad	21, 57 North Elmira, N. Y. Am; U S	20b Otego, N. Y. Natl
13 Netherwood, N. J.—Ad	40a North Fair Haven, N. Y. Ad	57 Otisville, N. Y. W F & Co
49 Newark, Del. Ad	14 North Ferrisburgh, Vt.—Natl	10b Ovid, N. Y.—Ad; U S
67, 13c, 21c, 57, 83 Newark, N. J. Ad	48 Northfield, Mass. Ad; Natl	57, 21, 40a, Owego, N. Y. Ad; U S
56, 95 Newark, N. J.—Ad; Am; Natl	14 Northfield, Vt. Natl	69 Oxford, Md. Ad
3 via 67 Newark, Ohio Ad	48 Northfield Farms, Mass. Ad	52 Oxford, Mass. Ad
69 Newark Centre, Del. Ad	58 Northford, Conn. Ad	21, 59 Oxford, N. Y.—U S
40a Newark Valley, N. Y.—Ad; U S	14 North Georgia, Vt. Natl	57 Oxford, Orange Co., N. Y.—Natl
95, 82 New Baltimore, N. Y. Natl	5 North Grafton, Mass. Ad	69 Oxford, Pa.—Ad
69, 83 New Bedford, Mass.—N Y & B	52 North Grosvenordale, Conn. Ad	21 Oxford Furnace, N. J. U S
59 New Berlin, N. Y. Natl	14 North Hartland, Vt. Natl	83 Oyster Bay, L. I.—L I
80 New Brighton, S. I. U S	66 North Harwich, Mass. N Y & B	84 Ozone Park, L. I. L I
58, 83 New Britain, Conn. Ad; Int'l	17 North Hatfield, Mass. Ad	52 Packerville, Conn.—Ad
67, 83 New Brunswick, N. J.—Ad	58 North Haven, Conn. Ad	via 56 Painesville, Ohio.—Am
95, 57, 82 Newburgh, N. Y. Ad; Am	29 North Hoosick, N. Y. Natl	57, 21 Painted Post, N. Y.—U S
via 58 Newburyport, Mass. Ad; Natl	36 North Kent, Conn. Ad	56 Palatine Bridge, N. Y.—Am
53 New Canaan, Conn. Ad	13g North Long Branch, N. J.—Ad	12 Palenville, N. Y. Am; Natl
49 New Castle, Del. Ad	66 North Middleboro, Mass. Ad	5, 48 Palmer, Mass. Ad
40, 48 New Castle, Pa.—Ad; Am	49 North Newark, N. J. W F & Co	67a Palmyra, N. J. Ad
47 New City, N. Y. U S	21, 59 North Norwich, N. Y. U S	95, 56 Palmyra, N. Y. Am; Natl
13c New Columbia, Pa.—Ad	52 North Oxford, Mass. Ad	68 Palmyra, Pa. Ad
1 Newcomb, N. Y. Natl	67a North Pemberton, N. J.—Ad	13 Pamrapo, N. J. Ad
80 New Drop, N. Y.—U S	38 North Petersburgh, N. Y. Natl	67 Paoli, Pa. Ad
63, 65, 95 New Durham, N. J.—Natl; W F	83 Northport, L. I. L I	71 Paradise, N. Y. W F & Co
75 New Fane, N. Y.—Am	57 North Providence, N. J. U S	57 Paramus, N. J. W F & Co
94 Newfield, N. J. Ad	1 North River, N. Y. Natl	21 Paris, N. Y. U S
40l, Newfield, N. Y.—Ad; U S	38 North Stephentown, N. Y. Natl	75 Parish, N. Y. Am
67 New Florence, Pa. Ad	21 Northumberland, Pa. Ad; U S	13c Parkdale, N. J. Ad
63 Newfoundland, N. J. Natl	65 Northvale, N. J. W F & Co	57 Parkersburg, W. Va. U S
56, 82 New Hamburgh, N. Y.—Am	21a North Vineland, N. J.—Ad	57 Parker's Glen, Pa. W F & Co
58c New Hartford, Conn. Ad; Natl	66 North Westport, Mass.—N Y & B	67 Parkersburgh, Pa. Ad
21, 59 New Hartford, N. Y.—Am ; U S	5 North Wilbraham, Mass. Ad	47 Park Ridge, N. J.—U S
58, 83 New Haven, Conn. Ad; Int'l	52 North Windham, Conn.—Ad	59 Parksville, N. Y.—Natl
75 New Haven, N. Y.—Am	36a, 83, 58 Norwalk, Conn.—Ad	52 Parkville, Conn. Ad
14 New Haven, Vt. Natl	48, 83 Norwich, Conn.—Ad	72, 7, 16 Parkville, L. I. Remsen
90 New Hurley, N. Y. Am	59, 21 Norwich, N. Y. U S; Natl	75 Parma, N. Y. Am
58, 52 Newington, Conn. Ad	52 Norwood, Mass. Ad	40, 13c Parryville, Pa. Ad
58 New Lebanon, N. Y.—Natl	65 Norwood, N. J. W F & Co	20a Parsons, Pa. U S
67a New Lisbon, N. J. Ad	75 Norwood, N. Y. Am	47 Peacock, N. J. U S
58, 83 New London, Conn. Ad	62 Norwood, R. I.—Ad	69 Paschall, Pa.—Ad
11c New Lots, L. I. Local	52 Norwood Central, Mass.—Ad	78 Pascoag, R. I. Ad
40 New Market, N. J. Ad	57 Nutley, N. J.—W F & Co	57, 21c, 63 Passaic, N. J. U S; Natl
36 New Milford, Conn. Ad	65, 95 Nyack, N. Y. Natl; W F & Co	57 Passaic Bridge, N. J.—U S
47 New Milford, N. J. U S	11 Oakdale, L. I. L I	41 Patchogue, L. I.—L I
39 New Milford, N. Y. W F & Co	95 Oakfield, N. Y Natl	57, 63, 21c, Paterson, N. J.—U S; Natl
21 New Milford, Pa. U S	3 Oakland, Md. Ad	40 Pattenburg, N. J. Ad
41 New Northport, L. I.—L I	40 Oakland, N. J.—Natl	56a Patterson, Essex Co., N. Y.—Natl
90 New Paltz, N. Y. U S	71 Oakland, N. Y. W F & Co	95 Pattersonville, N. Y.—Natl
68 New Philadelphia, Pa.—Ad	73 Oakland, R. I. Ad	63 Paulina, N. J. Natl
69 Newport, Del. Ad	62 Oakland Beach, R. I. Ad	64, 15 Paul Smith's, N. Y.—Natl
13g Newport, N. J. Ad	52 Oaklawn, R. I. Ad	9 Pavilion, N. J. Am
67 Newport, Pa. Ad	63 Oak Ridge, N. J. Ad	9 Pavilion Centre, N. Y. Am
62a, b, 66, 83 Newport, R. I.—Ad; N Y B	58a Oakville, Conn. Ad	56a Pawling, N. Y. Am
78 New Preston, Conn. Ad	50 Ocean Beach, N. J. Ad	74, 52 Pawtucket, R. I. Ad; Int'l
68 New Providence, Pa. Ad	91 Ocean City, N. J. Ad	62a Peace Dale, R. I. Ad
68 New Ringgold, Pa.—Ad	50 Ocean Grove, N. J. Ad	86 Peahala, N. J. Ad
58, 83 New Rochelle, N. Y.—Ad	87 Oceanic, N. J. Ad	21c, 13 Peapack, N. J. U S
5 New Salem, Mass.—Ad	41 Ocean Point, L. I. L I	9 Pearl Creek, N. Y. Am
95 New Scotland, N. Y.—Natl	13g Oceanport, N. J. Ad	47 Pearl River, N. Y. U S
80 New Springville, S. I.—U S	53 Odells, N. Y.—Am	11 Pearsall's, L. I. L I
83 New Suffolk, L. I.—L I	13 Ogden, N. J. Ad	59 Peekspuyt, N. Y. Natl
5 Newton, Mass.—Ad	68 Ogdensburgh, N. J. Natl	30a Peekville, Pa. U S; Natl
21f Newton, N. J. U S	75 Ogdensburgh, N. Y. Am; Natl	56, 82 Peekskill, N. Y. Am
36, 52 Newtown, Conn. Ad	via 57 Oil City, Pa.—Ad; Am; Natl	58 Pelham Manor, N. Y. Ad
67a Newtown, N. J.—Ad	67a Ohioville, N. Y.—Ad	58 Pelhamville, N. Y. Ad
6 New Utrecht, L. I.—Remsen	98 Old Chatham, N. Y.—Natl	13c Pen Argyle, Pa. Ad; U S
57 New Windsor, N. Y. W F & Co	5 Old Furnace, Mass.—Ad	68 Penceyd, Pa. Ad
57, 56, 95, 40 Niagara Falls, N. Y.—Am	41 Old Northport, L. I. L I	57 Pendleton Centre, N. Y. W F & Co
58 Niantic, Conn.—Ad	69 O'd Point Comfort, Va. Ad	56 Penfield, N. Y. Am
62 Niantic, R. I.—Ad	57 Olean, N. Y. Am; U S; W F & Co	67 Penn, Pa. Ad
21 Nichols, N. Y. U S	58 Olive Branch, N. Y. Am	59 Pennellville, N. Y. Natl
21 Nicholson, Pa. U S	73 Olneyville, R. I.—Ad	10, 13c Penn Haven Junc., Pa. Ad
20b Ninweh, N. Y. Natl	20a Olyphant, Pa. U S; Natl	13a Pennington, N. J. Ad
21 Noank, Conn. Ad	21 Onativia, N. Y. U S	67 Penn Valley, Pa. Ad
62 Noank, Conn. Ad	2 Oneco, Conn.—Ad	85 Penn Yan, N. Y. Ad; Am
65 Nordhoff, N. J. W F & Co	56, 59 Oneida, N. Y. Am; Natl	41c Penny Bridge, L. I.—Bowron
35 Norfolk, Conn.—Ad	59, 95 Oneida Castle, N. Y.—Natl	67 Pennspack, Pa. Ad
52 Norfolk, Mass. Ad	20b Oneonta, N. Y.—Natl	13a Penobscot, Pa. Ad
13g Normandie, N. J. Ad	75 Ontario, N. Y.—Am	49 Pequannock, N. J. W F & Co
58 Noroton, Conn. Ad	47 Oradell, N. J.—U S	21 Perkinsville, N. J.—U S
84 Norristown, Pa. Ad	2 Orange, Conn.—Ad	68 Perkiomen Junc., Pa. Ad
5, 58c, 29 North Adams, Mass.—Ad; Am	21c, 49 Orange, N. J.—U S; W F & Co	69 Perryman, Md. Ad
48 North Amherst, Mass. Ad	95, 65 Orangeburgh, N. Y. W F & Co	67a Perrysburg, N. Y. W F & Co
17, 58c Northampton, Mass. Ad; Natl	57 Orange Farm, N. Y. W F & Co	69 Perryville, Md. Ad
50 North Asbury Park, N. J. Ad	85 Ore Hill, Conn. Ad	24 Perryville, N. Y. Am; Natl
50 North Bay, N. Y. Natl	89 Orient, L. I.—L I	67, 13, 80, 83 Perth Amboy, N. J.—Ad

DIRECTIONS AND EXPRESS TO VARIOUS PLACES—Continued.

For Explanation of Abbreviations used, see page 112.

57 Peru, N. J. W F & Co	1 Pottersville, N. Y.—Natl	1 Riverside, N. Y. Natl
30 Peru, N. Y. Natl	68 Pottstown, Pa.—Ad	67a Riverton, N. J. Ad
40a Peruville, N. Y. Ad; U S	13c, 40, 68 Pottsville, Pa.—Ad	62 River View, R. I.—Ad
38 Petersburg, N. Y. Natl	56, 82 Poughkeepsie, N. Y.—Am.	75 River View, N. Y.—Am
67 Petersburg, Pa. Ad	67 Pouhquag, N. Y. Ad	68 Robesonia, Pa. Ad
56 Phelps, N. Y. Ad; Am	52 Pratt's, Conn. Ad	67 Robinvale, N. J.—Ad
62 Phenix, R. I. Ad	59 Pratts, N. Y. Natl	5 Rochdale, Mass.—Ad
75 Philadelphia, N. Y.—Am	21 Preble, N. Y. U S	68 Rochelle Park, N. J.—Natl
67, 13a, 67a, 84 Philadelphia, Pa. Ad	68 Prescott, Pa. Ad	56, 57, 85 Rochester, N. Y.—Am; U S
85 Phillips, Pa. Am	73 Primrose, R. I. Ad	21c, 13 Rockaway, N. J.—U S
13, 21c, 40 Phillipsburg, N. J. Ad; U S	80 Princess Bay, S. I.—U S	54, 83 Rockaway Beach, L. I.—L I
59 Phillipsport, N. Y. Natl	67 Princeton, N. J. Ad	59 Rockdale, N. Y. Natl
56a Philmont, N. Y. Am	11 Proctorsville, Vt. Am	10 Rockdale, Pa.—Ad
13a Philmont, Pa. Ad	39a Pompton, Pa. U S	58 Rockfall, Conn. Ad
87 Phœnicia, N. Y.—Am; Natl	75 Prospect, N. Y. Am	9 Rock Glen, N. Y. Am; W F
68 Phœnixville, Pa. Ad	67a Prospect Plains, N. J. Ad	11 Rockingham, Vt. Natl
75 Pierce's, N. Y.—Am	13c Prospect Rock, Pa Ad	via 58, 84 Rockland, Me. Natl
65 Piermont-on-the-Hill, N. Y. W F & Co	39a Providence, Pa. Ad; U S	59 Rockland, N. Y. Natl
	58, 62, 83 Providence, R. I. Ad; Int'l	83 Rock Landing, Conn.—Ad
75 Pierrepont Manor, N. Y. Am	66 Provincetown, Mass. N Y & B	82 Rockland Lake, N. Y. Ad
67 Pierson's, Pa. Ad	75 Pulaski, N. Y. Am	via 58 Rockport, Mass. Ad; Natl
56 Pierson's, N. Y.—Am	5 Putves, N. Y. Am	50 Rockport, Pa. Ad
9 Pike, N. Y. Am	9 Punxsutawney, Pa Ad; Am	59 Rock Rift, N. Y.—Natl
13g Pine Brook, N. J. Ad	50 Purdy's, Orange Co., N. Y. Am	85 Rock Stream, N. Y.—Ad; Am
57 Pine Bush, N. Y. W F & Co	56a Purdy's Westchester Co., N. Y.	59 Rock Tavern, N. Y. Natl
68 Pine Grove, Pa. Ad	52 Putnam, Conn. Ad	52 Rockville, Conn. Ad
87 Pine Hill, N. Y. Am; Natl	20 Putnam, N. Y. Natl	67 Rockville, Pa. Ad
57 Pine Island, N. Y.—W F & Co	30b Quaker Street, N. Y. Natl	41 Rockville Centre, L. I. L I
58c Pine Meadow, Conn. Ad	80 Quarantine, S. I. Brisk	59 Rockwell's Mills, N. Y.—Natl
58 Pine Orchard, Conn. Ad	67 Quarryville, N. J. Natl	58d Rocky Hill, Conn. Ad
51, 45 Pine Plains, N. Y.—Am	94 Quarryville, Pa. Ad	67 Rocky Hill, N. J. Ad
via 67 Piqua, Ohio Ad	40 Queen Ann, Md. Ad	62 Rocky Point, R. I. Ad
94 Pitman, N. J. Ad	11 Queens, N. Y.—L I	56 Rome, N. Y. Am; Natl
67 Pittsburg, Pa. Ad; Am; Natl	52 Quidnick, R. I. Ad	78 Romford, Conn. Ad
36, 5 Pittsfield, Mass. Ad; Am	58 Quinnipiack, Conn.—Ad	40b Romulus, N. Y. Ad; U S
56, 95 Pittsford, N. Y.—Am	41 Quogue, L. I. L I	82, 95, 56 Rondout, N. Y.—Am; Natl
20a, 21b, 10 Pittston, Pa. Ad; U S; W F	67 Raiway, N. J. Ad	41 Ronkonkoma, L. I.—L I
52 Plainfield, Conn. Ad	57 Ramapo, N. Y. W F & Co	75 Rance, N. Y.—Am
13 Plainfield, N. J. Ad	21 Ramsey's, N. J. W F & Co	68 Roseglen, Pa. Ad
67 Plainsboro, N. J. Ad	83 Randalls Island, N. Y. Local	13 Roselle, N. J. Ad
40 Plainsville, Pa. Ad	59 Randallsville, N. Y. Natl	13 Rosedale, N. Y.—U S
58c, 52 Plainville, Conn. Ad	66 Randolph, Mass. Ad	13g Rosenhayn, N. J. Ad
58c Plantsville, Conn. Ad	14 Randolph, Vt. Natl	71 Rose Point, N. Y. W F & Co
20 Plattsburgh, N. Y. Natl	40 Ransom, Pa. Ad	95 Roseton, N. Y. Natl
66 Pleasant Lake, Mass. N Y & B	75 Ransomville, N. Y. Am	21c Roselle, N. J. U S
80 Pleasant Plains, N. Y. U S	13 Raritan, N. J. Ad	75 Rosiere, N. Y. Am
51 Pleasant Valley, N. Y. Am	57 Rascelas, Pa. W F & Co	41, 83 Roslyn, L. I. L I
39a Pleasant Valley, Pa. Ad; U S	57 Rathbonville, N. Y. W F & Co	59 Roscoe, N. Y.—Natl
91 Pleasantville, N. J. Ad	41 Ravenswood, L. I. L I	83 Rossville, S. I. U S
56a Pleasantville, N. Y. Am	66 Raynham, Mass. N Y & B	20, 61 Round Lake, N. Y. Natl
83 Pleasure Bay, N. J. Ad	38 Rayville, N. Y. Natl	20, 14 Rouse's Point, N. Y. Natl
66 Plymouth, Mass. Natl	68 Reading, Pa. Ad	67b Roxbury, N. J.—Ad
21a Plymouth, Pa. U S	85 Reading Centre, N. Y. Am	78 Roxbury, Conn. Ad
66 Plympton, Mass. Ad	52 Redding, Conn. Ad	87 Roxbury, N. Y. Am; Natl
66 Pocasset, Mass N Y & B	56, 83 Red Bank, N. J. Ad	14 Roxbury, Vt. Natl
62 Pocasset, R. I. Ad	36a Redding, Conn. Ad	78 Roxbury Falls, Conn. Ad
69 Pocomoke, Md. Ad	35 Red Hook, N. Y. Am	14 Royalton, Vt. Natl
21 Pocono Summit, Pa. U S	10 Redington, Pa. Ad	68 Royer's Ford, Pa. Ad
41b Point Lookout, L. I.—L I	75 Redwood, N. Y.—Am	40 Rummerfield, Pa.—Ad
13c Point Phillipp, Pa. Ad	69 Rehoboth, Del. Ad	13g Rumson Beach, N. J. Ad
50 Point Pleasant, N. J. Ad	75 Remsen, N. Y. Am	21a Rupert, Pa. Ad; U S
52 Pomfret, Conn. Ad	75 Rensselaer Falls, N. Y. Am	57 Russell, N. Y. W F & Co
10 Pomona, N. J. Ad	39 Reynolds, N. Y. Natl	5 Russell, Mass.—Ad
17 Pomona, N. Y. U S	75 Reynoldsville, N. Y.—Ad	21c Rutherford, N. J.—U S; W F
67, 40 Pompton, N. J. Natl; W F & Co	56, 82 Rhinebeck, N. Y.—Am	20, 14 Rutland, Vt. Natl
39, 13 Pompton Junc. N. J. W F & Co	13 Ricefield, N. J. Ad	67 Ryde, Pa.- Ad
19 Pompton Plains, N. J. W F	75 Rice's, N. Y. Am	58 Rye, N. Y. Ad
57 Pond Eddy, N. Y. & Pa. W F	21 Richfield Springs, N. Y. U S	1 Sacandaga River, N. Y.—Natl
57, 52 Pontiac, N. J. W F & Co	40a Richford, N. Y. Ad; U S	58 Sackam Head, Conn. Ad
62 Pontiac, R. I. Ad	75 Richland, N. Y. Am	75 Sacketts Harbor, N. Y. Am
21 Poolville, N. Y. U S	68 Richland, Pa. Ad	via 58 Saco, Me. Ad
37 Portage, N. Y. Ad	5 Richmond, Mass.—Ad; Am	58 Sadds Mills, Conn.—Ad
95, 56 Port Byron, N. Y.—Am; Natl	via 13, 6 Richmond, Va. Ad	66 Sagamore, Mass. N Y & B
68 Port Carbon, Pa. Ad	14 Richmond, Vt. Natl	59 Sages Corners, N. Y. Natl
58, 83 Port Chester, N. Y. Ad	41 Richmond Hill, L. I. L I	41, 83 Sag Harbor, L. I. L I
68 Port Clinton, Pa. Ad	80 Richmond Valley, S. I. U S	80 Sailors' Snug Harbour, S.I. U S
20b Port Crane, N. Y. Natl	20b Richmondville, N. Y. Natl	11 St. Albans, Vt. Natl
69 Port Deposit, Md. Ad	56, 75 Richville, N. Y.—Am	40 St. Chair, Pa. Ad
95 Port Gibson, N. Y. Natl	57 Riderville, Pa. W F & Co	83 St. George, S. I.—U S; Brisk
20 Port Henry, N. Y. Natl	36a Ridgefield, Conn. Ad	11 St. James, L. I. L I
41 Port Jefferson, L. I. L I	13 Ridgefield, N. J.—W F & Co	41 St. Johnland, L. I. L I
57 Port Jervis, N. Y.—W F & Co	95, 68 Ridgefield Park, N. J.—Natl	14 St. Johns, Que. Natl
68 Port Kennedy, Pa. Ad	41 Ridgewood, L. I. L I	56, 95 St. Johnsville, N. Y. Am; Natl
20 Port Kent, N. Y.—Natl	57 Ridgewood, N. J.—W F & Co	via 57,3,67,56 St. Louis, Mo. Ad; Am; U S
58, 83 Portland, Conn. Ad	3 Ridley, Pa. U S	15 St. Regis, N. Y. Ad
via 58 Portland, Me. N Y & B	69 Ridley Park, Pa. Ad	57 Salamanca, N. Y.; Am; WF & Co
21 Portland, Pa. U S	67b Riegelsville, N. J. Ad	via 58 Salem, Mass. Ad; Natl
20b Portlandville, N. Y. Natl	67b Ringoes, N. J. Ad	94 Salem, N. J. Ad
75 Port Leyden, N. Y. Am	49 Ringwood, N. J. W F & Co	20 Salem, N. Y. Natl
13g, 83 Port Monmouth, N. J. Ad	49 Ringwood Junc., N. J. W F	75 Salina, N. Y. Am
58 Port Morris, N. J. Ad	94 Rio Grande, N. J. Ad	55 Salisbury, Conn. Ad
21c Port Murray, N. J. U S	13c Ritter, Pa. Ad	69 Salisbury, Md.—Ad
13g Port Norris, N. J. Ad	56 Riverdale, N. Y. Am	57 Salisbury, N. Y. W F & Co
21c, 13 Port Oram, N. J.—Ad	47 River Edge, N. J. U S	14 Salisbury, Vt. Natl
80 Port Richmond, S. I. U S	41 Riverhead, L. I. L I	51 Salt Point, N. Y. Am
41 Port Washington, L. I.—L I	13 Riverton, N. J. Ad	9 Saltvale, N. Y. Am
85 Post Creek, N. Y. Ad	58 Riverpoint, R. I. Ad	56 Sanborn, N. Y. Am
75 Potsdam, N. Y.—Am	58 Riverside, Conn. Ad	75 Sand Hills, N. Y. Am
85 Potter Brook, Pa.—Am	57, 67a Riverside, N. J.—Ad	

DIRECTIONS AND EXPRESS TO VARIOUS PLACES—Continued.

For Explanation of Abbreviations used, see page 112.

83	Sands Point, L. I.- L I	41 Shinnecock Hills, L. I. L I	57 Southport, L. I. L I
66	Sandwich, Mass. N Y & B	64 Shoemakersville, Pa. Ad	14 South Royalton, Vt. Ad
75	Sandy Creek, N. Y.- Am	57 Shohola Glen, Pa. W F & Co	95 So. Schenectady, N. Y. Natl
20	Sandy Hill, N. Y. Natl	87 Shokan, N. Y. Am; Natl	10 South Somerville, N. J. Ad
82	Sandy Hook, Conn. Ad	21c Short Hills, N. J.—U S	67 South Trenton, N. J. Ad
13g, 83	Sandy Hook, N. J. Ad; U S	56 Shortsville, N. Y.—Am	66 South Truro, Mass. N Y & B
36a	Sanford, Conn. Ad	13g Shrewsbury, N. J. Ad	17 South Vernon, Vt. Ad
75	Sandfords Corners, N. Y. Am	15 Shunpike, N. Y. Am	5 Southville, Mass. Ad
81	San Francisco, Cal. W. F. & Co	75 Shurtliffs, N. Y. Am	94 South Vineland, N. J. Ad
21	Sangerfield Centre, N. Y. U S	20 Shushan, N. Y.—Natl	66 South Wareham, Mass. N Y & B
95	Santa Clara, N. Y. Am	20b, 59 Sidney, N. Y. Natl	66 South Wellfleet, Mass. N Y & B
15, 64	Saranac Lake, N. Y. Natl	59 Sidney Centre, N. Y.—Natl	via 58 South West Harbor, Me. Ad
20	Saratoga, N. Y.- Natl	13c Siegfried, Pa.—Ad	58d South Wethersfield, Conn. Ad
66	Saucket, Mass. N Y & B	49 Silver Lake, N. J. W F & Co	58c Southwick, Mass. Ad
58	Saugatuck, Conn. Ad	57 Silver Springs, N. Y. Am	13c, 40 South Wilkesbarre, Pa. Ad
95, 82	Saugerties, N. Y. Am; Natl	58c Simsbury, Conn. Ad	48 South Wellington, Conn. Ad
74	Saundersville, Mass. Ad; Natl	49 Singac, N. J. W F & Co	36a South Wilton, Conn. Ad
21	Sanquoit, N. Y. U S	56, 82 Sing Sing, N. Y. Am	48, 52 South Windham, Mass. Ad
56, 95	Savannah, N. Y. Am; Natl	68 Sinking Spring, Pa.- Ad	52 South Windsor, Conn. Ad
21, 57	Savona, N. Y. W F & Co	56 Skaneateles, N. Y. Am	66 So. Yarmouth, Mass. N Y & B
58, 83	Saybrook, Conn. Ad	13a Skillman, N. J. Ad	65 Sparkill, N. Y. W F & Co
58d	Saybrook Point, Conn.- Ad	40 Skinner's Eddy, Pa. Ad	21a Sparta, N. J. Natl
40	Sayre, Pa. Ad	63 Slate Hill, N. Y. Natl	67 Spa Spring, N. J. Ad
80	Sayreville, S. I.- U S	40 Slatington, Pa. Ad	5 Spencer, Mass. Ad; Natl
41	Sayville, L. I.- L I	58 Sleepy Hollow, N. Y. Am	23, 40b Spencer, N. Y. Ad; Am; U S
56	Scarborough, N. Y. Am	20b Slingerlands, N. Y. Natl	56 Spencerport, N. Y. Am
56a	Searsdale, N. Y. Am	57 Sloatsburg, N. Y. W F & Co	11 Spoonk, L. I. L I
67	Schalks, N. J. Ad	40a, 57 Smithboro, N. Y. W F & Co	67a Spotswood, N. J. Ad
20	Schaghticoke, N. Y.—Natl	73 Smithfield, R. I.—Ad	21 Spragueville, Pa. U S
67	Schenck's, Pa. Ad	48 Smith's, Conn. Ad	56, 95 Sprakers, N. Y. Natl
66	Schenectady, N. Y. Am	5 Smiths, Mass.— Ad	64 Spring Cove, N. Y.- Natl
20b	Schenevus, N. Y.—Natl	20 Smiths Basin, N. Y.- Na l	58 Springdale, Conn. Ad
56	Schodack, N. Y.—Am	17 Smith's Ferry, Mass.- Ad	10 Springdale, N. J. Ad
21c, 13	Schooley's Mountain, N. J. Ad	57 Smith's Mills, N. Y. W F & Co	via 56, 57 Springfield, Ill. Am; U S
95	Schraalenburg, N. J. Natl	41 Smithtown, L. I.- L I	52, 58 Springfield, Mass Ad; Int'l
1	Schroon Lake, N. Y.- Natl	67a Smithville, N. J.- Ad	41 Springfield, L. I. L I
63	Schuetzen Park, N. J. Natl	69 Smyrna, Del. Ad	via 56 Springfield, Ohio. Ad
20	Schuylerville, N. Y. Natl	59 Smyrna, N. Y. Natl	51 Spring Lake, N. J. Ad
68	Schuylkill Haven, Pa.- Ad	75 Sodus, N. Y. Am	35 Spring Lake, N. Y. Am
57	Scio, N. Y.- W F & Co	49 Soho, N. Y. W F & Co	63 Spring Side, N. Y. Natl
20	Sciota, N. Y.- Natl	50 Soloville, N. Y.- Natl	13 Springtown, N. J. Ad
66	Scituate, Mass. Ad	56a Somers Centre, N. Y.-Am	40 Spring Town, N. Y. Natl
52	Scotland, Conn. Ad	66 Somerset, Mass. N Y & B	17, 65 Spring Valley, N. Y. U S
9, 57	Scottsville, N. Y. Am; W F & Co	67b Somerset, N. J. Ad	57 Spring Water, N. Y. W F & Co
21, 20a	Scranton, Pa. Ad; U S; Natl	75 Somerset, N. Y. Am	67 Spruce Creek, Pa.- Ad
75	Scriba, N. Y.- Am	57 Somer's Lane, Pa. W F & Co	56 Spuyten Duyvil, N. Y. Am
67b	Scudder's Falls, N. J.—Ad	91 Somers Point, N. J.- Ad	13g Squanknum, N. J - Ad
75	Sea Breeze, N. Y.- Am	13a Somerton, Pa.—Ad	56 Staatsburg, N. Y. Am
13g, 83	Sea Bright, N. J.- Ad	13 Somerville, N. J.- Ad	58 Stafford, Conn. Ad
41, 83	Sea Cliff, L. I. L I	20 Sonyea, N. Y.- W F & Co	56, 57 Stafford, N. Y.- Am; W F & Co
69	Seaforth, Del. Ad	58 Sound Beach, Conn.—Ad	86 Staffordville, N. J.- Ad
50, 67c	Sea Girt, N. J. Ad	20 South Acton, Mass. Ad; Natl	58, 83 Stamford, Conn. Ad
91	Sea Isle City, N. J.- Ad	59, 67a South Amboy, N. J. Ad	87 Stamford, N. Y.- Natl
51	Seaside, L. I.- L I	41 Southampton, L. I.- L I	40 Standing Stone, Pa. Ad
67a	Seaside Park, N. J. -Ad	58c Southampton, Mass. Ad	15 Standish, N. Y. Natl
91	Seaville, N. J. Ad	5 South Athol, Mass.- Ad	51 Stanfordville, N. Y. Am
21c, 57	Secaucus, N. J. W F & Co	10 South Atlantic, N. J. Ad	21c Stanhope, N. J.- U S
57	Seeley Creek, N. Y. W F & Co	57 South Avon, N. Y. W F & Co	68 Stanhope, Pa. Ad
65	Selkirk, N. Y.- Natl	20 South Ballston, N. Y. Natl	69 Stanton, Del. Ad
56	Seneca Falls, N. Y. Am	58 South Berlin, N. Y.- Natl	40 Stanton, N. J.—Ad
50	Seneca Hills, N. Y. Natl	83 South Bethlehem, N. Y. Ad	80, 83 Stapleton, S. I. U S
56	Sennett, N. Y. Am	66 South Braintree, Mass. -Ad	57 Starrucca, Pa W F & Co
41	Setauket, L. I. L I	50 Southbridge, Mass. Ad	58 State Line, Conn. Ad
20b	Seward, N. Y. Natl	12 South Cairo, N. Y.- Am; Natl	36 State Line, Mass.- Ad
13, 83	Sewaren, N. J.—Ad	17 South Charlestown, N. H.- Ad	57 State Line, Pa. Ad; Am
94	Sewell, N. J. Ad	66 South Chatham, Mass. N Y & B	68 Steelton, Pa - Ad
58a	Seymour, Conn.- Ad	21 South Columbia, N. Y. U S	67 Steiton, N. J Ad
57	Shaker Crossing, N. Y.-	1 South Corinth, N. Y. Natl	13c Steuton, Pa. Ad
5	Shaker Village, Mass.- Ad	48 South Coventry, Conn.- Ad	58 Stephentown, N. Y. Natl
92	Shaker Station, Conn.- Ad	17, 58c South Deerfield, Mass. Ad	36 Stepney, Conn. Ad
13c, 40	Shamokin, Pa.—Ad	66 South Dennis, Mass. N Y & B	52 Sterling, Conn. Ad
13g	Shamong, N. J.- Ad; U S	56a South Dover, N. Y.- Am	40a, 75 Sterling, N. Y. Ad; Am; U S
68	Shamrock, Pa - Ad	67 South Elizabeth, N. J.	19 Sterling Forest, N. J.- W F & Co
87	Shandaken, N. Y.—Am ; Natl	57 Southfields, N. Y. W F & Co	57 Sterlington, N. Y. W F & Co
62	Shamrock, R. I.—Ad	52 Southford, Conn. Ad	75 Sterling Valley, N. Y.- Am
13g	Shark River, N. J.- Ad ; U S	5 So. Framingham, Mass. Ad	75 Sterlingville, N. Y. Am
67a	Sharon, N. J. Ad	87 South Gilboa, N. Y.- Am	13c Steuben, Pa. Ad
14	Sharon, Vt.- Natl	82 South Glastonbury, Conn. Ad	58a Stevens, N. J. Ad
68	Sharon Hill, Pa.- Ad	21 South Granby, N. Y. U S	57 Stevens Point, Pa W F & Co
56a	Sharon Station, N. Y. Am	41 South Greenfield, L. I. L I	21c Stewartsville, N. J. U S
20b	Sharon Springs, N. Y.- Natl	66 South Harwick, Mass. N Y & B	21 Stiles, N. Y. U S
62	Shawomet Beach, R. I. Ad	58c Southington, Conn. Ad	63 Stillwater, N. J. Natl
7, 41c	Sheepshead Bay, L. I.- L I	36 South Kent, Conn. Ad	73 Stillwater, R. I. Ad
36	Sheffield, Mass. Ad	via 58 South Lawrence, Mass. Ad	21c Stirling, N. J.- U S
45	Shekomeka, N. Y. Am	36 South Lee, Mass. Ad	51 Missing, N. Y. Am
14	Shelburne, Vt. Natl	57 South Lavonia, N. Y.- W F & Co	75 Stittville, N. Y. Am
58c	Shelburne Falls, Mass.- Ad	13a South Londonderry, Vt. Ad	36 Stockbridge, Mass. Am
40b	Sheldrake, N. Y. Ad; U S	58 South Lyme, Conn.- Ad	36 Stockbridge, N. Y. Am
41, 83	Shelter Island, L. I. L I	66 South Middleboro, Mass. Ad	63 Stockholm, N. J. Natl
83	Shelton, Conn. Ad	59 South New Berlin, N. Y.- Natl	56, 82 Sto kport, N. Y. Am
13c, 40	Shenandoah, Pa. Ad	58, 83 South Norwalk, Conn. Ad	57 Stockport, N. Y. W F & Co
78	Shepang, Conn. Ad	63 South Ogdensburgh, N. J.—Natl	67b Stockton, N. J. Ad
13g	Sheppard's Mills, N. J.—Ad	41, 83 Southold, L. I. L I	40 Stockton, Pa. Ad
21	Sherburne, N. Y. U S	56 South Orange, N. J. U S	39 Stone Bridge, N. Y. W F & Co
59	Sherburne 4 Corners, N. Y. Natl	41 South Oyster Bay, L. I. L I	57 Stone Mill, Pa. W F & Co
68	Sheridan, Pa.- Ad	57 South Paterson, N. J.- W F & Co	11 Stony Brook, L. I. L I
57	Sheridan, N. Y. W F & Co	67a South Pemberton, N. J. Ad	62, 83 Stonington, Conn. Ad
21a	Shickshinny, Pa. Ad ; U S	40 South Plainfield, N. J. Ad	87b Stony Clove, N. Y. Am
13c	Shluser, Pa. Ad	58 Southport, Conn.- Ad	58 Stony Creek, Conn. Ad

DIRECTIONS AND EXPRESS TO VARIOUS PLACES—Continued.

For Explanation of Abbreviations used, see page 112.

1 Stony Creek, N. Y.—Natl	21 Tobyhanna, Pa.—U S	36 Van Dusenville, Mass.—Ad
59 Stony Ford, N. Y.—Natl	via 56, 57, 67 Toledo, Ohio—Ad	21, 40b Van Etten, N. Y.—Ad; Am; Natl
87 Stony Hollow, N. Y.—Am	48 Tolland, Conn.—Ad	57 Van Keuren, N. Y.—W F & CO
95 Stony Point, N. Y.—U S; Natl	52 Toles, Conn.—Ad	58 Van Nest, N. Y.—Ad
56 Storm King, N. Y.—Am	40 Tombicken, Pa.—Ad	72 Van Sicklen Sta., L. I.—Remsen
52 Stormville, N. Y.—Ad	82, 95 Tompkins Cove, N. Y.—Natl	51 Van Wagner's, N. Y.—Am
66 Stoughton, Mass.—Ad; Natl	80 Tompkinsville, S. I.—U S	41a Van Wicklen's, L. I.—L I
13a Stoutsburg, N. J.—Ad	13g, 67a Tom's River, N. J.—Ad	63 Van Whakles, N. J.—Natl
67 Strafford, Pa.—Ad	57 Tonawanda, N. Y.—Am	40a Venice Centre, N. Y.—Ad; U S
56, 58c Stratford, Conn.—Ad	68 Topton, Pa.—Ad	45 Verbank, N. Y.—Am
35 Stratton Brook, Conn.—Ad	67 Torresdale, Pa.—Ad	14 Vergennes, Vt.—Natl
21, 63 Stroudsburg, Pa.—U S; Natl	58a Torrington, Conn.—Ad	15 Vermontville, N. Y.—Natl
75 Stroughs, N. Y.—Am	80 Tottenville, S. I.—U S	52 Vernon, Conn.—Ad
56, 82 Stuyvesant, N. Y.—Am	40 Towanda, Pa.—Ad	39 Vernon, N. J.—W F & Co
21c Succasunna, N. J.—U S	52 Towantic, Conn.—Ad	95 Vernon, N. Y.—Natl
68 Sudberg, Pa.—Ad	80 Tower Hill, S. I.—U S	17 Vernon, Vt.—Ad
57, 63 Suffern, N. Y.—W F & Co	55a Towner's, N. Y.—Ad; Am	13 Vernoy, N. J.—Ad; U S
58 Suffield, Conn.—Ad	57 Town Line, N. Y.—W F & Co	56 Veron, N. Y.—Am
39 Sugar Loaf, N. Y.—W F & Co	39 Townsbury, N. J.—W F & Co	52 Versailles, Conn.—Ad
13c, 40 Sugar Notch, Pa.—Ad	68 Townsend, Del.—Ad	21 Vestal, N. Y.—U S
21c Summit, N. J.—U S	13c Township Line, Pa.—Ad	58 Victor, N. Y.—Am
9 Summit, N. Y.—W F & Co	67c Tracey's, N. J.—Ad	21 Vienna, N. Y.—Natl
52 Summit, R. I.—Ad	39 Tranquility, N. J.—U S	via 3, 67 Vincennes, Ind.—Ad
14 Summit, Vt.—Natl	56 Transit, N. Y.—Am	67a Vincentown, N. J.—Ad
47 Summit Park, N. J.—U S	14c Treichler, Pa.—Ad	13g, 94 Vine'and, N. J.—Ad
59 Summitville, N. Y.—Natl	13 Tremley, N. J.—Ad	67 Voorhees, N. J.—Ad
13c Sunbury, Pa.—Ad	66 Tremont, Mass.—N Y & B	20b, 95 Voorheesville, N. Y.—Natl
56, 57, 95 Suspension Bridge, N. Y.—Am	55a Tremont, N. Y.—Am	21 Wadham's Mills, N. Y.—Natl
37 Susquehanna, Pa.—W F & Co	68 Tremont, Pa.—Ad	52 Wadsworth, Mass.—Ad
57 Sutton, Mass.—Ad	13a, 67, 83 Trenton, N. J.—Ad	67a Wakefield, R. I.—Ad
67 Saydam Street, New Bruns.—Ad	75 Trenton, N. Y.—Am	90 Waldo, N. Y.—U S
94 Swain, N. J.—Ad	75 Trenton Falls, N. Y.—Am	57 Waldwick, N. J.—W F & Co
57 Swains, N. Y.—U S; W F & Co	56 Tribes Hill, N. Y.—Am	67 Wall, Pa.—Ad
via 58 Swampscott, Mass.—Ad; Natl	59 Trout Brook, N. Y.—Ad	21 Wallace, N. Y.—U S
94 Swansea, Mass.—N Y & B	57 Trowbridge, Pa.—W F & Co	57 Wallaceo, N. Y.—W F & Co
14 Swanton, Vt.—Natl	56, 82 Troy, N. Y.—Natl	58 Wallingford, Conn.—Ad
27 Swanzey, N. H.—Ad	40b Trumansburg, N. Y.—Ad; U S	75 Wallington, N. Y.—Ad; Am
63 Swartswood, N. J.—Natl	56 Trumbull Church, Conn.—Ad	90 Wallkill, N. Y.—U S
63 Swartwood, N. Y.—Am; Natl	66 Truro, Mass.—N Y & B	39 Walloomsac, N. Y.—Natl
68 Swartara, Pa.—Ad	21 Truxton, N. Y.—Am; Natl	13c Walnut Port, Pa.—Ad
68 Swedeland, Pa.—Ad	55a Tuckahoe, N. Y.—Am	52 Walpole, Mass.—Ad
94 Swedesboro, N. J.—Ad	86 Tuckerton, N. J.—Ad	9 Walston, Pa.—Am
59 Sylvan, N. Y.—Natl	68 Tuckerton, Pa.—Ad	29 Waltham, Mass.—Ad; Natl
45 Sylvan Lake, N. Y.—Am	21 Tully, N. Y.—U S	59 Walton, N. Y.—Natl
41 Syosset, L. I.—L I	67 Tullytown, Pa.—Ad	56 Walworth, N. Y.—Am
21, 56, 95 Syracuse, N. Y.—Am; U S; Natl	67b Tumble, N. J.—Ad	56, 95 Wampsville, N. Y.—Natl
67 Tacony, Pa.—Ad	40 Tunkhannock, Pa.—Ad	13c Wanakah, Pa.—Ad
52 Taft's, Conn.—Ad	20b Tunnel, N. Y.—Natl	57 Wanaque, N. J.—W F & Co
52 Talcottville, Conn.—Ad	13c Tunnel, Pa.—Ad	5 Ware, Mass.—Ad; Natl
65 Tallman's, N. Y.—W F & Co	57 Turner's, N. Y.—W F & Co	66 Warsaw, Mass.—N Y & B
58 Talmadge Hill, Conn.—Ad	58c Turner's Falls, Mass.—Ad; Natl	58 Warehouse Point, Conn.—Ad
13c Tamaqua, Pa.—Ad	58 Turnerville, Conn.—Ad	13g Watertown, N. J.—Ad
87a Tannersville, N. Y.—Am; Natl	20a Tuscarora, N. Y.—Am	56, 95 Warren, N. Y.—Am; Natl
65, 95 Tappan, N. Y.—Natl; W F & Co	68 Tuscarora, Pa.—Ad	5 Warren, Mass.—Ad; N Y & B
35 Tariffville, Conn.—Ad	57 Tuxedo, N. Y.—W F & Co	66 Warren, R. I.—N Y & B
73 Tarkiln, R. I.—Ad	35 Twin Lakes, Conn.—Ad	4 Warrensburgh, N. Y.—Natl
53, 94, 82 Tarrytown, N. Y.—Am	59 Twin Ponds, N. Y.—Natl	63 Warrington, N. J.—Natl
63 Tarrytown Hghts, N. Y.—Am	63 Two Bridges, N. J.—Natl	57 Warsaw, N. Y.—Am; W F
40b Tanghannock, N. Y.—U S	46 Tyler City, Conn.—Ad	39 Warwick, N. Y.—W F & Co
66 Taunton, Mass.—Int'l	65 Tyler Park, N. J.—Natl	62 Warwick, R. I.—Ad
21a Taylorville, Pa.—U S	67 Tyrone, Pa.—Ad	49 Warwick Wood'lds.—N. Y.—W F
95 Teaneck, N. J.—Natl	82 Ulster Landing, N. Y.—Am	78 Washington, Conn.—Ad
68 Tempe, Pa.—Ad	95 Ulster Park, N. Y.—Natl	via 13, 67, 81 Washington, D. C.—Ad; U S
65 Tenafly, N. J.—W F & Co	20b Unadilla, N. Y.—Natl	5 Washington, Mass.—Ad
67c Tremont, N. Y.—Ad	21 Unadilla Forks, N. Y.—U S	21c Washington, N. J.—U S
via 56, 57, 67 Terre Haute, Ind.—Am; U S	68 Union, Broome Co., N. Y.—W F	52 Washington, R. I.—Ad
52 Terryville, Conn.—Ad	52, 58a Union City, Conn.—Ad	72 Washington Cem., L. I.—Rem
18 Thamesville, Conn.—Ad	49 Union Course, N. Y.—W F & Co	57 Washington Mills, N. Y.—U S
1 The Glen, N. Y.—Natl	57 Uniondale, Pa.—W F & Co	67b Washington Crossing, N. J.—Ad
75 Theresa, N. Y.—Am	28 Union Hill, N. J.—Dodd & C.	63 Washingtonville, N. J.—Natl
47 Thiells, N. Y.—U S	75 Union Hill, N. Y.—Am	57 Washingtonville, N. Y.—W F
58a Thomaston, Conn.—Ad	40b Union Springs, N. Y.—Ad; U S	49 Watchung, N. J.—W F & Co
via 58 Thomaston, Me.—Ad	75 Union Square, N. Y.—Am	55a Wassaic, N. Y.—Am
66 Thomaston, Pa.—Ad	58c Unionville, Conn.—Ad	52, 58a Waterbury, Conn.—Ad; Int'l
52 Thompson, Conn.—Ad	41 Unionville, L. I.—Remsen	14 Waterbury, Vt.—Ad
57 Thompson, Pa.—Ad; W F & Co	63 Unionville, N. J.—Natl	58 Waterford, Conn.—Ad
56 Thompson Ridge, N. Y.—W F Co	56a Unionville, N. Y.—Am	74 Waterford, Mass.—Natl
67 Thompsontown, Pa.—Ad	67a Upper Bordentown, N. J.—Ad	40 Waterford, N. J.—Ad
58 Thompsonville, Conn.—Ad	13c Upper Lehigh, Pa.—Ad	20 Waterford, N. Y.—Natl
67 Thorndale, Pa.—Ad	49 Upper Mont Clair, N. J.—W F	21, 63 Water Gap, Pa.—U S
5 Thorndike, Mass.—Ad	64 Upper Saranac Lake, N. Y.—Nat	21c Waterloo, N. J.—U S
56, 75 Thousand Islands, N. Y.—Am	via 67 Urbana, Ohio—U S	56 Waterloo, N. Y.—Am
13, 40 Three Bridges, N. J.—Ad	20b Ushers, N. Y.—Natl	21 Water Mills, L. I.—L I
3 Three Mile Bay, N. Y.—Am	21, 56, 59, 95 Utica, N. Y.—Am; Natl	75 Watertown, N. Y.—Am
75 Three River Point, N. Y.—Am	74 Uxbridge, Mass.—Ad	58a Watertown, Conn.—Ad
5, 18 Three Rivers, Mass.—Ad	57 Vail's Gate, N. Y.—W F & Co	75 Watertown, N. Y.—Ad
69 Thurlow, Pa.—Ad	57 Vail's Gate Junc., N. Y.—W F	52, 58a Waterville, Conn.—Ad
1 Thurman, N. Y.—Natl	20 Valcour, N. Y.—Natl	5 Waterville, Mass.—Ad
14, 20 Ticonderoga, N. Y.—Natl	13 Valley, N. J.—Ad	via 58 Waterville, Me.—Ad
3 Tiffin, Ohio—Ad	59 Valley Cottage, N. Y.—Natl	21 Waterville, N. Y.—U S
3 Tilly Foster Mines, N. Y.—Am	95 Valley Falls, N. Y.—Natl	83 Watkin's Glen, N. Y.—Ad; Am
13a Tioga, Phila. Co., Pa.—Ad	52, 74 Valley Fal's, R. I.—Ad	21c Watseontog, N. J.—U S
57 Tioga, Tioga Co., Pa.—Am; WF Co	68 Valley Forge, Pa.—Ad	52 Wauregan, Conn.—Ad
57 Tioga Centre, N. Y.—W F & Co	59 Valley Mills, N. Y.—Natl	67 Waverly, N. J.—Ad
67 Tipton, Pa.—Ad	41 Valley Stream, L. I.—L I	41 Waverly, L. I.—L I
96 Titicut, Mass.—N Y & B	via 58 Vanceboro, Me.—Ad	21, 40, 57 Waverly, N. Y.—Ad; U S; W F
67b Titusville, N. J.—Ad	58 Van Cortlandt, N. Y.—Am	69 Wawa, Pa.—Ad
66 Tiverton, R. I.—N Y & B	57 Vandalia, N. Y.—W F & Co	
56, 82 Tivoli, N. Y.—Am	80 Vanderbilt Landing, S. I.—Brisk	21, 57 Wayland, N. Y.—U S; W F & Co

DIRECTIONS AND EXPRESS TO VARIOUS PLACES—Continued.

For Explanation of Abbreviations used, see page 112.

52	Wayland, R. I.—Ad	95	West Norwood, N. J.—Natl	40b	Willow Creek, N. Y.—Ad
20a	Waymart, Pa.—U S	95	West Nyack, N. Y.—Natl	21a	Willow Grove, Pa.—Ad; U S
49	Wayne, N. J.—W F & Co	13a	Weston, N. J.—Ad	21	Willow Point, N. Y.—U S
13a	Wayne Junc., Pa.—Ad	82, 95	West Park, N. Y.—Natl	20	Willsborough, N. Y.—Natl
95	Wayneport, N. Y.—Natl	21c	West Paterson, N. J.—U S	21	Willseyville, N. Y.—Natl
49	Weatherly, Pa.—Ad	52	West Patterson, N. Y.—Ad	69	Wilmington, Del.—Ad
58c	Wetogus, Conn.—Ad	20	West Pawlet, Vt.—Natl	81	Wilmington, N. C.—Ad
1	Weavertown, N. Y.—Natl	52	West Pawling, N. Y.—Ad	67	Willmore, Pa.—Ad
52	Webster, Mass.—Ad	21a	West Pittston, Pa.—U S	23	Wilseyville, N. Y.—U S; Natl
57	Webster, N. Y.—Natl; W F & Co	56, 82, 95	West Point, N. Y.—Am; Natl	75	Wilson, N. Y.—Am
85	Wedgewood, N. Y.—Am	81	West Point, Va.—Ad	30a, 83	Wilton Point, Conn.—Ad
40a, 56, 95	Weedsport, N. Y.—Ad; Natl	58	Westport, Conn.—Ad	58	Wilsons, Conn.—Ad
13c	Websport, Pa.—Ad	17	Westport, N. Y.—Ad	67a	Wilsons, N. J.—Ad
13	Welden, N. J.—Ad	20	Westport, N. Y.—Natl	39a	Wilton, Conn.—Ad
5	Wellesley, Mass.—Ad	62	West Providence, R. I.—Ad	via 58	Wilton, Me.—Ad
5	Wellesley Hills, Mass.—Ad	56	West Rush, N. Y.—Am	45	Winchells, N Y—Am
61	Wellfleet, Mass.—N Y & B	57	West Rutherford, N.J.—W F & Co	5	Winchendon, Mass.—Ad; Natl
57	Wells, N. Y.—W F & Co	20	West Rutland, Vt.—Natl	17	Winchester, N. H.—Ad
20b	Wellsbridge, N. Y.—Natl	58	West Somers, N. Y.—Am	52	Windemere, Conn.—Ad
via 67	Wellsburg, W. Va.—Ad	57	West Sparta, N. Y.—W F & Co	49	Windemere, N. Y.—W F & Co
57	Wellsville, N. Y.—U S; W F	5	West Springfield, Mass.—Ad	13c	Wind Gap, Pa.—Ad
67a	Wellwood, N. J.—Ad	36	West Stockbridge, Mass.—Ad	30	Windsor, Conn.—Ad
95	Wempler, N. Y.—Natl	1	West Stony Creek, N. Y.—Natl	67a	Windsor, N. J.—Ad
56	Wende, N. Y.—Am	21c	West Summit, N. J.—U S	20a	Windsor, N. Y.—Natl
94	Wenonah, N. J.—Ad	14	West Swanton, Vt.—Natl	17	Windsor, Vt.—Ad
68	Wernetsville, Pa.—Ad	52	West Thompson, Conn.—Ad	75	Windsor Bench, N. J.—Am
56	West Albany, N. Y.—Am	63	West Town, N. Y.—Ad	58	Windsor Locks, Conn.—Ad
14	West Alburgh, Vt.—Ad	20	West Troy, N. Y.—Natl	41	Winfield, L. I.—L I
95	West Athens, N. Y.—Natl	20	West Vienna, N. Y.—Natl	39a	Winnipauk, Conn.—Ad
13c	West Bangor, Pa.—Ad	94	Westville, N. J.—Ad	14	Winooski, Vt.—Natl
66	West Barnstable, Mass.—N Y & B	5	West Ware, Mass.—Ad	132	Winslow, N. J.—Ad
13c	West Bergen, N. J.—Ad	5	West Warren, Mass.—Ad	10, 13g	Winslow Junc., N. J.—Ad
56	West Bergen, N. Y.—Am	20	West Waterford, N. Y.—Natl	52	Winslow's, Mass.—Ad
56	West Bloomfield, N. Y.—Am	21	West Winfield, N. Y.—U S	58a	Winsted, Conn.—Ad
5	Westboro, Mass.—Ad	35	West Winsted, Conn.—Ad	59	Winterton, N. Y.—Natl
80	West New Brighton, S. I.—U S	17	Westwood, N. J.—Ad	20a	Winton, Pa.—Natl
5	West Brimfield, Mass.—Ad	52	West Wrentham, Mass.—Ad	67	Wissinoming, Pa.—Ad
58	Westbrook, Conn.—Ad	58d	Wethersfield, Conn.—Ad	75	Wolcott, N. Y.—Am
5	West Brookfield, Mass.—Ad	66	Weymouth, Mass.—Ad	15	Wolf Pond, N. Y.—Natl
6	West Brooklyn, L. I.—Remsen	20	Whallonsburgh, N. Y.—Natl	68	Womelsdorf, Pa.—Ad
41	Westbury, L. I.—L I	17	Whately, Mass.—Ad	75	Woodard, N. Y.—Am
75	West Camden, N. Y.—Am	13g	Wheatland, N. J.—Ad	94	Woodbine, N. J.—Ad
95	West Camp, N. Y.—Natl	52	Wheaton's, Conn.—Ad	13a	Woodbourne, Pa.—Ad
23	West Candor, N. Y.—Am; Natl	13g	Wheat Road, N. J.—Ad	14, 67,83	Woodbridge, N. J.—Ad
20	West Chazy, N. Y.—Natl	67	Wheat Sheaf, Pa.—Ad	94	Woodbury, N. J.—Ad
43	West Cheshire, Conn.—Ad	75	Wheeler's, N. Y.—Am	57	Woodburn, N. Y.—W F & Co
58	West Chester, Conn.—Ad	3 via 67	Wheeling, W. Va.—Ad	13	Woodfern, N. J.—Ad
58	Westchester, N. Y.—Ad	20	White Creek, Vt.—Ad	41a	Woodhaven, L. I.—L I
69	West Chester, Pa.—Ad	13c	White Face, L. I.—Local	55	Woodlawn, L. I.—Local
68	West Conshohocken, Pa.—Ad	21c	Whitehall, N. J.—U S	56a	Woodlawn, N. Y.—Am
30	West Cornwall, Conn.—Ad	20	Whitehall, N. Y.—Natl	13g	Woodmansie, N. J.—Ad
50	West Cornwall, N. Y.—Natl	40	White Hall, Pa.—Ad	58	Woodmont, Conn.—Ad
62	Wescott, R. I.—Ad	13c, 40	White Haven, Pa.—Ad	47	Woodridge, N. J.—U S
13g	Westcotts, N. J.—Ad	67a	White Hill, N. J.—Ad	13g	Woodruffs, N. J.—Ad
86	West Creek, N. J.—Ad	68	White Horse, Pa.—Ad	40a	Woods, N. Y.—Ad
43	West Cromwell, Conn.—Ad	19	Whitehouse, N. J.—Ad	41	Woodsburgh, L. I.—L I
40b	West Danby, N. Y.—Ad; U S	57	White Mills, Pa.—W F & Co	66	Wood's Holl, Mass.—N Y & B
41	West Deer Park, L. I.—L I	56	White Plains, N. Y.—Am	57	Woodside, N. J.—W F & Co
40a	West Dryden, N. Y.—Ad	90	Whitesport, N. Y.—Natl	41	Woodside, L. I.—L I
13c, 50	West End, L'g Branch, N.J.—Ad	11	White River Junc., Vt.—Ad	49	Woodside Park, N. J.—W F & Co
95	West Englewood, N. J.—Natl	59	White Shore, N. Y.—Natl	80	Woods of Arden, S. I.—U S
62	Westerly, R. I.—Ad	13g	White's, N. J.—Ad	74	Woonsocket, R. I.—Ad; N Y & B
68	West Falls, Pa.—Ad	56	Whitesboro, N. Y.—Natl	52, 58	Worcester, Mass.—Ad; Int'l
56	West Farmington, N. Y.—Am	56	Whitestone, N. Y.—Natl	20b	Worcester, N. Y.—Natl
56	West Farms, N. Y.—Ad	11, 83	Whitestone, Landing, L. I.—L I	63	Wurtendyke, N. J.—Natl
40b	West Fayette, N. Y.—Ad; U S	67	Whitford, Pa.—Ad	41b	Wreck Lead, L. I.—L I
58	Westfield, Conn.—Ad	13g	Whitings, N. J.—Ad	67a	Wrightstown, N. J.—Ad
5, 58c	Westfield, Mass.—Ad; Int'l	21	Whitney's Point, N. Y.—U S	20	Wrrtsboro, N. Y.—Natl
13	Westfield, N. J.—Ad	53	Wickford, R. I.—Ad	40	Wyalusing, Pa.—Ad
85	Westfield, Pa.—Am; U S; Natl	81	Wickatunk, L. I.—L I	41	Wyandance, L. I.—L I
41	West Hampton, L. I.—L I	62b	Wickford, R. I.—Ad	63	Wyckoff, N. J.—Natl
14	West Hartford, Vt.—Ad	62	Wickford Junc., R. I.—Ad	40a	Wyckoff, N. Y.—Ad
58	West Haven, Conn.—Ad	62b	Wickford Ldg., R. I.—Ad	21c	Wyoming, N. J.—Ad
17, 95	West Haverstraw, N. Y.—Natl	67b	Wilburtha Station, N. J.—Ad	9	Wyoming, N. Y.—Am
87	West Hurley, N. Y.—Am; Natl	13c, 40	Wilkesbarre, Pa.—Ad; U S	21a, 40	Wyoming, Pa.—Ad; U S
38	West Lebanon, N. Y.—Natl	67	Wilksburg, Pa.—Ad	10	Wysox, Pa.—Ad
68	West Manayunk, Pa.—Ad	40b	Willard, Seneca Co., N. Y.—Ad	58	Yantic, Conn.—Ad
13c	West Milton, Pa.—Ad	21	Willards, N. Y.—Ad	41	Yaphank, L. I.—L I
17	Westminster, Vt.—Ad	40b	Willets, N. Y.—Ad	13a	Yardly, Pa.—Ad
59	West Monroe, N. Y.—Natl	56a	Williams Bridge, N. Y.—Am	67a	Yardville, N. J.—Ad
67a	West Moorestown, N. J.—Ad	28	Williamsburg, L. I.—Weed & P	66	Yarmouth, Mass.—N Y & B
59	Westmoreland, N. Y.—Natl	58c	Williamsburgh, Mass.—Ad	58	Yatesville, Conn.—Ad
80	West New Brighton, S. I.—Brisk	48, 58	Willimantic, Conn.—Ad	67c	Yellowbrook, N. J.—Ad
54	West New Rochelle, N. Y.—Ad	14	Williston, Vt.—Ad	53, 56,82	Yonkers, N. Y.—Am; Fuller
5	West Newton, Mass.—Ad	21	Williwanna, Pa.—U S	21	York, N. Y.—Am; U S
35	West Norfolk, Conn.—Ad	51	Willow Brook, N. Y.—Am	58	Yorktown, N. Y.—Am

For $4.00 a year you will be supplied with the Weekly issue of this Guide, showing all changes in Time Tables, Foreign Mails, Steamship Sailings, etc.

BROOKLYN HORSE CAR LINES.

3d Avenue Line—From Fulton Ferry, through Fulton St., to Flatbush Av., to Third Av., to 25th St., to Greenwood Cemetery, connecting with trains to Fort Hamilton, Bay Ridge and Coney Island. Last car leaves Ferry at 12 16 a. m.

5th Avenue Line—From Fulton Ferry, through Furman St., passing Wall St. and South Ferries, to Atlantic and 5th Avs., to Greenwood Cemetery, connecting with Brooklyn, Bath & West End R. R. Night cars leave Fulton Ferry, 12 02, 12 22, 12 37, 12 52, 1 15, 2 15, 3 15, 4 15, 4 55, 5 00, 5 35 a. m.

7th Avenue Line—From Fulton Ferry, through Water, passing Catharine Ferry, to Fulton, Brooklyn Bridge, to Fulton, to Boerum Pl., to Atlantic Av., to 5th Av., to Flatbush Av., to 20th St., to 9th Av., to Greenwood, connecting with Prospect Park and Coney Island R. R. at 20th St. Last car leaves 39th St. and 9th Av. at 11 35; Fulton Ferry, 12 22 night.

9th and Vanderbilt Av. Line—From Brooklyn Bridge, through Washington St., to Concord St., to Navy St., to Park Av., to Vanderbilt Av., to 9th Av., to Greenwood Cemetery, connecting with Prospect Park & Coney Island R. R. Last car leaves Bridge Depot 11 45 night.

Adams St. Line—From Fulton Ferry, through Fulton to Front, to Catherine Ferry, to Adams St., to Brooklyn Bridge, to Fulton St., Boerum Pl., Atlantic Av., 5th Av. and 15th St., to Prospect Park at 9th Av., along 9th Av., to Greenwood, connecting with Prospect Park and Coney Island Railroad; also, 5th Av., to Greenwood Cemetery, main entrance. Last car leaves Fulton Ferry at 12 07 night.

Bergen St. Line—From South Ferry, Atlantic Av. to Boerum Pl., to Bergen, to Albany Av.; return via same route, or via Hoyt to Sackett, to Hamilton Ferry, or via Boerum Pl. to Fulton, to Adams, to Brooklyn Bridge, to Front, to Fulton Ferry. Last car leaves South Ferry at 12 55.

Brooklyn, Bay Ridge and Ft. Hamilton Steam Cars—From 36th St. and 3d Av., to Bay Ridge and Fort Hamilton via 3d Av.

Brooklyn, Bushwick and Queens County—From foot of Broadway, through Kent Av., North 2d St. and Metropolitan Av. to Lutheran Cemetery, Middle Village and St. John's Cemetery.

Bushwick Line—From Grand, Houston and Roosevelt St. Ferries, trough Kent Av., to Broadway, to Bedford Av., to South 6th St., to Meserole St., to Bushwick Av., to Myrtle Av., to City Line. Transfer at Graham Av. and Meserole St., to Flushing Av. line. Night cars leave Ferry depot at 12 17, 1 07, 1 37, 2 07, 2 45, 3 17, 3 47, 4 23, 4 57, 5 27 a. m.

Butler St. Line—From Fulton Ferry, Fulton to Front, Catharine Ferry to Adams, Brooklyn Bridge, to Boerum Pl., to Atlantic Ave.; or Wall and South Ferries, Atlantic Av. to Washington Av., to Butler, (connecting with Brighton Beach R. R.), to Nostrand Av. Last car leaves South Ferry at 12 00 night.

Calvary Cemetery Line—From foot Broadway, through Kent Av., to Grand St., to Humboldt, to Meeker Av., to Calvary Cemetery. Last car leaves Ferry, 1 02 a. m.

Calvary Cemetery, Greenpoint and Brooklyn Line—From Fulton Ferry to Concord St., to Navy St., to Park Av., to Throop Av., to Broadway, to Union Av., to Driggs St., to Van Cott Av., to Oakland St., to Box St., to Manhattan Av. Transfer Crosstown line at Park and Washington Avs.

Court St. Line—From Fulton Ferry, through Fulton to Court, to Hamilton Av., to 3d Av., to 25th St., to 5th Av., to Greenwood Cemetery, connecting with Coney Island and Fort Hamilton trains. Night cars from Fulton Ferry, 1 37, 2 07, 2 37, 3 07, 3 37, 4 07, 4 37, 5 07, 5 22 a. m.

Crosstown Line—From Erie Basin, through Richards St., to Woodhull, to Columbia, to Atlantic Av. (South Ferry), to Court St., to Joralemon, to Willoughby, to Raymond St., to Park Av., to Washington Av., to Kent Av., to Broadway (passing Grand, and Roosevelt Ferries), to Driggs St., to Van Cott Av., to Manhattan Av., to Newtown Creek. Branch to Long Island City, through Central Av. and Borden Av., to 31st St. Ferry, and Long Island R. R. Depot. Night cars leave depots, 1 00, 1 30, 2 30, 4 00 a. m.

Crosstown Line (Atlantic Av. R.R.) From Fulton Ferry, Fulton to Front, Catharine Ferry to Adams, Brooklyn Bridge, to Fulton, to Boerum Pl., to Bergen, to Hoyt (transfer at Hoyt St., to Bergen St. line to and from Albany Av.), to Sackett to Hamilton Ferry. Last car leaves Hamilton Ferry at 1 10, Bridge at 12 40 night.

Cypress Hills Line—From City line to St. Nicholas Av., to Myrtle Av., to Cypress Av., to Cypress Hills. Last car leaves City line at 9 15 p. m.

Cypress Hills Extension—From Fulton and Alabama Av., through Fulton Av., to Cypress Av., to main entrance Cypress Hills Cemetery.

DeKalb Av. Line—From Fulton Ferry, through Water St., to Washington St., to Fulton St., to DeKalb Av., to Myrtle Av., to Manhattan Beach Railroad. Night cars leave ferry, 12 17, 12 27, 12 37, 12 51, 1 06, 1 21, 1 36, 1 51, 2 06, 2 30, 3 06, 3 30, 4 20, 4 50, 5 20 a. m.

DeKalb and Franklin Av. Line—From Fulton Ferry, through Water, Washington and Fulton Sts. and DeKalb and Franklin Avs. to City line at Flatbush.

East New York Line—From Broadway ferries through Broadway to East New York; return same route. Night cars leave Ferry at 1 30, 2 30, 3 10, 3 50, 4 30, 5 10 a. m.

Fifteenth Street Line—From Hamilton Ferry, through Hamilton Av., to Fifteenth St., to 9th Av., to 20th St. (Culver's Depot). Last car leaves Ferry 11 39 night.

Flatbush Av. Line—From Fulton Ferry and Bridge Depot, through Fulton to Flatbush av., to Prospect Park and Flatbush. Night cars leave Fulton Ferry, 1 37, 2 07, 2 37, 3 07, 3 37, 4 07, 4 37, 5 07, 5 37, 6 07 a. m.

Flushing Av. Line—From Fulton Ferry, through Fulton to Sands, to Hudson Av., to Flushing Av., to Broadway and Graham Av., to Van Cott Av., to Manhattan Av., to Greenpoint, to 23d and 10th St. Ferries, Greenpoint. Transfers passengers to Greenpoint Line at Classon and Flushing Avs. and to Ridgewood and Grand St. and Broadway Ferries at Graham Av. and Messrole St. Night cars leave Fulton Ferry, 1 08, 1 23, 1 38, 1 53, 2 22, 2 52, 3 22, 3 52, 4 22, 4 52, 5 22, 5 38 a. m.

Franklin Av. Line—From foot Grand St., through Water St., to Kent Av., to South 8th, to Wythe Av., to Franklin Av., to Prospect Park, to Ocean Av., to Franklin Av. in Flatbush, to Greenwood Cemetery. Last car leaves Franklin and Flatbush Avs., 7 a. m.; Grand St. Ferry, 1 40 a. m.

Fulton St. and East New York—From Fulton Ferry through Fulton St. to East New York. Night cars leave Fulton Ferry, 1 08, 1 22, 2 08, 2 30, 3 00, 3 30, 4 00, 4 30, 5 00, 5 23.

Furman St. Line—From Fulton Ferry, Furman St., to Atlantic Av. (South Ferry), to Columbia St., to Sackett St., to Hamilton Ferry. Transfers to Van Brunt St. and Erie Basin line and to Hamilton Av. line from Hamilton Ferry.

Gates Av. Line—From Fulton Ferry, through Fulton St. to Greene Av., to Franklin Av., to Gates Av., to Broadway, to Ridgewood. Night cars leave Fulton Ferry, 1 52, 2 23, 3 07, 3 48, 4 06, 4 30 a. m.

Greenpoint Line—From Fulton Ferry, by Fulton St., to Myrtle Av., to Classon (or Washington) Av., to Kent Av., to Franklin St., to Commercial St., to Newtown Creek. Transfer to Flushing Avenue line at Classon and Flushing Avs. Night cars leave Fulton Ferry, 1 12, 1 37, 2 07, 3 07, 3 37, 4 37, 5 38 a. m.

Greenpoint and Bushwick Line—From depot through Bushwick Av., to Meserole St., to Graham Av., to Van Cott Av., to Manhattan Av., to Greenpoint Av. to 10th and 23d St. ferries, Greenpoint.

Greenpoint and Lorimer Street Line—From 10th St. Ferry, Greenpoint, to Lorimer St., to Park Av., to Nostrand Av., to Prospect Av.

Hamilton Avenue Line—From Hamilton Av. Ferry, through Hamilton Av. to 3d Av., to 25th St., to Greenwood Cemetery, connecting at 3d Av. and 25th St. for Fort Hamilton, Bay Ridge and Coney Island.

Hamilton Avenue and Prospect Park Line—From Hamilton Ferry, through Hamilton Av., to 9th St., to Prospect Park. Last car leaves ferry, 12 10 a. m.

Hicks Street Line—Through Hicks St., Atlantic Av., to Boerum Pl., to Adams St., to Brooklyn Bridge, Catharine and Fulton Ferries. Return by same route through Hicks St. to Hamilton Av., 15th St., to Prospect Park (5th Av. to Greenwood Cemetery and Ninth Av. to Prospect Park and Coney Island R. R. and Greenwood Cemetery.

Jamaica (Electric)—From Alabama Av. to Jamaica.

Lee and Nostrand Avenue Line—From foot of Broadway, to Driggs St., to Division Av., to Lee Av., to Nostrand Av., to Malbone St., to Willink entrance, Prospect Park. Night cars leave Broadway ferries, 12 18, 12 58, 1 22, 1 55 a. m.

BROOKLYN HORSE CAR LINES.—Continued.

Lutheran Cemetery Line From City line to Myrtle Av., to Palmetto, to Metropolitan Ave. (Lutheran Cemetery Middle Village). Last car leaves City line at 10 00 p. m.

Myrtle Av. Line From Fulton Ferry, through Fulton St., to Myrtle Av., to Ridgewood. Night cars leave Fulton Ferry, 1 22, 1 52, 2 22, 2 52, 3 22, 3 52, 4 22, 4 52, 5 22 a. m.

Newtown Line From foot of Broadway, through Kent Av., to Grand, to Newtown. Last car leaves ferry, 11 52 p. m.

Prospect Park and Flatbush Line Flatbush Av. (Willink entrance Prospect Park) to Greenwood Cemetery.

Prospect Park and Holy Cross Cemetery From Flatbush Av. and Malbone St., through Malbone St., Clove road, Clarkson St. (Almshouse, Hospital and Asylum), and Canarsie Lane, to Ho y Cross Cemetery.

Putnam Av. Line From Fulton Ferry, through Fulton St., to Putnam Av., to Nostrand Av., to Halsey St., to Broadway. Last car leaves Fulton Ferry, 12 40 a. m.

Ralph Av. Line From Broadway and Ralph Av., through Ralph Av., to Atlantic Av. East New York cars transfer both ways.

Reid Av. Line From Broadway ferries, Broadway, to Reid Av., to Fulton Av., to Utica Av., to Atlantic Av. Night cars leave Ferry at 2 00, 2 30, 3 00, 3 30, 4 00, 4 35 a. m.

Smith and Jay Street Line From Fulton Ferry through Water, to Main, to Prospect, to Jay, to Smith, to 9th Av., to 15th St., to City Line, connecting with horse cars to Coney Island. Last car leaves ferry depot, 12 44 a. m.

Sumner Av. Line From Broadway ferries, through Broadway, to Sumner Av., to Fulton St., to Troy Av., to Bergen St. Last night car leaves ferry at 1 10 night.

Tompkins Av. Line From Atlantic and Kingston Avs., through Kingston to Fulton, to Tompkins Av., to Harrison Av., to Division Av., to Roebling St., to Broadway, to Roosevelt and Grand St. ferries. Last car from ferry depot 1 18 a. m.

Van Brunt Street and Erie Basin Line—From Hamilton Ferry, through Hamilton Av. to Van Brunt St., to Erie Basin, through Elizabeth St. to Columbia St., Erie Basin Dry Docks. Transfer at Hamilton Ferry for South, Wall and Fulton Ferries, also by Sackett and Bergen Street Line to Albany Av., also, by South Brooklyn Central R. R. from Hamilton Ferry, through Sackett, Hoyt and Bergen Sts., to Albany Av.

Vanderbilt Avenue Line See "9th Av. and Vanderbilt Av. Line."

STEAMBOATS NOT RUNNING FROM NEW YORK CITY.

Romer & Tremper Steamboat Co., Steamboats J. H. Tremper and M. Martin **leave Newburgh** (for up Hudson River to Albany) daily, at 7 30 a. m., New Hamburgh 8 00 a. m., Marlborough 8 05 a. m., Milton 8 25 a. m., Poughkeepsie 8 50 a. m., Highland 8 55 a. m., Hyde Park 9 15 a. m., Esopus 9 25 a. m., Rondout 10 30 a. m., Rhinebeck 10 50 a. m., Barrytown 11 10 a. m., Tivoli 11 30 a. m., Saugerties 11 40 a. m., Malden 12 m., Smith Dock 12 15 p. m., Germantown 12 25 p. m., Catskill 12 45 p. m., Hudson 1 15 p. m., Coxsackie 1 45 p. m., Stuyvesant 2 05 p. m., New Baltimore 2 30 p. m., Coeymans 2 45 p. m., Castleton 3 15 p. m. **Arrive at Albany,** 4 00 p. m. (Trip from Albany to Troy on Tuesdays and Fridays only.)

Boats leave Albany (for down Hudson River) daily at 8 00 a. m., Castleton 8 40 a. m., Coeymans 9 10 a. m., New Baltimore 9 25 a. m., Stuyvesant 9 40 a. m., Coxsackie 10 00 a. m., Hudson 10 45 a. m., Catskill 11 40 a. m., Germantown 11 50 a. m., Smith Dock 11 40 a. m., Malden 11 50 a. m., Saugerties 12 05 p. m., Tivoli 12 15 p. m., Barrytown 12 40 p. m., Rhinebeck 1 10 p.m., Rondout 2 15 p. m., Esopus 2 50 p. m., Hyde Park 3 05 p. m., Highland 3 30 p. m., Poughkeepsie 4 00 p. m., Milton 4 10 p.m., Marlborough 4 25 p. m., New Hamburgh 4 40 p. m. **Arrive at Newburgh,** 5 30 p. m.

Nyack and Tarrytown Ferry Co., Steamboat Rockland leaves Nyack for Tarrytown daily, except Sundays, at 7 10 a. m., 8 00 a. m., 9 30 a. m., 11 30 a. m., 1 15 p. m., 2 15 p. m., 3 30 p. m., 5 05 p. m., 6 30 p. m. *On Sundays,* 9 15 a. m., 11 15 a. m., 1 15 p. m., 2 15 p. m., 3 30 p. m., 5 15 p. m., 6 30 p. m.

Returning leave Tarrytown for Nyack daily, except Sunday, 8 00 a. m., 9 00 a. m., 10 10 a. m., 12 20 p. m., 1 50 p. m., 3 20 p. m., 4 30 p. m., 6 00 p. m., 7 00 p. m. *On Sundays,* 10 05 a. m., 12 m., 1 50 p. m., 2 55 p. m., 4 15 p. m., 6 00 p. m., 7 00 p. m.

Ferry Boat leaves Garrison for West Point daily, except Sunday, 7 14 a. m., 8 00 a. m., 9 15 a. m., 9 30 a. m., 11 05 a. m., 12 10 p. m., 1 10 p. m., 1 53 p. m., 3 00 p. m., 4 05 p. m., 4 46 p. m., 5 30 p. m. *On Sundays,* 8 45 a. m., 9 11 a. m., 10 33 a. m., 4 20 p. m., 4 45 p. m., 5 28 p. m.

Returning leave West Point for Garrisons daily, except Sunday, 7 50 a. m., 8 56 a. m., 9 27 a. m., 11 00 a. m., 12 35 p. m., 1 14 p. m., 2 50 p. m., 3 53 p. m., 4 31 p. m., 5 16 p. m., 5 45 p. m. *On Sundays,* 9 00 a. m., 10 41 a. m., 1 33 p. m., 5 16 p. m. Fare 15c.

Newburgh and Fishkill Ferry, Ferryboat leaves Newburgh for Fishkill daily except Sundays, at 5 50 a. m., *6 40 a. m., *7 25 a. m., 8 00 a. m., *8 35 a. m., *9 15 a. m., *9 45 a. m., *10 20 a. m., *10 50 a. m., *11 20 a. m., *11 55 a. m., *12 20 p. m., *12 45 p. m., *1 15 p. m., 1 30 p. m., 2 15 p. m., 3 15 p. m., 3 45 p. m., *4 10 p. m., *4 45 p. m., *5 15 p. m., *5 35 p. m., 6 05 p. m., *6 15 p. m., *7 15 p. m., *7 45 p. m., *8 10 p. m., *8 40 p. m., 9 30 p. m., 10 15 p. m. *On Sundays,* 7 20 a. m., *8 35 a. m., 9 20 a. m., 9 50 a. m., 10 30 a. m., *11 00 a. m., *11 45 a. m., 12 15 p. m., 1 15 p. m., 1 30 p. m., 2 15 p. m., 2 45 p. m., 3 15 p. m., 3 45 p. m., *4 10 p. m., 4 30 p. m., 5 10 p. m., *5 35 p. m., 6 05 p. m., 6 45 p. m., *7 15 p. m., *7 45 p. m., *8 10 p. m., *8 40 p. m., *9 30 p. m., 10 15 p. m. *Trips marked * are from Depot Slip.*

Returning leaves Fishkill for Newburgh daily, except Sunday, at 5 45 a. m., 6 25 a. m., *7 00 a. m., *7 41 a. m., 8 30 a. m., *8 55 a. m., *9 30 a. m., *10 a. m., *10 35 a. m., *11 05 a. m., *11 35 a. m., *12 11 p. m., *12 34 p. m., *1 00 p. m., *1 35 p. m., 2 00 p. m., 2 30 p. m., 3 30 p. m., 3 55 p. m., *4 25 p. m., *5 02 p. m., 5 25 p. m., *5 50 p. m., 6 30 p. m., *7 01 p. m., *7 30 p. m., *7 55 p. m., *8 26 p. m., *9 05 p. m., 10 00 p. m. *On Sundays,* 5 50 a. m., 8 00 a. m., *9 00 a. m., 9 35 a. m., 10 10 a. m., 10 45 a. m., 11 45 a. m., 12 m., *1 00 p. m., 1 30 p. m., 2 00 p. m., 2 30 p. m., 3 00 p. m., 3 30 p. m., 3 55 p. m., *4 25 p. m., 4 55 p. m., 5 30 p. m., 5 50 p. m., 6 30 p. m., *6 45 p. m., 7 55 p. m., *8 26 p. m., 9 00 p. m., 10 00 p. m. *Trips marked * are from Depot Slip. Stages connect at Ferry landing for Matteawan every day.*

Ferry Boat Transport, Leaves Rondout for Rhinecliff daily except Sunday, at 6 35 a. m., 7 20 a. m., 8 15 a. m., 9 35 a. m., 10 45 a. m., 11 15 a. m., 11 55 a. m., 12 40 p. m., 2 15 p. m., 2 55 p. m., 4 30 p. m., 5 30 p. m., 6 35 p. m., 7 25 p. m. *On Sunday,* 7 15 a. m., 8 15 a. m., 1 30 p. m., 5 30 p. m., 6 30 p. m.

Leave Rhinecliffe for Rondout daily except Sunday, at 7 07 a. m., 7 47 a. m., 8 42 a. m., 10 00 a. m., 11 02 a. m., 11 35 a. m., 12 25 p. m., 1 00 p. m., 2 20 p. m., 3 19 p. m., 4 50 p. m., 6 02 p. m., 7 02 p. m., 7 55 p. m. *On Sunday,* 7 47 a. m., 8 42 a. m., 2 00 p. m., 6 02 p. m., 7 02 p. m.

Propeller Huntington leaves Huntington, L. I., for Norwalk, Conn., on Saturdays at 8 00 a. m. Returning leaves Norwalk on Saturdays, 3 00 p. m. Fare 50c.

Bridgeport and Port Jefferson Steamboat Co. On and after May 10th steamboat Nonowantuc leaves daily except Sunday, from Port Jefferson, L. I., for Bridgeport, Conn., at 8 30 a. m. Returning, leaves Bridgeport for Port Jefferson, 3 00 p. m. Fare 75c., excursion fare $1.

Greenport and Shelter Island Ferry Co. Until June 1st sail boats will make trips as often as winds will allow, leaving each side at the same time.

BROOKLYN ANNEX,

From foot Fulton St., Brooklyn Fare 10 cents

Connections are made at Jersey City with the following roads:

Pennsylvania R. R., New York, Susquehanna & Western R. R., West Shore R. R., Lehigh Valley R. R.

Leaves Fulton St., Brooklyn, for Jersey City *every day* at 6 30, 7 00, 7 30, 8 00, 8 30, 9 00, 9 30, 10 00, 10 30, 11 00, 11 30 a. m., 12 00 noon, 12 30, 1 00, 1 30, 2 00, 2 30, 3 00, 3 30, 4 00, 4 30, 5 00, 5 30, 6 00, 6 30, 7 00, 7 30, 8 00, 8 30, 9 00, 9 30, 10 00, 10 30, 11 00 p. m.

Leaves Jersey City for Brooklyn *every day* at 6 30, 7 00, 7 30, 8 00, 8 30, 9 00, 9 30, 10 00, 10 30, 11 00, 11 30 a. m., 12 00 noon, 12 30, 1 00, 1 30, 2 00, 2 30, 3 00, 3 30, 4 00, 4 30, 5 00, 5 30, 6 00, 6 30, 7 00, 7 30, 8 00, 8 30, 9 00, 9 30, 10 00, 10 30, 11 00 p. m.

Fall River Line for Boston, Newport, etc., Connections are made *every day* by the 4 30 p. m. trip from foot of Fulton St. direct to Pier. Connects also for Brooklyn on arrival of **Fall River Boat** at Pier.

Connection can also be made from Jersey City by the 4 00 p. m. trip to **Fall River Boat.**

BALTIMORE AND OHIO R. R.,

via Central R. R. of N. J., foot of Liberty St.
For "**Fares to all Places**," see Index.
Ticket Offices.—Depot, foot of Liberty St., 21, 71, 261, 415, 944, 1140, 1328 Broadway. 737 6th Avenue, 264 W. 125th St., 132 E. 125th St. Brooklyn: 4 Court St., 860 Fulton St., 98 Broadway.

To Washington.

STATIONS.	93	95	97	99	101	103	91
	a. m.	a. m.	a. m.	p. m.	p. m.	p. m.	Night
New York....lv.		8 30	11 00	1 30	2 30	4 45	12 00
foot Liberty st.							a. m.
Philadelphia.ar.	11 10	1 40	4 10	5 10	7 25	4 00	
Philadelphia.lv.	8 15	11 15	1 45	4 15	5 15	7 30	4 10
Chester....lv.	8 31	11 31	2 01	4 31	5 32	7 47	4 28
Wilmington.lv.	8 46	11 48	2 18	4 46	5 50	8 05	4 50
Newark. Del.lv.	9 01	12 04	2 34	5 01	6 06	8 21	5 30
Baltimore...ar.	10 35	1 40	4 10	6 35	7 45	10 00	7 00
Washington.ar.	11 45	2 30	5 00	7 15	8 45	10 55	8 15
	a. m.	p. m.	p. m.	p. m.	p. m.	p. m.	a. m.

To New York.

STATIONS.	90	92	94	96	98	102	104
	a. m.	a. m.	a. m.	p. m.	p. m.	p. m.	p. m.
Washington.lv.	8 00	9 30	11 25	2 30	4 15	8 00	10 30
Baltimore...lv.	8 30	10 20	12 15	3 20	4 54	8 55	11 50
Newark, Del.ar.	10 06	11 48	1 43	4 48	6 21	10 30	1 50
Wilmington.ar.	10 26	12 08	2 03	5 08	6 41	10 52	2 13
Chester.....ar.	10 42	12 26	2 21	5 26	6 57	11 09	2 37
Philadelphia.ar.	11 00	12 45	2 40	5 45	7 15	11 30	3 00
Philadelphia.lv.	11 05	12 50	2 45	5 50	7 20		3 10
New York...ar.	1 50	3 30	5 30	8 35	9 55		6 55
Foot Liberty St.	p. m.	p. m.	p. m.	p. m.	p. m.	p. m.	a. m.

Day coaches and Pullman buffet parlor cars attached to all day trains, and Pullman palace sleepers attached to night trains. Train No. 99 Vestibuled Limited, is composed entirely of Vestibuled Coaches and Pullman Buffet Parlor Cars. No extra fare is charged on this train.

New York, Philadelphia & Chicago Line.
WESTWARD.

STATIONS.	No. 5. Limited.		No. 7. Chic. Exp.
	Night.		
L've New York...	*12 00		*2 30 p. m.
" Newark, N.J. } B'd Br'k	*11 25 p. m.		2 35 "
" Trenton, " } Route.	*2 10 a. m.		3 46 "
Arr. Philadelphia.	4 00 "		5 10 "
L've Phila.(Eastern time).	*4 10 "		*5 15 "
Arr. Chester........	4 26 "		5 32 "
" Wilmington .	4 50 "		5 50 "
L've Baltimore....	8 00 "		8 05 "
" Washington .	8 55 "		9 05 "
Arr. Harper's Ferry.	10 27 "		10 40 "
" Martinsburg	11 00 "		11 11 "
L've Cumberland .			1 30 a. m.
Arr. Pittsburgh...			7 10 "
L've Pittsburgh .			7 30 "
L've Cumberland .	1 25 p. m.		
Arr. Piedmont .	2 15 "		
" Deer Park .			Runs
" Mountain Lake Park			via
" Oakland .	3 17 p. m.		Pittsburgh.
L've Grafton .	5 10 "		
Arr. Wheeling .	9 05 "		10 15 a. m.
L've Wheeling .	8 10 "		10 25 "
Arr. Bellaire (Central time) .	7 47 "		10 02 "
" Zanesville .	10 08 "		12 41 p. m.
" Newark, O.	10 55 "		1 40 "
Arr. Columbus .	3 25 a. m.		3 00 p. m.
Arr. Mt. Vernon .	11 45 p. m.		3 11 p. m.
" Mansfield .	12 19 a. m.		4 33 "
" Chicago Junction .	1 35 "		5 30 "
Arr. Tiffin .	2 15 a. m.		6 57 p. m.
" Sandusky .			7 01 "
Arr. Fostoria .	*2 55 "		7 30 "
" Defiance .	3 57 "		9 10 "
" Garrett .	5 00 "		11 25 "
" Chicago .	9 05 "		5 30 a. m.

Chicago, Philadelphia & New York Line.
EASTWARD.

STATIONS.	No. 6. Limited.		No. 8. Express.
L've Chicago (Central time)	*7 05 p. m.		*10 25 p. m.
Arr. Garrett .	11 45 "		3 20 a. m.
" Defiance .	12 42 a. m.		4 45 "
" Fostoria .	1 30 "		6 40 "
" Tiffin .	1 49 "		7 15 "
L've Sandusky .			7 10 a. m.
" Monroeville .			8 30 "
Arr. Chicago Junction .	2 25 a. m.		8 20 a. m.
" Mansfield .	3 14 "		9 58 "
" Mt. Vernon .	4 14 "		11 21 "
L've Columbus .	11 05 p. m.		11 20 a. m.
Arr. Newark .	5 00 a. m.		12 15 p. m.
" Zanesville .	5 53 "		1 33 "
" Bellaire .	8 42 "		4 40 "
" Wheeling (Eastern time).	9 50 "		6 20 "
L've Wheeling .			6 30 "
Arr. Grafton .	1 03 p. m.		
" Oakland .	3 01 "		
" Mountain Lake Park .			Runs
" Deer Park .			via
" Piedmont .	4 03 p. m.		Pittsburgh.
" Cumberland .	5 00 "		
Arr. Pittsburgh .			9 10 p. m.
L've Pittsburgh .			10 20 "
Arr. Cumberland .			3 55 a. m.
" Martinsburg .	7 25 p. m.		6 05 "
" Harper's Ferry .	8 01 "		6 47 "
" Washington .	9 35 "		8 35 "
" Baltimore .	10 45 "		9 45 "
" Wilmington .	2 13 a. m.		12 08 p. m.
" Chester .	2 37 "		12 26 "
" Philadelphia .	3 00 "		12 45 "
L've Philadelphia. }	3 10 "		12 50 "
Arr. Trenton, N.J. } B'd Br'k	4 19 "		2 09 "
" Newark, } Route	6 16 "		3 30 "
" New York.... }	6 55 "		3 30 "

* Daily.   † Except Sunday.   » Stop on Signal or notice to conductor.

Train No. 5 Vestibuled Limited has Day Coaches and Pullman Sleeper New York to Washington. Day Coaches and Pullman Buffet Sleeping Car Baltimore and Washington to Chicago. Pullman Sleeping Car Wheeling to Chicago.

Train No. 7 has Day Coaches and Pullman Palace Car New York to Washington. Day Coaches and Pullman Palace Sleeping Cars Baltimore and Washington to Pittsburgh, Wheeling and Chicago.

The List of Places on pages 112 to 123 includes over 3,000 towns in New York, Connecticut, New Jersey, Pennsylvania and adjacent states. The Express Company taking packages for these towns is given at each place.

BALTIMORE & OHIO R. R.—Continued.

New York, Cincinnati & St. Louis Line.
WESTWARD.

STATIONS.	No. 1. Limited.	No. 3. Express.
L've New York	*8 30 a. m.	†1 45 p. m.
" Newark, N. J. } B'd Br'k	8 50 "	4 35 "
" Trenton, } Route.	9 38 "	5 55 "
Arr. Philadelphia	11 10 "	7 25 "
L've Phila. (Eastern time)	*11 15 "	*7 30 "
" Chester	11 31 "	7 47 "
" Wilmington	11 48 "	8 05 "
" Newark, Del	12 08 p.m.	8 25 "
Arr. Baltimore	1 40 "	10 00 "
L've Baltimore	2 00 "	10 10 "
Arr. Washington	2 50 "	11 05 "
L've Washington	3 00 "	11 10 "
" Washington Junction	4 04 "	12 24 a. m.
" Harper's Ferry	4 28 "	12 51 "
" Martinsburg	5 00 "	1 25 "
" Cumberland	7 01 "	3 45 "
" Keyser	7 55 "	4 30 "
" Piedmont	8 10 "	4 45 "
" Oakland	9 11 "	5 50 "
Arr. Grafton	10 55 "	7 45 "
L've Grafton	11 00 "	8 05 "
Arr. Clarksburg	11 57 "	9 17 "
" Parkersburg	2 10 a. m.	11 30 "
L've Parkersburg (Central time)	1 20 "	10 10 "
Arr. Athens	2 34 "	11 58 "
" Chillicothe	4 25 "	1 55 p. m.
" Cincinnati	7 35 "	5 45 "
L've Cincinnati	8 15 "	8 30 "
" Vincennes	2 00 p. m.	2 13 a. m.
Arr. St. Louis	6 50 "	7 45 "
L've Cincinnati	8 15 a. m.	7 30 p. m.
Arr. Louisville	12 40 p. m.	11 45 "
L've Cincinnati C. H. & D. R. R	*8 00 a. m.	*7 15 p. m.
Arr. Indianapolis	11 40 "	10 55 "

St. Louis, Cincinnati & New York Line.
EASTWARD.

STATIONS.	No. 2. Limited.	No. 4. Express.
L've Indianapolis C. H. & D. R. R.	*3 30 p. m.	*3 55 a. m.
Arr. Cincinnati	7 30 "	7 45 "
L've St. Louis (Central time)	8 00 a. m.	8 05 p. m.
" Vincennes	12 57 p. m.	1 30 a. m.
" Louisville	2 25 "	2 20 "
Arr. Cincinnati	6 37 "	7 20 "
L've Cincinnati	7 30 "	8 25 "
" Chillicothe	10 42 "	11 36 p. m.
" Athens	12 31 a. m.	2 43 "
Arr. Parkersburg (Central time)	1 45 "	4 20 "
L've Parkersburg (Eastern time)	2 50 "	5 30 "
" Clarksburg	5 11 "	8 24 "
Arr. Grafton	5 55 "	9 15 "
L've Grafton	6 00 "	9 15 "
Arr. Oakland	7 45 "	11 43 "
" Piedmont	8 30 "	12 43 a. m.
" Keyser	8 50 "	12 55 "
" Cumberland	9 30 "	1 36 "
" Sir John's Run		2 57 "
" Martinsburg	11 47 a. m.	3 54 "
" Harper's Ferry	12 22 p. m.	4 31 "
" Washington Junction	12 45 "	5 05 "
" Washington	1 55 "	6 20 "
L've Washington	2 05 "	6 30 "
Arr. Baltimore	2 55 "	7 30 "
L've Baltimore	3 20 "	8 39 "
Arr. Newark	4 52 "	10 10 "
" Wilmington	5 08 "	10 26 "
" Chester	5 26 "	10 42 "
" Philadelphia	5 45 "	11 00 "
L've Philadelphia	5 50 "	11 05 "
Arr. Trenton, N. J. } B'd Br'k	7 15 "	12 35 p. m.
" Newark, N. J. } Route.	8 30 "	1 45 "
" New York	8 35 "	1 50 "

* Daily.   † Except Sunday.

Train No. 1 Vestibuled Limited has Day Coaches and Pullman Parlor Car New York to Washington. Day Coaches and Pullman Buffet Sleeping Car Baltimore and Washington to Cincinnati. Parlor Cars Cincinnati to Louisville and St. Louis. Pullman Vestibuled Sleeping Car Baltimore and Washington to Indianapolis, except Saturday.

Train No. 3 has Day Coaches and Pullman Parlor Car New York to Washington. Day Coaches and Pullman Buffet Sleeping Car Baltimore and Washington to St. Louis.

PHILADELPHIA, WILMINGTON AND BALTIMORE R. R.

Via Pennsylvania R. R. foot of Cortlandt and Desbrosses Sts.

For through trains to Baltimore see Pennsylvania R. R. Time Table.

M. Philadelphia.	9 More's.	23 Riverside.	48 Bacon Hill.	75 Edgewood.
1 South St. Station.	10 Ridley Park.	24 Edge Moor.	51 North East.	77 Magnolia.
3 Gray's Ferry.	11 Crum Lynne.	25 Landith.	54 Charlestown.	78 Gunpowder.
8 58th St.	12 Eddystone.	29 Wilmington.	57 Principio.	79 Harewood Park.
4 Mount Moriah.	13 Chester.	30 Newport.	59 Perryville.	81 Chase's.
4 Bonaffon.	14 Lamokin.	33 Stanton.	60 Havre de Grace.	83 Bengie.
5 Paschall.	15 Thurlow.	36 Ruthby.	63 Oakington.	85 Middle River.
6 Darby.	16 Trainer.	38 Pencador.	65 Swan Creek.	87 Stemmer's Run.
6 Academy.	17 Linwood.	38 Newark Center.	65 Aberdeen.	89 Back River.
7 Sharon Hill.	18 Claymont.	38 Newark.	67 Short Lane.	91 Bay View.
7 Folcroft.	20 Grubb's Landing.	41 Iron Hill.	69 Perryman's.	94 Biddle Street.
8 Glenolden.	21 Holly Oak.	43 Elkton.	71 Bush River.	95 Baltimore.
9 Norwood.	22 Bellevue.			

LOCAL TRAINS BETWEEN PHILADELPHIA, CHESTER AND WILMINGTON.

* Daily.   † Express trains.

Leave Philadelphia (Broad St. Station), for **Chester** and intermediate stations, 6 25, 7 27, 7 47, 8 31, *9 10, *10 28, 11 55 a. m., 12 37, 1 25, *2 02, 2 38, *3 01, 3 22, †4 05, 4 37, *†5 08, *5 21, 5 27, *†6 07, 6 12, 6 22, 6 38, *†6 57, 7 10, *8 35, 10 03, *10 10, *†11 20, *11 33 p. m. Sundays only, 8 35 a. m., 12 35, 2 05, 6 10, 10 00 p. m. Arrive Chester, Express trains, in 25 minutes; Accommodation trains in 37 minutes.

For **Wilmington**, *†3 50, 6 25, *†7 20, 7 27, *†8 31, *9 10, 10 29, *10 28, *†11 18, 11 55 a. m., †12 35, 1 25, †2 02, 2 28, *3 01, 3 22, †3 38, †4 05, †4 30, 4 37, *†5 08, 5 21, *5 12, †6 07, 6 22, *†6 57, 10, *11 30, *11 33, *†11 57 p. m. Sundays, 8 35 a. m., 12 35, 2 05, 6 10 p. m. Arrive Wilmington, Express trains, in 45 minutes; Accommodation trains in 1 hour 10 minutes.

Trains to Philadelphia.

Leave **Wilmington**, *†2 00, *†2 52, *†4 20, †6 30, 6 40, 6 55, 7 05, 7 50, 8 10, †8 50, 9 10, †9 47, *10 07, *10 40, 10 45, 11 33, *†11 51 a. m., †12 23, †12 30, 12 38, †1 30, *†2 27, 2 35, †00, *†5 21, 5 32, *†6 26, 6 40, *†7 05, *7 40, *10 00, *10 10, *10 45 p. m. Sundays, 7 00, 8 15 a. m., 12 10, 1 25, 4 10, 5 39 p. m. Arrive Philadelphia, Express trains, in 50 minutes; Accommodation trains in 1 hour 10 minutes.

Leave **Chester**, 5 34, 6 34, 6 55, 7 10, 7 26, 7 47, †8 16, 18 40, 8 48, *9 00, 9 30, 10 00, 10 31, 11 16 a. m., **†12 00 noon. *†12 10, †12 54, 1 07, 1 35, 3 07, †3 22, *†5 44, 6 01, 6 38, *7 10, *†7 30, 8 12, †3 33, 10 20, 11 11 p. m. Sundays, 7 28, 8 51 a. m., 12 44, 1 58, 4 43, 6 10, 8 03 p. m. Arrive Philadelphia, Express trains, in 23 minutes; Accommodation trains in 40 minutes.

THEATRES.

For Diagrams see following pages.

Academy of Music, E. 14th St. & Irving pl.
Amberg's, 15th St. & Irving Place.
Bijou, Broadway & 30th St.
Broadway, Broadway & 41st St.
Casino, Broadway & 39th St.
Comique, 125th St. & 3d Av.
Daly's, Broadway & 30th St.
Dockstader's, Broadway & 29th St.
Fifth Av., W. 28th St., n. Broadway.
Fourteenth St., 14th St., n. 6th Av.
Grand, 345 Grand St.
Grand Opera House, 8th Av. & 23d St.
Harrigan's Park, Broadway & 35th St.
Lexington Av. Opera House, 58th St., n. 3d Av.
London, 235 Bowery.
Lyceum, 4th Av. & 23d St.
Madison Square, 24th St., n. Broadway.
Metropolitan Opera House, Broadway & 49th St.
Miner's, Bowery n. Broome, and 8th Av. & 23d St.
Niblo's, 570 Broadway.
Old Bowery, Bowery, n. Canal.
Palmer's, Broadway & 30th St.
People's, 199 Bowery.
Poole's, 8th St., bet. Broadway & 4th Av.
Proctor's, 23d St., bet. 6th & 7th Avs.
Standard, Broadway & 33d St.
Star, Broadway & 13th St.
Thalia, 46 Bowery.
Theatre Comique, 125th St., n. 3d Av.
Third Ave., 445 3d Av.
Tony Pastor's, 14th St., n. 3d Av.
UnionSquare, Union Sq., 14thSt. & B'way.
Windsor, 45 Bowery.

OTHER PLACES OF AMUSEMENT.

American Institute, 3d Av., n. 64th St.
American Museum of Natural History, 77th St. & 8th Av. The Exhibition Halls of the Museum are open free to the public on Wednesdays, Thursdays, Fridays and Saturdays, and on all public holidays; also on Wednesday and Saturday evenings until 10 p. m. Mondays and Tuesdays are reserved for members and their friends, Students and Contributors, when admission is by ticket.
Chickering Hall, 5th Av. & W. 18th St.
Cyclorama Buildings, 19th St. & 4th Av., and Madison Av. & 59th St.
Cooper Union, 8th St. & 3d Av.
Eden Musee, 23d St. & 6th Av.
Hardman Hall, 19th St. & 5th Av.
Koster & Bial's Concert Hall, 23d St. & 6th Av.
Madison Square Garden, Madison Av. & E. 26th St.
Metropolitan Museum of Art, 5th Av. & 82d St. Open daily, except Sunday, from 10 a. m. to 4:30 p. m. Admission free, excepting Monday and Tuesday, when the charge is 25 cents.
National Academy of Design, 23d St. & 4th Av.
Steinway Hall, 14th St. & 4th Av.
Worth's Museum, E. 14th St., near Broadway.

HACK REGULATIONS AND LEGAL RATES OF FARE.

Distance is computed at 20 blocks to a mile, excepting through such streets that intersect the numeral and letter avenues, for example, 1st Ave. & Ave. A, when 7 blocks constitute a mile.

Sec. 89. The price or rates of fare to be asked or demanded by the owners or drivers of hackney coaches or cabs shall be as follows:

Cabs.

1. For conveying one or more persons any distance, sums not exceeding the following amount: fifty cents for the first mile or part thereof; and each additional half mile or part thereof, twenty-five cents. By distance, for "stops" of over five minutes and not exceeding fifteen minutes, twenty-five cents. For longer stops, the rate will be twenty-five cents for every fifteen minutes or fraction thereof, if more than five minutes. For a brief stop, not exceeding five minutes in a single trip, there will be no charge.

2. For the use of a cab, by the hour, with the privilege of going from place to place and stopping as often and as long as may be required, one dollar for the first hour or part thereof, and for each succeeding half-hour or part thereof, fifty cents.

Coaches.

3. For conveying one or more persons any distance, sums not exceeding the following amounts: one dollar for the first mile or part thereof, and each additional half mile or part thereof, forty cents. By distance for "stops" of over five minutes and not exceeding fifteen minutes, thirty-eight cents. For longer stops the rate will be thirty-eight cents for every fifteen minutes. For a brief stop, not exceeding five minutes in a single trip, there will be no charge.

4. For the use of a coach, by the hour, with privilege of going from place to place and stopping as often and long as may be required, one dollar and fifty cents for the first hour or part thereof, and for each succeeding half-hour or part thereof, seventy-five cents.

5. No cab or coach shall be driven by the time rate at a pace less than five miles an hour.

6. From "line balls," one or two passengers, to any point south of Fifty-ninth street, two dollars; each additional passenger, fifty cents; north of Fifty-ninth street each additional mile shall be charged for at a rate not to exceed fifty cents per mile.

7. Every owner or driver of any hackney coach or cab shall carry on his coach or cab one piece of baggage, not to exceed fifty pounds in weight without extra charge; but for any additional baggage he may carry, he shall be entitled to extra compensation at the rate of twenty-five cents per piece.

8. All disputes, as to prices or distance, shall be settled by the Mayor or such other person as he may designate.

9. In all cases, where the hiring of a hackney coach or a cab is not at the time thereof specified to be by the hour, it shall be deemed to be by the mile; and for any detention exceeding fifteen minutes, when so working by the mile, the owner or driver may demand at the rate of one dollar per hour.

It shall be the duty of the driver of every such hackney coach or cab, at the commencement of his employment, to present the passenger employing him with a printed card or slip, containing, in case of cabs, subdivisions 1 and 2, and in cases of coaches, subdivisions 3 and 4 of section 89 of this article.

Any person or persons who shall violate any or either of the provisions of above sections of this article, shall be liable to a penalty of ten dollars.

Complaints for violations of the above ordinances may be made at the office of the Mayor's Marshall, Room 1, City Hall.

DISTANCES.

From South Ferry.

To Wall Street	½	Mile.
" City Hall	1	"
" Canal Street	1½	"
" Houston Street	2	"
" 4th Street	2¼	"
" 14th Street	2¾	"
" 24th Street	3¼	"
" 37th Street	4	"
" 42d Street	4¼	"
" 62d Street	5¼	"
" 82d Street	6¼	"
" 102d Street	7¼	"
" 122d Street	8	"

East and West, from Broadway.

To East River, across	14th Street	1	Mile.
" " "	23d "	1	"
" " "	34th "	⅞	"
" " "	42d "	1	"
" " "	59th "	1¼	"
To North River, across	14th "	1¼	"
" " "	23d "	1⅛	"
" " "	34th "	1⅛	"
" " "	42d "	1	"
" " "	59th "	⅞	"

AMERICAN DISTRICT TELEGRAPH CO. OFFICES.

Main Office, 195 Broadway.

Street and number.
Broad St., 16.
Broadway, 120, 195, 276, 407, 599, 854, 1140, 1227, 1399.
Broome St., 114.
Cotton Exchange.
Canal & West St.
Church St., 151, 255.
Front St., 122.
Fulton St., 68.

Street and number.
Grand St., 233.
Grand Central Depot.
Greenwich St., 314.
Pearl St., 134.
Produce Exchange.
Stewart Building, B'way & Chambers.
West St., 112, 386.
3d Avenue, 300, 1080, 1369, 1616.

Street and number.
3d Avenue, cor. 47th St.
5th Avenue, 539.
6th Avenue, 686, 821, 998.
8th Avenue, 70, 985.
8th Avenue, cor. 34th St.
9th Avenue, cor. 73d St.
9th Avenue, cor. 93d St.
E. 14th St., 201.
W. 14th St., 110.

Street and number.
W. 23d St., 8, 270.
W. 34th St., 270.
W. 34th St. & North River.
E. 37th St., 2.
73d St., n. 9th Avenue.
93d St. & 9th Avenue.
E. 116th St., 205.
E. 125th St., 134.
W. 125th St., 62, 264.

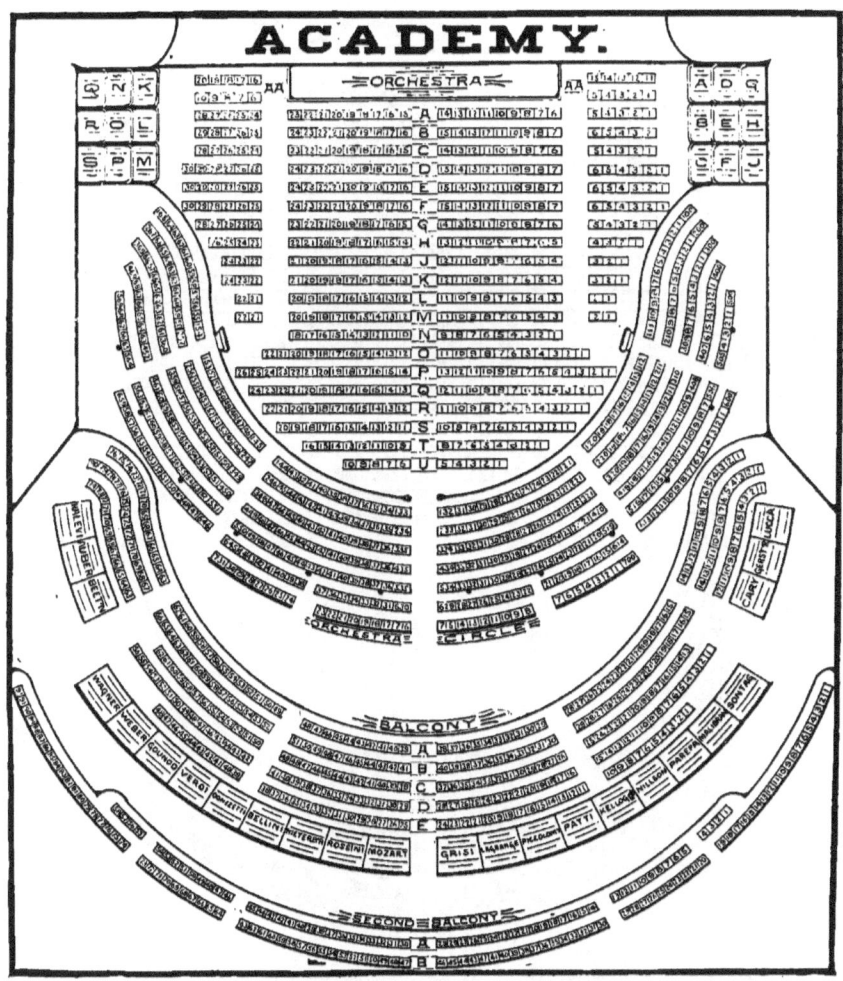

From plates prepared especially for Kenny's Guide, see page 128.

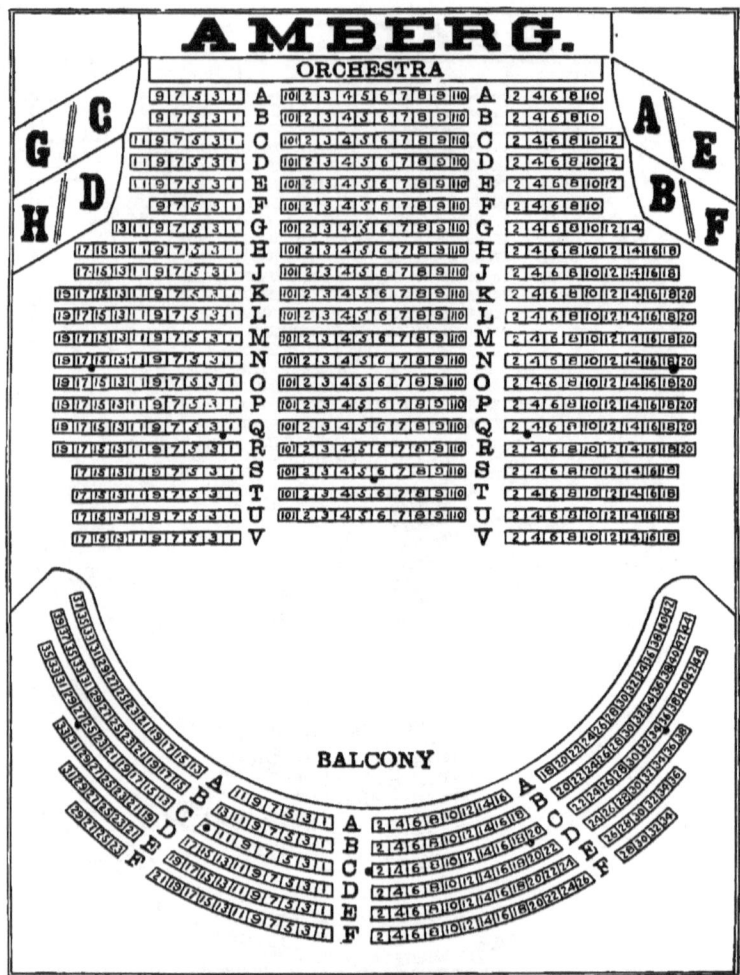

From plates prepared especially for Kenny's Guide, see page 128.

BIJOU.

ORCHESTRA

DRESS CIRCLE

From plates prepared especially for Kenny's Guide,
see page 128.

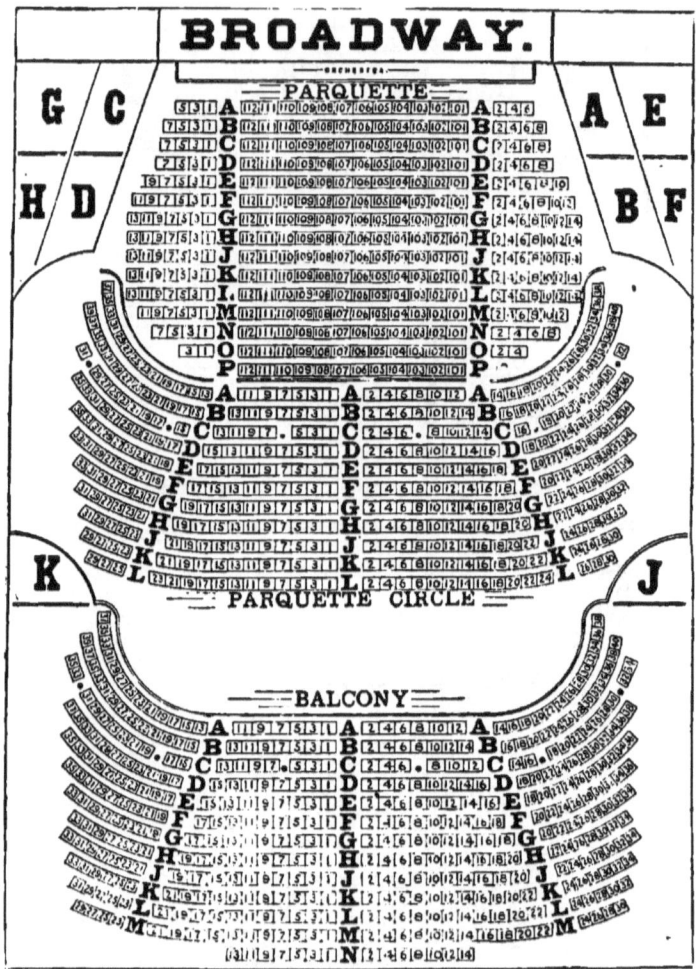

From plates prepared especially for Kenny's Guide, see page 128.

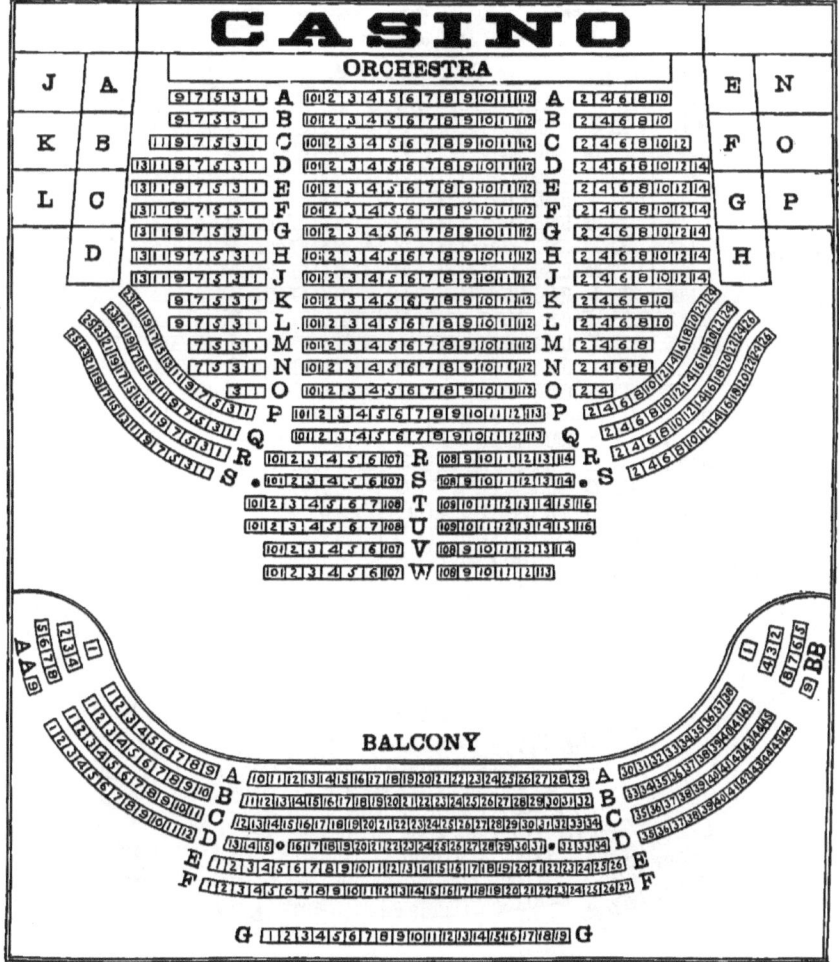

From plates prepared especially for Kenny's Guide, see page 128.

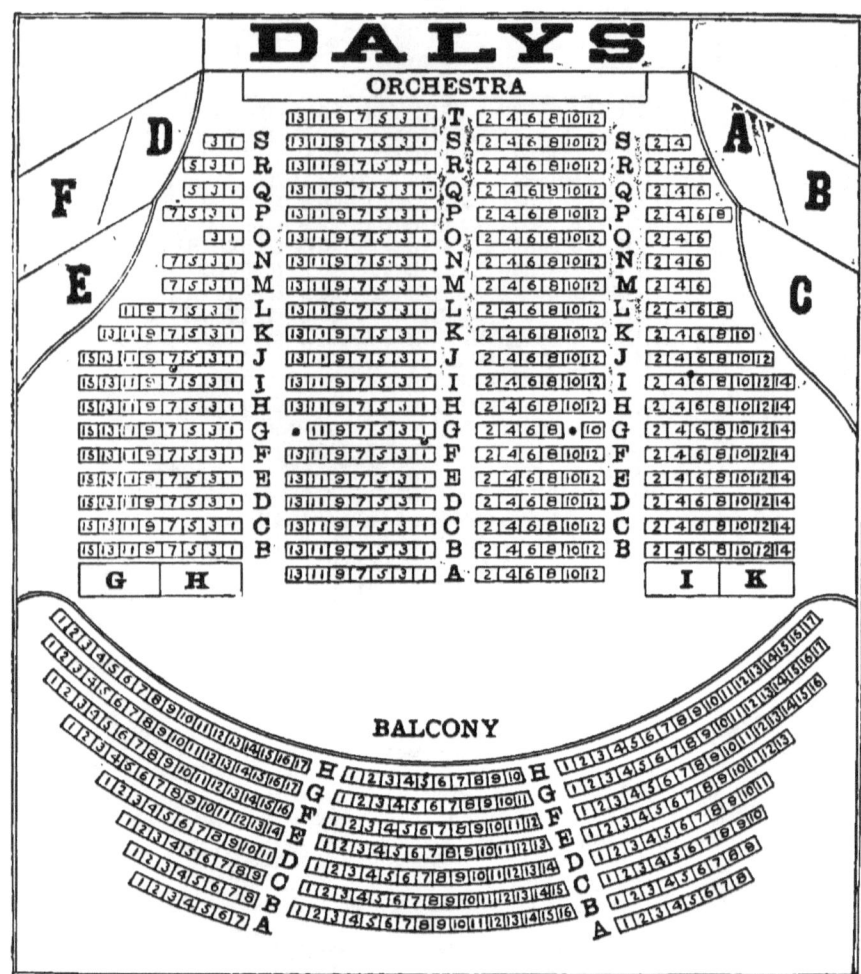

From plates prepared especially for Kenny's Guide, see page 128.

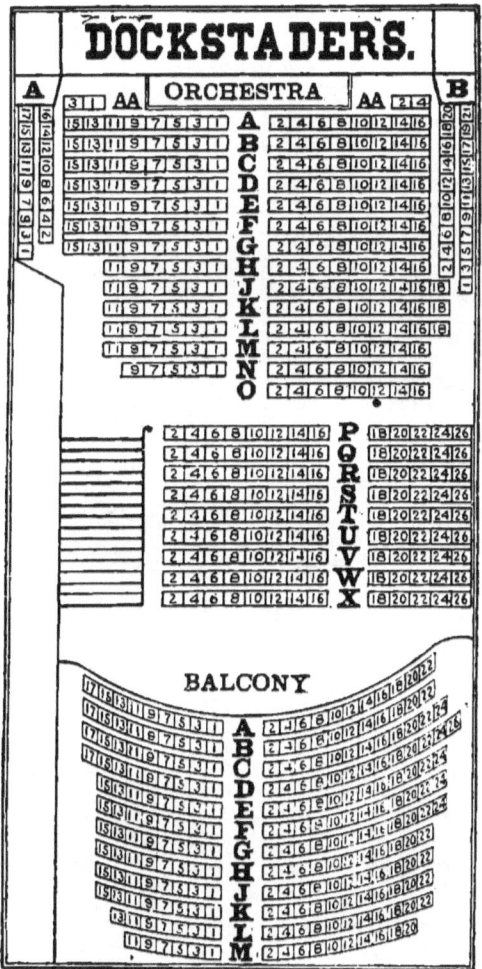

From plates prepared especially for Kenny's Guide, see page 128.

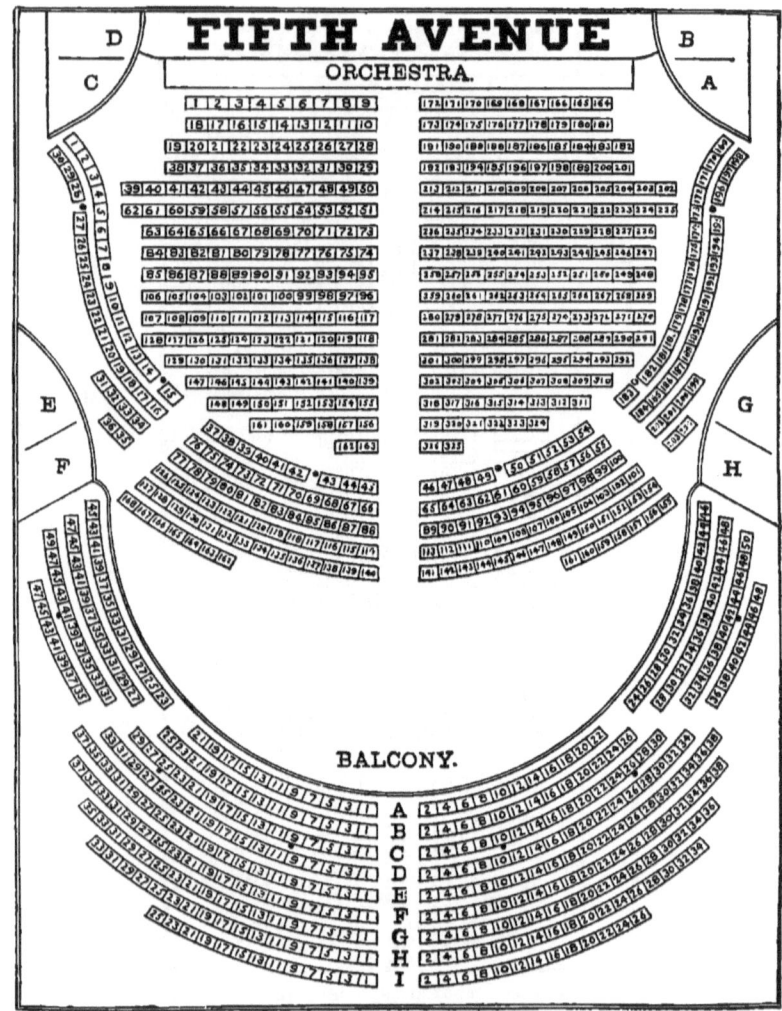

From plates prepared especially for Kenny's Guide. see page 128.

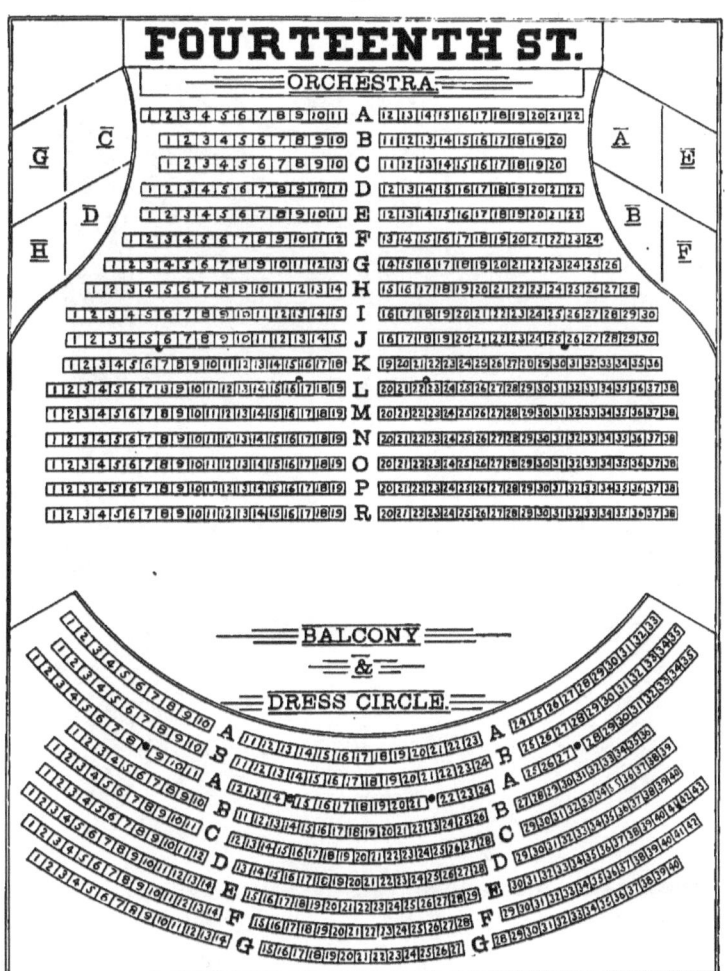

From plates prepared especially for Kenny's Guide, see page 128.

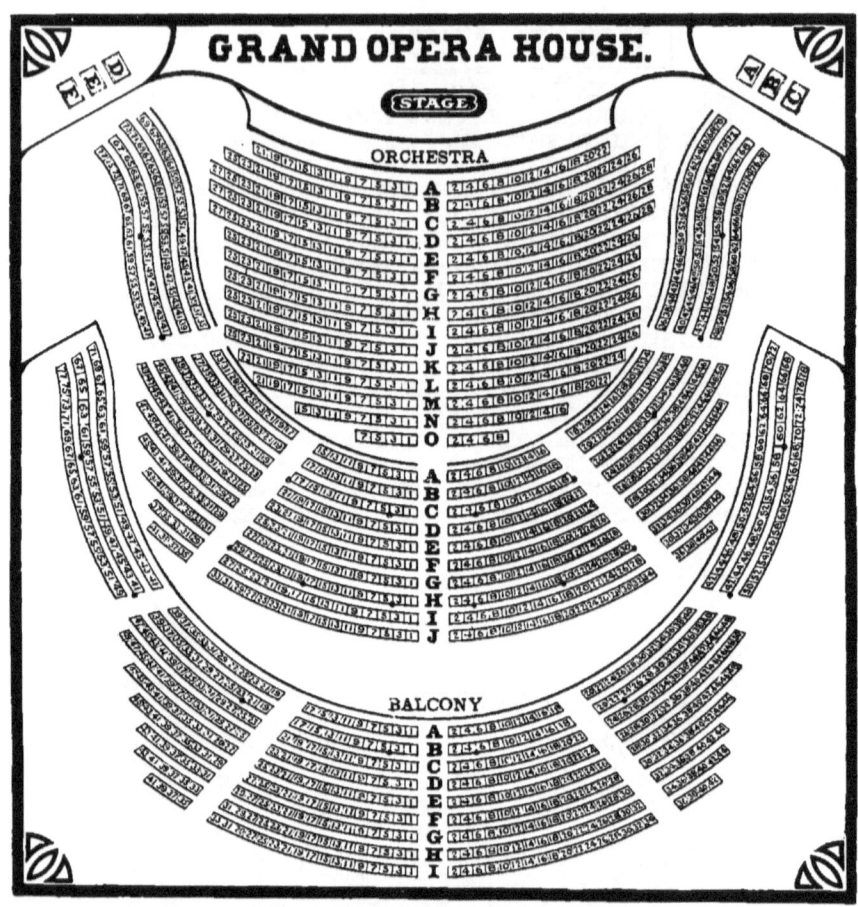

From plates prepared especially for Kenny's Guide, see page 128.

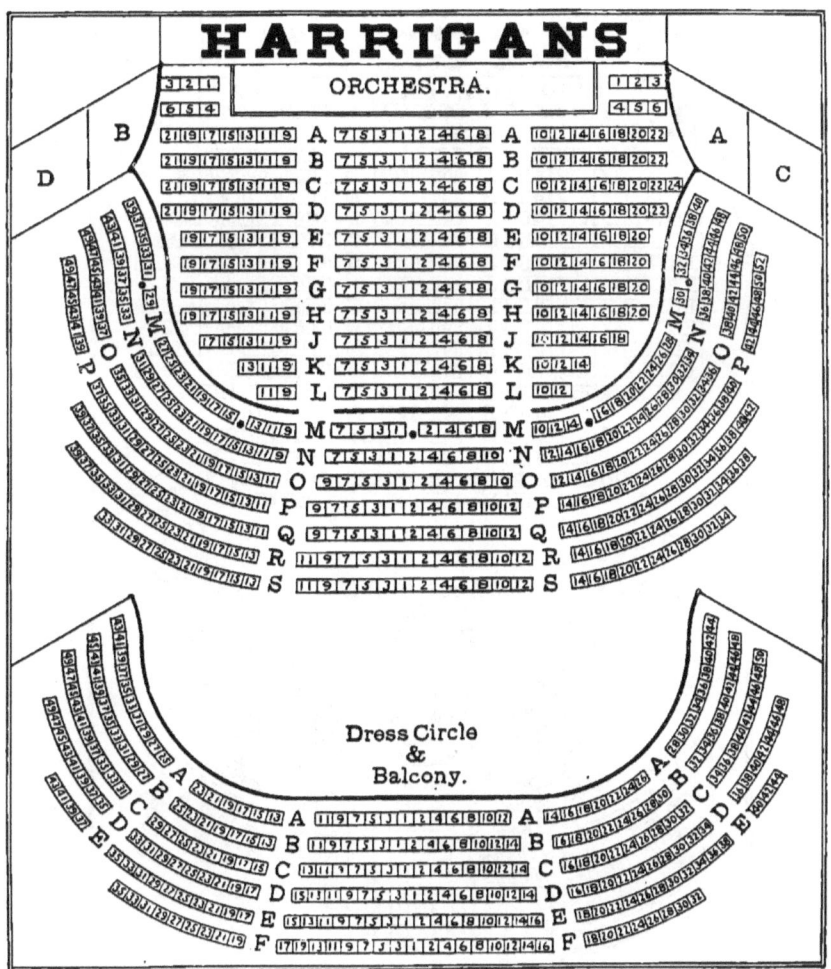

From plates prepared especially for Kenny's Guide, see page 128.

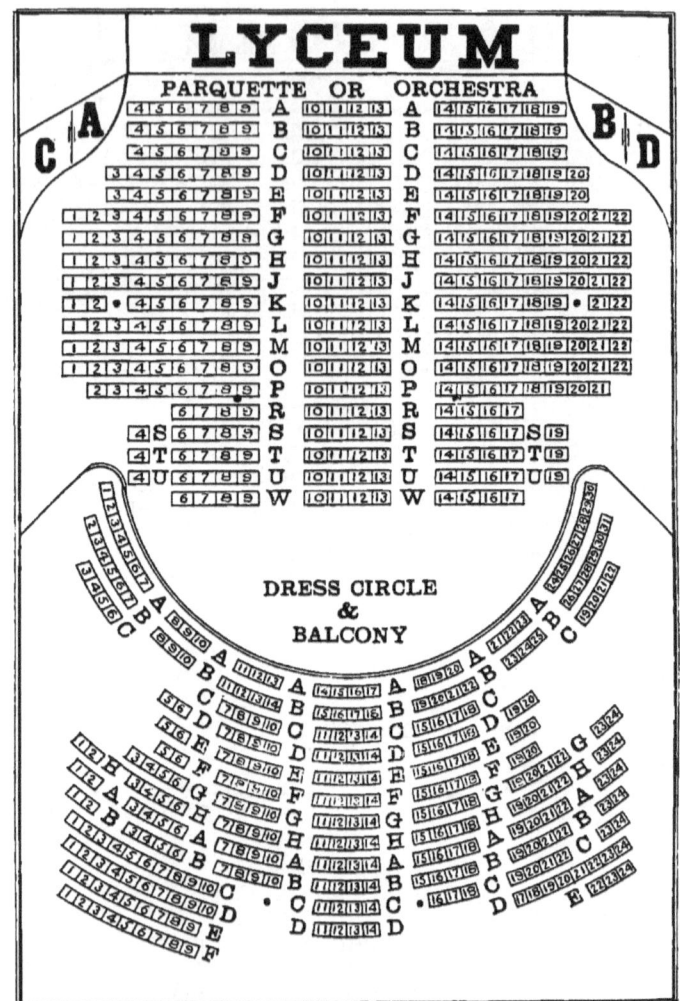

From plates prepared especially for Kenny's Guide, see page 128.

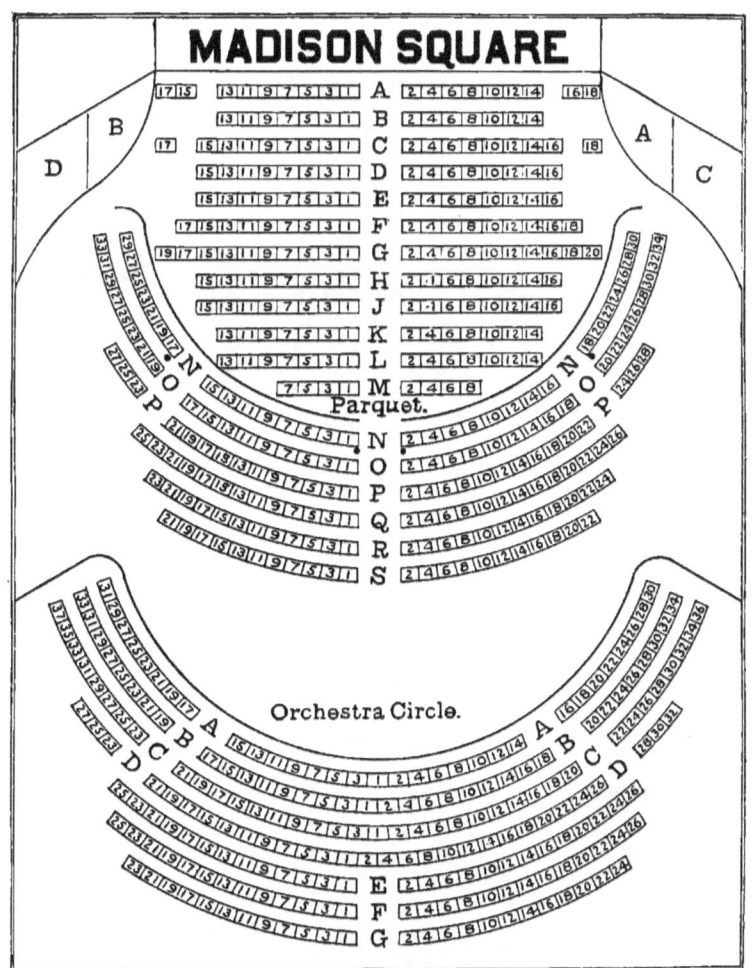

From plates prepared especially for Kenny's Guide, see page 128.

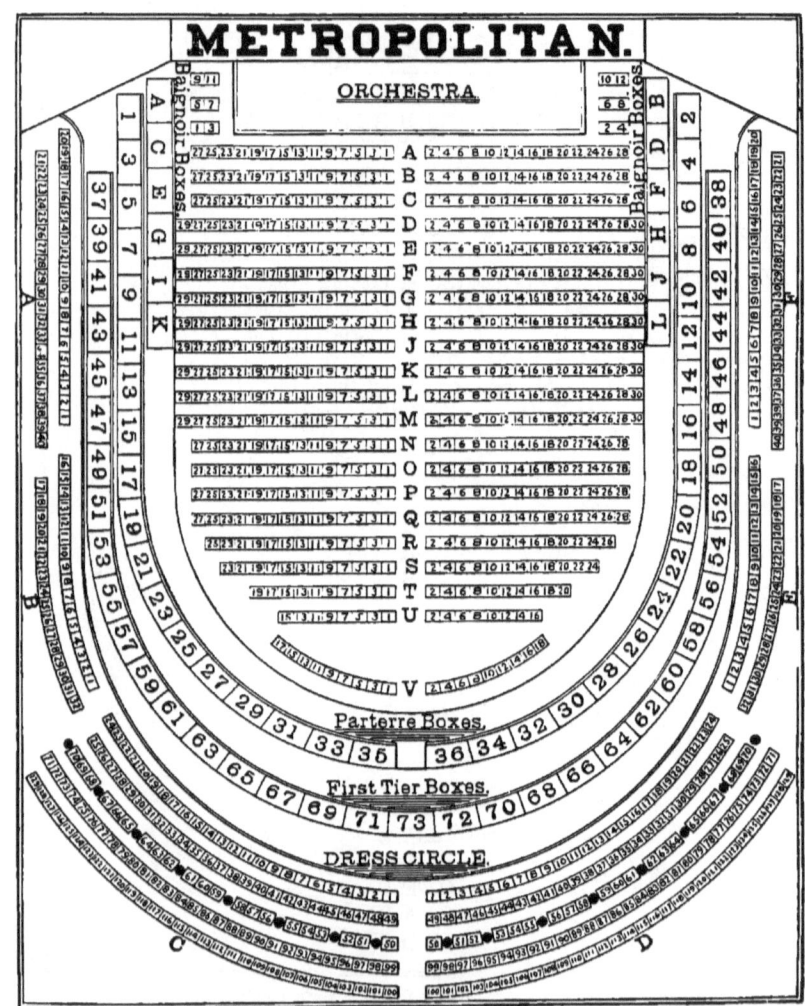

From plates prepared especially for Kenny's Guide, see page 128.

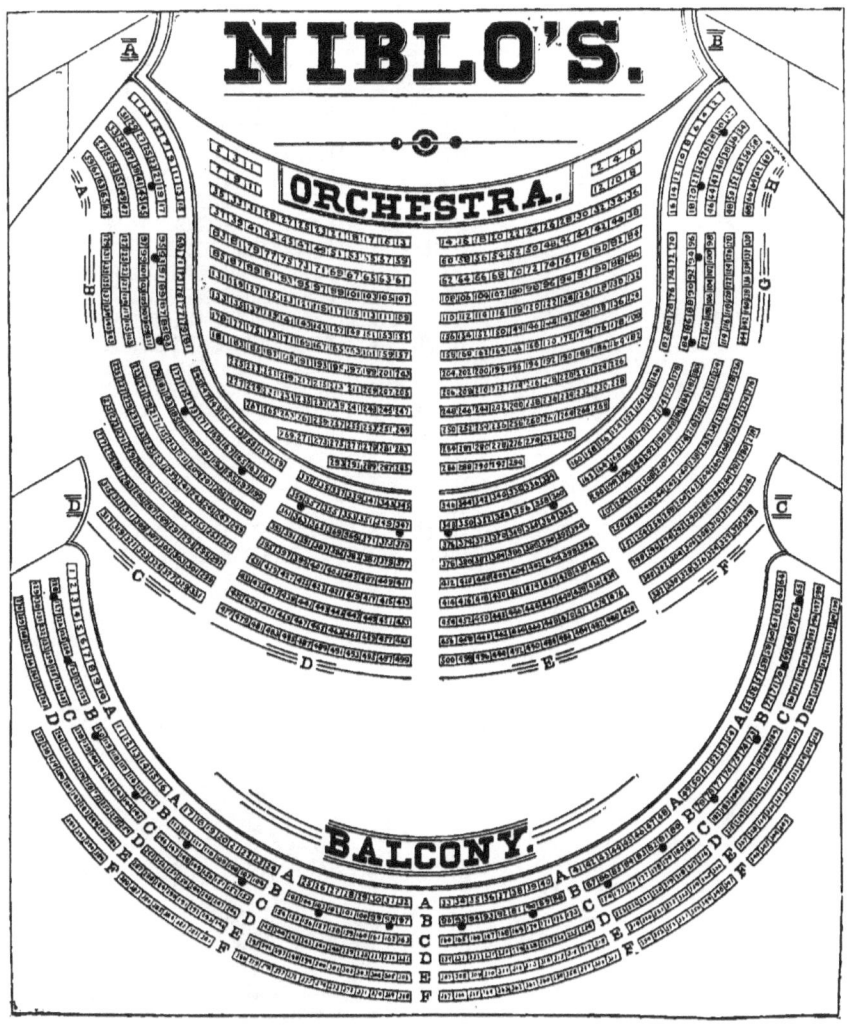

From plates prepared especially for Kenny's Guide, see page 128.

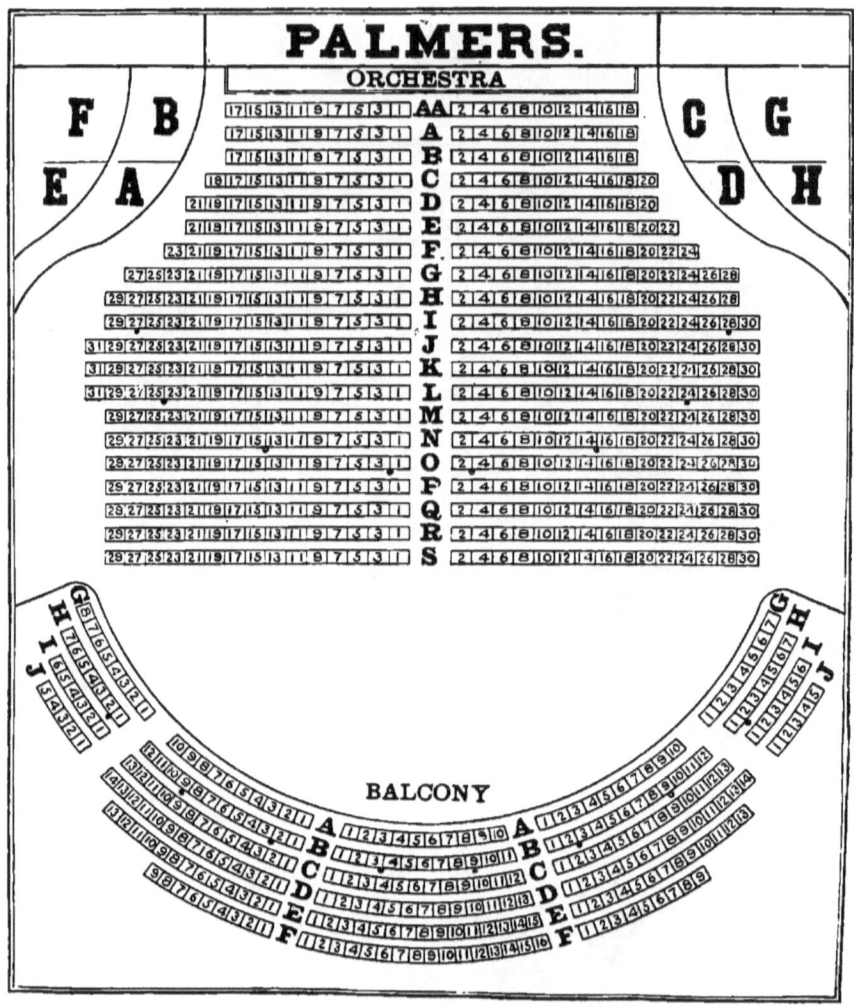

From plates prepared especially for Kenny's Guide, see page 128.

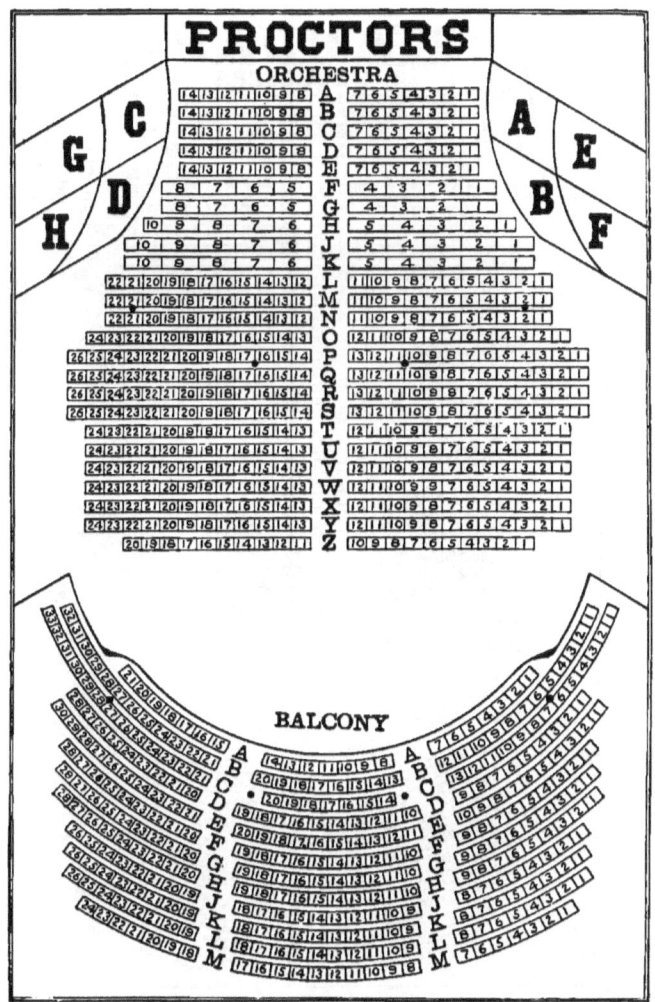

From plates prepared especially for Kenny's Guide, see page 128.

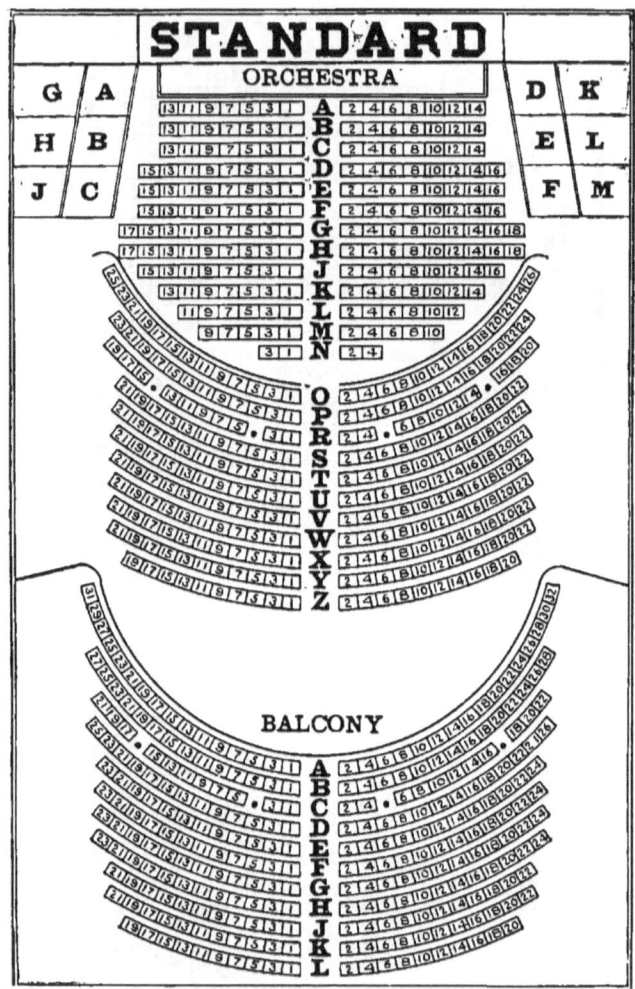

From plates prepared especially for Kenny's Guide, see page 128.

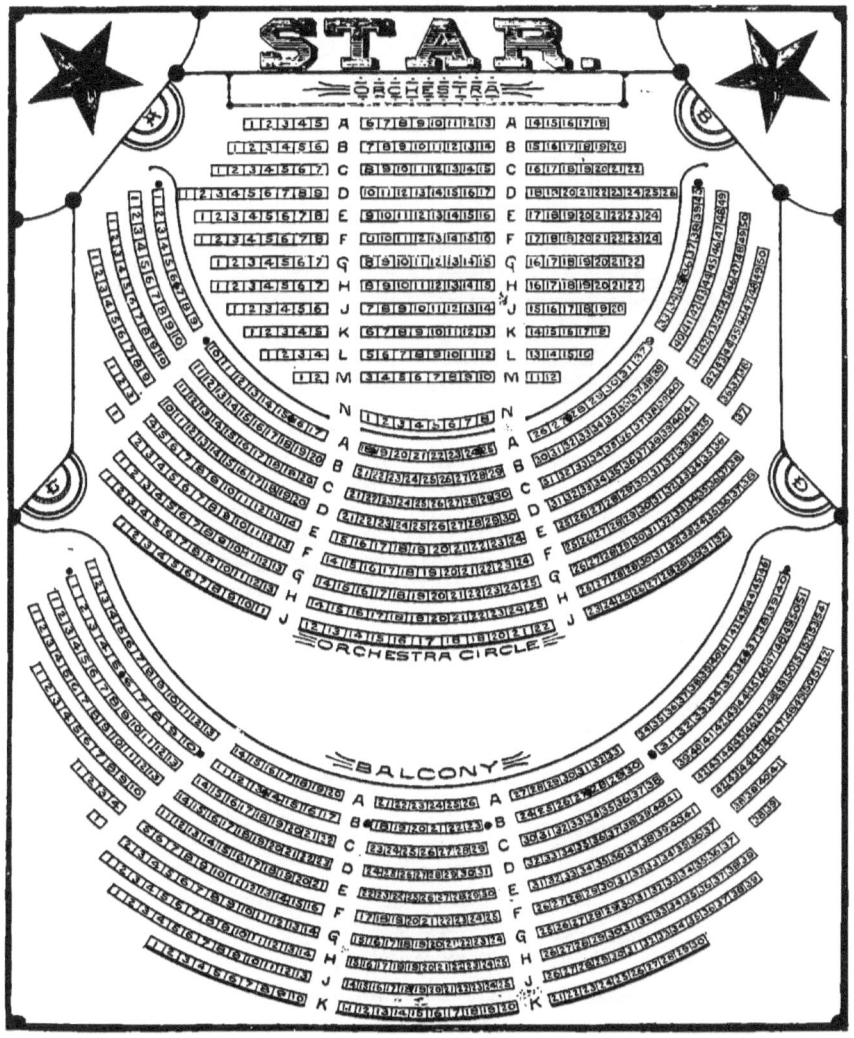

From plates prepared especially for Kenny's Guide, see page 128.

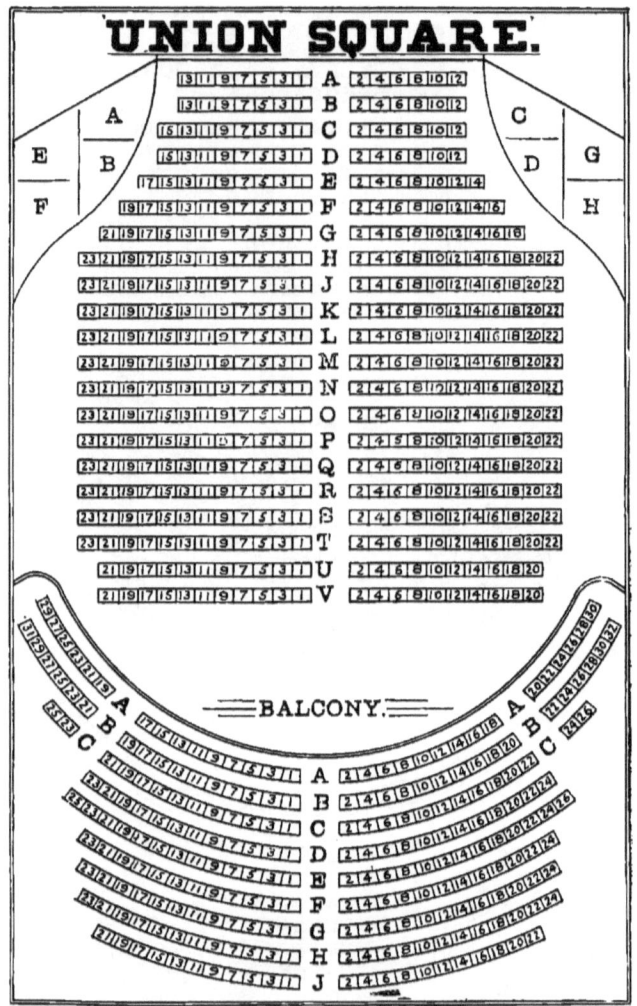

From plates prepared especially for Kenny's Guide, see page 128.

IMPORTANT CITIES WEST OF CHICAGO AND ST. LOUIS

Reached via Chicago and St. Louis.—For Fares to all Places see pages 65-69.
Trains leave New York for Chicago and St. Louis as follows:

PENNSYLVANIA R. R. Leave foot of Cortlandt and Desbrosses Sts. daily for **Chicago**, *19 00 a. m., *6 30 p. m., *8 00 p. m. Arrive Chicago, *6 05 p. m., *9 30 p. m., *7 00 a. m.
For **St. Louis**, leave New York daily, *9 00 a. m., *6 30 p. m. Arrive St. Louis, *7 30 p. m., *7 00 a. m.
*"Limited Express" (extra fare) also leaves New York at 9 00 a. m. and arrives Chicago 9 00 a. m. following day.

VIA NEW YORK CENTRAL AND "LAKE SHORE ROUTE."
Leave Grand Central Depot daily for **Chicago** at *9 50 a. m., *10 30 a. m. (except Sunday), *6 00 p. m., *10 00 p. m. Arrive Chicago, *9 50 a. m., *6 15 p. m., except Sunday), *9 30 p. m., *7 35 a. m.
For **St. Louis**, via " Bee Line." Leave Grand Central Depot daily, *9 50 a. m., *6 00 p. m. *10 00 p. m. Arrive St. Louis, *7 40 p. m., *7 30 a. m., *6 00 p. m.

VIA NEW YORK, LAKE ERIE AND WESTERN R. R. AND MICHIGAN CENTRAL R. R.
Leave foot of Chambers and West 23d Sts. daily for **Chicago**, *8 55 a. m., *4 55 p. m. *8 25 p. m. Arrive Chicago, *6 40 p. m., *10 30 p. m., *7 45 a. m.
For **St. Louis**. Leave New York daily, *11 55 p. m., *8 25 p. m. Arrive St. Louis, *7 45 p. m., *6 50 p. m.

TRAINS LEAVE CHICAGO AS FOLLOWS,
VIA CHICAGO AND NORTH WESTERN RY.:

For **Council Bluffs** and **Omaha** daily, *12 01 p. m., *5 30 p. m., *10 30 p. m. Arrive Council Bluffs, *8 52 a. m., *9 17 a. m., *6 05 p. m.; arrive Omaha, *10 00 a. m., *10 00 a. m., *7 05 p. m.
For **Milwaukee**, 8 00 a. m., 8 30 a. m., 11 30 a. m., 3 00 p. m., 5 00 p. m., 7 30 p. m., 9 05 p. m. Arrive Milwaukee in 3 hours.
For **St. Paul, Minneapolis and Duluth**, daily 5 30 p. m., 10 35 p. m. Arrive St. Paul, 7 30 a. m., 1 50 p. m.; arrive Minneapolis, 8 03 a. m., 2 30 p. m.; arrive Duluth, 5 25 p. m., 6 30 a. m.
For **Denver**, daily, 5 30 p. m., 10 30 p. m. Arrive Denver, 5 00 a. m., 3 30 p. m. (2d day).
For **DesMoines**, daily 12 01 p. m., 10 30 p. m. Arrive Des Moines, 3 00 a. m., 1 15 p. m.
For **Whitewood, Dak.**, 5 30 p. m. Arrive 9 30 a. m. Take stage at Whitewood for **Deadwood** and **Black Hills**,

Passengers holding first or second class tickets to points west of Council Bluffs will arrive as follows:

Leave Chicago 10 30 p. m.	Leave Council Bluffs 7 00 p. m.	Arrive Ogden 3 00 p. m.	Arrive Sacramento 3 05 a. m.	Arrive San Francisco 7 15 a. m.	Arrive Los Angeles 7 05 p. m.
Monday.	Tuesday.	Thursday.	Saturday.	Saturday.	Sunday.
Tuesday.	Wednesday.	Friday.	Sunday.	Sunday.	Monday.
Wednesday.	Thursday.	Saturday.	Monday.	Monday.	Tuesday.
Thursday.	Friday.	Sunday.	Tuesday.	Tuesday.	Wednesday.
Friday.	Saturday.	Monday.	Wednesday.	Wednesday.	Thursday.
Saturday.	Sunday.	Tuesday.	Thursday.	Thursday.	Friday.
Sunday.	Monday.	Wednesday.	Friday.	Friday.	Saturday.

Passengers holding first or second class tickets for points west of St. Paul will arrive as follows:

Leave Chicago 10 35 p. m.	Leave Saint Paul 4 00 p. m.	Arrive Bismarck 11 55 a. m.	Arrive Billings 5 50 a. m.	Arrive Helena 4 00 p. m.	Arrive Portland 6 30 a. m.
Monday.	Tuesday.	Wednesday.	Thursday.	Thursday.	Saturday.
Tuesday.	Wednesday.	Thursday.	Friday.	Friday.	Sunday.
Wednesday.	Thursday.	Friday.	Saturday.	Saturday.	Monday.
Thursday.	Friday.	Saturday.	Sunday.	Sunday.	Tuesday.
Friday.	Saturday.	Sunday.	Monday.	Monday.	Wednesday.
Saturday.	Sunday.	Monday.	Tuesday.	Tuesday.	Thursday.
Sunday.	Monday.	Tuesday.	Wednesday.	Wednesday.	Friday.

VIA CHICAGO, MILWAUKEE AND ST. PAUL RY.

For **Milwaukee**, 8 00 a. m., 11 30 a. m., 3 00 p. m., 5 30 p. m., 10 30 p. m. Arrive Milwaukee in 3 hours.
For **St. Paul, Minneapolis** and **Duluth**, daily 5 30 p. m., 10 30 p. m. Arrive St. Paul, 7 30 a. m., 1 50 p. m.; arrive Minneapolis 8 10 a. m., 2 35 p. m. Arrive Duluth, 3 20 p. m., 7 45 p. m.
For **Council Bluffs** and **Omaha**, daily 12 30 p. m., 10 40 p. m. Arrive Council Bluffs, 7 a. m. 6:35 p. m.; Omaha, 7 30 a. m., 7 05 p. m., next day.
For **Kansas City** and **St. Joseph**, daily 10 40 p. m. Arrive Kansas City 8 15 p. m.: arrive St. Joseph 8 55 p. m.
For **San Francisco**, daily 10 40 p. m. Arrive San Francisco 7 15 a. m.
For **Bismarck**, daily 5 30 p. m., 10 30 p. m. Arrive Bismarck, 5 10 a. m., 11 55 a. m. (2d day).
For **Portland**, daily 10 30 p. m. Arrive Portland, 7 00 a. m.

VIA "BURLINGTON ROUTE" C. B. & Q. R. R.

For **Burlington** and **Omaha**, daily at *12 01 p. m., *3 10 p. m., *1 00 p. m., *10 30 p. m. Arrive Burlington, *7 35 p. m., *7 15 p. m., *6 15 a. m.; arrive Omaha, *8 35 a. m., *3 20 a. m., *6 35 p. m.
For **Kansas City, St. Joseph** and **Atchison**, daily at 2 00 p. m., 10 30 p. m. Arrive Kansas City, 8 45 a. m., 7 40 p. m.; arrive St. Joseph, 8 00 a. m., 6 30 p. m.; arrive Atchison, 9 20 a. m., 8 00 p. m.
For **Denver**, daily 12 01 p. m., 1 00 p. m., 10 30 p. m. Arrive Denver, 7 10 a. m., 9 10 p. m., 2 25 p. m.
For **St. Paul** and **Minneapolis**, daily 3 55 p. m., 10 50 p. m. Arrive St. Paul, 7 55 a. m., 3 00 p. m.; arrive Minneapolis, 8 32 a. m., 3 40 p. m. next day.

VIA ATCHISON, TOPEKA AND SANTA FE R.R.

"**Santa Fe Route**" for **Kansas City, St. Joseph, Atchison** and **Topeka**, daily 1 40 p. m., 11 00 p. m. Arrive Kansas City, 8 25 a. m., 6 30 p. m.; arrive St. Joseph, 9 15 a. m., 8 30 p. m.; arrive Topeka, 11 50 a. m., 11 25 p. m.

TRAINS LEAVE ST. LOUIS AS FOLLOWS:
VIA "BURLINGTON ROUTE" C. B. AND Q. R. R.

For **St. Joseph, Kansas City** and **Denver**, daily at 8 05 p. m. Arrive St. Joseph, 8 00 a. m.; arrive Kansas City, 8 45 a. m.; arrive Denver 7 10 a. m. 2d day.
For **St. Paul** and **Minneapolis**, daily at 9 30 a. m. Arrive Minneapolis, 8 32 a. m. next day.

STEAMSHIPS FROM NEW YORK.

* *Mail Steamers.*

For Location of Piers, see page 70.

Destination.	FROM NEW YORK. Steamer and Date of Sailing.	Pier.	LEAVE FOR NEW YORK. Steamer and Date of Sailing.	Agent and Office.
Amsterdam	Edam, *May 16, 9 a. m.; Amsterdam, May 30, 6 a. m.	York St., J. C.	Edam & P. Caland, Apl. 27, May 18, due May 12, Jn. 2	Netherlands American Line, 39 B'way, 25 S. William St.
Antigua	Bermuda, *May 15.		Bermuda, April , due May 7	Quebec S. S. Co., A. E. Outerbridge & Co., 51 Broadway.
Antwerp	Pennland, *May 1, 6 30 a. m.; Illinois, May 1, 8 30 a. m	Sussex St., J. C.	Westernland*, April 27, due May 1, 8	Red Star Line, Peter Wright & Sons, 6 Bowling Green.
do.	Hermann, May 8	1th St., Hob'k'n.	Herman, April 12, due April 30	White Cross Line, Funch, Edye & Co., 27 S. William St.
Aux Cayes	A Steamer, May 4, 18	F't W. 25th St.	Claribel & Adirondack, Apl. 18, May 2, due May 1, 15	Atlas Line, Pim, Forwood & Co., 21 State St.
Bahia, *via Newport News*	Finance, *May 8; Allianca, June 5	RobertStrs., B'n	Allianca, *May 7, due May 26	U. S. & Brazil S. S. Co., P. F. Gerhard & Co., 84 Broad.
Baltimore	N. Y. & Balto. Trans. Line, daily, except Sunday, 5 p.m.	F't Rector St.	Daily, 5 p. m., due in 36 hours	H. C. Foster, Pier 7, N. R.
Bangor, Me	Lucy P. Miller, every Saturday, 12 m	Pier 15 E. R		F. H. Smith & Co., 31 South St.
Barbadoes, *via Newport News*	Finance, *May 8; Allianca, June 5.	RobertStrs., B'n	Allianca, *May 19, due May 26	U. S. & Brazil S. S. Co., P. F. Gerhard & Co., 84 Broad.
do.	Bermuda, *May 15		Bermuda, *April, due May 7	Quebec S. S. Co., A. E. Outerbridge & Co., 51 Broadway.
do.	Barracouta, May 11	18 E. R.	Barracouta, May , due May	Leacyraft & Co., 112 Pearl St.
Barcelona	Alesia, May 7			J. W. Ellwell & Co., 47 South St.
Belfast	S. of Nevada, May 2, 8 a. m.; S. of Nebraska, May 6, 12m	F't Canal St.	S. of Indiana & S. of Penn., due May 9, 16	State Line, A. Baldwin & Co., 53 Broadway.
Belize	Hondo, May 3; Aguan, May 21		Aguan, May, due May	Williams & Rankine, 19 Whitehall St.
Bermuda	A Steamer, May 2, 9, 16, 23, 30, 3 p. m		A Steamer, May, 2d, 9, 16, 23, 30, due in 3 days	Quebec S. S. Co., A. E. Outerbridge & Co., 51 Broadway.
Bordeaux	Panama, May 15			Funch, Edye & Co., 23 S. William St.
Bremen, *via Southampton*	Trave, *May 1, 7 a. m.; Fulda, May 1; Lahn, May 8	2d St., H'b'k'n.	Elbe, Eider, Apl. 27, 30, due May 6, 9	Norddeutscher Lloyd, Oelrichs & Co., 2 Bowling Green.
Bristol	Jersey City, May 4; Llandaff City, May 11	F't W. 26th St.	Llandaff City & Exeter City, May, due May	Bristol City Line, James Arkell & Co., 25 Whitehall St.
Brunswick, Ga.	Every Friday, 3 p. m	Burling Slip		C. H. Mallory & Co., Pier 20 E. R.
Campeche	City of Alexandria, *May 1; Saratoga, May 15, 3 p. m	F't Wall St	City of Alexandria, *May , due May 22	N. Y. & Cuba S. S. Co., J. E. Ward & Co., 113 Wall St.
Cardenas	City of Columbia, May 11, 3 p. m	F't Wall St	City of Columbia, May , due May 6	N. Y. & Cuba S. S. Co., J. E. Ward & Co., 113 Wall St.
Carthagena	A Steamer, May 9, 23	F't W. 25th St.	Alene & Athos, Apl. 29, May 13, due May 13, 27	Atlas Line, Pim, Forwood & Co., 21 State St.
Cienfuegos	Santiago, May 9; Cienfuegos, May 23, 3 p. m.	F't Wall St.	Santiago & Cienfuegos, Apl., May, due May 3, 17	N. Y. & Cuba S. S. Co., J. E. Ward & Co., 113 Wall St.
Charleston	Pioneer, May 1; Cherokee, May 3; Iroquois, May 7	Pier 29, E. R.	Seminole & Pioneer, May 3, 7, due May 5 & 10	W. P. Clyde & Co., 5 Bowling Green.
Clara	Basil*, May	MartinStrs., B'n	Basil, April – , due May —	Booth & Co., 15 Frankfort St.
Colon	A Steamer, May 1, 10, 20, 30, 12 m	F't Canal St.		Pacific Mail Line, foot of Canal St.
do.	Ailsa, *May 11; Alvena, May 25	F't W. 25th St.		Atlas Line, Pim, Forwood & Co., 21 State St.
Cherbourg	Rugia, May 2, 7 a. m., Wieland, May 9, 12 30 p. m	1st St., H'b'k'n.		Hamburg-American Packet Co., R. J. Cortis, 37 B'way.
Copenhagen	Polynesia, May 18	1st St., H'b'k'n.	Polynesia, April, May 12	Baltic Line, R. J. Cortis 37 Broadway.
Curacoa	Philadelphia, May 11; Cairngorm, May 16	Pier 36, E. R.	Cairngorm & Philadelphia, due May 2, 7	Red D Line, Boulton, Bliss & Dallett, 71 Wall St.
do.	Prinz Mauritz, May 1; Oranje Nassau, June 1	PrentissStrs. Bn	Oranje Nassau, May, due May	Kunhardt & Co. 32 Beaver St.
Dominica	Bermuda, *May 15		Bermuda, April, due May 7	Quebec S. S. Co., A. E. Outerbridge & Co., 51 Broadway.
Fernandina	Yemassee, May 4; Delaware, May 11, 3 p. m	Pier 29, E. R	Yemassee and Delaware, due May 15, 22	W. P. Clyde & Co., 5 Bowling Green.
do.	Every Friday, 3 p. m.	F't Burling Slip	Every Thursday, due Mondays	C. H. Mallory & Co., Pier 20, E. R., 317 Broadway.
Frontera	City of Alexandria, *May 1; Saratoga, May 15 3 p. m.	F't Wall St	City of Alexandria, May, due May 22	N. Y. & Cuba S. S. Co., J. E. Ward & Co., 113 Wall St.
Galveston	Every Wednesday and Saturday, 3 p. m.	F't Burling Slip	Lampasas and San Marcos, May, due May 8, 11	C. H. Mallory & Co., Pier 20, E. R., 317 Broadway.
do.	Every Thursday, 3 p. m.	North Moore St.		Southern Pacific Co., 343 Broadway.
Glasgow	Devonia, *May 4, 8 30 a. m.; Circassia, *May 11, 2 30 p.m.	F't Leroy St	Circassia, *Apl. 25, Ethiopia, May 2, due May 6, 13	Anchor Line, Henderson Bros., 7 Bowling Green.
do.	S. of Nevada, May 2, 8 00 a.m.; S. of Nebraska, May 9, 12m	F't Canal St.	S. of Indiana & S. of Penn., due May 9, 16	State Line, A. Baldwin & Co., 53 Broadway.
Halifax, N. S.	Portia, May 16		Sidonia and Portia, May 6, 11, due May 8 and 13.	Red Cross Line, Bowling & Archibald, 18 Broadway.
Hamburg	Rugia, May 2, 7 a. m.; Wieland, May 9, Bohemia, May 14	1st St., H'b'k'n.	Bohemia, Gellert Ap., Suevia, May, due May 9, 10, 16	Hamburg-Am. Packet Co., R. J. Cortis, 37 Broadway.
Havana	C. of Alexandria, May 1; C. of Washington, May 8, 3p.m	F't Wall St.	C. of Washington and Saratoga, due May 1 and 8.	N. Y. & Cuba S. S. Co., J. E. Ward & Co., 113 Wall St.
do.	Villaverde, May 4; a Steamer, May 11 and 24 3 p. m.	Foot of Dey St.	A Steamer, May, 4, 11 and 24, due in 5 days	Compania Transatlantica, J. M. Ceballos & Co., 80 Wall.
Havre	La Bourgogne, *May 4, 7 30 a. m.; La Gascogne, May 11	F't Morton St.	La Gascogne and Normandie, due May 5 and 12.	French Line, A. Forget, 3 Bowling Green.
do.		1st St., H'b'k'n.	Gellert, Apl. 30, Suevia, May 7, due May 10 and 18	Hamburg-Am. Packet Co., R. J. Cortis, 37 Broadway.
Hull	Colorado, May 4; Galileo, May 11	2d St., Hoboken	Galileo, May, due May	Wilson Line, Sanderson Bros., 21 State St.
Jacmel	A Steamer, *May 4, 18	F't W. 25th St.		Atlas Line, Pim, Forwood & Co., 21 State St.
Jacksonville	Cherokee, May 3; Iroquois, May 7, 3 p. m.	Pier 29, E. R.	Seminole and Cherokee, May 2, 9, due May 5, 12	W. P. Clyde & Co., 5 Bowling Green.
do.	Louis Bucki, about May 1			Warren Ray, 62 South St.
Jeremie	A Steamer, May 4, 18	F't W. 25th St.	Claribel and Adirondack, Apl., May, due May 1, 15	Atlas Line, Pim, Forwood & Co., 21 State St.
Kingston	Dorian, about May 1	PrentissStrs. Bn		Anchor Line, Henderson Bros., 7 Bowling Green.
do.	Ailsa, May 11; Adirondack, May 18	F't W. 24th St.	Claribel and Adirondack, Apl., May, due May 1, 15	Atlas Line, Pim, Forwood & Co., 21 State St.
La Guayra	Philadelphia, May 11; Cairngorm, May 16	Pier 36, E. R.	Cairngorm and Philadelphia, Apl., due May 2, 7	Red D Line, Boulton, Bliss & Dallett, 71 Wall St.
Leith	Critic, May 15	F't W. 26th St.	Critic, April, due May 15	Arrow Line, Simpson, Spence & Young, 78 Broad St.

151

Destination.	FROM NEW YORK. Steamer and Date of Sailing.	Pier.	LEAVE FOR NEW YORK. Steamer and Date of Sailing.	Agent and Office.
Liverpool, via Queenstown	New Y., *May 1, 6:30 a.m.; C. Chester, May 4, 8.30 a.m.	Christopher St.	C. of Paris & C. of Richmond, *May 1 & 1, due 2 & 13	Inman Line, F. Wright & Son, 6 Bowling Green.
do.	Germanic, May 1, 4 p.m.; Adriatic, May 8, 11 a. m.	ft W. 10th St.	Britannic & Celtic, May 1 & 8, due May 5 & 16.	White Star Line, J. H. Ismay, 41 Broadway
do.	City of Rome, May 7, 7 a.m., May 21, 6 a.m.	ft Leroy St.	City of Rome, May 15, due 23.	Anchor Line, Henderson Bros., 7 Bowling Green.
do.	Aurania, May 4, 8.30 a. m.; Gallia, May 8, 11 a. m.	ft Clarkson St.	Umbria & Servia, Ap. 27 & May 4, due M'y 4 & 12	Cunard Line, V. H. Brown & Co., 4 Bowling Green.
do.	Nevada, May 7, 7 a. m.; May 14, 4.30 p. m.	ft King St.	Alaska & Wyoming, Ap. 27 & May 4, due M'y 5 & 13	Guion Line, A. M. Underhill & Co.
do.	Egypt, May 2, 7 a. m.; The Queen, May 16, 6 a. m.	ft Houston St.	The Queen & Spain, Ap. 25 & M'y 2, due May 8 & 12	National Line, F. W. J. Hurst, 57 State St.
do. (Direct)	Hippucchus, May 2; Ptolemy, May 4.	Martin Strs. B'n		Bock & Jevons, 301 Produce Exchange.
do. do.	St. Romans, May 6.			Sumner Line, 18 Broadway.
Livingston.	Hasto, May 3; Agma, May 21			W'lliams & Hankine, 19 Whitehall St.
London	France, about May 2; Holland, May 8; Erin, May 15	ft Houston St.	Holland, April 15, Erin, April 22 due May 1 and 8	National Line, F. W. J. Hurst, 27 State St.
do.	Lydgate Hill, May 4; Richmond Hill, May 28	Prentice Strs. Bn	Richmond, May 7, due May 21.	Anchor Line, Henderson Bros., 7 Bowling Green.
Londonderry	Italia, May 11	W 24th St.		Wilson Line, Sanderson & Son, 21 State St.
Marseilles	Anchor Line steamers call here.	Pier 26 E. R.	Leave Londy next day after leaving Glasgow	Anchor Line, Henderson Bros., 7 Bowling Green
Marseilles vid Newport News	Philadelphia, May 11; Cairngorm, May 16	Robert Strs., Bn	*Cairngorn, *Apl , *Phila., Apl , due May 2 & 7	Red D. Brazil S. S. Co., F. F. Gerhard & Co., 81 Broad St. S
Martinique	Alesia, May 7		Alliance, *May 12, due May 26.	Cyprien Fabre & W. et India Line, Lusgrell & Co.
Martinique	Barracouta, May 7	Pier 16, E. R.		N. Y. & Cuba S. S. Co., J. E. Ward & Son, 90 Wall St.
Matanzas	Manhattan, May 4 and 25, 3 p. m.	Prentice Strs., Bn	Manhattan, May , due May	N. Y. & Cuba S. S. Co., J. E. Ward & Co., 113 Wall St.
Mediterranean Ports			Italia, April 14, due May 3.	Anchor Line, Henderson Bros., 7 Bowling Green.
Monte Video	Hampton, June 10	ft Wall St.	Santiago, *Ap. 28, Cienfuegos, May 13, due May3&17	N. Y. & Cuba S. S. Co., J. E. Ward & Son, 90 Wall St.
Nassau, N. P.	Santiago, *May 1; Cienfuegos, May 23, 3 p.m.	N. Moore St.		N. Y. & Cuba S. S. Co., J. E. Ward & Co., 113 Wall St.
New Orleans	Every Wednesday and Saturday, 3 p. m.	Pier 8 N. R.		Southern Pacific Co., 349 Washington St., 33 Broadway
Newport News		ft Beach St.		Cromwell Line, S. H. Seaman, 5 N. R.
Norfolk, Va	Old Dom. Line, Tues., Wed., Thurs., Sat., 3 p. m.	Robert Strs., Bn	Old Dominion Line, daily exc. Satur. & Sunday	Old Dominion S. S. Co., 25 West St.
Para	Finance, *May 8.	Martin Strs., Bn	Alliance, *May 14, due May 26.	U. S. & Brazil S. S. Co., F. F. Gerhard & Co., 81 Broad St.
do.	Basil, May	Martin Strs., Bn	Basil, May , due May	Booth & Co., 15 Frankford St.
do.	Marmulcusc, May 8	Martin Strs., Bn	Marmulcuse, April , due May	Red Cross Line, S. Green, 112 Pearl St.
do.	Marmulsen, May 8.	Martin Strs., Bn	Marmulsen, *April , due May	Red Cross Line, S. Green, 11½ Pearl St.
Pernambuco	Finance, *May 8.	Martin Strs. Bn	Alliance, *May 9, due May 26.	U. S. & Brazil S. S. Co., F. F. Gerhard & Co., 81 Broad St.
Plymouth	Paris, May 2, 7 a.m.; Wieland, May 9, 12.30 p.m.	1st St. Hoboken	Wed. and Satur. 5 p. m. , due in 33 hours	Hamburg Am. Packet Co., H. J. Cortis, 37 Broadway.
Portland, Me.	Maine S.S. Line, Wednesday and Saturday, 3 p. m.	ft W. 26th St.		Houston Hall, Pier
Port au Prince	Steamer, May 9, 23.	Prentice Strs. Bn	Athos & Athos Ap. 19 & M'y 4, due May 13 & 27.	Atlas Line, Fwd. Forwood & Co., 21 State St.
Porto Limon	Prinz Maurix, May 1; Orange N., June 1.	ft Dey St.		J. M. Ceballos & Co., 80 Wall St.
Port Limon	Athos, *May 11; Alveno, May 25.	ft W. 26th St.	Akros & Athos, May 4 and 16, due May 13 and 27	Atlas Line, Fun. Forwood & Co., 21 State St.
Progresso	C. of Alexandria, *May 1; C. of Washington, *May 8.	ft Wall St.	Saratoga & Niagara, *May 2 and 9, due May 8 & 5.	N.Y. & Cuba S. S. Co., J. E. Ward & Co., 113 Wall St.
do.	Villaverde, May 12; a Steamer, May 11 and 24, 3 p. m.	ft Dey St.	Steamer, May 4, 14, 24 due in 5 days.	J. M. Ceballos & Co., 80 Wall St.
Puerto Cabello	Philadelphia, May 11; Cairngorm, May 16.	Pier 26 E. R.	Cairngorn & Phila., *Ap. , due May 2 and 7.	Red D Line, Bouillon, Bliss & Dallett, 71 Wall St.
Queenstown	Liverpool			
Richmond	Old Dominion Line, Wednesday and Saturday, 3 p. m.	ft Beach St.	Tuesday and Friday, due in 2 days.	Old Dominion S. S. Co., 25 West St.
Rio de Janerio	Finance, *May 8	Robert Strs., Bn	Alliance, May 1, due May 24.	U. S. & Brazil S. S. Co., F. F. Gerhard & Co., 81 Broad St.
Rotterdam	Veendam, *May 1, 9 a. m.	York St., J. C.	Obdam & Amsterdam, M'y 1 & 11, due M'y 18 & 25	Neth. Am. Line, 39 Broadway, 25 S. William St.
Sagua	City of Atlanta, May 16, 3 p. m.	ft Wall St.	*City of Atlanta, May , due May 13.	N. Y. & Cuba S. S. Co., J. E. Ward & Co., 113 Wall St.
San Francisco, via Colon.	A Steamer, May	Canal St.		W. P. Clyde & Co., 5 Bowling Green.
Santiago de Cuba	C. of Para, May 7	ft Wall St.		Pacific Mail S. S. Co., foot of Canal St.
Santiago de Cuba	Santiago, *May 9; Cienfuegos, May 23 3 p. m.	ft Wall St.	Santiago, Cienfuegos, May 11, due May 2 & 17.	N. Y. & Cuba S. S. Co., J. E. Ward & Co., 113 Wall St.
Savannah, Ga.	Tuesday, Thursday, Saturday, 3 p. m.	Robert Strs., Bn	Alluoria, *April 30, due May 26.	Ocean S. S. Co., F. F. Gerhard & Co., 81 Broad St.
Savanilla	A Steamer, May 9, 23.	ft W. 26th St.	Sunday, Tuesday, Friday, due in 3 days.	Atlas S. S. Co., Pin. Walker, 21 State St.
Southampton	Augusta Victoria, May 23, 1 p. m.	1st St., Hoboken	Polynesia, April 27, due May 13.	Hamburg Am. Packet Co., H. J. Cortis, 37 Broadway.
Strettin	Polynesia, May 18.	1st St., Hoboken	Polynesia, April 27, due May 21.	Baltic Line, R. J. Curtis, 37 Broadway.
St. Josuo	Seminole, May 16.		Seminole, Fortia, May 3 & 8, due May 8 and 13.	Red Cross Line, Bowring & Archibald, 18 Broadway.

Destination.	FROM NEW YORK. Steamer and Date of Sailing.	Pier.	LEAVE FOR NEW YORK. Steamer and Date of Sailing.	Agent and Office.
St. Kitts	Bermuda, May 15		Bermuda, *April , due May 7	Quebec S. S. Co., A. E. Outerbridge & Co., 51 Broadway.
do.	Barracouta, May 11		Bermuda, *April , due May 7	Lesycraft & Co., 142 Pearl St.
St. Lucia	Bermuda, May 15		Barracouta, May , due May	Quebec S. S. Co., A. E. Outerbridge & Co., 51 Broadway.
do.	Barracouta, May 11	Pier 18 E. R.	Allianca, *May 30, due May 26	Mantic & West I. Line, Lesycraft & Co. 142 Pearl St.
St. Thomas	Finance, *May 8	Pier 18 E. R., lim.	C. of Washington, *May , due May 29	U. S. & Brazil S. S. Co., P. F. Gerland & Co., 81 Broad St.
Tampico	City of Washington, *May 8, 3 p. m	Robert Str., lim.	Bermuda, *April , due May 7	N. Y. & Cuba S. S. Co., J. E. Ward & Co., 113 Wall St.
Trinidad	Bermuda, May 15	Ft Wall St.	Barracouta, May , due May	Quebec S. S. Co., A. E. Outerbridge & Co., 51 Broadway.
do.	Barracouta, May 11	N E. R.		Lesycraft & Co., 112 Pearl St.
Tuxpan	Belair, May 2 ; Neptune, May 16		City of Washington, *May , due May 29	George Christall, 15 Exchange Place.
Vera Cruz	City of Washington, *May 8, 3 p. m	Ft Wall St.	Saratoga & Niagara, 25 & May 3, due May 8 & 15	N. Y. & Cuba S. S. Co., J. E. Ward & Co., 113 Wall St.
Washington, D. C.	C. of Alexandria, *May 1 ; C. of Washington, May 8	Ft Wall St.		N. Y. & Cuba S. S. Co., J. E. Ward & Co., 113 Wall St.
West Point, Va.	Old Dominion Line, Tues., Wed., Thurs., Sat., 3 p. m	Ft Beach St.		Old Dominion Line, 25 West St.
Wilmington, N. C.	Yromsoco, May 4 ; Beaufactor, May 8, 3 p. m	Pier 29 E. R.	Delaware & Beaufactor, May 2 & 3, due May 6 & 7	W. P. Clyde & Co., 5 Bowling Green.

COUPONS, DIVIDENDS, ELECTIONS, ETC.

COUPONS AND INTEREST PAYABLE MAY 1st UNLESS OTHERWISE STATED.

Atchison, Colorado & Pacific R. R., Union Trust Co., 73 Broadway.
Atchison, Jewell Co. & West'n R. R. Union Trust Co., 73 Broadway.
Atchison & Pike's Peak R. R., Union Trust Co., 73 Broadway.
Austin Electric Light Co., American Loan & Trust Co., 113 Broadway.
Albany City, Merchants' Bank, 42 Wall St.
Atlantic Ave. R. R., Brooklyn, Broadway Bank, 237 Broadway.
Aitkin Co., Minn. National Park Bank, 214 Broadway.
Big Level & Kinzua R. R. Co., Union Trust Co., 73 Broadway.
Bucyrus Water Co., Bank of Republic, 2 Wall St.
Buffalo Street R. R., Bank of Commerce, 29 Nassau St.
Boone Co. & Booneville R. R., Bank of Commerce, 29 Nassau.
Bellevue, Ohio, National Park Bank, 214 Broadway.
Boone Co., Iowa, Chemical Bank, 270 Broadway.
Chicago & Western Indiana, 1st Mtge., Drexel, Morgan & Co., 23 Wall St.
Cin., Indp., St. Louis & Chicago 1st Consolidated Mtge. 6s, Drexel, Morgan & Co., 23 Wall St.
Chicago & Ohio River 1sts., Corbin Banking Co. 192 Broadway.
Columbus, Ohio, National Park Bank, 214 Broadway.
Columbus, Ohio Board of Trade, National Park Bank, 214 Broadway.
Clifton Spring, N. Y., National Park Bank, 214 Broadway.
Canton City, Ohio, Chase National Bank, 15 Nassau St.
Cleveland & Pittsburgh R. R. Co.'s Consolidated Mtge. 7%, Farmers' Loan & Trust Co., 20 William St.
Consumers' Gas Works Co., Lt'd, Farmers' Loan & Trust Co., 20 William St.
Central Branch Union Pacific R. R., Union Trust Co., 73 Broadway.
Columbus & Indianapolis Cent'l 2d Mtge., Union Trust Co., 73 Broadway.
Cresson & Clearfield County & N. Y. Short Route R. R. Co., Morton, Bliss & Co., 28 Nassau st.
Central Crosstown R. R. Co., American Loan & Trust Co., 113 Broadway.
Citizens' Gas Light Co., American Loan & Trust Co., 113 Broadway.
Clinton County, Indiana (due May 15), Third National Bank, 20 Nassau St.
Clinton County, Indiana (due May 9th), Third National Bank, 20 Nassau St.
Chicago, Burlington & Quincy R. R., National Bank of Commerce, 29 Nassau St.
Connersville, Ind., Winslow, Lanier & Co., 17 Nassau St.
Cambridge, Ind. (due May 20th), Winslow, Lanier & Co., 17 Nassau St.
Detroit & Bay City R. R., Union Trust Co., 73 Broadway.
Dakota & Eastern Mtge. Co., Bank of Republic, 2 Wall St.
DesMoines Loan & Trust Co., American Loan & Trust Co., 113 Broadway.
Delaware County, Indiana (due May 15th) Third National Bank, 20 Nassau St.
Division Mortgage Co., Kansas, Merchants' Exchange National Bank, 257 Broadway.
DesMoines, Ia., Water Co., National Park Bank, 214 Broadway.
Denver & Rio Grande, Fourth National Bank, 14 Nassau St.
Delaware City, Ohio, Fourth National Bank, 14 Nassau St.
Equitable Mortgage Co., American Loan & Trust Co., 113 Broadway.
Elgin, Joliet & Eastern 1st Mtge., 5s., Drexel, Morgan & Co., 23 Wall.
East Tawas Village, Mich., Fourth National Bank, 14 Nassau St.
Evansville, Terre Haute & Chic. R. R. Co., Farmers' Loan & Trust Co., 20 William St.
Evansville, Terre Haute & Chic. R. R. 1st Mtge. Income, Farmers' Loan & Trust Co., 20 William St.
Elizabethtown Water Co., Farmers' Loan & Trust Co., 20 William St.
Fort Wayne, Indiana, City of, (due May 15th). Third National Bank, 20 Nassau St.
Foster Co., Dakota, National Park Bank, 214 Broadway.
Farmers' Loan & Trust Co., dividend payable at office, 20 William St.
Greencastle, Ind., Winslow, Lanier & Co., 17 Nassau St.
Grand Rapids & Indiana R. R., Winslow, Lanier & Co., 17 Nassau St.
Gardner, Coal City & Northern. 1st Mtge. 5s, Drexel, Morgan & Co., 23 Wall St.
Galveston Co., Texas, National Park Bank, 214 Broadway.
Greenpoint & Lorimer St. R. R. Co., National Park Bank. 214 Broadway.
Haverstraw Water Co., American Loan & Trust Co., 113 Broadway.
Hastings Imp't Co., Neb., Chemical Bank, 270 Broadway.
Hancock Co., Ind., Winslow, Lanier & Co., 17 Nassau St.
Housatonic R. R. Co., Consolidated Mtge. Farmers' Loan & Trust Co., 20 William St.
Indianapolis & St. Louis R'y "C." Union Trust Co., 73 Broadway.
Indiana, State Registered, Winslow, Lanier & Co., 17 Nassau St.
Indianapolis & Vincennes R. R. Co., 2d mtge. 6%. Farmer's Loan & Trust Co. 20 William St.
J. B. Watkins, Land Mtg. Co., National Bank of Commerce, 29 Nassau St.

Jersey City. Merchant's Exchange National Bank, 257 Broadway.
Jamaica, & Hunter's Point R. R., Corbin Banking Co., 192 Broadway.
Kalamazoo & South Haven R. R., Union Trust Co., 73 Broadway.
Kansas Pacific R. R., Consolidated, Union Trust Co., 73 Broadway.
Kansas Pacific R. R., Denver Extension, Union Trust Co., 73 Broadway.
Kings County Water Supply Co., American Loan & Trust Co., 113 Broadway.
Kansas City, Mo., National Bank of Commerce, 29 Nassau St.
Kansas City, Mo., Electric Light Co., Bank of Commerce, 29 Nassau St.
Kokomo, Ind., Winslow, Lanier & Co., 17 Nassau St.
Kokomo, Ind., (due May 15th) Winslow, Lanier Co., 17 Nassau St.
Kidder Co., Dakota, National Park Bank, 214 Broadway.
Kent Water Co., Farmer's Loan Co., 20 William St.
Lexington Water Works, Union Trust Co., 73 Broadway.
Louisville City, Bank of Republic, 2 Wall.
LaFayette, Ind. Street R'y Co., Winslow, Lanier & Co., 17 Nassau St.
Long Island R. R., pays quarterly dividend of 1%.
Long Island R. R. 1st mtg. Corbin Banking Co., 192 Broadway.
Long Island City & Flushing 1sts, Corbin Banking Co., 192 Broadway, 11 John St.
Long Island City & Flushing 2ds., Corbin Banking Co., 192 Broadway, 11 John.
Lincoln Mtg. & Trust Co., Ashland Kan., Fourth National Bank, 14 Nassau St.
Lawrence Co., Dakota, Fourth National Bank, 14 Nassau St.
Larchmont Yacht Club, 1st mtg. 7%, Farmer's Loan & Trust Co., 20 William St.
Michigan Central R. R., Union Trust Co., 73 Broadway.
Michigan Central R. R., 7%, Union Trust Co., 73 Broadway.
Michigan Air Line, Union Trust Co., 73 Broadway.
Moorhead, Minn., City of, Third National Bank, 20 Nassau St.
Milwaukee, Lake Shore & Western R'y. National Bank of Commerce, 29 Nassau St.
Moberly City, Mo., National Bank of Commerce, 29 Nassau St.
Marietta, Ohio, (due May 15th) Winslow, Lanier & Co., 17 Nassau St.
Miami County, Ind. (due May 17th) Winslow, Lanier & Co., 17 Nassau St.
Minneapolis & Duluth R. R., Bank of North America, 25 Nassau St.
Minneapolis, Minn., National Park Bank, 214 Broadway.
Minneapolis R'y. Co., 2d mtg. 6%, Farmer's Loan & Trust Co., 20 William St.
Middletown Gas & Electric Lt. Co., Farmer's Loan & Trust Co., 20 William St.
Mt. Vernon Water Works Co., Farmer's Loan & Trust Co., 20 William St.
Meridian Water Works Co., Farmer's Loan & Trust Co., 20 William St.
Marietta Mineral R'y Co., Farmer's Loan & Trust Co., 20 William St.
Maricopa & Phenix R. R. Co., Farmer's Loan & Trust Co., 20 William St.
Marshall Consolidated Coal Mining Co., Farmer's Loan & Trust Co., 20 William St.
N. Y. & Texas S. S. Co., Farmer's Loan & Trust Co., 20 William St.
Newark, Somerset & Straitsville, R. R., Union Trust Co., 73 Broadway.
New Philadelphia Village, Ohio Third National Bank, 20 Nassau St.
Newport & Wickford R. R., National Bank of Commerce, 29 Nassau St.
New England Loan & Trust Co., Bank of New York, 48 Wall St.
New York Mutual Gas Light Co.'s Bonds, Union Trust Co., 73 Broadway.
Newtown & Flushing R. R., Corbin Banking Co., 192 Broadway.
Norfolk Va. Water Loan, National Park Bank, 214 Broadway.
Ohio, & Miss. R'y., Springfield Div., Union Trust Co., 73 Broadway.
Ohio & W. Va., 1st mtg. 7%, Chase National Bank, 15 Nassau St.
Oregon & Transcontinental Co., 1st mtg. 6%, Farmer's Loan and Trust Co., 20 William St.
Omaha Gas Mfg. Co., Farmer's Loan & Trust Co., 20 William St.
Pullman Palace Car Co. (due May 15th), Farmers' Loan & Trust Co., 20 William St.
Phœnix Water Co., Union Trust Co., 73 Broadway.
Paola Water Co., American Loan & Trust Co., 113 Broadway.
Portsmouth, Ohio, Winslow, Lanier & Co., 17 Nassau St.
Pittsburg, Ft. Wayne & Chicago R'y. Co., Winslow, Lanier & Co., 17 Nassau St.
Prudential Fire Ass'n, 173 Broadway, pays 6% interest.
Pratt Coal & Iron Co., Fourth National Bank, 14 Nassau St.
Plattsburgh Town, N. Y., Fourth National Bank, 14 Nassau St.
Pittsburgh, Youngstown & Ashtabula R. R. Co. 1st Cons. Mtge. 5%, Farmers' Loan & Trust Co., 20 William St.
Richmond City & Seven Pines R. R. Co., American Loan & Trust Co., 113 Broadway.

MAILS TO FOREIGN COUNTRIES—MAY, 1889.
TRANS-ATLANTIC MAILS.

☞ *Mails for Great Britain, and for the Continent of Europe, to be dispatched from New York as per this schedule, are assigned to the fastest vessels available. Special directions on correspondence for Great Britain and the Continent for its dispatch from New York by particular vessels, merely with a view to celerity, are therefore unnecessary.*

Date.	Sailing Day.	Steamers.	Port of Destination.	Mails Close. A.M. P.M.	Mails to be Conveyed.
May 1	Wednesday.	Friesland.	Antwerp.	3.00	Specially addressed mail for Belgium.
1	Wednesday.	City of New York.	Queenstown.	3.30	Mails for Europe; also specially addressed mails for Europe.
1	Wednesday.	Trave.	South'mpton & Bremen.	3.30	Mails for Europe; also specially addressed mail for Ireland.
4	Saturday.	La Bourgogne.	Havre.	4.00	Mails for France direct; also Swiss, Italian, Spanish and Portuguese closed mails via Havre.
4	Saturday.	Aurania.	Queenstown.	5.00	Mails for Great Britain and Ireland; also Belgian, Netherlands and Austrian closed mails; also specially addressed mail for other European countries.
4	Saturday.	Fulda.	Southampton & Bremen.	5.00	Mails for Germany direct; also Danish, Swedish, Norwegian, Russian and Turkish closed mails via Bremen; also specially addressed mail for Great Britain, Ireland, Netherlands and Austria via Southampton.
4	Saturday.	Devonia.	Glasgow.	3.00	Specially addressed mail for Scotland.
4	Saturday.	Vesrniam.	Rotterdam.	6.00	Specially addressed mail for Netherlands.
8	Wednesday.	Gallia.	Queenstown.	7.30	Mails for Ireland; also specially addressed mail for Europe.
8	Wednesday.	Lahn.	Southampton & Bremen.	7.30	Mails for Europe; also specially addressed mail for Ireland.
8	Wednesday.	Belgenland.	Antwerp.	4.30	Specially addressed mail for Belgium.
9	Thursday.	Rotterdam.	Rott'rdam.	10.00	Specially addressed mail for Netherlands.
11	Saturday.	Ems.	Christiana.	10.00	Specially addressed mail for Norway.
11	Saturday.	La Gascogne.	Havre.	10.00	Mail for France direct; also Swiss, Italian, Spanish and Portuguese closed mails via Havre.
11	Saturday.	Elbe.	South'mpton & Bremen.	10.30	Specially addressed mail for Great Britain, Ireland, Belgium, Netherlands and Austria via Southampton, and for Germany, Denmark, Sweden, Norway, Russia and Turkey via Bremen.
11	Saturday.	Anchoria.	Glasgow.	11.00	Specially addressed mail for Scotland.
11	Saturday.		Queenstown.	11.00	Mails for Great Britain and Ireland; also Swiss, Italian, Spanish and Portuguese closed mails via Havre.
14	Tuesday.	Eider.	Southampton & Bremen.	3.00	Mails for Europe; also specially addressed mail for Ireland.
14	Tuesday.	Alaska.	Queenstown.		2.00 Mails for Great Britain and Ireland; also specially addressed mail for other European countries.
15	Wednesday.	Aller.	Southampton & Bremen.	3.30	Mails for Europe; also specially addressed mail for Ireland.
15	Wednesday.	Britannic.	Queenstown.		1.00 Specially addressed mail for Europe.
15	Wednesday.	City of Paris.	Queenstown.		2.00 Mails for Europe.
15	Wednesday.	Westernland.	Antwerp.		2.00 Specially addressed mail for Belgium.
16	Thursday.	Gellert.	Plymouth, Cherbourg & Hamburg.	3.30	Mails for Europe; also specially addressed mail for Ireland.
16	Thursday.	Edam.	Rotterdam.	1.30	Specially addressed mails for the Netherlands.
18	Saturday.	La Bretagne.	Havre.	6.30	Mail for France direct; also Swiss, Italian, Spanish and Portuguese closed mails via Havre.
18	Saturday.	Servia.	Queenstown.	3.30	Mails for Great Britain and Ireland; also Belgian, Netherlands and Austrian closed mails; also specially addressed mail for other European countries.
18	Saturday.	Ethiopia.	Glasgow.	1.30	Specially addressed mail for Scotland.
18	Saturday.	Werra.	Southampton & Bremen.	5.00	Mails for Germany direct; also Danish, Swedish, Norwegian, Russian and Turkish closed mails via Bremen; also specially addressed mail for Great Britain, Ireland, Belgium, Netherlands and Austria via Southampton.
21	Tuesday.	Wyoming.	Queenstown.	7.30	Mails for Ireland; also specially addressed mail for Great Britain and other European countries.
22	Wednesday.	Celtic.	Queenstown.	8.30	Mails for Ireland; also specially addressed mail for Great Britain and other European countries.
22	Wednesday.	Saale.	Southampton & Bremen.	8.30	Mails for Europe; also specially addressed mail for Ireland.
22	Wednesday.	Rhynland.	Antwerp.	5.30	Specially addressed mail for Belgium.
23	Thursday.	Obdam.	Rotterdam.	9.30	Specially addressed mail for the Netherlands.
23	Thursday.	Augusta Victoria.	Southampton & Bremen.	10.30	Mails for Europe; also specially addressed mail for Ireland.
25	Saturday.	La Champagne.	Havre.	10.30	Mail for France direct; also Swiss, Italian, Spanish and Portuguese closed mails via Havre.
25	Saturday.	Ems.	Southampton & Bremen.	11.00	Mails for Germany direct; also Danish, Swedish, Norwegian, Russian and Turkish closed mails via Bremen; also specially addressed mail for Great Britain, Ireland, Belgium, Netherlands and Austria via Southampton.
25	Saturday.	Anchoria.	Glasgow.	11.30	Specially addressed mail for Scotland.
25	Saturday.	Etruria.	Queenstown.	11.30	Mails for Great Britain and Ireland; also Belgian, Netherlands and Austrian closed mails; also specially addressed mail for other European countries.
28	Tuesday.	Arizona.	Queenstown.		2.00 Mails for Great Britain and Ireland; also French, Belgian, Netherlands, Swiss, Austrian, Italian, Spanish and Portuguese closed mails for Great Britain and other European countries.
29	Wednesday.	City of Rome.	Queenstown.	3.00	Mails for Ireland; also specially addressed mail for Great Britain and other European countries.
29	Wednesday.	Trave.	Southampton & Bremen.	4.00	Mails for Europe; also specially addressed mail for Great Britain and other European countries.
29	Wednesday.	City of New York.	Queenstown.		2.00 Mails for Great Britain and Ireland; also French, Belgian, Swiss, Austrian, Italian, Spanish and Portuguese closed mails for Great Britain and other European countries.
29	Wednesday.	Noordland.	Antwerp.		2.00 Specially addressed mail for Belgium.
30	Thursday.	Amsterdam.	Amsterdam.	3.30	Specially addressed mail for the Netherlands.
30	Thursday.	Hammonia.	Southampton & Hamburg.	3.30	Mails for Europe; also specially addressed mail for Ireland.

MAILS FOR THE WEST INDIES, MEXICO, AND FOR CENTRAL AND SOUTH AMERICA.

Date	Day	Steamer	Destination	Rate	Notes
May 1	Wednesday	City of Para	Aspinwall	10.60	Mails for Central America, except Costa Rica and Guatemala; and for South Pacific ports via Aspinwall; also specially addressed mails for Costa Rica and Guatemala.
1	Wednesday	Prins Mauritz	Port au Prince, &c.	11.00	Mails for Port au Prince and Jacmel; also specially addressed mails for Curacoa, Venezuela, Trinidad, British and Dutch Guiana.
1	Wednesday	City of Alexandria	Progreso, Campeche, &c.	1.00	Mails for the Mexican States of Yucatan, Campeche, Tabasco, and Chiapas; also specially addressed mails for other Mexican States.
2	Thursday	Orinoco	Hamilton		1.00 Mails for Bermuda.
4	Saturday	Alvo	Kingston, Jacmel & Aux Cayes	11.00	Mails for Jamaica, and for Jacmel and Aux Cayes, Hayti.
8	Wednesday	City of Washington	Progreso, Tampico, &c.	7.00	Mails for the Mexican States of Yucatan, Campeche, Tabasco and Chiapas; also specially addressed mails for other Mexican States.
9	Thursday	Alps	Port au Prince & Savanilla	11.00	Mails for Hayti; also specially addressed mails for the U. S. of Colombia, except Aspinwall and Panama.
9	Thursday	Trinidad	Hamilton		1.00 Mails for Bermuda.
9	Thursday	Santiago	Nassau & Santiago	1.10	Mails for the Bahama Islands and for Santiago, Cuba.
10	Friday	Newport	Aspinwall	10.00	Mails for Central America, except Costa Rica and Guatemala; and for the South Pacific ports via Aspinwall; also specially addressed mails for Costa Rica and Guatemala.
11	Saturday	Finance	St. Thomas, Barbadoes, &c.	1.00	Mails for St. Thomas, and St. Croix via St. Thomas; Barbadoes and for Trinidad and Demerara via Barbadoes; for Brazil direct; and for Argentine Republic, Uruguay, and Paraguay.
11	Saturday	Marsehense	Para & Pernambuco	2.30	Mails for Para and Pernambuco, Brazil.
11	Saturday	Barracouta	St. Kitts, Barbadoes, &c.	10.40	Mails for the Windward Islands.
11	Saturday	Alps	Kingston & Port Limon	11.00	Mails for Jamaica, and for Costa Rica via Port Limon.
11	Saturday	Philadelphia	Curacoa, Puerto Cabello, &c.	11.00	Mails for Curacoa and Venezuela; also specially addressed mails for the U. S. of Colombia via Curacoa.
15	Wednesday	Savoia	Rio de Janeiro & Santos	2.30	Mails for Brazil, any additional States; direct, and for the Argentine Republic, Uruguay, and Paraguay via Brazil.
15	Wednesday	Saratoga	Progreso, Campeche, &c.	1.00	Mails for the Mexican States of Yucatan, Campeche, Tabasco, and Chiapas; also specially addressed mails for other Mexican States.
16	Thursday	Cairnsmoor	Curacoa, Puerto Cabello, &c.	11.00	Mails for Curacoa and Venezuela; also specially addressed mails for the U. S. of Colombia via Curacoa.
16	Thursday	Orinoco	Hamilton		1.00 Mails for Bermuda.
18	Saturday	Bermuda	St. Croix, St. Kitts, Barbadoes, &c.	10.40	Mails for St. Croix, and for St. Thomas via St. Croix; also for the Windward Islands direct.
18	Saturday	Atene	Kingston, Jacmel & Aux Cayes	11.00	Mails for Jamaica, and for Jacmel and Aux Cayes, Hayti.
20	Monday	Colon	Aspinwall	10.00	Mails for Central America, except Costa Rica and Guatemala; and for the South Pacific ports via Aspinwall; also specially addressed mails for Costa Rica and Guatemala.
21	Tuesday	Elpira	Ciudad Bolivar		1.00 Mails for Ciudad Bolivar.
22	Wednesday	George W. Clyde	Cape Hayti, Puerto Plata, &c.	11.00	Mails for Cape Hayti, St. Domingo, and Turk's Island.
22	Wednesday	Niagara	Progreso and Vera Cruz	1.00	Mails for the Mexican States of Yucatan, Campeche, Tabasco, and Chiapas; also specially addressed mails for other Mexican States.
23	Thursday	Adirondack	Port au Prince & Savanilla	11.00	Mails for Hayti; also specially addressed mails for the U. S. of Colombia, except Aspinwall and Panama.
23	Thursday	Trinidad	Hamilton		1.00 Mails for Bermuda.
25	Saturday	Alvena	Kingston and Port Limon	11.00	Mails for Jamaica and for Costa Rica via Port Limon.
29	Wednesday	Valencia	Curacoa, Puerto Cabello, &c.	11.00	Mails for Curacoa and Venezuela; also specially addressed mails for the U. S. of Colombia via Curacoa.
29	Wednesday	Cienfuegos	Progreso & Vera Cruz	1.00	Mails for the Mexican States of Yucatan, Campeche, Tabasco, and Chiapas; also specially addressed mails for other Mexican States.
29	Wednesday	Islani	St. Kitts, Barbadoes, &c.	1.00	Mails for the Windward Islands.
30	Thursday	Orinoco	Hamilton		1.00 Mails for Bermuda.

FROM NEW ORLEANS. Allow three days from New York to connect.

Date	Day	Steamer	Destination	Rate	Notes
1	Wednesday	Prof. Morse	Livingston & Puerto Cortez	6.00	Mails for Guatemala and Republic of Honduras.
2	Thursday	City of Dallas	Belize, Livingston, &c.	7.00	Mails for British Honduras, Guatemala, and Republic of Honduras.
2	Thursday	Hutchinson	Havana	6.40	Specially addressed mails for Cuba and Porto Rico.
3	Friday	William G. Hewes	Bluefields	6.00	Mails for Nicaragua.
5	Sunday	S. Oteri	Truxillo and Roatan	6.00	Mails for Republic of Honduras and Bay Islands.
6	Monday	Foxhall	Port Limon	7.00	Mails for Costa Rica.
8	Wednesday	Breakwater	Belize, Livingston, &c.	7.00	Mails for British Honduras, Guatemala, and Republic of Honduras.
9	Thursday	Aransas	Havana	6.00	Specially addressed mails for Cuba and Porto Rico.
9	Thursday	Joseph Oteri, Jr.	Truxillo and La Ceiba	7.00	Mails for Republic of Honduras.
10	Friday	Harlan	Bluefields	6.00	Mails for Nicaragua.
10	Friday	S. Pizzatti	Truxillo and Roatan	6.00	Mails for Republic of Honduras and Bay Islands.
16	Thursday	City of Dallas	Belize, Livingston, &c.	7.40	Mails for British Honduras, Guatemala and Republic of Honduras.
16	Thursday	Hutchinson	Havana	6.00	Specially addressed mails for Cuba and Porto Rico.
17	Friday	Guseie	Bluefields	6.00	Mails for Nicaragua.
19	Sunday	Prof. Morse	Livingston and Puerto Cortez	6.00	Mails for Guatemala and Republic of Honduras.
19	Sunday	S. Oteri	Truxillo and Roatan	6.00	Mails for Republic of Honduras and Bay Islands.

Continued on next page.

MAILS TO FOREIGN COUNTRIES—MAY, 1889—Continued.

MAILS FOR THE WEST INDIES, MEXICO, AND FOR CENTRAL AND SOUTH AMERICA—Continued.

Date.	Sailing Day.	Steamers.	Port of Destination.	Mails Close. A.M. P.M.	Mails to be Conveyed.
			FROM NEW ORLEANS. Allow three days from New York to connect.		
May 22	Wednesday	Foxhall	Port Limon	7.00	Mails for Costa Rica.
23	Thursday	Breakwater	Belize, Livingston, &c	7.00	Mails for British Honduras, Guatemala, and Republic of Honduras.
23	Thursday	Annesec	Havana	7.00	Specially addressed mails for Cuba and Porto Rico.
24	Friday	William G. Hewes	Bluefields	6.00	Mails for Nicaragua.
25	Sunday	S. Vizzatti	Truxillo and Ruatan	6.00	Mails for Republic of Honduras.
27	Monday	Joseph Oteri, Jr.	Truxillo and La Ceiba	6.00	Mails for Republic of Honduras and Bay Islands.
30	Thursday	City of Dallas	Belize, Livingston, &c	7.00	Mails for British Honduras, Guatemala, and Republic of Honduras.
30	Thursday	Hutchinson	Havana	7.00	Specially addressed mails for Cuba and Porto Rico.
31	Friday	Harlan	Bluefields	6.00	Mails for Nicaragua.

TRANS-PACIFIC MAILS. Allow 7 days from New York to Connect.

From San Francisco.

Date.	Sailing Day.	Steamers.	Port of Destination.		Mails to be Conveyed.
May 2	Thursday	City of Rio de Janeiro	Yokohama and Hong Kong		Mails for Japan, Shanghai, Hong Kong and dependent Chinese ports; and for the East Indies, except Brit. India, Straits Settlements, Siam, and Dutch East Indies.
4	Saturday	Alameda	Honolulu, Auckland, Sydney		Mails for the Hawaiian Kingdom, New Zealand, and Australia; and for Fiji and Samoan Islands and New Caledonia via Sydney, New South Wales.
11	Saturday	Gaelic	Yokohama and Hong Kong		Mails for Japan, Shanghai, Hong Kong and dependent Chinese ports; and for the East Indies, except Brit. India, Straits Settlements, Siam, and Dutch East Indies.
18	Saturday	City of New York	Yokohama and Hong Kong		Mails for Japan, Shanghai, Hong Kong and dependent Chinese ports; and for the East Indies, except Brit. India, Straits Settlements, Siam, and Dutch East Indies.
24	Friday	Umatilla	Honolulu		Mails for the Hawaiian Kingdom.
25	Saturday	Belgic	Yokohama and Hong Kong		Mails for Japan, Shanghai, Hong Kong and dependent Chinese ports; and for the East Indies, except Brit. India, Straits Settlements, Siam, and Dutch East Indies.
31	Friday	Tahiti	Papeiti and Taiohae		Mails for Tahiti and Marquesas Islands.

COUPONS, ELECTIONS, ETC.—Continued.

Rochester, Ind. (due May 4th), Winslow, Lanier & Co., 17 Nassau St.
Ramsey Co., Minn., Chase National Bank, 15 Nassau St.
Rome City Street Ry. Co., Farmers' Loan & Trust Co., 20 William St.
San Antonio City, Texas, National City Bank, 52 Wall St.
Syracuse, Geneva & Corning R. R. Co., Coupons and Drawn Bonds (due May 15th), Farmers' Loan & Trust Co., 20 William St.
State Savings Ass'n, Ellsworth, Kan., Union Trust Co., 73 Broadway.
Shelbyville Waterworks Co., of Ind., American Loan & Trust Co., 113 Broadway.
Suburban & City R. R. & Improvement Co., American Loan & Trust Co., 113 Broadway.
San Marcos, Texas, Water Co. (May 3), Third National Bank, 20 Nassau St.
Santiago Cattle Co., National Bank of Commerce, 20 Nassau.
St. Louis City, Mo., National Bank of Commerce, 29 Nassau St.
St. Louis County, Mo., National Bank of Commerce, 15 Nassau St.
St. Paul & Northern Pacific Ry. Co. (Registered), Winslow, Lanier & Co., 17 Nassau St.
South Bend, Ind., National Park Bank, 214 Broadway.
Sheboygan City, Wis., Fourth National Bank, 11 Nassau St.
St. Paul City Bonds (due May 2d), Chase National Bank, 15 Nassau St.
St. Louis Cable & West'n R. R. Co., Farmers' Loan & Trust Co., 20 William St.
Somerset Ranche & Cattle Co., Farmers' Loan & Trust Co., 20 William St.
Tallahassee Gas & Electric Light Co., American Loan & Trust Co., 113 Broadway.
Terre Haute, Ind., Winslow, Lanier & Co., 17 Nassau St.
Texas State, Bank of New York, 48 Wall St.
Texas Loan Agency, National Park Bank, 214 Broadway.
Tenn. Coal, Iron & R. R. Co., consolidated 3d mtge., Fourth National Bank, 14 Nassau St.
Union Depot Co, Union Trust Co, 73 Broadway.
Union Security Co., Fourth National Bank, 14 Nassau St.
Virginia Electric Light & Power Co., American Loan and Trust Co., 113 Broadway.

Vermillion County, Indiana, Third National Bank, 20 Nassau St.
Warren Co., Iowa Chemical Bank, 270 Broadway.
Western Union Telegraph Co., Union Trust Co., 73 Broadway.
Western Trust & Security Co., American Loan and Trust Co., 113 Broadway.
Western R. R., Minn., Winslow, Lanier & Co., 17 Nassau St.
Wabash, Ind., Winslow, Lanier & Co., 17 Nassau St.
Whitley County, Ind. (due May 14th), Winslow Lanier & Co., 17 Nassau St.
Wabash County, Ind. (due May 15th), Winslow, Lanier & Co., 17 Nassau St.
Ward Consolidated Mining Co., 53 B'way, pays a dividend of 5 cents per share.
Wheeling & Lake Erie R'y., 2 Wall, pays a dividend of 1 %
Waterloo, Iowa, National Park Bank, 214 Broadway.
Wyoming Valley Coal Co., Farmers Loan & Trust Co., 20 William St.
Western Equipment & Car Co. Bonds, Farmers Loan and Trust Co., 20 William St.
Wellsville Water Co., Farmers Loan and Trust Co., 20 William St.
Yonkers Gaslight Co., National Park Bank, 214 Broadway.

MEETINGS OF STOCK COMPANIES.

May 1, N. Y. Chicago & St Louis R. R., at office in Cleveland, at 9 a. m.
May 1, Lake Shore & Michigan Sou. R'y, at office in Cleveland, 10 a. m.
May 2, Mich. Central R. R., at office in Detroit, 10 a. m.
May 6, Ouray Mining Co., 53 Broadway, 2 p. m.
May 6, Evening Star Mining Co., 53 Broadway, 2 p. m.
May 6, Morning Star Con. Mining Co., 53 Broadway, 2 p. m.
May 6, Ward Consolidated Mining Co., 53 Broadway, 2 p. m.
May 6, United States Tel. Co., 195 Broadway.
May 6, Oregon Short Line R'y. Annual, Cheyenne.
May 30, Central R. R. of N. J., at office in Jersey City, 12 to 2 p. m.
May 11, Del. & Hud. Co., cor. Cortlandt & Church Sts., at 12m.
May 15, Cleve, Col, Cin. & Ind. R'y, in Cleveland, 8 a. m.

FOREIGN MONEY EQUIVALENTS.

Their equivalent in American money, intrinsic value, without regard to rate of exchange.

Great Britain.

GOLD.

One Sovereign	$4 86
One-half Sovereign	2 43

SILVER.

Crown	$1 20
One-half Crown	60
One Florin	48
One Shilling	24
Six Pence	12
Four Pence	8
Three Pence	6

BANK NOTES.

£5 Bank of England	$24 25
£1 Irish and Scotch	4 84

Germany.

GOLD.

Twenty Marks	$4 74
Ten Marks	2 37
Five Marks	1 18

SILVER.

One Thaler	$0 69
One Mark	23

BANK NOTES.

One Hundred Marks	$23 62
Fifty Marks	11 81
Twenty Marks	4 72
Five Marks	1 18

Mexico.

Silver Dollar	$0 73
Gold Doubloon	15 55
$20.00 Gold	19 55

France, Belgium and Switzerland.

GOLD.

Twenty Francs	$3 86
Ten Francs	1 93
Five Francs	96

SILVER.

Five Francs	$0 93
Two Francs	36
One Franc	18
Half Franc (50 Centimes)	9

BANK NOTES.

Fifty Francs	$9 62
One Hundred Francs	19 12
Five Hundred Francs	95 60
One Thousand Francs	191 20

Spain.

GOLD.

Four Piasters	$3 88
Pistole	3 87
One-half Pistole	1 93
One-quarter Pistole	95

SILVER.

Spanish Dollar	$0 75
Five Pesetas	80
Twenty Reals	75
Ten Reals	37
Pistareen	16
Half Pistareen	8

FIRE INSURANCE COMPANIES.

Ætna of Hartford, 45 William.
Agricultural of Watertown, 71 Wall.
Albany of Albany, 156 Broadway.
Alliance Insurance Association, 32 Nassau.
American, 146 Broadway ; *for particulars see page 160.*
American of Boston, 141 Broadway.
American of Newark, 168 Broadway.
American of Philadelphia, 206 Broadway.
American Central of St. Louis, 71 Wall.
American Exchange, 115 Broadway.
Anglo-Nevada of San Francisco, 33 Pine.
Armenia of Pittsburg, 41 Pine.
Atlantic (F. & M.) of Providence, 44 Pine.
Board (N. Y.) of Fire Underwriters, 32 Nassau.
Board (National) of Underwriters, 156 Broadway.
Boatman's (F. & M.) of Pittsburg, 54 Pine.
Boston Underwriters, 120 Broadway.
Bowery, 141 Broadway and 124 Bowery.
Boylston of Boston, 206 Broadway.
British-America of Toronto, 32 Pine.
Broadway, 158 Broadway.
Brooklyn of Brooklyn, 168 Broadway.
Buffalo German of Buffalo, 155 Broadway.
Californian of San Francisco, 120 Broadway.
Citizens, 156 Broadway.
Citizens of Cincinnati, 41 Pine.
Citizens of Pittsburg, 155 Broadway.
Citizens of St. Louis, 54 Pine.
City, 111 Broadway.
City, of London, 33 Pine.
Clinton, 25 Pine.
Commerce of Albany, 44 Pine.
Commercial, in liquidation, 23 William.
Commercial of California, 33 Pine.
Commercial Mutual, 42 Wall.
Commercial Union of London, cor. Pine & William ; *for particulars see page 162.*
Commonwealth, 33 Nassau.
Concordia of Milwaukee, 25 Pine.
Connecticut of Hartford, 45 William.
Continental, 100 Broadway ; *for particulars see p. 164.*
County of Philadelphia, 120 Broadway.
Detroit (F. & M.) of Detroit, 54 Pine.
Eagle, 71 Wall.
Empire City, 166 Broadway.
Equitable (N. Y.), 58 Wall.
Equitable (F. & M.) of Providence, 146 Broadway.
Exchange, 41 Pine.
Farmers of York, Pa., 62 Liberty.
Farragut, 346 Broadway and 71 Liberty.
Fire Association of New York, 156 Broadway.
Fire Association of Philadelphia, 33 Pine.
Fire Insurance Association of London, 57 William.
Fireman's Fund of San Francisco, 33 Pine.
Firemens, 153 Broadway.
Firemens of Baltimore, 32 Nassau.
Firemens of Boston, 206 Broadway.
Firemens of Dayton, 44 Pine.
Firemens of Newark, 168 Broadway.
Franklin of Columbus, 170 Broadway.
Franklin of Philadelphia, 158 Broadway.
German American, 112 Broadway ; *for particulars see page 159.*
Germania, 177 Broadway ; *for particulars see page 160.*
German of Pittsburg, 155 Broadway.
Girard of Philadelphia, 170 Broadway.
Glens Falls of New York, 34 Pine.
Globe, 161 Broadway.
Greenwich, 161 Broadway.
Guardian, 153 Broadway.
Guardian of London, 50 Pine.
Hamburg-Bremen of Hamburg, 62 Cedar.
Hamilton, 155 Broadway.
Hanover, 40 Nassau.
Hartford of Hartford, 158 Broadway ; *for particulars see page 161.*
Hekla of Madison, Wis., 41 Pine.
Home, 119 Broadway.
Home Mutual of California, 34 Pine.
Howard, in liquidation, 54 Pine.
Imperial of London, 33 Pine.
Insurance Co. of North America (Philadelphia), 53 Liberty.
Insurance Co. of the State of Penn. (Philadelphia), 53 Liberty.
Jefferson, 111 Broadway.
Kings County of Brooklyn, 139 Broadway.
Knickerbocker, 64 Wall.
Lafayette of Brooklyn, 105 Broadway.
Lancashire of Manchester, 40 Pine.
Liberty, 120 Broadway.
Lion of London, 33 Pine.
Liverpool & London & Globe, 45 William ; *for particulars see page 162.*

London Assurance Co., 69 Wall St.
London & Lancashire, 36 Nassau.
Long Island, 172 Broadway.
Louisville Underwriters, 120 Broadway.
Mannheim (F. & M.) of Germany, 16 Exchange Place.
Manhattan Mutual, 111 Broadway.
Manufacturers & Builders, 152 Broadway.
Manufacturers & Merchants of Pittsburg, 41 Pine.
Mechanics of Philadelphia, 33 Pine.
Mechanics & Traders, in liquidation, 25 Canal.
Mercantile, 166 Broadway.
Mercantile (F. & M.) of Boston, 141 Broadway.
Mercantile of Cleveland, 120 Broadway.
Merchants, 151 Broadway.
Merchants of Newark, 83 Liberty.
Merchants of Providence, 146 Broadway.
Meriden of Meriden, 155 Broadway.
Metropolitan Board of Underwriters, cor. Cedar & William.
Michigan of Grand Rapids, 34 Pine.
Milwaukee Mechanics, 31 Pine.
Montauk of Brooklyn, 135 Broadway.
Mutual, 155 Broadway.
Nassau of Brooklyn, 173 Broadway.
National, 35 Pine.
National Board of Underwriters, 156 Broadway.
National Lloyds, 61 William.
Newark of Newark, 83 Liberty.
New Hampshire of Manchester, 155 Broadway.
New York, 72 Wall.
N. Y. Board of Fire Underwriters, 32 Nassau.
New York Bowery, 141 Broadway and 124 Bowery.
New York Equitable, 58 Wall.
New York & Boston, in liquidation, 61 William.
N. Y. Underwriters' Agency, 32 Nassau.
Niagara, 135 Broadway.
North American of Boston, 41 Pine.
North America Insurance Co. of Philadelphia, 53 Liberty.
North British & Mercantile, 54 William ; *for particulars see page 161.*
Northern Assurance Co. of London, 25 Pine.
North River, 173 Broadway.
Northwestern National of Milwaukee, 166 Broadway.
Norwich Union of Norwich, Eng., 67 Pine.
Orient of Hartford, 25 Pine.
Pacific, 470 and 173 Broadway.
Packers & Provision Dealers of Chicago, 141 Broadway.
Park, 156 Broadway.
Pennsylvania of Philadelphia, 206 Broadway.
People's, 168 Broadway and 363 Canal.
People of Manchester, 32 Pine.
People of Pittsburg, 54 Pine.
Peter Cooper, corner 9th St. and 3d Ave.
Phenix of Brooklyn, 195 Broadway ; *for particulars see page 162.*
Phenix of Hartford, 166 Broadway.
Phœnix of London, 67 Wall.
Providence Washington, 45 William.
Prudential Fire Association, 173 Broadway.
Queen of Liverpool, 60 Wall.
Reading of Reading, 54 Pine.
Reliance of Philadelphia, 34 Pine.
Rochester of Rochester, 89 Liberty.
Royal, 56 Wall.
Rutgers, 300 Park Row, 1295 Broadway and 58 Wall.
Safeguard, in liquidation, 32 Nassau.
St. Paul (F. & M.) of St. Paul, 32 Pine.
Scottish Union and N. of Edinburg, 44 Pine.
Security of Connecticut, 44 Pine.
Springfield (F. & M.) of Springfield, 45 William.
Spring Garden of Philadelphia, 120 Broadway.
Standard, 52 Wall.
Star, 34 Pine.
State of Pennsylvania Ins. Co. of Philadelphia, 53 Liberty.
Sterling, in liquidation, 167 Broadway.
Stuyvesant, 157 Broadway.
Sun, of London, 30 Nassau.
Sun Mutual of New Orleans, 155 Broadway.
Teutonia of New Orleans, 33 Pine.
The Fire Insurance Association of London, 57 William.
Transatlantic of Hamburg, 62 Liberty.
Underwriters' Agency, 32 Nassau.
Underwriters, National Board, 156 Broadway.
Underwriters, N. Y. Board, 115 Broadway.
Union of California, 44 Pine.
Union of Philadelphia, 16 Exchange Place.
United Firemen's of Philadelphia, 33 Pine.
United Fire Re-Insurance Co. of Manchester, 32 Nassau.
United States, 172 Broadway.
Westchester, 27 Pine.
Western of Pittsburg, 206 Broadway.
Western of Toronto, 44 Pine.
Williamsburg City, 150 Broadway.

EMIL OELBERMANN, President.
JOHN W. MURRAY, Vice President.

JAMES A. SILVEY, 2d Vice Pres't and Sec'y.
G. T. PATTERSON, Jr., 3d Vice President.

JANUARY 1st, 1889.

STATEMENT

OF THE CONDITION OF THE

German-American Insurance Company,
OF NEW YORK.

Par Value.		Market Value
$2,100,600	United States Registered 4% Bonds	$2,657,500
160,000	United States Currency 6% Bonds	208,000
25,000	Atlanta City 4½% Bonds	25,625
50,000	Chicago and Rock Island Railroad First Mortgage 6% Bonds	65,250
20,000	Chicago and Rock Island Railroad 5% Bonds	20,975
25,000	Cairo and Fulton Railroad First Mortgage 7% Bonds	25,750
30,000	Chi., Mil. and St. P. R. R. First Mort. 7% Bonds, I. & D. Div.	36,000
60,000	Chicago, Mil. and St. Paul 5% Bonds, Lacrosse Division	61,200
10,000	Chi., Mil. and St. P. First Mortgage 7% Bonds, I. & M. Div.	12,000
50,000	Central Pacific First Mortgage 6% Bonds	56,500
50,000	Union Pacific First Mortgage 6% Bonds	56,500
25,000	Kansas Pacific First Mortgage 6% Bonds, 1895	28,000
35,000	Kansas Pacific First Mortgage 6% Bonds, 1896	39,200
25,000	Kansas Pacific First Mortgage 6% Bonds, 1899	28,000
70,000	Chicago and Northwestern Sinking Fund 5% Bonds	76,300
40,000	Chicago and Northwestern Sinking Fund 6% Bonds	47,600
45,000	Chicago and Northwestern Debenture 5% Bonds	49,050
60,000	St. Louis, K. C. and North. First Mort. 7% Bonds, Real Estate	67,200
100,000	Erie Railway First Mortgage 7% Bonds, Consolidated	137,250
30,000	Syracuse, Binghamton & New York First Mortgage 7% Bonds	40,500
25,000	Little Miami First Mortgage 5% Bonds	25,750
25,000	Louisville and Nashville General Mortgage 6% Bonds	28,000
25,000	Louisville and Nashville Trust Bonds 6%	27,500
100,000	New York, Lack. and Western First Mortgage 6% Bonds	129,000
55,000	Chicago, Burlington and Quincy Debenture 5% Bonds	57,200
50,000	Missouri Pacific First Mortgage 6% Bonds	55,000
50,000	Missouri, Kansas and Texas First Mortgage 7% Bonds	45,750
100,000	New York Central and Hudson River Debenture 5% Bonds	111,000
75,000	Albany and Susquehanna First Consolidated Mortgage 6% Bonds	92,250
30,000	St. P., Minn. and Manitoba First Consolidated Mortgage 6% Bonds	35,400
30,000	Chi., Mil. & St. Paul First Mortgage 5% Bonds, C. & P. W. Division	30,750
55,000	Pennsylvania Company 4½% Bonds	59,950
25,000	Dakota and Great Southern First Mortgage 6% Bonds	25,000
25,000	Fargo and Southern First Mortgage 6% Bonds	25,000
181,650	New York and Harlem Railway Stock, 2,638 shares	310,694
55,000	Chicago, Rock Island and Pacific R. R. Stock, 550 shares	53,900
48,000	Omaha and St. Louis preferred stock, 480 shares	12,000
50,000	Consolidated Gas Company stock, 500 shares	41,125
10,000	American Exchange National Bank stock, 100 shares	14,500
$3,974,650		

	Cash in Banks	$222,346.00
	Cash in Trust Company	5,000.00
	Cash in Office	117.79
	Cash in hands of Managers	8,589.05
	Balance in hands of Agents	129,716.67
	Premiums uncollected, Home Office	60,901.80
	Accrued Interest	550.00

Total Assets, - - $5,345,293.70

	Capital Stock	$1,000,000.00
	Re-Insurance Reserve	1,890,351.32
	Losses Adjusted and Unadjusted	198,764.92
	Commissions and other Liabilities	12,188.98

Net Surplus, - - $2,243,985.48

Office: Nos. 113 and 115 Broadway.

American Fire Insurance Company

OF NEW YORK,

MUTUAL LIFE OLD BUILDING.   146 BROADWAY.

STATEMENT, JANUARY 1st, 1889.

Cash Capital,	$400,000 00
Unearned Premiums and other Liabilities,	360,176 41
Net Surplus,	548,337 91
Total Assets,	**$1,308,514 32**

INVESTED AS FOLLOWS:

Cash,	$66,683 51
Bonds and Mortgages,	55,220 00
Demand Loans,	153,250 00
U. S. Bonds owned by the Company,	614,250 00
Other Bonds and Stocks owned by the Company,	390,750 00
Interest Accrued, Premiums Due, &c.,	28,360 81
	$1,308,514 32

DAVID ADEE, President.

CHAS. P. PEIRCE, Ass't Sec'y   W. H. CROLIUS, Secretary.

SILAS P. WOOD, Agency Manager.

GERMANIA FIRE INSURANCE COMPANY

OF NEW YORK,

177 & 179 BROADWAY.

STATEMENT, JANUARY 1st, 1889.

ASSETS.

Cash Capital.	$1,000,000 00
Reserve for Re-Insurance,	1,015,054 30
Reserve for Losses under adjustment,	67,219 29
Net Surplus,	726,445 08
Total,	$2,808,718 67

RUDOLPH GARRIGUE, - - - - - - - President.

HUGO SCHUMANN, - - - - - - Vice-Pres. & Sec'y.

North British and Mercantile Insurance Company

Of London and Edinburgh.

UNITED STATES BRANCH: 54 WILLIAM STREET, N. Y.

NEW YORK BOARD OF MANAGEMENT.

SOLON HUMPHREYS, Esq., Chairman.
(E. D. Morgan & Co.)

J. J. ASTOR, Esq.

H. W. BARNES, Esq.

CHAS. H. COSTER, Esq.
(Drexel, Morgan & Co.)

DAVID DOWS, Jr., Esq.
(David Dows, Jr., & Co.)

JACOB WENDELL, Esq.
(Jacob Wendell & Co.)

CHAS. EZRA WHITE, Esq.

SAM. P. BLAGDEN, Manager.
WM. A. FRANCIS, Asst. Manager.

ROBT. H. WASS, General Agent.　　WM. R. ECKER, Asst. Gen'l Agent.

H. M. JACKSON, Secretary.

INCORPORATED 1810.　　　　　　　CHARTER PERPETUAL.

Hartford Fire Insurance Co.

OF HARTFORD, CONN.

STATEMENT, JANUARY 1st, 1889.

Cash Capital,	$1,250,000 00
Assets,	5,750,080 47
Surplus,	2,233,982 59

GEO. L. CHASE, President.

P. C. ROYCE, Secretary.　　　　THOS. TURNBULL, Ass't Secretary.

OFFICE OF METROPOLITAN DISTRICT,

158 BROADWAY, NEW YORK CITY.

GEO. M. COIT, Manager.

Liverpool and London and Globe
INSURANCE COMPANY.

ENTERED U. S. 1848.

PROGRESS IN UNITED STATES.
FIRE PREMIUMS.

1848,	$ 4,519 00
1858,	471,988 00
1868,	1,739,620 00
1878,	2,422,126 00
1888,	3,928,010 27

Fire Losses Paid in the United States Exceed $44,300,000.

CHIEF OFFICE: 45 WILLIAM STREET,
NEW YORK CITY.

PHENIX INSURANCE COMPANY
Of Brooklyn, N. Y.
CASH CAPITAL, - - $1,000,000.

Insures against Losses by Fire, Windstorms, Tornadoes, Cyclones and Lightning.

NEW YORK OFFICES: 195 BROADWAY.

GEORGE P. SHELDON, President.
ARTHUR B. GRAVES, Vice-President.   GEORGE INGRAHAM, 2d Vice-President.
PHILANDER SHAW, Secretary.   CHARLES C. LITTLE, Asst. Secretary.

Western and Southern Department, Phenix Building, Chicago, Ill., T. R. Burch, General Agent.
South Eastern Department, H. C. Stockdell, General Agent, Atlanta, Ga.
J. W. Barley, General Agent, Eastern Department and Middle States, Office in New York.

Commercial Union Assurance Company, Limited,

OF LONDON,

Cor. Pine and William Sts., New York.

STRUTHERS & CO.,

Map Engravers and Printers,

24, 26, 28, 30, 32 & 34 NEW CHAMBERS STREET,

NEW YORK.

Relief Plates of Maps, Diagrams, Color Plates, etc.

FINE COLOR PRINTING A SPECIALTY.

THE FRANKLIN PHOTO-ELECTROTYPE CO.,

305 PEARL STREET, NEW YORK,

Designers, Engravers, Photo-Electrotypers.

SPECIAL FACILITIES FOR THE MANUFACTURE OF

Cuts for Catalogues, Books, Magazines, Newspapers,

AND FOR ALL ADVERTISING AND ILLUSTRATIVE PURPOSES.

PROMPTNESS AND QUALITY ASSURED.

FOREIGN EXCHANGE QUOTATIONS.

	April 13.		April 15.		April 16.		April 17.		April 18.	
Bankers' sterling, 60 days nominal.....	$4 87½	$4 88	$4 87½	$4 88	$4 87½	$4 88	$4 87½	$4 88	$4 87½	$4 88
Bankers' sterling, sight, nominal.......	4 89½	4 90	4 89½	4 90	4 89½	4 90	4 89½	4 90	4 89½	4 90
Bankers' sterling, 60 days, actual	4 86¾	4 87	4 86¾	4 87	4 86¾	4 87	4 86¾	4 87	4 86¾	4 87¼
Bankers' sterling, sight, actual........	4 88¾	4 89	4 88¾	4 89	4 88¾	4 89	4 88¾	4 89	4 88½	4 88¾
Cable transfers.	4 89¼	4 89¾	4 89¼	4 89½	4 89	4 89½	4 89	4 89½	4 87	4 89¼
Prime commercial sterling, long.......	4 87	4 86½	4 86	4 86½	4 86	4 86½	4 86	4 86½	4 86¼	4 86½
Documentary sterling, 60 days.........	4 85½	4 86	4 85½	4 86	4 85½	4 86	4 85½	4 86	4 85¾	4 86¼
Paris bankers' 60 days	5 18⅛	5 17½	5 18⅛	5 17½	5 18⅛	5 17½	5 18⅛	5 17½	5 18⅛	5 17½
Paris bankers' sight..........	5 16¼	5 15⅝	5 16¼	5 15⅝	5 16¼	5 15⅝	5 16¼	5 15⅝	5 16¼	5 20⅝
Paris commercial, 60 days..	5 20⅝	5 20	5 20⅝	5 20	5 20⅝	5 20	5 20⅝	5 20	5 20⅝	5 20
Paris commercial, sight.	5 18⅛	5 17½	5 18⅛	5 17½	5 18⅛	5 17½	5 18⅛	5 17½	5 18⅛	5 17½
Antwerp commercial, 60 days...........	5 21⅞	5 21¼	5 12⅞	5 21¼	5 21⅞	5 21⅜	5 21⅞	5 21¼	5 21⅞	5 20⅝
Swiss bankers', 60 days..................	5 19⅜	5 18¾	5 19⅜	5 18¾	5 19⅜	5 18¾	5 19⅜	5 18¾	5 19⅜	5 18¾
Swiss bankers', sight.....................	5 16⅞	5 16¼	5 16⅞	5 16¼	5 16⅞	5 16¼	5 16⅞	5 16¼	5 16⅞	5 16¼
Reichsmarks (4), bankers', 60 days.....	95¼	95⅝	95¼	95⅝	95¼	95⅝	95¼	95⅝	95¼	95⅝
Reichsmarks (4), sight	95⅝	95¾	95⅝	95¾	95⅝	95¾	95⅝	95¾	95½	95¾
Reichsmarks (4), commercial, 60 days..	94⅞	95⅛	94⅞	95⅛	94⅞	95⅛	94⅞	95⅛	94⅞	95⅛
Reichsmarks (4), sight	95⅜	95½	95⅜	95½	95⅜	95½	95⅜	95½	95¼	95⅜
Guilders, bankers', 60 days	40 3-16	40¼	40 3-16	40¼	40 3-16	40¼	40 3-16	40¼	40 3-16	40¼
Guilders, bankers', sight................	40⅜	40 7-16	40⅜	40 7-16	40⅜	40 7-16	40⅜	40 7-16	40⅜	40 7-16
Guilders, commercial, 60 days..........	40	40 1-16	40	40 1-16	40	40 1-16	40	40 1-16	40	40 1-16
Guilders, commercial, sight............	40 3-16	40¼	40 3-16	40¼	40 3-16	40¼	40 3-16	40¼	40 3-16	40¼
Copenhagen, Stockholm and Christiania, krona, 60 days	26¾	26⅞	26¾	26⅞	26¾	26⅞	26¾	26⅞	26¾	26⅞
Copenhagen, Stockholm and Christiania, krona, sight..........	27	27⅛	27	27⅛	27	27⅛	27	27⅛	27	27⅛

THE CONTINENTAL FIRE INSURANCE CO.

has a Cash Capital of

ONE MILLION OF DOLLARS,

Cash Assets of over

FIVE MILLIONS OF DOLLARS,

a Reserve for the security of Insurance in force amounting to over

TWO MILLIONS AND A HALF OF DOLLARS,

and a Net Surplus, above the Capital and all liabilities, of over

TWELVE HUNDRED THOUSAND DOLLARS.

It has paid Losses to date amounting to the large sum of over

TWENTY-THREE MILLIONS OF DOLLARS.

It conducts its business under the provisions of the Safety Fund Law of the State of New York, and has in the two Safety Funds

ONE MILLION OF DOLLARS.

Its gain in Net Surplus for the year just closed (1888) was the largest of any American company.

In the great Chicago fire, which occurred in the year 1871, it paid, in cash, losses amounting to nearly Two Millions of Dollars, and so strong were its reserves that *it did this without impairing its Capital.* Thirteen months later, it paid in consequence of the large fire in the city of Boston nearly Three-Quarters of a Million of Dollars.

Such facts as these should recommend the Company to all having property to insure. Why should you select a weak Company when you can just as well select a strong one, which has been tried by passing through conflagrations in consequence of which one hundred Companies failed? The best is the cheapest. Especially is it incumbent upon trustees, guardians, executors, agents and others acting in a fiduciary capacity to select for those whose interests are entrusted to their charge, unquestioned indemnity.

If you desire insurance on property of any kind, and will send us a postal card we will save you all trouble by having our representative call on you. An examination of the list of Directors of this Company should be satisfactory evidence to any one, that the connection with it by men of such standing in the community is further evidence of its reliability.

TOTAL ASSETS.

Reserve for re-Insurance	2,501,884.39
Reserve for losses	204,763.24
Reserve for Commissions, Taxes, &c	54,495.00
Reserve for Scrip dividends and all other claims	40,510.40
Cash Capital	1,000,000.00
Net Surplus	1,226,691.66
	5,028,344.69

PRINCIPAL OFFICE, 100 BROADWAY, NEW YORK.

BRANCH OFFICES: 1273 Broadway, 10 Cooper Institute, 121 E. 125th St.
BROOKLYN: Cor. Court and Montague Sts., and 126 Broadway.

DIRECTORS.

WILLIAM L. ANDREWS.	JAMES FRASER.	ALFRED RAY
SAMUEL D. BABCOCK.	AURELIUS B. HULL.	WM. M. RICHARDS.
HIRAM BARNEY.	WILLIAM H. HURLBUT.	JOHN L. RIKER.
GEORGE BLISS.	BRADISH JOHNSON.	HENRY F. SPAULDING.
CHARLES H. BOOTH.	H. H. LAMPORT.	WILLIAM H. SWAN.
HENRY C. BOWEN.	WILLIAM G. LOW.	LAWRENCE TURNURE.
JOHN CLAFLIN.	EDWARD MARTIN.	THEO. F. VAIL.
E. W. CORLIES.	RICHARD A. McCURDY.	J. D. VERMILYE.
JOHN H. EARLE.	ALEX. E. ORR.	JACOB WENDELL.

F. C. MOORE, President,

CYRUS PECK, Vice-Pres't & Secretary,

HENRY EVANS, 2d Vice-Pres't & Sec'y Agency Dep't.

EDWARD LANSING, Ass't Sec'y.   C. H. DUTCHER, Sec'y Brooklyn Dep't.

www.ingramcontent.com/pod-product-compliance
Lightning Source LLC
Chambersburg PA
CBHW030244170426
43202CB00009B/620